Cognitive Psychology

Cognitive Psychology

Edited by Helen Kaye

This publication forms part of the Open University module DD303 *Cognitive psychology*. Details of this and other Open University modules can be obtained from the Student Registration and Enquiry Service, The Open University, PO Box 197, Milton Keynes MK7 6BJ, United Kingdom (tel. +44 (0)845 300 60 90; email general-enquiries@open.ac.uk).

Alternatively, you may visit the Open University website at www.open.ac.uk where you can learn more about the wide range of modules and packs offered at all levels by The Open University. To purchase a selection of Open University materials visit www.ouw.co.uk, or contact Open University Worldwide, Walton Hall, Milton Keynes MK7 6AA, United Kingdom for a brochure (tel. +44 (0)1908 858793; fax +44 (0)1908 858787; email ouw-customer-services@open.ac.uk).

The Open University, Walton Hall, Milton Keynes MK7 6AA

First published 2005. Second edition 2010.

The second edition is based on the first edition edited by Nick Braisby and Angus Gellatly.

Edited and designed by The Open University.

Typeset in India by Alden Prepress Services, Chennai.

Printed in the United Kingdom by TJ International Ltd, Padstow.

ISBN 978 1 8487 3467 8

2.1

The paper used in this publication contains pulp sourced from forests independently certified to the Forest Stewardship Council (FSC) principles and criteria. Chain of custody certification allows the pulp from these forests to be tracked to the end use (see www.fsc-uk.org).

Mixed Sources
Product group from well-managed forests and other controlled sources
www.fsc.org Cert no. SGS-COC-2482
© 1996 Forest Stewardship Council
FSC

Preface

This book has been produced as the core text for The Open University's Level 3 module in *Cognitive psychology* (DD303). However, it has been designed to serve students taking other courses of study in cognitive psychology as well, either as essential or recommended reading. There are a number of features of the design of this text that we hope will serve well both students learning about cognitive psychology and educators teaching the subject.

Book structure

The chapters in this book are organized in five parts. The first four parts focus on broad and well-established topic areas within cognitive psychology, such as perceptual processes and memory. The fifth considers topics that have been thought to present challenges to the cognitive approach, such as emotion and consciousness; as well as how cognitive psychology can be applied outside the laboratory.

The first chapter is not located in one of these parts. It attempts to give a historical and conceptual introduction to cognitive psychology, laying out the foundations of the subject, and raising some of the important themes and issues that are revisited in later chapters. Some of these themes are developed also in the introductions to each of the subsequent parts; we recommend that students read these introductions prior to reading their associated parts, and re-read them afterwards.

Chapter structure

Each chapter has been structured according to certain conventions.

An **emboldened term** signifies the introduction of a key concept or term that is either explicitly or implicitly defined in the surrounding text. The locations of these defined terms are also flagged in bold in the index.

Each chapter contains a number of **activities**. Often these may be simple thought exercises that may take no more than a minute or so. Others are more involved. Each activity has been integrated into the design of the chapter, and is aimed at enhancing students' understanding of the material. We recommend that student readers attempt as many of these activities as possible and, where appropriate, revisit them after completing each chapter.

The chapters in this book also make use of **text boxes**. Each box has been written to amplify a particular aspect of the material without interrupting the ongoing narrative. Though the boxes illuminate a wide range of issues, many focus on aspects of **research studies** and **methods**. Students may find they wish to finish a section before reading a particular box.

Each substantive main section finishes with a **section summary**, often a bullet point list reminding the student of the key points established in that section. We hope that students will use these as useful barometers of their understanding and re-read sections where the summary points are not clearly understood.

Each chapter makes a number of explicit **links** to other chapters in the book, often to specific numbered sections. It would be tedious in the extreme to continually follow each and every link, flicking to the relevant pages and reading the relevant 'linked' section. Rather, these links are intended to help students perceive the interconnected nature of cognitive psychology, identifying connections between topics that otherwise might seem disparate. Of course, we hope that students will be motivated to follow some of these links either on first reading, or on a later reading, perhaps as a revision aid.

Each chapter ends with an invitation for you to visit the DD303 website and access an original journal article relevant to the chapter. The precise article is specified on the website and will extend and deepen your knowledge of a particular topic in cognitive psychology. These supplementary articles are part of your core reading and will also develop your skills in locating and reading primary source material. Finally, as well as a list of references each chapter concludes with some specific suggestions for **further reading**. Within each chapter some issues get less attention than they deserve, and so interested readers may wish to pursue some of these suggestions for a more in-depth treatment. Moreover, it is always worth approaching a topic from more than one direction – consulting different texts, including other general texts on cognitive psychology, can help achieve a richer understanding and we recommend this approach to all students.

Supporting a module in cognitive psychology

There are few restrictions on how one might use this text to support the teaching of a module in cognitive psychology. The chapters in this book may be tackled in a number of different orders. Depending on the focus of the module, particular parts may be omitted, or particular chapters omitted from a given part or parts. The book as a whole presupposes relatively little prior knowledge of cognitive psychology on the part of a student. However, in some instances, later chapters may presuppose some limited knowledge of related earlier chapters, though this is usually explicitly indicated. Similarly, while all chapters are designed to be taught at the same level, later chapters may tackle issues considered too complex in the earlier chapters. By focusing more on earlier or later chapters, modules can vary somewhat the degree of difficulty of the material they present.

Companion volume

Accompanying this book is a companion publication, *Cognitive Psychology: Methods Companion*, also designed as a key teaching text for The Open University's Level 3 module in *Cognitive psychology*. The *Methods Companion* considers in detail a number of key methodological issues in cognitive psychology.

Acknowledgements

Finally, developing The Open University's Level 3 module in *Cognitive psychology* (DD303) has been a major undertaking, involving the production of two books, various pieces of software and associated files, audio materials, websites and web-based materials, and numerous other additional items and activities. To say that such a module, and that this text, could not have been produced without the help and cooperation of a large number of people is an understatement. The following pages list those who have made this enterprise possible, and to each we extend our grateful and sincere thanks, as we do to anyone we have omitted in error.

Nick Braisby and Angus Gellatly, updated for the second edition by Helen Kaye

Cognitive Psychology Module Team

This book was designed and produced for The Open University module DD303 *Cognitive psychology*. The editor gratefully thanks all those people, listed below, who have been involved in the process (based at The Open University, unless otherwise stated).

ORIGINAL DD303 TEAM:

    Module Chair: Nick Braisby

    Curriculum Manager: Ingrid Slack

    Core Team Members: Sandy Aitkenhead; Nicola Brace; Angus Gellatly; Alison J. K. Green; Martin Le Voi; Bundy Mackintosh; Peter Naish; Graham Pike

Curriculum Manager (rights): Ann Tolley

Curriculum Assistants: Marie Morris; Elaine Richardson

Additional Authors: Jackie Andrade (University of Sheffield); Peter Ayton (City University; Chris Barry (University of Essex); Simon Bignell (University of Essex); Martin A. Conway (University of Durham); Graham Edgar (University of Gloucestershire); Simon Garrod (University of Glasgow); Gareth Gaskell (University of York); Ken Gilhooly (University of Paisley); Olaf Hauk (MRC Cognition and Brain Sciences Unit); Graham J. Hitch (University of York); Emily A. Holmes (MRC Cognition and Brain Sciences Unit); Ashok Jansari (University of East London); Helen Kaye; Paul Mulholland; Mike Oaksford (Cardiff University); Mike Pilling; John Richardson; Andrew Rutherford (Keele University); Anthony J. Sanford (University of Glasgow); Stella Tickle; Tony Stone (London South Bank University); Stuart Watt (Robert Gordon University); Jenny Yiend (MRC Cognition and Brain Sciences Unit)

Module Reader: Matt Lambon Ralph (University of Manchester)

External Assessor: James Hampton (City University)

Media Project Manager: Lynne Downey

Production and Presentation Administrator: Richard Golden

Copublishing Adviser: Jonathan Hunt

Lead Editor: Chris Wooldridge

Editors: Alison Edwards; Kathleen Calder; Winifred Power (Freelance)

Designers: Tammy Alexander; Alison Goslin; Diane Mole

Graphic Artists: Janis Gilbert; Sara Hack

Picture Researcher: Celia Hart

eMedia Quality Promoter: Roger Moore

Software Designers: Ian Every; Maurice Brown; David Morris

Rights Adviser: Alma Hales

Contracts Executives: Katie Meade; Sarah Gamman

Compositors: Pam Berry; Lisa Hale; Phillip Howe

Print Buyer Controller: Lene Connolly

Assistant Print Buyer: Dave Richings

Contents in brief

Contents

Chapter 16: Applying cognitive psychology *Hayley Ness*

Foundations of cognitive psychology

Chapter 1

Helen Kaye, based on an earlier version by
Nick Braisby and Angus Gellatly

1   Introduction

Why do we forget some things but clearly remember others? How do we perceive our environment? How do we infer from patterns of light or sound the presence of objects in our environment, and their properties? How do we understand language, and produce it so that others can understand? How does our use of language affect the ways we reason, and solve problems? How do we think?

These are some of the foundational questions that cognitive psychology examines. They are foundational partly because they concern the nature of basic psychological abilities – abilities that we often take for granted, yet which are vital to our normal, healthy functioning and are key to our understanding of what it means to be human. And they are foundational partly because they are important for psychology as a whole, and its application in everyday life. For example, how can we hope to understand the behaviour of employees in an organization unless we first understand their perceptions and how they reason and attempt to solve problems? How can we understand the way in which people interact to shape one another's opinions, if we do not understand how people understand and process language, and how they make judgements? How can we assess the reliability of an eyewitness account of a crime without appreciating the factors that affect our ability to remember events?

Throughout this book, the various authors tackle these and other questions, and show you how much of these foundations cognitive psychologists have so far uncovered. The book begins with an exploration of perceptual processes, moves to a discussion of memory, considers language and how we classify things and then tackles thinking processes. The last part of the book is devoted to topics that present a challenge to cognitive psychology – consciousness and emotion – and to applications of cognitive psychology in the 'real world'.

In this chapter, we try to answer the question 'What is cognitive psychology?' and, in so doing, examine some of the different ways psychologists have approached cognition. We touch upon the relations between cognitive psychology and other sub-disciplines of psychology, and those between cognitive psychology and other disciplines (such as philosophy, linguistics and neuroscience).

2   What is cognitive psychology?

Well, as with most questions, there can be short or long answers. The short answer is that cognitive psychology is the branch of psychology devoted to the scientific study of the mind. But what does 'studying the mind' entail, what do cognitive psychologists actually study and how do they do it? A quick way to answer these questions would be to scan the contents page of this book. This will give you a good idea of the topics cognitive psychologists typically study. Certainly the topics of perception, attention, language, categorization, reasoning, problem solving and memory are central to the study of cognition. Cognition has also broadened to include the topics of consciousness and emotion, which have not always been seen as readily amenable to a cognitive approach. Subsequent chapters will have much more to say about these issues than we have space for here. One way to demonstrate the sorts of things that interest cognitive psychologists is to have a go at studying a mind as it works – your mind.

ACTIVITY 1.1

At this moment you are involved in getting information from this book. Your eyes are moving across the page and detecting patterns of black and white and light and shade; or, if you are listening to this book on audio, or read out from an electronic copy, your ears will be detecting sound waves of varying intensity and pitch. Those are the behaviours that could be observed by an outsider. Take a few minutes to jot down the explanation you would give for what you are doing right now, if that outsider were to ask why you are behaving in the way you are. Try to think of many different ways of answering the question and list the processes that you think might be going on in your mind – how would you describe them?

COMMENT

The first thing to note is that there are lots of different sorts of explanations. For example, you might have noted that your reading is bound up with a feeling of elation – perhaps you love studying cognitive psychology – or a feeling of anxiety – perhaps you are uncertain of obtaining a good module grade. You are reporting the **emotion** that's on your mind. Perhaps you jotted down as an answer that you reasoned you ought to read this book since you want to do well on your module. Perhaps doing well on your module is part of a strategy to reach a goal, or solve a problem. You might also have suggested that you decided to read this book – perhaps faced with different ways of spending your time, you judged that this would be the most beneficial and enjoyable (we'll try not to let you down!). Correspondingly, you might have thought there are processes going on in your mind to do with **reasoning**, **problem solving** and **decision making**.

It might be that you are reading this chapter for a second time because you want to make sure you **remember** it. So, there may be feelings of **recognition** and anticipation – or maybe an awareness of how much we forget.

You might have suggested that you were trying to make sense of the chapter; you were involved in understanding words, phrases and sentences. You might have indicated that there must be processes for **understanding language**. Perhaps you offered other explanations. Maybe you explained your reading of the book by saying 'That is what books are for' – because you **categorized** it as a book. Maybe you suggested you were scanning your eyes across the page in order to **perceive** and recognize words. And perhaps you were aware that you were paying **attention** to the text and not being distracted by the sounds of traffic or a doorbell. In fact you may realize that you were **conscious** of only some aspects of your environment while you were concentrating on the book.

The words in bold type in the previous paragraphs are major topics discussed in this book and are all part of cognitive psychology.

Activity 1.1 identifies many different kinds of cognitive process that may be operating simultaneously while we are carrying out a task. However, a corollary is that cognitive psychologists try to devise studies that isolate the particular cognitive processes under investigation – for example, a researcher interested in language processing will try to design their studies so that they measure language processes only, and are not unwittingly influenced by other processes, such as emotion or reasoning. This approach of fractionating cognition into different components has led to great advances in our understanding of how specific cognitive abilities operate, particularly in laboratory conditions. However, there has always been interest in how cognition happens in real life, and in DD303 we will also explore how what we know about cognitive psychology from laboratory studies helps us to understand how people behave in everyday situations.

ACTIVITY 1.2

Psychology students have a bit of an advantage over those of other disciplines in that they can apply some of the knowledge they're gaining to the processes they need to follow. For example, think for a moment about what you need to do to pass an exam. Jot down a few key words.

COMMENT

You probably jotted down something about remembering what you read during the module – cognitive psychology has a lot to say about how remembering works. You may have mentioned answering the question (if you've ever marked an exam, you'll know that it's a crucial skill) – which involves categorizing the module material appropriately, and making a judgement about what to include. Even understanding the relationship between anxiety and performance can help you judge what constitutes 'good' exam nerves.

Summary of Section 2

- Cognitive psychology can be characterized as the scientific study of the mind.
- Cognitive psychology can be characterized in terms of its subject matter (see the table of contents for this book).
- Cognitive psychology tends to isolate individual processes for study – it is important to acknowledge that everyday behaviour involves the integration of multiple cognitive processes.

3   A brief history of cognitive psychology

Cognitive psychology did not begin at any one defining moment, and there are many antecedents to its evolution as a branch of inquiry. In this section we will briefly sketch some of those antecedents and try to indicate how and why they resulted in the development of what today we call cognitive psychology. However, all written history is necessarily selective and simplified, and a historical account as brief as the one we are about to give must be especially so.

3.1   Origins of cognitive psychology

Although philosophers such as Descartes and Locke developed arguments regarding the nature and function of the mind, it wasn't until the nineteenth century that experimental evidence began to emerge.

Wilhelm Wundt established the first dedicated psychology laboratory in Leipzig in 1879. He took consciousness to be the proper subject matter of psychology. According to Wundt, physical scientists study the objects of the physical world either directly or, more often, through observation of the readings on instruments. In either case, observation is mediated by conscious experience but for physical scientists things in the world are the object of study not the conscious experience by means of which we know them. Psychology would be different in that it would take as its subject matter conscious experience itself.

Wundt adopted introspection as a research method, believing that properly trained psychologists should be able to make observations of their own experience in a manner similar to the way properly trained physicists make selective observations of the world. Wundt fully understood the need to design experiments with adequate controls and to produce replicable results. He also made use of objective measures of performance, such as reaction time (RT). The focus of his interest, however, was the conscious experience that preceded the response. For example, if one condition in an experiment yielded longer RTs (i.e. people were slower) than another, he wanted to know how the two preceding conscious experiences differed. Wundt was not concerned with the unconscious processes involved in responding to a simple stimulus, the rapid information-processing operations that, as you will find in the following chapters, form much of the subject matter of modern cognitive psychology. He considered these to lie in the realm of physiology rather than of psychology. Although introspection has fallen out of favour to some extent, there are areas of cognitive psychology where it is still a useful tool. For example, in Chapter 11 you will be introduced to 'protocol analysis', which involves people verbalizing their thoughts as they tackle tricky problems.

Also in Germany in the nineteenth century, Hermann Ebbinghaus pioneered the use of experimentation to understand mental phenomena such as memory and perception. In experimentation Ebbinghaus identified the need to control potential confounding variables, to manipulate an independent variable systematically and to measure its effects on a dependent variable. So, with his classic memory experiments Ebbinghaus selected items to memorize that were novel and had no pre-existing meaning – these were short letter strings such as FOS or JIK. The independent variable he manipulated was the delay between his memorizing the strings and testing his memory for them. The dependent variable he measured was how quickly he could relearn the letter string list after the delay. This doesn't sound like the most exciting experiment ever, and in fact Ebbinghaus carried out all of the trials only on himself, perhaps to spare others the tedium. Equally, though, using a single participant controlled for individual differences. In 1885 Ebbinghaus published a book entitled *On Memory*, where he documented findings that are still being explored today. For example, he observed that how well a particular item is remembered can depend where in a list of items it is situated. Chapter 5 of this book describes contemporary research into serial order effects.

We have mentioned experiments in passing, and Box 1.1 describes the characteristics of an experiment.

1.1 ──────────────────────────────── **Methods**

The characteristics of an experiment

Psychologists use experiments as a way of testing a hypothesis that is typically derived from a theory or model of cognition. To do so involves control and measurement. An experimenter typically attempts to manipulate one or two factors while holding everything else constant and measures the effect of those manipulations. For example, in an experiment to assess the effect of word length on the number of words that can be memorized, the experimenter would prepare a series of lists of words, each of different numbers of syllables. Hence there would be a two-syllable list and a three-syllable list, etc., the number of syllables being the independent variable. Apart from the number of syllables, all of the lists would be as similar as possible: words would be drawn from the same categories (for example animal names or food types) and would be matched for familiarity, ease of pronunciation and so on. Participants would be exposed to each list for an equal length of time with minimal, but equal amounts of external distraction. The dependent variable measured would be the number or percentage of words correctly recalled. This experiment and its implications for our understanding of memory are presented in Chapter 5.

Ebbinghaus also researched perception and is credited with discovering the visual illusion demonstrated in Figure 1.1.

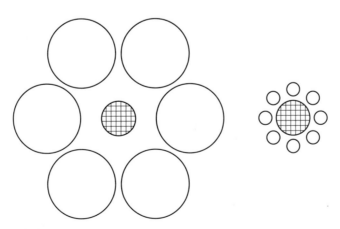

Figure 1.1 Which of the cross-hatched circles appears larger? (They are actually the same size)

ACTIVITY 1.3

How might you investigate which factors affect the magnitude of the effect of the Ebbinghaus illusion? Jot down independent variables you could manipulate.

COMMENT

Independent variables that researchers have investigated include the size of the surrounding circles, the distance between the central and surrounding circles, whether the outer circles contain pictures (Van Ulzen *et al.*, 2008) and so on. One particularly ingenious study by Muise *et al.* (1997) represented the inner circle as an 'Oreo cookie' to manipulate the value of the circle that was being judged.

Cognitive psychology also has roots in the USA, where Harvard professor William James established the first dedicated psychology teaching laboratory in the same year as Wundt's laboratory was founded, 1879. James's work complemented Wundt's emphasis on the contents of mind and Ebbinghaus's mechanisms of mind by concentrating on the function of the mind. Sounding remarkably like an exponent of what is now called evolutionary psychology, James focused on the purpose of consciousness and behaviour. His major concern was how our behaviour, including our emotions, helps us to live and function in the 'real world'. James coined the term 'stream of thought, of consciousness' (1981 [1890], p.239) and used introspection to study his own stream of consciousness. James carried out very few empirical studies, but rather concentrated on the observation and analysis of human behaviour. Many of James's observations have gained contemporary empirical evidence and their influence is evident throughout this book. In memory, for example, he noted that thinking over and elaborating on an event improves memory of it (James, 1981 [1890], p.662). Chapters 5 and 6 discuss how rehearsal and elaborative processing enhance retention. James discussed the role of one's self as an agent in re-experiencing past life events, and in Chapter 7 you will be introduced to the 'working self' which acts to construct our autobiographical memory. In Chapter 14 you will study William James's views on the relationship between emotion and behaviour.

3.2   Behaviourism and cognitive psychology

John B. Watson, the principal standard bearer for the new kind of psychology, redefined the subject matter of psychology away from the study of the mind, explaining that 'Behaviorism ... holds that the subject matter of human psychology is the behavior of the human being' (Watson, 1930, p.2). Watson was especially keen to move psychological research out of the laboratory and into the 'real world'. He was less interested in fine distinctions of conscious experience than in how people act in everyday life, and in how they can be influenced. He wanted to see psychological knowledge applied to education, clinical problems and advertising, and he initiated work in all these areas. Not all behaviourists were as zealous as Watson when it came to applying psychology, but one belief they did have in common was that psychology should be scientific and objective; and by this they meant that its subject matter should be publicly observable. However, consciousness is by its nature only privately observable – that is, by the person experiencing it.

What is publicly observable – that is, evident to everyone – is the behaviour or response emitted by the subject and any stimulus presented to them by the investigator. So, psychologists such as Edward Thorndike, Watson and, later, B.F. Skinner, Hans Eysenck and others argued that psychology should be scientific in its approach, and should seek to explain behaviour through reference only to those things that may be observed and measured. The emphasis on public observation was intended to place psychology on an objective footing, akin to natural sciences like physics and chemistry, and reflected a wider philosophical consensus as to the proper nature of scientific inquiry.

Behaviourists were concerned to show how even complex phenomena might be understood in terms of principles of learning, with behaviour seen as made up of learned responses to particular stimuli. More complex behaviour could be seen as a chain of stimulus–response pairs, in which each response also serves as the stimulus that leads to the production of the next response. For example, in navigating a maze your first response may be to turn right. This act can then serve as a stimulus to turn left at the next decision point; that response in turn becomes a stimulus for a response of going left again; and so on. One view of language production, for example, was that the utterance of a word could be seen as a learned response: a child might be rewarded for making a noise that approximated to 'Mummy' (a response) when their mother appeared (a stimulus), and this would increase the likelihood of repeating the response in the presence of the stimulus. The utterance of a whole sentence could be seen as involving a chain of stimulus–response pairs, in which each response (the utterance of a word) also served as the stimulus that led to the production of the next response (the next word).

Despite the possibility of giving behaviourist explanations of complex activities such as the utterance of a sentence, behaviourists tended not to offer accounts of what we now refer to as higher mental processes – processes such as producing and understanding language, planning, problem solving, remembering, paying attention, consciousness and so on. Of course many of these are things that cannot be observed and measured but nevertheless are major topics of interest to cognitive psychologists.

3.3 The problems with behaviourism

In 1948, at a meeting known as the Hixon symposium, Karl Lashley gave a talk entitled 'The problem of serial order in behaviour'. In this, he gave prominence to the problems posed for behaviourist accounts by complex actions in which behaviour segments are somehow linked together in a sequence, and where two segments depend upon one another, even though they may be separated by many intervening segments. Language, as you might have guessed, provides a prime example. In fact, the last sentence illustrates the point nicely: when I came to write the word 'provides' in the previous sentence I chose to end it with the letter 's'. I did so, of course, because this verb has to agree grammatically with the singular noun 'language', the subject of the sentence. In my actual sentence, these two words were separated by a clause, and so my action at the time of writing the word 'provides' depended upon a much earlier behaviour segment – my writing of the word 'language'. Lashley argued that since the production of some words in a sequence could be shown to depend upon words produced much earlier, the simple view that each word is the stimulus that produces the subsequent word as a response could not properly explain language production.

Lashley also argued that many behaviour sequences are executed simply too rapidly for feedback from one segment to serve as the trigger for the next. He cited examples such as the speed with which pianists and typists sometimes move their fingers, or with which tennis players adjust their whole posture in response to an incoming fast service. Lashley's alternative to the chaining of behaviour segments was to suppose that complex sequences are planned and organized in advance of being initiated.

Lashley's view that behaviourism could not properly explain how people produce (or comprehend) language was later reinforced by a review of Skinner's book *Verbal Behavior* (Skinner, 1957) by the linguist Noam Chomsky (Chomsky, 1959). Chomsky argued that, contrary to the behaviourist claims, language could not be thought of as a set of learned responses to a set of stimulus events. His argument had a number of different aspects. For example, he argued that children seem to acquire their first language too effortlessly – certainly more easily than adults learn a second language. He also argued that if the behaviourists were right then exposing children to impoverished or ungrammatical language should hinder their learning of the correct stimulus–response relationships. Yet studies show that much of the speech to which young children are exposed is indeed ungrammatical and otherwise impoverished, and this in no way prevents them from learning the grammar of their native tongue. Similarly, Chomsky argued that general intelligence ought to influence the learning of stimulus–response relationships. Again, however, intelligence does not seem to influence whether or not children learn the underlying grammatical rules of their language. Chomsky presented many other arguments to the same effect, and though many of these have been thought to be contentious, his position was extremely influential in setting up an alternative, cognitive conception of language. Most significantly, Chomsky proposed that language is rule-based and that, far from children learning language by learning how to respond to particular stimuli, their acquisition of language involves acquiring its rule-base. On this view, my being able to write grammatical sentences involves deploying my (generally implicit, or unconscious) knowledge of the rules of language. In referring to such implicit knowledge, Chomsky proposed that an understanding of how people produce, comprehend or acquire language will necessarily involve reference to something that cannot be observed directly – their knowledge of the underlying rules, or organization, of the language.

A challenge to strict behaviourism also came from work with non-human animals. Edward C. Tolman, himself a behaviourist, exposed hungry rats to a maze which contained food (see Figure 1.2) (Tolman, 1948). The rats rapidly learned to find the food following the series of left and right turns as would be predicted by stimulus–response theory. However, Tolman demonstrated that the rats had learned more than this: later, when the maze was modified so that the original arm was blocked and other arms were opened, animals ran along the arm that led directly to the food rather than along the one closest to the original arm. This suggested that the rats had learned where food was located, not just a chain of responses to obtain it. Tolman proposed that the rats had constructed a cognitive map, a mental construct that is neither directly observable nor measurable. Subsequently, many animal experiments have suggested that even non-human behaviour cannot all be explained adequately by strict behaviourist mechanisms. This book refers briefly to work involving animals, but if you are interested in finding out about the cognitive abilities of non-human species see Pearce (2008).

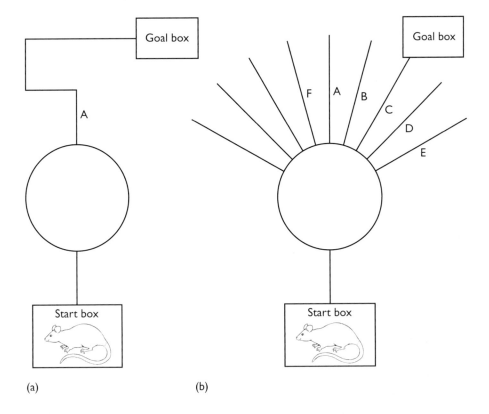

(a)   (b)

Figure 1.2   Rats are first trained in maze (a) and rapidly run from the start box to the food. The maze is then modified to become test maze (b) so that A is closed but a number of alternative paths are opened. If the rat had learned to run straight ahead it would choose arm B or arm F, which are closest to A; if it had learned the spatial location of the food it would choose the route that leads to the previous location of the food, route C. Results indicated that rats selected the direct route, C, rather than one of the routes closest to A

ACTIVITY 1.4

Imagine you carried out this experiment. Why do you think you would not put food in the goal box when you tested the animals in the second part of the experiment?

COMMENT

If the rat ran the most direct route it could be argued that, rather than responding to its representation of where in space the goal box was located, it smelt the food and simply followed its nose.

Although behaviourism was and indeed continues to be influential, interest in cognition continued in Britain. Frederic Bartlett investigated how what we remember depends on the type of internal mental representation we create and our desire to find meaning in what we've experienced. He typically presented fables reflecting different cultural ideas and narrative structures (such as the 'War of the ghosts' story; Bartlett, 1995 [1932]) and asked participants to recall the story as accurately as they could. Bartlett demonstrated that participants' recall was patchy and distorted, concentrating on aspects that would fit with their own preconceptions and knowledge. Rather than the verbatim recall Ebbinghaus was interested in, Bartlett was concerned with the way we extract the gist of what was experienced. This work has obvious implications for the way we interpret an eye-witness account of a crime – we need to appreciate the extent to which the witnesses' recall depends on preconceptions and expectations as well as on what actually happened. This is explored further in Chapter 16.

A major event during Bartlett's career was the Second World War, and its attendant technological developments. There was a practical need to train people to use the new devices and this required an understanding of human cognitive processes, particularly in attention and perception. Bartlett, along with Kenneth Craik, established the Applied Psychology Unit at the University of Cambridge, where much research into topics such as vigilance in radar operators and perception in pilots was carried out – and indeed the unit continues to contribute greatly to understanding of how cognition can be applied to the 'real world'. You can learn more about its work, past and present, from its website, at www.mrc-cbu.cam.ac.uk. Bartlett's student, Donald Broadbent, himself a Second World War pilot and later director of the Applied Psychology Unit, published highly influential work on how we attend to aspects of our environment. Chapter 2 considers this work and its development.

3.4 Cognition and the brain

Contemporary cognitive psychology has been greatly influenced by brain research as well as by the study of thought and behaviour. In the eighteenth century, Franz Gall proposed that different parts of the brain performed different functions, an idea that still has currency today, and that personality traits could be deduced from the shape of the skull, reflecting differently sized brain areas. This is known as phrenology, which has largely fallen out of favour, though replicas of Fowler's phrenologist's head (Figure 1.3) continue to be best-sellers. L.N. Fowler founded the British Phrenological Society, which continued to operate until the 1960s.

Gall proposed that language was controlled by the front part of the brain, and in 1860 Paul Broca, a French physician, reported the cases of two patients with severe aphasia who were found at post-mortem to have damage to their cerebral cortex, specifically the left frontal lobes. These brains have been preserved, and recent brain imaging (magnetic resonance imaging, MRI) has revealed that other, subcortical areas were damaged too (Dronkers *et al.*, 2007). Carl Wernicke, who was working in Germany at around the same time as Broca, documented aphasia cases where damage to a different area of the cortex resulted in slightly different symptoms. He developed a model of language production where different aspects were attributed to different anatomical areas of the brain. Although the exact detail of the model may

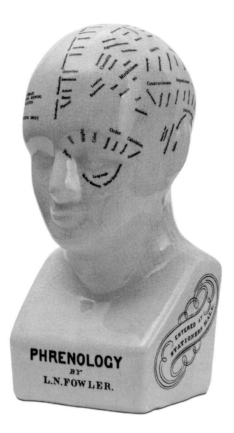

Figure 1.3   Fowler's phrenologist's head

not be correct, the idea that different parts of the brain contribute to particular cognitive abilities is accepted today.

Cognitive neuropsychology takes as its premise that studying a damaged system can help us to understand how the intact system works, so a close examination of the altered cognitive abilities of a person with brain damage can tell us much about normal cognition. A commonly drawn analogy is with a car. A person who doesn't know much about what goes on under the bonnet may only begin to understand how the parts of an engine work together when the car develops a fault. Studying damaged brains can inform us in two ways. First, it can tell us about possible functions of different brain structures, which Ward (2010) refers to as classical neuropsychology. Second, it can inform us about the involvement of different cognitive components in cognition (cognitive neuropsychology). For example, Henry Molaison (HM) had a particular part of his brain, the medial temporal lobes, removed as treatment for severe epilepsy. Following the operation HM was found to have severe memory problems: in particular, he was impaired in his ability to remember new information for any length of time. This case and others like it, as well as findings from animal experiments, have led to theories of the function of medial temporal lobe structures – an example of classical neuropsychology. During the intensive study that HM was subject to, it became clear that he was able to learn new motor skills such as mirror drawing and retain the ability over a long period of time. Interestingly, though, he had no conscious memory of the practice he'd had in acquiring the skills. This evidence of dissociation between motor skill memory and memory of the practice sessions supports models of cognition that propose that there are different types of long-term memory, and is an example of cognitive neuropsychology.

Henry Molaison died in December 2008 aged 84. During 2009 his brain underwent dissection into microscopically thin slices. These will be examined to build up a full picture of the exact size and position of the lesions, and results of the analyses will be posted on the Web.

Both classical and cognitive neuropsychology are the subject matter of neuroscience, though perhaps not surprisingly this module will mostly consider the contribution of cognitive neuropsychology to our understanding of cognition.

We have introduced two major methods of investigation in cognitive psychology, experimentation and cognitive neuropsychology. Box 1.2 lists similarities and differences between the two.

1.2   **Methods**

Some similarities and differences between experimentation and cognitive neuropsychology

Similarities

- Both assume that there is a commonality among people; that is, that everyone's cognitive system functions in basically the same way. So both methods rely on generalizing from the sample of people under investigation to the whole population.

- Both assume that cognition can be fractionated; that is, that it is possible to separate one aspect, such as memory, from the rest of cognition and that it will function normally when isolated in that way.

- Both methods involve testing people on a set of tasks the investigator has decided upon. These are often rather artificial, perhaps requiring participants to memorize a word list or carry out a reasoning task.

Differences

- Experiments typically test large numbers of participants; cognitive neuropsychology studies often rely on single-subject designs and investigate only one person with a particular type of brain damage.

- Experiments usually collect a specific piece of quantitative data from each participant, for example a reaction time or an error rate. Investigations involving a brain-damaged individual may collect more data, often qualitative as well as quantitative.

→

- In an experiment the experimenter decides what will be manipulated and randomly allocates participants to groups. In a well-controlled experiment it is possible to identify causes and effects; that is, to demonstrate that manipulating the independent variable causes changes in the dependent variable. In neuropsychology brain damage occurs accidentally, so the brain-damaged person or group is 'preselected'. This means that in neuropsychological studies the investigator can never be sure that the brain-damaged person was 'normal' before the accident and so can't be confident that unusual behaviour after the accident was caused by the damage to the brain.

- In an experiment participants are usually volunteers who are fully aware of the commitments they are making. It could be argued that participants who have suffered brain damage are less able to give fully informed consent.

3.5 Computers and the mind

In 1943 Kenneth Craik, a former research student of Bartlett's, published a book entitled *The Nature of Explanation* in which he developed the idea that people construct mental models of the world and that it is these models, or representations, that direct behaviour. In the book he draws parallels between the way people mentally model the world and physical models we might build to predict how, for example, a bridge might withstand a heavy weight being placed on it. This mechanistic way of considering how cognitive processes work fits with another development in the mid twentieth century that influenced the development of cognitive psychology: the possibility of designing and then building computers to process information. Alan Turing was a mathematician working at Bletchley Park, where he played a central role in developing ways of decrypting Enigma codes. In 1936 he developed an abstract specification for a machine (a Turing machine) that could compute any mathematical function that in principle could be computed. Technological progress was rapid, and within ten years John von Neumann articulated a set of architectural proposals for designing programmable, general-purpose computers. These developments carry important implications for our understanding and study of the mind. They appeared to show, for example, that reasoning, a central feature of the human mind, could be implemented in a digital computer. If that were the case, then not only could the computer be used as a tool to aid our understanding of the mind, but the question would also arise as to whether minds and computers are essentially alike. Indeed, in 1950, Turing proposed a test – the Turing test – by which he thought we should judge whether two entities have the same intelligence. Turing believed that should the situation ever arise whereby we could not distinguish the intelligence of a human from the 'intelligence' of a computer, then we ought to concede that both were equally intelligent. Moreover, since we are in agreement that humans are capable of thought, we ought to concede that computers too are capable of thought.

Box 1.3 outlines the Turing test and considers what it might take for it to be passed.

1.3

The Turing test: can computers think?

Turing proposed that we could determine whether a computer can think by judging whether it succeeds in what he called the imitation game. In the game there are three participants, two humans (A and B) and a computer (C). The arrangement of the participants and the communication flow between them is schematically indicated in Figure 1.4.

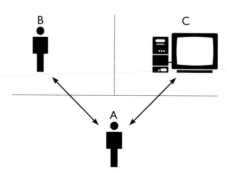

Figure 1.4   The arrangement of the participants in Turing's imitation game

The participants are positioned in separate rooms, so each one is unable to see, hear or touch the others. However, one of the human participants (A) is connected via a VDU terminal connection to the other human participant (B) and also to the computer (C). A can communicate electronically with both B and C. The goal for A is to ascertain which of B and C is the computer, and which the human. The goal of B, the other human, is to assist A in making the correct identification (perhaps by trying to appear as human as possible). C's goal, by contrast, is to lead A into making the wrong identification (by imitating human behaviour). C wins the game if A cannot reliably identify C as the computer. Turing's claim was that if a computer could simulate human behaviour so successfully that another human could not tell that it was a computer, then the computer could legitimately be said to think.

Turing's position remains controversial, of course, though it certainly captured the imagination of the time. In 1956, at the Dartmouth Conference (held in Dartmouth, New Hampshire), John McCarthy coined the phrase 'Artificial Intelligence' (or AI). He founded AI labs at the Massachusetts Institute of Technology in 1957, and then another at Stanford in 1963, and so began a new academic discipline, predicated on the possibility that humans are not the only ones capable of exhibiting human-like intelligence.

The notion that computer models can demonstrate intelligent behaviour was further explored by David Marr in the 1970s, and his influential book *Vision* was published posthumously in 1982. Marr's computer model of vision is described in Chapter 3; here we will outline his argument that in order to understand a cognitive system three levels of analysis need to be considered. The first of these is the **computational** or functional level. By this Marr meant what the system needs to compute – that is, what its output needs to be, and what input it is provided with. To draw on one of Marr's examples, we as humans have binocular stereopsis, the ability to put together the information collected by our two eyes to form a three-dimensional image. So, the inputs to the system are two slightly different 2D images (one on the retina of each eye) and the output is a 3D image where we can appreciate the spatial relationships between objects. The **algorithmic** or process level of analysis specifies how a computation can be achieved – what processes and calculations need to be applied to the input to achieve the output. In the example of stereoptic vision, the images from our two eyes need to be compared, the same features identified on each and the distance between those features calculated. Finally, the **implementational** level specifies how the algorithm is realized physically – the way the 'hardware' works. In human or animal vision this level involves understanding how retinal receptors affect neurons in the visual pathways. In a computer model of vision the implementational level might involve transistors, diodes and the like (or at least in Marr's time it did). Cognitive psychologists tend to explain cognition at the computational and algorithmic levels – that is, they consider the functions and processes of cognition. The implementational level tends to be the domain of neuroscientists, though undoubtedly biological factors constrain the algorithms that can be used. This is a very brief description of what is involved in the different levels of analysis, and a fuller account is provided by Glennerster (2007), who considers Marr's legacy to cognitive psychology.

You have now been introduced to a variety of the influences that have contributed to contemporary cognitive psychology and may appreciate that cognitive psychology has inherited some of the behaviourist concerns with scientific method.

Throughout this book you will see that almost constant reference is made to systematic observations of human behaviour (and sometimes animal behaviour too). Almost every chapter will present the results of empirical investigations of normal individuals and those who have suffered brain damage – these studies are fundamental in guiding our understanding. But cognitive psychology rejects the exclusive focus on what is observable. As Lashley and Chomsky implied, understanding the mind requires us to consider what lies behind behaviour – to ask what rules or processes govern the behaviour we observe. Each chapter will also consider the extent to which we understand how the mind processes information, and how that information is represented. The application of research is also a major part of cognitive psychology and most chapters of this book will consider how far what is learned in the laboratory is used and useful in the 'real world'.

Cognitive psychology also has a major commitment to the use of computers as a device for aiding our understanding of the mind. Computers are used as research equipment to control experiments, to present stimuli, to record responses and to tabulate and analyse data.

Computers in DD303

In DD303 you will use computers to carry out experimental procedures and to analyse your data. The software you will use provides a handy shortcut to presenting stimuli and recording the responses precisely, as well as carrying out accurate mathematical operations on the data. Knowing exactly how the software works is not required and it is certainly unlikely that the calculations use the same processes that you would use if you were to do the maths by hand.

Computers are also used as a research tool – if we can implement reasoning in a computer, for example, we may gain insight into how reasoning might be implemented in the brain. This is a different situation: here we are interested in how similar the processes used by the computer software and the person might be. So, most of the chapters in this book will also discuss ways in which researchers have used computer models to help us understand how the mind processes and represents information when people perform certain behaviours.

Yet the difficulty remains that if cognitive psychology is concerned with the processes and representations of the mind, and these cannot be directly observed, how can cognitive psychologists bridge the gap? How do we speculate about the nature of something we cannot observe, while remaining scientific?

Summary of Section 3

- Cognitive psychology inherits some of the behaviourist concerns with scientific method. Each chapter in this book presents the results of empirical investigations – investigations that are fundamental in guiding our understanding.
- Cognitive psychology rejects an exclusive focus on what is observable. Almost every chapter considers the extent to which we understand how the mind processes information, and how that information is represented.
- Studying abnormal cognitive performance can aid our understanding of normal cognition.
- Cognitive psychology is committed to using computers as a tool for aiding our understanding of the mind.
- Computers are used as research equipment to control experiments, to present stimuli, to record responses and to tabulate and analyse data.
- Computers are used as a research tool – if we can implement reasoning in a computer, for example, we may gain insight into how reasoning might be implemented in the brain.

4   Science, models and the mind

So, how *can* cognitive psychologists bridge the gap? How *do* we speculate about the nature of something we cannot observe, while remaining scientific? There are broadly three kinds of answer.

First, scientific theories commonly invoke unobservable theoretical entities to account for observational data (e.g. force fields, electron energy levels, genes or cognitive operations). So, postulating the unobservable is not of itself unscientific.

The second answer builds on the first. When a theory hypothesizes an unobservable, theoretical construct, a model needs to be specified of the relationship between the construct and the behaviour to be explained. It would have been insufficient for Newton to have tried to explain why things fall to Earth by simply invoking the notion of gravitation. He went further and derived equations to model the effects of gravity, and which can be used to generate predictions about how gravity ought to work for things whose motion has not yet been systematically observed. So physicists could then perform studies in order to confirm the predictions (that is, until Einstein's theories of relativity, but that is another story). Cognitive psychology proceeds in a similar way. Consider again the example of language. Cognitive psychologists have made numerous detailed observations of the production (and comprehension) of language. Explaining these observations, however, seems to require positing things internal to the mind that are involved in producing the observed behaviour. These are the unobservable, theoretical constructs of mental processes and structures. Positing these, of course, is just the starting point. The challenge for cognitive psychologists has been to say more. They have to develop models of these mental structures and processes and show how they give rise to the observed behaviour and, importantly, how successfully they predict behaviour that has not yet been systematically studied in experiments.

Now, developing a model is not an easy task. Newton apparently needed the inspiration provided by an apple falling to Earth (or so the story goes ...). And much of the challenge facing cognitive psychologists is to harness their creativity and imagination in order to suggest plausible models. Throughout your reading of this book, you might wish to consider how you would have responded to some of the problems described. You might want to consider what would constrain your choice of model, what kinds of model you would have developed, and how you would have set about doing this. Without doubt, these are difficult questions – so don't lose too much sleep over them! – but at least they serve to show how creative cognitive psychology is. Creative, too, is the matter of devising studies in order to evaluate a model. By working out the predictions a model might make, psychologists can evaluate models by devising studies to test the predictions, and by then making the relevant behavioural observations.

Creating models and designing studies to test them is not easy, but cognitive psychologists can use computers to help. The previous section suggested two ways in which computers are important to cognitive psychology other than as experimental equipment: computers might be things capable of thought; and they can also serve as tools for implementing models such as a model of language processes. Now, perhaps, you can see how they might contribute to the scientific objectives of cognitive psychology – researchers can use computers in order to create cognitive models. Just as computer programmers can build programs to do things such as word processing or financial accounts, so researchers in cognitive psychology can program computers to behave according to a particular model of the mind. Using computers to program particular models can be helpful on a number of counts.

Models can rapidly become very complicated, and too complicated to be expressed verbally, or for one person to hold all the relevant details in mind. This problem affects others too – meteorologists increasingly use computer models of weather systems, and economists use computer models of the economy. The phenomena involved are so complicated that, without computers, they would be almost impossible to model.

It is not always easy to work out the predictions of a model. Programming a model can allow researchers to simulate the effects of different conditions and so find out how the model behaves, and whether this behaviour accurately predicts how humans will behave. Perhaps most importantly of all, by programming a cognitive model into a computer researchers can determine whether the model is internally consistent (whether there are statements in the model that contradict one another), and whether the model is already stated clearly and precisely. If it is, the computer program will run; otherwise, it will crash.

1.4

When is a model a good model?

Source: adapted from Mulholland and Watt in an earlier edition of this book

In this box we consider three evaluative criteria against which a cognitive model can be judged:

- the extent to which the behaviour of the model fits human performance

- the validity of the model from the viewpoint of psychological theory

- the parsimony of the model – the extent to which unnecessary complication is avoided.

Cognitive modelling can be described as building a model of a cognitive process and comparing the behaviour of the model against human performance. If the model behaves in the same way as humans, then the structure of the model and the way it works may give some insight into how humans perform the task. Clearly, if the behaviour of the model does not mirror human performance, then there is no support for the hypothesis that the internal workings of the model reflect human cognitive processes. And, of course, this failure of a model to fit the data can itself be an important and useful lesson learned.

This leads us to our second criterion. The internal structure of the model, by which it produces behaviour, needs to be defensible in terms of the psychological literature. We could, for example, build a model of how chess players select a move that involves a process of comparing multiple images of possible boards. There is no evidence from experimental studies that humans possess such an ability. However, a model that incorporated a limited-capacity working memory would fit with empirical evidence.

Our third criterion is parsimony. The law of parsimony or **Ockham's Razor** states that an explanation of a phenomenon should not contain any unnecessary detail. Specifically, and in relation to cognitive modelling, a model should contain only the minimum number of components and so should not contain components that do not impact on the behaviour of the model. Therefore, any component of a model has to provide explanatory significance that justifies the additional complexity that it also brings. So, Ockham's Razor requires that a model is as simple as it can be.

Thus cognitive psychology can posit the existence of unobservable (cognitive) processes and structures and still be scientific. Not only is this true of other disciplines, such as physics and chemistry, but, like those disciplines, the gap between observable behaviour and unobservable processes and structures can be bridged via the creation and evaluation of models.

There is, however, a new possibility for linking cognitive processes with a focus on observation, and this leads to the third answer to the question with which this section began: a way to bridge the gap. The advent of new techniques for imaging the brain suggests that, just possibly, mental processes and structures may not be entirely unobservable (as the behaviourists once believed).

4.1   Cognitive neuroscience and the mind

The end of the twentieth century and the beginning of the twenty-first has seen huge technological advances in our ability to observe and measure brain activity while we are performing cognitive tasks. We are able to detect which parts of the brain become active, and in what order when a particular task is performed, and we can compare brain activity in cognitive tasks that we believe involve similar mechanisms. Functional MRI (fMRI), positron emission tomography (PET) and other kinds of imaging detect minute changes in the brain and, again with the aid of computers, allow us to see which parts of the brain become especially active when people are engaged in a certain task (relative to when they are engaged in some control task or tasks). There is considerable debate in the cognitive community as to the usefulness of imaging techniques for helping researchers to develop theories of cognition. Activity 1.5 will help you get a sense of the issues involved.

ACTIVITY 1.5

Consider the images in colour Plate 1. These are images of the brain of a person who is taking part in a semantic categorization task. In the experiment a trial consists of presenting three words serially then requiring the participant to judge whether the fourth word belongs to the same category as the first three. The control trials involve presenting three strings of letters and asking whether a fourth string is composed of the same letter. The experiment investigated whether categorizing living and non-living things involves different brain areas. Using fMRI, Devlin *et al.* (2000) found no systematic differences in brain activation when judgements involved inanimate or animate categories. The orange colouring on the brain images illustrates the extent and location of activation in the semantic task compared with that during the letter string control trials.

While you are looking at the images consider the following questions:

- What can you infer from the images alone?

- What does the indication of activity in particular brain regions tell you? Think about the processes going on inside participants' minds.

- What additional information would you need to be able to say what the brain activity represents? Suppose you were given very detailed anatomical descriptions of the active regions: what would that enable you to conclude?

COMMENT

It is one thing to say that there is activity in particular regions of the brain, but quite another to say exactly what cognitive processes and structures are involved. An image of brain activity, on its own, does not help very much. Seemingly, what is crucially needed is the further information as to what information each brain region processes – that is, we need to know the function of the active regions. One way of trying to identify the function of different brain regions is to compare brain images for different kinds of task – regions that are active for all tasks may be implicated in information processing that is common to those tasks. This assumes we have good models for the information-processing characteristics of different tasks. If so, and also using anatomical and neuropsychological evidence, researchers can then tentatively begin to identify particular regions with particular functions. This in turn can help researchers to interpret and design further brain imaging studies.

One criticism of imaging studies is that, at best, they help researchers to localize a particular function – that is, researchers can identify the function with a particular region of the brain – but they do not improve our theories of cognition. However, this is a bit like saying that being able to see chromosomes and genes using a very powerful microscope does not improve the theory of genetic inheritance. Well, in one sense that is true. But making visible entities that were previously only theoretical does increase overall confidence in the theory. For example, in Chapter 6 there is a discussion of how, when people recognize a stimulus as having been presented previously, they may indicate that they remember the exact circumstances when it was previously presented, or they may just have a strong feeling of familiarity without being able to tie it down to a particular time or event. Tulving (1985) referred to these types of responses as 'remember' or 'know', and there is considerable debate, summarized in Chapter 6, about the distinction between the two. Studies by Henson and colleagues (reviewed by Henson, 2005) using fMRI have found that different brain areas are active when participants report remembering or 'just knowing' that a stimulus was presented previously. Colour Plate 2 illustrates the differences, which provide support for models that propose that the two responses reflect different types of memory.

Imaging techniques continue to improve technologically and will contribute to cognitive theory in various ways. At one level, brain activity can be treated as a dependent variable – a measurable response to an independent variable. At another level, understanding the structure and processes of the brain may help us appreciate why our cognitive processing works in particular ways; for example, why do some attentional processes appear to operate serially and others in parallel? To continue with the genetic analogy, when genes were first made visible, genetic engineering was a very distant prospect, but it is hard to imagine the latter without the former. The advances in cognitive sciences to which neuroimaging will contribute are equally hard to predict, but we will be surprised if they do not prove to be many and varied.

Summary of Section 4

- Cognitive psychology can be scientific, while being interested in what goes on, unseen, inside the mind for a number of reasons.
- Other natural sciences invoke unobservable entities and are not as a consequence rendered unscientific.
- Like other sciences, cognitive psychology proceeds by modelling what cannot be observed, to produce predictions that can be tested by conducting appropriate studies.
- The advent of imaging technology, though undoubtedly contentious, raises the prospect of observing processes that were previously unobservable.

5   Conclusions

In this chapter we have attempted to outline some of the history of cognitive psychology and its subject matter. As we have seen, cognitive psychology has a relatively long history, and has made and continues to make many connections with other disciplines. To understand the nature of cognitive psychology, we have had to consider a wide range of issues, from computation to neuroimaging; from mundane but complex behaviour such as understanding language to the skills involved in tracking aircraft on a radar screen. Our survey has touched on action, perception, thinking, language, problem solving, categorization and consciousness. We have considered the nature of scientific investigation, the importance of observation and the need for, and practice of, sciences to posit theoretical entities that cannot be observed. The breadth of the many issues we have raised testifies to the importance of developing a systematic and rigorous understanding of the mind. It also, we believe, points to the fascination and enjoyment that we hope you will gain from studying cognitive psychology.

Nonetheless, we do not mean to suggest that cognitive psychology does not present any real challenges or problems – far from it. Most, if not all, of the topics we will consider in this book are still not fully understood. Though cognitive psychology has proved remarkably successful so far, it remains to be seen just how well it will deliver a full understanding. Indeed, while there are topics such as attention and perception where cognitive psychologists have made great progress, others, such as consciousness and emotion, still present real challenges. In this short chapter we have had to omit much of importance, and this chapter should be regarded as simply a partial survey of the foundations of cognitive psychology, intended to help you make the most of the chapters that follow.

Further reading

Mandler, G. (2007) *A History of Modern Experimental Psychology: From James and Wundt to Cognitive Science*, Cambridge, MA, MIT Press. In this book George Mandler provides a much more detailed account of the roots of cognitive psychology than we are able to give in this chapter.

Pearce, J.M. (2008) *Animal Learning and Cognition: An Introduction* (3rd edn), Hove, Psychology Press. In this book John Pearce provides a fascinating review of the cognitive abilities of non-human animals that complements the emphasis on human cognition in DD303.

Ward, J. (2010) *The Student's Guide to Cognitive Neuroscience* (2nd edn), Hove, Psychology Press. Here, Jamie Ward provides a comprehensive and student-friendly guide to neuroscience that extends the biological aspects of psychology that you'll study in DD303.

References

Bartlett, F.C. (1995 [1932]) *Remembering: A Study in Experimental and Social Psychology* (2nd edn), Cambridge, Cambridge University Press.

Chomsky, N. (1959) 'A review of B.F. Skinner's "Verbal Behavior"', *Language*, vol.35, no.1, pp.26–58.

Devlin, J.T., Russell, R.P., Davis, M.H., Price, C.J., Wilson, J., Moss, H.E., Matthews, P.M. and Tyler, L.K. (2000) 'Susceptibility induced loss of signal: comparing PET and fMRI on a semantic task', *NeuroImage*, vol.11, pp.589–600.

Dronkers, N.F., Plaisant, O.M., Iba-Zizen, T. and Cabanis, E.A. (2007) 'Paul Broca's historic cases: high resolution MR imaging of the brains of Leborgne and Lelong', *Brain*, vol.130, no.5, pp.1432–41.

Glennerster, A. (2007) 'Marr's vision: twenty five years on', *Current Biology*, vol.17, no.11, pp.397–9.

Henson, R.N.A. (2005) 'What can functional neuroimaging tell the experimental psychologist?', *Quarterly Journal of Experimental Psychology*, vol.58A, pp.193–233.

James, W. (1981 [1890]) *The Principles of Psychology*, Cambridge, MA, Harvard University Press.

Marr, D. (1982) *Vision: A Computational Investigation into the Human Representation and Processing of Visual Information*, New York, W.H. Freeman.

Muise, J.G., Brun, V. and Porelle, M. (1997) 'Salience of central figure in the Ebbinghaus illusion: the Oreo cookie effect', *Perceptual and Motor Skills*, vol.85, pp.1203–08.

Pearce, J.M. (2008) *Animal Learning and Cognition: An Introduction* (3rd edn), Hove, Psychology Press.

Skinner, B.F. (1957) *Verbal Behavior*, New York, Appleton-Century-Crofts.

Tolman, E.C. (1948) 'Cognitive maps in rats and men', *Psychological Review*, vol.55, pp.189–208.

Tulving, E. (1985) 'Memory and consciousness', *Canadian Psychology*, vol.26, pp.1–12.

Turing A.M. (1950) 'Computing machinery and intelligence', *Mind*, vol.59, pp.433–60.

Van Ulzen, N.R., Semin, G.R., Oudejans, R.D. and Beek, P.J. (2008) 'Affective stimulus properties influence size perception and the Ebbinghaus illusion', *Psychological Research*, vol.72, no.3, pp.304–10.

Ward, J. (2010) *The Student's Guide to Cognitive Neuroscience* (2nd edn), Hove, Psychology Press.

Watson, J.B. (1930) *Behaviorism* (revd edn), Chicago, IL, University of Chicago Press.

PART 1
PERCEPTUAL PROCESSES

Introduction

In Part 1 you will find chapters on attention, perception and recognition. Why do we begin with these particular topics? Well, there is a fairly strong tradition of placing these topics early in books on cognition, and there are at least two reasons for this. First, there is a strong applied psychology theme to all these topics, whether it is finding better ways to present relevant information to people in safety-critical occupations, such as aircraft pilots, devising techniques for improving eye-witness identification, or designing machines that can 'see' and 'recognize'. Second, attention, perception and recognition are all topics that concern the relationship between the mind and the world, which seems a good place to start trying to understand the mind itself. Other chapters – for example, Chapter 8 on language processing – also address the issue of how information from the world gets 'into' the mind, but the topics of attention, perception and recognition provide particularly direct questions relating to it. Why do we become aware of some aspects of the environment rather than others? How is it that we manage to perceive those things we do become aware of? And for those things we do consciously perceive, how do we come to recognize what they are?

As you will see, these turn out to be far from simple questions and to require far from simple answers. A key issue that comes up in all three chapters has to do with distinguishing between aspects of the world (physics), how these aspects affect the body and especially the nervous system (physiology), and what mental representations result (cognitive psychology). In Chapter 2, you will learn what kinds of physical energy the auditory system uses to represent the location of a sound source; in Chapter 3 you will encounter a theory of how the visual system comes to represent Gestalt organization, which is easily mistaken for a property of the world rather than of the mind; in Chapter 4 you will see how different aspects of the same physical face – familiarity, identity, emotional tone – are processed by different physiological pathways and have separate cognitive representations.

A further key issue that emerges in all three chapters is the fractionation of functions. It turns out that there is not just one sort of attention but many different forms of it. Similarly, it transpires that visual perception is far from being a unitary function; in fact, vision is made up of such a multitude of component processing streams that Chapter 3 has space to mention only some of them. As indicated in the previous paragraph, recognition can also be analysed into different processes, and a similar fractionation will recur in later chapters in relation to other mental functions such as memory. (How we should conceptualize all these cognitive functions and their subcomponents is something it might be useful to consider in the light of Chapter 9 on categorization.) Allied to the issue of how cognitive functions can be analysed into component processes are questions as to which of these processes result in representations that are or are not consciously experienced, and which can be carried out in parallel and which only one at a time.

A common theme across all the chapters is the use of neuropsychological evidence to help elucidate key issues such as those we have just identified. Injury to the brain can affect attention, perception and recognition in quite unexpected ways. Studying the behavioural and phenomenological consequences of injury to specific parts of the brain, relating neuroanatomy to behaviour and conscious experience, throws light upon the structure of cognition by providing both tests of psychological theories and grounds from which theories may be derived.

Another issue common to all the chapters is the extent to which stored knowledge enters into the functions of attention, perception and recognition. These functions might be purely stimulus-driven; that is, driven by physical properties of the world. But if they are not, then at what stage in processing does prior knowledge exert its influence? Do we, for example, necessarily identify a plant *before* picking it? If not, why would we tend to avoid picking stinging nettles with bare hands? Do we perceive familiar faces in the same way that we perceive unfamiliar faces? If not, does familiarity also affect perception of other classes of object? It is important that answers to such questions are given within a theoretical context. When you have read the chapters, you should reflect on how well or how badly cognitive psychological theories have fared in recent decades.

In Chapter 2, Peter Naish describes such different forms of attention as attention to regions of space, attention to objects and attention for action, but attempts finally to summarize them all under a single fairly abstract definition of the term. He shows how ideas about attention have changed and diversified over the last fifty years and considers how well the early theories have stood up to examination. In Chapter 3, Graham Pike and Graham Edgar consider top-down and bottom-up theories of perception, and propose a resolution in terms of perception for recognition and perception for action. They also introduce and evaluate Marr's computational framework for a bottom-up theory of perception. Lastly, in Chapter 4, Graham Pike and Nicola Brace describe and contrast two theories of object perception, as well as a model of face perception that has been implemented as a connectionist network. Across the chapters you will encounter theories being tested and sometimes confirmed and sometimes found wanting. You will also meet the idea that different theories may be complements of one another rather than simply alternatives. One theory may succeed in one domain but fail in another, and vice versa for a second theory. You will also see how confidence in a theory varies with its range of application, and how confidence can be boosted if it proves possible to implement the theory as a working computer model. The challenge for the future is for theorists to develop more detailed and implementable theories of attention, perception and recognition whilst allowing that different people may find distinct ways of doing the same thing.

Attention

Chapter 2

Peter Naish

1   Auditory attention

For many of us the concept of attention may have rather negative connotations. At school we were told to pay attention, making us all too aware that it was not possible to listen to the teacher while at the same time being lost in more interesting thoughts. Neither does it seem possible to listen effectively to two different things at the same time. How many parents with young children would love to be able to do that! One could be excused for feeling that evolution has let us down by failing to enable us to process more than one thing at a time. If that is how you feel, then this chapter might add insult to injury, because it will cite evidence that we do in fact process a good deal of the material to which we are not attending. Why, you might ask, do we go to the trouble of analysing incoming information, only to remain ignorant of the results? To attempt an answer it is necessary to consider a range of issues, stretching from registration of information by the sense organs, through the processes of perception, to the nature of awareness and consciousness. Attention is a broad and intriguing topic. That breadth makes it very difficult to offer a simple definition of the term, so I will not attempt to do so until the end of the chapter.

To cover some of this topic (we have only a chapter, and there are whole books on the subject) I shall follow an approximately historical sequence, showing how generations of psychologists have tackled the issues and gradually refined and developed their theories. You will discover that initially there seemed to them to be only one role for attention, but that gradually it has been implicated in an ever-widening range of mental processes. As we work through the subject, two basic issues will emerge. One is concerned with the mechanisms of attention, and raises questions such as:

- How much material can we take in at once?
- What happens to information to which we did not attend?
- In what circumstances does attention fail, allowing unwanted information to influence or distract us?

The other theme has a more philosophical flavour, and raises questions concerning why we experience the apparent limitations of attention:

- Are the limitations simply an inevitable characteristic of a finite brain?
- Have we evolved to exhibit attention – that is, does it confer advantages?

We shall begin to explore these issues by looking at the ways in which one of our senses (hearing) has developed to facilitate attention.

1.1   Disentangling sounds

If you are still feeling aggrieved about the shortcomings of evolution, then you might take heart from the remarkable way in which the auditory system has evolved so as to avoid a serious potential problem. Unlike our eyes, our ears cannot be directed so as to avoid registering material that we wish to ignore; whatever sounds are present in the environment, we must inevitably be exposed to them. In a busy setting such as a party we are swamped by simultaneous sounds – people in different parts of the room all talking at the same time. An analogous situation for the visual system would be if several people wrote superimposed messages on the same piece of paper, and we then attempted to pick out one of the messages and read it. Because that kind of visual superimposition does not normally occur, there have been no evolutionary pressures for the visual system to find a solution to the problem (though see below). The situation is different with hearing, but the possession of two ears has provided the basis for a solution.

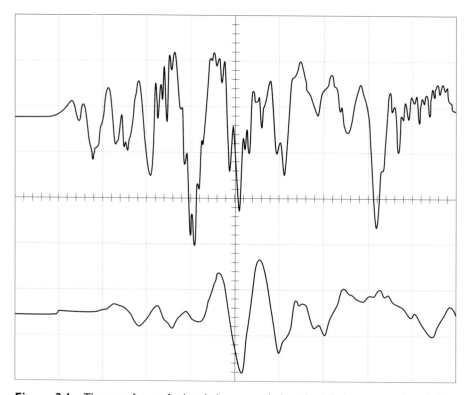

Figure 2.1   The waveform of a hand clap, recorded at the left (upper trace) and right (lower trace) ears. Horizontal squares represent durations of 500 microseconds (a microsecond is one-millionth of a second); vertical divisions are an arbitrary measure of sound intensity

Figure 2.1 shows a plot of sound waves recorded from inside a listener's ears. You can think of the up and down movements of the wavy lines as representing the in and out vibrations of the listener's ear drums. The sound was of a single hand clap, taking place to the front left of the listener. You will notice that the wave for the right ear (i.e. the one further from the sound) comes slightly later than the left (shown by the plot being shifted to the right). This right-ear plot also goes up and down far less, indicating that it was less intense, or in hearing terms that it sounded less loud at that ear. These differences, in timing and intensity, are important to the auditory system, as will be explained.

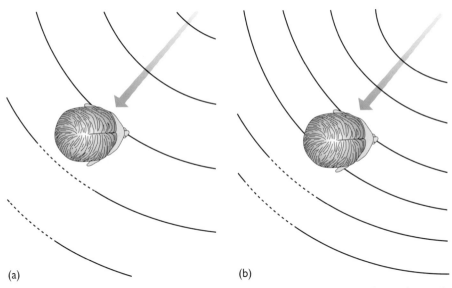

(a)   (b)

Figure 2.2 Curved lines represent wave crests of a sound approaching from a listener's front left. In (b) the sound has a shorter wavelength (higher pitch) than in (a), so waves are closer together, with a crest at each ear

Figure 2.2(a) represents sound waves spreading out from a source and passing a listener's head. Sound waves spread through the air in a very similar way to the waves (ripples) spreading across a pond when a stone is thrown in. For ease of drawing, the figure just indicates a 'snapshot' of the positions of the wave crests at a particular moment in time. Two effects are shown. First, the ear further from the sound is slightly shadowed by the head, so receives a somewhat quieter sound (as in Figure 2.1). The head is not a very large obstacle, so the intensity difference between the ears is not great; however, the difference is sufficient for the auditory system to register and use it. If the sound source were straight ahead there would be no difference, so the size of the disparity gives an indication of the sound direction. The figure also shows a second difference between the ears: a different wave part (crest) has reached the nearer left ear than the further right ear (which is positioned somewhere in a trough between two peaks). Once again, the inter-aural difference is eliminated for sounds coming from straight ahead, so the size of this difference also indicates direction.

Why should we make use of both intensity and wave-position differences? The reason is that neither alone is effective for all sounds. I mentioned that the head is not a very large obstacle; what really counts is how large it is compared with a **wavelength**. The wavelength is the distance from one wave crest to the next. Sounds which we perceive as low pitched have long wavelengths – longer in fact than the width of the head. As a result, the waves pass by almost as if the head was not there. This means that there is negligible intensity shadowing, so the intensity cue is not available for direction judgement with low-pitched sounds. In contrast, sounds which we experience as high-pitched (e.g. the jingling of coins) have wavelengths that are shorter than head width. For these waves the head is a significant obstacle, and shadowing results. To summarize, intensity cues are available only for sounds of short wavelength.

In contrast to the shadowing effect, detecting that the two ears are at different positions on the wave works well for long-wavelength sounds. However, it produces ambiguities for shorter waves. The reason is that if the wave crests were closer than the distance from ear to ear, the system would not be able to judge whether additional waves should be allowed for. Figure 2.2(b) shows an extreme example of the problem. The two ears are actually detecting identical parts of the wave, a situation which is normally interpreted as indicating sound coming from the front. As can be seen, this wave actually comes from the side. Our auditory system has evolved so that this inter-ear comparison is made only for waves that are longer than the head width, so the possibility of the above error occurring is eliminated. Consequently, this method of direction finding is effective only for sounds with long wavelengths, such as deeper speech sounds.

You will notice that the two locating processes complement each other perfectly, with the change from one to the other taking place where wavelengths match head width. Naturally occurring sounds usually contain a whole range of wavelengths, so both direction-sensing systems come into play and we are quite good at judging where a sound is coming from. However, if the only wavelengths present are about head size, then neither process is fully effective and we become poor at sensing the direction. Interestingly, animals have evolved to exploit this weakness. For example, pheasant chicks (which live on the ground and cannot fly to escape predators) emit chirps that are in the 'difficult' wavelength range for the auditory system of a fox. The chicks' mother, with her bird-sized head, does not have any problems at the chirp wavelength, so can find her offspring easily. For some strange reason, mobile telephone manufacturers seem to have followed the same principle. To my ears they have adopted ringtones with frequencies that make it impossible to know whether it is one's own or someone else's phone which is ringing!

ACTIVITY 2.1

1   Set up a sound source (the radio, say), then listen to it from across the room. Turn sideways-on, so that one ear faces the source. Now place a finger in that nearer ear, so that you can hear the sound only via the more distant ear. You should find that the sound seems more muffled and deeper, as if someone had turned down the treble on the tone control. This occurs because the shorter wavelength (higher-pitched) sounds cannot get round your head to the uncovered ear. In fact you may still hear a little of those sounds, because they can reflect from the walls, and so reach your uncovered ear 'the long way round'. Most rooms have sufficient furnishings (carpets, curtains, etc.) to reduce these reflections, so you probably will not hear much of the higher sounds. However, if you are able to find a rather bare room (bathrooms often have hard, shiny surfaces) you can use it to experience the next effect.

2   Do the same as before, but this time you do not need to be sideways to the sound. If you compare your experiences with and without the finger in one ear you will probably notice that, when you have the obstruction, the sound is more 'boomy' and unclear. This lack of clarity results from the main sound, which comes directly from the source, being partly smothered by slightly

later echoes, which take longer routes to your ear via many different paths involving reflections off the walls, etc. These echoes are still there when both ears are uncovered, but with two ears your auditory system is able to detect that the echoes are coming from different directions from the main sound source, enabling you to ignore them. People with hearing impairment are sometimes unable to use inter-aural differences, so find noisy or echoing surroundings difficult.

1.2   Attending to sounds

From the above, you will appreciate that the auditory system is able to separate different, superimposed sounds on the basis of their different source directions. This makes it possible to attend to any one sound without confusion, and we have the sensation of moving our 'listening attention' to focus on the desired sound. For example, as I write this I can listen to the quiet hum of the computer in front of me, or swing my attention to the bird song outside the window to my right. Making that change feels almost like swinging my eyes from the computer to the window and the term **spotlight of attention** has been used to describe the way in which we can bring our attention to bear on a desired part of the environment.

My account so far has explained the mechanisms that stop sounds becoming 'jumbled' and reminds us that, subjectively, we listen to just one of the disentangled sounds. It seems obvious that they would need disentangling to become intelligible, but why do we then attend to only one? That question leads us into the early history of attention research.

One of the first modern researchers formally to investigate the nature of auditory attention was Broadbent (1952, 1954), who used an experimental technique known as **dichotic listening**. This offers a way of presenting listeners with a simplified, more easily manipulated version of the real world of multiple sounds. Participants wear a pair of headphones, and receive a different sound in each ear; in many studies the sounds are recorded speech, each ear receiving a different message. Broadbent and others (e.g. Treisman, 1960) showed that, after attending to the message in one ear, a participant could remember virtually nothing of the unattended message that had been played to the other, often not even the language spoken.

Broadbent's experiments showed that two refinements should be made to the last statement. First, if the two messages were very short, say just three words in each ear, then the participant could report what had been heard by the unattended ear. The system behaved as if there were a short-lived store that could hold a small segment of the unattended material until analysis of the attended words was complete. Second, if the attended message lasted more than a few seconds, then the as yet unprocessed material in the other ear would be lost. The store's quality of hanging on to a sound for a short time, like a dying echo, led to it being termed the **echoic memory**.

It was also shown that people would often be aware of whether an unattended voice had been male or female, and they could use that distinction to follow a message. Two sequences of words were recorded, one set by a woman, the other by a man. Instead of playing one of these voice sequences to each headphone, the words were made to alternate. Thus, the man's voice jumped back and forth, left to right to left, while the woman's switched right to left to right. In this situation participants were able to abandon the normal 'attending by ear' procedure, and instead report what a particular speaker had said; instead of using location as a cue for attention, they were using the pitch of the voice.

The explanation for these findings seemed straightforward. Clearly the brain had to process the information in a sound in order to understand it as speech. In this respect, the brain was rather like a computer processing information (computers were beginning to appear at that time), and everyone knew that computers could only process one thing at a time – that is, **serially**. Obviously (theorists thought) the brain must be serial too, so, while processing the information of interest, it needed to be protected from all the rest: it needed to attend and select. However, the earliest stages of processing would have to take place in **parallel** (i.e. taking in everything simultaneously), ensuring that all information would potentially be available, but these initial processes would have to utilize very simple selection procedures; anything more complex would demand serial processing. The procedures were indeed simple: attention was directed either on the basis of the direction of a sound, or on whether it was higher- or lower-pitched. Broadbent's (1954) theory was that, after the first early stage of parallel information capture, a 'gate' was opened to one stream of information and closed to the rest.

2.1   Research study

Application of research on auditory attention

Donald Broadbent's early career included research for the UK Ministry of Defence, and his findings often led to innovation. One problem he addressed was the difficulty pilots experienced, when trying to pick out a radio message from a number of interfering stations (radio was less sophisticated then). Pilots' headphones delivered the same signals to each ear, so it was not possible to use inter-aural differences to direct attention to the wanted message. Broadbent devised a stereo system, which played the desired signal through *both* headphones, while the interference went only to one or the other. This made the interference seem to come from the sides, while the signal sounded as if it was in the middle (identical waves at the two ears). In effect, this was dichotic listening, with a third (wanted) signal between the other two. The improvement in intelligibility was dramatic, but when Broadbent played a recording to officials they decided that it was so good that he must have 'doctored' the signal! The system was not adopted. Decades later, I demonstrated (Naish, 1990) that using stereo, and giving a directional quality to the headphone warning sounds used in aircraft cockpits, could result in significantly shorter response times. Thus, the warning indicating an approaching missile could be made to seem as if coming from the missile direction, so speeding the pilot's evasive measures. The next generation of fighter aircraft may at last incorporate '3D' sound.

1.3 Eavesdropping on the unattended message

It was not long before researchers devised more complex ways of testing Broadbent's theory of attention, and it soon became clear that it could not be entirely correct. Even in the absence of formal experiments, common experiences might lead one to question the theory. An oft-cited example is the **cocktail party effect**. Imagine you are attending a noisy party, but your auditory location system is working wonderfully, enabling you to focus upon one particular conversation. Suddenly, from elsewhere in the room, you hear someone mention your name! If you were previously selecting the first conversation, on the basis of its direction and the speaker's voice, then how did your 'serial' brain manage to process another set of sounds in order to recognize your name?

Addressing this puzzle, Treisman (1960) suggested that, rather than the all-or-nothing selection process implied by Broadbent, the ability to pick out one's name could be explained by an **attenuation** process. The attenuation process would function as if there were a **filter**, 'turning the volume down' for all but the attended signal. Although that would leave most unattended material so attenuated as to be unnoticed, for a signal to which we were very sensitive, such as our own name, there would be sufficient residual information for it to be processed and hence attract our attention. Treisman devised a series of ingenious experiments which supported this idea. Many of her studies involved **shadowing**, a dichotic listening technique which requires the participant to repeat aloud everything that is heard in one ear, following like a shadow close behind the spoken message. (NB this is not to be confused with the very different 'head shadowing' referred to earlier.) This task demands concentration, and when the shadowed message ceases the participant appears to be completely ignorant of what was said in the other ear.

In one experiment Treisman actually made the storylines in the messages swap ears in the middle of what was being said. Thus, the left ear might hear:

Little Red Riding Hood finally reached the cottage, but the wicked wolf was in * beds; one was large, one medium and one small.

Meanwhile, the right ear would receive:

When she had finished the porridge, Goldilocks went upstairs and found three * bed, dressed in the grandmother's clothes.

The asterisks indicate where the storylines swap ears. The interesting finding is that when asked to shadow one ear participants tend to end by shadowing the other, because they follow the sense of the story. Broadbent's position could not explain that, since the listener could not know that the story continued in the other ear, if that ear had been completely ignored. Treisman, on the other hand, claimed that the story temporarily sensitized the listener to the next expected words, just as with the permanent sensitization associated with our own name. Sensitization of this temporary kind is known as **priming**, and many experimental techniques have demonstrated its existence. For example, in a **lexical decision task** (a task that requires participants to indicate as quickly as possible whether or not a string of letters spells a real word), people can respond much more quickly to a word if it is preceded by another related to it. For example, the 'Yes' is given to *doctor* (yes, because it is a word) more quickly when presented after the word *nurse* than when following the word *cook*.

Treisman's ideas stimulated a succession of experiments, some seeming to show that information could 'get through' from a wider range of stimuli than one's own name or a highly predictable word in a sentence. For example, Corteen and Wood (1972) carried out a two-part experiment. Initially they presented their participants with a series of words, and each time a word from a particular category (city name) appeared the participant was given a mild electric shock. In this way, an association was formed between the shock and the category. Although the shocks were not really painful, they inevitably resulted in something like mild apprehension when one of the critical words was presented. This response (which once learned did not require the shocks in order for it to continue) could be detected as a momentary change in skin electrical resistance. The sweat glands of a nervous person begin to secrete, and the salty fluid lowers the resistance to a small (non-shocking) electric current. The change is known as the **galvanic skin response (GSR)** and has been used in so-called lie detectors. Corteen and Wood connected their participants to GSR apparatus when they started the second part of the experiment: a dichotic listening task. As usual, participants could later remember nothing about the unattended message, but the GSR showed that each time the ignored ear received one of the 'shocked' words there was a response. Moreover, a GSR was detected even to words of the same category, but which had not been presented during the shock-association phase. This generalizing of the response to un-presented words strengthens the claim that their meanings were established, even when not consciously perceived.

Not surprisingly, at this stage of research into auditory attention a number of psychologists began to question the idea that the brain could not process more than one signal at a time. Deutsch and Deutsch (1963) suggested that *all* messages received the same processing, whether they were attended or not; Norman (1968) proposed that unattended information must at least receive sufficient processing to activate relevant semantic memories (i.e. the memory system that stores the meanings of words; see Chapter 6). These suggestions certainly explained the intriguing dichotic listening results, showing people to be influenced by material of which they seemed to have no knowledge. However, the ideas, if true, would require the brain to be far more parallel in its function than had been supposed. At that time there was neither an analogue by which parallel processing could be conceptualized, nor sufficient neuroanatomical information to contribute to the debate. Today there is ample evidence of the parallel nature of much of the brain's processing and, additionally, computers have advanced to the stage where brain-like parallel processing can be emulated. Thus, modern researchers have no difficulty in conceptualizing parallel processing and the nature of the attention debate has shifted somewhat. Nevertheless, recent studies have also revealed that early stages of analysis are modified by attention, effects that Broadbent would have immediately recognized as examples of filtering. We shall explore these issues in more depth, after first considering the nature of attention in visual processing.

Summary of Section 1

The auditory system is able to process sounds in such a way that, although several may be present simultaneously, it is possible to focus upon the message of interest. However, in experiments on auditory attention, there have been contradictory results concerning the fate of the unattended material:

- The auditory system processes mixed sounds in such a way that it is possible to focus upon a single wanted message.
- Unattended material appears not to be processed:
  - The listener is normally unable to report significant details concerning the unattended information.
  - Only the most recent unattended material is available, while still preserved in the echoic memory.
- These results suggest parallel acquisition of all available information, followed by serial processing to determine meaning for one attended message.
- Although there is little conscious awareness of unattended material, it may receive more processing than the above results imply:
  - Words presented to the unattended ear can produce priming and physiological effects.
  - Participants trying to 'shadow' one ear will follow the message to the other ear.
- These results imply that processing takes place in parallel, to the extent that meaning is extracted even from unattended material.

2 Visual attention

I introduced Section 1 by suggesting that the auditory system had a special problem: unlike the visual system, it needed processes which would permit a listener to attend to a specific set of sounds without being confused by the overlap of other, irrelevant noises. The implication of that line of argument was that vision had no need of any such system. However, although we do not see simultaneously *everything* that surrounds us, we can certainly see more than one thing at a time. Earlier, I wrote of attending to the sound of the computer in front of me, or of the birds to one side. I can do much the same visually. While keeping my eyes directed to the computer screen, I can either attend to the text I am typing or, out of the corner of my eye, I can be aware of the window and detect a bird when it flies past. If our eyes can receive a wide range of information in parallel, does that give the brain an attentional problem analogous to that of disentangling sounds? If visual information is handled in much the same way as auditory information seems to be, then we might expect the various items in the field of view to activate representations in memory simultaneously. That should lead to effects equivalent to those found in listening experiments; in other words, it might be possible to show that we are influenced by items which we did not know we had seen. We shall examine evidence of this shortly, but I shall first draw your attention to another area of similarity between hearing and seeing.

I pointed out at the start of Section 1.1 that, whereas we often have to follow one speech stream while ignoring others, we do not normally have to disentangle overlapping handwriting. However, it is worth bearing in mind that visual objects do overlap and hide parts of each other, and the brain certainly has the problem of establishing which components of the image on the retina 'go together' to form an object. This issue is examined in more depth in Chapter 3.

As with hearing, a variety of cues is available to help in directing visual attention. Taking my window again as an example, I can either look at the glass and see a smear (I really must get round to washing the window!), or I can look through that, to the magpie sitting chattering in the apple tree. In this kind of situation we use distance to help separate objects, in much the same way as we use direction in hearing. However, we can deploy our attention in a more sophisticated way than simply on the basis of distance, as can be demonstrated by another aircraft-related example.

Military jets are often flown very fast and close to the ground (to avoid radar detection), requiring the pilot to attend intently to the outside view. At the same time, there are various pieces of information, traditionally displayed on instruments within the cockpit, which the pilot must check frequently. To avoid the pilot having to look down into the cockpit, the 'head-up display' (HUD) was developed. This comprises a piece of glass, just in front of the pilot, in which all the vital information is reflected. The pilot can read the reflection, or look through it to the outside world, just as one can look at reflections in a shop window, or look through to the goods on display. With a simple reflection, the pilot would still have to change focus, like me looking at the smear or the bird. However, modern HUDs use an optical system which makes the information reflected in the display appear to be as far away as the outside scene. This saves valuable refocusing time. Nevertheless, although the numerals in the HUD now appear to be located at the same distance as, say, a runway, pilots still have the sensation of focusing on one or the other; if they are reading their altitude they are relatively unaware of the scene on which it is superimposed. This suggests (as we shall see in more detail later) that visual attention can be linked to specific objects rather than to general regions of space, very much as auditory attention can follow a particular speaker's voice, or the sense of a sentence.

2.1   Knowing about unseen information

An obvious difference between hearing and seeing is that the former is extended in time, while the latter extends over space. So, for example, we can listen to a spoken sentence coming from one place, but it takes some time to hear it all. In contrast, a written sentence is spread over an area (of paper, say) but, as long as it is reasonably short, it can be seen almost instantly. Nevertheless, seeing does require some finite time to capture and analyse the information. This process can be explored by presenting letters or words for a short, measured period of time; nowadays they are shown on a computer screen, but early research used a dedicated piece of apparatus, called a tachistoscope. Just how long was required to register a small amount of information was investigated by Sperling (1960), who showed participants grids of letters, arranged as three rows of four letters each. If such a display was presented for 50 ms (i.e. 50 milliseconds, which is one twentieth of a second), people were typically able to report three or four of the letters; the rest seemed to have remained unregistered in that brief period of time.

Sperling explored this further. He cued participants with a tone, indicating which of the three rows of letters they should try to report: a high note for the top row, lower for middle and deep for bottom. Crucially, the tones were not presented until just *after* the display had disappeared, meaning that participants were not able to shift their attention in preparation for the relevant row of letters when presented: it already had been presented. Strange as it seemed, people were still able to report three or four items from the cued row. Since they did not know until after the display had gone which row would be cued, this result implied that they must have registered most of the letters in *every row*; in other words, between nine and 12 letters in total. This apparent paradox, of seeming to know about a larger proportion of the items when asked only to report on some of them, is called the **partial report superiority effect**. The effect was also observed if letters were printed six in red and six in black ink, then two tones used to indicate which colour to report. Participants seemed to know as much about one half (the red, say) as they did about all 12, implying that, although they could not report all the letters, there was a brief moment when they did have access to the full set and could choose where to direct their attention. The 'brief moment' was equivalent to the echoic memory associated with dichotic listening experiments, so the visual counterpart was termed an **iconic memory** (an icon being an image). All the material seemed to be captured in parallel, and for a short time was held in iconic memory. Some was selected for further, serial processing, on the basis of position or colour; these being analogous to position and voice pitch in dichotic listening tasks. Unselected material (the remaining letters) could not be remembered.

With the close parallels between these auditory and visual experiments, you will not be surprised to learn that the simple selection and serial-processing story was again soon challenged, and in very similar ways. Where the hearing research used shadowing to prevent conscious processing of material, the visual experiments used **backward masking**. Masking is a procedure in which one stimulus (the target) is rendered undetectable by the presentation of another (the mask); in backward masking the mask is presented after the target, usually appearing in the order of 10–50 ms after the target first appeared. The time between the onset of the target display and the onset of the mask is called the **stimulus onset asynchrony** (SOA). The target might be an array of letters or words; this disappears after a few tens of milliseconds, to be replaced by the mask, which is often a random pattern of lines. The SOA can be adjusted until participants report that they do not even know whether there has been a target, let alone what it was. In such circumstances the influence of the masked material seems sometimes still to be detected via priming effects. Thus, Evett and Humphreys (1981) used stimulus sequences containing two words, both of which were masked. The first was supposed to be impossible to see, while the second was very difficult. It was found that when the second word was related to the first (e.g. 'tiger' following 'lion') it was more likely to be reported accurately; the first, 'invisible' word apparently acted as a prime.

Claims such as these have not gone unchallenged. For example, Cheesman and Merikle (1984) pointed out that although participants say they cannot see masked words, they often do better than chance when forced to guess whether or not one had actually been presented. These researchers insisted that proper conclusions about extracting meaning from unseen material could be made only if the material was truly unseen; that is, when the participants could do no better than chance. Under these conditions they found no evidence for priming by masked words. However, more recently researchers have provided persuasive evidence that meaning *can* be extracted from material of which the participant is unaware. This is worth examining in more detail.

Pecher *et al.* (2002) used the Evett and Humphreys (1981) technique, but with modifications. As in the earlier study, they showed a potential prime (e.g. 'lion'), followed by a hard-to-see masked target (e.g. 'tiger'). However, there were two changes in this study. First, the priming word could be displayed either for a very short time, so that it was allegedly undetectable, or it was shown for a duration of 1 second, giving ample time for reading and guaranteeing a priming effect.

The second change was to use two sets of trials. In one, the following target was almost always (90 per cent of the time) related to the prime (e.g. 'lion' followed by 'tiger'). In the other set of trials only 10 per cent of trials used related words. For remaining trials the stimuli were unrelated, so that the first word was not strictly a prime (e.g. 'list' followed by 'tiger'). The results of this study are summarized in Table 2.1.

Table 2.1 The percentage of targets correctly reported under various priming conditions

	Short duration prime		1 second prime	
	10% related	90% related	10% related	90% related
Related words	56	52	70	91
Unrelated words	49	43	55	51
Priming advantage	7	9	15	40

Source: adapted from Pecher et al., 2002

The effects are best appreciated by looking first at the final two columns of figures, showing the results when the first word was displayed for 1 second. For the condition where only 10 per cent of targets were related to the preceding word, 70 per cent of those targets were correctly identified when there was a relationship. The hit rate fell to 55 per cent when the targets were not related, so the priming effect produced a 15 per cent advantage (70 – 55 = 15). The last column shows a massive 91 per cent hit rate for related words, when there was a 90 per cent chance that they would be related to the preceding prime. The priming advantage in this condition has risen to 40 per cent. Why does the benefit of a related prime jump from 15 per cent to 40 per cent when the targets are more likely to be related to the primes? The answer is that, when there is a high chance that they will be related, participants spot the connection and try to guess what the target must have been: they often guess correctly. Notice that they can do this only because the prime word was clearly visible. Look now at the corresponding figures, for when the prime was displayed very briefly. Here the priming advantages (7 per cent and 9 per cent) are far more modest (but statistically significant). However, the important result is that the change from 10 per cent to 90 per cent relatedness does not produce the large increase in the priming effect observed in the 1 second condition. The small increase from 7 per cent to 9 per cent was not statistically significant. It can be concluded that participants were unable to guess in the brief condition, so presumably had not been able to identify the prime words. Nevertheless, those words did produce a small priming effect, so they must have received sufficient analysis to activate their meaning.

2.2   Towards a theory of parallel processing

When people are asked to guess about masked material, they are commonly able to provide some information, but it often lacks detail. For example, if participants in a Sperling-type experiment have recalled three letters, but are pressed for more, then they can often provide one or two. However, they generally do not know information such as whereabouts in the display the letters occurred, or what colour they were. These, of course, are exactly the kinds of detail that can be used to select items for report, and were believed to be usable in that role because they were characteristics which could be processed quickly and in parallel. The guessing results seem to turn the logic on its head, because the presumed complex information, such as letter identities, is discovered, while the simple colour and position information is unavailable. Coltheart (1980) offered an elegant solution to this problem, built around the semantic/episodic distinction used when describing memory (see Chapter 6). In the context of letters, semantic information would be the basic knowledge of letter identity. Episodic detail links the general identity to a specific occurrence: detail such as the fact that 'N' is in large, upper-case type, and is printed in red and at the start of the sign 'NO SMOKING'. Coltheart proposed that items do not normally reach conscious awareness unless both the semantic and episodic detail are detected. So, for example, one would not expect to be having an 'N-feeling' (semantic) in the absence of a letter with some specific characteristics (size, colour, etc.) in the field of view!

It has become clear from electrophysiological studies that visual item identification occurs in a different region of the cortex from the areas which respond to colour or location. These different kinds of information have to be united, and this process, Coltheart (1980) suggests, takes time and attention. According to this account, Sperling's 12 letters, or even Evett and Humphrey's *lion*, are indeed processed in parallel to cause semantic activation, but the viewer will not become aware of this, unless able to assign the corresponding episodic details. Nevertheless, if pressed, the participant may sometimes admit to 'having a feeling' that an item might have been presented, although not know what it looked like (see also Chapter 6 for a discussion of the semantic–episodic distinction).

The important point to note in the above account is that attention is no longer being described as the process that selects material for complex serial processing (e.g. word identification). Instead, Coltheart suggests that attention is required to join the products of two parallel processes: the identification and the episodic characterization. This idea that attention is concerned with uniting the components of a stimulus is not unlike a theory which Treisman has been developing (after her early auditory attention work, she now researches visual attentive processes). We shall consider Treisman's work (which does not involve backward masking), but first we should look a little further at what masking actually does to the processing of a stimulus.

2.3 Rapid serial visual presentation

It has been known for a long time that backward masking can act in one of two ways: **integration** and **interruption** (Turvey, 1973). When the SOA between target and mask is very short, integration occurs; that is, the two items are perceived as one, with the result that the target is difficult to report, just as when one word is written over another. Of more interest is masking by interruption, which is the type we have been considering in the previous section. It occurs at longer SOAs, and interruption masking will be experienced even if the target is presented to one eye and the mask to the other. This dichoptic (two-eyed) interaction must take place after information from the two eyes has been combined in the brain; it could not occur at earlier stages. In contrast, integration masking does not occur dichoptically when target and mask are presented to separate eyes, so presumably occurs quite early in analysis, perhaps even on the retina. On this basis, Turvey (1973) described integration as peripheral masking, and interruption as central masking, meaning that it occurred at a level where more complex information extraction was taking place.

Another early researcher in the field (Kolers, 1968) described the effect of a central (interruption) mask by analogy with the 'processing' of a customer in a shop. If the customer (equivalent to the target) comes into the shop alone, then s/he can be fully processed, even to the extent of discussing the weather and asking about family and holidays. However, if a second customer (i.e. a mask) follows the first, then the shopkeeper has to cease the pleasantries, and never learns about the personal information. The analogy was never taken further, and of course it is unwise to push an analogy too far. Nevertheless, one is tempted to point out that the second customer is still kept waiting for a while. Where does that thought take us? It became possible to investigate the fate of following stimuli, in fact whole queues of stimuli, with the development of a procedure popularized by Broadbent (Broadbent and Broadbent, 1987), who, like Treisman, had moved on from auditory research. The procedure was termed rapid serial visual presentation, in part, one suspects, because that provided the familiar abbreviation RSVP; participants were indeed asked to *répondez s'il vous plaît* with reports of what they had seen.

Unlike the traditional two-stimulus, target–mask pairing, **rapid serial visual presentation (RSVP)** displayed a series of stimuli in rapid succession, so each served as a backward mask for the preceding item. SOAs were such that a few items could be reported, but with difficulty. Typical timings would display each item for 100 ms, with a 20 ms gap between them; the sequence might contain as many as 20 items. Under these conditions stimuli are difficult to identify, and participants are certainly unable to list all 20; they are usually asked to look out for just two. In one variation, every item except one is a single black letter. The odd item is a white letter, and this is the first target; the participant has to say at the end of the sequence what the white letter had been. One or more items later in the sequence (i.e. after the white target), one of the remaining black letters may be an 'X'. As well as naming the white letter, the participant has to say whether or not X was present in the list. These two targets (white letter and black X) are commonly designated as T1 and T2. Notice that the participant has two slightly different tasks: for T1 (which will certainly be shown) an unknown letter has to be identified, whereas for T2 the task is simply to say whether a previously designated letter was presented. These details, together with a graph of typical results, are shown in Figure 2.3.

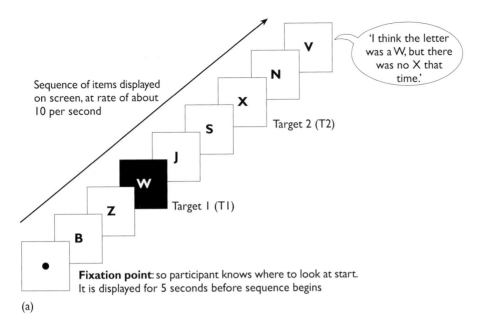

(a)

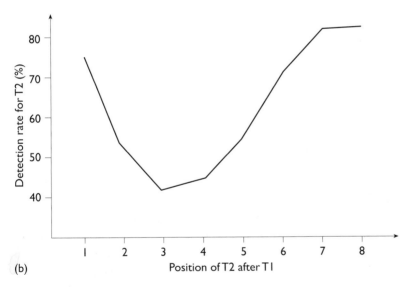

(b)

Figure 2.3 The RSVP technique: (a) the sequence of stimuli, shown in the same location on a computer screen, in which the participant has to identify a white letter, then decide whether an X was also present; (b) typical results, showing the likelihood of detecting the X, when presented in the first and subsequent positions following the white target

As can be seen from the graph in Figure 2.3(b), T2 (the X) might be spotted if it is the item immediately following T1, but thereafter it is less likely that it will be detected unless five or six items separate the two. What happens when it is not detected? As you may be coming to expect, the fact that participants do not report T2 does not mean that they have not carried out any semantic analysis upon it. Vogel *et al.* (1998) conducted an RSVP experiment that used words, rather than single letters. Additionally, before a sequence of stimuli was presented, a clear 'context' word was displayed, for a comfortable 1 second. For example, the context word might be *shoe*, then the item at T2 could be *foot*. However, on some presentations T2 was not in context; for example, *rope*. While participants were attempting to report these items, they were also being monitored using EEG (electroencephalography). The pattern of electrical activity measured via scalp electrodes is known to produce a characteristic 'signature', when what might be called a mismatch is encountered. For example, if a participant reads the sentence *He went to the café and asked for a cup of tin*, the signature appears when *tin* is reached. The Vogel *et al.* (1998) participants produced just such an effect with sequences such as *shoe – rope*, even when they were unable to report seeing *rope*. This sounds rather like some of the material discussed earlier, where backward masking prevented conscious awareness of material that had clearly been detected. However, the target in the RSVP situation appears to be affected by something that happened *earlier* (i.e. T1), rather than by a following mask. The difference needs exploring and explaining.

Presumably something is happening as a result of processing the first target (T1), which temporarily makes awareness of the second (T2) very difficult. Measurements show that for about 500–700 ms following T1, detection of T2 is lower than usual. It is as if the system requires time to become prepared to process something fresh, a gap that is sometimes known as a **refractory period**, but that in this context is more often called the **attentional blink**, abbreviated to AB. While the system is 'blinking' it is unable to attend to new information.

Time turns out not to be the only factor in observing an AB effect ('AB effect' will be used as a shorthand way of referring to the difficulty of reporting T2). Raymond *et al.* (1992) used a typical sequence of RSVP stimuli, but omitted the item immediately following the *first* target. In other words, there was a 100 ms gap, rather than another item following. Effectively, this meant that the degree of backward masking was reduced, and not surprisingly resulted in some improvement in the report rate for T1. Very surprisingly, it produced a considerable improvement in the reporting of T2; the AB effect had vanished (see Figure 2.4(a)). How did removing the mask for one target lead to an even larger improvement for another target that was yet to be presented? To return to our earlier analogy, if the shopkeeper is having some trouble in dealing with the first customer, then the second is kept waiting and suffers. That doesn't explain *how* the waiting queue suffers (if it were me I should probably chat to the person behind, and forget what I had come for), but that question was also addressed by removing items from the sequence.

Giesbrecht and Di Lollo (1998) removed the items following T2, so that it was the last in the list; again, the AB effect disappeared (see Figure 2.4(b)). So, no matter what was going on with T1, T2 could be seen, if it was not itself masked. To explain this result, together with the fact that making T1 easier to see also helps T2, Giesbrecht and Di Lollo developed a two-stage model of visual processing. At Stage 1, a range of information about target characteristics is captured in parallel: identity, size, colour, position and so on. In the second stage, they proposed, serial processes act upon the information, preparing it for awareness and report. While Stage 2 is engaged, later information cannot be processed, so has to remain at Stage 1. Any kind of disruption to T1, such as masking, makes it harder to process, so information from T2 is kept waiting longer. This has little detrimental impact upon T2 unless it

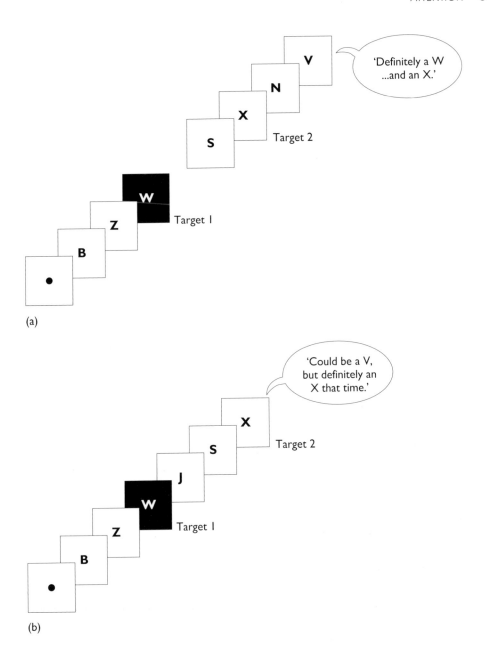

Figure 2.4   (a) Target 2 is seen more easily when Target 1 is made easier to see by removing the following item; (b) Target 2 is also seen easily when items following it are omitted

too is masked by a following stimulus (I don't forget what I came to buy, if there is no-one else in the queue to chat with). When T2 is kept waiting it can be overwritten by the following stimulus. The overwriting process will be damaging principally to the episodic information; an item cannot be both white and black, for example. However, semantic information may be better able to survive; there is no reason why *shoe* and *rope* should not both become activated. Consequently, even when there is insufficient information for Stage 2 to yield a fully processed target, it may nevertheless reveal its presence through priming or EEG effects. There is an obvious similarity between this account and Coltheart's (1980) suggestion: both propose the need to join semantic and episodic detail.

2.4   Masking and attention

Before I summarize the material in this section, and we move on to consider attentional processes with clearly seen displays, it would be appropriate to consider the relevance of the masking studies to the issue of attention. We began the whole subject by enquiring about the fate of material which was, in principle, available for processing, but happened not to be at the focus of attention. Somehow we have moved into a different enquiry, concerning the fate of material that a participant was trying to attend to, but did not have time to process. This seemed a natural progression as the chapter unfolded, but are the two issues really related? Merikle and Joordens (1997) addressed this very question; they characterized it as a distinction between perception without awareness (such as in masking studies) and perception without attention (as with dichotic listening). They carried out a number of studies, in which processing was rendered difficult either by masking, or by giving the participants two tasks, so that they could not focus on the target. They concluded that the results were entirely comparable, and that the same underlying processes are at work in both kinds of study.

Summary of Section 2

The results of the visual attention experiments we have considered can be interpreted as follows.

- Attention can be directed selectively towards different areas of the visual field, without the need to refocus.
- The inability to report much detail from brief, masked visual displays appears to be linked to the need to assemble the various information components.
- The visual information is captured in parallel, but assembly is a serial process.
- Episodic detail (e.g. colour, position) is vulnerable to the passage of time, or to 'overwriting' by a mask.
- Semantic information (i.e. identity/meaning) is relatively enduring, but does not reach conscious awareness unless bound to the episodic information.
- Attention, in this context, is the process of binding the information about an item's identity to its particular episodic characteristics.
- 'Unbound' semantic activation can be detected by priming and electrophysiological techniques.

3   Integrating information in clearly seen displays

The binding of features emerges as being a very significant process when displays are brief, because there is so little time in which to unite them. With normal viewing, such as when you examine the letters and words on this page, it is not obvious to introspection that binding is taking place. However, if, as explained above, it is a necessary precursor to conscious awareness, the process must also occur when we examine long-lived visual displays. Researchers have attempted to demonstrate that the binding process does indeed take place.

3.1   Serial and parallel search

Examine the three sections of Figure 2.5 and in each case try to get a feel for how long it takes you to find the 'odd one out'. The figure is a monochrome version of the usual form of these stimuli; you can see a coloured example in colour Plate 3.

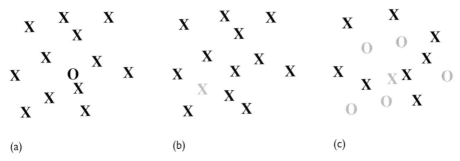

(a)   (b)   (c)

Figure 2.5   Find the odd item in each of the groups, (a), (b) and (c)

You probably felt that the odd items in Figures 2.5(a) and 2.5(b) simply 'popped out', and were immediately obvious, whereas the grey X in Figure 2.5(c) took you slightly longer to find. These kinds of effect have been explored formally by Treisman (e.g. Treisman and Gelade, 1980). The odd item is referred to as the target and the others as the distractors. Treisman showed her participants a series of displays of this nature, and measured how long it took them to decide whether or not a display contained a target. She was particularly interested in the effect of varying the number of distractors surrounding the targets. It was found that for displays similar to Figures 2.5(a) and 2.5(b) it made no difference to decision times whether there were few or many distractors. In contrast, with the 2.5(c) type of display, participants took longer to decide when there were more distractor items; each additional distractor added approximately 60 ms to the decision time.

How is that pattern of results to be explained? Treisman pointed out that the first two displays have target items which differ from the rest on only one dimension; the target is either a round letter (O), among 'crossed-line' letters (X), or a grey letter among black letters. The 2.5(c) display type is different; to identify the target it is necessary to consider two dimensions. It has to be an X (but there are others, so on its own being an X does not define the target), and it has to be grey (but again, there are other grey letters). Only when X and grey are combined does it become clear that this is an 'odd one out'. All these features (various colours and shapes) are quite simple and are derived in the early stages of visual processing, but importantly different types of analysis (e.g. of shape or colour) take place in different parts of the brain. To see whether there is just 'greyness', or just 'roundness' in a display is easy, so easy in fact that the whole display seems to be taken in at a glance, no matter how many items there are. In other words, all the different items are processed at the same time, in parallel. The situation is very different when shape and colour have to be combined because they are determined in different brain areas; somehow the two types of information have to be brought together. You will recall from Section 2 that attention appears necessary to unite episodic and semantic information. Treisman proposed that it is also required to link simple features. Each item in the display has to receive attention just long enough for its two features (shape and colour) to be combined, and this has to be done one item at a time until the target is found. In other words, the processing is serial, so takes longer when there are more items to process.

It has been known for some time that the parietal region of the brain (part of the cortex that sits like a saddle across the top of the brain) is one of the areas involved in attention. A fuller account of the problems that result from damage to this area will be given in Section 5.1; at this point it is relevant to mention that Treisman (1998) reports investigations with a patient who had suffered strokes in that region. He was shown simple displays, containing just two letters from a set of three (T, X and O); they were printed in different colours, from a choice of three (red, blue or yellow). He was asked to describe the first letter he noticed in the display. On a particular occasion he might be shown a blue T and a red O. Although he often made mistakes, he would rarely respond 'Yellow X' to that display; that is, he did not claim to see features that were not there at all, so he was not simply guessing. What he did say quite often would be something like 'Blue O'. He had correctly identified features that were present, but was unable to join them appropriately. The implication of this is that both the detection and the integration of features are necessary steps in normal perception, and that integration requires attention.

3.2   Non-target effects

Treisman's **feature integration theory** has been very influential, but it does not appear to explain all experimental observations, and there have been alternative accounts of the feature-binding process. Duncan and Humphreys (1989) reported effects which do not fit too well within the basic Treisman account. They required participants to search for the letter 'L' (the target) within a number of 'Ts' (the non-targets). You may get a feel for the relative difficulty of different versions of their task by examining Figure 2.6.

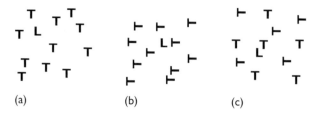

Figure 2.6   Examples of the kinds of stimuli used by Duncan and Humphreys (1989). Find the letter L in each of the groups, (a), (b) and (c)

The task can be conceptualized as looking for two lines that meet at a corner (the L), rather than forming a T-junction. It should not make much difference whether the T-junctions are vertical or horizontal (as in Figure 2.6(a) and 2.6(b)), and, indeed, the search times for these two sorts of display are similar. However, when the Ts are mixed, as in Figure 2.6(c), it takes longer to find the target. This finding would not have been predicted by a simple feature integration theory. Duncan and Humphreys (1989) argued that part of finding the target actually involves rejecting the non-targets and that this is a harder task when they come in a greater variety.

This explanation does not rule out the idea that features need to be integrated to achieve recognition, but it does suggest that non-targets, as well as targets, need to be recognized. The following section also describes evidence that non-targets are recognized, but in this case the recognition appears to take place in parallel.

3.3   The 'flanker' effect

A potential problem for the feature integration theory is the fact that the time taken to understand the meaning of a printed word can be influenced by other, nearby words. Of itself, this is not surprising, because it is well known that one word can prime (i.e. speed decisions to) another related word; the example *nurse – doctor* was given in Section 1.3. However, Shaffer and LaBerge (1979) found priming effects, even when they presented words in a way which might have been expected to eliminate priming. For their experiment a word was presented on a screen, and as quickly as possible a participant had to decide to what category it belonged: for example an animal or a vegetable. The participant was required to press one button for animal names, and another for vegetables. This sounds straightforward, but the target word was not presented in isolation; above and below it another word was also printed, making a column of three words. The target, about which a decision was to be made, was always in the centre. The words repeated above and below the target were termed the 'flankers'. Before the three words were displayed, markers in the field of view showed exactly where the target would appear. Figure 2.7 shows examples of possible displays.

cat   pea

dog   dog

cat   pea

(a)   (b)

Figure 2.7   The flanker effect. It takes longer to decide 'dog' is an animal when surrounded by words of another category, as in (b)

You will probably not be surprised to learn that people make category judgements more quickly for examples such as that shown in Figure 2.7(a) than for the 2.7(b) type of stimulus. Presumably, while the target information is being processed, details about the flankers are also being analysed, in parallel. When they turn out to be from the category associated with pressing the other button they slow the response. This slowing is very much like the impact of the conflicting colour names in the Stroop effect (see Box 2.2). However, recall that Treisman's theory suggests that focused, *serial* attention is required to join features together. A printed word has many features, and it would be thought that they require joining before the word can be recognized; it should not be possible to process the three words simultaneously. A participant focusing on the target could not (according to the theory) also be processing the flankers.

2.2   **Research study**

The Stroop effect

Stroop (1935) reported a number of situations in which the processing of one source of information was interfered with by the presence of another. The best known example uses a list of colour names printed in non-matching coloured inks (see colour Plate 4).

A variant is the 'emotional Stroop task', which can be used in therapeutic diagnoses. For example, severe depression produces cognitive impairment and, in the elderly, it is difficult to distinguish this from the effects of the onset of dementia. Dudley *et al.* (2002) used colours to print a list of words, some of which were associated with negative emotions (e.g. the word *sadness*). Depressed people have an attentional bias towards such depression-related material. Patients were required to name the ink colours for each word, as quickly as possible. Both depressed patients and those in the early stages of Alzheimer's disease were slower than a control group, but only the patients with depression were extra slow in responding to negative words. The technique permits an appropriate diagnosis.

Broadbent addressed this problem (Broadbent and Gathercole, 1990), and produced an explanation to 'save' the feature integration theory. He suggested that the central target word primed the flankers so effectively that they could be detected with the minimum of attention. Taking the items in Figure 2.7 as an example, if this explanation were true it would have to be argued that 'dog' primes 'cat', which, being another animal, leads to faster decision times. 'Dog' cannot prime 'pea', as they are unrelated, so there is nothing to make the decision any quicker. In other words, it is not that 'pea' makes responses to 'dog' harder; rather, 'cat' makes them easier. Broadbent and Gathercole tested this explanation with an ingenious modification to the usual way of presenting targets and flankers. Instead of displaying all three words simultaneously, the target appeared first, to be joined by the flankers 40 ms later. The sequence is represented in Figure 2.8.

The reasoning behind this change was as follows. If Broadbent and Gathercole were correct that the flankers were analysed only because of priming from the target word, then giving the target a 'head start' should enable it to prime even more effectively; the flanker effect would be even stronger. On the other hand, if interference from the flankers were merely an example of processing not being as 'serial' as Treisman supposed, then making flankers arrive late, when target processing had already started, should *reduce* their impact. The results showed a strong flanker effect (i.e. faster responses with same-category flankers), suggesting that the priming idea was correct. However, there is another interpretation of the

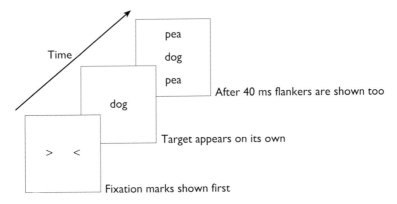

Figure 2.8   The Broadbent and Gathercole (1990) modification: the flankers are delayed for 40 ms

Broadbent and Gathercole results. It has been well established that an item suddenly appearing in the visual field will capture attention (e.g. Gellatly *et al.*, 1999). By making the flankers appear later, Broadbent and Gathercole may have ensured that they would attract attention away from the target. This could explain why the flankers showed a particularly strong effect with this style of presentation. Although the Broadbent and Gathercole idea of staggering the display times of the stimuli was ingenious, a convincing demonstration of parallel processing requires all the different stimuli to be presented at the same time.

Summary of Section 3

When consciously perceiving complex material, such as when looking for a particular letter of a particular colour:

- Perception requires attention.
- The attention has to be focused upon one item at a time, thus ...
- processing is serial.
- Some parallel processing may take place, but ...
- it is detected indirectly, such as by the influence of one word upon another.

4   Attention and distraction

The above account of having attention taken away from the intended target reminds us that, while it may be advantageous from a survival point of view to have attention captured by novel events, these events are actually distractions from the current object of attention. Those who have to work in open-plan offices, or try to study while others watch TV, will know how distracting extraneous material can be. Some try to escape by wearing headphones, hoping that music will be less distracting, but does that work? Are some distractors worse than others? These kinds of question have been addressed by research and the answers throw further light upon the nature of attention.

4.1 The effects of irrelevant speech

Imagine watching a computer screen, on which a series of digits is flashed, at a nice easy rate of one per second. After six items you have to report what the digits had been, in the order presented (this is called serial recall – see also Chapter 5). Not a very difficult task, you might think, but what if someone were talking nearby? It turns out that, even when participants are instructed to ignore the speech completely, their recall performance drops by at least 30 per cent (Jones, 1999).

In the context of dichotic listening (Section 1.2), it was shown that ignored auditory material may nevertheless be processed, and hence its meaning influences perception of attended material. However, meaning appears to have no special impact, when speech interferes with memory for visually presented material. Thus, hearing numbers spoken, while trying to remember digits, is no more damaging than listening to other irrelevant speech items (Buchner *et al.*, 1996). In fact, even a foreign language, or English played backwards, are no less disruptive than other irrelevant speech items (Jones *et al.*, 1990). On the other hand, simple white noise (a constant hissing like a mis-tuned radio) is almost as benign as silence. Interference presumably results from speech because, unlike white noise, it is not constant: it is broken into different sounds.

The importance of 'difference' in the speech can be shown by presenting lists of either rhyming or non-rhyming words. It turns out that a sequence such as 'cat, hat, sat, bat ...' is less disruptive than a sequence such as 'cat, dog, hit, bus ...' (Jones and Macken, 1995). Jones (1999) proposes that, whether listening to speech, music, or many other types of sound, the process requires the string of sounds to be organized into perceptual 'objects'. To recognize an auditory object, such as a word or melody, requires that the segments of the stream of sounds are identified, and it is also necessary to keep track of the order of the segments. This ordering process, which occurs automatically, interferes with attempts to remember the order of visually presented items. When the sounds contain simple repetitions (as with the rhyming 'at' sound) the ordering becomes simpler, so the memory task is less disrupted. This was demonstrated in a surprising but convincing way by Jones *et al.* (1999). Their participants attempted to remember visually presented lists, while listening through headphones to a repeating sequence of three syllables, such as the letter names 'k ... l ... m ... k ... l ... m'. These were disruptive, since the three letters have quite different sounds. The experimenters then changed the way in which the speech was delivered. The 'l' was played through both headphones, so sounded in the middle (see Section 1.2, Box 2.1), but the 'k' was played only to the left ear and the 'm' was heard in the right. This manipulation results in the perception of three 'streams' of speech, one on the left, saying 'kay, kay, kay ...', one in the middle, repeating 'ell', and the last on the right saying 'em'. The significant point is that instead of hearing a continually changing sequence, the new way of playing *exactly the same sounds* results in them sounding like three separate sequences each of which never changes. Remarkably, the result is that they are no longer as disruptive to the visual recall task.

This section has taken the concept of attention into a new area. Previously we have seen it as a means of separating information, or of directing the assembly of different aspects of the attended item. In most of the earlier examples it has appeared that a great deal of processing can take place in parallel, although the results may not all reach conscious awareness. The impact of irrelevant speech shows that parallel processing is not always possible. It seems to break down in this case because demands are made on the same process – the process that places items in a sequence. Here it would seem that we have a situation where there really is a 'bottleneck', of the sort envisaged in early theories of attention (see Sections 1.2 and 1.3).

What of trying to study with music? Undoubtedly, 'Silence is Golden', but if music is to be played, then my suggestion is that it should perhaps be something that changes very slowly, such as the pieces produced by some of the minimalist composers.

4.2   Attending across modalities

The preceding section raised the issue of attention operating (and to some extent failing) across two sensory modalities. By focusing on distraction we ignored the fact that sight and sound (and other senses) often convey mutually supporting information. A classic example is lip-reading. Although few of us would claim any lip-reading skills, it turns out that, particularly in noisy surroundings, we supplement our hearing considerably by watching lip movements. If attention is concerned with uniting elements of stimuli from within one sense, then we might expect it to be involved in cross-modal (i.e. across senses) feature binding too. In this section we will look briefly at one such process.

A striking example of the impact of visual lip movements upon auditory perception is found in the **ventriloquism effect**. This is most commonly encountered at the cinema, where the loudspeakers are situated to the side of the screen. Nevertheless, the actor's voice appears to emanate from the face on the screen, rather than from off to the side. Driver (1996) demonstrated just how powerful this effect could be. He presented participants with an auditory task that was rather like shadowing in dichotic listening (Section 1.3) – only much harder! The two messages, one of which was to be shadowed, did not go one to each ear: they both came from the same loudspeaker, and were spoken in the same voice. To give a clue as to which was to be shadowed, a TV monitor was placed just above the loudspeaker, showing the face of the person reading the to-be-shadowed message. By lip-reading, participants could cope to some extent with this difficult task. Driver then moved the monitor to the side, away from the loudspeaker. This had the effect of making the appropriate message seem to be coming from the lips. Since the other message did not get 'moved' in this way, the two now *felt* spatially separate and, although in reality the sounds had not changed, the shadowing actually became easier!

These kinds of effects have further implications at a practical level. The use of mobile telephones while driving a car has been identified as dangerous, and the danger is not limited to the case where the driver tries to hold the phone in one hand and steer with the other. If a hands-free headset is used of the type which delivers sound via an earpiece to just one ear, the caller's voice sounds as if it is coming from one side. Attending to this signal has the effect of pulling visual attention towards the lateral message, reducing the driver's responsiveness to events ahead (Spence, 2002).

Summary of Section 4

We have seen that attentive processes will 'work hard' to unite information into a coherent whole.

- Even spatially separate visual and auditory stimuli can be joined if they appear to be synchronous (the ventriloquism effect).
- When stimuli are not synchronous the system attempts to order the segments of the stimuli independently, resulting in distraction and lost information.
- It is a 'bottleneck' in the ordering process that results in one stream of information interfering with the processing of another.

5   The neurology of attention

Modern techniques for revealing where and when different parts of the brain become active have recently provided a window on the processes of attention. For example, one of these brain-scanning techniques, functional magnetic resonance imaging (fMRI), has been used to show the behaviour of an area of the brain that responds to speech. It turns out also to become activated in a person viewing lips making speech movements *in the absence of sound*. For this to happen there must be connections between relevant parts of the visual and auditory areas.

5.1   The effects of brain damage

Before the advent of 'brain mapping', such as by fMRI, it was nevertheless possible to discover something of the part played by different regions of the brain, by observing the problems resulting from brain damage (such as following a stroke). One such area was mentioned in Section 3.1 – the parietal lobe. Damage to a single lobe (there is one on either side) leads to what is called **sensory neglect**, or sometimes simply neglect. A patient is likely completely to ignore the doctor if s/he stands on the neglected side (the side opposite to the site of the damage). When eating, the patient will probably leave any food that is on the 'wrong' side of the plate, and if asked to draw a flower will put petals on only one side. The problem is not simply blindness to all that lies on the neglected side. A patient asked to draw a whole vase of flowers may draw only those hanging over the 'preserved' side, but with each individual flower itself only half complete. It appears sometimes to be half the *object* which is neglected, rather than half the field of view. Figure 2.9 shows a typical attempt, by a patient with visual neglect, to draw a clock face.

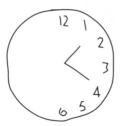

Figure 2.9   The typical appearance of a clock face, as drawn by a patient with visual neglect

That neglect may be associated with the object rather than the scene was demonstrated formally by Driver and Halligan (1991). They showed patients pairs of pictures that looked rather like silhouettes of chess pieces. Patients had to say whether the two pictures were the same or different. Where there *were* differences, they comprised an addition to one side, near the top of the figure (as if the chess queen had something attached to one ear!). When the addition was on the neglected side patients were unable to detect the difference. Suppose the 'problem' side was the left. The question is whether the patient has difficulty with processing information to the left of the page, or to the left of the object. Driver and Halligan tested this by tilting the pictures to the right (see Figure 2.10), so that the one-sided feature, although still on the left of the figure, was now in the right half of the page. Still the patients experienced difficulty: neglect was object-related.

We have been describing attention as a mechanism for assembling the sub-components of items in a scene, so it is not difficult to conceptualize a fault leading to some components being omitted. This account sees attention as an essential element of the perceptual process, helping to organize incoming information. However, neglect is not limited to objects that are physically present. Bisiach and Luzzatti (1978) asked their patient to imagine standing in the cathedral square of the Italian city where he grew up. He was to imagine looking towards the cathedral and to describe all that was in the square. He did this very well, except that he failed to mention any of the buildings down the left-hand side of the square (his brain injury was on the right). He was then asked to imagine standing on the cathedral steps, looking back towards his previous viewpoint. Again, he only reported details from the right. However, with the change of view, this meant that he was now describing

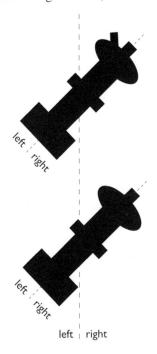

left | right

Figure 2.10 Same or different? The feature that distinguishes the two figures is to the left of the object, but on the right of the page

previously ignored buildings! Clearly his memory was intact, but in some way not entirely accessible. Equally clearly, attentive processes are involved in the assembly of remembered material as well as of physically present stimuli.

An even more extreme form of neglect is encountered in a condition known as Balint's syndrome. It occurs when a patient is unfortunate enough to suffer damage to both parietal lobes, which results in it being extremely difficult to shift attention from one object to another. Thus, when trying to light a cigarette, the patient may find that his attention has been 'captured' by the flame, to the extent that he can no longer see the cigarette. One patient complained, 'When I see your spectacles I cannot see your face.' This is reminiscent of the experience of pilots using a head-up display (HUD) (see Section 2), where focusing on flight information displayed in the HUD makes the outside scene feel less 'visible'. Surprising as it may sound, it seems necessary to deduce from these effects that we *all* experience the world as a series of objects. However, unless our attentive process has been damaged, we can shift the attention so rapidly from one object to another that we perceive them all as being present simultaneously. Exactly what constitutes an object depends upon the situation; Balint patients are revealing here, because they see only one object at a time. Baylis *et al.* (1994) described a patient who could not report the letters making up an isolated word. Viewed in this way, each letter was a small object and it was not possible to switch attention from one to the next. However, the patient could read the whole word, since for this purpose it was a single object.

Early visual processing takes place in two major pathways in the brain, known as the ventral and dorsal streams (these are described in Section 6 of Chapter 3); the parietal region is part of the dorsal pathway. Damage to the ventral stream results in different kinds of integration problems; patients are aware of all aspects of a scene, but to the patient they remain segmented into small elements. For example, an individual shown a photograph of a paint-brush described seeing a wooden stick and a black object (the bristles) which he could not recognize. Humphreys (2001) suggests that the varieties of different problems are evidence that the binding together of different features takes place in several different stages and brain locations.

5.2   Event-related potentials

When a sense organ (eye, ear, etc.) receives a stimulus, the event eventually causes neurons to 'fire' (i.e. produce electrical discharges) in the receiving area of the brain. The information is sent on from these first sites to other brain areas. With appropriate apparatus and techniques it is possible to record the electrical signals, using electrodes attached to the scalp. The electrical potentials recorded are called **event-related potentials (ERPs)**, since they dependably follow the triggering sensory event. In fact a whole series of electrical changes are detected, first from the receiving brain areas, then later from subsequent sites. The timing of the ERPs gives a clue as to where in this sequence they are being generated.

Woldorff *et al.* (1993) examined ERPs evoked by sounds. These included signals occurring as soon as 10 ms after the auditory event. To generate a response so quickly, these ERPs must have originated in the brain stem, in the first 'relay' between ear and auditory cortex. The earliest stages of registration at the auditory cortex were detected after about 20–50 ms. It was of particular interest that, whereas the 10 ms signal was not affected by attention, the magnitude of the electrical activity in the cortex was smaller when the sounds were played to an unattended ear. This shows that, at a very early stage of cortical analysis, attending away from a stimulus actually reduces the intensity of the signal in the brain. The result lends a good deal of support to the theory that attention is exercised by controlling a filter early in the processing sequence (see Section 1.3). Note, however, that the unattended signal is only attenuated, not eliminated.

Summary of Section 5

Many familiar themes have re-emerged in this section, together with the recognition that attention is involved in the assembly of remembered material as well as of current perceptions.

- Attention is associated with the generation of perceptual objects.
- In addition to being an essential part of external stimulus processing, attention influences remembered experiences.
- ERP data show that cortical signals derived from unattended external stimuli are attenuated.

6   Concluding thoughts

We seem to have come a long way and covered a great deal of ground since I approached this subject by explaining that a mechanism must exist to help us focus on one sound out of many. That clearly is one function of attention, but attention seems to have other functions too. The results of visual search experiments show that attention is a vital factor in joining together the features that make up an object, and the experiences of brain-damaged patients suggest that this feature-assembly role ensures that our conscious perceptions are generally of objects, rather than of their constituent parts. Cross-modal research has demonstrated that the gathering together of related information from different senses is also controlled by attention.

Attention has a role to play in dealing with competition. The early researchers believed that attention was vital, because the brain would be able to deal with only one signal at a time; a 'winning' signal had to be picked from among the competitors. Although we have shown that a good deal of analysis can actually take place in parallel, there are also results which suggest that more complex analysis is largely serial, thus requiring a mechanism to select from the competing stimuli. Often, the parallel processes have to be demonstrated rather obliquely, since their results do not become consciously available. Thus attention has to do with what reaches conscious awareness. Why should this be so? Why should we not be equally aware of several items simultaneously?

Allport (1987) offered an answer that suggests yet another role for attention: it is to direct actions. Although we might, in principle, be able to perceive many things at once, there are situations where it would be counterproductive to attempt to *do* more than one thing. Allport gave fruit gathering as an example. When we look at a bush of berries we need to focus attention upon one at a time, since that is how they have to be picked. If animals had not evolved this ability to select, if all the food items remained equally salient, they would starve as they hovered over them all, unable to move toward any one! From this perspective, attention is the process that saves us from trying to carry out incompatible actions simultaneously. However, everyday experience reminds us that the issue of consciousness remains relevant. For example, novice drivers experience considerable difficulty in trying simultaneously to perform all the actions needed to control a vehicle; in Allport's view they are trying to 'attend-for-action' to more than one thing at a time. However, this could be restated as an attempt to be *conscious* of more than one thing at a time. Once the driver has become more skilful, the difficulty of combining actions disappears, but so too does the driver's conscious awareness of performing them: they have become automatic.

2.3 ─────────────────────────── **Research study**

Hypnosis, time and attention

Brain scanning has revealed that regions of the brain known to be involved in attention show unusual activity when hypnotized participants become tolerant of pain (Crawford *et al.*, 1998), or experience hallucinations (Szechtman *et al.*, 1998).

Many people are unable to achieve such extreme effects in hypnosis, but there is one phenomenon that almost everyone experiences: hypnosis sessions usually feel they have lasted for far less time than the actual duration. I have explained this observation (Naish, 2001, 2002) by linking it to Gray's (1995) theory of consciousness, which involves some of the same brain regions. He proposed that we maintain the content of our conscious awareness by registering repeated 'snapshots' of our environment. Our sense of time may be linked to the rate at which the environment is sampled.

To become hypnotized usually involves an induction in which one is asked to relax and focus attention on internal feelings, such as the heaviness of limbs or the rate of one's breathing. Subsequently, one is invited to imagine and attend to a pleasant, relaxing scene. Neither of these activities produces fast-changing streams of stimuli; the bodily feelings change only slowly and the relaxing scene is self-generated, so changes only when one wants it to change. I propose that in these circumstances there is no need to take such frequent snapshots, since little will change from one to the next. Consequently, we are less aware of the passage of time. In support of this claim, it turns out that participants who rate themselves as more successful at attending to their self-generated experiences and ignoring the real world are those who make larger underestimates of the session duration (Naish, 2003).

One might well ask how the term 'attention' has come to be applied to so many roles and processes; it might have been better to use different labels to distinguish between them. To use one word with so many aspects certainly makes a unitary definition very difficult to formulate. I suspect that the single term has stuck because ultimately all these facets of attention do lead to one result: conscious awareness. Even in so-called altered states of consciousness, such as hypnosis, attention appears to be a vital component (see Box 2.3). To conclude with a personal view, I will offer the following definition:

Attention is the process which gives rise to conscious awareness.

I promised at the start of this chapter that attention was a broad and intriguing topic. I am sure you will agree that it was broad – and we haven't covered half of it – but I hope you are now intrigued too. It is generally accepted that readers cannot continue to devote attention to text that goes on too long, so I trust that I have stimulated, rather than sated, your attention!

Now that you have read this chapter you can reinforce and extend your learning by reading an original journal article associated with it, available online from the DD303 website. Remember, these are original journal articles, so the style is different from this textbook, and don't be too concerned if you can't follow every detail.

Further reading

Styles, E.A. (1997) *The Psychology of Attention*, Hove, Psychology Press. A very readable textbook, which covers and extends the topics introduced in this chapter.

Pashler, H. (ed.) (1998) *Attention*, Hove, Psychology Press. An edited book, with contributors from North America and the UK. Topics are dealt with in rather more depth than in the Styles book.

References

Allport, D.A. (1987) 'Selection for action: some behavioural and neurophysiological considerations of attention and action', in Heuer, H. and Sanders, A.F. (eds) *Perspectives on Perception and Action*, Hillsdale, NJ, Lawrence Erlbaum Associates.

Baylis, G.C., Driver, J., Baylis, L. and Rafal, R.D. (1994) 'Reading of letters and words in a patient with Balint's syndrome', *Neuropsychological*, vol.32, pp.1273–86.

Bisiach, E. and Luzzatti, C. (1978) 'Unilateral neglect of representational space', *Cortex*, vol.14, pp.129–33.

Broadbent, D.E. (1952) 'Listening to one of two synchronous messages', *Journal of Experimental Psychology*, vol.44, pp.51–5.

Broadbent, D.E. (1954) 'The role of auditory localization in attention and memory span', *Journal of Experimental Psychology*, vol.47, pp.191–6.

Broadbent, D.E. and Broadbent, M.H.P. (1987) 'From detection to identification: response to multiple targets in rapid serial visual presentation', *Perception and Psychophysics*, vol.42, pp.105–13.

Broadbent, D.E. and Gathercole, S.E. (1990) 'The processing of non-target words: semantic or not?', *Quarterly Journal of Experimental Psychology*, vol.42A, pp.3–37.

Buchner, A., Irmen, L. and Erdfelder, E. (1996) 'On the irrelevance of semantic information for the "irrelevant speech" effect', *Quarterly Journal of Experimental Psychology*, vol.49A, pp.765–79.

Cheesman, J. and Merikle, P.M. (1984) 'Priming with and without awareness', *Perception and Psychophysics*, vol.36, pp.387–95.

Coltheart, M. (1980) 'Iconic memory and visible persistence', *Perception and Psychophysics*, vol.27, pp.183–228.

Corteen, R.S. and Wood, B. (1972) 'Autonomous responses to shock associated words in an unattended channel', *Journal of Experimental Psychology*, vol.94, pp.308–313.

Crawford, H.J., Horton, J.E., Hirsch, T.B., Harrington, G.S., Plantec, M.B., Vendemia, J.M.C., Shamro, C., McClain-Furmanski, D. and Downs, J.H. (1998) 'Attention and disattention (hypnotic analgesia) to painful somatosensory TENS stimuli differentially affects brain dynamics: a functional magnetic resonance imaging study', *International Journal of Psychophysiology*, vol.30, p.77.

Deutsch, J.A. and Deutsch, D. (1963) 'Attention: some theoretical considerations', *Psychological Review*, vol.70, pp.80–90.

Driver, J. (1996) 'Enhancement of selective listening by illusory mislocation of speech sounds due to lip-reading', *Nature*, vol.381, pp.66–8.

Driver, J. and Halligan, P.W. (1991) 'Can visual neglect operate in object centred co-ordinates? An affirmative case study', *Cognitive Neuropsychology*, vol.8, pp.475–96.

Dudley, R., O'Brien, J., Barnett, N., McGuckin, L. and Britton, P. (2002) 'Distinguishing depression from dementia in later life: a pilot study employing the emotional Stroop task', *International Journal of Geriatric Psychiatry*, vol.17, pp.48–53.

Duncan, J. and Humphreys, G.W. (1989) 'Visual search and visual similarity', *Psychological Review*, vol.96, pp.433–58.

Evett, L.J. and Humphreys, G.W. (1981) 'The use of abstract graphemic information in lexical access', *Quarterly Journal of Experimental Psychology: Human Experimental Psychology*, vol.33A, pp.325–50.

Gellatly, A., Cole, G. and Blurton, A. (1999) 'Do equiluminant object onsets capture visual attention?', *Journal of Experimental Psychology: Human Perception and Performance*, vol.25, pp.1609–24.

Giesbrecht, B. and Di Lollo, V. (1998) 'Beyond the attentional blink: visual masking by object substitution', *Journal of Experimental Psychology: Human Perception and Performance*, vol.24, pp.1454–66.

Gray J.A. (1995) 'The contents of consciousness – a neuropsychological conjecture', *Behavioural and Brain* Sciences, vol.18, pp.659–76.

Humphreys, G.W. (2001) 'A multi-stage account of binding in vision: neuropsychological evidence', *Visual Cognition*, vol.8, pp.381–410.

Jones, D.M. (1999) 'The cognitive psychology of auditory distraction', *British Journal of Psychology*, vol.90, pp.167–87.

Jones, D.M. and Macken, W.J. (1995) 'Phonological similarity in the irrelevant speech effect: within- or between-stream similarity?', *Journal of Experimental Psychology: Learning, Memory and Cognition*, vol.21, pp.103–15.

Jones, D.M., Miles, C. and Page, J. (1990) 'Disruption of reading by irrelevant speech: effects of attention, arousal or memory?', *Applied Cognitive Psychology*, vol.4, pp.89–108.

Jones, D.M., Saint-Aubin, J. and Tremblay, S. (1999) 'Modulation of the irrelevant sound effect by organizational factors: further evidence from streaming by location', *Quarterly Journal of Psychology*, vol.52A, pp.545–54.

Kolers, P.A. (1968) 'Some psychological aspects of pattern recognition', in Kolers, P.A. and Eden. M. (eds) *Recognizing Patterns*, Cambridge, MA, MIT Press.

Merikle, P.M. and Joordens, S. (1997) 'Parallels between perception without attention and perception without awareness', *Consciousness and Cognition*, vol.6, pp.219–36.

Naish, P.L.N. (1990) 'Simulating directionality in airborne auditory warnings and messages', in Life, M.A., Narborough-Hall, C.S. and Hamilton, W.I. (eds) *Simulation and the User Interface*, London and New York, Taylor and Francis.

Naish, P.L.N. (2001) 'Hypnotic time distortion: busy beaver or tardy time-keeper', *Contemporary Hypnosis*, vol.18, pp.118–30.

Naish, P.L.N. (2002) 'Perceiving, misperceiving, and hypnotic hallucinations', in Roberts, D. (ed.) (2002).

Naish, P.L.N. (2003) 'The production of hypnotic time-distortion: determining the necessary conditions', *Contemporary Hypnosis*, vol.20, pp.3–15.

Norman, D.A. (1968) 'Towards a theory of memory and attention', *Psychological Review*, vol.75, pp.522–36.

Pecher, D., Zeelenberg, R. and Raaijmakers, G.W. (2002) 'Associative priming in a masked perceptual identification task: evidence for automatic processes', *Quarterly Journal of Experimental Psychology: Human Experimental Psychology*, vol.55A, pp.1157–73.

Raymond, J.E., Shapiro, K.L. and Arnell, K.A. (1992) 'Temporary suppression of visual processing in an RSVP task: an attentional blink?', *Journal of Experimental Psychology: Human Perception and Performance*, vol.18, pp.849–60.

Roberts, D. (ed.) (2002) *Signals and Perception: The Fundamentals of Human Sensation*, Basingstoke, Palgrave/The Open University.

Shaffer, W.O. and LaBerge, D. (1979) 'Automatic semantic processing of unattended words', *Journal of Verbal Learning and Verbal Behaviour*, vol.18, pp.413–26.

Spence, C. (2002) 'Multisensory integration, attention and perception', in Roberts, D. (ed.) (2002).

Sperling, G. (1960) 'The information available in brief visual presentations', *Psychological Monographs*, 74 (Whole Number 498), 29.

Stroop, J.R. (1935) 'Studies of interference in serial verbal reactions', *Journal of Experimental Psychology*, vol.18, pp.643–62.

Szechtman, H., Woody, E., Bowers, K.S. and Nahmias, C. (1998) 'Where the imaginal appears real: a positron emission tomography study of auditory hallucinations', *Proceedings of the National Academy of Sciences*, vol.95, pp.1956–60.

Treisman, A. (1960) 'Contextual cues in selective listening', *Quarterly Journal of Experimental Psychology*, vol.12, pp.242–8.

Treisman, A. (1998) 'Feature binding, attention and object perception', *Philosophical Transactions of the Royal Society of London*, Series B, vol.353, pp.1295–1306.

Treisman, A. and Gelade, G. (1980) 'A feature-integration theory of attention', *Cognitive Psychology*, vol.12, pp.97–136.

Turvey, M.T. (1973) 'On peripheral and central processes in vision: inferences from an information-processing analysis of masking with patterned stimuli', *Psychological Review*, vol.80, pp.1–52.

Vogel, E.K., Luck, S.J. and Shapiro, K.L. (1998) 'Electrophysiological evidence for a postperceptual locus of suppression during the attentional blink', *Journal of Experimental Psychology: Human Perception and Performance*, vol.24, pp.1656–74.

Woldorff, M.G., Gallen, C.C., Hampson, S.A., Hillyard, S.A., Pantev, C., Sobel, D. and Bloom, F.E. (1993) 'Modulation of early sensory processing in human auditory cortex during auditory selective attention', *Proceedings of the National Academy of Sciences of the USA*, vol.90, pp.8722–6.

Perception

Chapter 3

Graham Pike and Graham Edgar

1   Introduction

If you have ever searched frantically for an object that turns out to have been right in front of you all along, then this chapter may make you feel better. For, as you will see, perception of even the simplest object is actually a very complex affair. So, next time you turn the house upside down looking for your keys and then find them in the first place you looked, remember that your brain is using extremely sophisticated processes, many of which are beyond even the most advanced computer programs available today (not that computer programs ever lose their keys!).

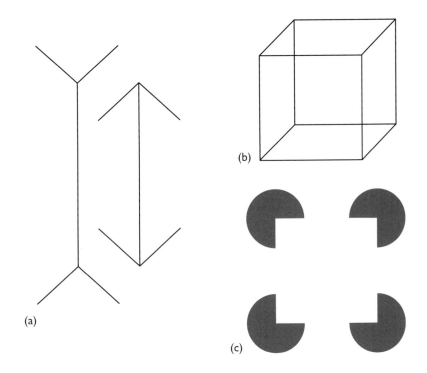

Figure 3.1   Three visual phenomena: (a) Müller-Lyer illusion; (b) Necker cube; (c) Kanizsa's illusory square

The sophistication of the cognitive processes that allow us to perceive visually is perhaps, if perversely, revealed best through the errors that our perceptual system can make. Figure 3.1 contains three very simple images that illustrate this. Image (a) is the Müller-Lyer illusion, in which the vertical line on the left is perceived as being longer even though both lines are of an identical length. Image (b) is a Necker cube, in which it is possible to perceive the cube in either of two perspectives (although you can never see both at the same time so please do not strain your eyes trying).

Image (c) is Kanizsa's (1976) illusory square, in which a square is perceived even though the image does not contain a square but only four three-quarter-complete circles.

ACTIVITY 3.1

Look at each of the three visual illusions in Figure 3.1 and try to work out why it occurs. If you can't think of an answer, it may help to look at Figure 3.2.

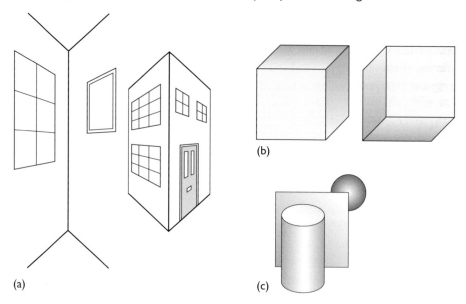

(b)

(a)   (c)

Figure 3.2 Some clues to why the illusions in Figure 3.1 may occur

COMMENT

One explanation for the Müller-Lyer illusion is that the arrowheads provide clues as to the distance of the upright line. For example, the inward-pointing arrowheads suggest that the vertical line might be the far corner of a room whilst the outward-pointing arrowheads suggest the vertical line could be the near corner of a building. We therefore see the first vertical line as longer because we assume it is further away from us than the second vertical line, though it makes the same size image on the retina.

The Necker cube can be seen in two different ways, as there are no clues as to which is the nearest face. Most cube-like objects that we encounter are solid and contain cues from lighting and texture about which is the nearest face. As the Necker cube does not contain these cues, we are unable to say for certain which face is closest.

Kanizsa's illusory square occurs due to a phenomenon known as perceptual completion. When we see an object partly hidden behind (occluded by) another object, we represent it to ourselves as a whole object rather than as missing its hidden parts. In the same way, we assume that four black circles are being occluded by a white square.

If the cognitive processes involved in perception were simple, then it would be hard to see how the effects in Figure 3.1 could occur. After all, they are all based on very straightforward geometric shapes that should be easy to perceive accurately. As we saw in Activity 3.1, there must be more sophisticated processes that have been developed to perceive the complex visual environment, which get confused or tricked by elements of these images. In fact the three effects above are likely to be caused because our visual system has evolved to perceive solid, three-dimensional (3D) objects and attempts to interpret the two-dimensional (2D) shapes as resulting from 3D scenes.

Perceptual errors arising from localized damage to the brain also demonstrate the complexities involved in visual perception. Some of the problems faced by people suffering from specific neuropsychological conditions include: being able to recognize objects but not faces (prosopagnosia); being able to perceive individual parts of the environment but not to integrate these parts into a whole; believing that one's family has been replaced by robots/aliens or impostors of the same appearance (Capgras syndrome); and only being able to perceive one side of an object (visual, or sensory, neglect – see Chapter 2, Section 5.1).

1.1 Perceiving and sensing

The term perception has different meanings, although a common element in most meanings is that perception involves the analysis of sensory information. When cognitive psychologists talk about perception, they are usually referring to the basic cognitive processes that analyse information from the senses. Throughout this chapter we shall be examining research and theories that have attempted to reveal and describe the cognitive processes responsible for analysing sensory information and providing a basic description of our environment; basically, how we make sense of our senses!

There has been considerable debate about the role played by sensory information in our perception of the world, with some philosophers rejecting the idea that it plays any part at all in the perception of objects. Atherton (2002) suggested that this may be because the notion of a sensation is rather problematic: 'Sensations seem to be annoying, extra little entities ... that somehow intervene between the round dish and our perception of it as round' (Atherton, 2002, p.4). We will not delve into this philosophical debate here, other than to note the distinction between sensation and perception. Throughout this chapter we will use the term 'sensation' to refer to the ability of our sense organs to detect various forms of energy (such as light or sound waves). However, to sense information does not entail making sense of it. There is a key difference between being able to detect the presence of a certain type of energy and being able to make use of that energy to provide information as to the nature of the environment surrounding us. Thus we use the term 'sensation' to refer to that initial detection and the term 'perception' to refer to the process of constructing a description of the surrounding world. For example, there is a difference between the cells in a person's eye reacting to light (sensation) and that person knowing that their module tutor is offering them a cup of tea (perception).

You may have noticed that we have begun to focus on visual perception rather than any of the other senses. Although the other senses, particularly hearing and touch, are undoubtedly important, there has been far more research on vision than on the other modalities. This is because when we interact with the world we rely more on vision than on our other senses. Far more of the primate brain is engaged in processing visual information than in processing information from any of the other senses. We use vision both in quite basic ways, such as avoiding objects, and in more advanced ways, such as in reading or recognizing faces and objects. So, although the previous chapter examined auditory perception and Chapter 4 will explore haptic perception (touch) as well as visual perception, we will devote the present chapter to examining research into, and theories of, visual perception.

1.2 The eye

The logical place to start any consideration of visual perception is with the eye. A cross-section of the human eye is presented in Figure 3.3. Incoming light passes through the cornea into a small compartment called the anterior chamber (filled with fluid termed aqueous humour) and then through the lens into the major chamber of the eye that is filled with a viscous jelly called vitreous humour. The light is focused by the lens/cornea combination onto the retina on the back surface of the eye. It is the receptor cells in the retina that 'sense' the light.

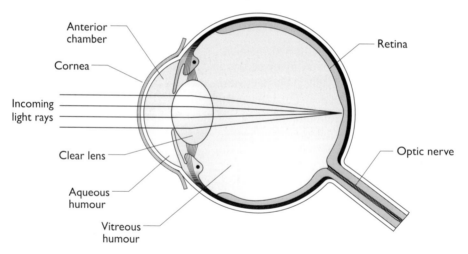

Figure 3.3   The human eye

The retina consists of two broad classes of receptor cell, rods and cones; so called for their shapes. Both rods and cones are sensitive to light, although the rods respond better than the cones at low light levels and are therefore the cells responsible for maintaining some vision in poor light. The cones are responsible for our ability to detect fine detail and different colours and are the basis of our vision at higher (daylight) light levels. Many animals, such as dogs and cats, have a higher ratio of rods to cones than humans do. This allows them to see better in poor light, but means that they are not so good at seeing either colour or fine detail.

One area of the retina that is of particular interest is the central portion known as the macula lutea (as it is yellow in colour and 'lutea' derives from a Latin word that means yellow), which contains almost all of the cones within the human retina. Within the macula, there is a small indentation called the fovea. The fovea is the area of the retina that contains the highest density of cones and is responsible for the perception of fine detail.

ACTIVITY 3.2

Place your thumbs together and hold them out at arm's length from your eyes. Now slowly move your left thumb to the left whilst keeping your eyes focused on your right thumb. You will find that, after you have moved your left thumb more than about two thumb widths away from where your eyes are focused, it appears to go out of focus. This is because the light being reflected into your eyes from the left thumb is no longer striking the fovea, meaning that you cannot perceive it in fine detail.

1.3   Approaches to perception

Psychologists have taken many different approaches to studying perception. One important distinction between approaches is whether the 'goal' of perception is assumed to be action or recognition. It is possible to conceive of recognition and action as being stages in the same perceptual process, so that action would only happen once recognition had taken place. However, our reaction to objects in the environment sometimes has to be very quick indeed, so that first having to work out what an object may be would be inconvenient to say the least. For example, if I see a moving object on a trajectory that means it will hit me in the head, the most important thing is to move my head out of the way. Working out that the object is the crystal tumbler containing vodka and tonic that was only moments ago in the hand of my somewhat angry looking partner is, for the moment at least, of secondary importance. I need to act to get out of the way of the object regardless of what the object actually is or who threw it.

As we shall see, there is evidence that perception for action and perception for recognition are quite different processes that may involve different neural mechanisms (Milner and Goodale, 1998). But, although it is important to make the distinction between perception for action and perception for recognition, we should not see them as being entirely independent. Sometimes the object that is about to hit your head could be the football that David Beckham has just crossed from the wing, requiring a very different response from that to the crystal tumbler.

Another way of differentiating approaches to perception is to consider the 'flow of information' through the perceptual system. To see what we mean by this phrase, try Activity 3.3.

ACTIVITY 3.3

Consider these two scenarios:

1   A blindfolded student trying to work out what the unknown object they have been handed might be.

2   A blindfolded student searching for their textbook.

Imagine you are the blindfolded student. What strategies do you think you might employ to complete the above two tasks successfully? Can you identify any key differences in these strategies?

COMMENT

A common strategy to employ for the first scenario is to try to build up a 'picture' of the object by gradually feeling it. A common strategy to employ for the second scenario is to hold in your mind the likely shape and texture of the book and to search the environment for an object that shares these characteristics. The key difference between these scenarios is the direction in which information about the object is 'flowing', demonstrated by how the student's existing knowledge of what objects look like is being utilized. In the first scenario, information is flowing 'upward', starting with an analysis of the information derived from the senses (in this case via touch). In the second scenario, information is flowing 'downward', starting with the knowledge of what books tend to feel like.

So, in the case of touch, perception of the environment can involve information 'flowing' through the relevant perceptual system in two directions. But what about vision? If we were to remove the blindfold from our student in Activity 3.3, they would instantly be able to tell what the unknown object was or to spot the book in front of them. Does this mean that there is not a similar flow of information when the sense being used is vision?

To answer this question, let's try to formulate the stages involved in the student perceiving that there is a book in front of them. One approach might be:

- Light reflected from the book strikes the retina and is analysed by the brain.

- This analysis reveals four sudden changes in brightness (caused by the edges of the book against whatever is behind it).

- Two of these are vertical edges and two are horizontal edges (the left/right and top/bottom of the book).

- Each straight edge is joined (by a right angle at each end) to two others (to form the outline of the book).

- Within these edges is an area of gradually changing brightness containing many small, much darker areas (the white pages with a growing shadow toward the spine and the much darker words).

- A comparison of this image with representations of objects seen previously suggests that the object is an open book.

As this approach starts with the image formed on the retina by the light entering the eye and proceeds by analysing this pattern to gradually build up a representation of the object in view, we refer to it as involving **bottom-up processing**. This means that the flow of information through the perceptual system starts from the bottom – the sensory receptors – and works upward until an internal representation of the object is formed.

There is, however, another way of recognizing the book. It is very likely that the student has seen many books in the past and has a fair idea of what a book should look like. This existing knowledge regarding book appearance could come in very useful in finding the textbook. Instead of building up a picture of the environment by analysing sensory information alone, it could be that the student uses existing knowledge of what books look like to find this particular book. For example, they might progress like this:

- I know that books are rectangular in shape and have light pages with dark words.
- I can see something in front of me that matches this description, so it must be a book.

The flow of information in this latter example has been reversed. The student started with existing knowledge regarding the environment and used this to guide their processing of sensory information. Thus the flow of information progressed from the top down as it started with existing knowledge stored in the brain, and we refer to it as involving **top-down processing**.

So both haptic and visual perceptual processes may operate both by building up a picture of the environment from sensory information and by using existing knowledge to make sense of new information. In other words, the flow of information through the perceptual system can be either bottom-up or top-down. These concepts will be explored throughout this chapter and we shall examine theories that concentrate on one or other of these processes and also look at how they might interact.

Summary of Section 1

- Even the perception of simple images involves sophisticated cognitive processing, as demonstrated by visual illusions and neuropsychological disorders.
- We use the term sensation to refer to the detection of a particular form of energy by one of the senses and the term perception to refer to the process of making sense of the information sent by the senses.
- In the human eye the lens and cornea focus light onto the retina, which contains receptor cells that are sensitive to light.
- Perception can have different goals. The most common goals are perception for action and perception for recognition.
- The bottom-up approach to perception sees sensory information as the starting point, with perception occurring through the analysis of this information to generate an internal description of the environment.
- The top-down approach to perception involves making greater use of prior knowledge, with this guiding the perceptual process.

2   The Gestalt approach to perception

As with Chapter 2, we are going to examine the various approaches that have been taken to studying visual perception in a more or less historical order. One of the principal approaches to perception in the first half of the twentieth century was that of the **Gestalt** movement, which was guided by the premise 'The whole is greater than the sum of its parts'. In perceptual terms, this meant that an image tended to be perceived according to the organization of the elements within it, rather than according to the nature of the individual elements themselves.

It is easy to see **perceptual organization** at work as it tends to be a very powerful phenomenon. In fact it appears as if both visual and auditory stimuli can be grouped according to similar organizing principles (Aksentijevic *et al.*, 2001).

ACTIVITY 3.4

Look at Figure 3.4 and describe your first impression of what you see.

Figure 3.4   Two examples of perceptual organization

You probably described seeing a circle and two crossing lines. But the image on the left is not a circle as it contains a gap at the top. This is the Gestalt perceptual organizational phenomenon of **closure** at work, in which a 'closed' figure tends to be perceived rather than an 'open' one. Likewise, the image on the right is not necessarily crossing lines, as it could be two pen-tips touching (in the middle of the image). The reason you see a cross is due to what the Gestalt researchers called **good continuation**, by which we tend to interpret (or organize) images to produce smooth continuities rather than abrupt changes.

Other Gestalt organizational laws include **proximity** and **similarity**.

ACTIVITY 3.5

As before, look at Figure 3.5 and describe your first impressions.

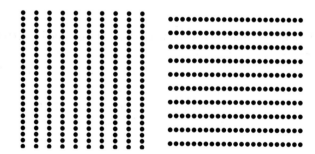

Figure 3.5   The organizational law of proximity

At one level you probably see two squares, due to the law of closure. However, you will also probably have seen the square on the left as consisting of columns of dots and the one on the right as consisting of rows of dots. The reason for this is that, in the left-hand image, the horizontal spacing between the dots is greater than the vertical, and vice versa for the image on the right. Thus, the proximity of the individual elements is being used to group them into columns in the left-hand square and rows in the right-hand one.

ACTIVITY 3.6

Now describe what you see in Figure 3.6.

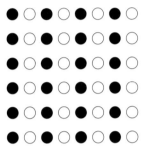

Figure 3.6   The organizational laws of similarity and proximity

As well as again seeing a square due to the law of closure, you perhaps saw the square as consisting of columns of circles. If so, this was an example of the organizational law of similarity (of colour). However, the spacing of the circles is such that the law of proximity encourages you to see rows not columns. For many people the law of similarity takes precedence and they see columns, while others may tend to see rows. Most people can readily switch between one organization (or interpretation) and the other because each conforms with a particular Gestalt law.

The Gestalt researchers (including Koffka, 1935; Kohler, 1947 and Werthiemer, 1923) formulated other organizational laws, but most were deemed to be manifestations of the **Law of Pragnanz**, described by Koffka as: 'Of several geometrically possible organizations that one will actually occur which possesses the best, simplest and most stable shape' (Koffka, 1935, p.138).

So, you can see that a number of organizational laws can be used in order to work out which individual components of an image should be grouped together. Now look around the room in which you are sitting. How many squares composed of dots can you see? How many nearly complete circles and crossing lines are there? Your immediate response was probably to say 'none' or 'only those in this book'. However, if you look carefully you will see that the stimuli used in the Gestalt demonstrations do have counterparts in the real world. For example, when I look out of my window I see a football that is partly hidden by a post and provides an example of closure, as I perceive a complete sphere rather than an incomplete circle. The figures that you have seen in this section can therefore be seen as simplified 2D versions of real-world objects and scenes. Because they are simplified, some information that would be present in real-world scenes is discarded. This lack of realism is a disadvantage. On the other hand, however, it is possible to control and manipulate features of these figures, such as the proximity or similarity of elements, to see how they may contribute to perception.

As we shall see in the next section, there is considerable tension in the field of visual perception as to the usefulness of simplified stimuli such as those used by the Gestaltists. Some approaches are based on laboratory experimentation in which simplified scenes or objects are shown to participants, whilst proponents of other approaches claim that perception can only be studied in the real world, by examining how people perceive solid, 3D objects that are part of a complex 3D environment.

Summary of Section 2

- The Gestalt approach to perception involved studying the principles by which individual elements tend to be organized together.
- Organizing principles include closure, good continuation, proximity and similarity.
- The stimuli used by Gestalt researchers tended to be quite simple, two-dimensional geometric patterns.

3   Gibson's theory of perception

In Section 1.3 we stated that one way of classifying different approaches to perception was according to whether they were primarily bottom-up or top-down. If visual perception is based primarily around bottom-up processing, we must be capable of taking the information from the light waves that reach our eyes and refining it into a description of the visual environment. Bottom-up perception requires that the light arriving at the retina is rich in information about the environment. One bottom-up approach to perception, that of J.J. Gibson (1950, 1966), is based on the premise that the information available from the visual environment is so rich that no cognitive processing is required at all. As Gibson himself said:

> When the senses are considered as a perceptual system, all theories of perception become at one stroke unnecessary. It is no longer a question of how the mind operates on the deliverances of sense, or how past experience can organize the data, or even how the brain can process the inputs of the nerves, but simply how information is picked up.
>
> *(Gibson, 1966, p.319)*

If you are thinking to yourself, 'What does picked up mean?' or 'How is this information *picked up*?', you are expressing a criticism that is often levelled at Gibson's theory (e.g. Marr, 1982). The Gibsonian approach concentrates on the information present in the visual environment rather than on how it may be analysed. There is a strong link between perception and action in Gibson's theory, and action rather than the formation of an internal description of the environment can be seen as the 'end point' of perception.

Gibson conceptualized the link between perception and action by suggesting that perception is **direct**, in that the information present in light is sufficient to allow a person to move through and interact with the environment. One implication of this is that, whereas perception of a real environment is direct, perception of a 2D image in a laboratory experiment (or any 2D image come to that) would be *indirect*. When confronted with an image, our direct perception is that it is an image; that it is two-dimensional and printed on paper, for example. Our perception of that which it depicts is only indirect. For this reason, Gibson thought that perception could never be fully explored using laboratory experiments.

Figure 3.7 *Ceci n'est pas une pipe*, 1928, by René Magritte

When you look at Figure 3.7, what do you see? Your first reaction is probably to say 'a pipe'. But, if what you are seeing is a pipe, then why can't you pick it up and smoke it? As Magritte informs us, what you are seeing is not a pipe, but a picture of a pipe. Like Gibson, Magritte is drawing a distinction between direct perception (paint on canvas) and indirect perception (that the painting depicts a pipe).

3.1 An ecological approach

At the heart of Gibson's approach to perception is the idea that the world around us structures the light that reaches the retina. Gibson believed perception should be studied by determining how the real environment structures the light that reaches our retina. From the importance placed on the 'real world' it is clear why Gibson's is seen as an **ecological approach** to perception. Gibson referred to theories that were based on experiments employing artificial, isolated, flat (or plane) shapes as 'air' theories, whilst he referred to his own as a 'ground' theory, as it emphasized the role played by the real, textured surface of the ground in providing information about distance. As Gibson stated: 'A surface is substantial; a plane is not. A surface is textured; a plane is not. A surface is never perfectly transparent; a plane is. A surface can be seen; a plane can only be visualized' (Gibson, 1979, p.35).

The impetus for Gibson's theory came from his work training pilots to land and take off during the Second World War. When approaching a runway, it is very important that a pilot is able to judge accurately the distance between plane and ground. The perceptual skill involved in this judgement is that of 'depth perception', this being the ability to judge how far you are from an object or surface. However, Gibson found that tests based on pictorial stimuli did not distinguish good from bad pilots and that training with pictorial stimuli had little impact on actual landing performance (Gibson, 1947). Extrapolating from this problem, Gibson suggested that psychological experimentation based on the use of pictorial stimuli is not an apt method for studying perception.

His point was that the experience of perception in the real world is very different from the experience of looking at 2D experimental stimuli in a laboratory. In the real world, objects are not set against a blank background, but against the ground, which consists of a very large number of surfaces that vary in their distance from and orientation to the observer. In their turn, these surfaces are not perfectly smooth planes, but consist of smaller elements, such as sand, earth and stone, which give them a textured appearance. In addition, the objects themselves will consist of real surfaces that also contain texture. To explain perception, we need to be able to explain how these surfaces and textures provide information about the world around us.

3.2 The optic array and invariant information

The structure that is imposed on light reflected by the textured surfaces in the world around us is what Gibson termed the **ambient optic array**. The basic structure of the optic array is that the light reflected from surfaces in the environment converges at the point in space occupied by the observer (see Figure 3.8). As you can see from Figure 3.9, as you stand up, the position of your head with respect to the environment is altered and the optic array changes accordingly.

You can see from Figures 3.8 and 3.9 that the primary structure of the optic array is a series of angles that are formed by light reflecting into the eyes from the surfaces within the environment. For example, an angle may be formed between the light that is reflected from the near edge of a table and that from the far edge.

In addition to the primary structure of the optic array, Gibson maintained that there were additional, higher-order features that could provide unambiguous information as to the nature of the environment. He referred to these higher-order features as **invariants**, and believed that an observer could perceive the surrounding world by actively sampling the optic array in order to detect invariant information.

One of the most commonly cited forms of invariant information was explored by Sedgwick (1973). Sedgwick demonstrated the 'horizon ratio relation', which specifies that the ratio of how much of an object is above the horizon to how much is

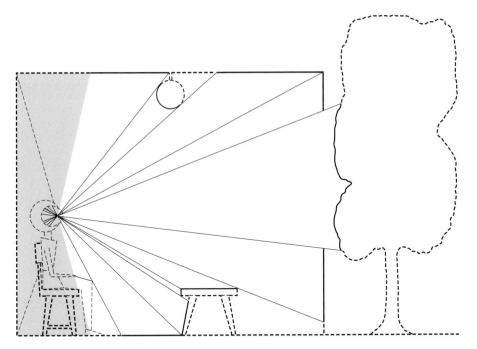

Figure 3.8 The ambient optic array

Source: Gibson, 1979, Figure 5.3

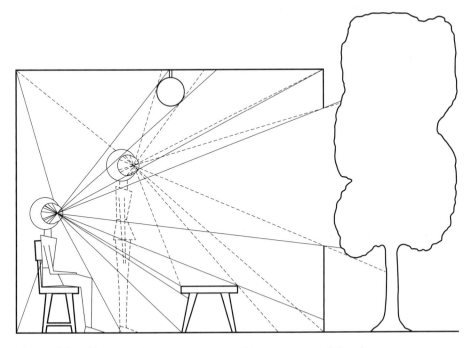

Figure 3.9 Change in the optic array caused by movement of the observer

Source: Gibson, 1979, Figure 5.4

below remains constant (or invariant) as the object travels either toward or away from you (see Figure 3.10). This form of invariant information allows you to judge the relative heights of different objects regardless of how far away they are. The proportion of the object that is 'above' the horizon increases with the overall height of the object (see Figure 3.11).

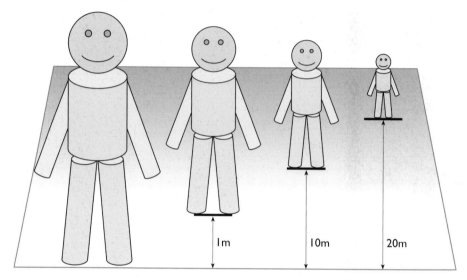

Figure 3.10   The horizon ratio relation: same height objects at different distances

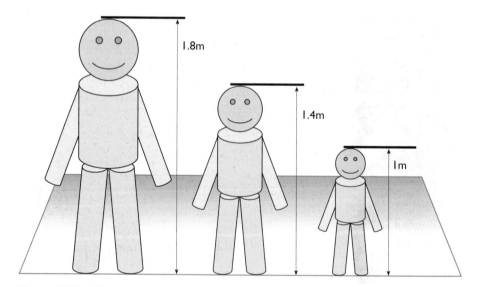

Figure 3.11   The horizon ratio relation: different height objects at same distance

One of the most important forms of invariant information in Gibson's theory is **texture gradient**, although he also discusses gradients of colour, intensity and disparity. There are three main forms of texture gradient relating to the density, perspective and compression of texture elements. The exact nature of a texture element will change from surface to surface (see Figure 3.12); in a carpet the elements are caused by the individual twists of material; on a road they are caused by the small stones that make up the surface. In making use of texture gradients, we assume that the texture of the surface is uniform; for example, that the road surface consists of stones of similar size throughout its length. Therefore, any change in the apparent nature of the texture provides us with information regarding the distance, orientation and curvature of the surface.

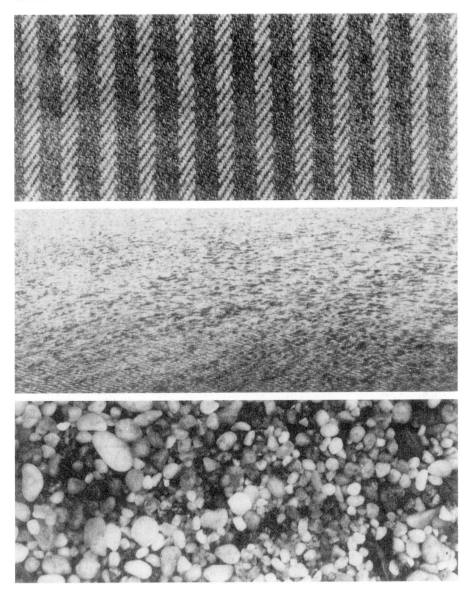

Figure 3.12   Examples of texture elements

Source: Gibson, 1979, Figure 2.1

Using texture gradients as a guide, we can tell if a surface is receding because the density of texture elements (number of elements per square metre) will increase with distance. For example, the surface in Figure 3.13(a) appears to recede as the density of texture elements (the individual squares) increases toward the top of the image.

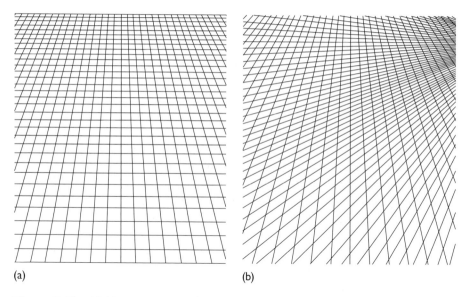

(a)   (b)

Figure 3.13   (a) How texture gradient can reveal that a surface is receding; (b) how perspective and compression gradients reveal the shape and orientation of a surface

In a similar fashion, the perspective gradient (the width of individual elements) and the compression gradient (the height of individual elements) can reveal the shape and orientation of a surface. As you can see from Figure 3.13(b), we do not see this surface as flat because the width and height of the individual texture elements change, making the surface appear to be slanting and curved.

Without texture, considerable ambiguity about shape and orientation can be introduced into the stimulus and this poses a problem for experiments that make use of planar geometric shapes (as you saw with the Necker cube in Activity 3.1). So, texture gradient is a powerful source of invariant information provided by the structure of light within the optic array. It furnishes us with a wealth of information regarding the distance, size and orientation of surfaces in the environment.

3.3   Flow in the ambient optic array

What is clear to me now that was not clear before is that structure as such, frozen structure, is a myth, or at least a limiting case. Invariants of structure do not exist except in relation to variants.

(Gibson, 1979, p.87)

In the above quotation Gibson is highlighting the importance of another intrinsic aspect of perception that is often missing from laboratory stimuli – that of motion. His argument is that invariant information can only be perceived in relation to variant information. To put it another way, in a static view all information is invariant because it never changes. To perceive invariant information, we have to see the environment change over time.

There are two basic forms of movement: motion of the observer and motion of objects within the environment. Motion of the observer tends to produce the greatest degree of movement as the entire optic array is transformed (see Figure 3.9). Gibson suggested that this transformation provided valuable information about the position and shape of surfaces and objects. For example, information about shape and particularly position is revealed by a phenomenon known as **motion parallax**. The principle of motion parallax is that the further an object is from an observer, the less it will *appear* to move as the observer travels past it. Imagine the driver of a moving inter-city train looking out of their side-window at a herd of cows grazing in a large field next to the line. The cows near the train will *appear* to move past much faster than the cows at the back of the field. Thus, the degree of apparent motion is directly related to the distance of the object from the observer.

A second means by which observer motion can provide information about the shape and position of objects is through **occlusion**. Imagine the same observer described above travelling past the same field of cows. Their motion will cause the cows nearest to the train to pass in front of, or *occlude*, the cows grazing further away. This allows the observer to deduce that the *occluded* cows (i.e. the ones that become hidden by other cows) are further away than those doing the *occluding*.

Gibson dealt with the motion of the observer through reference to **flow patterns** in the optic array. As our train driver looks at the grazing cows by the side of the track, the entire optic array will appear to flow past from left to right, assuming that the driver looks out of the right-hand window (see Figure 3.14).

Figure 3.14 Flow patterns in the optic array parallel to the direction of the observer's motion

When the train driver becomes bored with cow watching and returns their attention to the track in front of the train, the flow patterns in the optic array will change so that the texture elements appear to be radiating from the direction in which the train is travelling (the apparent origin of this radiating flow pattern is known as the **pole**). The texture elements that make up the surfaces in the environment will appear to emerge from the pole, stream toward the observer and then disappear from view (see Figure 3.15).

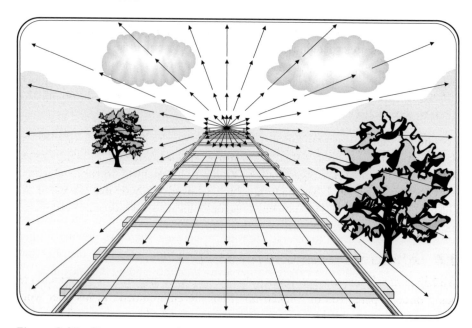

Figure 3.15   Flow patterns in the optic array in the direction of the observer's motion

This pattern would be completely reversed if the guard at the rear of the train were to look back toward the direction from which the train had come (see Figure 3.16).

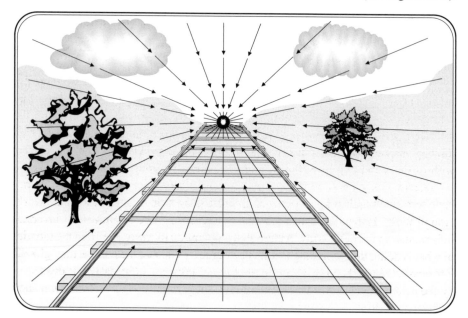

Figure 3.16   Flow patterns in the optic array in the opposite direction to the observer's motion

Gibson proposed a set of rules that linked flow in the optic array to the movement of the observer through the environment (Gibson, 1979):

* If there is flow in the ambient optic array, the observer is in motion; if there is no flow, the observer is not moving.

- Outflow of the optic array from the pole specifies approach by the observer and inflow to the pole specifies retreat.

- The direction of the pole specifies the direction in which the observer is moving.

- A change in the direction of the pole specifies that the observer is moving in a new direction.

For Gibson, the movement of the observer was a critical part of perception. In fact he deemed it of such importance that he saw the *perceptual system* as not being limited to the eyes and other sense organs but constituting a hierarchy of organs in which the eyes are linked to a head that can turn, which is linked to a body that can move. As Gibson said: 'perceiving is an act, not a response, an act of attention, not a triggered impression, an achievement, not a reflex' (Gibson, 1979, p.21).

3.4   Affordances and resonance

We began our discussion of Gibson's theory by stating that he saw information as being directly perceived or 'picked up' from the environment. In his later work Gibson (1979) took this idea of information being 'picked up' one step further and suggested that the end point of the perceptual process was not a visual description of the surrounding world, but rather that objects directly 'afforded' their use.

At its simplest (and least controversial level) the concept of **affordance** builds on earlier research conducted by the Gestalt psychologists, in which the features of objects were seen as providing information as to their use. For instance, the features of a rock would suggest that it could be stood upon, the features of a fallen branch that it could be picked up, and the features of a fruit that it could be eaten.

However, Gibson makes two claims regarding affordances that are rather harder to accept and have proven to be far more controversial. First, he states that affordances act as a bridge between perception and action and do not require the intervention of any cognitive processes. Just as the nature of the environment can be directly 'picked up' from the structure of the optic array, the observer can interact with surfaces and objects in the environment directly through affordance.

Second, Gibson saw no role for memory in perception, as the observer does not have to consult their prior experience in order to be able to interact with the world around them. Instead he states that the perceptual system **resonates** to invariant information in the optic array. Although the definition of 'resonates' and the identity of what is doing the resonating is left very vague by Gibson, the point is that 'global' information about the optic array (in the form of invariant information) is dealt with by the perceptual system without the need to analyse more 'local' information such as lines and edges.

These assertions may seem unreasonable to you, as they have done to other researchers. If we are studying psychology, then surely the cognitive processes that allow us to perceive must be one focus of our attention. In addition, if when perceiving the world we do not make use of our prior experiences, how will we ever learn from our mistakes? In the next two sections we shall turn to theories that attempt to deal with these issues and to explain exactly how the brain makes sense of the world around us.

However, even if Gibson's theory does not enlighten us as to the nature of the cognitive processes that are involved in perception, his theory has been extremely influential, and researchers in perception still need to bear in mind his criticisms of the laboratory approach which makes use of artificial stimuli:

> Experiments using dynamic naturalistic stimuli can now be conducted, virtual scenes can be constructed, and images of brain activity while viewing these can be captured in a way that would have been difficult to envisage a century ago. However, the simulated lure of the screen (or even a pair of screens) should not blind experimenters and theorists to the differences that exist between the virtual and the real.
>
> *(Wade and Bruce, 2001, p.105)*

Summary of Section 3

- Gibson developed an ecological approach to perception and placed great emphasis on the way in which real objects and surfaces structure light – he termed this the ambient optic array.
- He suggested that invariant information (such as texture gradient) could be 'picked up' from the optic array to provide cues as to the position, orientation and shape of surfaces.
- Invariant information could also be revealed by motion, which produces variants such as flow patterns in the optic array.
- The importance of real surfaces and of motion led Gibson to suggest that perception could not be studied using artificial stimuli in a laboratory setting.
- Gibson did not see perception as a product of complex cognitive analysis, but suggested that objects could 'afford' their use directly.
- Interaction with the environment is at the heart of Gibson's theory; action is seen as the 'goal' of perception.

4   Marr's theory of perception

> ... the detection of physical invariants, like image surfaces, is exactly and precisely an information-processing problem, in modern terminology. And second, he [Gibson] vastly underrated the sheer difficulty of such detection ... Detecting physical invariants is just as difficult as Gibson feared, but nevertheless we can do it. And the only way to understand how is to treat it as an information-processing problem.
>
> *(Marr, 1982, p.30)*

As we stated previously, one criticism that has been levelled at Gibson's approach is that it does not explain in sufficient detail *how* information is picked up from the environment. To address this problem, a theory was needed that attempted to explain exactly how the brain was able to take the information sensed by the eyes and turn it into an accurate, internal representation of the surrounding world. Such a theory was proposed by David Marr (1982).

Before we look at Marr's theory, it is worth pointing out some of the similarities and differences between the approaches taken by Marr and Gibson. Like Gibson, Marr's theory suggests that the information from the senses is sufficient to allow perception to occur. However, unlike Gibson, Marr adopted an information-processing approach in which the processes responsible for analysing the retinal image were central. Marr's theory is therefore strongly 'bottom-up', in that it sees the retinal image as the starting point of perception and explores how this image might be analysed in order to produce a description of the environment. This meant that, unlike Gibson, who saw action as the end point of perception, Marr concentrated on the perceptual processes involved in object recognition.

Marr saw the analysis of the retinal image as occurring in four distinct stages, with each stage taking the output of the previous one and performing a new set of analyses on it. The four stages were:

1   *Grey level description* – the intensity of light is measured at each point in the retinal image.

2   *Primal sketch* – first, in the raw primal sketch, areas that could potentially correspond to the edges and texture of objects are identified. Then, in the full primal sketch, these areas are used to generate a description of the outline of any objects in view.

3   *2½D sketch* – at this stage a description is formed of how the surfaces in view relate to one another and to the observer.

4   *3D object-centred description* – at this stage object descriptions are produced that allow the object to be recognized from any angle (i.e. independent of the viewpoint of the observer).

More generally, Marr concentrated his work at the computational theory and algorithmic levels of analysis and had little to say about the neural hardware that might be involved. One reason for this is that he developed his theory largely by designing computer-based models and algorithms that could perform the requisite analyses.

4.1   The grey level description

One way of describing the first stage in Marr's theory is to say that it gets rid of colour information. This is not because Marr thought that colour was unimportant in perception. Rather, he thought that colour information was processed by a distinct **module** and need not be involved in obtaining descriptions of the shape of objects and the layout of the environment. In fact, the modular nature of perception was a fundamental part of Marr's theory:

> Computer scientists call the separate pieces of a process its modules, and the idea that a large computation can be split up and implemented as a collection of parts that are as nearly independent of one another as the

overall task allows, is so important that I was moved to elevate it to a principle; the principle of modular design.

(Marr, 1982, p.102)

This meant that the perception of colour could be handled by one 'module' and the perception of shape by another.

The first stage in Marr's theory acts to produce a description containing the intensity (i.e. the brightness) of light at all points of the retina. A description composed solely of intensity information is referred to as 'greyscale', as, without the information provided by analysing the wavelength of light, it will consist of nothing but different tones of grey. If you turn down the colour on your TV, the resulting picture will be a greyscale image – although we call it 'black and white', it actually consists of many shades of grey.

Without going into too much detail, it is possible to derive the intensity of the light striking each part of the retina, because as light strikes a cell in the retina, the voltage across the cell membrane changes and the size of this change (or **depolarization**) corresponds to the intensity of the light. Therefore, a greyscale (or grey level) description is produced by the pattern of depolarization on the retina. In other words it is possible to derive the greyscale description simply by analysing the outputs of the receptor cells in the retina.

4.2   The primal sketch

The next part in Marr's theory, the generation of the primal sketch, occurs in two stages. The first stage consists of forming a raw primal sketch from the grey level description by identifying patterns of changing intensity.

ACTIVITY 3.7

Find a wooden table or chair and place it where it is both well-illuminated and against a light background. Describe how the intensity of the light reflected from the table/chair changes across its surface and in comparison with the background.

COMMENT

You should be able to see that the edges of the table/chair are marked by a quite large, sharp change in the intensity of the reflected light caused by the object in question being darker than the background. In addition, there are smaller changes in intensity caused by the individual parts of the table/chair and by the texture of the wood. You may also have noticed other changes in the intensity of the reflected light that did not correspond to the edge of the object, its parts or texture.

It is possible to group changes in the intensity of the reflected light into three categories:

- Relatively large changes in intensity produced by the edge of an object.

- Smaller changes in intensity caused by the parts and texture of an object.

- Still smaller changes in intensity due to random fluctuations in the light reflected.

Marr and Hildreth (1980) proposed an algorithm that could be used to determine which intensity changes corresponded to the edges of objects, meaning that changes in intensity due to random fluctuations could be discarded. The algorithm made use of a technique called **Gaussian blurring**, which involves averaging the intensity values in circular regions of the greyscale description. The values at the centre of the circle are weighted more than those at the edges in a way identical to a normal (or Gaussian) distribution.

By changing the size of the circle in which intensity values are averaged, it is possible to produce a range of images blurred to different degrees. Figure 3.17 shows images that have been produced in this manner. The original (i.e. unblurred) image is shown in (a). As you can see, using a wider circle (b) produces a more blurred image than using a narrower circle (c).

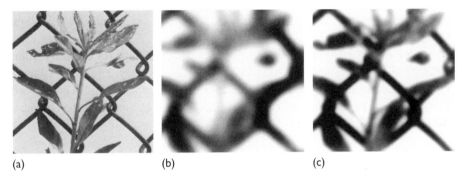

(a)   (b)   (c)

Figure 3.17   Examples of Gaussian blurred images

Source: Marr and Hildreth, 1980, p.190

Marr and Hildreth's algorithm works by comparing images that have been blurred to different degrees. If an intensity change is visible at two or more adjacent levels of blurring, then it is assumed that it cannot correspond to a random fluctuation and must relate to the edge of an object. Although this algorithm was implemented by Marr and Hildreth on a computer, there is evidence that retinal processing delivers descriptions that have been blurred to different degrees.

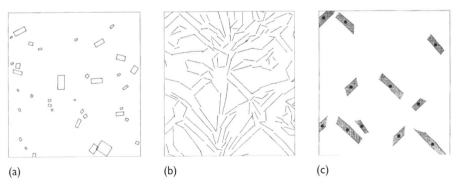

(a)   (b)   (c)

Figure 3.18   Primitives used in the raw primal sketch: (a) blobs, (b) edge-segments and (c) bars

Source: Marr, 1982, Figure 2.21, p.72

By analysing the changes in intensity values in the blurred images, it is possible to form a symbolic representation consisting of four **primitives** corresponding to four types of intensity change. Marr referred to these primitives as 'edge-segments', 'bars', 'terminations' and 'blobs'. An edge-segment represented a sudden change in intensity; a bar represented two parallel edge-segments; a termination represented a sudden discontinuity; and a blob corresponded to a small, enclosed area bounded by changes in intensity. In Figure 3.18, you can see how the image shown in Figure 3.17(a) would be represented using three of these primitives, whilst Figure 3.19 shows how three simple lines would be represented in the raw primal sketch.

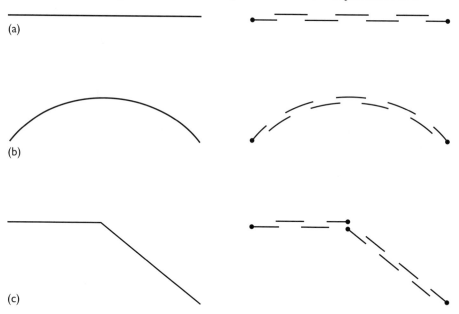

(a)

(b)

(c)

Figure 3.19   Representation of three simple lines in the raw primal sketch: 'The raw primal sketch represents a straight line as a termination, several oriented segments, and a second termination (a). If the line is replaced by a smooth curve, the orientations of the inner segments will gradually change (b). If the line changes its orientation suddenly in the middle (c), its representation will include an explicit pointer to this discontinuity. Thus in this representation, smoothness and continuity are assumed to hold unless explicitly negated by an assertion' (Marr, 1982, p.74)

Source: Marr, 1982, Figure 2.22, p.74

As you can see from Figure 3.19, although the raw primal sketch contains a lot of information about details in the image, it does not contain explicit information about the global structure of the objects in view. The next step is therefore to transform the raw primal sketch into a description, known as the **full primal sketch**, which contains information about how the image is organized, particularly about the location, shape, texture and internal parts of any objects that are in view.

Basically, the idea is that **place tokens** are assigned to areas of the raw primal sketch based on the **grouping** of the edge-segments, bars, terminations and blobs. If these place tokens then form a group themselves, they can be aggregated together to form a new, higher-order place token.

Imagine looking at a tiger. The raw primal sketch would contain information about the edge of the tiger's body, but also about the edges and pattern of its stripes and the texture of its hair. In the full primal sketch, place tokens will be produced by the grouping of the individual hairs into each of the stripes. The place tokens for each stripe would then also be grouped (because they run in a consistent vertical pattern along the tiger) into a higher-order place token, meaning that there will be at least two levels of place tokens making up the tiger.

Various mechanisms exist for grouping the raw primal sketch components into place tokens and for grouping place tokens together. These include **clustering**, in which tokens that are close to one another are grouped in a way very similar to the Gestalt principle of proximity, and **curvilinear aggregation**, in which tokens with related alignments are grouped in a similar fashion to the Gestalt principle of good continuation.

As we saw in Section 2, perceptual grouping is a robust, long-established and powerful effect. Marr saw algorithms expressing laws such as those formulated by the Gestalt approach as being responsible for turning the ambiguous raw primal sketch into the full primal sketch in which the organization of objects and surfaces was specified.

4.3   The 2½D sketch

In Marr's theory, the goal of early visual processing is the production of a description of the environment in which the layout of surfaces and objects is specified in relation to the particular view that the observer has at that time. Up until now we have been looking at how the shape of objects and surfaces can be recovered from the retinal image. However, in order to specify the layout of surfaces, we need to now include other information, specifically cues that tell us how far away each surface is.

Marr's modular approach to perception means that while the full primal sketch is being produced, other visual information is being analysed simultaneously. Much of this has to do with establishing depth relations, the distance between a surface and the observer and also how far objects extend. We saw in Section 3 that motion cues and cues from texture can be used to specify the distance to an object, and it is also possible to make use of the disparity in the retinal images of the two eyes (known as **stereopsis**), and shading cues that are represented in the primal sketch.

Marr proposed that the information from all these 'modules' was combined together to produce the 2½D sketch. It is called the 2½D sketch, rather than the 3D sketch, because the specification of the position and depth of surfaces and objects is done in relation to the observer. Thus, the description of an object will be **viewer-centred** and will not contain any information about the object that is not present in the retinal image. How the viewer-centred 2½D sketch is turned into a fully 3D, **object-centred** description is one of the topics dealt with in the next chapter.

Marr saw the 2½D sketch as consisting of a series of primitives that contained vectors (a line depicting both size and direction) showing the orientation of each surface. A vector can be seen as a needle, in which the direction the needle is pointing tells us in which direction the surface is facing, and its length tells us by how much the surface is slanted in relation to the observer. A cube would therefore be represented like the one shown in Figure 3.20. In addition to the information shown in Figure 3.20, Marr suggested that each vector (or needle) would have a number associated with it that indicated the distance from the observer.

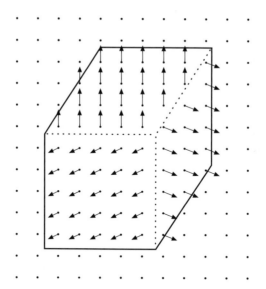

Figure 3.20   A 2½D sketch of a cube

Source: Marr, 1982, Figure 4.2, p.278

The 2½D sketch therefore provides an unambiguous description of the size, shape, location, orientation and distance of all the surfaces currently in view, in relation to the observer.

4.4   Evaluating Marr's approach

Marr's theory was the catalyst for a great deal of computational and psychological research. Some of this research has reported findings consistent with the mechanisms proposed by Marr, whilst some has found that Marr's theory does not offer a good explanation for the results obtained. We will not attempt to review every single study here, but instead describe a few studies that have tested elements of Marr's theory.

Marr and Hildreth (1980) attempted to test their idea that the raw primal sketch was formed by searching for changes in intensity values in adjacent levels of blurring, by implementing this algorithm in a computer program. They found that when applied to images of everyday scenes the algorithm was reasonably successful in locating the edges of objects. However, as with all computer-simulation research, it is important to remember that, just because a specific program yields the expected results, it does not necessarily follow that this is what is happening in the human perceptual system.

It seems as if Marr's approach to the formation of the full primal sketch was flawed in that it was limited to grouping strategies based on the 2D properties of an image. Enns and Rensick (1990) showed that participants could easily determine which one of a series of figures consisting of blocks was the odd-one-out, even though the only difference between the figures was their orientation in three dimensions. Thus, some grouping strategies must make use of 3D information.

One area in which Marr's theory does seem to fit the results of experimentation is in the integration of depth cues in the 2½D sketch. This phenomenon has been studied in experiments that have attempted to isolate certain forms of depth cue and then determine how they interact. For example, Young *et al.* (1993) looked at how motion cues interacted with texture cues. They concluded that the perceptual system does process these cues separately, and will also make selective use of them depending on how 'noisy' they are. In other words, in forming the 2½D sketch, the perceptual system does seem to integrate different modules of depth information, but will also place more emphasis on those modules that are particularly useful for processing the current image.

As well as the success of the specific processes suggested by Marr, it is also possible to evaluate his theory according to broader concepts. As we shall see in Section 6, there is evidence that there are two visual pathways in the brain that appear to process separately 'what' information and 'where' information. It seems that there exist different perceptual processes according to whether the goal of perception is action or object recognition. Although Marr's theory is a modular approach, so that different types of visual information are processed separately, it did not predict the separation of visual pathways into action and object recognition and indeed it is hard to incorporate this into the theory (Wade and Bruce, 2001). However, although the precise nature of the processes suggested by Marr may not map exactly onto those actually used by the brain to perceive the world, the impact of Marr's theory should not be underestimated: 'Thus it is not the details of Marr's theory which have so far stood the test of time, but the approach itself' (Wade and Bruce, 2001, p.97).

Summary of Section 4

- Marr proposed a theory of vision that was based on bottom-up processing of information.
- His approach was to see perception as being composed of a series of stages, with each stage generating an increasingly sophisticated description.
- Marr saw the end point of the perceptual process as object recognition rather than action.
- The first stage involves producing a grey level description based on the activation of retinal cells.
- This description is analysed by blurring it to different degrees. Changes in intensity value that are present in two or more adjacent levels of blurring are assumed to correspond to the 'edge' of an object (or part of an object).
- The raw primal sketch is generated by assigning one of four primitives (edge-segment, bar, termination or blob) to each change in intensity values.

- The full primal sketch is generated by using perceptual organizational principles such as clustering and similarity to group these primitives together and assign each group a place token.
- Information from different modules (such as stereopsis and motion) is combined with the full primal sketch to produce the 2½D sketch. This contains primitives consisting of vectors that reveal the distance and orientation, in relation to the observer, of the visible surfaces.

5   Constructivist approaches to perception

The previous sections of this chapter should have given you some idea of how we can see and interpret sensory information. The emphasis so far has been on 'bottom-up' processes. As discussed previously, there is also information flowing 'top-down' from stored knowledge. This makes intuitive sense. To be able to perceive something as 'a bus', you need to access stored knowledge concerning what the features of a bus actually are (big object with wheels, etc.).

Thus, what you see a stimulus *as* depends on what you know. This notion that perceiving something involves using stored knowledge as well as information coming in from the senses is embodied in an approach referred to as the **constructivist approach**. The approach is described as 'constructivist' because it is based on the idea that the sensory information that forms the basis of perception is, as we have already suggested, incomplete. It is necessary to *build* (or 'construct') our perception of the world from *incomplete* information. To do this we use what we already *know* about the world to interpret the incomplete sensory information coming in, and to 'make sense' of it. Thus stored knowledge is used to aid in the recognition of objects.

ACTIVITY 3.8

Look back at Activity 3.1. Can you explain any of the visual illusions in terms of what you now know about the bottom-up approach to perception?

COMMENT

Gibson would tell us that the Necker cube is a geometric figure that contains none of the information (particularly texture gradients) that we would usually use when perceiving an object. Marr's theory can help us to explain Kanizsa's illusory square, as the four areas of intensity change corresponding to the missing parts of the circles would be grouped together to form a square.

But what about the Müller-Lyer illusion? There are a number of alternative explanations for this illusion, one of which is that we group each vertical line with its set of arrowheads to form a single object. This of course results in the object with the inward-pointing arrowheads being larger than the one with the outward-pointing arrowheads; basically, due to perceptual grouping we cannot separate the vertical line from the overall size of the object. However, as the Müller-Lyer illusion is reduced if the straight arrowheads are replaced with curved lines (see Figure 3.21), it could be that we also need to look at an explanation based on top-down perception.

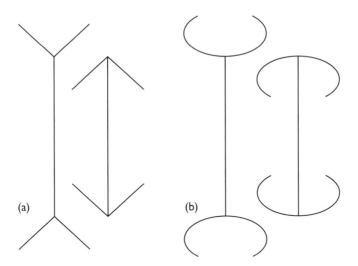

Figure 3.21   The original Müller-Lyer illusion (a), and with curved arrowheads (b)

As we saw in Activity 3.1, another explanation of the Müller-Lyer illusion is that we make use of top-down information and see the outward-pointing arrowheads as an indication that the vertical line is nearer to us than the line with the inward-pointing arrowheads.

Two of the foremost proponents of the constructivist approach are Irvin Rock (1977, 1983, 1997) and Richard Gregory (1980). Gregory suggested that individuals attempt to recognize objects by generating a series of **perceptual hypotheses** about what that object might be. Gregory conceptualized this process as being akin to how a scientist might investigate a problem by generating a series of hypotheses and accepting the one that is best supported by the data (in perception, 'data' would be the information flowing 'up' from the senses).

We are forced to generate hypotheses, according to Gregory's argument, because the sensory data are incomplete. If we had perfect and comprehensive sensory data we would have no need of hypotheses as we would *know* what we perceived. Stored knowledge is assumed to be central to the generation of perceptual hypotheses as it allows us to fill in the gaps in our sensory input. The influence of stored knowledge in guiding perceptual hypotheses can be demonstrated by the use of impoverished figures such as the one in Figure 3.22 (Street, 1931).

At first glance this picture may be difficult to perceive as anything other than a series of blobs. So the resulting hypothesis might be that it is just 'a load of blobs'. If, however, you are told that it is a picture of an ocean liner (coming towards you, viewed from water level) then the picture may immediately resolve into an image of an ocean liner. The sensory information has not changed, but what you know about it has, allowing you to generate a reasonable hypothesis of what the figure represents. Similarly, in the example, used in Activity 3.3, of trying to

Figure 3.22   An example of an impoverished figure
Source: Street, 1931

identify an object by touch alone, if you are given some clues about the function of the object (i.e. your knowledge related to the object is increased), it is likely to be easier to identify it.

The use of knowledge to guide our perceptual hypotheses may not always lead to a 'correct' perception. There are some stimuli with which we are so familiar (such as faces) that there can be a strong bias towards accepting a particular perceptual hypothesis, resulting in a 'false' perception. For instance, look at the faces in Figure 3.23.

  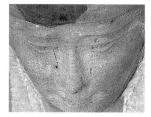

Figure 3.23   The mask of Hor

This is the mask of Hor, an Egyptian mummy. The first view is the mask from the front and the second two are of the back of the mask. Although the face viewed from the back is 'hollow' it still appears perceptually as a normal face. Our knowledge of how a face is supposed to look is (according to Gregory, 1980) so strong that we cannot accept the hypothesis that a face could be 'hollow'. This effect is interesting in that it provides an example of a perceptual hypothesis conflicting with what Gregory terms 'high-level' knowledge. You *know* at a conceptual level that the mask is hollow, yet you still *perceive* it as a 'normal' face. This, as Gregory suggests, represents a tendency to go with the most *likely* hypothesis. The Penrose triangle (Penrose and Penrose, 1958) in Figure 3.24 demonstrates a similar point.

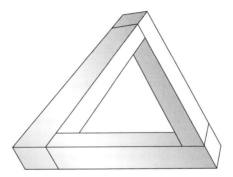

Figure 3.24   An impossible triangle

Source: Penrose and Penrose, 1958

It would be impossible to construct the object in Figure 3.24 so that the three sides of the triangle were joined. At one level, we 'know' that this must be true. Yet whichever corner of the triangle we attend to suggests a particular 3D interpretation. Our interpretation of the figure changes as our eyes (or just our attention) jumps from corner to corner. These data-supported interpretations, or hypotheses, tend to overwhelm the conceptual knowledge that we are viewing a flat pattern.

Although the constructivist approach in general, and Gregory's theories in particular, provide an attractive explanatory framework for perception, there are areas of the theory (as there were with Gibson's approach) that are left rather vague. For instance, how do we actually generate hypotheses and how do we know when to stop and decide which is the 'right' one? Why does knowledge sometimes but not always help perception? How can we 'know' something is wrong, and yet still perceive it as wrong (as with the hollow face)? Although these are difficult questions to answer, progress is being made in explaining how human perception may be based, at least in part, on constructivist principles; some of this work will be discussed below.

Thus, there appears to be evidence that perceptions of the outside world can be 'constructed' using information flowing 'up' from the senses combined with knowledge flowing 'down'. However, this seems to be in direct contrast to the theories of Gibson and Marr discussed earlier which suggest that there is no need to use stored knowledge to interpret the information flowing in from the senses. Indeed, the impossible triangle above shows that we do not always make use of knowledge that may be relevant and available. So, just how important is knowledge to the process of perception, and is there any way in which we can reconcile theories of perception that see knowledge as being essential with those that see it as unnecessary? The following section considers how these different theories may be reconciled through consideration of the way in which the brain processes sensory information.

Summary of Section 5

- What you see a stimulus *as* depends on what you *know*. This means that perception must involve top-down processing.
- The constructivist approach to perception is based on the idea that sensory data are often incomplete, so a description can only be constructed by making use of stored knowledge.
- Gregory suggested that sensory data are incomplete and we perceive by generating a series of perceptual hypotheses about what an object might be.
- The use of stored information can lead to perceptual hypotheses that are inaccurate, which is why we may be fooled by some visual illusions.

6   The physiology of the human visual system

There appear to be at least two (and maybe more) partially distinct streams of information flowing back from the retina (via the optic nerve) into the brain (e.g. Shapley, 1995). The characteristics of these streams and their relation to the theories of perception already described is the topic of this section. It should be emphasized that the distinction between the two streams is fairly loose. There is overlap in the types of information that the streams carry and there are numerous interconnections between them, but they may conveniently be conceptualized as distinct. The following subsections trace these streams of information from the retina to the brain.

6.1   From the eye to brain

You may remember from Section 1.2 that there are two types of light-sensitive cells in the retina, called rods and cones. Both rods and cones are connected to what are termed retinal ganglion cells that essentially connect the retina to the brain. Ganglion cell axons leave the eye via the 'blind spot' (the concentration of blood vessels and nerve axons here means that there is no room for any receptors, hence this region is 'blind'). These cells then project (send connections) to an area termed the lateral geniculate nucleus (LGN), and from there to the area of the brain known as the 'primary visual cortex' (also known as V1). Even at the level of retinal ganglion cells, there is evidence of two distinct streams or 'pathways', referred to as the parvocellular pathway, and the magnocellular pathway (e.g. Shapley, 1995). These names derive from the relative sizes of the cells in the two pathways: larger cells in the magnocellular pathway, and smaller cells in the parvocellular one. This distinction is maintained up to, and within, the primary visual cortex, although there are interconnections between the two pathways.

Information travelling onward from the primary visual cortex is still maintained in two distinct streams (see Figure 3.25). One stream, leading to the inferotemporal cortex, is termed the **ventral stream**, and the other, leading to the parietal cortex, is known as the **dorsal stream**.

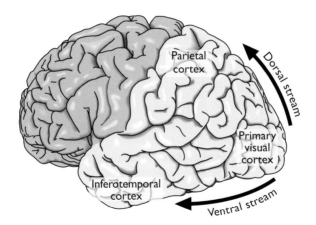

Figure 3.25   The dorsal and ventral streams

6.2   The dorsal and ventral streams

The *ventral* stream projects to regions of the brain that appear to be involved in pattern discrimination and object recognition, whilst the *dorsal* stream projects to areas of the brain that appear to be specialized for the analysis of information about the position and movement of objects. Schneider (1967, 1969) carried out work with hamsters which suggested that there were two distinct parts of the visual system, one system concerned with making pattern discriminations, the other involved with orientation in space. Schneider suggested that one system is concerned with the question, 'What is it?', whereas the other system is concerned with the question, 'Where is it?'. This, and later, work (Ungerleider and Mishkin, 1982) led to the ventral pathway being labelled a 'what' system, and the dorsal pathway a 'where' system.

Although the two streams appear to be specialized for processing different kinds of information, there is ample evidence of a huge degree of interconnection between the systems at all levels. Also, the streams appear to converge in the prefrontal cortex (Rao *et al.*, 1997), although there is still some evidence that the dorsal–ventral distinction is maintained (Courtney *et al.*, 1996). It has been suggested that it is in the prefrontal cortex that meaning is associated with the information carried by the two streams.

Although describing the two streams as 'what' and 'where' is convenient, there is a large body of work that suggests that the distinction is not quite that straightforward. For instance, Milner and Goodale (1995) report a number of studies with a patient, DF, who suffered severe carbon monoxide poisoning that appeared to prevent her using her ventral system for analysing sensory input. She could not recognize faces or objects, or even make simple visual discriminations such as between a triangle and a circle. She could draw objects from memory but not recognize them once she had drawn them. DF did, however, appear to have an intact dorsal stream. Although unable to tell if two discs were of the same or different widths (or even *indicate* the widths by adjusting the distance between her fingers), if she was asked to pick the discs up then the distance between her index finger and thumb as she went to pick them up was highly correlated with the width of the discs.

In other words, she did *not* have size information available to conscious perception (via the ventral stream), but it *was* available to guide *action* (via the dorsal stream).

Norman (2002), following on from similar suggestions by Bridgeman (1992) and Neisser (1994), has drawn on the ongoing debate concerning the characteristics of the dorsal and ventral streams and suggested a dual-process approach. In this approach, the two streams are seen as acting synergistically so that the dorsal stream is largely concerned with perception for action and the ventral stream essentially concerned with perception for recognition. The dual-process approach is supported by some of the characteristics of the two streams (Norman, 2001, 2002):

1   There appears to be evidence (Goodale and Milner, 1992; Ungerleider and Mishkin, 1982) to suggest that the ventral stream is primarily concerned with recognition whilst the dorsal stream drives visually guided behaviour (pointing, grasping, etc.).

2   The ventral system is generally better at processing fine detail (Baizer *et al.*, 1991) whereas the dorsal system is better at processing motion (Logothesis, 1994).

3   The studies on patient DF (Milner and Goodale, 1995) suggest that the ventral system is knowledge-based and uses stored representations to recognize objects, whilst the dorsal system appears to have only very short-term storage available (Bridgeman *et al.*, 1997; Creem and Proffitt, 1998).

4   The dorsal system receives information faster than the ventral system (Bullier and Nowak, 1995).

5   A limited amount of psychophysical evidence suggests that we are much more conscious of ventral than of dorsal stream functioning (Ho, 1998).

6   It has been suggested (Goodale and Milner, 1992; Milner and Goodale, 1995) that the ventral system recognizes objects, and is thus object-centred. The dorsal system is presumed to be used more in driving some action in relation to an object and thus uses a viewer-centred frame of reference (this distinction arises again in the next chapter).

6.3   The relationship between visual pathways and theories of perception

We have already seen that Gibson's approach to perception concentrated more on perception for the purposes of action, whilst Marr's theory was principally concerned with object recognition. In addition, the constructivist approach is also more concerned with perception for recognition than perception for action, as it concentrates on how we may use existing knowledge to work out what an object might be. Although these approaches have their differences, it is undoubtedly the case that we need to both recognize objects and perform actions in order to interact with the environment. It could be, then, that the type of perception discussed by Gibson is principally subserved by the dorsal system, whilst the ventral system is the basis for the recognition approach favoured by Marr and the constructivists.

For example, Gibson's notion of 'affordance' emphasizes that we might need to detect what things are *for* rather than what they actually *are*. That is, affordances are linked to actions ('lifting' or 'eating', for example). The dorsal system appears to be ideally suited to providing the sort of information we need to act in the environment. In addition, if a system is to be used to drive action, it really needs to be fast, as the dorsal stream seems to be.

The earlier discussion of Gibson's ecological approach also stated that Gibson saw no need for memory in perception. Certainly, one of the characteristics of the dorsal stream is that it appears to have no more than a very short 'memory' (at least for representations of objects). Thus, there appear to be some grounds for suggesting that the dorsal stream is Gibsonian in operation.

In contrast, the ventral stream appears to be ideally suited to the role of recognizing objects. It is specialized in analysing the sort of fine detail that Marr saw as essential to discriminating between objects, and it also seems able to draw on our existing knowledge (top-down information) to assist in identifying them. In addition, it is slower than the dorsal stream; but then recognizing what an object may be is not necessarily an immediate priority. For example, knowing *that* an object is moving toward you quickly is initially more important than knowing *what* it is.

6.4   A dual-process approach?

Norman's proposal discussed above does provide an attractive way of reconciling two of the classic approaches to visual perception. There is perhaps a danger, however, in trying to 'shoehorn' what is known about the dorsal and ventral streams into the framework provided by previous theories. Given that both the constructivist and Gibsonian theories are rather vague on how the processes they describe could be implemented, it is questionable how useful they are as a theoretical framework in which to interpret the workings of the dorsal and ventral streams. Attempting to explain the streams in the light of the previous theories does tend to emphasize the way in which they work separately rather than the way in which they work together. Undoubtedly, the two streams *can* operate independently (as demonstrated by the case of DF discussed earlier), but this is rather like saying that you can take the steering column out of a car and both the car and the steering wheel will still function to some degree! In fact, Norman (2002) describes the two streams as synergistic and interconnected, rather than independent.

Binsted and Carlton (2002), in a commentary on the proposal put forward by Norman, provide an illustration of the interaction between the dorsal and ventral streams using the example of skill acquisition. Previous work (Fitts, 1964) suggests that the early stages of learning a skill (such as driving) are characterized by cognitive processes of the sort associated with the ventral stream, whereas once the task is well practised it is characterized by learned motor actions of the sort associated with the dorsal stream.

The question is, if these two streams function in such different ways, how is learning transferred from one to the other? It is possible, of course, that learning occurs in both streams at the same time and that whichever is most effective 'leads' in performance of the task, but this still implies a high degree of interaction between them and a blurring of the boundaries between their functions. The issue (which is as yet unresolved) then becomes whether the two streams interact to such an extent that it is meaningless to consider them to be functionally separate and representative of different theoretical approaches to visual processing (as Norman suggests). Thus, rather than questioning whether both Gibsonian and constructivist principles are operating in visual processing, the debate centres on whether it is appropriate to ascribe these types of processing to discrete pathways. Whatever the outcome of the debate, Norman does present a compelling argument that visual processing does *not* have to be either for action *or* for recognition; it can be both.

6.5   Combining bottom-up and top-down processing

As we have shown, approaches to perception can be differentiated according to whether they are primarily concerned with perception for action or recognition, or with bottom-up or top-down processing. It may have occurred to you when reading about these approaches that it is likely that perception must in fact contain elements of both types of processing. A key question, then, is whether there is any evidence that this is in fact the case.

   You were introduced to the idea of visual masking in the last chapter, particularly the concept of backward masking, in which the presentation of a second image disrupted the perception of an initial image. In Figure 3.26 you can see sets of stimuli that have been used to demonstrate two different types of visual masking. In each case, the mask is presented after a very brief presentation of the target. The task facing the participant is to report which corner of the diamond target is missing.

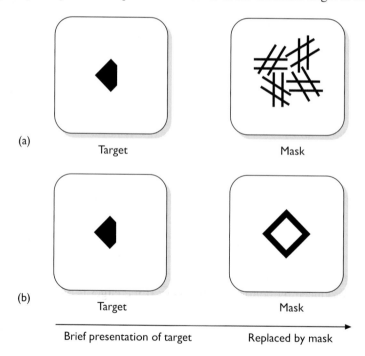

Figure 3.26   Stimuli used to demonstrate backward masking

   Standard explanations of why masking occurs with the stimuli in Figure 3.26 require that the mask contains contours that either overlap (Figure 3.26(a)) or exactly coincide with (Figure 3.26(b)) those of the target (Enns and Di Lollo, 2000). But, if masking is a product of the close similarity between the contours of target and mask, it is hard to account for the fact that a masking effect is also found for the images in Figure 3.27 (Di Lollo *et al.*, 1993).

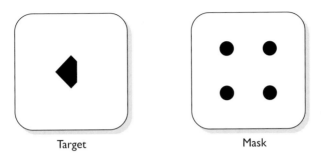

Target   Mask

Figure 3.27   An example of a four-dot mask

Enns and Di Lollo (1997) reported that the four-dot pattern shown in Figure 3.27 appeared to mask the target if target and mask were presented together and the target displayed very briefly, or if the mask was displayed very soon after a brief presentation of the target. Enns and Di Lollo (2000) explained the masking observed using the four-dot pattern by reference to **re-entrant processing**. We know from neuroscience research that communication between two different regions of the brain is never unidirectional. If one region is sending a signal to another, then the second region also sends a signal back through what are referred to as **re-entrant pathways** (Felleman and Van Essen, 1991).

Hupe *et al.* (1998) suggested that re-entrant pathways could be used to allow the brain to check a perceptual hypothesis against the information in an incoming signal. In other words:

- Bottom-up processing produces a low-level description.

- This is used to generate a perceptual hypothesis at a higher level.

- Using re-entrant pathways, the accuracy of the perceptual hypothesis is assessed by comparing it with the (perhaps now changed) low-level description.

Di Lollo *et al.* (2000) used this idea as the basis for an explanation of visual masking. The idea is that each part of the displayed image(s) is perceived in terms of a combination of high-level descriptions similar to a perceptual hypothesis and low-level codes produced by bottom-up processes. If the target is only presented very briefly, then masking can occur because by the time the high-level perceptual hypothesis is compared with the low-level bottom-up description, the target will have been replaced by the mask. Thus, the perceptual hypothesis will be rejected because it is based on a pattern (the target) that is different from the pattern currently being subjected to bottom-up processing (the mask) – see Figure 3.28.

The re-entrant processing explanation of visual masking is based upon the presumed interaction of bottom-up processes with top-down processes. This is consistent with the idea that perception is neither entirely bottom-up nor entirely top-down, but is actually reliant on both forms of processing.

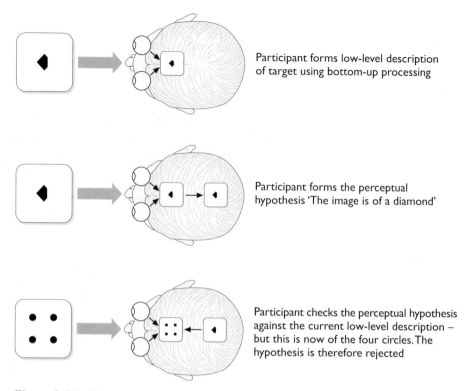

Participant forms low-level description of target using bottom-up processing

Participant forms the perceptual hypothesis 'The image is of a diamond'

Participant checks the perceptual hypothesis against the current low-level description – but this is now of the four circles. The hypothesis is therefore rejected

Figure 3.28   The re-entrant processing explanation of backward masking

Summary of Section 6

- There appear to be at least two partially distinct, but interconnected streams of information flowing back from the retina to the primary visual cortex.
- From here, a ventral stream leads to the inferotemporal cortex and a dorsal stream to the parietal cortex.
- There is evidence that the ventral stream may be involved in perception for recognition and the dorsal stream in perception for action.
- Thus the dorsal stream would be better at dealing with the type of perception dealt with by Gibson and the ventral stream with the type of perception dealt with by Marr and the constructivist approach.
- Enns and Di Lollo's re-entrant processing explanation of backward masking was based on a combination of bottom-up and top-down perception.

7   Conclusion

We started this chapter by promising to show you just how complex even the perception of simple objects can be. We hope you now have some idea of these complexities and of the problems that face any potential theory of visual perception. You have also seen how rich the field of perception is. There are many influential theories that have had a profound impact on both our understanding of perception and the way we approach cognitive psychology more generally. For example, Gibson showed us the importance of considering how we interact with the real world and Marr demonstrated the advantages of the modular approach to information processing. So, next time you are hunting in vain for your keys, do not be too hard on yourself. Remember all the computations, descriptions and hypotheses that your brain is having to process in order to perceive the environment around you.

Now that you have read this chapter you can reinforce and extend your learning by reading an original journal article associated with it, available online from the DD303 website. Remember, these are original journal articles, so the style is different from this textbook, and don't be too concerned if you can't follow every detail.

Further reading

Bruce, V., Green, P.A. and Georgeson, M.A. (2003) *Visual Perception: Physiology, Psychology and Ecology*, Hove, Psychology Press.

Gibson, J.J. (1986) *The Ecological Approach to Visual Perception*, Hillsdale, NJ, Lawrence Erlbaum Associates.

Gregory, R.L. (1997) *Eye and Brain: The Psychology of Seeing*, Oxford, Oxford University Press.

Marr, D. (1982) *Vision: A Computational Investigation into the Human Representation and Processing of Visual Information*, New York, W.H. Freeman & Company.

References

Aksentijevic, A., Elliott, M.A. and Barber, P.J. (2001) 'Dynamics of perceptual grouping: similarities in the organization of visual and auditory groups', *Visual Cognition*, vol.8, pp.349–58.

Atherton, M. (2002) 'The origins of the sensation/perception distinction', in Heyer, D. and Mausfeld, R. (eds) *Perception and the Physical World: Psychological and Philosophical Issues in Perception*, Chichester, John Wiley & Sons Ltd.

Baizer, J.S., Ungerleider, L.G. and Desimone, R. (1991) 'Organization of visual inputs to the inferior temporal and posterior parietal cortex in macaques', *Journal of Neuroscience*, vol.11, pp.168–90.

Binsted, G. and Carlton, L.G. (2002) 'When is movement controlled by the dorsal stream?', *Behavioral and Brain Sciences*, vol.25, pp.97–8.

Bridgeman, B. (1992) 'Conscious vs unconscious processing: the case of vision', *Theory & Psychology*, vol.2, pp.73–88.

Bridgeman, B., Peery, S. and Anand, S. (1997) 'Interaction of cognitive and sensorimotor maps of visual space', *Perception and Psychophysics*, vol.59, pp.456–69.

Bullier, J. and Nowak, L.G. (1995) 'Parallel versus serial processing: new vistas on the distributed organization of the visual system', *Current Opinion in Neurobiology*, vol.5, pp.497–503.

Courtney, S.M., Ungerleider, L.G., Keil, K. and Haxby, J.V. (1996) 'Object and spatial visual working memory activate separate neural systems in human cortex', *Cerebral Cortex*, vol.6, pp.39–49.

Creem, S.H. and Proffitt, D.R. (1998) 'Two memories for geographical slant: separation and interdependence of action and awareness', *Psychonomic Bulletin and Review*, vol.5, pp.22–36.

Di Lollo, V., Bischof, W.F. and Dixon, P. (1993) 'Stimulus-onset asynchrony is not necessary for motion perception or metacontrast masking', *Psychological Science*, vol.4, pp.260–3.

Di Lollo, V., Enns, J.T. and Rensink, R.A. (2000) 'Competition for consciousness among visual events: the psychophysics of re-entrant pathways', *Journal of Experimental Psychology: General*, vol.129, pp.481-507.

Enns, J.T. and Di Lollo, V. (1997) 'Object substitution: a new form of masking in unattended visual locations', *Psychological Science*, vol.8, pp.135–9.

Enns, J.T. and Di Lollo, V. (2000) 'What's new in visual masking?', *Trends in Cognitive Science*, vol.4, pp.345–52.

Enns, J.T. and Rensick, R.A. (1990) 'Sensitivity to three-dimensional orientation from line drawings', *Psychological Review*, vol.98, pp.335–51.

Felleman, D.J. and Van Essen, D.C. (1991) 'Distributed hierarchical processing in primate visual cortex', *Cerebral Cortex*, vol.1, pp.1–47.

Fitts, P.M. (1964) 'Perceptual-motor skills learning', in Melton, A.W. (ed.) *Categories of Human Learning*, New York, Academic Press.

Gibson, J.J. (1947) 'Motion picture testing and research', *AAF Aviation Psychology Research Report No. 7*, Washington, DC, Government Printing Office.

Gibson, J.J. (1950) *The Perception of the Visual World*, Boston, MA, Houghton Mifflin.

Gibson, J.J. (1966) *The Senses Considered as Perceptual Systems*, Boston, MA, Houghton Mifflin.

Gibson, J.J. (1979) *The Ecological Approach to Visual Perception*, Hillsdale, NJ, Lawrence Erlbaum Associates.

Goodale, M.A. and Milner, A.D. (1992) 'Separate visual pathways for perception and action', *Trends in Neurosciences*, vol.15, no.1, pp.20–5.

Gregory, R.L. (1980) 'Perceptions as hypotheses', *Philosophical Transactions of the Royal Society of London*, Series B, vol.290, pp.181–97.

Ho, C.E. (1998) 'Letter recognition reveals pathways of second-order and third-order motion', *Proceedings of the National Academy of Sciences of the United States of America*, vol.95, no.1, pp.400–4.

Hupe, J.M., James, A.C., Payne, B.R., Lomber, S.G., Girard, P. and Bullier, J. (1998) 'Cortical feedback improves discrimination between figure and ground by V1, V2 and V3 neurons', *Nature*, vol.394, pp.784–7.

Kanizsa, G. (1976) 'Subjective contours', *Scientific American*, vol.234, no.4, pp.48–52.

Koffka, K. (1935) *Principles of Gestalt Psychology*, New York, Harcourt Brace.

Kohler, W. (1947) *Gestalt Psychology: An Introduction to New Concepts in Modern Psychology*, New York, Liveright Publishing Corporation.

Logothesis, N.K. (1994) 'Physiological studies of motion inputs', in Smith, A.T. (ed.) *Visual Detection of Motion*, London, Academic Press.

Marr, D. (1982) *Vision: A Computational Investigation into the Human Representation and Processing of Visual Information*, New York, W.H. Freeman & Company.

Marr, D. and Hildreth, E. (1980) 'Theory of edge detection', *Proceedings of the Royal Society of London*, Series B, vol.207, pp.187–217.

Milner, A.D. and Goodale, M.A. (1995) *The Visual Brain in Action*, Oxford, Oxford University Press.

Milner, A.D. and Goodale, M.D. (1998) 'The visual brain in action', *Psyche*, vol.4, pp.1–14.

Neisser, U. (1994) 'Multiple systems: a new approach to cognitive theory', *European Journal of Cognitive Psychology*, vol.6, no.3, pp.225–41.

Norman, J. (2001) 'Ecological psychology and the two visual systems: not to worry', *Ecological Psychology*, vol.13, no.2, pp.135–45.

Norman, J. (2002) 'Two visual systems and two theories of perception: an attempt to reconcile the constructivist and ecological approaches', *Behavioral and Brain Sciences*, vol.25, no.1, pp.73–96.

Penrose, L.S. and Penrose, R. (1958) 'Impossible objects: a special type of illusion', *British Journal of Psychology*, vol.49, p.31.

Rao, S.C., Rainer, G. and Miller, E.K. (1997) 'Integration of what and where in the primate prefrontal cortex', *Science*, vol.276, pp.821–4.

Rock, I. (1977) 'In defense of unconscious inference', in Epstein, W. (ed.) *Stability and Constancy in Visual Perception: Mechanisms and Processes*, New York, Wiley.

Rock, I. (1983) *The Logic of Perception*, Cambridge, MA, MIT Press.

Rock, I. (1997) *Indirect Perception*, Cambridge, MA, MIT Press.

Schneider, G.E. (1967) 'Contrasting visuomotor functions of tectum and cortex in the golden hamster', *Psychologische Forschung*, vol.31, pp.52–62.

Schneider, G.E. (1969) 'Two visual systems', *Science*, vol.163, no.3870, pp.895–902.

Sedgwick, H.A. (1973) *The Visible Horizon*, Unpublished PhD thesis, Cornell University Library.

Shapley, R. (1995) 'Parallel neural pathways and visual function', in Gazzaniga, M.S. (ed.) *The Cognitive Neurosciences*, Cambridge, MA, MIT Press.

Street, R.F. (1931) *A Gestalt Completion Test*, New York, Bureau of Publications, Teachers College, Columbia University.

Ungerleider, L.G. and Mishkin, M. (1982) 'Two cortical visual systems', in Ingle, D.J., Goodale, M.A. and Mansfield, R.J.W. (eds) *Analysis of Visual Behaviour*, Cambridge, MA, MIT Press.

Wade, N.J. and Bruce, V. (2001) 'Surveying the scene: 100 years of British vision', *British Journal of Psychology*, vol.92, no.1, pp.79–113.

Werthiemer, M. (1923) 'Untersuchungen zur Lehre von der Gestalt, II', *Psychologische Forschung*, no.4, pp.301–50. Translated as 'Laws of organization in perceptual forms', in Ellis, W.D. (ed.) (1955) *A Source Book of Gestalt Psychology*, London, Routledge and Kegan Paul.

Young, M.J., Landey, M.S. and Maloney, L.T. (1993) 'A perturbation analysis of depth perception from combinations of texture and motion cues', *Vision Research*, vol.33, pp.2685–96.

Recognition

Chapter 4

Graham Pike and Nicola Brace

1 Introduction

In the last chapter, on perception, we explored some of the cognitive processes involved in forming a mental description of the environment based on input from the senses. As well as being able to determine the position and shape of the objects around us, it is also possible to recognize *what* we are seeing. Unless we fully accept Gibson's concept of affordance (and it's safe to say that we don't), there must be another step: another set of processes that transform the basic descriptions of objects generated by analysing the retinal image into objects that are familiar to us and which we can recognize.

The same is, of course, true of our other senses; for example, when we listen we may hear music, car engines and voices. Again, there must be cognitive processes that somehow transform the auditory input of sound waves into what we recognize as an environment of voices, music and cars.

Let's stop for a moment and consider the basic steps that might be involved in the process of visually recognizing an object:

- First, there must be processes that are able to construct an internal representation (referred to as a 'description') of the object, based on the information in the retinal image.

- Second, there must be processes that are able to store this description so that we can recognize the object if we see it again.

- Third, there must be processes that somehow compare the description of the object that we can currently see to the descriptions of objects that we have stored.

- Lastly, it is very likely that we have seen objects from many different angles, yet are able to recognize them regardless of the current angle of view. As we shall see, the nature of the mechanism that allows us to do this is an important and much debated point.

A basic diagram displaying the recognition process is provided in Figure 4.1 (overleaf).

In one sense, the process of recognition is the process of generating and comparing descriptions of objects that are currently in view with descriptions of objects that we have seen previously. It is worth noting that this is a very simplistic way of viewing and describing recognition, and in Section 2 we shall look at some of the problems with this simplistic approach.

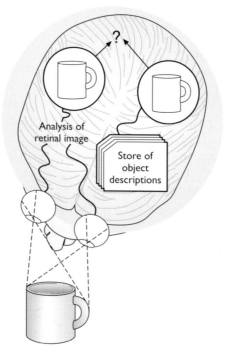

Figure 4.1   The basics of the recognition process

1.1   Recognition in the wider context of cognition

In Figure 4.2, we can see how Humphreys and Bruce (1989) summarized the way in which object recognition fits into a wider context of cognition that includes perception (perceptual classification), categorization (semantic classification) and naming. As you can see from Figure 4.2, the first stage in the process is the early visual processing of the retinal image. One example of this form of processing is that which produces Marr's full primal sketch (Marr, 1982). In the second stage a

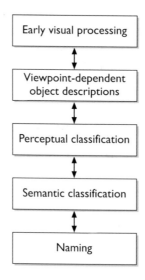

Figure 4.2   Model of object recognition suggested by Humphreys and Bruce (1989)

description of the object is generated, but this description is dependent on the viewpoint of the observer. This stage is therefore similar to what Marr (1982) referred to as the 2½D sketch.

Humphreys and Bruce refer to the next stage as 'perceptual classification' and it is really this stage that we have been discussing so far in this chapter. Perceptual classification involves a comparison of the information regarding the object in view with descriptions of objects that have been stored previously. It is at this stage that the object is 'recognized'.

Once the object has been recognized, or perceptually classified, it can then be 'semantically classified'. This process, also referred to as 'categorization', is examined in the next chapter. Once this stage has been achieved, the object can then be named, aspects of which will be examined in the later chapters on language.

Summary of Section 1

- As well as being able to determine the location and shape of an object, or the location and pitch of a sound, we also have to be able to recognize what they are.
- A basic model of recognition requires that a description from sensory input is generated and compared with descriptions stored in memory.
- Recognition must come after the initial processes of perception and before the stages in which an object can be first semantically classified and then named.

2   Different types of recognition

As we have stated above, the view that recognition involves comparing an object description generated from the retinal image to descriptions stored in long-term memory is very simplistic. In fact there are quite different *types* of recognition, depending on what it is we are trying to recognize and how we go about trying to recognize it. Throughout this chapter we shall be exploring these different types of recognition and examining some of the issues that suggest the process of recognition is far more complex than the simplistic model presented in Figure 4.1 suggests.

2.1   Object and face recognition

The end point of Humphreys and Bruce's (1989) model of recognition (Figure 4.2) is the naming stage. Naming, of course, is not a necessary component of being able to recognize an object: even if an animal has no capacity for language, it can still recognize objects. But the names we give things do provide a clue to the fact that there are different types of recognition.

ACTIVITY 4.1

Figure 4.3 shows two images. See if you can name them.

Figure 4.3

You probably provided the names 'apple' and 'Sigmund Freud'. These are evidently two different types of name, but can you describe why these two types of name are so different? *Hint: think about how many different apples and Sigmund Freuds there are.*

In completing Activity 4.1, you may have realized that the name you provided for the left-hand image was the category to which the object belonged, whilst the name for the right-hand image corresponded to an individual rather than a category (i.e. you did not name the image 'a face').

Naming reveals that it is possible to recognize objects in different ways. When we see objects such as fruit and furniture we tend to concentrate on which category they belong to, and when we provide names for them, these are usually the name for that category. Thus, we are making **between-category** distinctions such as 'that object is an orange and that one is a table'. However, when we see a face, we often do more than recognize that the object belongs to the category of objects known as 'faces': we also work out *whose* face it is. In other words, we make a **within-category** distinction.

The difference between within- and between-category recognition is one reason why **face recognition** is generally researched as a separate topic from **object recognition**. In addition, there are some issues that are unique to face recognition such as:

- The internal features of a face can move, which changes the appearance of the face.

- This movement can serve to express emotional and social cues.
- Faces can change quite dramatically over time, due to ageing or haircuts for instance.

ACTIVITY 4.2

Can you identify the person depicted in the three images shown in Figure 4.4?

Figure 4.4

COMMENT

The images are of Paul McCartney and you were (probably) able to recognize him from all three images, even though there are some quite obvious differences in appearance. In fact, you were probably able to recognize the E-fit image of him (right-hand image), even though this is constructed by combining together features from several other faces. So, we can recognize a face that is familiar to us even when quite large changes have been introduced.

As well as distinguishing between face and more general object recognition, it is possible to identify a number of different types of face recognition. One such distinction is between recognizing familiar and unfamiliar faces. Pike *et al.* (2000) reported that people were often able to identify E-fit images even when other participants had rated them as a poor likeness. However, like the E-fit in Activity 4.2, these were images of famous people, whose faces would have been familiar to the participants. Considerable evidence suggests we are not so accurate at recognizing even real faces that are not so familiar to us. For example, many witnesses express uncertainty when asked to identify the perpetrator of a crime from a line-up (Pike *et al.*, 2001). Even when the anxiety of the witness is reduced by using a video identification parade, identification accuracy is far from perfect (Kemp *et al.*, 2001).

A second distinction that applies to types of face recognition is that between recognizing whose face you are looking at and recognizing what emotion it may be portraying. You can imagine that the importance of faces in conveying emotional state and in facilitating social interactions has led us to develop some very sophisticated cognitive processes for interpreting facial expressions. In fact, we are able to judge the emotion being displayed on a face with great accuracy (the cognition involved in perceiving emotion is considered in Chapter 14) and are very sensitive to eye movements in those around us. It is tempting to think that we may have evolved a specific set of cognitive processes for recognizing faces and the emotions they express because of the social importance of this information. However, there is evidence (Young *et al.*, 1993) that although we do have specific processes for recognizing emotions, these processes are not involved in recognizing identity. We shall return to the difference between emotion and identity recognition later in this chapter, but logically you can see that you need to be able to tell whether someone is angry or happy regardless of whether you can recognize them or not. Likewise, you need to be able to recognize who someone is regardless of whether they appear happy or angry.

The question of whether faces are recognized by the same cognitive processes that are used to recognize other objects has been at the centre of a great deal of research. Although a definitive answer as to just how different face recognition is from general object recognition has yet to be provided, the two have tended to be treated as different areas of research. Because of this, we have divided this chapter into two main areas of discussion. The first (the rest of Section 2 and Section 3) will look at theories of how we recognize objects, and the second (Sections 4 to 7) will look at models of face recognition and examine in more depth the question of whether faces are recognized by special processes.

2.2 Active processing – recognizing objects by touch

One limitation of the basic recognition procedure we suggested in Section 1 is that it treats recognition as a passive process. Gibson (1986) stressed that perception is an active process and that we are beings who interact with and investigate the environment. In examining how Gibson's idea of active perception might apply to recognition, we will temporarily switch modalities from vision to touch. One reason for concentrating on touch is that purely passive object recognition through touch would be almost impossible. Although there may be some objects that you can recognize if they were simply placed on your hand, most objects would require exploration. We have evolved sophisticated processes for exploring the environment and objects using touch in very exact and careful ways.

First, we have tremendous control over our hands, so that we can both move our fingers precisely and also apply varying degrees of pressure to objects in a very measured way. This is done by employing a **feedback** system, whereby information from touch receptors allows the brain to control the location and amount of pressure applied by the fingers. As well as being able to regulate touch precisely, we can also pinpoint the location of our limbs with great accuracy via receptors inside our muscles and joints. This information about limb location is known as **kinesthesis**, and it can be combined with information from the touch receptors to guide our hands and fingers. Of particular importance are the relative positions of your fingers as they touch the object, their orientation to your hand, and the position of your hand in relation to your arm and of your arm in relation to your body. The processes that allow us to keep track of the relative locations of all our limbs are known as **proprioception**.

So, at every moment that we are touching an object, we know the exact position of our fingers (kinesthesis) and what the object feels like at that point (touch receptor information). The information gained from this combination is referred to as **haptic information** and it can be used to generate a description of an object.

Lederman and Klatzky (1987) found that there was considerable consistency in the way in which people used their hands in order to gather haptic information. They described how participants tended to use a series of **exploratory procedures** when investigating an object with their hands. Lederman and Klatzky (1990) went on to study these exploratory procedures in more depth and described how each particular procedure could be used to derive a certain type of information that was useful for recognizing an object. For example, if shape was important in recognizing the object people tended to move their fingers around the object's contours, and if texture was important they would move their fingers across the surface of the object.

ACTIVITY 4.3

Ask someone to place a variety of objects within easy reach of you (you can do this yourself if you wish). Ask them to choose objects that differ in shape, texture and weight. Close your eyes and pick up each object in turn and try to work out what it is. As you do this, try to make a mental note of the different movements that your hands make and what each movement tells you about the object.

Table 4.1 gives a list of some of the hand movements reported by Lederman and Klatzky (1987), along with the information that these exploratory procedures tend to reveal. Did you find yourself using these movements?

Table 4.1   The information revealed by exploratory hand movements

Movement	Information
Enclose object in hand(s)	Overall shape
Following contours with fingers	More exact shape
Lateral motion with fingers	Texture
Press with fingers	Hardness
Static contact with fingers	Temperature
Unsupported holding	Weight

Source: based on Lederman and Klatzky,1987, Table 1, p.345

Although haptic perception can be used to recognize objects, visual recognition has the obvious advantage that it can be used for distant objects that are out of reach and tends to be far quicker and more accurate in processing information about shape, particularly complex 3D shape (Lederman *et al.*, 1993). But visual perception is not so useful when it comes to judging the weight and texture of an object.

So, haptic perception is a very useful source of information and can be used to recognize certain objects. The study of haptic perception also serves to demonstrate that recognition is not necessarily passive and that much can be gained from considering it as an active process. Nor is active perception limited to touch. You saw in the last chapter how your interpretation of the impossible triangle (Figure 3.24) kept changing as you visually explored the object, corner by corner.

2.3   Recognizing two-dimensional objects

Another way of distinguishing between types of recognition is according to whether the object in question is three-dimensional (3D), such as the book in front of you, or two-dimensional (2D), such as the words in front of you. The difference between 2D and 3D object recognition takes on added significance when you consider that the description generated from the retinal image will in essence be 2D, whilst most objects tend to be 3D. In fact, much of the early research conducted on recognition processes was focused on how simple, two-dimensional 'patterns' are recognized. Although it can be argued that this work tells us little about how complex, three-dimensional objects are recognized, it does serve to highlight some of the problems that are inherent in any approach to object recognition.

By far the simplest model of visual pattern recognition postulates **template matching**. This is the idea that we have a large number of templates stored in long-term memory against which we compare the patterns we come across. For example, a template would exist for every number from 0 to 9 and for every letter from A to Z. The problem with this theory is that it cannot cope with the enormous variation in the actual patterns that are used to represent even simple things such as alphanumeric characters. For example, in Figure 4.5 the top row contains examples of the letter 'R' and the bottom row contains examples of letters, each of which shares many similar properties with the specific example of an 'R' immediately above it. Although we do not have any great difficulty in reading these letters, it is hard to see how a simple template could be created that would accept every example in the top row as a letter 'R' and reject every example in the bottom row.

Figure 4.5   Different alphanumeric characters that share similar properties

If the problem with template matching is that the template cannot deal with variation in the stimulus it has to recognize, we have to look at some way of representing objects that is not so reliant on the exact visible pattern. One way of doing this is to try to extract the key characteristics or features of an object. In the case of alphanumeric characters, these features could be the number of curved and straight lines and the relationship between them. An 'O' might therefore be represented as a single continuous curve, a 'P' as one vertical line and one discontinuous curve, and a 'T' as one horizontal and one vertical line that form two right angles.

One of the most influential **feature recognition theories** is the Pandemonium system, so called because processing units known as 'demons' were used to detect each feature. This system was designed as the basis for a computer program to decode Morse code signals (Selfridge, 1959) and was later adapted by Neisser (1967) to recognize alphanumeric characters. Although Pandemonium systems have been useful in recognizing simple, highly constrained patterns, they do not provide a particularly useful model of human object recognition. A central flaw in feature recognition theories is that describing an object in terms of a list of key features does not capture the structural relations *between* features. If you look back at the feature-based descriptions provided for an 'O', 'P' and 'T' above, you will see that these three descriptions could also apply to the figures presented to the right of each letter in Figure 4.6, meaning that these shapes would be misidentified as letters.

Figure 4.6   Examples of different patterns described by the same key features

An approach that has had more success in explaining how both simple patterns and more complex objects might be recognized is that based on **structural descriptions**. Structural descriptions are made up of a series of propositions, based on both a description of the elements that comprise the object and the structural relations between them. Thus, the structural description of a letter 'L' might contain the following propositions:

- There are two lines.
- There is one horizontal line.
- There is one vertical line.
- The horizontal line supports the vertical line.
- The horizontal line extends to the right of the vertical line.
- The horizontal and vertical lines are joined at a right angle.

Although the propositions stated above are expressed in language, they can be equally well expressed in other forms of symbolic representation, such as that used in a computer program.

One key advantage that structural descriptions have is that it is possible to see how they could be applied to three-dimensional objects. Consider the three representations of the character 'L' in Figure 4.7. Both template matching and feature recognition theories would recognize the representation to the left as being an 'L', but would immediately reject the other two. However, the two forms of the letter 'L' on the right of Figure 4.7 do share a similar structural description once we consider their three-dimensional properties.

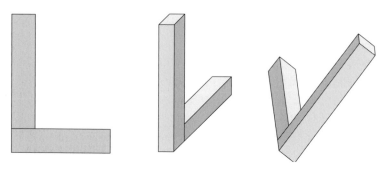

Figure 4.7 Three representations of a 3D 'L' shape

But, in order to obtain a description that includes elements of three-dimensional structure, we must be able to turn the 2D retinal image, that is dependent on the particular view that the observer has of the object, into a 3D description that is centred not on the viewer but on the object itself. This, as you might expect, requires an even more sophisticated means of describing objects, and is the focus of the second half of Marr's theory of vision – which we shall look at in Section 3.

2.4 Object-centred vs viewer-centred descriptions

One of the most fundamental problems in recognizing an object is that it is possible to view an object from many angles. As we have seen, any theory that treats an object as a simple pattern is likely to fail when applied to a 3D object (as with the 'L' in Figure 4.7). Consider writing a very simple computer program based on recognizing an object by matching patterns. As an example, Figure 4.8 contains a conceptual diagram of how a computer might be programmed to recognize a coffee mug.

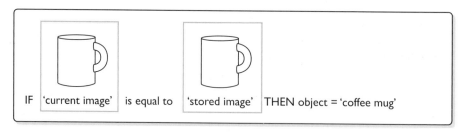

Figure 4.8 A simple program for recognizing an object

But coffee cups are actually 3D objects and can be viewed from many angles. Let's see how our simple computer program would cope if we turned our coffee cup so it was facing the other way. As you can see from Figure 4.9, the program has decided that, as the patterns do not match, the object is NOT a coffee cup.

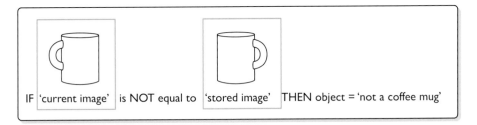

IF 'current image' is NOT equal to 'stored image' THEN object = 'not a coffee mug'

Figure 4.9   A simple program failing to recognize an object from a different viewpoint

The failure of the simple program to deal with a small change in viewpoint is obviously an unacceptable flaw in any system that wishes to interact with its environment. Instead of being reliant on seeing objects from just a single viewpoint, the process of object recognition must somehow be based on descriptions of objects that allow recognition to take place *independent* of viewpoint. In fact, these processes must be tolerant of any naturally occurring change, not just changes in viewpoint. This is a very important point and one that is central to the study of object recognition.

Marr (1982) conceptualized the problem of viewpoint as that of turning the **viewer-centred description** of the object that was formed in the 2½D sketch (see Chapter 3, Section 4.3) into a **3D object-centred description** that would allow the object to be recognized despite changes in viewpoint. In the next section we shall look at how Marr suggested this might happen.

Summary of Section 2

- There are different types of recognition, that depend on what is being recognized and how.
- Object recognition tends to be based on making between-category distinctions and face recognition on making within-category distinctions.
- Face recognition tends to be researched apart from more general object recognition because faces can convey social and emotional information and their appearance can change.
- Recognition is not entirely a 'passive' process and can involve an active exploration of the environment. This is particularly true of haptic recognition, in which objects are recognized by touch.
- One key problem facing any theory of visual recognition is that the retinal image is essentially 2D, but objects are 3D.
- Early theories that concentrated on recognizing 2D patterns, such as template matching and feature recognition theories, are therefore not particularly useful models of human recognition.
- Theories based on abstracting a structural description of an object are better able to cope with 3D objects.
- As a 3D object can be viewed from many angles, our recognition system must be able to turn an object description centred on the viewer into one centred on the object.

3   Recognizing three-dimensional objects

As we saw in the previous chapter, in the first part of Marr's theory of perception, early visual processing of the retinal image eventually leads to the generation of the 2½D sketch. But the surfaces and objects in the 2½D sketch are described in relation to the viewpoint of the observer and are therefore viewer-centred descriptions. As we saw in the previous section, viewer-centred descriptions are of little use in recognizing real objects that can be seen from any angle and any distance. The second half of Marr's theory was therefore concerned with how the information in the 2½D sketch might be used in order to construct a 3D object-centred description of each object.

If it were not possible to generate a 3D object-centred description, the only way of accurately recognizing objects would be to store a very large number of viewer-centred descriptions. Although there are theories that have taken this approach, for now we will concentrate on the idea that recognition is best subserved by a single representation of an object that can be used to recognize it from any angle.

Marr and Nishihara (1978) suggested that objects could be represented by generating a 3D object-centred description that would allow the object to be recognized from virtually any angle. They proposed that this description was based on a **canonical coordinate frame**. This basically means that each object would be represented within a framework that was about the same shape as the object. You could imagine the representation of a carrot as being a cylinder that tapered toward one end.

This procedure appears at first glance to be somewhat paradoxical, as it would be necessary to know the approximate shape of the object before you could begin to recognize it! However, remember that the formation of the 3D object-centred description occurs after considerable analysis of the retinal image has already taken place, so some information as to the shape/outline of the object will already exist.

3.1   Marr and Nishihara's theory

Marr and Nishihara saw the first step in establishing a canonical coordinate frame as defining a central axis for the object in question. This is relatively easy to do if the object in question either has a natural line of symmetry or has a length that is noticeably greater than its width and depth (see Figure 4.10).

In fact, the generation of the central axis is so important in Marr and Nishihara's theory that it is restricted to specific objects that can be easily described by one or more **generalized cones**. A generalized cone is any 3D shape that has a cross-section of a consistent shape throughout its length. The cross-section can vary in size, but not in shape. All of the objects shown in Figure 4.11 are examples of generalized cones. Although restricting the theory to generalized cones is undoubtedly one weakness of Marr and Nishihara's theory, the basic shape of many natural objects, particularly those that grow (such as animals and plants), can be described, albeit rather loosely, in this way.

To locate the central axis of an object, it is first necessary to make use of the information contained within the 2½ D sketch in order to work out what shape the object has. Marr (1977) suggested that it is possible to work out the shape of an

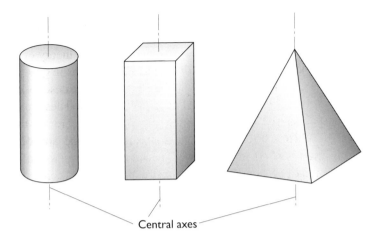

Figure 4.10   Locating the central axis of an object

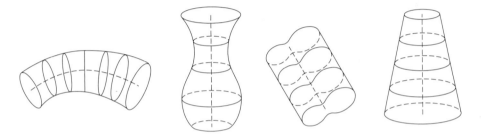

Figure 4.11   Three generalized cones
Source: Marr, 1982, Figure 3.59, p.224

object based on the object's **occluding contours** (these are basically the object's silhouette). The points on the object's surface that correspond to the boundary of its silhouette are of particular importance in Marr's theory, and he referred to them as the **contour generator** – because they can be used to generate the contour of the object.

As Marr (1982) points out, we seem to have no problems in deriving 3D shapes from silhouettes such as those used in Picasso's *Rites of Spring* (see Figure 4.12).

However, as the silhouette of an object is two-dimensional, it is possible that it could be caused by more than one 3D object. Consider the circular silhouette (a) in Figure 4.13. This could be caused by any of the 3D objects below it (if they were sufficiently rotated), yet we tend to interpret the silhouette as being produced by the sphere (b).

Marr suggested that the problem of how we can derive 3D shape from 2D silhouettes is solved by the visual system making certain assumptions about what it is seeing. As Marr himself said, 'Somewhere buried in the perceptual machinery that can interpret silhouettes as three-dimensional shapes, there must lie some source of additional information that constrains us to see the silhouettes as we do' (Marr, 1982, p.219). Marr conceptualized this 'additional information' as coming in the form of three basic assumptions built into the computational processes:

Figure 4.12   *Rites of Spring* by Picasso

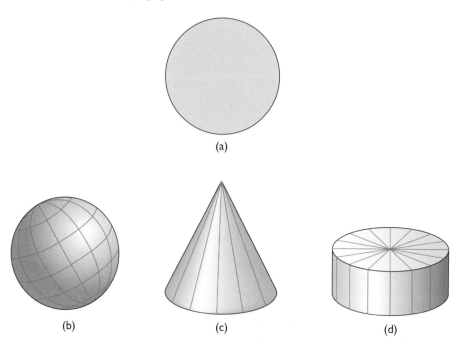

Figure 4.13   A silhouette (a) and three objects that could cause it (b, c and d)

- Each point on the contour generator corresponds to a different point on the object.

- Any two points that are close together on the contour in an image are also close together on the contour generator of the object.

- All the points on the contour generator lie in a single plane (i.e. are planar).

The first two points are relatively straightforward and the third assumption has been illustrated in Figure 4.14.

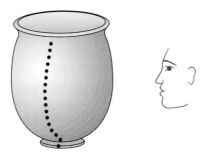

Figure 4.14 The black dots indicate points that lie in the same plane with respect to the viewer

Source: Marr, 1982, Figure 3.57(d), p.220

The third assumption, that all of the points on the contour generator are planar, is a vital component in Marr's theory, but it can be problematic. As we have seen, it is possible for two quite different objects to share the same silhouette and for the points on the silhouette to vary in their distance from the observer. We tend to interpret the contour on the left in Figure 4.15 as being a hexagon. However, this contour will be produced by the cube to the right. The problem is that the assumption that all the points on the contour are planar is violated by this view of the cube, as point (A) is further away than point (B). As the points on the cube's occluding contour are not planar, we tend to interpret its silhouette incorrectly.

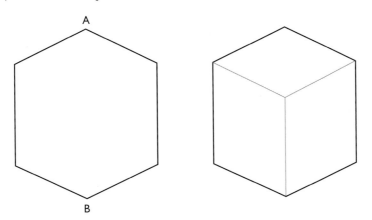

Figure 4.15 The contour of a cube may not be planar

Source: based on Marr, 1982, Figure 3.58, p.221

Once the shape of the object has been derived using its contour generator, the next step is to locate the axis/axes necessary to represent the object. It is fairly straightforward to do this when the shape is simple as symmetry usually tells us where its axis is located, but what about more complex shapes? The answer is that we often need to represent the shape using several axes, so that the object is divided into components and one axis is used for each component (these are referred to as **component axes**).

In Figure 4.16, one method of locating axes suggested by Marr and Nishihara (1978) is illustrated. As you can see, the object in question is a toy donkey (a). The first step (b) involves working out areas of **concavity** (these correspond to parts of the contour that include a bend inwards and are represented in the figure by a '−') and **convexity** (parts of the contour that include a bend outwards and are represented by a '+'). The shape can then be divided into sections by finding areas of sharp concavity (c) and using these to divide the object into smaller parts (d). Once the shape has been divided in this way, it is possible to represent each section via a component axis (e).

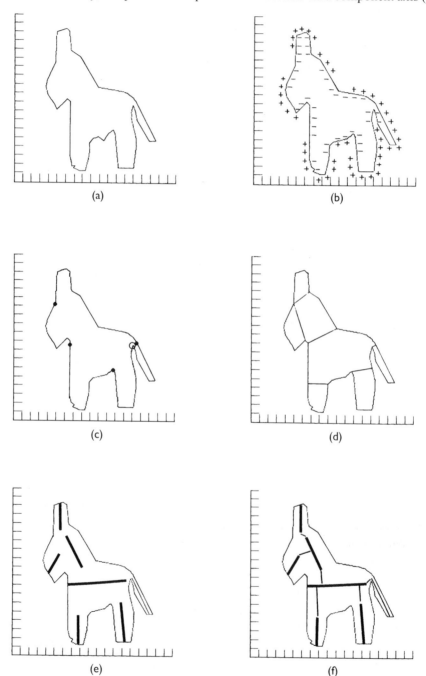

Figure 4.16   Locating the component axes of an object

Source: Marr and Nishihara, 1978, Figure 6

These component axes can then be represented in relation to the horizontal axis of the body (f).

Figure 4.17 illustrates how it is possible to represent a quite complex object using several components or **primitives** as Marr called them. The description of the object must allow recognition at a global level, such as being able to tell that an object is a human body, and also incorporate more detailed information, such as the fact that a human hand has five fingers. It is therefore necessary for there to be a hierarchy of 3D models, in which each subsequent level contains a more detailed description of a specific part of the object. This means that fewer primitives will be used to represent each part of the object at the higher levels of the hierarchy.

For example, consider the description of the human body provided in Figure 4.17. At the highest level, the entire human body is described in relation to a single axis that runs through the centre of the body (a). This 3D model also contains the relative length and orientation of the axes that describe the head, torso, arms and legs (b). However, no details regarding smaller parts (such as the fingers) are provided.

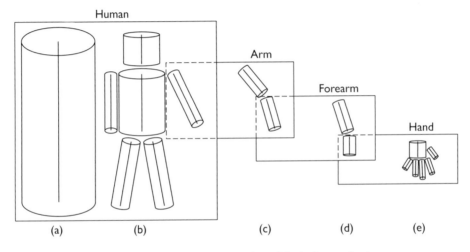

Figure 4.17 Marr and Nishihara's hierarchical model of a human body

Source: Marr and Nishihara, 1978, Figure 3

The axis that corresponds to each limb (b) is then used as the major axis for a more detailed description of that limb (c). For example, the axis of the cylinder representing the right arm is then used as the major axis to represent the upper and lower part of that arm (c). The axis of the cylinder used to describe the lower part of the arm (c) is used as the major axis to describe the forearm and hand (d). Finally, the axis of the cylinder used to describe the hand (d) is used as the major axis in order to describe the five fingers (e). Thus we have a 3D model description that can be used to recognize an entire human body as well as any of its parts.

Having derived a 3D description of the object, Marr and Nishihara (1978) saw the next step in the process of recognition as comparing this to a **catalogue of 3D models**, formed from the 3D descriptions of all previously seen objects. The catalogue is organized hierarchically according to the amount of detail present in the model (see Figure 4.18). At the highest level the catalogue consists of descriptions devoid of any decomposition into components. The next level contains more detail, corresponding to the number and basic layout of limbs as in Figure 4.17. At the next level even more detail is contained, such as that relating to the angles and lengths of component axes.

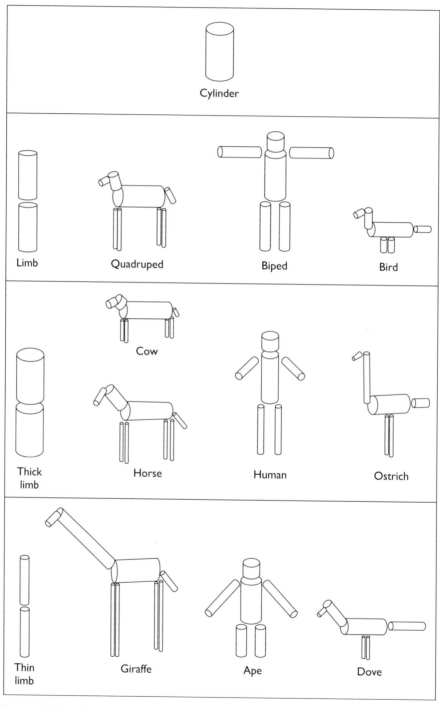

Figure 4.18   3D model catalogue

Source: Marr and Nishihara, 1978, Figure 8

The 3D model generated of a new object (the target) is related to the catalogue, starting at the highest level. The target is compared to the stored models and the example it best matches is used as the basis for the next level of detail. The process stops when a level is reached that corresponds to the level of detail present in the target. At this point, assuming the target contains sufficient detail, a match should have been found that allows the object to be recognized.

So, the generation of a 3D model description solves several problems inherent to object recognition. As the model is 3D, it allows recognition of the object from many angles and its hierarchical nature allows recognition of the entire object whilst maintaining more detailed information about the components.

3.2   Evaluating Marr and Nishihara's theory

Although it can be difficult to study the cognition involved in object recognition, there is evidence for some of the suggestions made by Marr and Nishihara.

One of the key predictions of their theory arises from the fact that they see establishing a central axis as a vital stage in the recognition process. This means that it should be very difficult to recognize an object if it is also difficult to establish the location of its central axis. Some support for this notion comes from a study, conducted by Lawson and Humphreys (1996), in which participants had to recognize objects (line drawings in this case) that had been rotated. Rotation did not appear to have an effect on recognition unless the major axis of the object was tilted toward the observer. Presumably, the disruption to recognition was due to the major axis appearing foreshortened and therefore harder to locate.

More powerful evidence in support of Marr and Nishihara's theory comes from neuropsychological case studies. Warrington and Taylor (1978) reported that patients with damage to a particular part of the right hemisphere could recognize objects when they were presented in a typical view but not when presented in an unusual view. These patients also found it very difficult to say whether two photographs (presented simultaneously) were of the same object when one image was a typical view of that object and one an unusual view.

One explanation for this effect is that the patients could not transform the two-dimensional representation of the unusual view of the object into a 3D model description. However, as well as it being difficult to establish the central axis of an object presented in an unusual view, it is also likely that rotation would cause some key features of the object to become hidden. Humphreys and Riddoch (1984) prepared images of objects in which *either* a critical feature was obscured *or* where the central axis had been foreshortened through rotation. These images were presented to patients similar to those tested by Warrington and Taylor. The patients had far more problems recognizing the axis-foreshortened objects than those with a key feature hidden. The results of these studies do offer some evidence that axis location may play a central role in generating a 3D model description of an object.

3.3   Biederman's theory

Marr and Nishihara's work has been extended and adapted in several related theories of object recognition. The most influential of these was proposed by Biederman in 1987. Biederman's theory (1987a) was also based on representing complex objects using a series of more simple primitives. Unlike Marr and Nishihara, Biederman did not restrict these primitives to generalized cones. Instead he proposed that the basic building blocks for describing an object were a set of basic shapes such as cylinders and cubes known as **geons** (an abbreviated form of the phrase 'geometric ions'). Many of these geons are generalized cones, but they also include other 3D shapes that are very useful in representing common objects. A subset of geons is shown in the top part of Figure 4.19.

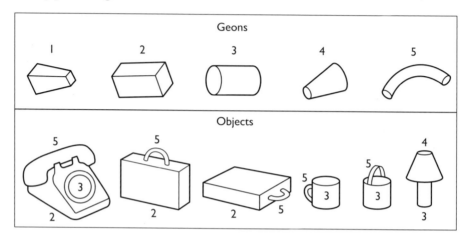

Figure 4.19   A selection of geons

Source: Biederman, 1987b

Biederman suggested that approximately 36 geons are needed in order to produce descriptions of all common objects. As with Marr and Nishihara's theory, more complex objects are represented by several different components and the division into components is based on areas of concavity.

The principal way in which Biederman's theory diverges from Marr and Nishihara's approach is the way in which a 3D description is formed from information in a 2D image – in other words, how the information in the primal sketch can be used to generate a 3D object-centred description. Biederman proposed that Marr's contour generators are not necessary to recover 3D shape, as each geon will have a key feature that remains invariant across different viewpoints. Thus, all that needs to be done is to locate these key features in the 2D primal sketch. Each feature can then be matched to a geon so that a 3D structural description of the object is generated. This description is then matched against those stored in memory.

Behind the concept of key features that remain invariant across viewpoint is the idea that some regular aspects of a 3D shape will tend to remain constant in any 2D image that is formed of that object. Biederman termed these 'non-accidental' properties to distinguish them from any regularity that was due simply to a particular viewpoint.

Biederman listed five non-accidental properties:

Curvilinearity – a curve in the 2D image is produced by a curve on the object.

Parallelism – lines that are parallel in the 2D image will be parallel on the object.

Cotermination – two or more edges that terminate at the same point in the 2D image will terminate at the same point on the object.

Symmetry – if the 2D image is symmetrical then the object will contain the same axis of symmetry.

Collinearity – a straight line in the 2D image is caused by a straight line on the object.

Choosing which geon to use in order to represent an object (or part of an object) is then simply a matter of detecting these non-accidental properties and selecting a geon that shares them. For example, the 2D image of a ball will be a circle and will therefore contain no parallelism, cotermination or collinearity, but will contain curvilinearity and an almost infinite degree of symmetry. The only geon to share these properties is a sphere, so the 3D shape of the ball is correctly described by a spherical geon.

Although these assumptions allow apparently ambiguous 2D images to be turned into an accurate 3D description, they can also lead to misinterpretation. For example, if you look at the wheel of a bicycle that is directly in front of you so that the wheel is viewed edge-on, its edges will appear to have the following non-accidental properties (see Figure 4.20):

Collinearity – the two vertical edges will appear as straight lines.

Symmetry – there will be two lines of symmetry, one horizontal and one vertical.

Parallelism – the two vertical edges will appear parallel.

However, the first of these non-accidental properties (collinearity) will be incorrect as a wheel does not contain any straight edges. We only see straight edges because of the viewpoint.

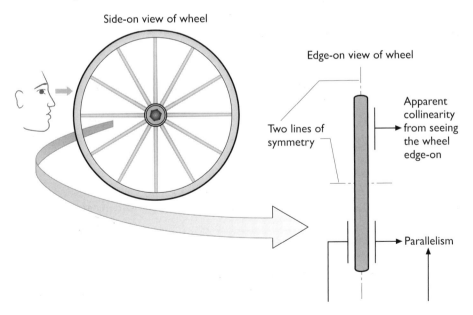

Figure 4.20 Apparent non-accidental properties of a wheel viewed edge-on

Although describing an object using non-accidental properties to select geons can lead to problems, there is evidence that supports Biederman's theory. The premise that concavities are used to divide the object into components (this premise was also used by Marr and Nishihara) was studied by presenting participants with images of objects that had part of their contours deleted. Deleting the part of the contour that corresponded to a concavity (that therefore occurred between components) resulted in a greater disruption to recognition than deleting part of the contour from elsewhere on the object (Biederman, 1987a).

The production of an object description that is independent of viewpoint is a crucial stage in the theories of both Marr and Nishihara and of Biederman. So is there evidence that recognition does involve the generation of an object-centred description rather then relying purely on viewer-centred descriptions?

To investigate the extent to which recognition is object-centred, Biederman and Gerhardstein (1993) used a technique known as repetition priming, where the presentation of one stimulus will make recognition of a related stimulus faster and/or more accurate. The idea behind their experiment was that if an object-centred description were being formed, then presenting one particular viewpoint of an object should facilitate (or prime) recognition of the same object presented in a different view. Their results showed that one viewpoint of an object did prime recognition of a separate viewpoint, as long as the change in the angle of viewpoint was not more than 135 degrees. However, even if the viewpoints were less than 135 degrees apart, if one or more geon was hidden between the first and second view, then the amount of priming was reduced. This result supports both the idea that an object-centred description is generated (otherwise different viewpoints should not prime each other), and that this makes use of geons.

However, other researchers have reported results that do not appear consistent with Biederman and Gerhardstein's findings. Bulthoff and Edelman (1992) found that participants were generally unable to recognize complex objects that were presented in a novel viewpoint, even if the view of the object was one that should have allowed the generation of an object-centred description. In the end, it is unlikely that recognition is *completely* reliant upon the generation of object-centred descriptions such as those suggested by Marr and Nishihara (1978) and by Biederman (1987a), and there may well be tasks that involve viewpoint-dependent recognition (Tarr, 1995).

One task that it is hard to incorporate into either Marr and Nishihara's or Biederman's theory is that of within-category discrimination. By representing objects as models consisting of either generalized cones or geons, a wealth of information is inevitably lost. For example, it is very likely that two collie-shaped canines would be represented as identical 3D models, yet it is possible to tell a border collie from a rough collie and even to tell specific dogs apart.

It makes sense that there should be more than a single way of arriving at such a complex cognitive achievement as object recognition. In the theories we have examined in this section, the process of recognition has been conceived of as almost wholly passive and based on a single retinal 'snapshot' or view. As we have stated previously, there are different types of recognition and different ways of achieving it, including taking a more active approach.

Summary of Section 3

- Objects can be recognized from many different angles, suggesting that the process of recognition may be based on the generation of a 3D object-centred description.
- Marr and Nishihara (1978) suggested a theory of object recognition based on generating 3D models. This was achieved by: deriving the shape of an object from the 2½D sketch; dividing it into 'primitives' using areas of sharp concavity; generating an axis for each of these components; and representing each component via a generalized cone.
- The 3D models were hierarchical in nature, and so include both global and detailed information stored in a hierarchically organized catalogue.
- Biederman (1987) suggested a similar theory based on using the non-accidental properties of an object to generate a description in terms of a series of basic volumetric forms known as geons.
- Although there is evidence that supports the approach taken by Marr and Nishihara and by Biederman, there are some forms of recognition which are difficult to explain using their theories.

4   Face recognition

Another type of recognition, and one that is very problematic for the 3D model approaches we have looked at so far, is that of recognizing faces. If we return to Humphreys and Bruce's model of object recognition shown in Figure 4.2, we can see that these theories have concentrated on the 'perceptual classification' stage of the process. Although this stage may provide information useful for navigation and basic interaction with the objects we find in the environment, more complex interaction is often necessary. For example, when you are confronted by a person, you want to know not only that there is a human face in front of you, but *whose* face it is. This requires a much finer level of distinction than simply recognizing a sphere as a sphere; you must be able to tell which *specific* face is in front of you. As we shall see in Sections 4 to 7 of this chapter, the need to recognize individual faces has led to theories and research concentrating on different issues from that conducted within the area of more general object recognition.

Faces can be categorized at several different levels. At one level, we decide that the stimulus is a face as opposed to some other object. At another level, we decide that the face is female or male or derive other semantic information such as ethnic origin. We may even make attractiveness judgements. Importantly, we also decide whether the face is familiar or unfamiliar. If the face is familiar, there is also the need to decide to whom the face belongs and it is at this level that faces are rather different from other objects. It is this within-category judgement, which is like recognizing a specific cat or a specific cup, that sets face recognition apart from object recognition more generally and is regarded as more visually demanding because the differences between faces can be fairly minimal.

Tanaka (2001) has found evidence to liken this level of face recognition to expert recognition – for example, the expertise that certain individuals acquire through training at bird-watching or X-ray analysis. But whereas only some specifically trained people achieve object expertise, face expertise is a general expertise that we all share and acquire without specific training. Whether or not this face expertise is the result of an innate processing system or the expression of a learned skill is a matter of debate and an issue we will return to in Section 7 of this chapter.

4.1   Recognizing familiar and unfamiliar faces

So how good are we at recognizing faces and identifying people? You already saw in Activity 4.2 that it was possible to recognize a face that was familiar to you (Paul McCartney) despite quite large changes in appearance. In fact, when you think about it, you are able to recognize your family and friends from any angle, under different lighting conditions and even when they age or change their hairstyle, and you are still likely to be able to do this in 30 years' time. There is evidence to suggest that we can remember the names and faces of school-friends over long periods of time; recognition tests revealed hardly any forgetting over a 35-year period (Bahrick *et al.*, 1975). This is not the case with all the faces we encounter though. Later work by Bahrick investigated the ability of college teachers to recognize former students taught over a 10-week period (Bahrick, 1984). The teachers had met these students three to five times a week. Although the level of correct face recognition for those taught recently was reasonably high at 69 per cent, this dropped as the number of intervening years increased so that after 8 years only 26 per cent of the former students were correctly recognized.

What about faces that are not so familiar and that we've only seen once? A number of face-learning experiments have been conducted (e.g. Yin, 1969) and these have found that, when given an immediate recognition test, participants performed extremely well. (For example, Yin observed that participants correctly recognized 93 per cent of the faces previously shown to them.) However, if the picture of the face shown in the recognition test depicted a different viewpoint or expression, then recognition rates dropped (e.g. Bruce, 1982), suggesting that what is being tested is 'recognition of a specific picture of a face' rather than 'face recognition' as we encounter it in everyday life.

Indeed, as you will see in Box 4.1, research has demonstrated that unfamiliar face recognition appears to be quite different from familiar face recognition.

┌───┐
4.1 ─────────────────────────────────── **Research study**

Recognizing unfamiliar faces in matching tasks

Even matching unfamiliar faces that are presented simultaneously (a task that does not test our memory) appears to be surprisingly difficult. In a field experiment, Kemp *et al.* (1997) looked at how well cashiers could match shoppers to credit cards bearing their photographs. They found that cashiers would frequently accept credit cards depicting a photograph of someone who bore a resemblance to the shopper (the correct decision rate to reject the card was only 36 per cent). Even when the photograph was of someone who bore no particular resemblance to the shopper but was of the same sex and ethnic background, the correct decision rate to reject the card was only 66 per cent (see Activity 4.1).

Other studies have demonstrated that we are not very good at matching two similar high-quality photographic images when the face is unfamiliar. Bruce *et al.* (1999) showed participants a high-quality video still of an unfamiliar young male target which was then presented in a line-up of similar images of nine other young men. Even when told that the target was definitely present in the line-up, participants picked it out accurately on only 80 per cent of the trials. If not told that the target was present, or if the pose of the target was varied between initial presentation and test, then performance was still worse. In fact the performance of these participants has been matched or even exceeded by that of an automatic face recognition system tested on the same images (Burton *et al.*, 2001).

Of interest too are the findings of a study looking at our ability to recognize unfamiliar faces by touch. Kilgour and Lederman (2002) found that when participants explored the faces both visually and tactually, performance was no better than when the faces were explored by touch alone.
└───┘

ACTIVITY 4.4

Look at the images of three faces shown in Figure 4.21. Which of the images to the left (a or b) do you think is of the same woman as that in the right-hand image (c)? These images are examples of images that were used on photo-credit cards in the study conducted by Kemp *et al.* (1997).

(a)   (b)   (c)

Figure 4.21   Three faces

COMMENT

The correct answer is that the left-hand image (a) is of the same woman shown in (c), but cashiers often refused to accept it due to the change in hairstyle. However, the image in the centre (b) was often incorrectly accepted as being of the woman to the right (c).

We will focus the rest of our discussion of face recognition largely on our ability to identify familiar faces and will start our discussion by considering some of the errors people make. These errors provide us with important information about the different systems and processes that may be involved in face recognition. Importantly, models of face recognition need to be able to account for such errors.

Summary of Section 4

- Face recognition is an example of a within-category judgement task.
- Our ability to identify familiar faces is extremely good and relatively unaffected by pose, lighting or viewpoint.
- Recognition of unfamiliar faces is much poorer and is influenced by changes in pose, lighting or viewpoint.

5   Modelling in face recognition

The theories of object recognition we have looked at previously centred on matching the description of an object that is in view with a stored representation. Although face recognition also involves similar matching processing, this is not usually considered the end point. In addition to matching the face we also need to access relevant semantic information and, preferably, the person's name.

ACTIVITY 4.5

Although we may have face expertise, we do make mistakes. Before reading on, reflect for a moment and recall the last time you discovered that you failed to recognize someone you know or you mistakenly thought you recognized someone you didn't know.

In a diary study, Young *et al.* (1985) asked 22 participants to make a record of the mistakes they made in recognizing people over an eight-week period. The recorded errors or difficulties tended to fall into different categories as shown in Table 4.2.

Table 4.2 The main types of everyday errors in face recognition revealed by Young *et al.* (1985)

Types of everyday errors	Number of errors
Person misidentified	314
Person unrecognized	114
Person seemed familiar only	223
Difficulty in retrieving full details of the person	190
Decision problems	35

What do these different categories mean? '*Person misidentified*' refers to those occasions when someone unfamiliar is misidentified as someone familiar and '*Person unrecognized*' refers to occasions when someone familiar was thought to be someone unfamiliar. Both may arise because of poor viewing conditions (i.e. it is a bit dark) or because we know the person only slightly. '*Person seemed familiar only*' refers to those occasions when you recognize someone as being familiar but no other information comes to mind immediately, and '*Difficulty in retrieving full details of the person*' refers to occasions when only some semantic information is retrieved and not, for example, their name. These errors often occur when the familiar person is seen outside the context in which they are usually encountered. Finally, '*Decision problems*' refer to those occasions where you think you recognize the person but decide it cannot be them, perhaps because you believe they are currently in another country.

The pattern of these errors suggests that, although we might retrieve previously learned semantic information about a person without recalling their name, we will never recall their name without also retrieving relevant semantic information. However, before we can recall either semantic information or a name, we must realize the face is familiar.

These findings on everyday errors are consistent with the notion that the recognition of faces involves a sequence of processes using different types of information. Hay and Young (1982), Young *et al.* (1985) and then Bruce and Young (1986) refined a cognitive theoretical framework or model of person recognition involving such a sequence of stages. On meeting people, we encode their faces. This encoded information may activate **face recognition units** (FRUs) that contain stored information about the faces we are familiar with. If there is a reasonable match between what has been encoded and what is stored in the recognition unit, then the recognition unit will be activated and allow access to semantic information about the person's identity, such as their occupation, stored in **person identity nodes** (PINs). It is only once the PIN for a face has been activated that their name can be generated. A **cognitive system** is also involved, as the information provided by the recognition system must be evaluated. As the diary study above indicated, errors in face recognition can arise because of decision problems. For example, if we know that the person doesn't live or work nearby, that knowledge may override what our recognition system is telling us and hence we may doubt that we have correctly identified the person.

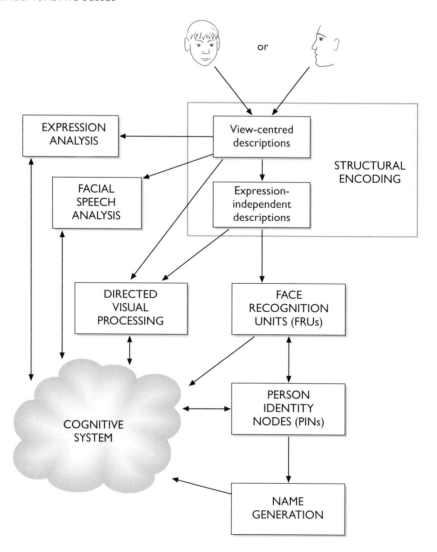

Figure 4.22   Bruce and Young's functional model for face recognition

Source: Bruce and Young, 1986, p.312

The Bruce and Young (1986) functional model for face recognition is presented in Figure 4.22. As you can see, there are separate routes for facial expression analysis, facial speech analysis and face recognition; and face recognition progresses through a sequence of stages from FRUs to PINs to name generation.

The notion that different types of information are sequentially accessed is also supported by the results of experiments conducted in the laboratory. For example, Hay *et al.* (1991) showed participants 190 famous and unfamiliar facial images and asked them to decide whether or not each face was familiar and to state the person's occupation and the person's name. Participants did not retrieve a name without also being able to name the occupation, thus supporting the notion that semantic 'person identity' information is retrieved *before* the person's name. Other studies (e.g. Johnston and Bruce, 1990), looking at how quickly we can complete a particular task, have shown that faces can be classified as familiar more quickly than they can be classified by occupation, and furthermore that classifications that require accessing the person's name take longer than classifications involving a person's occupation or other semantic properties. These findings support the notion that perceptual classification, judging the familiarity of a person, takes place *before* semantic classification and that a person's name is accessed last. They also provide a nice demonstration of how the findings from the laboratory may support those derived in a more everyday study of face recognition, such as Young *et al.*'s (1985) diary study.

5.1   A connectionist model of face recognition

The **IAC model** (e.g. Burton *et al.*, 1990; Burton and Bruce, 1993) is a connectionist model (recall the discussion of connectionism in Chapter 1) of face recognition and an extension and implementation of the Bruce and Young model described above. IAC stands for 'interactive activation and competition network'. As this model is a computer simulation of face recognition it has been tested by seeing how compatible it is with the available evidence, and by looking at the predictions it generates.

The model comprises units which are organized into pools (see Figure 4.23). These pools contain:

- *FRUs (face recognition units):* For every familiar person, there is one FRU in the model. These are view-independent and seeing any recognizable view of a face will activate the appropriate FRU. These representations allow perceptual information to be mapped onto stored memories. (This is basically what was suggested in the Bruce and Young model.)

- *PINs (person identity nodes):* This is where a face is classified as belonging to a person, and there is one unit per known person.

- *SIUs (semantic information units):* Relevant semantic information is stored here, e.g. occupational category.

- *Lexical output:* Units representing output as either words or name.

The IAC model also includes a route based on word recognition. The pool of WRUs (word recognition units) represents an input lexicon containing both specific names and more general information, such as nationality or occupation. Words which are names have direct links to a pool of NRUs (name recognition units), which are linked to PINs in the same way as FRUs. The WRUs which do not correspond to names are linked to SIUs.

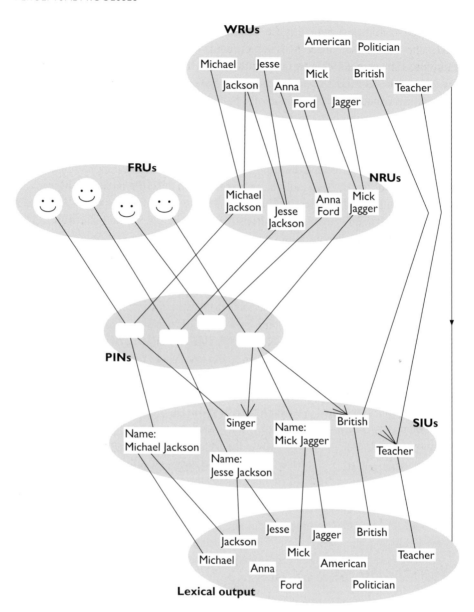

Figure 4.23   The central architecture of the IAC model

Figure 4.23 shows how the pools are connected. The input systems (FRUs and NRUs) join to a common set of person identity nodes (PINs) and these are linked to units containing semantic information (SIUs). Each of the pools is illustrated here with just a few examples of the units they might contain. Many SIUs will be shared and here many people will be represented with such information as 'teacher' or 'British'.

Recognizing a face is modelled in the following way: seeing a face will activate an FRU which in turn increases activation in the relevant PIN. As PINs are linked to SIUs, activation of the PIN will bring about activation in the relevant SIU. The notion that different types of information are sequentially accessed is therefore still present in this connectionist model. If a certain threshold is achieved in the PIN, then this signals familiarity. An important point to note is that different types of information come together at the PIN stage, including information from recognition systems specialized for faces as well as those specialized for the recognition of written or spoken names, and familiarity is judged on this pooled information.

We mentioned before that IAC stood for 'interactive activation and competition network'. The 'interactive activation' arises from the links between units in different pools which are *excitatory*: the FRU for Mick Jagger's face excites or activates the PIN for Mick Jagger which in turn excites semantic information units for the name 'Mick Jagger', the occupation 'singer' and the nationality 'British'. These excitatory links are bidirectional so that excitation also runs in the opposite direction from 'singer' to Mick Jagger's PIN and Mick Jagger's FRU. However, within each pool, links between units are *inhibitory* (these links are not shown in Figure 4.23), so this is where 'competition' arises. Excitement in the FRU for Mick Jagger will inhibit activity in the other FRUs, just as excitement in Mick Jagger's PIN will inhibit activity in the other PINs and excitement in one SIU will inhibit activity in another SIU. But the SIU for Mick Jagger (which might be 'singer') will also excite many other PINs (in this example, those belonging to all other singers). This means that activation of PINs will not be limited solely to the specific person in question but that some activation will also occur for anyone who is semantically related (e.g. shares the same occupation). Thus, the model incorporates the results of experiments that have shown priming effects – that you are quicker to recognize Bill Wyman if you have already seen Mick Jagger. Generally, the strength of this connectionist model is that it can account for findings from laboratory studies as well as for the everyday errors described by Young *et al.* (1985).

Summary of Section 5

- Everyday errors suggest that recognizing faces involves sequential access to different types of information.
- A cognitive model of person recognition involving such an idealized sequence of stages has been developed (Bruce and Young, 1986).
- IAC is a connectionist model of face recognition which is an extension and implementation of this cognitive model.

6 Neuropsychological evidence

Prosopagnosia, the inability to recognize faces whilst maintaining the ability to recognize other objects, is a well-documented phenomenon. However, cases of 'pure' prosopagnosia are exceptionally rare. It is more common to see deficits affecting other visual categories too. The recognition of all familiar faces is affected, regardless of their semantic categories (so it is not the case that the failure to recognize a face is restricted to faces of celebrities or politicians). However, as recognition from other cues, for example voice, usually remains unaffected, the condition is specific to visual recognition of faces and is not a more general impairment of the recognition of personal identity. Also, the ability to distinguish between faces is often preserved.

In this section, we shall focus on two key findings that have emerged from investigations of prosopagnosia: first, that identification of expression appears to be independent from face identification; and, second, that face recognition and awareness of face recognition might also be independent of one another. It is possible that although prosopagnosics are unable to recognize faces consciously or overtly, certain types of non-conscious response may be preserved. We shall examine how the IAC model may account for this.

As mentioned in Section 5, models of face recognition have proposed a route for face identification that is independent of emotional expression, and this independence has received support from experimental work and from neuropsychological research. In many cases of prosopagnosia, the ability to recognize facial expressions may be unaffected. Young et al. (1993) looked at ex-servicemen with unilateral brain injuries and tested familiar face recognition, unfamiliar face matching and analysis of emotional facial expressions. Analysis of accuracy data showed evidence of selective impairments in each of these three abilities. For example, one participant with a right hemisphere lesion was selectively impaired in identifying familiar faces, whereas a different participant, also with a right hemisphere lesion, had problems only with matching unfamiliar faces. A number of other participants with left hemisphere lesions were only impaired on the facial expression tasks. Response latency data also supported the notion of a selective deficit of facial expression processing but suggested that impairments of familiar face recognition and unfamiliar face matching were not entirely independent from one another. The findings from this study thus provide strong support for the notion that facial expression analysis and face identification seem to proceed independently of each other (and also some support for the notion that the ability to recognize familiar faces and to match unfamiliar faces may be selectively and independently impaired).

Previously, when describing models of face recognition, we did not draw a distinction between face recognition and awareness of recognition. However, neuropsychological research on prosopagnosia suggests that the distinction is important. Bauer (1984) monitored changes in autonomic nervous system activity via changes in **skin conductance response (SCR)**. These changes signal an affective or emotional reaction (you may remember reading in Chapter 2 on attention how a closely related response, GSR, was measured to look at unconscious processes). Bauer showed LF, a participant with prosopagnosia, a face and read out a list of five names, whilst simultaneously measuring SCR. If LF was asked to pick the correct name, he performed no better than at chance. In other words, LF was overtly unable to recognize familiar people from their faces. However, LF showed a greater SCR when the correct name was read aloud compared with the incorrect names. Thus, LF was showing an affective or emotional response, but this response was not a conscious one. The term **covert recognition** is used to describe this non-conscious recognition or emotional response to the faces.

Since Bauer's work, many studies have investigated covert recognition and the issue is not whether this type of face recognition exists but how to interpret it. Bauer proposed that separate neural pathways are responsible for two independent routes to recognition, one for conscious overt recognition and one for non-conscious covert recognition. Although questions remain over exactly how overt and covert recognition processes are mediated and how these processes normally become integrated, there is support for the involvement of the two major neural pathways (see Box 4.2).

4.2   **Research study**

Capgras delusion

Capgras delusion usually occurs as part of a psychiatric illness although it can result from brain injury. A person with Capgras delusion believes firmly that someone they know, usually a relative or close friend, has been replaced by an impostor, double, robot or alien. Sometimes the delusion relates to objects; for example, the sufferer may believe that tools, ornaments or other household objects have been replaced by doubles. Face and object Capgras delusion do not usually coexist, and the disorder tends to be specific to one domain. The key point here is that individuals with a face Capgras delusion recognize a face but simultaneously refute its authenticity. Exactly why those with Capgras delusion adhere to the belief that the person must be an impostor is still being debated.

Ellis and Young (1990) suggested that Capgras delusion may be a 'mirror image' of the impairments underlying prosopagnosia. Bauer (1984) proposed that the neuroanatomical pathway involved in overt recognition was the 'ventral visual-limbic pathway' whereas the pathway involved in covert recognition was the 'dorsal visual-limbic pathway'. Ellis and Young suggested that the Capgras delusion resulted from damage to such a dorsal route, so that sufferers would recognize the familiar person but not receive supporting affective information. Their prediction that individuals with Capgras delusion would recognize familiar faces but would fail to show an autonomic emotional response to these familiar faces has received support from several studies (e.g. Hirstein and Ramachandran, 1997). Whilst overt recognition is intact, covert recognition seems to be impaired.

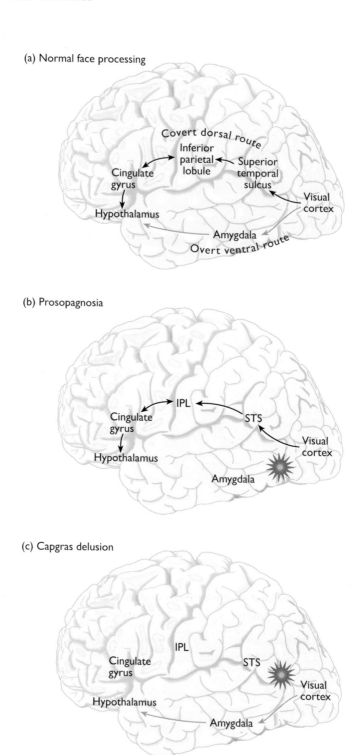

Figure 4.24 The dorsal and ventral routes in normal face processing (a), prosopagnosia (b) and Capgras delusion (c)

Source: Ellis and Lewis, 2001, Figure 3, p.154

Figure 4.24 shows normal face processing (a), with a darker arrow showing the covert dorsal route and a lighter arrow the overt ventral route. In prosopagnosia (b) the overt ventral route is thought to be damaged, and in Capgras delusion (c) the covert dorsal route is thought to be damaged.

A different issue is whether those individuals who retain covert recognition can be helped to overcome their disorder. Could covert recognition be turned into overt recognition? Sergent and Poncet (1990) were the first to demonstrate such provoked overt recognition. In their study, PV was shown eight faces of famous people from the same semantic category and she was unable to identify them. However, when she was told that they all had the same occupation and she looked at the faces again, she was able to say that they were all politicians, name seven of the people, and recall biographical information about the eighth person. This and other later studies (e.g. Diamond *et al.*, 1994) have shown that provoked overt recognition can occur under certain experimental conditions, and this provides some hope for rehabilitative work.

Can the IAC model accommodate the pattern of deficits described here? Covert without overt recognition is explained in terms of attenuation (or weakening) in the connections between the FRUs and PINs. This means that when a face is seen, and the FRU is activated, the weakened FRU–PIN connection strength means that excitation of the corresponding PIN is not raised above the threshold for the face to be recognized overtly. However, this weakened activation may be sufficient to raise the excitation of the PIN above its resting level, mediating covert recognition. Provoked overt recognition is explained in the following way. Telling PV that the faces are related is equivalent to strengthening the PIN–SIU connections. Unlike FRU–PIN connections, PIN–SIU links are assumed to remain intact in instances of prosopagnosia where covert recognition is observed. Once these connections are strengthened, activation is passed back from the shared SIUs to the relevant PINs. These then achieve threshold and the faces are recognized overtly. Simulations with the model confirmed this particular prediction – provoked overt recognition was successfully modelled (Morrison *et al.*, 2001).

So, as a model of face recognition, the IAC model is impressive in that it can account for a wide range of data from studies on face recognition. Whilst there are other models of face recognition, some of these are based on a narrower range of evidence; for example, they may have sought only to account for the findings from neuropsychological studies. As we have seen here, IAC is compatible with everyday, laboratory and neuropsychological findings.

Summary of Section 6

- Prosopagnosia is the inability to recognize faces although expressions and other objects may still be correctly identified.
- Covert face recognition, shown by autonomic responses to faces, may however be spared.

- Overt conscious face recognition and covert non-conscious face recognition are different types of face recognition that may be mediated by different neural pathways.
- Capgras delusion may be a mirror image of prosopagnosia in terms of which system remains intact and which system is damaged.
- Provoked overt recognition has been achieved in some studies and has been successfully modelled using the IAC model.

7   Are faces 'special'?

In this last section we return to the issue of the difference between face recognition and object recognition, and in particular to face expertise and how we are able to discriminate so readily between faces. There are several important issues that the literature has addressed:

1   Is there a neuroanatomical location that underlies face processing and, if so, does this mean that face processing is unique and qualitatively different from the processing of other types of visual stimuli?

2   Is face processing an innate or learned skill? Have we developed a face expertise because of constant exposure to faces and practice at differentiating between them or is there an innate ability?

3   How important are the individual features of the face, the relationships between the features or the three-dimensional structure? Do we process the individual facial features or the face as a whole?

In the last section, we looked at the syndrome of prosopagnosia and found that research implicated several neurological pathways. Of particular interest is that prosopagnosia can leave object recognition relatively intact and, in turn, face recognition has been spared in cases where object recognition has been impaired (a double dissociation). Studies using the technique of functional magnetic resonance imaging (fMRI) have found facial stimuli to activate an area in the fusiform gyrus in the posterior temporal lobes (especially in the right hemisphere) whilst non-face objects activated a different area. There is also the observation of cells specialized for faces within the monkey temporal lobe – these cells respond selectively to faces of humans and/or monkeys but not to other stimuli (e.g. geometrical shapes and bananas). There is, therefore, evidence to suggest that the processing of faces is mediated by specific areas of the brain, that there is cortical specialization for faces. But does this mean that face recognition is *unique*, that the processes used for recognizing faces are qualitatively different from those used for recognizing other visual stimuli?

There is support for the notion that there is a special mechanism from birth for processing facial information, as newborn babies show a preference for face-like visual patterns. Rather than an innate neural mechanism that processes faces, Johnson and Morton (1991) suggested that there is a mechanism that makes newborns attentive to faces, and this innate attentional bias then ensures that any system for learning visual stimuli receives a lot of face input and learns about the individual characteristics of faces. Although there is a 'kick-start' mechanism which gives face processing in newborns a special status, this serves to guide subsequent learning and soon other processing systems will come into play (these may or may not be unique to faces).

One reason to think that face recognition is a special type of recognition, distinct from other object recognition, is that faces all tend to look alike in that they have similar features in similar positions. Given this similarity, it could be that we have to make use of a different form of visual information to recognize a face from that used to recognize, for example, a table. Some evidence that this is indeed the case comes from studies that have demonstrated that inverting, or turning upside down, visual stimuli disproportionately impairs our ability to recognize faces compared with our ability to recognize objects. This is known as the **inversion effect**. Yin (1969) and other studies since (e.g. Johnston *et al.*, 1992) have shown that inverting a photograph of a face disrupts recognition more than does inverting an image of an object. Yin looked at the influence of inversion on faces and other stimulus material including houses and aeroplanes. Although recognition memory was better for upright faces than for other material, when the stimuli were turned upside down, recognition for faces was worse than that for other material. The key question is whether this peculiar reversal of recognition accuracy for faces (from best upright to worst inverted) supports the notion that faces are processed differently from other stimuli or whether there is an alternative explanation.

Diamond and Carey (1986) investigated an alternative hypothesis, namely that the effect of inversion on faces was a result of our perceptual mechanisms becoming 'tuned' to seeing this special type of visual stimulus in the usual upright orientation. This 'tuning' or expertise would then be 'lost' when we see them inverted. Their research considered whether the inversion effect was indeed specific to human faces or whether it would in fact arise when using any class of visual stimulus with which we have a large amount of experience. To investigate this, Diamond and Carey selected participants to include both people who were not interested in dogs and people who were dog experts (mainly dog-show judges, breeders/handlers or people with a sustained interest in dogs). These participants were shown photographs of both human faces and dogs (body profiles – see Figure 4.25) and told to look at each photograph and try to remember it. Analysis revealed that whereas all participants recognized upright faces better than inverted faces, dog experts also recognized upright dogs better than inverted dogs. This finding has been interpreted as supporting the notion that the inversion effect is acquired as a result of expertise and is not a 'face-specific' effect.

What changes then in the way we process faces as we acquire this expertise? Diamond and Carey proposed a distinction between first-order and second-order relational properties. *First-order relational properties* refer to the spatial relation-ships among parts of the face; for example, the eyes are above the nose and the mouth below the nose. Faces cannot be distinguished according to their first-order relational properties as they all share the same basic arrangement or configuration. However, first-order relational properties help us detect that a visual stimulus is a face – a necessary step before identifying the face. *Second-order relational properties* refer to the differences in this basic configuration. This refers to the differences in the way the features are arranged in relation to each other; for example,

(a) Inspection items that participants were
asked to remember

(b) Recognition items: participants were asked to judge which of the stimulus items they
had seen previously

Figure 4.25   Examples of the dog stimuli used by Diamond and Carey

Source: Diamond and Carey, 1986, p.112

wide-set eyes with a low forehead versus narrow-set eyes and a high forehead. Expertise results in a greater sensitivity to these second-order relational properties, as it is these properties that individuate members of the same class, such as human faces.

There is support for the notion that inversion influences our sensitivity to second-order relational properties. For example, Searcy and Bartlett (1996) presented participants with photographs of grotesque looking faces. They created images where they had either distorted individual facial features (eyes and mouths) or they had distorted the spatial relations between the features (see Figure 4.26). They then presented these manipulated images in upright and inverted orientations. Participants rated the grotesqueness of the images and results showed that images of faces with distortions to the spatial relations between the features were rated as less grotesque when presented inverted rather than upright; inversion failed to reduce ratings of grotesqueness when the distortions were performed on the features.

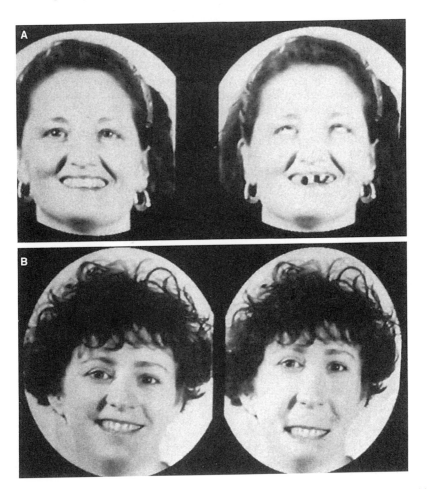

Figure 4.26 Examples of stimuli used by Searcy and Bartlett (1996): the pair labelled 'A' shows a normal image and one with distorted facial features; the pair labelled 'B' shows a normal image and one with spatial distortion

Source: Searcy and Bartlett, 1986, Figure 1, p.907

These findings support the notion that inversion disrupts our processing of spatial relationships between the features.

Research like this suggests our expertise in (upright) face recognition stems from the way in which these upright faces are processed as 'configurations', rather than as an assemblage of independent features. The term **configural processing** has been used, although this has been interpreted in a number of ways: to refer to the spatial relationships between features (i.e. second-order relational properties); to refer to the way facial features interact with one another (i.e. the way the shape of the mouth influences how the shape of the nose is perceived); to refer to holistic processing of the face (i.e. the face is perceived as a whole face pattern and not broken down into separate features); or even to refer to the basic arrangement of the facial features (i.e. first-order relational properties).

A considerable amount of research has been devoted to investigating the relative importance of this type of processing as compared with the processing of the facial features (known as featural processing or piecemeal processing). Although it is not always clear what different researchers mean by the term 'configural', there is agreement that configural information plays an important role in the perception and representation of upright faces. The suggestion that this reliance on configural processing is the result of learning to recognize lots of faces, and hence the result of expertise, does not rule out any input from an innate mechanism, which may have 'kick-started' this learning by biasing attention towards faces. However, it does not suggest that face perception and recognition involve *unique* processes which are qualitatively different from those used to process other types of stimuli. Finally, it is worth noting that research has yet to clarify the different processes involved in recognizing familiar faces as opposed to unfamiliar faces, or fully to specify the overlap between the processes involved in face identification and those used in object recognition.

In sum, although there is physiological and neuropsychological evidence supporting the existence of areas specialized for processing faces, and although there is evidence suggesting an innate ability to pay attention to faces, the processes involved in face recognition do not appear to be unique.

Summary of Section 7

- Neuropsychological and physiological evidence suggests that there are specific areas of the brain that mediate face processing.
- Research on newborn babies suggest an innate ability to attend to faces.
- The inversion effect appears to be linked to our expertise in processing upright faces using configural information.
- We may develop expertise at distinguishing members of other categories of visual stimuli that also involves configural processing.
- Evidence does not suggest that the processes involved in the perception and recognition of faces are unique.

8   Conclusion

In this chapter we have explored different types of recognition and looked at some of the mechanisms that allow us to recognize objects and faces. In reading about recognition, you may well have got the idea that cognitive psychologists still have a lot to learn about how object and face recognition may occur. This is undoubtedly the case and a great deal of research is still being conducted in order to provide a more comprehensive and detailed theory of the cognition involved in recognition. Just as there are different types of recognition, there are also different ways of recognizing faces and objects – for example, visually or by touch – and these different ways may involve different processes. So, rather than see the theories discussed here as providing a final answer, the best way to view them is as taking some of the initial steps in this complex but interesting field.

Now that you have read this chapter you can reinforce and extend your learning by reading an original journal article associated with it, available online from the DD303 website. Remember, these are original journal articles, so the style is different from this textbook, and don't be too concerned if you can't follow every detail.

Further reading

Bruce, V., Green, P.R. and Georgeson, M.A. (2003) *Visual Perception: Physiology, Psychology and Ecology*, Hove, Psychology Press.

Marr, D. (1982) *Vision: A Computational Investigation into the Human Representation and Processing of Visual Information*, New York, W.H. Freeman & Company.

Rakover, S.S. and Cahlon, B. (2001) *Face Recognition: Cognitive and Computational Processes* (Advances in Consciousness Research), Philadelphia, PA, John Benjamins Publishing Co.

References

Bahrick, H.P. (1984) 'Memory for people', in Harris, J.E. and Morris, P.E. (eds) *Everyday Memory, Actions and Absent-mindedness*, Academic Press, London.

Bahrick, H.P., Bahrick, P.O. and Wittlinger, R.P. (1975) 'Fifty years of memory for names and faces: a cross-sectional approach', *Journal of Experimental Psychology: General*, vol.104, pp.54–75.

Bauer, R.M. (1984) 'Autonomic recognition of names and faces in prosopagnosia: a neuropsychological application of the guilty knowledge test', *Neuropsychologia*, vol.22, pp.457–69.

Biederman, I. (1987a) 'Recognition by components: a theory of human image understanding', *Psychological Review*, vol.94, pp.115–47.

Biederman, I. (1987b) 'Matching image edges to object memory', *Proceedings of the First International Conference on Computer Vision*, IEEE Computer Society, pp.384–92.

Biederman, I. and Gerhardstein, P.C. (1993) 'Recognizing depth-rotated objects: evidence and conditions for three-dimensional viewpoint invariance', *Journal of Experimental Psychology: Human Perception and Performance*, vol.19, pp.1162–82.

Bruce, V. (1982) 'Changing faces: visual and non-visual coding processes in face recognition', *British Journal of Psychology*, vol.73, pp.105–16.

Bruce, V. and Young, A. (1986) 'Understanding face recognition', *British Journal of Psychology*, vol.77, pp.305–27.

Bruce, V., Henderson, Z., Greenwood, K., Hancock, P.J.B., Burton, A.M. and Miller, P. (1999) 'Verification of face identities from images captured on video', *Journal of Experimental Psychology: Applied*, vol.5, pp.339–60.

Bulthoff, H.H. and Edelman, S. (1992) 'Psychophysical support for a two-dimensional view interpolation theory of object recognition', *Proceedings of the National Academy of Sciences of the USA*, vol.89, pp.60–4.

Burton, A.M. and Bruce, V. (1993) 'Naming faces and naming names: exploring an interactive activation model of person recognition', *Memory*, vol.1, pp.457–80.

Burton, A.M., Bruce, V. and Johnston, R.A. (1990) 'Understanding face recognition with an interactive activation model', *British Journal of Psychology*, vol.81, pp.361–80.

Burton, A.M., Miller, P., Bruce, V., Hancock, P.J.B. and Henderson, Z. (2001) 'Human and automatic face recognition: a comparison across image formats', *Vision Research*, vol.41, pp.3185–95.

Diamond, B.J., Valentine, T., Mayes, A.R. and Sandel, M.E. (1994) 'Evidence of covert recognition in a prosopagnosic patient', *Cortex*, vol.28, pp.77–95.

Diamond, R. and Carey, S. (1986) 'Why faces are and are not special: an effect of expertise', *Journal of Experimental Psychology: General*, vol.115, pp.107–17.

Ellis, H.D. and Lewis, M.B. (2001) 'Capgras delusion: a window on face recognition', *Trends in Cognitive Sciences*, vol.5, no.4, pp.149–56.

Ellis, H.D. and Young, A.W. (1990) 'Accounting for delusional misidentifications', *British Journal of Psychiatry*, vol.157, pp.239–48.

Gibson, J.J. (1986) *The Ecological Approach to Visual Perception*, Hillsdale, NJ, Lawrence Erlbaum Associates.

Hay, D.C. and Young, A.W. (1982) 'The human face', in Ellis, A.W. (ed.) *Normality and Pathology in Cognitive Functions,* London, Academic Press.

Hay, D.C., Young, A.W. and Ellis, A.W. (1991) 'Routes through the face recognition system', *Quarterly Journal of Experimental Psychology*, vol.43A, pp.761–91.

Hirstein, W. and Ramachandran, V.S. (1997) 'Capgras syndrome: a novel probe for understanding the neural representation of identity and familiarity of persons', *Proceedings of the Royal Society*, London, Series B, vol.264, pp.437–44.

Humphreys, G.W. and Bruce, V. (1989) *Visual Cognition: Computational, Experimental and Neuropsychological Perspectives*, Hove, Lawrence Erlbaum Associates Ltd.

Humphreys, G.W. and Riddoch, M.J. (1984) 'Routes to object constancy: implications from neurological impairments of object constancy', *Quarterly Journal of Experimental Psychology*, vol.36A, pp.385–415.

Johnson, M.H. and Morton, J. (1991) *Biology and Cognitive Development: The Case of Face Recognition*, Oxford, Blackwell.

Johnston, A., Hill, H. and Carmen, N. (1992) 'Recognizing faces: effects of lighting direction, inversion and brightness reversal', *Perception*, vol.21, pp.365–75.

Johnston, R.A. and Bruce, V. (1990) 'Lost properties? Retrieval differences between name codes and semantic codes for familiar people', *Psychological Research*, vol.52, pp.62–7.

Kemp, R., Pike, G. and Brace, N. (2001) 'Video-based identification procedures: combining best practice and practical requirements when designing identification systems', *Psychology, Public Policy and Law*, vol.7, no.4, pp.802–7.

Kemp, R., Towell, N. and Pike, G. (1997) 'When seeing should not be believing: photographs, credit cards and fraud', *Applied Cognitive Psychology*, vol.11, no.3, pp.211–22.

Kilgour, A.R. and Lederman, S.J. (2002) 'Face recognition by hand', *Perception and Psychophysics*, vol.64, pp.339–52.

Lawson, R. and Humphreys, G.W. (1996) 'View-specificity in object processing: evidence from picture matching', *Journal of Experimental Psychology: Human Perception and Performance*, vol.22, pp.395–416.

Lederman, S.J. and Klatzky, R.L. (1987) 'Hand movements: a window into haptic object recognition', *Cognitive Psychology*, vol.19, pp.342-8.

Lederman, S.J. and Klatzky, R.L. (1990) 'Haptic classification of common objects: knowledge-driven exploration', *Cognitive Psychology*, vol.22, pp.421–59.

Lederman, S.J., Klatzky, R.L. and Pawluk, D.T. (1993) 'Lessons from the study of biological touch for robot haptic sensing', in Nichols, H. (ed.) 'Advanced tactile sensing for robotics', in *World Scientific Series in Robotics and Automated Systems*, vol.5, Singapore, World Scientific Publishing.

Marr, D. (1977) 'Analysis of occluding contour', *Proceedings of the Royal Society of London*, Series B, vol.197, pp.441–75.

Marr, D. (1982) *Vision: A Computational Investigation into the Human Representation and Processing of Visual Information*, New York, W.H. Freeman and Company.

Marr, D. and Nishihara, H.K. (1978) 'Representation and recognition of the spatial organization of three-dimensional shapes', *Proceedings of the Royal Society of London*, Series B, vol.211, pp.151–80.

Morrison, D.J., Bruce, V. and Burton, A.M. (2001) 'Understanding provoked overt recognition in prosopagnosia', *Visual Cognition*, vol.8, pp.47–65.

Neisser, U. (1967) *Cognitive Psychology*, New York, Appleton-Century-Crofts.

Pike, G., Brace, N. and Kynan, S. (2001) 'The visual identification of suspects: procedures and practice', *A Publication of the Policing and Reducing Crime Unit, Home Office Research, Development and Statistics Directorate*.

Pike, G., Kemp, R. and Brace, N. (2000) 'The psychology of human face recognition', *IEE Electronics and Communications: Visual Biometrics*, 00/018, pp.12/1–12/6.

Searcy, J.H. and Bartlett, J.C. (1996) 'Inversion and processing component and spatial-relational information in faces', *Journal of Experimental Psychology: Human Perception and Performance*, vol.22, pp.904–15.

Selfridge, O.G. (1959) 'Pandemonium: a paradigm for learning', in *The Mechanisation of Thought Processes*, London, HMSO.

Sergent, J. and Poncet, M. (1990) 'From covert to overt recognition of faces in a prosopagnosic patient', *Brain*, vol.113, pp.989–1004.

Tanaka, J.W. (2001) 'The entry point of face recognition: evidence for face expertise', *Journal of Experimental Psychology: General*, vol.130, pp.534–43.

Tarr, M.J. (1995) 'Rotating objects to recognize them: a case study on the role of viewpoint dependency in the recognition of three-dimensional objects', *Psychonomic Bulletin and Review*, vol.2, pp.55–82.

Warrington, E.K. and Taylor, A.M. (1978) 'Two categorical stages of object recognition', *Perception*, vol.7, pp.695–705.

Yin, R.K. (1969) 'Looking at upside down faces', *Journal of Experimental Psychology*, vol.81, pp.141–5.

Young, A.W., Hay, D.C. and Ellis, A.W. (1985) 'The faces that launched a thousand slips: everyday difficulties and errors in recognizing people', *British Journal of Psychology*, vol.76, pp.495–523.

Young, A.W., Newcombe, F., De Haan, E.H.F., Small, M. and Hay, D.C. (1993) 'Face perception after brain injury', *Brain*, vol.116, pp.941–59.

PART 2
MEMORY

Introduction

In Part 2 you will find three chapters dedicated to the topic of memory. You have already encountered explicit references to and implicit assumptions regarding memory processes and/or memory stores. In Part 1, the activation and utilization of stored knowledge was frequently invoked in trying to comprehend the processes of attention, perception and recognition. In fact, memory of one sort or another is integral to every form of cognition and you will find references throughout this book. However, the chapters in Part 2 differ from the other chapters in that they take memory as their focus of interest rather than as an important incidental to some other major topic.

In Chapter 5, 'Working memory', the focus of interest is on the memory stores and/or processes involved simply in maintaining whatever information an individual has in mind, or in executing whatever tasks they are engaged upon at a particular moment. As the chapter explains, the notion of working memory elaborates and extends upon the older and simpler idea of a short-term memory store. Working memory is conceived as a workspace with a limited capacity that is composed of a number of component parts. Evidence for these separate components comes from studies employing various techniques for selectively interfering with cognitive performance. Neuropsychological data bear strongly upon the issues, and evidence is also adduced from studies employing neuroimaging techniques.

Chapter 5 also considers individual differences in working memory. As described in Chapter 1, cognitive psychology as a whole tends to play down individual differences in favour of an emphasis on what it is that people have cognitively in common. This is similar to the way in which anatomists emphasize the considerable similarities in people's bodies ahead of their individual variations. But psychology, to an even greater degree than anatomy, cannot afford to overlook individuality for long. In Chapter 5 you will see how cognitive psychologists can make use of individual differences to test their theories, and also utilize their theories to explain individual differences in cognition.

In Chapter 6, 'Long-term memory: encoding to retrieval', the concern is to understand how information gets into and is withdrawn from more permanent memory. The chapter lays emphasis on understanding how different types of encoding and retrieval operations determine what gets remembered and in what form. The quality of memory, it turns out, results from interactions between encoding processes, the kinds of cognitive representations that are constructed, and types of retrieval operations that act upon those representations in fulfilling whatever goals a person is intent upon. One theme of the chapter is the sheer difficulty of knowing how best to conceptualize memory. A major distinction is seen between the noun 'memory' and the verbs 'memorizing' and 'remembering'. That is, on the one hand, memory can be conceived as a set of stores and, on the other, memory can be thought of as a set of systems or processes. As you will see there are arguments and data that favour and count against both conceptualizations. Whichever one opts for, there is then a problem of deciding how many stores or how many processes to postulate.

One reason these questions can be so hard to answer is introduced at the start of the chapter. It is that the functions of memory in normal everyday cognition are so vast and diverse, and for the most part so reliable and smooth-running, that – as with the processes of vision – they are really quite hard to think about. It is perhaps on account of this that this chapter builds on Chapter 5 by further emphasizing the importance of neuropsychological observations and studies for understanding the cognitive psychology of memory. Of course, it is the case that any memory impairment will itself be open to a variety of interpretations. Despite this, however, you will see in Chapter 6 that neuropsychological data have played an important part in the development of theories about the nature of memory.

Chapter 7 introduces the notion of autobiographical memory, the personal memories people have of events and experiences relating to themselves. This leads into a consideration of the relationship between autobiographical memory and our sense of self. The chapter builds on the distinctions between remembering specific events and our general knowledge that are considered in Chapter 6. However, research into autobiographical memories cannot rely on the same kinds of laboratory-based, experimental methods used to investigate other types of memory – think of the difficulties of running a memory experiment where participants will be tested for recall decades later! Research in this area tends to rely on particular distinctive methods aimed at eliciting memories of actual episodes from our past, and the chapter activities invite you to take part in some of these procedures.

Chapter 7 develops ideas about how autobiographical memory relates to the 'working self', a concept that has parallels with that of working memory discussed in Chapter 5. The working self is conceived as a hierarchy of interconnected goals, some but not all of which can enter consciousness. The chapter also examines the disruptive effects of affectively charged trauma memories in post-traumatic stress syndrome.

Autobiographical memory has a self-evident bearing on consciousness; much of our stream of consciousness features episodes of autobiographical memory or is derived from such episodes and from our individual sense of self. You have already encountered the relationship between cognition and consciousness in Part 1 and you will continue to do so throughout the book, culminating in Chapter 15, which is simply entitled 'Consciousness'.

Working memory

Chapter 5

Graham J. Hitch

1 Introduction

Working memory refers to our ability to coordinate mental operations with transiently stored information during cognitive activities such as planning a shopping trip or reading a newspaper. This chapter begins with a brief discussion that places the concept of working memory within the context of memory as a whole, then moves on to deal with distinctions between the concepts of working memory, short-term memory (STM) and long-term memory (LTM). Having done this, we are in a position to consider the architecture of working memory, that is, the unchanging features that account for its operation in different cognitive activities. We shall see that – in common with many other aspects of the cognitive system – identifying structure is no trivial task. The discussion is organized around the influential account of working memory presented by Baddeley (1986), tracing some of the developments in this model in the light of new evidence and noting alternative accounts where appropriate. The material covered has been chosen to illustrate the increasing diversity of phenomena that are seen as relating to working memory and includes evidence from laboratory experiments, individual differences, normal and abnormal development, neuropsychology and neuroimaging. We go on to focus in more detail on the particular topic of phonological working memory and vocabulary acquisition, where the convergence of different kinds of evidence is particularly striking. Finally, we take a short look at recent developments in computational modelling that attempt to make theories of working memory more precise. Overall, we shall see that, although we are beginning to understand more about working memory, many questions still have to be answered.

1.1 Human memory as a multifaceted system

When someone tells us they have a poor memory, they may be referring to any of a range of specific problems. For example, they may have difficulties in recalling past events, remembering to do things or perhaps retrieving facts or names. In everyday life we tend to talk about memory as if it is a single faculty. However, there are many grounds for thinking that memory is multifaceted, made up of a number of separate but interlinked systems (this will be discussed in more detail in Chapter 6). Probably the oldest theoretical distinction of this kind is between a system for holding information over long periods of time and a system that deals with information over much shorter intervals, of the order of seconds or at most a few minutes. STM refers to our ability to retain temporary information over such intervals, as in looking up a telephone number and then dialling it. Working memory is a related concept but, as our earlier examples of reading and planning make clear, it goes beyond the mere retention of information. More specifically, working memory keeps track of transient information and coordinates mental operations in a variety of cognitive tasks. The classic illustration of working memory in action is complex mental arithmetic, where we typically break the task down into a series of operations. For example, $26 + 37$ might be broken down into the stages $20 + 30 = 50$ and $6 + 7 = 13$ and $50 + 13 = 63$ in order to get the answer. It can be seen here how the various stages have to be coordinated, and how early stages generate transient information that has to be maintained for eventual use in later stages. Experimental studies show that errors of mental arithmetic are mainly due to forgetting transient information during delays imposed by the sequencing of operations (Hitch, 1978). Written calculation overcomes this limitation of working memory by providing a durable external record. Other everyday examples of situations placing demands on working memory are talking to a group of unfamiliar people while trying to remember their names or taking notes while following a presentation. In such cases the combined demands of attending to mental operations while remembering transient information can cause difficulty and may result in errors, suggesting that working memory has a limited capacity. In order to discuss working memory in greater detail, it is necessary to sharpen the distinction between it and STM. This will be done in Section 1.3, but, in order to get closer to the roots of this distinction, we need first to go back to the origins of the historically earlier distinction between STM and LTM.

1.2   Distinction between short-term and long-term memory

Although William James first introduced the concept of 'primary memory' in 1890, it was not until the 1960s that an interest in memory over brief intervals of less than a minute became firmly established. Memory researchers at that time were pre-occupied with the question of whether or not human memory is a unitary mental faculty, as a number of different kinds of evidence were emerging that pointed to the idea of separate systems for short-term and long-term recall. One of these was evidence that memory for verbal stimuli has different properties over short and long intervals. For example, Baddeley (1966a) showed that immediate recall of a list of briefly presented words is poor when the items are phonemically similar to each other (e.g. share the same vowel, as in *man, can, cad*, etc.) but is unaffected when they are semantically similar (e.g. share the same meaning, as in *huge, big, large*, etc.). However, when the same materials are presented more than once and memory is tested after a longer retention interval, the accuracy of recall is lower for semantically similar items and is unaffected by phonemic similarity (Baddeley, 1966b). These observations pointed to two separate storage systems that code information in different ways. Information in STM is held in an acoustic or speech-based form whereas information in LTM is coded in terms of its meaning. Other evidence showed that the rate of forgetting briefly presented stimuli was unusually rapid when compared with forgetting rates for better-learned material, consistent with the idea that STM is much more labile than LTM (Brown, 1958). Over and above these observations, it had been known for quite some time that the so-called 'span of immediate memory' is limited to just a few items, whether these are digits, letters or words (e.g. Miller, 1956). Memory span is the longest sequence that can be recalled accurately after a single presentation. The low limit on span suggested that STM can be distinguished from LTM on the grounds of its limited capacity.

So compelling was all this evidence at the time that several two-store models of memory were proposed. Reflecting this unanimity, their common features were referred to as the 'modal' model (Murdock, 1967). The main assumptions of this model were (1) that STM is a limited-capacity store of short duration, (2) that control processes, such as subvocal rehearsal, can be used to maintain information in STM, and (3) that information in STM is gradually transferred to LTM. Atkinson and Shiffrin (1971) provide the best-known example of this type of account (see Figure 5.1).

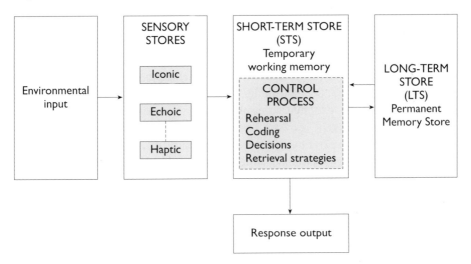

Figure 5.1 The modal model of memory, redrawn from Atkinson and Shiffrin (1971). Note how information has to pass through the short-term store in order to access the long-term store. Note also that the sensory stores are not discussed in the text. They are very short-lived and are specific to the various sensory pathways that feed information into the short-term store

Source: Atkinson and Shiffrin, 1971

You will see from the diagram that Atkinson and Shiffrin (1971) labelled their short-term store as a working memory that serves other functions besides acting as a temporary store. These functions include the regulation of control processes such as rehearsal or retrieving information from LTM. Note that control processes are optional and are conceptually different from involuntary, automatic processes. At about the same time that the Atkinson and Shiffrin model was enjoying its popularity, numerous other authors argued that the transient storage provided by STM was crucial for cognitive activities such as sentence comprehension or problem solving. In other words, there was a general assumption that STM behaves as some form of working memory. You can gain some insight into the plausibility of supposing that these activities require keeping track of temporary information within a stream of ongoing mental operations by trying one for yourself (see Box 5.1 on the comprehension of garden-path sentences).

5.1 ─── **Methods**

Understanding 'garden-path' sentences

Garden-path sentences are sentences that lead the comprehender 'up the garden path' towards an incorrect interpretation, as in *We painted the wall with cracks* (see Chapter 8). It is the ambiguity of such sentences that makes them difficult. One explanation assumes that multiple interpretations of ambiguous sentences are held in working memory (Just and Carpenter, 1992). Just and Carpenter support their view with evidence that individuals with low working memory capacity are less able to maintain multiple interpretations than individuals with high working memory capacity. However, an alternative theory is that comprehension draws on more specialized resources than working memory (e.g. Caplan and Waters, 1999).

Despite the fact that the modal model captures some important insights, the consensus it reflected was somewhat fleeting. One concern was whether the various strands of evidence for distinguishing STM and LTM converged on a coherent account. For example, different ways of estimating the capacity of the short-term store gave quite different answers and the reasons for this were unclear. The immediate consequence of this challenge was a resurgence of interest in LTM (e.g. the 'levels of processing approach' proposed by Craik and Lockhart, 1972) rather than attempts to revise and refine the concept of the short-term store. Another concern was whether the short-term store does in fact act as a working memory. One example causing difficulty for this position was some intriguing neuropsychological evidence from a patient known in the literature as KF who sustained brain damage as a result of a road accident (Shallice and Warrington, 1970). KF's auditory digit span was only two items which is way below the normal range of seven plus or minus two items identified by Miller (1956). However, despite having such a severe deficit, KF performed normally on tests of long-term learning and memory, he had normal intelligence and no major difficulties in understanding spoken language (Shallice and Warrington, 1970). In one respect KF's pattern of memory performance was consistent with the modal model: it could be explained in terms of selective damage to his STM while his LTM was intact. Moreover, the fact that damage to part of the brain could have this effect suggested a separate neuroanatomical localization of the short-term store. However, the absence of a general impairment in KF's learning, comprehension and reasoning presents obvious difficulties for the idea that STM acts as a working memory that is necessary for supporting such activities.

1.3   Working memory as more than STM

Given difficulties such as those presented by KF, Baddeley and Hitch (1974) made an empirical investigation of whether STM does indeed act as a working memory. One technique they used was the **dual-task paradigm** in which people perform two tasks at the same time. The logic of this paradigm is that two tasks will interfere with one another if they require access to a common resource and if their combined demands exceed its capacity. Baddeley and Hitch (1974) examined the effect of requiring people to perform an irrelevant STM task at the same time as a cognitive task that involved either reasoning, comprehending language or learning new information. For example, in one experiment people carried out a verbal reasoning task while remembering sequences of random digits (see Box 5.2 for an outline of the experimental procedure). Reasoning was impaired when the STM load was increased by making the digit sequences longer. Similar results were obtained when the cognitive task was either comprehending prose or learning a list of words for free recall. Baddeley and Hitch (1974) drew two main conclusions from these observations. First, the finding that an irrelevant STM task interferes with a range of cognitive tasks is consistent with the idea of a common working memory system that combines temporary information storage with ongoing mental operations. Second, working memory goes beyond the concept of STM. Thus, even when the load on STM approached memory span, and therefore 'filled' short-term storage capacity, there was no catastrophic breakdown in concurrent cognition. This suggests the idea that working memory includes an additional resource that is not shared with STM.

5.2 ———————————————————— **Research study**

Studying the effect of an irrelevant memory load on verbal reasoning

The verbal reasoning task used by Baddeley and Hitch (1974) involved deciding whether a sentence gave a true or a false description of the order of a letter pair. Examples are, *A precedes B – AB* (true), and *B does not follow A – AB* (false). Varying the verb, the grammar, the letter order and the truth-value of the answer gave a total of 32 problems of varying difficulty. Each problem was shown individually, performance being measured by the speed and accuracy of pressing 'true' and 'false' response keys.

One experiment involved a comparison between the effect on reasoning of concurrently repeating a sequence of six random digits and counting repeatedly from one to six. The rationale was that a sequence of six random digits is close to the span of immediate memory, whereas the counting sequence is stored in long-term memory. Repeating random digits slowed solution times in the reasoning task, relative to a control condition, but the counting task had very little effect. Furthermore, the interference produced by random digits was greater for the more difficult versions of the reasoning task. The conclusion Baddeley and Hitch (1974) drew was that reasoning and short-term retention compete for a limited-capacity 'workspace' that can be flexibly allocated to either the storage demands of the memory load or the processing demands of the reasoning task.

Further evidence for a distinction between STM and working memory came from studies of individual differences. The logic behind this approach is that if two tasks involve similar underlying psychological processes, a person who performs well on one should do well on the other. In statistical terms, the two abilities should be positively correlated. In an influential study, Daneman and Carpenter (1980) argued that standard measures of STM, such as word span and digit span, tax storage capacity but do not assess the capacity to combine storage with ongoing processing operations. In order to provide a better assessment of the latter, and therefore of working memory, Daneman and Carpenter devised a novel reading span task. In this task, participants were required to read aloud a set of unrelated sentences and immediately afterwards to recall the last word of each sentence. Box 5.3 gives further information about the procedure. As you will see if you try it for yourself, the task rapidly becomes very demanding as the number of sentences increases. To assess the limit on reading span, Daneman and Carpenter (1980) prepared three sets each of two, three, four, five and six sentences. Participants were presented with increasingly longer sets of sentences until they failed all three sets at a particular level. An individual's reading span was taken as the maximum level at which they were correct on at least two of the three sets. The procedure is analogous to standard measures of STM span in that it assesses the longest sequence of items that can be maintained over a short interval. However, in reading span, the items have to be remembered at the same time as performing the processing operations required for reading sentences, whereas in STM span there is no simultaneous processing requirement.

5.3   **Research study**

Procedure for determining reading span

The materials for Daneman and Carpenter's (1980) reading span task were a set of unrelated sentences, each of which was typed on a separate card. The two examples they gave are:

When at last his eyes opened there was no gleam of triumph, no shade of anger.

The taxi turned up Michigan Avenue where they had a clear view of the lake.

Cards were arranged in sets of two, three, four, five and six sentences, there being three instances of each set-size. Participants were shown one card at a time and read it aloud at their own pace, starting at set-size two. The second card was presented as soon as the first was read. A blank card signalled recall of the final word on each card in their order of occurrence (i.e. *anger, lake* in the above example of set-size two). Three trials were given at each set-size, and set-size was increased until all three trials at a particular level were failed. At this point testing was ended. Reading span was taken as the level at which the participant was correct on two out of three sets. As with memory span, there are many variants on this basic procedure.

Daneman and Carpenter (1980) compared reading span with word span as predictors of reading comprehension skills in a group of college students. Reading comprehension was measured in three ways: fact questions, pronoun questions and verbal SATs (see Table 5.1). It turned out that reading span was a very good predictor of all three measures and a much better predictor than word span. Daneman and Carpenter went on to show that a listening span measure gave similar results, showing that the correlation is not specific to reading. They interpreted their findings as showing that working memory capacity is an important source of individual differences in language comprehension, the key characteristic of working memory being combining temporary storage with information processing, in line with the approach taken by Baddeley and Hitch (1974).

Table 5.1   Correlations between spans and various measures of reading comprehension

	Reading comprehension measure		
	Fact questions	Pronoun questions	Verbal SAT
Reading span	.72	.90	.59
Word span	.37	.33	.35

Source: Daneman and Carpenter, 1980, experiment 1

You are probably already well aware that correlations can be interpreted in many ways. Thus, a criticism often made of Daneman and Carpenter is that their correlations might be an artefact of similarities in processing operations in the various tasks they used. Reading span, listening span and language comprehension all involve language processing whereas word span does not. The potential force of this criticism is substantial and called into question whether Daneman and Carpenter's results have anything to do with working memory as a general-purpose resource. To address it, other investigators have looked at patterns of correlation using different measures of working memory span to which the criticism does not apply. For example, Turner and Engle (1989) devised an operation span task in which participants solved sets of arithmetical calculations. After each calculation was completed a word was presented and at the end of the set all the words had to be recalled. Operation span was the limit on how many words could be recalled under these conditions. Turner and Engle (1989) found that operation span was a superior predictor of reading comprehension than was standard STM span, despite involving dissimilar processing operations. Their results therefore provide support for the idea of a general working memory system that is common to a range of different activities involving the combination of information processing with temporary storage. Subsequent work by Engle *et al.* (1999b) has expanded this picture by showing that working memory span is more closely related to general intelligence than is STM.

Summary of Section 1

- Human memory can be seen as a multifaceted system whose distinct components have different characteristics and functions.
- An important distinction is that between a transient, limited-capacity, STM system and a more stable LTM system.
- Atkinson and Shiffrin (1971) suggested that STM acts as a working memory responsible for a variety of control processes.
- Baddeley and Hitch (1974) explored and expanded this idea and concluded that STM is better regarded as a component of working memory.
- Converging evidence that working memory and STM are not identical comes from studies of individual differences: e.g. Daneman and Carpenter (1980) found that reading span was much better than word span for predicting verbal abilities.

2   The structure of working memory

We have seen some of the evidence suggesting that working memory differs from STM, but so far little about how it differs beyond referring to evidence that working memory includes STM. This section covers the structure of working memory in more detail.

2.1   A multicomponent model

In their original investigation, Baddeley and Hitch (1974) studied whether irrelevant STM loads affected reasoning, language comprehension and list learning. Their aim was to examine whether these cognitive activities involve the same limited capacity as STM. Although high STM loads did cause interference, people could retain low loads of two or three items without much disruption to the primary task. This observation was seen as consistent with the suggestion that working memory can be partitioned into two components, one that can hold small amounts of temporary information and another that is more concerned with cognitive processing. In further experiments Baddeley and Hitch (1974) looked at the effects of varying the phonemic similarity of the materials in reasoning and comprehension tasks. Adverse sensitivity to phonemic similarity is a characteristic feature of STM (see Section 1.2), and showing that reasoning and comprehension are also sensitive would suggest that they share a common factor. In the reasoning task, subjects were asked to verify relationships such as 'A is not preceded by B – AB', where the letters used were either phonemically similar (e.g. TD) or dissimilar (e.g. MC). In the comprehension task, subjects were asked to say whether the words of a sentence were presented in a meaningful or jumbled order. The words either rhymed (e.g. *Red headed Ned said Ted fed in bed*) or did not rhyme (e.g. *Dark skinned Ian thought Harry ate in bed*). The results showed that phonemic similarity did disrupt reasoning and comprehension, but only somewhat mildly.

To account for their results, Baddeley and Hitch (1974) assumed that one of the components of working memory is a limited-capacity, speech-based store capable of storing two to three items. This subsystem was described as an **articulatory rehearsal loop** and can be viewed as roughly equivalent to the earlier concept of STM (more detail about the articulatory loop is given in Section 2.2). The articulatory loop could be used to store small memory loads during cognitive tasks and was responsible for the effect of phonemic similarity on performance. The second component was described as a **central executive**, responsible for the control and coordination of mental operations in a range of activities including but extending beyond reasoning, comprehension, learning and memory. The executive was seen as a limited-capacity workspace that can be flexibly allocated to control processes or temporary information storage, depending on the nature of the task in hand. Thus a small irrelevant memory load could be stored in the articulatory loop without taxing the central executive, but a larger memory load would take up extra resources in the executive. Given a limit on the capacity of the workspace, this theoretical account maintains that there will be a trade-off such that fewer resources are available to support processing operations when temporary storage demands increase.

In reflecting on their results, Baddeley and Hitch noted that the tasks they had investigated were all primarily verbal. The question arose as to whether tasks involving visual memory and visual imagery also draw on working memory and, if so, how. The information available from dual-task studies indicated that combining two visuo-spatial activities (such as tracking a moving object while performing a mental imagery task) or combining two verbal activities is more difficult than combining one of each. This observation suggests there are separate resources specialized for dealing with verbal and visuo-spatial information. Nevertheless, as there is some mutual interference when a visuo-spatial and a verbal task are combined, the data are also consistent with the involvement of a common resource. One way of accounting for these observations is to assume that the central executive controls visual and verbal tasks and that there is a separate subsystem for storing visuo-spatial information, analogous to the articulatory loop. This tripartite model, in which the extra subsystem is referred to as the visuo-spatial sketchpad, was developed further by Baddeley (1983, 1986) and is illustrated in Figure 5.2.

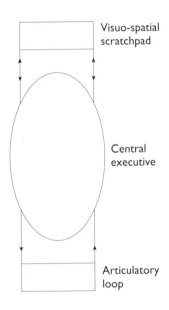

Visuo-spatial scratchpad

Central executive

Articulatory loop

Figure 5.2   The structure of working memory

Source: based on Baddeley, 1983

Unfortunately there is not the space to deal with the visuo-spatial sketchpad in the detail it deserves. However, one interesting observation is that neurological patients can show selective impairments in visuo-spatial STM and imagery tasks suggestive of a separate brain location for visuo-spatial function. Corsi span is a test of visuo-spatial STM in which a set of nine identical cubes is mounted at haphazard locations on a horizontal board. The experimenter points to a selection of cubes and the task is to reproduce the sequence immediately by pointing. Sequence length is progressively increased and the limit beyond which performance breaks down defines span. De Renzi and Nichelli (1975) found that Corsi span and auditory digit span could be impaired independently in patients with different lesions. Evidence such as this is strongly indicative of a separate, non-verbal store. Such a store may underpin the use of visual coding to remember verbal items. The formation of mental images as mnemonics to aid recollection has a long history going back at least as far as Ancient Greece. Using the dual-task methodology, Baddeley and Lieberman (1980) made the interesting observation that use of a visual imagery mnemonic was disrupted by a spatial task (tracking a moving loudspeaker while blindfold) but not by a visual task (detecting changes in the brightness of a blank field). This pattern was not observed when the mnemonic strategy was rote rehearsal instead of imagery, suggesting it was not a function of the relative difficulty of the spatial and visual interfering tasks. Baddeley and Lieberman (1980) interpreted their results as evidence that mental imagery is spatial rather than visual.

However, this somewhat counterintuitive conclusion does not generalize to all forms of imagery. Hitch *et al.* (1995) studied people's ability to perform an imagery task in which they were shown two separate line drawings. They then had to superimpose mental images of the drawings in order to reveal a novel percept. For example one drawing looked like two ice cream cones and the other showed a curved line whose ends coincided with the locations of the tops of the cones. When mentally superimposed, the drawings combined to reveal a skipping rope. Hitch *et al.* (1995) found that imagery performance was better when the drawings were visually congruent (i.e. both consisted of a black figure on a white ground) than when they were incongruent (i.e. their contrasts were reversed). Thus in this particular imagery task, there is clear evidence that the images preserve information about visual appearances. It is interesting to note in passing that if you were able to 'see' the skipping rope in your mind's eye after reading the above descriptions, you achieved this using conceptually driven images rather than the perceptually driven images studied in Hitch *et al.*'s (1995) experiment. The visual characteristics of the two types of image are not necessarily the same.

In a review of visuo-spatial working memory, Logie (1995) suggested that there are separate spatial and visual systems, such that a spatial movement system can be used to rehearse the contents of a visual store. This proposal corresponds to a visuo-spatial analogue of the articulatory loop. However, the full story about imagery and working memory is still unfolding and may be considerably more complex. For example, Smyth and Waller (1998) asked rock climbers to imagine tackling familiar routes while performing a variety of secondary tasks designed to disrupt their ability to use visual, spatial or kinaesthetic information. The results implicated multiple forms of representation and pointed to the complexity of imagery for skilled movement.

In conclusion, the work of Baddeley and Hitch (1974) led to a tripartite model of working memory that was subsequently developed by Baddeley (1986). This model appears to have been the first substantive account of working memory and has been influential within the field. However, an increasing number of alternative accounts have emerged subsequently, many of which are described in a volume edited by Miyake and Shah (1999). Several theoretical issues divide these approaches. One of the principal questions concerns the relationship between working memory and LTM. Baddeley and Hitch (1974) assumed that the two were separate systems. However, a number of authors take a different view, maintaining that working memory corresponds to an activated region of LTM (e.g. Ericsson and Kintsch, 1995; Cowan, 1988). Part of the motivation for this alternative approach comes from the effects of a person's degree of knowledge in a specific domain on their working memory capacity in that domain. For example, chess experts display superior working memory skills when given tasks within the chess domain. There is much more to be discovered about effects such as these and their interpretation. However, it is interesting to note that Cowan (1988) still assumes a separate executive system, making the difference of view one concerning the nature of back-up storage (that is, specialized buffer stores versus activated LTM) (see also Engle *et al.*, 1999a). The idea of specialized buffer stores has also been challenged by the work of Jones (see Section 2.3.4). In the remainder of this chapter we stay within the Baddeley and Hitch framework for the purpose of organizing the discussion, raising problems for it where appropriate. We begin with the relatively well-specified concept of the articulatory loop, before moving on to the central executive, the most important but still least well understood aspect of working memory.

2.2   Phonological working memory

One reason the articulatory loop is relatively well understood is the existence of a cluster of experimental manipulations that affect its operation. We have already encountered one of these, namely the phonemic similarity of items presented in tests of immediate recall (see Section 1.2). A second variable was the word length of the items. In an important series of experiments, Baddeley *et al.* (1975) showed that the limit on STM span for verbal stimuli was not a fixed number of items or chunks, as Miller (1956) had claimed. They showed instead that memory span varies with the length of the items, being higher for shorter items (e.g. *harm, wit*) than for longer items (e.g. *university, hippopotamus*). Box 5.4 describes one of their procedures and results. One of many interesting observations was that there was a systematic relationship between how many words could be recalled and the time it took to say them out loud. Thus, people could recall the number of words that could be spoken in about two seconds. This is consistent with the idea of a rehearsal loop in which rehearsing items refreshes their decaying memory traces. Longer words take longer to rehearse so fewer can be refreshed within two seconds, the time limit set by the rapidity of the decay process. Baddeley *et al.* (1975) also examined individual differences and found that faster speakers tended to recall more information than slower speakers. This is consistent with the model if one assumes that faster speakers can rehearse more rapidly. The model could also account for the phonemic similarity effect, as a given amount of decay would have a greater effect on the ability to discriminate the memory traces of items that share phonological features. To appreciate this point, suppose you have been presented with the sequence of phonemically similar letters BTCG to recall. If, as a result of partial forgetting of the third item, you could only remember that it contained an /e/ sound, this would not be very helpful as it leaves many options open. Compare this with a sequence of dissimilar items such as *RJQL*, where being able to remember that the third item had a /u/ sound would be of much more help.

This model of the articulatory loop was also able to explain the results of dual-task experiments in which immediate serial recall was combined with **articulatory suppression** (a secondary task involving the repetition of a redundant and irrelevant word such as *the the the the*). Articulatory suppression simply requires the participant to repeat a word over and over again. This low-level **secondary task** is intended to occupy the articulatory loop with irrelevant (but unavoidable) activity, so that performance on the **primary task** has to manage without the assistance of the articulatory loop (or at least without a large part of its functioning). Baddeley *et al.* (1975) found that articulatory suppression disrupted recall, consistent with it disrupting use of the articulatory loop. Suppression also removed differences between the recall of longer and shorter words and between phonemically similar and dissimilar items. These further effects are also consistent with disruption of the loop. However, the effects of word length and phonemic similarity only disappeared

┌───┐

5.4 ──────────────────────────────────── **Research study** ──

The word-length effect

In one of their experiments, Baddeley *et al.* (1975) constructed five pools of 10 words of one, two, three, four or five syllables. The pools were matched for semantic category and familiarity. To illustrate, the one-syllable pool included *Stoat, Mumps, School, Greece,* and corresponding items in the five-syllable pool were *Hippopotamus, Tuberculosis, University, Yugoslavia.* Ten lists of five words were made up of random permutations within each pool. The lists were presented in a random order, words being shown one after another at a two-second rate. Immediately after list presentation, participants spoke their recall. In a second part of the experiment, reading rate was measured. This was achieved by timing participants reading aloud a typed list of the words in each pool as quickly as they could.

The results showed that the percentage of words recalled dropped as the number of syllables increased. Moreover, as the graph shows (see Figure 5.3), the plot of percentage correct recall against articulation rate formed a straight line. The slope of the line was about two seconds, demonstrating that the faster a person can say a list of words out loud (that is, the faster they can rehearse), the more effective they prove in subsequently recalling those words.

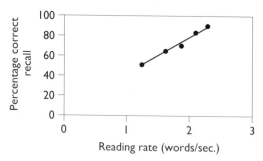

Figure 5.3 Results obtained by Baddeley *et al.* (1975). Percentage of words recalled is plotted as a function of the rate at which the same words could be read aloud, for five different word lengths. The point furthest to the right corresponds to one-syllable words, the next point to the left represents two-syllable words, and so on

└───┘

when items were presented visually and not when they were presented auditorily. This unexpected effect of presentation modality was for some time something of a puzzle. The position was eventually clarified in experiments carried out by Baddeley *et al.* (1984) where suppression was continued during recall as well as item presentation. Under these conditions, suppression removed the word-length effect for auditory items, but still did not remove the phonemic similarity effect. Baddeley *et al.* (1984) explained these results in terms of a modified theoretical account in which the articulatory loop is seen as consisting of a decaying phonological store (the locus of the phonemic similarity effect) and a control process of subvocal rehearsal (the locus of the word-length effect) (see Figure 5.4). According to this account, spoken stimuli access the loop automatically whereas visual inputs have to be verbally recoded, an optional control process that involves **subvocalization**. Suppression eliminates the word-length effect for both visually and auditorily

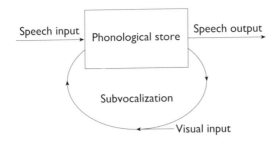

Figure 5.4 The structure of the phonological loop, according to the ideas developed by Baddeley *et al.* (1984)

presented stimuli by disrupting rehearsal, but only eliminates the effect of phonemic similarity for visually presented stimuli as only this type of stimulus requires verbal recoding. In this way, specification of different pathways by which visual and spoken stimuli access the loop explains an otherwise obscure pattern of findings. Nowadays, it is more common to use the term **phonological loop** to refer to this more developed, two-component account of the articulatory loop. The next section shows how this model of the phonological loop generates useful insights into developmental changes in verbal STM as children grow up.

2.2.1   Developmental and cross-linguistic differences

The two-part model of the phonological loop is interesting in a number of different ways. Not least is that the model can be applied to phenomena outside its initial scope. One example is the developmental growth of memory span during childhood, for which many competing explanations have been proposed (Dempster, 1981). Thinking in terms of the phonological loop model suggests it would be informative to measure children's recall of lists of words of different lengths and the speed at which they can articulate the words, as in Baddeley *et al.*'s (1975) study of adults. The results of doing this are quite striking. As children's ages increase, their average level of recall increases in proportion to the rise in their average speech rate (Nicolson, 1981; Hulme *et al.*, 1984; see Figure 5.5). Furthermore, the size of the word-length effect in children of different ages reflects the time it takes to articulate words of different lengths. Finding such a clear empirical relationship is informative and suggests a possible explanation for the developmental growth in memory span. Thus, if older children can rehearse faster, then they can maintain more items within the approximately

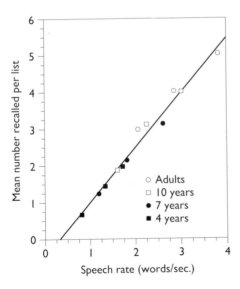

Figure 5.5 Results obtained by Hulme *et al.* (1984). Percentage of words recalled is plotted as a function of their speech rate for three different word-lengths and four age-groups

two-second time limit set by trace decay in the phonological store. Notice, however, that this is a causal interpretation of a correlation and therefore difficult to prove conclusively. Yet another phenomenon to which the concept of the phonological loop has been applied is cross-linguistic differences in digit span. For example systematic differences in mean digit span in English (7.2 digits), Spanish (6.4 digits), Hebrew (6.5 digits) and Arabic (5.8 digits) that would otherwise be difficult to explain turn out to be highly correlated with differences in the rates at which the digits can be articulated in these languages (Naveh-Benjamin and Ayres, 1986).

The phonological loop model has prompted further discoveries about developmental change. One of these discoveries concerns the effect of word length when children remember a sequence of stimuli presented as either spoken words or nameable pictures. Older children aged around seven upwards show the standard tendency for poorer recall of items with longer names for both types of stimulus, but younger children show this only for spoken stimuli (Hitch et al., 1989). Moreover, when recalling nameable pictures, younger children find it harder when the pictures are visually similar to one another whereas older children find it harder when the names of the pictures are phonemically similar (Hitch et al., 1988). These observations are consistent with the assumption that auditory stimuli gain automatic access to the loop but that phonological recoding is necessary for visual stimuli. They suggest further that the process of recoding is somewhat slow to develop and that younger children are more reliant on visuo-spatial working memory. Subsequent research has confirmed the developmental progression from visual to phonological coding and suggests that it is related to learning to read, being markedly delayed in dyslexic children (Palmer, 2000a, 2000b).

2.2.2 The irrelevant speech effect

Yet another application of the phonological loop model was to explain why the presence of background speech disrupts STM for visually presented verbal stimuli. Salamé and Baddeley (1982) showed that having to ignore irrelevant speech was more interfering than ignoring irrelevant noise, leading them to suggest that unattended speech enters the phonological store whereas non-speech sounds do not. Consistent with such an interpretation, blocking people's ability to verbally recode visual stimuli by having them suppress articulation removes the disruptive effect of irrelevant speech (Salamé and Baddeley, 1982). However, this account has been challenged by evidence that unattended non-speech sounds can cause interference, and that the amount of interference is determined by the same factors as for speech. One such common factor is that steady-state streams (where the irrelevant stimuli remain the same) cause less disruption than changing-state streams (where the irrelevant stimuli vary over time) (Macken and Jones, 1995). Such observations have been used to question the assumption that irrelevant speech has an effect that is specific to the phonological loop. They suggest a broader explanation of the interference caused by irrelevant sounds in terms of general memory mechanisms that are not specific to the verbal domain. The irrelevant speech (or sound) phenomenon has developed into an area of considerable controversy (see, for example, Baddeley and Larsen, 2003). However, the two theoretical approaches are not mutually exclusive and it may be, for example, that irrelevant speech affects both a general mechanism (e.g. for serial ordering) as well as the phonological store.

2.2.3 Neural basis

Before closing this part of the discussion, we shall consider some evidence about the neural basis of the phonological loop. An obvious challenge for any model is to explain neuropsychological cases of selective impairment of memory span of the type demonstrated by Shallice and Warrington (1970). Vallar and Baddeley (1984) made a detailed investigation of one such patient, known as PV. Following a stroke that left her with damage that included her left parietal cortex, PV's auditory digit span was reduced to only two items. However, her other abilities were relatively unimpaired. For example, her speech was fluent and her rate of articulation was normal. Vallar and Baddeley (1984) found that PV's memory span for spoken sequences was poorer when the items were phonemically similar but was unaffected by their word length. They interpreted these observations as indicating that her phonological store was damaged. Thus, if the store was functioning at a reduced level, spoken inputs would access it automatically and immediate recall would be sensitive to the phonemic similarity of the items. However, given a damaged phonological store, PV would not find subvocal rehearsal a useful strategy. Hence, she would not show the normal word-length effect. Like other patients of this type, PV's memory span for visually presented verbal stimuli was higher than her auditory span. Moreover, her visual span was unaffected by either phonemic similarity or word length of the materials. These observations suggest that PV may have been relying on visuo-spatial working memory to remember visual stimuli. There may be an interesting parallel to be drawn here with children's reliance on visuo-spatial working memory for remembering visual stimuli early on in development when, albeit for different reasons, their ability to use the phonological loop is restricted (see Section 2.2.1).

Research on patients raises the question of the neuroanatomical localization of the phonological loop. Neuroimaging techniques provide the opportunity to study this in the normal brain. In an early study, Paulesu *et al.* (1993) investigated which areas of the brain are active in tasks thought to involve the phonological loop. Such experiments depend on a subtraction logic whereby brain activation observed in one experimental task is compared with that in another. By arranging that the two tasks differ solely in the process of interest, the neural activation specific to that particular process can be obtained by subtraction. This of course is not as simple as it sounds and typically involves making theoretical assumptions about the tasks under consideration. Paulesu *et al.* (1993) compared activation patterns in a verbal memory task requiring storage and rehearsal, a rhyme judgement task that required rehearsal but not storage, and a control task requiring neither storage nor rehearsal (Box 5.5 (overleaf) describes the experiment in more detail). The results suggested separate localization of storage and rehearsal, consistent with the theoretical distinction between these two aspects of the phonological loop. Furthermore, localization of the store to an area in the left parietal cortex corresponded approximately to the locus of damage in patients like PV. Other neuroimaging studies converge with – but also complicate – this simple picture, especially with regard to the involvement of other brain areas (e.g. Henson, 2001). My purpose here is merely to illustrate an early success in using the phonological loop model to guide the collection and interpretation of neuroimaging data.

5.5   **Research study**

Neural correlates of the phonological loop

Paulesu *et al.* (1993) used positron emission tomography (PET) to measure blood flow in different regions of the brain. This technique involves making an intravenous injection of radioactive water and then scanning the brain to record the spatial distribution of radioactivity. Scanning is performed during matched tasks that differ with regard to a feature of interest. Subsequent comparison of the two activation patterns allows brain regions associated with the feature of interest to be identified. (A similar logic applies to functional magnetic resonance imaging (fMRI), a more recent technique that does not involve radioactivity.)

Paulesu *et al.* compared brain activation patterns in phonological and non-phonological memory tasks. The phonological task involved showing a sequence of six consonants followed by a probe letter. Participants indicated whether the probe item had appeared in the sequence. The non-phonological memory task was identical except that the items were unfamiliar Korean characters. The two tasks were therefore closely matched, but only remembering consonants engaged the phonological loop. Subtracting activation patterns revealed that the consonant memory task was associated with increased blood flow in left hemisphere regions corresponding to Broca's area and the supramarginal gyrus of the parietal cortex (see colour Plate 5).

A second comparison was between a rhyme judgement task and a shape judgement task. In the rhyme task participants saw a series of consonants and indicated whether each one rhymed with the letter B, which was always present. The shape task was identical except that the stimuli were Korean characters and the judgement was one of shape similarity. Previous research suggested that the rhyme judgement task would engage the subvocal rehearsal system but not the phonological store. Subtraction of the scans indicated that the rhyme task activated Broca's area, but not the left supramarginal gyrus. Thus, the subvocal rehearsal system can be identified with Broca's area and, by revisiting the subtraction for the memory tasks, the phonological store can be identified with the left supramarginal gyrus.

2.2.4 Theoretical issues

We have seen how a simple model of the phonological loop has proved productive in ways that extend beyond its initial remit. These applications cover a surprisingly extensive range that includes developmental and cross-linguistic differences, effects of irrelevant speech, cases of neuropsychological impairment and results of neuroimaging studies. The model has turned out to be remarkably successful – it has evidently 'travelled well'. However, some of its limitations are steadily becoming more apparent. as in its explanation of the effects of irrelevant speech. Other recent evidence suggests that the word-length effect may not be due to differences in items' spoken duration. Thus, there is little or no effect of word duration when the phonological complexity of items is carefully controlled (Lovatt *et al.*, 2000). In addition, developmental studies suggest that rehearsal is not necessary for the word-length effect. Specifically, children as young as four show a word-length effect when recalling spoken stimuli, an age when it is generally agreed they have not acquired the ability to use rehearsal strategies (Hulme *et al.*, 1984). Other authors have shown that output delays are sufficient to cause word-length effects, without appealing to rehearsal (Brown and Hulme, 1995; Cowan *et al.*, 1992).

Whether the limitations of the phonological loop as a model count as falsifications is an interesting scientific issue that might send us back to the drawing board for an entirely new account. Some authors have taken this approach (Nairne, 2002). The alternative strategy is to revise the model to overcome its limitations, while at the same time preserving its original insights. We saw an earlier example of this in the elaboration of the account of the phonological loop to explain why the effects of articulatory suppression differ when the memory items are seen rather than heard (see Section 2.2). A more recent example is the effort to develop the concept of the phonological loop through more detailed computational modelling (see Section 4). It is probably too soon to say which of these strategies will be the more productive – a totally new approach or development based on the present model. Only time will tell. For the present we note that, despite its limitations, the phonological loop continues to provide a simple, usable framework for linking a robust set of psychological phenomena, and is still widely used. However, before continuing with further discussion of the phonological loop, we turn to the main aspect of working memory in the tripartite model: the central executive.

2.3   Executive processes

The central executive is, in general terms, responsible for controlling and co-ordinating mental operations in working memory. Baddeley and Hitch (1974) suggested that the functions of the executive included supervising slave stores such as the phonological loop and the visuo-spatial sketchpad, as well as interactions with LTM. However, as we shall see, more precise identification of executive functions is a matter of continuing debate. The executive is at once the most important component of working memory, the most controversial and the least understood. At various times it has been described as a 'ragbag' or an area of 'residual ignorance' and, in a review, Andrade (2001) referred to it as 'problematic'. There are good reasons for these remarks. One is that the executive could be seen as merely a reinvention of the somewhat derided concept of the homunculus, a person inside the head. The well-known problem here is that of explaining what controls the homunculus without appealing to an infinite regress of homunculi. Another difficulty is that, at an intuitive level, executive processes clearly have links to our sense of conscious awareness. This is another difficult concept, with a long history of intractability (see Chapter 15 on consciousness). However, rather than allowing themselves to be put off by these problems, researchers have attempted to understand what aspects of executive control they can, with the long-term goal of steadily reducing the area of residual ignorance.

2.3.1   Central workspace

We read earlier how Baddeley and Hitch (1974) conceptualized the executive as a limited-capacity central workspace with resources that could be flexibly allocated to various combinations of mental operations and temporary information storage. We also saw how Daneman and Carpenter's (1980) reading span task was designed as a method for assessing the capacity of such a workspace. Thus, given the assumption that resources for processing and storage trade off against each other, reading span can be interpreted as a measure of residual storage capacity when the workspace is also occupied in supporting reading processes. However, further evidence is needed to confirm that it is useful to think of the limited span of working memory as reflecting the capacity of a workspace or 'mental blackboard'.

Several investigators have tried to examine more precisely what limits the span of working memory in tasks such as reading span and listening span. Given that the number of items in store increases from the start to the end of a trial, the workspace hypothesis predicts a corresponding decline in the resources available to support processing. This would follow from the trade-off between resources within the workspace. Towse *et al.* (1998) tested this prediction by studying the performance of children on reading span, operation span and counting span in a series of parallel experiments. (Counting span involves presenting a set of visual displays showing random dots that must be counted. At the end of the set, the totals must be recalled and counting span is the maximum number of totals successfully recalled.) The results gave no clear support for the prediction, in that there was no systematic change in the speed of processing operations within trials. Towse *et al.* (1998) also entertained an alternative hypothesis according to which, rather than sharing attention between processing and storage, children switch attention back and forth between processing and storage. Thus, in reading span for example, children might read a sentence, store the final word, read the next sentence, store its final word and so on. According to this 'task-switching' account, reading span is limited by the rate of forgetting sentence-final words during the time intervals spent in reading. This is similar to the way in which errors in mental arithmetic were explained (Hitch, 1978) and is quite different from the resource-sharing account. To test the task-switching hypothesis, Towse *et al.* (1998) manipulated the time intervals over which information had to be stored in different conditions in which the total amount of processing was held constant. This was achieved by altering the order of presentation of the items within a set, some of the items being designed to take longer to process than others. In line with the prediction from task switching, spans were lower when the intervals over which information had to be maintained were longer. This was true for all three tasks, reading span, operation span and counting span, suggesting a result of some generality. Subsequent research confirmed this by showing that manipulating the order of presentation of items has similar effects in adults (Towse *et al.*, 2000).

Other investigators have also found an effect of the length of the intervals devoted to processing operations in working memory span tasks, but have shown also that span is lower when the operations themselves are more complex (Barrouillet and Camos, 2001). Moreover, Hitch *et al.* (2001) found some evidence for a trade-off in the form of a weak tendency for processing operations to become slower as storage load increased. Effects such as these lead us towards a mixed model that involves both attention switching and resource sharing. Further evidence suggests that other factors may also be involved in limiting working memory span. For example, de Beni *et al.* (1998) found that individuals with low spans made more intrusion errors where they erroneously recalled items from previous trials. This observation suggests that the ability to inhibit potentially interfering information is an important aspect of the span task. Other studies have also suggested a link between working memory capacity and inhibitory processes (e.g. Conway and Engle, 1994).

Taking all these observations together, it seems that a simplistic interpretation of working memory span as reflecting the capacity of a central workspace is unlikely to be correct. Working memory span may involve a central workspace, but it is clearly a complex task requiring a more complex theoretical account. Such a conclusion points to the difficulty of sustaining any simple conceptualization of executive processes. Indeed, an important issue to emerge in recent studies of executive function is whether the executive is a single, unified entity or a system that is fractionated into distinct subcomponents. This question of fractionation has led to an interest in tasks other than working memory span that capture different aspects of executive function.

2.3.2 Attention

The view of the executive put forward by Baddeley (1986) was substantially different from that proposed earlier by Baddeley and Hitch (1974), stemming in part from difficulties with the idea of resource trade-off. It was inspired by an imaginative attempt of Norman and Shallice (1986) to provide a unified explanation for slips of action in everyday life and the more serious disturbances of behaviour seen in patients with frontal lesions (frontal patients). One rather striking example of such a disturbance is 'utilization behaviour' (Lhermitte, 1983) where frontal patients show particular difficulty inhibiting stereotyped responses. For instance when a glass and then a bottle of water are merely placed in front of such a patient, the glass is picked up, filled with water and drunk. Similar behaviour is seen with other familiar objects such as a comb or a spoon.

Norman and Shallice (1986) proposed a model in which the control of cognition and action involves two levels. At the lower level is a set of learned schemata for routine sequences of actions or mental operations each of which fires automatically to a specific 'trigger stimulus'. For example, if we overhear someone mention our own name we automatically orient our attention towards the speaker. These schemata are arranged in parallel, so that at any moment there is competition among those that potentially might fire. At the higher level sits a supervisory attentional system (SAS), a limited-capacity resource capable of intervening at the lower level. A typical example would be the SAS intervening to stop a schema from firing despite the presence of its trigger stimulus. This model explains the difficulties of frontal patients in terms of a deficit in the resources available for executive control. Thus in utilization behaviour, strongly triggered schemata fire even when they lead to contextually inappropriate behaviour. Diary studies of slips and lapses in everyday life reveal that these too often involve making an inappropriate but familiar action in a familiar context. For example, one diarist recorded intending to get his car out but as he passed through the back porch on his way to the garage he stopped to put on his Wellington boots and gardening jacket, as if to work in the garden (Reason, 1984). Such errors tended to occur when the diarists reported their attention was distracted elsewhere. The Norman and Shallice (1986) model would explain such errors in terms of distraction rendering the SAS temporarily unavailable to inhibit the strongly triggered habit of going into the garden.

Baddeley (1986) adopted the SAS as a model of executive control, thus moving away from the notion of the executive as a workspace combining both processing and storage to that of a purely attentional system. This move led more or less directly to a search for fresh ways of investigating executive processes. One such task involves generating a random stream of responses using only the digits 0–9, a surprisingly difficult task (see Box 5.6). The major source of difficulty in random generation seems to be the avoidance of stereotyped sequences such as ascending or descending series of digits, or, in the case of letters, alphabetical runs. This type of error is consistent with a theoretical analysis in which the requirement for randomness involves pitting the capacity for supervised inhibitory control against the tendency to execute strongly learned habits, sometimes called 'pre-potent' responses. Experimental evidence confirms that random generation is a demanding task, but shows also that it is a very complex task, suggesting that it is unlikely to be a pure measure of executive function (see Towse, 1998).

5.6 **Methods**

Random generation

In the random generation task, participants are asked to select items repeatedly at random from a restricted pool such as the digits 0–9 or the letters of the alphabet. Generation is usually required at a specified rate, such as one per second. Some idea of the difficulty of the task can be gained by asking someone to try it for a minute and noting down their responses. Most people soon start hesitating or repeating themselves, typically emitting stereotypical sequences such as alphabetic runs (e.g. ABC) or familiar acronyms (e.g. ITN). The degree of randomness can be estimated in various ways, one of the simplest being to count the proportion of stereotyped pairs produced. Baddeley (1986) described evidence that randomness declines systematically when either the pace of generation or the difficulty of a secondary card-sorting task was increased. These observations are consistent with the suggestion that random generation taxes a limited-capacity system.

2.3.3 Fractionation

In an attempt to develop the concept of the executive yet further, Baddeley (1996) proposed that the system could be fractionated into a number of separate but related functions dealing with different aspects of attention. These were focusing, dividing and switching attention, and using attention to access information in LTM. To give a general idea of these distinctions, focusing attention is required when irrelevant information has to be ignored whereas dividing is necessary when attention has to be shared between different tasks. Thus attention is focused when listening to one message and ignoring another, but divided when two messages have to be monitored simultaneously, or when different activities have to be combined, as in dual-task experiments. Attention switching on the other hand refers to situations where attention must be repeatedly shifted from one process to another. For example, in generating a random sequence of digits, attention must constantly shift between different retrieval plans in order to avoid stereotypical patterns of responses. This in turn is somewhat different from the role of attention within a retrieval plan when actively searching for information in LTM. Baddeley (1996) described a certain amount of empirical support for the separability of executive functions. For example, patients with Alzheimer's disease have an exaggerated difficulty in combining concurrent tasks whereas normal ageing is associated with increasing difficulty in focusing attention. However, in general the paper was theoretical and was in essence an attempt to set the agenda for future research.

One way the agenda has been taken forward is through the study of individual differences in executive function in the normal population. In one such study, Miyake *et al.* (2000) gave a large sample of students a range of tasks designed to involve different facets of attentional control. These were shifting attention, monitoring and updating information and inhibiting pre-potent responses. Analysis of the data showed that a three-factor statistical model based on these three components gave a better account of relationships among abilities than simpler (i.e. one- or two-factor) models. This outcome is consistent with the general idea that executive function is fractionated, but it will be noted that the number of functions and their identity differ from Baddeley's (1996) proposal. Such a discrepancy is difficult to interpret, especially as a limitation of factor analysis is that it can only reveal the structure in the variables that are entered into the analysis. Miyake *et al.* (2000) went on to assess individual differences in a number of other tasks that are widely used as tests of executive function. The results showed that these tasks mapped onto the three putative components of executive function in different and sometimes unexpected ways. This is an interesting finding because it emphasizes the need for further development towards purer and better-understood measures of executive function.

As a general conclusion, the present state of knowledge is that executive function appears to fractionate, but it is not clear how (compare this with Chapter 2 on multiple types of attention). Thus, we still need to separate out and identify the various components of executive control. Whatever the outcome, there is a further issue of how such a diverse executive can operate in a unitary way. That is, how do the components of a many-faceted executive system interact coherently and avoid conflict in the control of perception, thought and action?

2.3.4   Coherence and the binding problem

It is interesting to note that the problem of coherence is not restricted to executive processes and applies to working memory more generally. Thus, if any system consists of a number of separate subsystems, then the question arises as to how the subsystems interact to ensure that the system as a whole operates in an integrated manner. For example, if visuo-spatial information about multiple objects is stored separately from verbal information about the same objects, the system must have a way of keeping track of which information refers to what object. This is sometimes referred to as the **binding problem**. Indeed, one critique of the working memory model of Baddeley and Hitch (1974) and its subsequent development by Baddeley (1986) is that by assuming separate subsystems it creates a binding problem that it fails to address (Jones, 1993). We encountered Jones' work when discussing the disruptive effect of irrelevant speech on immediate memory for verbal sequences

(Section 2.2 and Chapter 2). Salamé and Baddeley (1982) suggested that irrelevant speech enters the phonological loop, where it competes with the information to be remembered. However, Macken and Jones (1995) showed that irrelevant tones also disrupt immediate memory for verbal sequences. The amount of interference increased when the irrelevant tones or speech varied (or 'changed state'), suggesting a common mechanism. Jones and colleagues also showed that irrelevant speech disrupts memory for spatial sequences and that, here too, variability of the unattended stimuli determines the amount of interference (Jones *et al.*, 1995). Given these observations, Jones *et al.* (1995) argued that the interference due to various types of irrelevant stimuli is best explained in terms of a common level of representation within a unitary memory system. They regarded this common 'episodic record' as solving the binding problem by storing combinations of features together rather than having those features dispersed over separate stores.

Do the foregoing considerations imply that the unitary view proposed by Jones is correct and that attempts to fractionate working memory should be abandoned? The answers to these two questions seem to be probably 'not necessarily' and 'no'. The first answer is based on the argument that, while the similar patterns of interference across modalities suggest a common mechanism, such a mechanism could supplement rather than replace modality-specific stores. For example, the effect of variability of irrelevant stimuli might be explained in terms of the attention-grabbing property of stimulus change. Another possibility is suggested by evidence that irrelevant stimuli disrupt order information (Beaman and Jones, 1997). Thus, there might be a common serial-ordering mechanism that interacts with separate stores holding the various types of information being ordered. Perhaps the strongest reason for not abandoning fractionation is that a unitary account cannot explain the large amount of evidence for dissociations from sources other than the irrelevant sound paradigm. Nevertheless, by suggesting an alternative interpretation of the irrelevant speech effect and thereby drawing attention to the binding problem, the approach of Jones and his colleagues has made an important contribution.

In his most recent attempt to address the problem of executive control, Baddeley (2000) discusses a number of shortcomings of the tripartite 1986 model. One of these was an explicit acknowledgement that fractionation generates a binding problem. In a major revision to the model, Baddeley (2000) retained the notion of the executive as an attentional system but added to this a second component consisting of a multimodal **episodic buffer** that integrates information across modalities and is closely associated with consciousness. This new proposal is an attempt to account for both the unitary nature of conscious experience and the coherence with which the system as a whole operates. It is too soon to evaluate the episodic buffer. For the present we note that it has much in common with Jones' episodic record and may in part be regarded as an attempt to reconcile the tension between the two approaches of fractionation vs integration.

Summary of Section 2

- Working memory is a multicomponent model, which fractionates (or partitions) cognitive activities into a series of components.
- The original fractionation was into the articulatory rehearsal loop and central executive.
- The articulatory loop is further fractionated into the phonological store and a control process of subvocal rehearsal and is now more usually termed the 'phonological loop'.
- The central executive is an area of some ignorance, perhaps awaiting further fractionation.
- Corroborative evidence for fractionation comes from neuropsychological studies on patients with selective cognitive impairments.
- The binding problem refers to how the cognitive system keeps track of information processing about an object or task when that information is spread out over multiple independent subsystems.
- Central control needs to ensure multiple processes do not result in incoherence.
- Concepts such as episodic records (Jones) and the episodic buffer (Baddeley) attempt to solve the binding problem.
- The problem of understanding executive function in the context of working memory is actually part of a much wider field of enquiry that encompasses attention and conscious awareness.

3   Vocabulary acquisition

So far we have mentioned some but by no means all of the many functions of working memory and its subsystems. One that has been studied particularly closely is the role of the phonological loop in learning new vocabulary. The ability to store the sequence of phonemes making up a word must be important when encountering the word for the first time and retaining its spoken form long enough to learn it. The evidence comes from a variety of sources that include neuropsychological impairment, studies of individual differences in vocabulary size and experimental studies of word learning.

3.1   Neuropsychological evidence

Some of the clearest evidence that the phonological loop must play a role in vocabulary acquisition comes from the patient, PV, whose phonological store had a reduced capacity. Although PV had a normal long-term memory for familiar items, she encountered profound difficulty in learning novel word forms. Baddeley *et al.* (1988) showed this experimentally by testing her ability to learn pairings such as *Rosa–Svieti*, where the first word was in her native Italian and the second was an unfamiliar word derived from Russian. The result was dramatic: PV showed no learning at all. However, when the members of the pairs were both Italian words she performed normally. These observations establish a clear distinction between the processes involved in learning the two types of pairing and demonstrate a relationship between short-term phonological memory and long-term phonological learning. They also resurrect a classic debate about the relationship between short- and long-term memory. Patients like PV, such as KF (see Section 1.2), who had normal LTM but extremely impaired STM, were important to the argument for separate stores. That dissociation still stands, but the fact that PV can only learn pairings of familiar items (whose phonetic structure is already stored in LTM) indicates that there is also some association between STM and LTM in the phonological domain. How should we interpret this association? One possibility is that short-term and long-term phonological memory are different aspects of the same neuroanatomical and functional system. As with Cowan's (1988) view that working memory corresponds to an activated region of long-term memory, one could think of the phonological loop as the currently active area within a phonological long-term memory system that is separate from other long-term memory systems such as semantic memory.

3.2   Individual differences

If learning new vocabulary items depends on the capacity to hold a phonological sequence over a short interval, then the two abilities should correlate within individuals. A number of studies have shown that children's auditory digit span correlates with their performance on tests of vocabulary (see Baddeley *et al.*, 1998). Further evidence has come from studies that assess the child's ability to repeat a non-word they have just heard (e.g. *Blonterstaping*). Non-word repetition was devised as a more demanding test of memory for phonological form than digit span, and non-word repetition is typically more highly correlated with vocabulary scores than is digit span. Of course, with a correlation it is possible the causal relationship is in the reverse direction, such that it is vocabulary knowledge that underpins the ability to repeat non-words rather than phonological ability facilitating vocabulary acquisition. However Gathercole *et al.* (1997) found that, consistent with the latter interpretation, individual differences in the capacity of the phonological loop predict children's performance on a simulated vocabulary learning task.

As a postscript, it is interesting to note that measures of the phonological loop also correlate with vocabulary in second-language learning. Service (1992) found that Finnish children's ability to repeat English-sounding non-words before starting to learn English predicted their English vocabulary some two years later. Moreover, Papagno and Vallar (1995) showed that polyglots selected for being fluent in at least three languages had superior auditory digit span and non-word repetition when compared with controls. The polyglots were especially good at learning word–non-word pairs but were no better than controls at learning word–word pairs.

3.3   Experimental studies

Yet another way of assessing the involvement of the phonological loop in new word learning is to take an experimental approach. In a series of studies, Papagno and her colleagues investigated adults learning sets of either word–non-word pairs or word–word pairs. Papagno and Vallar (1992) showed that increasing the phonemic similarity of the non-words in a set, or the number of syllables in the non-words, impaired learning. However, corresponding manipulations in the word–word learning task had no effect. Papagno *et al.* (1991) found that articulatory suppression impeded the learning of word–non-word pairs but had no effect on learning word–word pairs. The absence of effects on the word–word learning task provides confirmation that the role of the loop is specific to learning novel words. These experimental differences between word–word and word–non-word learning fit well with the data on individual differences in these same tasks. However, we must bear in mind that experimental evidence that the phonological loop is necessary for learning non-words in adults leaves open the question of whether there are stages in development when the phonological loop drives vocabulary acquisition.

Summary of Section 3

- The phonological loop is involved in learning new word forms but not new associations between familiar words. These two tasks show a neuropsychological dissociation. They have also been dissociated experimentally in healthy adults.
- Individual differences in vocabulary size and vocabulary correlate with the capacity of the phonological loop in children and adults.
- However, the causal nature of the relationship between the phonological loop and vocabulary during development may be complex.

4   Modelling the phonological loop

A number of attempts have been made to develop mathematical and computational models of the phonological loop (Brown *et al.*, 2000; Burgess and Hitch, 1992, 1999; Page and Norris, 1998). Part of the impetus behind these efforts is the need to explain important phenomena that the two-component model fails to address. For example, the phonological loop is only an account of immediate recall and does not say anything about learning and long-term phonological memory. Clearly, extra assumptions are needed to account for how phonological forms of newly learnt words are acquired. Even within immediate recall, the phonological loop is far from providing a complete account. Thus, an important feature of digit span and other immediate serial recall tasks is the need to remember the order of the items. Indeed, for closed sets of familiar items such as digits or letters, the most common errors are order errors. However, the phonological loop does not explain how information about order is encoded nor how order errors are generated. These omissions make a case for extending the two-component model of the phonological loop to account for long-term learning and serial ordering, while at the same time attempting to preserve its essential insights.

One argument for using modelling techniques such as computer simulation to develop and express theories is the increasing complexity of our current knowledge. As should be evident from the present discussion, one strength of the two-component account of the phonological loop is its simplicity and the ease with which it can be used to generate testable predictions. In passing we may also note that this same strength has also allowed investigators to show where some of its assumptions are wrong (see Section 2.2.4). This is an important part of the scientific process. However, revising and extending the two-component account of the phonological loop to cope with errors and omissions runs the risk of ending up with an increasingly unwieldy theory. In particular, adding capabilities for serial ordering and learning would almost certainly render the model too unwieldy to generate clear predictions. Moving from an informal, verbal–conceptual level of theorizing to a more explicit, computational account is one way of overcoming this problem.

The most basic test of the adequacy of a computational model is whether it reproduces the same behaviour as humans when presented with the same tasks. However, this is not necessarily a very convincing test as the model-builder knows in advance the phenomena of interest and in general will have made sure the model succeeds in reproducing them. A more powerful test is to run further simulations in which the model is presented with novel experiments. The model's pattern of behaviour corresponds to its prediction about human behaviour in the same circumstances. The experiments can then be run with human participants to see whether the model's predictions are upheld. Unfortunately, it is not quite as simple as this sounds, and there are many reasons for being cautious before embarking on computational modelling. One is that developing a mechanistic account involves making extra assumptions sufficient to allow the model to 'run'. Sometimes the challenge of justifying these assumptions is hard to meet. We are fortunate in the case of auditory–verbal STM that there is a wealth of published data with which to constrain model-building. The same cannot be said, however, for executive function, and detailed computational modelling would almost certainly be premature in this case. In the following section, we describe briefly some constraints that influence the solution to the problem of how to handle serial order in the context of a detailed model of the phonological loop. Note that we do not discuss models in detail, nor evaluate their ability to explain existing experimental and neuropsychological data. Nor do we examine their ability to make novel predictions. These are all important aspects of modelling, but unfortunately there is not space to go into them here.

4.1 Serial order

The general problem of explaining serial order in behaviour is well known and several types of mechanism have been proposed. We will briefly describe some of these, bearing in mind that what interests us here is the specific question of what type of ordering mechanism underpins the operation of the phonological loop. According to the **chaining hypothesis**, serial order is coded by forming associations between consecutive items (e.g. Jones, 1993; Wickelgren, 1965). However, although chaining might seem highly plausible, it encounters some basic problems. One is explaining recall of a sequence containing repeated items, such as the number *2835867*. If order is encoded as a chain of associations, then the repeated item (*8*) will be associated with not one but two following items (*3* and *6*). Consequently sequences containing repeated items should be difficult to recall and errors should occur after each occurrence of the repeated item. Although sequences containing repeats are more difficult to recall in verbal STM tasks, errors tend to occur on rather than after the repeated item (Jahnke, 1969). Further evidence against chaining comes from errors in recalling sequences in which phonemically similar items alternate with phonemically dissimilar items, such as *BXDJTQVR*. These errors show a characteristic zig-zag pattern as one goes through the list, with more errors on the similar-sounding items (i.e. *BDTV*) and fewer on the dissimilar items (Baddeley, 1968; Henson *et al.*, 1996). Furthermore, dissimilar items are recalled with the same accuracy in alternating lists as in pure lists where all the items are dissimilar (see Figure 5.6). According to chaining theories, extra errors ought to occur on the dissimilar items, as these follow similar cues. For these reasons, chaining seems unlikely to explain how the phonological loop deals with serial order (though there are mathematical models that nevertheless adopt this approach, for example Lewandowsky and Murdock, 1989).

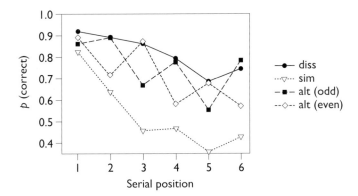

Figure 5.6   Serial position curves for the recall of six-item lists that varied in their phonemic composition. Diss: all items phonemically dissimilar, sim: all items phonemically similar, alt (odd)/alt (even): alternating phonemically similar and dissimilar items with similar items in odd- or even-numbered serial positions

Source: Baddeley, 1968, experiment v

One alternative to chaining is the positional hypothesis, according to which order is coded by associations between each item and a representation of its position within the sequence. In the simplest example of this type of model, Conrad (1965) assumed that verbal STM is composed of an ordered array of slots each containing a successive item in a list. To remember the sequence, the contents of the slots are simply read out. This simple model has no problem explaining how sequences containing repeated items are recalled. However, it cannot account for typical order errors in serial recall, where a common failure consists of an exchange between two adjacent items (e.g. recalling the sequence *318476205* as *318746205*: this is known as a transposition error). More generally the probability of transposition errors decreases with their distance from the correct position (Healy, 1974). Estes (1972) proposed a mathematical model to account for this distribution of order errors, according to which positional information is encoded for each item and becomes less precise as a function of forgetting. In a related approach, computational models by Burgess and Hitch (1999) and Brown *et al.* (2000) propose that order is coded by associations between each item and a timing signal that varies with its position. The timing signal provides an approximate coding of position and is used to explain the distribution of order errors in a somewhat similar way to Estes. One success of this approach is that it can explain the zig-zag variation of recall with position for lists of alternating phonemically similar and dissimilar items (e.g. *BXDJTQVR*). The Burgess and Hitch model (1999) achieves this by assuming that recall of each item is a two-stage process involving, first, using positional information to select a candidate item and, second, retrieving the phonemic content of the selected item. Phonemic similarity of items is assumed to make the second of these two stages less efficient, but has no effect on the first stage. Figure 5.7 shows simulations generated by the Burgess and Hitch (1999) model. These have the same zig-zag form as the experimental data (even though the simulations do not give enough 'primacy', i.e. decline in recall from the start of the list).

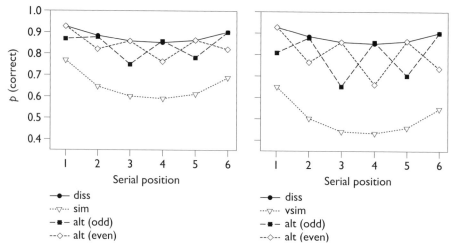

Figure 5.7   Serial position curves obtained by using the Burgess and Hitch (1999) model to simulate the experimental conditions of Baddeley (1968, experiment v). The left-hand panel shows simulations in which the similar items had one of two phonemes in common. The right-hand panel shows simulations in which the similar items had three of four phonemes in common (i.e. a higher degree of phonemic similarity)

A third point of view comes from non-associative models according to which encoding the order of a sequence does not involve forming novel associations. For example, in the primacy model of Page and Norris (1998), differences in the activation levels of items in memory are used to encode information about their order. Page and Norris assume that each successive item in a sequence is encoded with a lower level of activation than its predecessor. This process forms a 'primacy gradient' of activation levels over the list. Recall of the items in the correct serial order involves an iterative process of choosing the most strongly activated item, then the next and so on. Although this model is radically different from positional accounts, it passes the test of being able to simulate zig-zag patterns in the recall of lists of phonemically similar and dissimilar items. It is interesting to note that the model achieves this by assuming that the primacy gradient is used to select each item for recall but that a second phonological stage is used to retrieve the item's phonemic composition. Thus the primacy model and the positional model of Burgess and Hitch (1999) share the idea of two stages in recall, but differ in how they assume these stages work.

So far then we can see that data on alternating lists are useful for ruling out chaining models but do not discriminate between positional and non-associative models. Fortunately, there are further data that help discriminate between these two classes of model. These relate to the **temporal grouping effect**, whereby presenting a sequence of items in rhythmic temporal groups brings about a marked reduction in order errors in immediate recall (Ryan, 1969). Thus, recall of a sequence such as *318476205* is more accurate if it is presented as groups of three items, i.e. *318,476,205* (where the commas denote pauses). Moreover, grouping changes the pattern of order errors. Instead of the most common mistake being to transpose an item to an adjacent position, errors of recalling an item in a corresponding position in a different group become much more frequent, as in *31͟6 47͟8 205*. These effects of grouping suggest a positional coding system in which position can be encoded at different levels. That is, a higher level codes the position of groups within a list and a lower level codes the position of items within groups. Hitch *et al.* (1996) show how their computational model captures these hierarchical effects of position in memory. Insofar as Page and Norris's (1998) primacy model encodes order on a single dimension, it cannot explain evidence for the coding of order on different levels. However, it would not be impossible to extend the model to include combinations of primacy gradients at different levels.

Summary of Section 4

- One of the arguments for modelling is to go beyond the concept of a two-component phonological loop and address a wider range of phenomena such as serial ordering and non-word learning.
- Modelling is appropriate when we have a reasonably good conceptual understanding of the system we are trying to model and there are extensive data with which to constrain modelling.
- Some of the issues in modelling serial order in the phonological loop illustrate how existing data can be used to help make decisions about the underlying mechanisms.
- The chaining hypothesis cannot explain certain aspects of serial order recall. However, other hypotheses have had more success, for example the positional hypothesis and non-associative accounts.

5   Conclusion

We have examined the concept of working memory, with particular emphasis on phonological working memory and executive control. Taking a somewhat historical approach, we have traced how the concepts of the phonological loop and the central executive emerged from previous research and how they have subsequently been developed as researchers have found out more about them. As we have seen, progress in tackling these two aspects of working memory has developed at different rates. In the case of the phonological loop, experimental evidence from a variety of sources converged on a relatively simple two-component model. In turn, this model led to insights into a range of phenomena, including the development of STM, its neuropsychological impairment and children's learning of vocabulary. Although the simple model has been shown to be inadequate in a number of details it nevertheless preserves sufficient insights to have encouraged computational modellers to develop more detailed accounts that explain a greater range of phenomena. Such models are fairly recent and only time will tell whether this approach will prove productive.

In the case of the central executive the story is quite different. Here progress has been much slower and has consisted of various attempts to get an adequate conceptual handle on the problem. In this context the difficulty of devising satisfactory and reasonably well-understood tests of the various aspects of executive function that have been proposed should perhaps not surprise us. What is needed is a greater conceptual understanding of the various functions of executive control, one that goes beyond the promising beginning made by Norman and Shallice (1986) and develops the sorts of ideas discussed by Baddeley (1996).

In closing, we note that specifying the architecture of working memory is useful but cannot be the whole story. Thus, two important issues emerged when considering the evidence that working memory can be fractionated into a variety of subsystems. These concern how the system functions in a coherent and coordinated way and how it makes use of learned schemata and knowledge in LTM. Only when broader issues such as these are addressed can we start to give a coherent account of the role of working memory in such apparently ordinary everyday activities as planning a shopping trip or reading a newspaper.

Now that you have read this chapter you can reinforce and extend your learning by reading an original journal article associated with it, available online from the DD303 website. Remember, these are original journal articles, so the style is different from this textbook, and don't be too concerned if you can't follow every detail.

Further reading

Andrade, J. (ed.) (2001) *Working Memory in Perspective*, Hove, Psychology Press. Chapters by experienced researchers present a critical assessment of the Baddeley and Hitch (1974) model of working memory.

Baddeley A.D. (2000) 'Is working memory still working?', *American Psychologist*, vol.56, pp.851–64. In 2001 Alan Baddeley received the American Psychological Association's Award for Distinguished Scientific Contributions. This article presents his award address, which took the form of a personal review of the current state of the Baddeley and Hitch (1974) model of working memory.

Miyake, A. and Shah, P. (1999) *Models of Working Memory: Mechanisms of Active Maintenance and Executive Control*, Cambridge, Cambridge University Press. Proponents of competing theoretical approaches to working memory were invited to present their views in a format that was designed to help clarify areas of agreement and disagreement.

References

Andrade, J. (2001) 'The working memory model: consensus, controversy, and future directions' in Andrade, J. (ed.) *Working Memory in Perspective*, Hove, Psychology Press.

Atkinson, R.M. and Shiffrin, R.M. (1971) 'The control of short-term memory', *Scientific American*, vol.225, pp.82–90.

Baddeley, A.D. (1966a) 'Short-term memory for word sequences as a function of acoustic, semantic and formal similarity', *Quarterly Journal of Experimental Psychology*, vol.18, pp.362–5.

Baddeley, A.D. (1966b) 'The influence of acoustic and semantic similarity on long-term memory for word sequences', *Quarterly Journal of Experimental Psychology*, vol.18, pp.302–9.

Baddeley, A.D. (1968) 'How does acoustic similarity influence short-term memory?', *Quarterly Journal of Experimental Psychology*, vol.20, pp.249–64.

Baddeley, A.D. (1983) 'Working memory', *Philosophical Transactions of the Royal Society London*, B 302, pp.311–24.

Baddeley, A.D. (1986) *Working Memory*, Oxford, Oxford University Press.

Baddeley, A.D. (1996) 'Exploring the central executive', *Quarterly Journal of Experimental Psychology*, 49A, pp.5–28.

Baddeley, A.D. (2000) 'The episodic buffer: a new component of working memory?', *Trends in Cognitive Sciences*, vol.4, pp.417–23.

Baddeley, A., Gathercole, S. and Papagno, C. (1998) 'The phonological loop as a language learning device', *Psychological Review*, vol.105, pp.158–73.

Baddeley, A.D. and Hitch, G.J. (1974) 'Working memory' in Bower, G. (ed.) *The Psychology of Learning and Motivation: Advances in Research and Theory*, vol.8, New York, Academic Press.

Baddeley, A.D. and Larsen, J.D. (2003) 'The disruption of STM: a response to our commentators', *Quarterly Journal of Experimental Psychology*, 56A, pp.1301–6.

Baddeley, A.D., Lewis, V.J. and Vallar, G. (1984) 'Exploring the articulatory loop', *Quarterly Journal of Experimental Psychology*, 36A, pp.233–52.

Baddeley, A.D. and Lieberman, K. (1980) 'Spatial working memory' in Nickerson, R.S. (ed.) *Attention and Performance*, VIII, Hillsdale, NJ, Erlbaum.

Baddeley, A.D., Papagno, C. and Vallar, G. (1988) 'When long-term learning depends on short-term storage', *Journal of Memory and Language*, vol.27, pp.586–96.

Baddeley, A.D., Thomson, N. and Buchanan, M. (1975) 'Word length and the structure of short-term memory', *Journal of Verbal Learning and Verbal Behavior*, vol.14, pp.575–89.

Barrouillet, P. and Camos, V. (2001) 'Developmental increase in working memory span: resource sharing or temporal decay?', *Journal of Memory and Language*, vol.45, pp.1–20.

Beaman, C.P. and Jones, D. (1997) 'The role of serial order in the irrelevant speech effect: tests of the changing-state hypothesis', *Journal of Experimental Psychology: Learning, Memory and Cognition*, vol.23, pp.459–71.

Brooks, D.N. and Baddeley, A.D. (1976) 'What can amnesic patients learn?', *Neuropsychologia*, vol.14, pp.111–22.

Brown, J. (1958) 'Some tests of the decay theory of immediate memory', *Quarterly Journal of Experimental Psychology*, vol.10, pp.12–21.

Brown, G.D. and Hulme, C. (1995) 'Modelling item length effects in memory span: no rehearsal needed?', *Journal of Memory and Language*, vol.34, pp.594–621.

Brown, G.D., Preece, T. and Hulme, C. (2000) 'Oscillator-based memory for serial order', *Psychological Review*, vol.107, pp.127–81.

Burgess, N. and Hitch, G.J. (1992) 'Toward a network model of the articulatory loop', *Journal of Memory and Language*, vol.31, pp.429–60.

Burgess, N. and Hitch, G.J. (1999) 'Memory for serial order: a network model of the phonological loop and its timing', *Psychological Review*, vol.106, pp.551–81.

Caplan, D. and Waters, G.S. (1999) 'Verbal working memory and sentence comprehension', *Behavioural and Brain Sciences*, vol.22, pp.77–126.

Cohen, N.J. and Squire, L.R. (1980) 'Preserved learning and retention of pattern-analysing skill: dissociation of "knowing how" and "knowing that"', *Science*, vol.210, pp.207–9.

Conrad, R. (1965) 'Order errors in immediate recall of sequences', *Journal of Verbal Learning and Verbal Behavior*, vol.4, pp.161–9.

Conway, A.R.A. and Engle, R.W. (1994) 'Working memory and retrieval: a resource-dependent inhibition model', *Journal of Experimental Psychology: General*, vol.123, pp.354–73.

Cowan, N. (1988) 'Evolving conceptions of memory storage, selective attention, and their mutual constraints within the human information processing system', *Psychological Bulletin*, vol.96, pp.341–70.

Cowan, N., Day, L., Saults, J.S., Keller, T.A., Johnson, T. and Flores, L. (1992) 'The role of verbal output time in the effects of word length on immediate memory', *Journal of Memory and Language*, vol.31, pp.1–17.

Craik, F.I.M. and Lockhart, R.S. (1972) 'Levels of processing: a framework for memory research', *Journal of Verbal Learning and Verbal Behavior*, vol.11, pp.671–84.

De Beni, R., Palladino, P., Pazzaglia, F. and Cornoldi, C. (1998) 'Increases in intrusion errors and working memory deficit of poor comprehenders', *Quarterly Journal of Experimental Psychology*, 51A, pp.305–20.

Daneman, M. and Carpenter, P.A. (1980) 'Individual differences in working memory and reading', *Journal of Verbal Learning and Verbal Behavior*, vol.19, pp.450–66.

de Renzi, E. and Nichelli, P. (1975) 'Verbal and non-verbal short term memory impairment following hemisphere damage', *Cortex*, vol.11, pp.341–53.

Dempster, F.N. (1981) 'Memory span: sources of individual and developmental differences', *Psychological Bulletin*, vol.89, pp.63–100.

Engle, R.W., Kane, M.J. and Tuholski, S.W. (1999a) 'Individual differences in working memory capacity and what they tell us about controlled attention, general fluid intelligence and the functions of the prefrontal cortex' in Miyake, A. and Shah, P. (eds) *Models of Working Memory: Mechanisms of Active Maintenance and Executive Control*, Cambridge, Cambridge University Press.

Engle, R.W., Tuholski, S.W., Laughlin, J.E. and Conway, A.R.A. (1999b) 'Working memory, short-term memory and general fluid intelligence: a latent variable approach', *Journal of Experimental Psychology: General*, vol.128, no.3, pp.309–31.

Ericsson, K.A. and Kintsch, W. (1995) 'Long-term working memory', *Psychological Review*, vol.102, pp.211–45.

Estes, W.K. (1972) 'An associative basis for coding and organization in memory' in Melton, A.W. and Martin, E. (eds) *Coding Processes in Human Memory*, Washington, DC, Winston.

Gathercole, S.E., Hitch, G.J., Service, E. and Martin, A.J. (1997) 'Phonological short-term memory and new word learning in children', *Developmental Psychology*, vol.33, pp.966–79.

Healy, A.F. (1974) 'Separating item from order information in short-term memory', *Journal of Verbal Learning and Verbal Behavior*, vol.13, pp.644–55.

Henson, R. (2001) 'Neural working memory' in Andrade, J. (ed.) *Working Memory in Perspective*, Hove, Psychology Press.

Henson, R.N.A., Norris, D.G., Page, M.P.A. and Baddeley, A.D. (1996) 'Unchained memory: error patterns rule out chaining models of immediate serial recall', *Quarterly Journal of Experimental Psychology*, 49A, pp.80–115.

Hitch, G.J. (1978) 'The role of short-term working memory in mental arithmetic', *Cognitive Psychology*, vol.10, pp.302–23.

Hitch, G.J., Brandimonte, M.A. and Walker, P. (1995) 'Two types of representation in visual memory: evidence from the effects of stimulus contrast on image combination', *Memory and Cognition*, vol.23, pp.147–54.

Hitch, G.J., Burgess, N., Towse, J.N. and Culpin, V. (1996) 'Temporal grouping effects in immediate recall: a Working Memory analysis', *Quarterly Journal of Experimental Psychology*, 49A, pp.116–39.

Hitch, G.J., Halliday, M.S., Dodd, A. and Littler, J.E. (1989) 'Development of rehearsal in short-term memory: differences between pictorial and spoken stimuli', *British Journal of Developmental Psychology*, vol.7, pp.347–62.

Hitch, G.J., Halliday, M.S., Schaafstal, A. and Schraagen, J.M. (1988) 'Visual working memory in young children', *Memory and Cognition*, vol.16, pp.120–32.

Hitch, G.J., Towse, J.N. and Hutton, U. (2001) 'What limits children's working memory span? Theoretical accounts and applications for scholastic development', *Journal of Experimental Psychology: General*, vol.130, pp.184–98.

Hulme, C., Thomson, N., Muir, C. and Lawrence, A. (1984) 'Speech rate and the development of short-term memory span', *Journal of Experimental Child Psychology*, vol.38, pp.241–53.

Jahnke, J.C. (1969) 'The Ranschburg effect', *Psychological Review*, vol.76, pp.592–605.

Jones, D. (1993) 'Objects, streams and threads of auditory attention' in Baddeley, A. and Weiskrantz, L. (eds) *Attention, Awareness and Control*, Oxford, Oxford University Press.

Jones, D., Farrand, P., Stuart, G. and Morris, N. (1995) 'Functional equivalence of verbal and spatial information in serial short-term memory', *Journal of Experimental Psychology: Learning, Memory and Cognition*, vol.21, pp.1008–18.

Just, M.A. and Carpenter, P.A. (1992) 'A capacity theory of comprehension: individual differences in working memory', *Psychological Review*, vol.99, pp.122–49.

Lewandowsky, S. and Murdock, B.B., Jr (1989) 'Memory for serial order', *Psychological Review*, vol.96, pp.25–57.

Lhermitte, F. (1983) '"Utilization behaviour" and its relation to lesions of the frontal lobes', *Brain*, vol.106, pp.237–55.

Logie, R.H. (1995) *Visuo-spatial Working Memory*, Hove, Lawrence Erlbaum Associates.

Lovatt, P.J., Avons, S.E. and Masterson, J. (2000) 'The word-length effect and dysllabic words', *Quarterly Journal of Experimental Psychology*, 53A, pp.1–22.

Macken, W.J. and Jones, D.M. (1995) 'Functional characteristics of the "inner voice" and the "inner ear": single or double agency?', *Journal of Experimental Psychology: Learning, Memory and Cognition*, vol.21, pp.436–48.

Miller, G.A. (1956) 'The magical number seven plus or minus two: some limits on our capacity for processing information', *Psychological Review*, vol.63, pp.81–97.

Miyake, A., Friedman, N.P., Emerson, M.J., Witzki, A.H. and Howerter, A. (2000) 'The unity and diversity of executive functions and their contributions to complex "frontal lobe" tasks: a latent variable analysis', *Cognitive Psychology*, vol.41, pp.49–100.

Miyake, A. and Shah, P. (1999) *Models of Working Memory: Mechanisms of Active Maintenance and Executive Control*, Cambridge, Cambridge University Press.

Murdock, B.B., Jr (1967) 'Recent developments in short-term memory', *British Journal of Psychology*, vol.58, pp.421–33.

Nairne, J.S. (2002) 'Remembering over the short-term: the case against the standard model', *Annual Review of Psychology*, vol.53, pp.53–81.

Naveh-Benjamin, M. and Ayres, T.J. (1986) 'Digit span, reading rate, and linguistic relativity', *Quarterly Journal of Experimental Psychology*, 38A, pp.739–52.

Nicolson, R.S. (1981) 'The relationship between memory span and processing speed' in Friedman, M., Das, J.P. and O'Connor, N. (eds) *Intelligence and Learning*, New York, Plenum Press.

Norman, D.A. and Shallice, T. (1986) 'Attention to action: willed and automatic control of behavior' in Davidson, R.J., Schwartz, G.E. and Shapiro, D.E. (eds) *Consciousness and Self-regulation: Advances in Research and Theory*, vol.4, New York, Plenum Press.

Page, M.P.A. and Norris, D.G. (1998) 'The primacy model: a new model of immediate serial recall', *Psychological Review*, vol.105, pp.761–81.

Palmer, S. (2000a) 'Working memory: a developmental study of phonological recoding', *Memory*, vol.8, pp.179–94.

Palmer, S. (2000b) 'Phonological recoding deficit in working memory of dyslexic teenagers', *Journal of Research in Reading*, vol.23, pp.28–40.

Papagno, C., Valentine, T. and Baddeley, A.D. (1991) 'Phonological short-term memory and the foreign-language vocabulary learning', *Journal of Memory and Language*, vol.30, pp.331–47.

Papagno, C. and Vallar, G. (1992) 'Phonological short-term memory and the learning of novel words: the effect of phonological similarity and item length', *Quarterly Journal of Experimental Psychology*, 44A, pp.47–67.

Papagno, C. and Vallar, G. (1995) 'Short-term memory and vocabulary learning in polyglots', *Quarterly Journal of Experimental Psychology*, 48A, pp.98–107.

Paulesu, E., Frith, C.D. and Frackowiack, R.S.J. (1993) 'The neural correlates of the verbal component of working memory', *Nature*, vol.362, pp.342–4.

Reason, J. (1984) 'Lapses of attention in everyday life' in Parasuraman, R., Davies, R. and Beatty, J. (eds) *Varieties of Attention*, Orlando, FL, Academic Press.

Ryan, J. (1969) 'Grouping and short-term memory: different means and patterns of grouping', *Quarterly Journal of Experimental Psychology*, vol.21, pp.137–47.

Salamé, P. and Baddeley, A.D. (1982) 'Disruption of short-term memory by unattended speech: implications for structure of working memory', *Journal of Verbal Learning and Verbal Behavior*, vol.21, pp.150–84.

Service, E. (1992) 'Phonology, working memory, and foreign-language learning', *Quarterly Journal of Experimental Psychology*, 45A, pp.21–50.

Shallice, T. and Warrington, E.K. (1970) 'Independent functioning of verbal memory stores: a neuropsychological study', *Quarterly Journal of Experimental Psychology*, vol.22, pp.261–73.

Smyth, M.M. and Waller, A. (1998) 'Movement imagery in rock climbing: patterns of interference from visual, spatial and kinaesthetic secondary tasks', *Applied Cognitive Psychology*, vol.12, pp.145–57.

Towse, J.N. (1998) 'On random generation and the central executive of working memory', *British Journal of Psychology*, vol.89, pp.77–101.

Towse, J.N., Hitch, G.J. and Hutton, U. (1998) 'A reevaluation of working memory capacity in children', *Journal of Memory and Language*, vol.39, no.2, pp.195–217.

Towse, J.N., Hitch, G.J. and Hutton, U. (2000) 'On the interpretation of working memory span in adults', *Memory and Cognition*, vol.28, no.3, pp.341–8.

Turner, M.L. and Engle, R.W. (1989) 'Is working memory capacity task dependent?', *Journal of Memory and Language*, vol.28, pp.127–54.

Vallar, G. and Baddeley, A.D. (1984) 'Fractionation of working memory: neuropsychological evidence for a phonological short-term store', *Journal of Verbal Learning and Verbal Behavior*, vol.23, pp.151–61.

Wickelgren, W.A. (1965) 'Short-term memory for repeated and non-repeated items', *Quarterly Journal of Experimental Psychology*, vol.17, pp.14–25.

Long-term memory: encoding to retrieval

Chapter 6

Andrew Rutherford

1 Introduction

Everyone appreciates how useful it is to have a good memory. However, fewer people appreciate that having a good memory is not just useful – it is vital to the way we live our lives and it is vital to our psychological functioning. Quite literally, our memory contains all that we know. Yet, despite the vast amount of information stored, memory almost always provides accurate and rapid access to the pertinent information we require. It is memory that tells us who we are and what we have done, it is memory that provides us with the words and grammar required to construct comprehensible sentences and it is memory that holds the information that lets us recognize different types of cars, dogs or sporting events, or make a cup of tea or coffee. Given the essential role of memory in our lives, it is not surprising that memory has been an active area of research in psychology since its first scientific investigation by the German philosopher Hermann Ebbinghaus in the 1880s.

This chapter focuses on long-term memory, particularly episodic memory, although there will be some mention of semantic memory too. As the name suggests, **episodic memory** is a record of the episodes that constitute our lives. Episodic memory provides a description of what you have experienced (and thought) over the days, weeks and years of your life. This chapter presents some of the accounts of how episodic memory operates and some pertinent experimental evidence. Researchers interested in normal memory usually examine people with normal memories, but they also may examine people with abnormal memory resulting from physical damage to the brain. Examining the memory operation of people with brain damage may seem a peculiar way of finding out about normal memory, but an accurate account of normal memory operation also should be able to explain why and how its manner of operation changes when damage is sustained. Just as a car mechanic's understanding of the normal operation of a car engine will explain why a particular engine is not running properly, so an accurate account of normal memory should explain abnormal memory operation. More formally, it can be said that data from neuropsychological studies provide useful constraints on psychological accounts of normal memory. Of course, such studies also provide beneficial insight into the memory problems experienced by brain-damaged people.

Memory may be regarded as involving three logical stages, **encoding**, **storage** and **retrieval** (getting information in, keeping it there and then getting it back out). Typically, psychologists examine memory by presenting material and then, later, observing what can be remembered. Different manipulations can be applied at the encoding, storage and retrieval stages, depending on the purpose of the study. Investigation of any particular stage is a matter of theoretical emphasis and experimental method, but irrespective of whether encoding, storage or retrieval is of interest, all stages will have been involved when information is remembered.

Summary of Section 1

- Our long-term memory contains all that we know and all that makes us who we are.
- Usually our memory operation is very efficient.
- Episodic memory is the record of our life experiences.
- Neuropsychological findings can constrain psychological accounts of normal memory.
- Memory involves three logical stages: encoding, storage and retrieval.
- Examination of any particular stage is a matter of theoretical emphasis and experimental method.

2 Encoding

Encoding is the label given to the way in which objects and events in the world come to be represented in memory. Our normal perception of objects and events requires considerable encoding. However, the application of further encoding processes can produce memory representations of objects and events that differ considerably from those arising solely from perceptual processes.

2.1 Levels of processing

An article by Craik and Lockhart (1972) had a huge influence on memory research. At the time, the major theoretical vehicle for explaining memory performance was Atkinson and Shiffrin's (1968) '**multi-store**' or '**modal**' memory model. The 'multi-store' label referred to the assumption of separate sensory registers for each sense modality, a short-term store and a long-term memory store. (This description of different memory stores in which different memory processes operate has much in common with the multiple memory systems perspective discussed in Section 3.) The 'modal' label was due to the model encapsulating most accounts of the memory data collected up to that time (Murdock, 1967). Nevertheless, then and soon after, a number of problems were identified with the multi-store model (see Baddeley, 1997). Craik and Lockhart reviewed these problems and argued that the major determinant of the memorability of an item was not the store in which the item was held, as proposed by the multi-store model, but the level of processing that it received at encoding. Craik and Lockhart presumed that processing proceeded through a fixed sequence of levels, from early perceptual processes, through pattern recognition to the extraction of meaning. The greater the depth of processing applied to an item, the more likely it was to be remembered (see Box 6.1). Craik and Lockhart considered that, although a 'spread of elaborative coding' provided a good description of processing at the semantic level, they referred to '**depth of**

6.1 ── Research study

Levels of processing

Craik and Tulving (1975, experiment 1) reported an experiment that manipulated participants' level of processing and tested recognition memory. Participants were presented with a question followed by a word. They had to answer 'yes' or 'no' to the question and then, later on, their memory for the words was tested (see Table 6.1).

Table 6.1

Question	Yes	No
1 Is the word in capital letters?	TABLE	table
2 Does the word rhyme with WEIGHT?	crate	market
3 Is the word a type of fish?	shark	heaven
4 Does the word fit in the sentence? "the man peeled the _____"	orange	roof

Perceptually oriented processing must be engaged to provide answers to questions 1 and 2: graphemic for question 1 and phonetic for question 2. As the words were presented visually, visual processes always were engaged. Graphemic processing alone was engaged by question 1. To answer question 2, however, phonetic processing also must be engaged. Therefore, greater of levels of processing were required to answer question 2. Questions 3 and 4 both required deeper levels of semantically oriented processing, but still more elaborative semantic processing was required to answer question 4 than question 3. The proportion of words correctly recognized as a function of the level of processing engaged at encoding is presented below.

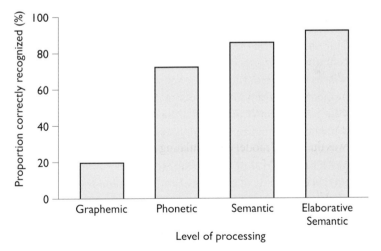

Figure 6.1   Recognition as a function of level of processing from Craik and Tulving, 1975

As predicted, participants' recognition memory performance increased with deeper levels of processing.

processing' to convey the essence of their argument. As 'deeper' levels of processing are implemented, more elaborate, longer lasting and stronger memory traces are produced. In Craik and Lockhart's conception, the processing operations both modify and leave a trace in the system. Rather than there being items that are constructed specially to be stored in memory, memories (i.e. memory traces) are simply the after-effects of processing.

Of course, processing need not proceed through all levels. The processing of information may stop at any point due to attention being diverted elsewhere or, at any given level, the processing already engaged may simply repeat rather than proceed through further levels. A common example of this sort of repetitive processing is verbally rehearsing a telephone number to keep it 'in mind' before calling the number. Craik and Lockhart labelled this **Type I processing** and considered it to manifest primary memory, as had been described by James (1890). **Type II processing** was the label applied to processing that proceeded through further levels. Craik and Lockhart also assumed that while Type II processing would benefit memory, no further benefit to long-term memory would accrue from repetitive Type I processing beyond that bestowed initially by the form of processing engaged.

The levels of processing framework changed the nature of psychological accounts of memory. Prior to Craik and Lockhart's (1972) article, most accounts of memory emphasized the nature of the structures holding the information to explain memory performance. Subsequently, however, most accounts of memory have emphasized the processes or mental operations carried out with respect to the material presented to explain memory performance. In the early to mid seventies, the emphasis on processing also was supported by seminal developments at the intersection of a number of cognate disciplines, such as artificial intelligence, linguistics, philosophy and neuroscience. This area of intersection is now called cognitive science and adopts a strong computational (i.e. formal processing) perspective. Nevertheless, despite all of the benefits and advantages of the levels of processing framework, it was never intended as the perfect account of memory. Objectively defining which processing levels were 'deeper' than others (and in what circumstances) was found to pose a substantial problem (Baddeley, 1978). A lack of an objective definition of levels of processing means that processing level may end up being defined in a circular fashion. Specifically, deeper levels of processing are predicted to improve memory performance, but without an objective definition of what constitutes deeper levels, improved memory performance is taken to indicate a deeper level of processing. A problem with defining processing level in this circular fashion is that the levels of processing framework predictions cannot be tested properly, as any lack of memory performance improvement can be interpreted as indicating a failure to deepen the level of processing at encoding.

Also the levels of processing framework does not provide explanations of all memory phenomena. For example, independently, Glenberg et al. (1977) and Rundus (1977) developed the same technique to examine Type I processing (maintenance rehearsal). Numbers were presented for participants to remember, but to stop them rehearsing the numbers, they had words to rehearse for various intervals. However, rather than being asked to recall the numbers at test, the participants were asked to free-recall the words they had been led to believe were irrelevant. In these circumstances, participants should be expected only to maintenance-rehearse the words. As predicted by Craik and Lockhart's levels of processing account, it was found that the length of time spent maintenance rehearsing the words had no effect on memory as measured by free recall (Rundus, 1977). Glenberg *et al.* (1977) observed the same with free recall, but they also found that maintenance rehearsal improved recognition memory. Levels of processing can give no account of the benefit recognition memory obtains from maintenance rehearsal, not least because the levels of processing framework focuses on encoding operations and not retrieval operations. Later in the chapter we shall see how models of memory have developed to provide an account of the findings of Glenberg *et al.* (1977) and Rundus (1977).

2.2   Relational and item-specific processing

Psychologists have long been aware that distinctive items are well remembered (e.g. Koffka, 1935). The levels of processing framework considered that a more unique or distinctive memory trace resulted from greater depth of processing and semantic elaboration (e.g. Lockhart *et al.*, 1976). However, there is also a large body of research in psychology indicating that memory benefits from organizing items at encoding – categorizing or arranging them on the basis of properties they share (e.g. Elio and Reutener, 1970; Deese, 1959; Tulving, 1962) (see Box 6.2). These findings create something of a paradox. Establishing items' distinctiveness emphasizes their differences, while organizing items emphasizes their similarities. As Hunt and McDaniel (1993) ask, 'how can both similarity and difference be beneficial to memory?'

6.2   **Research study**

Distinctive processing benefits memory independently of the level of processing

Eysenck and Eysenck (1980) conducted an experiment where distinctive processing was manipulated independently of level of processing. (Distinctive processing focuses on unique aspects of the stimulus item.)

Participants were presented with nouns that they had to process in a semantically distinct (S-D) fashion by providing a descriptor (for example, an adjective) that would be used infrequently to modify the noun. Semantically non-distinct processing (S-ND) was fostered by having participants provide a descriptor that was used frequently to modify the noun. Phonetically distinct processing (P-D) was achieved by presenting participants with nouns that are pronounced differently to the way their spelling suggests, but participants had to pronounce the words in line with their spelling. For example, the usually silent 'b' in comb would have to be pronounced at the end of the word. Phonetically non-distinct processing (P-ND) was obtained by having subjects say nouns which have conventional spelling and pronunciation.

→

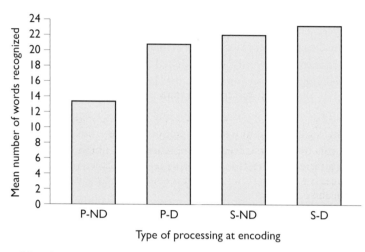

Figure 6.2   Correct recognition as a function of experimental conditions

The results showed there was very little difference between recognition performance after semantic and distinctive, semantic and non-distinctive, and phonetic and distinctive processing, but there was a significant drop in recognition performance after phonetic and non-distinctive processing. Therefore, semantic processing enhances memory performance, but distinctive processing, even with phonetic processing, can lift memory performance to the level observed with semantic processing. In other words, it seems that distinctive processing can benefit memory performance independently of the level or depth of processing engaged.

Hunt and McDaniel (1993) resolve this paradox by referring to the different forms of processing underlying the detection of similarity and difference. **Relational processing** underlies similarity, whereas **item-specific processing** underlies distinctiveness. Mandler (1979) provides a useful description and illustration (see Figure 6.3) of the way in which memory representations are affected (organized in Mandler's terminology) by these two forms of processing. Item-specific processes focus specifically on the item's mental representation, enhancing the operation and coherence of the cognitive processes that carry the mental representation. Mandler calls this sort of enhancement 'integration'. Practising saying a word provides one example of item-specific processing, the consequence of which is greater fluency of pronunciation. In fact, enhancing the operation and coherence of cognitive processes (their integration) often is expressed as an increase in processing fluency. Relational processes establish connections between different entity representations. Mandler refers to this as 'elaboration'. Seeing a cat and thinking of it being chased by a dog is a simple example of relational processing – a relation (chasing) is drawn between two entities (cat and dog). According to Mandler (1979), maintenance rehearsal results in integration (i.e. employs item-specific processing), while semantic processing results in elaboration (i.e. employs relational processing).

(a) Item

(b) Item after integration

(c) Item after elaboration

Figure 6.3 A graphic analogy of integration (due to item-specific processing) and elaboration (due to relational processing) (Mandler, 1979). Item-specific processing (b) enhances the coherence of the cognitive processes carrying the mental representation components (depicted by the links between the components of the representation). Relational processing (c) establishes connections between the mental representations of the target item and other items

2.2.1 Encoding processing and Mandler's (1980) dual-process model of recognition

Soon after his account of integration and elaboration in memory representations, Mandler presented a very influential dual-process model of recognition (Mandler, 1980). In this model, one process runs very quickly and is based on familiarity. The sense of familiarity is thought to result from processing fluency, that is, the more fluently an item can be processed (or encoded) the more familiar it feels. Familiarity depends upon the degree of integration of the entity representation: greater integration makes the presented item feel more familiar and facilitates subsequent processing of the same or similar items (Jacoby and Dallas, 1981). The other process runs more slowly and employs more involved and extensive search and retrieval operations used in recall to determine if the entity was presented before. The search and retrieval process benefits from elaboration – the greater the elaboration, the greater the benefit to the retrieval process. Presumably, the connections between representations established by relational processing provide a variety of different routes (cues) to the representation of the target. (See Box 6.3 for a more detailed discussion of item-specific relational processing.)

Mandler also distinguishes between simple recognition and identification. Simple recognition is based only upon an evaluation of the familiarity of an entity and, therefore, provides a context-free judgement of prior occurrence. In contrast, identification employs a search and retrieval stage, as well as a familiarity evaluation. Search and retrieval processes first provide and then employ contextual information. This is used to restrict the memory search on subsequent retrieval cycles. For example, if someone is trying to remember a person's name, usually they know (i.e. can retrieve) if it is a male or female name, and they may even know (or guess) the place where they frequently encounter this person. Both gender and place provide contexts that are able to restrict or focus the memory search. Mandler also assumes that both familiarity and search and retrieval processes are initiated simultaneously and operate in parallel. However, as the speedy familiarity-based process will finish first, time-pressured recognition is most likely based on simple recognition.

┌─ 6.3 ──────────────────────────────────── Research study ─┐

Effects of item-specific and relational processing on free recall and recognition

Hunt and Einstein (1981, experiment 1) presented participants with either a categorized list of 36 words (6 words from each of 6 categories) or 36 unrelated words. It was assumed that participants would process the categorized words spontaneously in a relational fashion (but not necessarily in an item-specific fashion), while participants receiving the unrelated words would process them spontaneously in an item-specific fashion (but not necessarily in a relational fashion).

For both categorized and unrelated lists, free recall and recognition were tested. However, prior to these tests, participants were required either to sort the words into specified categories (a relational processing task), or to rate the pleasantness of the words (an item-specific processing task). Participants read a short story for one minute before trying to free-recall the 36 words. Recognition was tested after free recall. Table 6.2 below presents the average free recall and recognition scores.

Table 6.2

	Categorized list		Unrelated list	
	Relational processing	Item-specific processing	Relational processing	Item-specific processing
Free recall[1]	.42	.48	.47	.33
Recognition[2]	.73	.93	.89	.91

[1] Correct free recall as a proportion of total number of items presented (i.e. 36).

[2] AG scores – a non-parametric measure of recognition sensitivity (Pollack et al., 1964).

Free recall of the categorized list was greater after item-specific processing (.48) than after relational processing (.42), but free recall of the unrelated list was greater after relational processing (.47) than after item-specific processing (.33). Therefore, free recall benefits from task processing that is different from that facilitated by the type of list. This shows that both relational and item-specific processing contribute to free recall.

Although considerable research has shown that recognition memory benefits from relational processing (e.g. Craik and Tulving, 1975), Hunt and Einstein's recognition data do not simply replicate the free recall data. Recognition of categorized list items was greater after item-specific processing (.93) than after relational processing (.73) but, unlike free recall, recognition of unrelated list items was the same irrespective of relational (.89) or item-specific processing (.91). It seems additional item-specific processing may become redundant for free recall, but it continues to benefit recognition.

└──┘

Mandler's (1979, 1980) descriptions provide an explanation for the findings obtained by Glenberg *et al.* (1977) and Rundus (1977). Free recall derives greatest benefit from relational processing, but little benefit from maintenance rehearsal (i.e. item-specific processing), which promotes integration. In contrast, familiarity-based simple recognition depends upon the degree of integration. Therefore, a high degree of item-specific processing, maintenance rehearsal or Type I processing, will benefit recognition to a greater degree than it will benefit free recall.

To explain the effects on memory performance of different forms of encoding requires consideration of the relations between memory encoding, memory representation and memory tests. This illustrates the point made in Section 1: whether interest is in encoding, storage or retrieval, all stages of memory are involved when information is remembered.

Summary of Section 2

- The levels of processing framework was presented as a counter to the multi-store memory model.
- The levels of processing framework asserted that memorability was due to the level of processing received at encoding and not the store in which the item was held.
- Distinctive processing can benefit memory independently of the level of processing.
- Relational and item-specific are two important types of processing.
- Mandler's dual-process model of recognition memory assumes item-specific processing enhances processing fluency or familiarity, as well as the distinctiveness, of an item, while relational processing supports context-based retrieval.
- Recall derives greater benefit from relational processing, while recognition derives greater benefit from item-specific processing.

3   Memory stores and systems

A memory store is where non-active memory representations are held. For example, imagine your favourite item of clothing. When not in use, the memory representation upon which this image depends will be held in a memory store. Memory systems include memory stores, but memory systems also include all the processes that operate when memory representations are active, such as the processes that generate the image of your favourite item of clothing. The memory systems perspective is that memory stores and memory processing are localized in the same part of the brain. This view receives support from research on connectionist systems, where representation and processing are intimately related. The accounts to be presented in this section certainly assume that memory and its associated processing are localized within the brain. However, as will be described, these accounts have tended to focus on identifying different types of memory systems and their apparent locations in the brain, rather than on describing the processing and nature of the memory representation.

3.1 Multiple memory systems

Tulving and associates (e.g. Tulving and Schacter, 1990; Schacter *et al.*, 2001) are strong advocates of a multiple memory systems perspective. (Table 6.3 presents the various systems and subsystems of human learning and memory proposed by Schacter and Tulving, 1994.) Although Schacter and Tulving present five long-term memory (LTM) systems and eleven subsystems, discussion here will concentrate on the distinction between episodic and semantic memory.

Episodic memory is considered to be a record of a person's experiences. It stores information about the events and occurrences that make up a person's life and, crucially, according to Wheeler *et al.* (1997), the subjective experiences that accompany the information retrieved from episodic memory. Therefore, the answers to questions such as 'What did you do yesterday afternoon?' and 'Have you seen this picture before?' would tax episodic memory. **Semantic memory** is considered to be our general knowledge store. In short, it contains all the information underlying our understanding of the world. For example, it provides the information we use to recognize or describe different types of animals, objects, etc., it provides the information for using and understanding language and it stores the sort of information we would employ to choose our ideal summer holiday destination. Questions such as 'What is the capital of Scotland?' and 'Did Plato own a car?' would tax semantic memory. However, no personal experience accompanies the information retrieved from semantic memory.

Table 6.3 Schacter and Tulving's (1994) systems and subsystems of human learning and memory

System	Other labels	Subsystems	Retrieval type
Procedural	Non-declarative	(i) Motor skills (ii) Cognitive skills (iii) Simple conditioning (iv) Simple associative learning	Implicit
Perceptual representation	Non-declarative	(i) Visual word form (ii) Auditory word form (iii) Structural description	Implicit
Semantic	General Factual Knowledge	(i) Spatial (ii) Relational	Implicit
Primary	Working	(i) Visual (ii) Auditory	Explicit
Episodic	Personal Autobiographical Events		Explicit

In terms of research focus, a distinction certainly exists between episodic and semantic memory. Most psychology texts identify Collins and Quillian's (1969) research as seminal work on the topic of semantic memory. They converted a system for representing information in computer systems into a model of human knowledge and examined its psychological reality. This and further investigation established the study of human knowledge, or semantic memory, as a distinct research area with its own issues, paradigms and measures.

One criticism of Tulving's distinction between episodic and semantic memory systems is the need for substantial communication between them. This is illustrated by the fact that information encoded in episodic memory usually is comprehended fully, yet our knowledge of the world, upon which this comprehension is based, would be stored in semantic memory. To provide episodic memory with easy access to semantic memory information, Tulving (1984) suggested episodic memory was embedded within semantic memory. A study reported by Anderson and Ross (1980) is relevant to this issue. They investigated the independence of semantic and episodic memory systems, and were interested in whether episodic memory information affected semantic memory. Two types of task can be used to examine semantic and episodic memory. A sentence *verification* task requires participants to state whether a sentence is true or false and is regarded as a test of semantic memory. A sentence *recognition* task requires participants to state whether or not a sentence was presented earlier and is regarded as a test of episodic memory. Anderson and Ross measured how long participants took to verify a sentence. For example: a spaniel is a dog. (Here 'dog' is the category and 'spaniel' is an exemplar of that category; we will look at this in more detail in Chapter 9.) Beforehand, participants were allocated to one of five conditions. In four of these conditions, participants were presented with episodic information about the categories and exemplars. This information was presented in the form of simple sentences that participants had to learn (for example: a plumber pets a dog, a spaniel retrieves a ball). In the fifth control condition, participants received no information about the category or the exemplar. The results revealed that the time taken to verify sentences (that is, to make semantic judgements) was affected by the nature of the episodic information about the exemplar and category presented in the previous sentences. Contrary to there being a distinct separation between episodic and semantic memory, episodic information affected retrieval from semantic memory.

The need to facilitate transfer of information from the semantic memory system to the episodic memory system led Tulving (1984) to suggest episodic memory was embedded within semantic memory, while the results of the Anderson and Ross study reveal that information also transfers from the episodic memory system to the semantic memory system. Such transfer between systems raises the question, why should there be separate episodic and semantic memory systems? Anderson and Ross note that semantic memory must respond to experience, but the manner in which this occurs is not specified. This last point is related to another criticism of distinct episodic and semantic memory systems dealt with below.

The multiple memory systems perspective, especially the episodic and semantic memory distinction, has been criticized as lacking theoretical development (e.g. McKoon *et al.*, 1986; Neely, 1989). In particular, the way in which different variables differentially affect the operation of episodic and semantic memory systems has not been described. For example, Anderson (1974) demonstrated the fan effect. The fan effect is the name given to the phenomenon where participants' recognition times for sentences about a particular concept increase as more information about the concept is acquired (see Anderson, 2000). As a recognition task is employed, it is episodic memory that is tested and, indeed, the fan effect is observed in tests of episodic memory but not in tests of semantic memory (Shoben *et al.*, 1978). McKoon *et al.* (1986) point out that although these observations could be presented as support for a distinction between episodic and semantic memory systems, the theoretical account of these systems provides no basis for predicting the fan effect in episodic rather than semantic memory tests. Indeed, the completely opposite result (i.e. detecting the fan effect in semantic, but not in episodic memory tests) also could be presented as support for the distinction between semantic and episodic memory systems. A model cannot be specified sufficiently when both of two contradictory patterns of effects can be interpreted as supporting the model.

Rather than develop the theory underlying the proposed multiple memory systems, so that unambiguous theoretical predictions can be made, the tendency has been simply to categorize memory systems and subsystems by identifying them with particular types of memory performance. However, another criticism of multiple memory systems is the lack of agreement, even among multiple memory systems proponents, on the criteria by which systems and subsystems are distinguished and classified. For example, Johnson and Chalfonte (1994) consider episodic and semantic memory to be two subsystems rather than two separate systems. Yet another criticism is that a lack of agreement on the criteria by which systems are distinguished and classified may lead to a spurious proliferation of systems (e.g. Roediger *et al.*, 1999).

Frequently, neuroimaging techniques are used to identify the brain regions associated with performance on these different tasks and memory tests. These brain regions have been interpreted, somewhat simply, as the neuroanatomical sites of the particular memory systems underlying the different tasks and tests. Recently, however, there has been an increase in the application of more sophisticated neuroanatomical network analysis approaches. These examine the interactions between different memory 'systems' underlying performance on different tasks and memory tests (e.g. Nyberg and Cabeza, 2001). As discussed in Section 5.2.2, interactions between systems raise interesting questions about what constitutes a system.

Neuropsychological data obtained from the study of amnesic patients (see Box 6.4) also have been presented to support the distinction between episodic and semantic memory. Tulving (e.g. Tulving, 1983) argues that the amnesic syndrome is due to a severe deficit in episodic memory combined with an intact semantic memory. The retention of amnesics' intellect and language skills is strong evidence that a substantial part of their semantic memory operates normally. However, the apparently normal operation of semantic memory appears to arise from the use of semantic information acquired prior to the amnesic trauma. Gabrieli *et al.* (1988) noted that HM (see Box 6.4) continued to use many of the verbal expressions common at the time of his operation in the 1950s, and was only mildly successful in explaining words and phrases that had come into use since then. Even after considerable practice learning the meaning of ten unfamiliar words, HM was exceedingly poor at matching the words to their definitions. Grossman (1987) reported similar problems in amnesic patients suffering from Korsakoff syndrome (in which patients have damage to their brains in similar areas to HM), while Cermak and O'Connor (1983) describe how an amnesic patient, who had been a laser expert, was able to explain new developments in laser technology after reading a recent article. However, a little later, he could not remember anything of what he had read and could not provide answers to questions based on what he had read. Contrary to Tulving and Schacter's claims, therefore, the amnesic syndrome cannot be attributed to a severe deficit in just episodic memory. As deficits are observed across both semantic and episodic memory tasks, the nature of the amnesic syndrome does not support a distinction between independent episodic and semantic memory systems.

6.4   **Research study**

The amnesic syndrome

Milner (1966) described the case of HM. In 1953, when he was 27, HM underwent brain surgery in an attempt to treat intractable epilepsy. The aim was to remove those parts of his brain considered to be the focus of the epileptic seizures. The operation was a success in that subsequently the epilepsy could be controlled by drugs, but a tragic and unforeseen result of the operation was that HM became profoundly amnesic. The removal of the anterior two-thirds of the hippocampus from both sides of the brain (bilaterally) is thought to have been responsible for his amnesia (e.g. Squire, 1987). Although HM retained his memory for events occurring up to a short time before the operation, he seemed to have lost most of his ability to form new memories. HM stayed with his parents for some time after the operation. However, as HM's memory problems make it impossible for him to live without supervision, he has lived in a nursing home since 1980. HM's father died in 1967 and his mother died ten years later. Yet, six years after moving to the nursing home, HM thought he still lived with his mother and was unsure if his father was alive (Parkin, 1993). HM can read the same book or magazine repeatedly without any recollection of having done so before and, typically, after spending all morning with psychologists doing various tests, he cannot remember the testing session, nor recognize the psychologists when they return in the afternoon.

As even this brief account might suggest, despite his substantial memory impairment, and in common with other amnesics, HM is able to interact and converse quite normally. He also retains a normal immediate memory span and demonstrates memory for a variety of perceptual and motor tasks, although he reports no memory of the learning episodes.

The amnesic syndrome seems to manifest whenever there is bilateral hippocampal damage. Although there may be a variety of different reasons for such damage, Korsakoff syndrome provides the largest group. Korsakoff syndrome is caused by a thiamine deficiency, often associated with chronic alcoholism, which leads to damage to parts of the brain, including the hippocampus.

As we have seen, a distinction between episodic and semantic memory is a very useful heuristic for distinguishing between types of memory task and research areas, but it is unlikely that Tulving's description of separate episodic and semantic memory systems is correct. A simpler conception is that semantic memory is an abstraction of episodic experience. Common aspects of episodes are, by definition, experienced repeatedly. In contrast, there is an inconsistent association between the common aspects of the episodes and the various contexts in which they occur. As a result, the common aspects of the episodes will be well learned and will be able to be retrieved easily and speedily, while the associated contexts, without the benefit of such repetition, will become inaccessible or will fade from memory (e.g. Baddeley, 2002; Hintzman, 1986). An account almost identical to this, based on connectionist memory research, has been presented by McClelland *et al.* (1995).

3.2   Declarative and procedural memory

One influential systems account of the amnesic syndrome was presented by Squire (e.g. Cohen and Squire, 1980). Squire proposes two separate LTM systems: a *declarative* system and a *procedural* system (see Figure 6.4). The declarative–procedural distinction was made with respect to knowledge by the philosopher Ryle (1949) and is much used in cognitive science (e.g. Winograd, 1975).

Declarative knowledge corresponds to 'knowing that'. Responses to semantic and episodic memory tasks typically provide declarative information, such as '(I know that) the capital of Scotland is Edinburgh', or '(I know that) I have seen that picture before'. Cohen (1984) described declarative knowledge as being represented in a system '... in which information is ... first processed or encoded, then stored in some explicitly accessible form for later use, and then ultimately retrieved upon demand'.

Procedural knowledge corresponds to 'knowing how'. For example, the type of information underlying the ability to ride a bicycle is procedural knowledge. Cohen (1984) describes procedural knowledge as being involved when 'experience serves to influence the organization of processes that guide performance without access to the knowledge that underlies the performance'. One way to access this information is to observe performance of a procedure that employs the information: try riding a bike and observe what you do and when, and consider why you do it.

It has been known for some time that amnesics are able to exhibit normal or close to normal learning on a variety of different tasks. For example, the time HM takes to complete a jigsaw puzzle declines with practice. Squire organizes the tasks on which amnesics demonstrate learning under the headings of skills and habits, priming, simple classical conditioning and non-associative learning (see Figure 6.4). Although amnesics' performance on these sorts of tasks demonstrates that learning occurs, typically amnesics cannot remember having carried out any of the tasks before.

According to Squire, it is a failure of the declarative memory system that produces the deficits observed in amnesic memory performance (for example, the

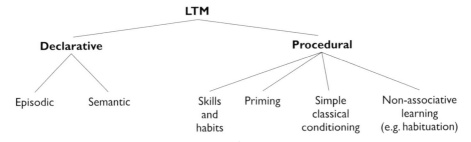

Figure 6.4   Squire's LTM distinctions and their relation to LTM tasks. Declarative memory involves conscious remembrance of events and facts. Procedural memory encompasses a variety of different abilities where experience alters behaviour without there being conscious access to the memory content

Source: adapted from Squire, 1992

inability to remember having practised the task), while the continued operation of the procedural memory system explains the learning amnesics are able to exhibit. However, procedural memory is considered to be 'a heterogeneous collection of separate abilities that can be additionally dissociated from each other' (Squire *et al.*, 1993). A number of different processes or memory systems seem necessary to serve the variety of different tasks labelled as examples of procedural memory. Achieving an understanding of the different components underlying procedural memory is an important contemporary goal (Baddeley, 1997).

Summary of Section 3

- Non-active memory representations are held in a memory store.
- The memory systems perspective regards memory storage and processing as occurring within a system that is localized within the brain.
- The multiple memory systems perspective advocates a large number of memory systems and subsystems, including episodic and semantic memory.
- Evidence from normal participants and amnesics, as well as theoretical concerns, argues against the multiple memory systems perspective, particularly regarding episodic and semantic memory.
- Semantic memory may develop from abstracted episodic memory information.
- The less elaborate distinction between procedural and declarative memory systems may provide a more accurate account of long-term memory.
- It is likely that procedural memory fractionates into a number of different memory systems.

4 Retrieval

Retrieval is the label given to the way in which information held in memory is made available for use. Retrieval involves finding, activating and sometimes further processing pertinent memory representations.

4.1 Encoding specificity and transfer appropriate processing

The notions of **encoding specificity** (e.g. Tulving, 1983) and **transfer appropriate processing** (e.g. Bransford *et al.*, 1979) continue to influence research and accounts of memory retrieval. The encoding specificity hypothesis was introduced by Tulving and Osler (1968) in relation to a study of the role of cues in memory retrieval. They presented participants with target words written in capitals. Also presented with each target word were zero, one or two weakly associated words written in lower case (for example, MUTTON, fat, leg; CITY, dirty, village). Participants were told that the words in lower case might help them remember the capitalized target words and to try and think about how the lower-case words were related to the target words. Tulving and Osler found a single weak associate aided recall of the target word, provided the weak associate had been presented at learning. Neither one nor two weak associates aided recall if they had not been presented at learning – recall was not assisted by the provision of these cues at test alone. Tulving and Osler concluded that specific retrieval cues facilitate recall only if information about them and their relation to the target item is stored along with the target item. Successful retrieval of the target item increases with the overlap between the information stored in memory and the information employed at retrieval (Tulving, 1979).

The transfer appropriate processing (TAP) account also emphasizes the overlap between encoding and retrieval. Morris *et al.* (1977) presented TAP as an adjunct to Craik and Lockhart's (1972) levels of processing framework to give proper emphasis to retrieval processing, which they believed had been neglected. Therefore, TAP focuses on the overlap between the *processes* engaged at encoding and the *processes* engaged at retrieval. Specifically, it predicts that the best memory performance will be observed when the processes engaged at encoding transfer appropriately to retrieval (see Box 6.5).

Although encoding specificity deals with information and TAP deals with processing, these distinctions may be different sides of the same coin. Both accounts emphasize the relationship between encoding and retrieval, and the benefit to memory performance when encoding conditions are recapitulated at retrieval. As information at encoding and at retrieval is manifest within the cognitive system by psychological processes, it may be more a matter of expression rather than psychological substance whether information or processes are recapitulated.

6.5   Research study

An experimental test of transfer appropriate processing

Morris *et al.* (1977) conducted an experiment to test the TAP hypothesis. All participants were presented with a list of words, such as CAT and TABLE. For half of the participants the orienting questions were of the form, Does the word rhyme with hat? Does the word rhyme with label? (phonetic processing), while the other participants received questions of the form, Is it an animal? Do you sit at it? (semantic processing). The next day, half of the participants in the phonetic orienting condition were given a standard, semantically oriented recognition test (for example, identify which of the following words were presented previously: CAT, ROAD, POUND, TABLE, BALL and so on), while the other half were shown another set of words and asked to identify (that is, recognize) which words rhymed with the words presented the day before (for example, identify which of the following words rhyme with those presented previously: FIRE, MAT, STAIR, CABLE, PAPER, etc.). Similarly, half of the semantic orienting condition participants received a standard, semantically oriented recognition test, while the others received the rhyme test. Figure 6.5 below presents the mean proportion of correctly recognized words as a function of orienting and recognition tasks.

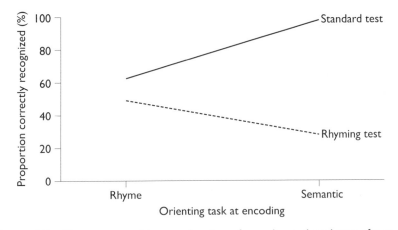

Figure 6.5   Correct recognition as a function of encoding task and type of test

When rhyme/phonetic processing was employed at encoding and test, memory performance was better than when semantic processing was employed at encoding but rhyme/phonetic processing was employed at test. Likewise, when semantic processing was employed at encoding and test, memory performance was better than when rhyme/phonetic processing was employed at encoding and semantic processing was employed at test. As TAP predicts, memory performance was better when there was a match between the processes engaged at encoding and the processes engaged at retrieval.

Summary of Section 4

- Retrieval involves finding, activating and sometimes further processing pertinent memory representations.
- Both encoding specificity and TAP emphasize the relationship between encoding and retrieval, such that performance is enhanced by increasing similarity of information (encoding specificity) or processing (TAP).

5   Implicit memory

Free recall, cued recall and recognition memory tests are explicit tests of memory. When any of these techniques are employed, it is clear to participants that their memory is being tested – it is plain that memory must be used to do the task. However, it is also possible to test participants' memory without them appreciating that their memory is being used. When this is done, the memory test is said to be implicit. This terminology follows Roediger *et al.* (1992), who define the learning task as either incidental or intentional and the memory test as either explicit or implicit. Unfortunately, however, the terms applied in this research area have been varied and mixed. For example, Schacter and Tulving (1994) refer to both task and test as being explicit or implicit, Jacoby (1984) refers to the test as being incidental or intentional, while both Johnson and Hasher (1987) and Richardson-Klavehn and Bjork (1988) refer to the test as being direct or indirect and label the type of memory taxed as being explicit or implicit. Just to make things a little more complicated, there is also an area of research labelled *implicit learning*. This is concerned with the way in which rule-governed relations between stimulus items are learned without conscious awareness. Although it seems that work in implicit learning should have consequence for implicit memory, these two research areas remain quite separate. In the following sections, only implicit memory research will be considered and the terminology of Roediger *et al.* (1992) will be employed.

5.1   Perceptual and conceptual implicit memory

Roediger and McDermott (1993) list a variety of tests used to investigate *perceptual* and *conceptual* incidental memory. The word-fragment task employed in the Tulving *et al.* (1982) study (see Box 6.6) is an example of a perceptual implicit memory test. Perceptual (or data-driven) implicit tests require participants to resolve perceptually impoverished displays (McDermott and Roediger, 1996). A display is perceptually impoverished if it presents a version of the stimulus that is not as easily identified as is usual, due to the relatively poor quality of the stimulus, the short duration of the stimulus presentation or the stimulus presented being incomplete. To identify the stimulus, it is assumed that processes involving the analysis of perceptual or surface-level features are engaged, although other representations needed for stimulus identification also may be involved (Mulligan, 1998). In addition to word-fragment completion, other tests of perceptual implicit memory include: word-stem completion, where a whole word has to be completed from only the first few letters (e.g. Graf *et al.*, 1984); word (perceptual) identification, where participants have to identify words presented very swiftly (for example, for 35 milliseconds; Jacoby and Dallas, 1981); anagram solution (e.g. Srinivas and Roediger, 1990); and lexical decision (e.g. Duchek and Neely, 1989). In contrast, conceptual implicit tests require participants to employ their semantic knowledge to answer questions or provide responses to a cue (McDermott and Roediger, 1996) and so they are assumed to engage processes that involve the analysis of semantic information (Mulligan, 1998). Although less research has been carried out on conceptual implicit memory, a number of tests have been developed. They include word association (Shimamura and Squire, 1984) and category instance generation – where participants have to generate examples of a particular category (e.g. Srinivas and Roediger, 1990) – and answering general knowledge questions (Blaxton, 1989). Irrespective of whether the tests are perceptual or conceptual, implicit memory is demonstrated when better performance occurs with recently presented items compared with items not presented recently.

6.6   **Research study**

Empirical evidence of implicit memory

Tulving et al. (1982) conducted an experiment in which participants were asked to try to learn a list of 96 words. One hour later, the participants were asked to carry out a recognition test that used 24 of the presented words (targets) and 24 similar words that had not been presented before (distractors), and a word-fragment completion test, where 24 word fragments were based on another set of 24 presented words and 24 word fragments were based on words not presented before. (Word-fragment completion involves the presentation of real words with certain letters removed. For example, the word fragment F_ O _ _ A _ L might be presented and participants would complete the fragment by replacing the empty slots with O, T, B and L to provide the real word, FOOTBALL. In this study, each word fragment had only one real word solution. For word fragments based on presented words, the presented words were the only real word solutions.) Seven days later, participants received recognition and word-fragment completion tests, as described above, for the remaining 48 words presented originally.

Participants were expected to carry out the word-fragment task without realizing that half of the solutions to the word fragments are words that they had been presented with before. On this basis, it is assumed that the word-fragment task is an implicit test of memory. The interesting measure for the word-fragment test is how many word fragments were completed correctly when the corresponding full word had been presented previously compared with the number of correct completions when a corresponding full word had not been presented previously. Tulving et al. found more word fragments were completed when the corresponding full word had been presented previously and labelled this a word repetition priming effect. Figure 6.6 presents the probability of correct response as a function of type of test (word fragment or recognition) after one hour and after 7 days.

→

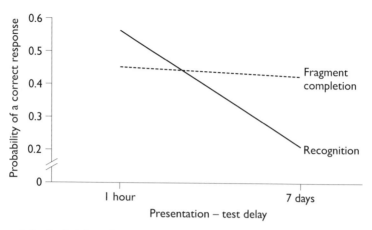

Figure 6.6 Probability of a correct response as a function of the presentation–test delay and type of test

While explicit memory performance on the recognition test declined substantially between the test that occurred one hour after and the test that occurred 7 days after the stimulus presentation, there was no significant decline in implicit memory performance between the word-fragment completion tests at one hour and at 7 days after stimulus presentation.

The word-fragment priming effect could occur because participants realize the words shown originally also complete the word fragments. Participants then might try to recall words and try to match them to the word fragments, converting the implicit test into an explicit test. However, if this occurred, then performance on the word-fragment completion test after 7 days should have declined in line with the explicit recognition test performance.

5.2 Accounts of implicit memory

The distinction between implicit and explicit memory tasks provides a *description* of a person's psychological experience of memory use as different tasks are done (Schacter, 1987). It does not provide an *explanation* of the different effects observed with perceptual implicit memory tests, conceptual implicit memory tests and explicit memory tests. So far, most research has focused on transfer appropriate processing or memory systems accounts to explain these phenomena. These accounts will be outlined and considered in turn, but it soon will be appreciated that neither of these accounts is able to accommodate all of the research findings. Nevertheless, as research continues it is important to know the strengths and weaknesses of previous accounts, so new theoretical formulations may retain the former and avoid the latter.

5.2.1 TAP account

Roediger and associates (e.g. Roediger *et al.*, 1989) have been the strongest advocates for applying Morris *et al.*'s (1977) TAP account to explain the differences in performance on implicit and explicit memory tests. According to Roediger and associates, the important distinction is not between implicit and explicit retrieval from different memory stores, but the match between the type of (perceptual or conceptual) processing engaged when stimuli are tested. Roediger and associates argued that in most experiments on implicit memory, the processing required at memory test often was confounded with the implicit–explicit memory test distinction. TAP predicts that perceptual implicit tests will benefit most from encoding that engaged similar perceptual processes. Likewise, performance on conceptual implicit memory tests will benefit from encoding that engaged similar conceptual processes. Therefore, TAP predictions regarding performance on conceptual implicit memory tests are identical to TAP predictions for explicit memory tests. Indeed, Roediger and Blaxton (1987) state that performance on all implicit conceptual tests should match that observed with free recall, as free recall is the definitive conceptual test. In free recall, no retrieval cues are provided, so participants must rely exclusively on top-down conceptual processing.

However, there are research findings at odds with the TAP account. For example, Hunt *et al.* (1990) noted that orthographic distinctiveness (a perceptual factor) affected both (perceptual) implicit memory test performance and free recall. McDermott and Roediger (1996) also report that while presenting words that were conceptually related to each target word (conceptual repetition) enhanced the free recall of the target words, it did not enhance performance in the category exemplar generation test. Similarly, conceptual repetition by virtue of a picture followed by a corresponding word (or vice versa) also enhanced free recall, but again had no effect on priming in the category exemplar generation test. McDermott and Roediger did obtain enhanced priming in the category exemplar generation test after verbal conceptual repetition when participants were given relational processing instructions. However, the difference between participants' perfor- mance on the implicit conceptual memory test (category exemplar generation) and on the explicit memory test (free recall) contradicts the TAP prediction of equivalent (conceptual processing-based) memory performance. Therefore, TAP is able to give a good account of much, but not all, of the implicit and explicit memory test data.

In an attempt to deal with these problems, Roediger and associates modified the TAP account and relabelled it *components of processing* (e.g. Roediger *et al.*, 1999). Essentially, this view considers performance on different memory tests to involve different sets of processes. The sets of processes employed by different memory tests may share some processes (i.e. component processes), but different processing components will be employed in any two tests that dissociate. Roediger's TAP account of implicit memory has been very influential in focusing research on the nature of the processing underlying encoding at learning and retrieval when memory is tested. However, the TAP account has been criticized for being circular. For example, the TAP account states that repetition priming occurs when there is appropriate transfer of processing, but, unfortunately, the mark of appropriate transfer of processing is considered to be repetition priming. (As mentioned in Section 2.1, Baddeley (1978) criticized levels of processing for a similar circularity of account.) Greater detail on the mechanisms operating in these circumstances is necessary to avoid this circularity and, indeed, this is one of the requirements placed on the components of processing account by McDermott and Roediger (1996).

5.2.2 Memory systems accounts

Both Tulving and associates' multiple memory systems perspective and Squire's declarative and procedural memory systems have been applied to give account of the differences observed between explicit and implicit memory test performance. In both cases, the differences in explicit and implicit memory test performance are regarded as being due to the tests taxing different memory systems (see Table 6.3 and Figure 6.4). Squire simply attributes performance on explicit memory tasks to the declarative memory system and performance on implicit memory tasks to the procedural memory system. As procedural memory is very likely to fractionate into a number of different memory systems, there is greater similarity between Squire's account and the multiple memory systems perspective than may appear at first glance. The multiple memory systems perspective attributes performance on perceptual implicit memory tasks such as word priming and fragment completion to the visual word form subsystem of the perceptual representation system, while picture priming is attributed to the structural description subsystem of the perceptual representation system (e.g. Schacter *et al.*, 2001). Also within this perspective, Gabrieli (1999) attributes performance on conceptual implicit memory tests to yet another system – the conceptual representation system (this compares with the perceptual representation system; see Table 6.3). Schacter (1990) attempted to shed some light on the operation of the perceptual representation system by suggesting that it operates according to TAP principles.

  In Section 3.1, one of the criticisms of the multiple memory systems perspective was that a lack of agreement on the criteria by which systems are distinguished and classified may lead to a spurious proliferation of systems. In fact, as more and more memory systems are postulated, so the difference between a processing perspective and the multiple memory systems perspective diminishes. A 'system' has to be more than just the brain structures that carry out the cognitive operations for a specific task. As, ultimately, all cognitive processes have a neural basis, simply defining a memory system as the brain structures that carry out the cognitive operations for a specific task goes no further than stating where in the brain these processes run. Identifying where a process runs does not distinguish between the processing perspective and the multiple memory systems perspective (e.g. Crowder, 1993). Similarly, as neuroanatomical network analysis reveals that the brain structures involved in memory are highly interactive, rather than being stand-alone systems (e.g. Nyberg and Cabeza, 2001), so the difference between the multiple memory systems and processing perspectives diminishes.

5.3 Implicit memory and amnesia

While amnesics perform poorly on explicit memory tests, their performance on implicit memory tests is similar to that of controls. For example, Graf *et al.* (1984) presented lists of words to amnesics and controls who had to judge how much they liked each word. Later, participants received four memory tests: three explicit (free recall, cued recall, recognition) and one implicit (word-stem completion). As expected, amnesics performed much more poorly on the explicit memory tests than controls, but they exhibited as much implicit memory as controls on the word-stem completion test.

Vaidya *et al.* (1995) found no difference between amnesics and controls in either perceptual implicit memory performance (word-fragment completion) or conceptual implicit memory (word association). However, amnesics' performance on explicit perceptual and conceptual memory tests was as poor as expected. Similar findings were reported by Cermak *et al.* (1995).

These results present problems for the TAP account of implicit memory. According to the TAP account, the reason amnesics are able to perform implicit memory tests on a par with normal controls is because they retain their perceptual processing capability. Therefore, amnesics' poor memory performance should be due to impaired conceptual processing. However, the ability of amnesics to perform conceptual implicit memory tests on a par with normal controls contradicts this account. Moreover, the fact that amnesics exhibited their usual poor memory performance on explicit perceptual and conceptual memory tests indicates that the distinction between implicit and explicit memory tests is more important than the distinction between perceptual and conceptual processing.

Cermak *et al.* (1995) explained their findings in terms of dual memory processes, such as underlie Mandler's account of recognition outlined earlier. According to Cermak *et al.*, amnesics will exhibit normal memory performance whenever the memory task can be accomplished on the basis of item familiarity-processing fluency. Usually, implicit memory tasks can be accomplished on this basis, whereas explicit tasks usually require more context-based discriminations. Likewise, perceptual tasks often can be accomplished on the basis of item familiarity, while conceptual tasks typically require context-based discrimination processing. However, both familiarity and context-based processing may be applied to any task. Of course, the exact nature of the task will determine how successfully it can be accomplished using familiarity or context-based processing. It is the varying degrees of success in applying familiarity or context-based processing to a task that give rise to the differences between some implicit and explicit memory tasks, and between some perceptual and conceptual processing tasks.

Summary of Section 5

- An explicit memory task taxes memory with participants' awareness, but an implicit memory task taxes memory without participants' awareness.
- Free recall, cued recall and recognition are standard explicit memory tasks.
- There are conceptual and perceptual implicit memory tasks.
- Perceptual implicit memory tasks include word-fragment completion, word-stem completion, word identification, anagram solution and lexical decision.

- Conceptual implicit tests include word association, category instance generation and answering general knowledge questions.
- Amnesics exhibit normal memory performance on implicit tasks.
- The multiple memory systems perspective and Squire's declarative and procedural memory systems attribute the differences between explicit and implicit memory test performance to these tasks being served primarily by different memory systems.
- The TAP account attributes the differences between explicit and implicit memory test performance to perceptual implicit tests benefiting most from perceptual encoding at presentation, while conceptual implicit memory tests and standard explicit memory tests benefit from conceptual encoding at presentation.
- Cermak et al. suggest implicit memory tasks can be accomplished on the basis of item familiarity/processing fluency, whereas explicit tasks usually require more context-based discriminations.

6   Jacoby's process-dissociation framework

Although some tasks and memory tests are regarded as providing good measures of certain encoding and retrieval processes, it would be wrong to think they provide pure measures of these processes. Irrespective of the task and memory test employed, it is likely that the specific memory processes under investigation will be contaminated to some extent by the operation of other memory processes. This point is especially relevant with respect to implicit and explicit memory performance.

It was mentioned in Box 6.6 that participants might convert the implicit test into an explicit test if they realized that many of the word fragments (or word stems or anagrams) corresponded with words shown earlier. One approach to this issue was presented by Jacoby (e.g. Jacoby, 1991), who assumes that implicit memory performance is based primarily on automatic (familiarity-based) processes (see the discussion of Mandler's dual-process model in Section 2.2.1), while explicit memory depends most on conscious recollective memory processes. Box 6.7 outlines Jacoby's process-dissociation procedure and also shows how the measures of automatic and recollective processes derived from the procedure not only confirm theoretical expectations, but also provide some insight into the mechanisms underlying memory effects.

Although Jacoby's inventive approach and its developments (e.g. Yonelinas, 2002) offer new and attractive methods for understanding and investigating memory, the validity of Jacoby's assumption that recollective and automatic processes are independent has provoked considerable debate and research. Joordens and Merikle (1993) claim that only automatic processes retrieve items from memory. Recollective processes only operate to acquire further information about these words. As only automatic processes are involved in the retrieval of items from memory, recollective processes do not contribute to memory retrieval *per se*. According to Joordens and Merikle, therefore, with respect to memory retrieval, rather than recollective processes being independent of automatic processes, recollective processes are redundant in relation to automatic processes. Jacoby (e.g. Jacoby *et al.*, 1997) strongly disputes this claim and has provided a description of the conditions necessary for the implementation of a tenable process-dissociation procedure (Jacoby, 1998). Research continues on this and other issues, such as whether all automatic familiarity-based retrieval is unconscious and whether all controlled recollective retrieval is conscious (e.g. Gardiner *et al.*, 1998).

6.7   **Research study**

Process-dissociation procedure

Jacoby *et al.* (1993) presented words to participants under a full attention condition, where they just read the words, and under a divided attention condition, where they also had to listen to a tape-recorded list of numbers and indicate each time a sequence of three odd numbers was presented. The aim of the divided attention task was to reduce the influence of recollective processes at memory test, but to leave automatic processes unaffected. Later, participants received a word-stem completion memory test where half of the word stems were coloured green and half were red. When presented with a green word stem, participants had to use it as a cue to remember one of the words presented earlier. If they could not remember a word, they were asked to complete the word stem with the first word that came to mind. When presented with a red word stem, participants again were asked to use it as a cue to remember one of the words presented earlier, but they were not to provide this as a response – instead they were to complete the stem to make some other word that came to mind. The green stem task is an inclusion test and the red stem task is an exclusion test (see below). Jacoby *et al.* found that the probabilities of responding with a previously presented word were as follows:

Attention	Probability of responding with a previously presented word	
	Inclusion test	**Exclusion test**
Full	0.61	0.36
Divided	0.46	0.46

On an inclusion test, the probability of responding with a presented word equals the probability of conscious recollection (R), plus the probability that this word is remembered automatically (A) when there is a failure of conscious recollection ($1 - R$). However, remembering the word automatically, *given* a failure of conscious recollection, is a conditional probability that is obtained by multiplying the probability of automatic remembering and the probability of a failure of conscious

$\longrightarrow$

recollection. Therefore, the probability of responding with a presented word on an inclusion test is:

Equation one

Inclusion = $R + A(1 - R)$

On an exclusion test, the probability of providing a presented word equals the probability of remembering automatically when there is a failure of conscious recollection. Therefore, the probability of providing a presented word on an exclusion test is:

Equation two

Exclusion = $A(1 - R)$

Equations one and two may be rewritten to obtain the probabilities of conscious recollection (R) and of remembering automatically (A). That is:

R = Inclusion − Exclusion

$$A = \frac{\text{Exclusion}}{(1 - R)}$$

R and A estimates for the words presented in the second part of the experiment, based on the data presented above, are as follows:

Attention	R	A
Full	0.25	0.47
Divided	0.00	0.46

These estimates are consistent with the view that automatic memory processes are unaffected by changes in the attentional resource available at encoding, whereas recollective processes suffer severely if focused attentional resources are not deployed at encoding. Nevertheless, the calculation of R as zero should be interpreted only as indicating that participants' recollective component may have been insufficient to register under these particular experimental conditions (Baddeley, 1997).

Summary of Section 6

- Jacoby's process-dissociation framework assumes that two independent processes contribute to memory performance: automatic and recollective memory processes.
- Automatic (familiarity-based) processes are assumed to be unconscious.
- Recollective (search-and-retrieval-based) memory processes are assumed to be under conscious control.
- Implicit memory performance is based primarily on automatic processes.
- Explicit memory performance is based primarily on recollective memory processes.

7   Remember and know judgements

Tulving (1985) carried out the first experiment requiring a distinction to be made between items recalled due to *remembering* that the item was presented (you have a conscious recollection of the item appearing in the study) and *knowing* the item was presented (you simply know that the item appeared but you have no conscious recollection of its occurrence). According to Tulving, remembering should reflect retrieval from episodic memory, while knowing should reflect retrieval from semantic memory. In his typical neologistic fashion, Tulving created and applied the label *autonoetic* (self-knowing) to the form of consciousness accompanying retrieval from episodic memory and the label *noetic* (knowing) to the form of consciousness accompanying retrieval from semantic memory (see Box 6.8).

Tulving's (1985) study employed free recall and cued recall, but most other studies of remember and know judgements have focused on recognition for two reasons. First, there was an initial presumption that remember and know judgements were relevant to dual-process accounts of recognition (see Section 2.2). Second, while both recall and recognition tests provide a good proportion of remember judgements, only recognition tests provide a good proportion of know judgements – few know judgements are obtained with recall.

The subjective nature of remember and know judgements should be highlighted. In a memory experiment employing recall, participants provide remember and know judgements only after they have recalled an item. When recognition is employed, a one-step or two-step procedure can be applied. With one-step procedures, participants straight away judge whether they remember, know or were not presented with an item. All items judged as remember or know are deemed to be recognized. With two-step procedures, remember or know judgements are made only after the participant positively recognizes an item. (Know judgements seem to be more accurate when a two-step procedure is used; Eldridge *et al.*, 2002.) As the experimenter knows which words have been presented, an objective decision can be made about the accuracy of the recalled or recognized item. However, remember and know judgements cannot be assessed objectively, as they are based on the extent to which participants *believe* their introspections concord with the remember and know descriptions provided. Remember and know judgements are employed because they provide information on states of awareness that it seems impossible to obtain from more conventional, objective measures. For example, experimental groups may obtain identical recognition scores, but they may differ in terms of their proportions of remember and know judgements (Gardiner and Richardson-Klavehn, 2001). To improve the accuracy of remember and know judgements, Gardiner (e.g. Gardiner *et al.*, 1998) suggests that participants should be provided with the opportunity to indicate that the recalled or recognized item was a guess. Without this facility, guesses will be placed in the know category by default, so affecting the validity of the remember and know procedure.

Empirical evidence of a distinction between remembering and knowing

Tulving (1985) reported two experiments. In experiment 1, participants studied pairs of words. The first word of the pair specified a category and this was followed by an exemplar of that category (for example, *fruit* – PEAR). Three memory tests then were presented: free recall of each exemplar (in any order), cued recall with the category name as the cue, and cued recall with the category name and the first letter of the exemplar as the cue. In all tests, participants had to judge whether their responses were accompanied by a feeling of *remembering* or a feeling of *knowing*. Item recall was scored in a particular fashion: all of the items free-recalled were scored, but with the category name cued recall test, only items not free-recalled were scored, and with the category name and first letter cued recall test, only items not free-recalled nor recalled on the basis of category name cues were scored.

Tulving reasoned that items free-recalled had the richest representation in episodic memory as they had been recalled without any cues. Items recalled only on the basis of category name cueing had a less rich representation in episodic memory because they required cueing. Items recalled only on the basis of category name and first letter cueing had the poorest representation in episodic memory because they required most cueing. As feelings of remembering (indicated by remember judgements) arise as a consequence of the representational richness of episodic memory, remember judgements should be most prevalent with free recall items, less prevalent with category name cued recall items and least prevalent with category name plus first exemplar letter cued recall items. Data analysis revealed that the probability of a recalled item receiving a remember judgement was a function of the type of memory test, just as Tulving had predicted.

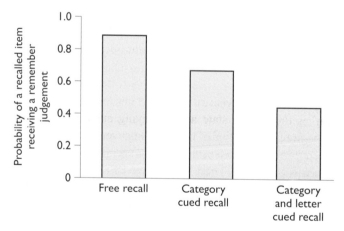

Figure 6.7 Probability of a recalled item receiving a remember judgement as a function of the recall test

In experiment 2, Tulving presented participants with the same tasks, but while testing on half of the stimulus items occurred immediately, the other stimulus items were tested after eight days. Compared with immediate testing, the probability of a remember judgement decreased after an eight day presentation–test gap. All of these findings are consistent with Tulving's view that remember judgements reflect the rich information available in episodic memory, which diminishes over longer retention intervals.

Gardiner (2002) identifies four types of variable in terms of their effect on remember and know judgements. There are variables that increase the number of remember responses, but do not affect know responses (for example, levels of processing; Gardiner, 1988). There are variables that increase know responses, but do not affect remember responses (for example, suppression of focal attention during stimulus presentation prior to test; Mantyla and Raudsepp, 1996). There are variables that increase know responses and decrease remember responses (non-word versus word presentation; Gardiner and Java, 1990). Finally, there are variables that have similar effects on remember and know responses (for example, long and short response deadlines; Gardiner *et al.*, 1998). Gardiner claims that as some variables exert similar effects on remember and know responses, while other variables exert different effects on remember and know responses, distinct memory processes must underlie know and remember responses.

7.1   Do remember and know judgements reflect different response criteria?

Donaldson (1996) argued that remember and know judgements simply reflect decisions based on different response criteria. Rather than reflecting qualitatively different memory processes, Donaldson's detection theory account attributes remember and know judgements to different criterial points on a single quantitative dimension of memory strength. Gardiner *et al.* (2002) have presented considerable evidence contradicting this account. However, the focus here will be on a different strand of contradictory evidence.

According to Donaldson's detection model, the strongest memories are associated with remember judgements. Yet, as Gardiner and Conway (1999) point out, 'knowing' is the natural state accompanying answers to semantic memory questions – conscious recollection of the encoding event(s) very rarely accompanies the retrieval of information from semantic memory. Does this mean that semantic memory information has less strength than episodic-type information? A good indication of the answer to this question was provided by a large-scale naturalistic study conducted by Conway *et al.* (1997). They examined changes in awareness as psychology knowledge was acquired by undergraduates. Psychology students took a three-alternative multiple choice test (MCT) and six months later, they took the same test again. For each question, the MCT correct answer involved information presented directly in a lecture, while the plausible but incorrect MCT answers involved information also presented in the same lecture. The students had to select one of the MCT answers and then indicate whether they (i) remembered a learning episode where they encountered this information, (ii) just knew that this was the correct answer, that is, they had a strong feeling of knowing but did not remember a learning episode, (iii) neither remembered the learning episode nor knew the answer but felt the chosen answer was more familiar, or (iv) felt they were guessing, for example, choosing the example that looked least unlikely. (The familiarity category was included to separate aspects of the know judgement, but it has no bearing on the results discussed here.) Table 6.4 presents the response probabilities for correct answers over the two tests.

Table 6.4   Response probabilities for correct answers over the two multiple choice tests

Response	Probability of correct answers in test 1	Probability of correct answers in test 2
Remember	.39	.14
Know	.19	.43
Familiar	.25	.26
Guess	.17	.17

Source: Table 1 in Conway et al., 1997

Over the two tests, the proportion of familiar (iii) and guess (iv) judgements remained the same. However, there was an interesting pattern of change for the proportion of remember and know judgements over the two tests. In test 1, remember judgements dominated, with a low proportion of know judgements. However, six months later, in test 2, know judgements dominated, with a low proportion of remember judgements. There is a substantial 'remember to know' shift in the proportion of judgements made about correct answers over the six month gap between tests. This finding applied to all of the students participating in the study, but the shift from remember to know judgements was most pronounced for students who attained the highest grades.

Contrary to Donaldson's detection theory account, these data indicate that know (and not remember) judgements are associated with the stronger type of memory (the information most likely to be remembered). Conway et al. (1997) interpret the 'remember to know' shift as revealing the way in which memories are modified by the loss of detail, so that a more abstract version is retained as conceptual knowledge in semantic memory. These data and their interpretation are consistent with the view that semantic memory is an abstraction of episodic memory regularities and contrast with Tulving's (1984) conception that the episodic memory system is embedded within the semantic memory system (see Section 3.1).

Summary of Section 7

- Remembered items may be given a remember judgement (you have a conscious recollection of the item appearing in the study) or a know judgement (you simply know the item appeared but you have no conscious recollection of its occurrence).

- Remember and know judgements are based on the extent to which participants believe their introspections concord with remember and know descriptions – they are subjective judgements.
- Contrary to Donaldson's detection theory account, know judgements appear to reflect stronger memories than remember judgements.

8 Conclusion

Craik and Lockhart's levels of processing article stimulated a great deal of research on memory encoding processes. This work emphasized that the mental operations carried out on presented material had great consequence for the memorability of this material. However, work by Mandler, Tulving, and Morris, Bransford and Franks demonstrates that good memory performance relies upon the interaction between memory encoding, memory representation and retrieval operations.

Around the same time as Craik and Lockhart's levels of processing article, Tulving provided a description of separate semantic and episodic memory systems, but it was not until the 1980s that memory systems research began to exert a substantial theoretical influence. This influence seems to have arisen as a consequence of a number of somewhat related factors, including a renaissance in connectionist research and developments in cognitive neuroscience, particularly with respect to neuroimaging techniques, and cognitive neuropsychological investigation of abnormal memory as a consequence of brain damage. Tulving and associates' multiple memory systems perspective, particularly the distinction between episodic and semantic memory, was criticized heavily by cognitive psychologists, the majority of whom found greater evidence for Squire's simpler procedural–declarative distinction. The multiple memory systems perspective was more warmly received in the field of neuropsychology. Nevertheless, enthusiasm for the multiple memory systems perspective has waned for a variety of reasons. One reason is the observation that amnesics' performance on tasks that tax new semantic information and new episodic information seems to be affected equally. Another reason is the lack of development of the theoretical accounts of the various multiple memory systems. Yet another reason is the weakening of the conception of distinct memory systems, as a result of the number of memory systems proposed and the substantial system interactions identified by neuroanatomical network analysis.

In recent years, there has been a marked increase in research activity focusing on retrieval operations. Initially, this interest was prompted by two phenomena: implicit memory and remember and know judgements. Research on these topics reveals the benefit of the theoretical constraints imposed by neuropsychological findings. Meanwhile Jacoby and associates' work on the process-dissociation procedure not only provides theoretical insight into these phenomena, but also has introduced new methods to investigate memory. Due to the nature of the phenomena considered, retrieval research has had to confront and accommodate issues of consciousness, as well as the fact that people can modify and change how they retrieve information from memory. Each of these factors has contributed to an overall improvement in theoretical accounts of memory.

An aim of this chapter was to present an overview of research in the psychology of memory that not only reflects these influences and changes, but also demonstrates the exciting advances in understanding that these perspectives have provided. Memory research continues to be one of the most active research areas in psychology, where useful and interesting theoretical and methodological developments are leading to a more accurate appreciation of memory operation.

Now that you have read this chapter you can reinforce and extend your learning by reading an original journal article associated with it, available online from the DD303 website. Remember, these are original journal articles, so the style is different from this textbook, and don't be too concerned if you can't follow every detail.

Further reading

Yonelinas, A.P. (2002) 'Components of episodic memory: the contribution of recollection and familiarity' in Baddeley, A., Conway, M. and Aggleton, J. (eds) *Episodic Memory: New Directions in Research*, Oxford, Oxford University Press.

Tulving, E. (2002) 'Episodic memory and common sense: how far apart?' in Baddeley, A., Conway, M. and Aggleton, J. (eds) *Episodic Memory: New Directions in Research*, Oxford, Oxford University Press.

Baddeley, A. (2002) 'The concept of episodic memory' in Baddeley, A., Conway, M. and Aggleton, J. (eds) *Episodic Memory: New Directions in Research*, Oxford, Oxford University Press.

Yu, J. and Bellezza, F.S. (2000) 'Process dissociation as source monitoring', *Journal of Experimental Psychology: Learning, Memory and Cognition*, vol.26, no.6, pp.1518–33.

References

Anderson, J.R. (1974) 'Retrieval of propositional information from long-term memory', *Cognitive Psychology*, vol.6, pp.451–74.

Anderson, J.R. (2000) *Cognitive Psychology and its Implications*, New York, Worth Publishers.

Anderson, J.R. and Ross, B.H. (1980) 'Evidence against a semantic–episodic distinction', *Journal of Experimental Psychology: Human Learning and Memory*, vol.6, pp.441–65.

Atkinson, R.C. and Shiffrin, R. (1968) 'Human memory: a proposed system and its control processes' in Spence, K. and Spence, J. (eds) *The Psychology of Learning and Motivation Vol.2*, New York, Academic Press.

Baddeley, A.D. (1978) 'The trouble with levels: a re-examination of Craik and Lockhart's framework for memory research', *Psychological Review*, vol.85, pp.139–52.

Baddeley, A.D. (1997) *Human Memory: Theory and Practice* (revised edn), Hove, Psychology Press.

Baddeley, A.D. (2002) 'The concept of episodic memory' in Baddeley, A., Conway, M. and Aggleton, J. (eds) *Episodic Memory: New Directions in Research*, Oxford, Oxford University Press.

Blaxton, T.A. (1989) 'Investigating dissociations among memory measures: support for a transfer-appropriate processing framework', *Journal of Experimental Psychology: Learning, Memory and Cognition*, vol.15, pp.657–68.

Bransford, J.D., Franks, J.J., Morris, C.D. and Stein, B.S. (1979) 'Some general constraints on learning and memory research' in Cermak, L.S. and Craik, F.I.M. (eds) *Levels of Processing in Human Memory*, Hillsdale, NJ, LEA.

Cermak, L.S. and O'Connor, M. (1983) 'The anterograde and retrograde retrieval ability of a patient with amnesia due to encephalitis', *Neuropsychologia*, vol.21, pp.213–34.

Cermak, L.S., Verfaelie, M. and Chase, K.A. (1995) 'Implicit and explicit memory in amnesia: an analysis of data-driven and conceptually driven processes', *Neuropsychology*, vol.9, pp.281–90.

Cohen, N.J. (1984) 'Preserved learning capacity in amnesia: evidence for multiple memory systems' in Squire, L.R. and Butters, N. (eds) *Neuropsychology of Memory*, New York, Guilford Press.

Cohen, N.J. and Squire, L.S. (1980) 'Preserved learning and retention of pattern-analysing skill in amnesia using perceptual learning', *Cortex*, vol.17, pp.273–8.

Collins, A.M. and Quillian, M.R. (1969) 'Retrieval time from semantic memory', *Journal of Verbal Learning and Verbal Behavior*, vol.8, pp.240–7.

Conway, M.A., Gardiner, J.M., Perfect, T.J., Anderson, S.J. and Cohen, G. (1997) 'Changes in memory awareness during learning: the acquisition of knowledge by psychology undergraduates', *Journal of Experimental Psychology: General*, vol.126, pp.393–413.

Craik, F.I.M. and Lockhart, R.S. (1972) 'Levels of processing: a framework for memory research', *Journal of Verbal Learning and Verbal Behavior*, vol.11, pp.671–84.

Craik, F.I.M. and Tulving, E. (1975) 'Depth of processing and the retention of words in episodic memory', *Journal of Experimental Psychology: General*, vol.104, pp.268–94.

Crowder, R. (1993) 'Systems and principles in memory theory: another critique of pure memory' in Collins, A.F., Gathercole, S.E., Conway, M.A. and Morris, P.E. (eds) *Theories of Memory*, Hove, LEA.

Deese, J. (1959) 'Influence of inter-item associative strength upon immediate free recall', *Psychological Reports*, vol.5, pp.305–12.

Donaldson, W. (1996) 'The role of decision processes in remembering and knowing', *Memory and Cognition*, vol.24, pp.523–33.

Duchek, J.M. and Neeley, J.H. (1989) 'A dissociative word frequency × levels of processing interaction in episodic recognition and lexical decision tasks', *Memory and Cognition*, vol.17, pp.148–62.

Eldridge, L.L., Sarfatti, S. and Knowlton, B.J. (2002) 'The effect of testing procedure on remember–know judgements', *Psychonomic Bulletin and Review*, vol.9, pp.139–45.

Elio, R.E. and Reutener, D.B. (1970) 'Colour context as a factor in encoding and as an organization device for retrieval of word lists', *Journal of General Psychology*, vol.99, pp.223–32.

Eysenck, M.W. and Eysenck, M.C. (1980) 'Effects of processing depth, distinctiveness and word frequency on retention', *British Journal of Psychology*, vol.71, pp.263–74.

Gabrieli, J.D.E. (1999) 'The architecture of human memory' in Foster, J.K. and Jelic, M. (eds) *Memory: Systems, Process or Function?*, Oxford, Oxford University Press.

Gabrieli, J.D.E., Cohen, N.J. and Corkin, S. (1988) 'The impaired learning of semantic knowledge following bilateral medial-temporal lobe resection', *Brain*, vol.7, pp.157–77.

Gardiner, J.M. (1988) 'Functional aspects of recollective experience', *Memory and Cognition*, vol.16, pp.309–13.

Gardiner, J.M. (2002) 'Episodic memory and autonoetic consciousness: a first person approach' in Baddeley, A., Conway, M. and Aggleton, J. (eds) *Episodic Memory: New Directions in Research*, Oxford, Oxford University Press.

Gardiner, J.M. and Conway, M.A. (1999) 'Levels of awareness and varieties of experience' in Challis, B.H. and Velichkovsky, B.M. (eds) *Stratification in Cognition and Consciousness*, Amsterdam, John Benjamins Publishing.

Gardiner, J.M. and Java, R.I. (1990) 'Recollective experience in word and nonword recognition', *Memory and Cognition*, vol.18, pp.23–30.

Gardiner, J.M., Ramponi, C. and Richardson-Klavehn, A. (1998) 'Experiences of remembering, knowing and guessing', *Consciousness and Cognition*, vol.7, pp.1–26.

Gardiner, J.M., Ramponi, C. and Richardson-Klavehn, A. (2002) 'Recognition memory and decision processes: a meta-analysis of remember, know and guess responses', *Memory*, vol.10, pp.83–98.

Gardiner, J.M. and Richardson-Klavehn, A. (2001) 'Remembering and knowing' in Tulving, E. and Craik, F.I.M. (eds) *The Oxford Handbook of Memory*, Oxford, Oxford University Press.

Glenberg, A.M., Smith, S.M. and Green, C. (1977) 'Type 1 rehearsal: maintenance and more', *Journal of Verbal Learning and Verbal Behavior*, vol.16, pp.339–52.

Graf, P., Squire, L.R. and Mandler, G. (1984) 'The information that amnesic patients do not forget', *Journal of Experimental Psychology: Learning, Memory and Cognition*, vol.10, pp.164–78.

Grossman, M. (1987) 'Lexical acquisition in alcoholic Korsakoff psychosis', *Cortex*, vol.23, pp.631–44.

Hintzman, D.L. (1986) '"Schema abstraction" in a multiple-trace memory model', *Psychological Review*, vol.93, pp.411–28.

Hunt, R.R. and Einstein, G.O. (1981) 'Relational and item-specific information in memory', *Journal of Verbal Learning and Verbal Behavior*, vol.20, pp.497–514.

Hunt, R.R., Humphrey, N. and Toth, J.P. (1990) 'Perceptual identification, fragment completion and free recall: concepts and data', *Journal of Experimental Psychology: Learning, Memory and Cognition*, vol.16, pp.282–90.

Hunt, R.R. and McDaniel, M.A. (1993) 'The enigma of organization and distinctiveness', *Journal of Memory and Language*, vol.32, pp.421–45.

Jacoby, L.L. (1984) 'Incidental versus intentional retrieval: remembering and awareness as separate issues' in Squire, L.R. and Butters, N. (eds) *Neuropsychology of Memory*, New York, Guilford Press.

Jacoby, L.L. (1991) 'A process dissociation framework: separating automatic from intentional uses of memory', *Journal of Memory and Language*, vol.30, pp.513–41.

Jacoby, L.L. (1998) 'Invariance in automatic influences on memory: toward a user's guide for the process dissociation procedure', *Journal of Experimental Psychology: Learning, Memory and Cognition*, vol.24, pp.3–26.

Jacoby, L.L. and Dallas, M. (1981) 'On the relationship between autobiographical memory and perceptual learning', *Journal of Experimental Psychology: General*, vol.3, pp.306–40.

Jacoby, L.L., Toth, J.P. and Yonelinas, A.P. (1993) 'Separating conscious and unconscious influences of memory: measuring recollection', *Journal of Experimental Psychology: General*, vol.122, pp.139–54.

Jacoby, L.L., Yonelinas, A.P. and Jennings, J.M. (1997) 'The relation between conscious and unconscious (automatic) influences: a declaration of independence' in Cohen, J.D. and Schooler, J.W. (eds) *Scientific Approaches to Consciousness*, Mahwah, NJ, LEA.

James (1890) *The Principles of Psychology*, New York, Henry Holt and Company.

Johnson, M.K. and Chalfonte, B.L. (1994) 'Binding complex memories: the role of reactivation and the hippocampus' in Schacter, D.L. and Tulving, E. (eds) *Memory Systems*, Cambridge, MA, MIT Press.

Johnson, M.K. and Hasher, L. (1987) 'Human learning and memory', *Annual Review of Psychology*, vol.38, pp.631–68.

Joordens, S. and Merikle, P.M. (1993) 'Independence or redundancy? Two models of conscious and unconscious influences', *Journal of Experimental Psychology: General*, vol.122, pp.462–7.

Koffka, K. (1935) *Principles of Gestalt Psychology*, New York, Harcourt Brace.

Lockhart, R.S., Craik, F.I.M. and Jacoby, L.L. (1976) 'Depth of processing, recognition and recall' in Brown, J. (ed.) *Recall and Recognition*, London, Wiley.

Mandler, G. (1979) 'Organization and repetition: organizational principles with special reference to rote learning' in Nilsson, L-G. (ed.) *Perspectives on Memory Research*, Hillsdale, NJ, LEA.

Mandler, G. (1980) 'Recognizing: the judgement of previous occurrence', *Psychological Review*, vol.87, pp.252–71.

Mantyla, T. and Raudsepp, J. (1996) 'Recollective experience following suppression of focal attention', *European Journal of Cognitive Psychology*, vol.8, pp.195–203.

McClelland, J.L., McNaughton, B.L. and O'Reilly, R.C. (1995) 'Why there are complimentary learning systems in the hippocampus and neocortex: insights from the successes and failures of connectionist models of learning and memory', *Psychological Review*, vol.102, pp.419–57.

McDermott, K.B. and Roediger, H.L. (1996) 'Exact and conceptual repetition dissociate conceptual memory tests: problems for transfer appropriate processing theory', *Canadian Journal of Experimental Psychology*, vol.50, pp.57–71.

McKoon, G., Ratcliff, R. and Dell, G.S. (1986) 'A critical examination of the semantic/episodic distinction', *Journal of Experimental Psychology: Learning, Memory and Cognition*, vol.12, pp.295–306.

Milner, B. (1966) 'Amnesia following operation on the temporal lobes' in Whitty, C.W.M. and Zangwill, O.L. (eds) *Amnesia*, London, Butterworths.

Morris, C.D., Bransford, J.D. and Franks, J.J. (1977) 'Levels of processing versus transfer appropriate processing', *Journal of Verbal Learning and Verbal Behavior*, vol.16, pp.519–33.

Mulligan, N.W. (1998) 'The role of attention during encoding in implicit and explicit memory', *Journal of Experimental Psychology: Learning, Memory and Cognition*, vol.24, pp.27–47.

Murdock, B.B. (1967) 'Recent developments in short-term memory', *British Journal of Psychology*, vol.58, pp.421–33.

Neely, J.H. (1989) 'Experimental dissociations and the semantic/episodic memory distinction' in Roediger, H.L. and Craik, F.I.M. (eds) *Varieties of Memory and Consciousness: Essays in Honor of Endel Tulving*, Hillsdale, NJ, LEA.

Nyberg, L. and Cabeza, R. (2001) 'Brain imaging of memory' in Tulving, E. and Craik, F.I.M. (eds) *The Oxford Handbook of Memory*, Oxford, Oxford University Press.

Parkin, A. (1993) *Human Memory*, Oxford, Blackwell.

Pollack, I., Norman, D.A. and Galatner, E. (1964) 'An efficient nonparametric analysis of recognition memory', *Psychonomic Science*, vol.1, pp.327–8.

Richardson-Klavehn, A. and Bjork, R.A. (1988) 'Measures of memory', *Annual Review of Psychology*, vol.39, pp.475–543.

Roediger, H.L. and Blaxton, T.A. (1987) 'Retrieval modes produce dissociations in memory for surface information' in Gorfein, D. and Hoffman, R.R. (eds) *Memory and Cognitive Processes: The Ebbinghaus Centennial Conference*, Hillsdale, NJ, LEA.

Roediger, H.L., Buckner, R.L. and McDermott, K.B. (1999) 'Components of processing' in Foster, J.K. and Jelic, M. (eds) *Memory: Systems, Process or Function?*, Oxford, Oxford University Press.

Roediger, H.L. and McDermott, K.B. (1993) 'Implicit memory in normal human subjects' in Spinnler, H. and Boller, F. (eds) *Handbook of Neuropsychology*, Amsterdam, Elsevier.

Roediger, H.L., Weldon, M.S. and Challis, B.H. (1989) 'Explaining dissociations between implicit and explicit measures of retention: a processing account' in Roediger, H.L. and Craik, F.I.M. (eds) *Varieties of Memory and Consciousness: Essays in Honour of Endel Tulving*, Hillsdale, NJ, LEA.

Roediger, H.L., Weldon, M.S., Stadler, M.L. and Riegler, G.L. (1992) 'Direct comparison of two implicit memory tests: word fragment and word stem completion', *Journal of Experimental Psychology: Learning, Memory and Cognition*, vol.18, pp.1251–69.

Rundus, D. (1977) 'Maintenance rehearsal and single level processing', *Journal of Verbal Learning and Verbal Behaviour*, vol.16, pp.665–81.

Ryle, G. (1949) *The Concept of Mind*, London, Hutchinson.

Schacter, D.L. (1987) 'Implicit memory: history and current status', *Journal of Experimental Psychology: Learning, Memory and Cognition*, vol.13, pp.501–18.

Schacter, D.L. (1990) 'Perceptual representation systems and implicit memory: toward a resolution of the multiple memory systems debate' in Diamond, A. (ed.) *The Development and Neural Bases of Higher Cognitive Functions*, New York, New York Academy of Sciences.

Schacter, D.L. and Tulving, E. (1994) 'What are the memory systems of 1994?' in Schacter, D.L. and Tulving, E. (eds) *Memory Systems*, Cambridge, MA, MIT Press.

Schacter, D.L., Wagner, A.D. and Buckner, R.L. (2001) 'Memory systems of 1999' in Tulving, E. and Craik, F.I.M. (eds) *The Oxford Handbook of Memory*, Oxford, Oxford University Press.

Shimamura, A.P. and Squire, L.R. (1984) 'Paired associate learning and priming effects in amnesia: a neuropsychological approach', *Journal of Experimental Psychology: General*, vol.113, pp.556–70.

Shoben, E.J., Wescourt, K.T. and Smith, E.E. (1978) 'Sentence verification, sentence recognition and the semantic–episodic distinction', *Journal of Experimental Psychology: Human Learning and Memory*, vol.4, pp.304–17.

Squire, L.R. (1987) *Memory and Brain*, New York, Oxford University Press.

Squire, L.R. (1992) 'Declarative and nondeclarative memory: multiple brain systems supporting learning and memory', *Journal of Cognitive Neuroscience*, vol.4, pp.232–43.

Squire, L.R., Knowlton, B. and Musen, G. (1993) 'The structure and organization of memory', *Annual Review of Psychology*, vol.44, pp.453–95.

Srinivas, K. and Roediger, H.L. (1990) 'Classifying implicit memory tests: category association and anagram solution', *Journal of Memory and Language*, vol.29, pp.389–412.

Tulving, E. (1962) 'Subjective organization in free recall of "unrelated" words', *Psychological Review*, vol.69, pp.344–54.

Tulving, E. (1979) 'Relation between encoding specificity and levels of processing' in Cermak, L.S. and Craik, F.I.M. (eds) *Levels of Processing in Human Memory*, Hillsdale, NJ, LEA.

Tulving, E. (1983) *Elements of Episodic Memory*, Oxford, Clarendon Press.

Tulving, E. (1984) 'Précis of elements of episodic memory', *Behavioral and Brain Sciences*, vol.7, pp.223–68.

Tulving, E. (1985) 'Memory and consciousness', *Canadian Psychology*, vol.26, pp.1–12.

Tulving, E. and Osler, S. (1968) 'Effectiveness of retrieval cues in memory for words', *Journal of Experimental Psychology*, vol.77, pp.593–601.

Tulving, E. and Schacter, D.L. (1990) 'Priming and human memory systems', *Science*, vol.247, pp.301–6.

Tulving, E., Schacter, D.L. and Stark, H.A. (1982) 'Priming effects in word-fragment completion are independent of recognition memory', *Journal of Experimental Psychology: Learning, Memory and Cognition*, vol.8, pp.336–42.

Vaidya, C.J., Gabrieli, J.D.E., Keane, M.M. and Monti, L.A. (1995) 'Perceptual and conceptual memory processes in global amnesia', *Neuropsychology*, vol.10, pp.529–37.

Wheeler, M.A., Stuss, D.T. and Tulving, E. (1997) 'Toward a theory of episodic memory: the frontal lobes and autonoetic consciousness', *Psychological Bulletin*, vol.121, pp.331–54.

Winograd, T. (1975) 'Frame representations and the declarative procedural controversy' in Bobrow, D. and Collins, A. (eds) *Representation and Understanding: Studies in Cognitive Science*, New York, Academic Press.

Yonelinas, A.P. (2002) 'Components of episodic memory: the contribution of recollection and familiarity' in Baddeley, A., Conway, M. and Aggleton, J. (eds) *Episodic Memory: New Directions in Research*, Oxford, Oxford University Press.

Autobiographical memory and the working self

Chapter 7

Martin A. Conway and Emily A. Holmes

1   What are autobiographical memories?

Consider the following memories:

1   A memory freely recalled by a 54-year-old recalling memories from any point in his life:

> I remember a bright sunny morning walking down a hill near our house. I had on a red jacket, red shirt, blue jeans, and brown suede boots. I was seventeen. I was going into town and I felt great ... it was a feeling of being sort of utterly calm, utterly well, a feeling of expectancy: interesting things were about to happen. It was a feeling I don't think I have had in such a 'pure' form since.
>
> *(Taken from an unpublished study by Martin A. Conway)*

2   A response made by a person asked to recall a memory to the (cue) word 'ship':

> We were going on holiday to France. I remember that we stayed at a boarding house in Dover and went down to the ferry very early the following morning. My brother and I were wildly excited it was the first time we had been abroad and the first time we had been on a ship of any sorts. I have a vivid memory of looking back at the White Cliffs as the boat pulled out of the harbour – they seemed immensely tall.
>
> *(Conway, 1996)*

3   A memory recalled when reading about 'flashbulb' memories – vivid memories of one's personal circumstances when learning an item of news (Brown and Kulik, 1977):

> My own memory for the declaration of the Second World War, from September 1939, occurred when I was aged 6 years and 6 months. I have a clear image of my father standing on the rockery of the front garden of our house waving a bamboo garden stake like a pendulum in time with the clock chimes heard on the radio which heralded the announcement. More hazily, I have an impression that neighbours were also out in the adjoining

gardens listening to the radio and, although my father was fooling around, the feeling of the memory is one of deep foreboding and anxiety.

(Gillian Cohen, personal communication, 1994, see Conway and Pleydell-Pearce, 2000)

4   A memory reported by David Pillemer in a study of what have been termed 'self-defining' memories (Singer and Salovey, 1993; see too Pillemer, 1998):

I remember sitting in 'X''s class on the day that a midterm ... was handed back. I was a freshman and felt that I was in over my head. The professor gave a stern lecture on the values of good writing before she handed back the papers. As she reproached us, my terror grew because her comments seemed to be personally directed at me. I was from a small town, did not have the same background as anyone in my class, and had immediately felt my inadequacies when class began in September. Then she said 'But 'Y' has answered the questions well and has an unusual lyrical and personal style that enhanced her answer'. I couldn't believe that she was talking about my paper, but she was. I can still envision that dimly lit little room in the bottom of Z and smell its peculiar musty odour. I can still picture her stern but kind face and feel the relief and pride I felt at that moment.

(Pillemer, 1998)

5   A memory for a traumatic experience reported by a person suffering from post-traumatic stress disorder (PTSD):

A man who drove cars for a living was involved in a road traffic accident. He was a back seat passenger in a car when it was in a high speed collision with another vehicle; activation of the air bags in the front of the car produced a cloud of powder, which he thought at the time was smoke. At the time he could smell petrol and thought the car might ignite and remembered thinking 'I will be burned alive'. His wife was unconscious after the impact and he thought that she had died. He remembered thinking to himself 'what am I going to do now?' as he thought about his future alone without his wife. He had been experiencing terrific guilt about this as it suggests to him that he is a selfish person. In addition, he was an experienced driver and anticipated the crash, but did not cry out. He felt that he could have averted the crash if he had done this. He experienced intrusive thoughts, such as 'I should have shouted' (to warn the driver) and he relived the feeling he felt when he thought his wife had died, which he believed to be his fault because he had not shouted out.

(Conway et al., 2004, see also Ehlers et al., 2004)

Autobiographical memories like these, from the mundane to the profound, help form the self, they provide a personal historical context or personal biography for who we are now; they are in essence the 'database' of the self (Conway and Pleydell-Pearce,

2000; McAdams, 2001; see too Hollway and Jefferson, 2000). They help us integrate with each other, with the history of our times, and give a continuity to experience that would not otherwise be possible. Such a central form of cognition is, much as one might expect, highly complex and engages processes in many different parts of the brain. Because of this, autobiographical memory is highly susceptible to changes in brain function and is easily disrupted by brain injury (the experience of trauma) and by psychiatric illnesses. Complexity is also present in the nature of those memories that are freely retrieved and those that are recalled to cues, i.e. memory 2 above, and this is particularly evident in the distribution of memories across the lifespan. You might have already noticed in the example memories listed above that several date to when the rememberers would have been in their late teens and early twenties (memories 1, 2 and 4). This seems to be a time when particularly enduring memories are formed and memories from this period remain highly accessible, in contrast to memories from childhood and infancy, which are difficult to access. Indeed, in the example memories above none date to when the rememberers were five years or younger. In Section 2 we first consider the accessibility of memories across the lifespan. Section 3 concentrates on the psychological nature of autobiographical memories, their representation in long-term memory and their relation to the self. In Section 4 we review findings on disruptions of autobiographical memory following brain injury and the experience of trauma.

2 Autobiographical memory across the lifespan

ACTIVITY 7.1

The lifespan retrieval curve

We are going to do an autobiographical memory retrieval experiment and you will need the following equipment: a pen, a stack of plain paper (say 20 to 40 sheets of A4 cut in half) and a watch (a stopwatch would be best but it is not essential).

You will need a quiet room to work in for about an hour. When you are ready read the instructions and start immediately.

Instructions

1   In the next 10 minutes recall as many memories as you can. The memories should be specific and detailed as in the examples at the start of the chapter. Try to sample from across your life and avoid recalling memories all from one period (for example, a recent holiday). No memories from the past 12 months are allowed.

2   Each time you recall a memory write down a short title on a piece of paper. The title should be designed so that if you read it again you would know exactly what you recalled. IMPORTANT: turn the sheet face down and do not look at the title again during this recall phase.

3   When the 10 minutes is up STOP.

4   DO NOT READ FURTHER UNTIL YOU HAVE RECALLED YOUR MEMORIES. THEN RETURN TO THE INSTRUCTIONS BELOW.

Now go back through and date each of the memories by recording how old you were, in months, when the recalled event took place (age at encoding or AaE). If you really want to simulate an autobiographical memory experiment you could also rate each of the memories on the rating scales used in Activity 7.2, ahead.

Now we want to plot AaE. To do this, have a scale ranging from '0' (birth) to your actual age now. Then divide the scale into five-year time bins (any size of 'bin' will do and I have chosen five-year 'bins' or periods of time simply because this is often used in published reports). This AaE scale will form the 'X' axis running along the bottom of the graph. The 'Y' axis will simply be a count of the number of memories falling in each five-year time bin and will run from 0 to about 10 (it is unlikely that you will have more than 10 memories falling in any one time bin but if you do, increase the 'Y' axis scale to, say, 15 or 20, or whatever number best suits your data). For each bin in which memories occur mark an 'X' to indicate how many memories fall in that time bin. For example, maybe six memories date to the period when you were 20 to 25 years of age. The 'X' marked in this bin will then map on to '6' on the 'Y' axis. Next join up the 'X's and compare your lifespan retrieval curve to Figure 7.1.

Autobiographical memories are complex mental constructions that take time to bring to mind and once in mind have to be effortfully maintained. Although, of course, in abnormal remembering, such as occurs in PTSD (post-traumatic stress disorder, see Section 4), exactly the reverse may occur and some details of a trauma may be spontaneously and intrusively recalled and prove difficult to keep out of mind (such as the experience of guilt in memory 5, at the beginning of this chapter). Clearly, some set of central or executive processes must operate to construct memories appropriately, to keep irrelevant knowledge out of mind where it would intrude and take up resources needed for other tasks, and to ensure that what is recalled is relevant to the task or goal currently active. We have found it useful to postulate a structure we call the **working self** (Conway and Pleydell-Pearce, 2000). The choice of name is deliberate and it is intended to make an explicit connection to the concept of 'working memory' (Baddeley, 1986, 2000; see Chapter 5). The working self is conceived as a hierarchy of currently active goals (**goal hierarchy**) and self-conceptions through which current experience is encoded and in which memories are constructed. Because of this, we believe that the self has a profound influence on the accessibility of autobiographical knowledge and therefore upon the process of memory construction. This influence may extend across the lifespan, so that periods of change and development of the self, which contain self-defining memories that are crucial to the working self, may be particularly marked in autobiographical memory. The distinguishing aspect of memories and knowledge from these times may lie in their raised accessibility relative to other more dormant periods: in other words memories from these periods readily come to mind.

The working self – goal hierarchy and self-conceptions – probably first emerges in some more or less coherent form as the infant develops the ability for objective and subjective self-awareness, i.e. conceptions of 'I' and 'Me', in its second year (Howe and Courage, 1997). Certainly children as young as 30 months have detailed autobiographical memories (Fivush *et al.*, 1996) although these typically are not accessible in adulthood. Undoubtedly the working self and its relation to autobiographical memory changes over the course of childhood and perhaps only stabilizes into an enduring form in late adolescence and early adulthood (Erikson and Erikson, 1982/1997). These periods of development of the self are reflected in the **lifespan retrieval curve**, which is observed when older adults (about 35 years and older) recall autobiographical memories in free recall or in a variety of cued recall conditions (Franklin and Holding, 1977; Fitzgerald and Lawrence, 1984; Rubin *et al.*, 1986; Rubin *et al.*, 1998). Memories are plotted in terms of age at encoding of the remembered experiences, and the resulting lifespan retrieval curve typically takes a form similar to that shown in Figure 7.1 (did your own lifespan retrieval curve take this form?). As can be seen in Figure 7.1 the lifespan retrieval curve consists of three components: the period of childhood amnesia (from birth to approximately five years of age), the period of the reminiscence bump (from 10 to 30 years) and the period of recency (which declines from the present back to the period of the reminiscence bump).

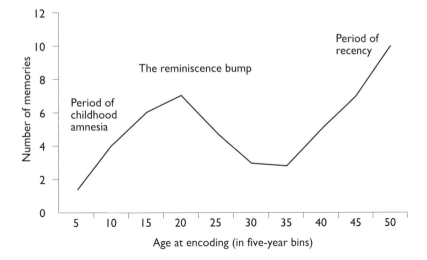

Figure 7.1   An idealized representation of the lifespan retrieval curve

2.1   Childhood amnesia

There are many theoretical explanations of the period of childhood amnesia (see Pillemer and White, 1989), but most founder on the fact that children below the age of five years have a wide range of specific and detailed autobiographical memories (Fivush *et al.*, 1996). Explanations that postulate childhood amnesia to be related to general developmental changes in intellect, language, emotion, etc. fail simply because apparently normal autobiographical memories were in fact accessible when the individual was in the period of childhood amnesia. It seems unlikely that an increase in general functioning would make unavailable already accessible memories.

From the perspective of the Conway and Pleydell-Pearce (2000) model of autobiographical memory this period is seen as reflecting changes in the working self's goal hierarchy. The goals of the infant and young child, through which experience is encoded into memory, are so different, so disjunct, from those of the adult that the adult working self is unable to access those memories. Another possibility, one much more in line with Freudian thinking on childhood amnesia (Freud, 1955, first published in 1899), is that the working self of infancy and early childhood is much less able to control the occurrence and intensity of emotional experience. Episodic memories encoded during this period are then saturated with intense emotions and, if recalled in maturity, could destabilize the adult working self by reinstating intense infant emotions. This view suggests that access to autobiographical memories encoded during this period might be quite powerfully limited by the adult working self, leading to the lack of memories from this period. Currently, however, there is no generally accepted explanation for this component of the lifespan retrieval curve. Although it is not as mysterious as it once was, the period of childhood amnesia continues to present a challenge to autobiographical memory researchers.

2.2   The reminiscence bump

The second, and also very interesting, component of the lifespan retrieval curve is the period when rememberers were aged 10 to 30 years, which is known as the **reminiscence bump** (RB). The RB is distinguished by an increase in recall of memories relative to the period that precedes it and those that follow it. (Was it present in your curve?) The RB has been observed in dozens of studies leading David Rubin (a leading researcher in this area) to describe it as one of the most 'reliable' empirical observations in cognitive psychology (Conway and Rubin, 1993; Rubin, 2002). Nonetheless, care must be taken in collecting memories for the RB. If memories are given dates as they are recalled then rememberers have a tendency to become 'stuck' in a time period. Then they may not produce a RB, or may produce an exaggerated RB depending on which time period the rememberer adheres to. Similarly, some rememberers can become 'stuck' in the very recent past and recall only memories from the last few months, again obscuring the RB and period of childhood amnesia.

In general, these types of retrieval strategies need to be minimized and access to memories should be open (rather than constrained or directed). The rememberer should therefore respond with the first memories to come to mind, i.e. those that are most accessible, for the full lifespan retrieval curve to be observed. When these conditions are met the RB is frequently observed. Interestingly, however, the RB is present not just in the recall of specific autobiographical memories but also emerges in a range of different types of autobiographical knowledge. For example, the RB has been observed in the recall of: films (Sehulster, 1996); music (cf. Rubin *et al.*, 1998); books (Larsen, 1998); and public events (Holmes and Conway, 1999; Schuman *et al.*, 1997). Memories recalled from the period of the RB are more accurate (Rubin *et al.*, 1998). They are judged as more important, by the individual, than memories from other time periods, and are rated as highly likely to be included in one's autobiography (Fitzgerald, 1988, 1996; Fromholt and Larsen, 1991, 1992; Rubin and Schulkind, 1997). The autobiographical memories of middle-aged and older adults are therefore characterized by a high degree of accessibility to autobiographical memories dating to the period when they were 10 to 30 years of age, and this is typically most marked for the narrower period 15 to 25 years of age.

In a rather similar manner to the period of childhood amnesia the RB also has several plausible explanations (see Rubin et al., 1998). Some obvious explanations can, however, be ruled out. Memories from the RB period are not dominated by first-time experiences, but rather appear to consist of memories of experiences that are idiosyncratic to individual rememberers. Similarly, the suggestion that memories from the RB are more vivid – the idea being that memory encoding is at peak efficiency during this period – turns out to be incorrect (Holmes and Conway, 1999; Rubin and Schulkind, 1997). Also incorrect are explanations that either postulate preferential effort to recalling memories from this period, or suggest RB memories are of more pleasant experiences. It has been found that no special effort is made to recall RB memories, and they are not of more pleasant events than memories from other parts of the lifespan (Rubin and Schulkind, 1997).

Instead, it seems that a more complex explanation is required and two candidate explanations currently exist. One comes from Rubin and colleagues (Rubin, 2002), a central hypothesis of which is that 'Events from the bump period are remembered best because they occur when rapid change is giving way to relative stability that lasts at least until retrieval' (Rubin, 2002, p.14). By this view a period of rapid change is dominated by novel experiences which more fully engage encoding processes, and so become represented in memory in a highly accessible way and lead to the RB. An alternative to the 'novelty' hypothesis is that the high accessibility of memories from this period may be related to their enduring relation to the self (Conway and Pleydell-Pearce, 2000). Possibly, many memories from the period of the RB are of **self-defining** experiences (Fitzgerald, 1988; Singer and Salovey, 1993), and have a powerful effect in binding the working self to a specific reality. The 'novelty' of RB experiences lies in their newness and uniqueness *for the self*, and they may play a crucial role in the final formation of a stable self system during late adolescence and early adulthood. Memories from this period help to define identity (Conway, 1996) and, because of this, they endure in memory in a highly accessible form. Which of these two hypotheses (the novelty hypothesis, or the self hypothesis) is the correct explanation is currently unknown but, as with so many supposedly 'alternate' explanations in psychology, it may turn out that both are required in order to develop a full theoretical account of the RB.

2.3 Recency

The final component of the lifespan retrieval curve, the 'recency' component (see Figure 7.1), can be simply explained as a period of forgetting older memories: memories recently encoded remain accessible, memories retained over a longer retention interval are subject to decay and/or interference and so become progressively less accessible. This pattern of retention is familiar from laboratory studies and is one that has been observed many times. On the other hand it might be questioned why such memories or salient experiences should be 'forgotten' in this way. Moreover, it might also be noted that when people are specifically instructed to recall older autobiographical memories, there are apparently plenty of available memories (see Holmes and Conway, 1999, for example). Thus, what is of importance here is not the forgetting but rather a bias or preference in access. It may be that the recency portion of the lifespan retrieval curve reflects a lowering in self-relevance of memory for experiences from the recent past and, hence, a corresponding lowering of accessibility rather than complete forgetting. Thus, as recently acquired autobiographical memories become less relevant to the working self's goals, their accessibility is attenuated, but not lost, and can be restored by direct attempts to retrieve recent information. Of course, as the retention interval lengthens access may actually become lost, rather than just attenuated, and in that case forgetting would occur.

Summary of Section 2

- The 'lifespan retrieval curve' illustrates how frequently autobiographical memories are recalled over different periods in someone's life. The lifespan retrieval curve is characterized by periods of childhood amnesia, the reminiscence bump and recency.
- The concept of the 'working self' (Conway and Pleydell-Pearce, 2000) can be thought of as a hierarchy of currently active goals and self-concepts through which experience is encoded and memories constructed.

3   Autobiographical knowledge, episodic memory, the working self and memory construction

ACTIVITY 7.2

Taking part in an autobiographical memory experiment: retrieving memories to cue words

Before reading further, it will be useful to retrieve a few more of your own memories, and reflect on what comes to mind both while forming a memory and when it is fully constructed. To do this, imagine that you are a participant in an autobiographical memory experiment. The experimenter tells you that you will have to bring to mind memories of specific experiences of events that you yourself experienced, and that took place over periods of seconds, minutes, hours, but no longer than one day – as with the example memories listed at the start of the chapter. This means that responses such as 'last summer', 'when I was little', or 'holiday in Italy' are too general and do not count as memories. Instead you are required to recall detailed memories, memories of specific events. These can be from any part of your life, indeed sampling widely would be good, but they should not be of events experienced in the last 12 months.

You are asked to recall specific memories by reading 'cue' words, then bringing to mind the first memory about which the cue word reminds you – bearing in mind the constraints of sampling widely and not from the past 12 months. Once you have the memory in mind, write down a description of it and provide a title. You should also rate each memory on the following scales:

Table 7.1   Memory vividness

	1	2	3	4	5
Memory vividness	No imagery	Some imagery	Usual image vividness	Vivid imagery	Extremely vivid imagery
Valence of the remembered experience	Very negative	Negative	Neutral/ positive	Very positive	
Emotional intensity of the remembered experience	Very mild	Some emotion	Emotional	Intense	As intense as any emotional experience I have ever had
Rehearsal. How frequently have you thought and/or talked about this event?	Very rarely	Sometimes	With about average frequency	Above average	Very frequently

Okay let's create a response sheet now. On a sheet of paper write the following:

Memory 1					
Title:					
Memory description:					
Ratings (circle a number):					
Vividness:	1	2	3	4	5
Valence:	1	2	3	4	5
Intensity:	1	2	3	4	5
Rehearsal:	1	2	3	4	5

AaE: _____ (leave this blank for now)

Do this three times so you have three memory response sheets (in an actual experiment far more memories would be collected, usually 20 or more).

Assuming you are now ready:

- Recall your first memory to the cue word CHAIR and then complete the response sheet.

- Now recall a memory to the word ILLNESS and complete the response sheet.

- Finally recall a memory to the cue SUMMER and complete the response sheet.

Now, go back and at the bottom of each response sheet on the line that says 'AaE' write (in months and as exactly as you can) your age when the remembered event occurred (age at encoding or 'AaE').

Keep the response sheets handy while you read the rest of this chapter, as we will often refer back to them. For now try to answer the following questions. Keep a record of your answers and come back to them when you have finished the chapter.

(i) Did your memories always contain both abstract autobiographical knowledge as well as very detailed records of actual experiences?

(ii) Were the details always or predominantly in the form of visual mental images? If not, what form were they in?

(iii) Did you feel any emotions? Particularly with respect to the last two memories in comparison to the first memory.

(iv) Did the memories just 'pop' into mind when you read the cue words, or did you have to elaborate the cue, for example think about a chair at home and some incident associated with it, such as when you bought it?

(v) Did it take longer to retrieve a memory to cue two than to cues one and three?

(vi) How complete a record of the actual event would you say the memory is?

(vii) Did you notice how 'time compressed' the memory was? That is, it almost certainly took far less time to recall the event than the experience itself took.

(viii) How accurate, as a record of the experiences, were the memories?

(ix) At some point in the attempt to retrieve/construct the memories you must have decided that you had an appropriate memory in mind. Was this associated with any feelings? Did you have a sort of 'aha' experience when the memory came to mind? Did you feel as though you were almost reliving at least a small part of the past (memory researchers call this *recollective experience*)?

The pattern of memories retrieved over the lifespan has a particular shape, as shown in Figure 7.1, and one which strongly implicates the self in memory retrieval. The lifespan retrieval curve is, however, just one aspect of this complex higher-order form of cognition. Another and equally important aspect is the *constructive* nature of autobiographical remembering. We know from the experience of our own memories that when knowledge of the past comes to mind, intentionally or spontaneously, it often features facts about ourselves and our lives, images of people, locations, activities and, of course, detailed (episodic) memories of specific events may be recalled (as in the cue word experiment you have just completed). It is this coming together of conceptual autobiographical knowledge, generic images and episodic memories that is the major form of construction in autobiographical remembering. In this section the nature and organization of autobiographical knowledge in long-term memory is considered first, followed by an account of episodic memories. The role of the working self in memory construction is then reviewed and, finally, the process of memory construction itself is outlined.

3.1   Autobiographical knowledge

One way in which autobiographical knowledge has been thought about is in terms of event specificity. Two broad types of autobiographical knowledge have been identified along this dimension: general events and lifetime periods (Conway and Pleydell-Pearce, 2000).

3.1.1   General events

General events, as the term implies, are more strongly event-specific than lifetime periods, but not as event-specific as sensory–perceptual episodic memories, which are directly derived from actual experience (Conway, 2001) (see the discussion of episodic memories in Chapter 6). **General events** refer to a variety of autobiographical knowledge structures such as single events (e.g. the day we went to London), repeated events (e.g. work meetings) and extended events (e.g. a holiday in Spain). General events may themselves be organized in several different ways. For example, there may be 'mini-histories' structured around detailed and sometimes vivid episodic memories of goal attainment in developing skills, knowledge and personal relationships (Robinson, 1992). Some general events may be of experiences of particular significance for the self and act as reference points for other associated general events (Pillemer, 1998; Singer and Salovey, 1993). Other general events may be grouped together because of their emotional similarity (McAdams *et al.*, 2001), and it is likely that there are yet other forms of organization at this level that await investigation (Brown and Schopflocher, 1998). However, the research currently available indicates that organization of autobiographical knowledge at the level of general events is extensive, and it appears to virtually always refer to progress in the attainment of highly self-relevant goals.

Conway and Pleydell-Pearce (2000), in a review, conclude that general events contain knowledge about locations, others, activities, feelings and goals common to an event, as well as some specific episodic memories that help organize the general event knowledge. This autobiographical knowledge may be represented in several different ways and consist of images, feelings, verbal statements, associated together in a mental model (cf. Johnson-Laird, 1983 and Chapter 13). However, autobiographical knowledge in general events predominantly takes the form of generic visual images, i.e. images derived from repeated experiences (Brewer, 1986, 1988, 1996; Conway, 1996, 2001; Rubin and Greenberg, 1998). General event autobiographical knowledge can be used to access associated sensory–perceptual episodic memories and, when it is used in this way, a specific and detailed autobiographical memory (AM) can be formed. Thus, a specific AM will usually, if not always, contain some general event knowledge and this will often be in the form of generic images (was this the case with the memories you recalled earlier?).

3.1.2 Lifetime periods

In one of the few studies of this type of knowledge Robinson (1992) examined people's memories for the acquisition of skills (e.g. riding a bicycle or driving a car) and for aspects of personal relationships. These general events were found to be organized around a series of vivid memories relating to **goal attainment**. Consider two examples from Robinson's study: 'Ever agreeable, and eager to do anything that would get me out of the doldrums of inferiority, my father rented a bike and undertook to help me to learn. ... I shall always remember those first few glorious seconds when I realized I was riding on my own ...' (Quinn, 1990, cited in Robinson, 1992, p.224).

> The first time I flew an airplane was one of the best firsts. It marked a sense of accomplishment for myself, and it also started me on the career path I have always wanted to follow. The day was warm and hazy, much as summer days in Louisville are. My nervousness didn't help the situation, as I perspired profusely. But as we took off from runway 6 the feeling of total euphoria took over, and I was no longer nervous or afraid. We cruised at 2,500 feet and I worked on some basic manoeuvres for approximately 45 minutes. We then returned to the airport, where I realized that this will soon be a career.
>
> *(Robinson, 1992, p.226)*

These 'first time' memories can cue other related memories and the whole general event carries powerful self-defining evaluations that persist over long periods of time. Importantly, Robinson found many memories featured goal-related evaluative knowledge or self-defining memories (Singer and Salovey, 1993) along with more general knowledge and specific episodic memories. General event autobiographical knowledge can also be used to access related **lifetime periods** that contain associated knowledge. Lifetime periods, like general events, contain representations of locations, others, activities, feelings and goals common to the period they represent. They effectively encapsulate a period in memory and in so doing may provide ways in which access to autobiographical knowledge can be limited, channelled or directed. As with general events there is evidence that lifetime periods contain evaluative knowledge, negative and positive, of progress in goal attainment (Beike and Landoll, 2000), and it seems likely that lifetime periods may play an important role in what Bluck and Habermas (2000) call the **life story**.

A life story is some more or less coherent theme or set of themes that characterize, identify and give meaning to a whole life. A life story consists of several life story **schema**, which associate together selective autobiographical knowledge to define a theme (Bluck and Habermas, 2000). A schema is a memory structure that encapsulates an event such that common parts are fixed, while variable parts occur as 'slots'. Thus a schema for 'going to the cinema' would have predefined common parts (such as queuing for tickets, buying popcorn) and slots for variable parts (which cinema we went to, who I was with, what film we saw). Lifetime periods might provide the autobiographical knowledge that can be used to form life story schema and thus support the generation of themes. This may be particularly so because of the goal-evaluative information they contain. For example, a lifetime period such as 'when I was at university' will consist of representations of people, locations, activities, feelings and goals common to the period, but will also contain some general evaluation of the period, i.e. this was an anxious time for me, living away from home was difficult, I was lonely, I found the work too difficult, etc.

Lifetime period evaluations access related general events and, in turn, episodic memories that, when formed, provide the 'evidence' justifying the evaluations (see Beike and Landoll, 2000, and Conway and Pleydell-Pearce, 2000 for more on how autobiographical knowledge 'grounds' the self in memories of experience). They could also form the basis of a life story schema and, in the example above, 'when I was at university', this might perhaps centre on the unsuitability of the individual to higher education. This in turn might support a theme of an individual more suited to 'practical' as opposed to 'academic' activities (cf. McAdams, 2001). Thus, lifetime period autobiographical knowledge is less event-specific than general event autobiographical knowledge; it is also more conceptual and abstract. It encapsulates significant parts of the life story and may form an important bridge from autobiographical memory to core aspects of the self. Figure 7.2 (overleaf) depicts this scheme of autobiographical knowledge organization, and shows how such knowledge may be represented at different levels to form hierarchical **partonomic** knowledge structures. Partonomic refers to the way that a specific episodic memory is *part of* a general event, which in turn is *part of* a lifetime period, which is part of a life schema (Conway, 1996).

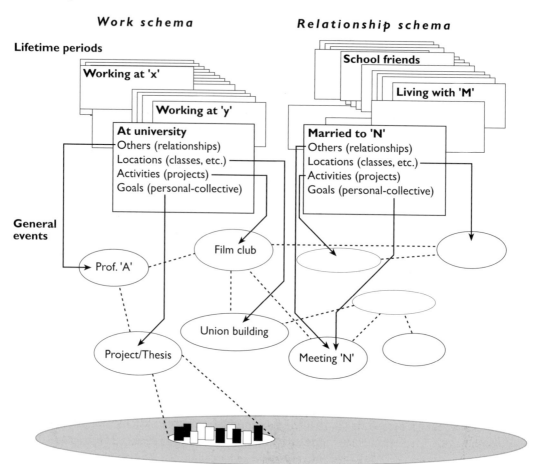

Life story

Life story schema

Work schema   *Relationship schema*

Lifetime periods

Working at 'x'   School friends

Working at 'y'   Living with 'M'

At university   Married to 'N'
Others (relationships)   Others (relationships)
Locations (classes, etc.)   Locations (classes, etc.)
Activities (projects)   Activities (projects)
Goals (personal-collective)   Goals (personal-collective)

General
events
          Film club
Prof. 'A'
          Union building   Meeting 'N'
Project/Thesis

Sensory-perceptual episodic memories

Figure 7.2   Autobiographical knowledge and episodic memories

3.2 Episodic and semantic memory

In Tulving's (1972) original distinction between episodic and semantic memory, the defining feature of episodic memory was that it contained spatio-temporal information (see Chapter 6, Section 3.1). Episodic memories were of specific events that occurred at unique times, while semantic knowledge was of abstract, conceptual, context-free knowledge not linked to any specific place, time or learning episode. The reference for episodic memory was then individual personal experience, whereas the reference of semantic knowledge was social and universal (Tulving, 1983). So, for example, if you now remember Activity 7.1, in which you recalled some memories, that is an episodic memory of part of the experience of reading this chapter. In contrast, recalling that two broad classes of knowledge in long-term memory are termed 'episodic' and 'semantic' memory, with the former referring to memory for experiences and the latter to memory for conceptual knowledge, is a form of semantic memory. Attractive though this fractionation of long-term knowledge into episodic and semantic memory may be, it unfortunately has problems.

One problem is that episodic memories must, of course, contain semantic knowledge and this raises the question of how easily the two types of knowledge can be distinguished. A second problem is that there are knowledge representations in long-term memory that on Tulving's (1972) original definition we would want to term 'semantic', but which contain spatio-temporal information. For example, a schema for 'breakfast', which specifies the location, time, actions, order of actions and objects involved of a typical breakfast (Schank and Abelson, 1977): is this a semantic or episodic representation? A third problem relates to autobiographical knowledge. For instance, a person may know that last year they took a holiday in Italy – no other information needs to be brought to mind. But the reference of this knowledge (namely holiday) is both personal and universal and, moreover, it clearly contains spatio-temporal knowledge (see also Dritschel *et al.*, 1992). The fourth problem is that Tulving himself has revised the concept of 'episodic'. In its latest incarnation the distinguishing feature is that episodic memories when recalled cause recollective experience, i.e. the feeling of experiencing the past, and this does not occur when other types of long-term knowledge are brought to mind (Wheeler *et al.*, 1997).

The episodic–semantic distinction is then a difficult one to sustain and this is especially true when we consider autobiographical memory. However, in an attempt to retain the concept of episodic memory, Conway (2001) put forward a revised view of the concept that was closer in spirit to Tulving's original conception, but which sought to refine it to meet the main points of later criticisms and revisions. According to this new view, knowledge contained in episodic memories is very largely *sensory–perceptual* in nature. Figure 7.2 conveys this by depicting episodic memories in an undifferentiated pool of representations of sensory–perceptual experiences. Thus, episodic memory is a repository of 'experience-near', highly event-specific sensory–perceptual details of recent experiences: experiences that lasted for comparatively short periods of time (seconds, minutes or at most hours). These sensory–perceptual episodic memories do not endure in memory unless they become linked to more permanent autobiographical memory knowledge structures. Conway (2001) argues that access to sensory–perceptual episodic memories is rapidly lost. This is because most episodic memories do not become linked to more stable and permanent autobiographical knowledge in long-term memory and, as a consequence, they rapidly decay and become permanently inaccessible. As a simple demonstration, cast your mind back over the events of today. They will be extremely detailed and numerous. If you try the same exercise, remembering today's events, in a day or so, or perhaps next week, few episodic memories will have been retained relative to the number available on the day of experience, although rather more may be retained in the way of general event autobiographical knowledge. Only those episodic memories integrated with or consolidated in long-term memory close in time to the actual experience will later be accessible and available to enter into the subsequent formation of autobiographical memories.

3.2.1 Recollective experience

Experience-near sensory–perceptual knowledge when accessed during memory construction supports **recollective experience** and, consequently, episodic memory has a unique affinity for this type of memory awareness (Wheeler *et al.*, 1997). Recollective experience is the sense or experience of the self in the past and is induced by images, feelings and other memory details that come to mind during remembering (see Gardiner and Richardson-Klavehn, 2000, for a review). This memory awareness or feeling state (the sense of the self in the past) signals to a rememberer that the mental representation it is associated with is in fact a memory of an experience that actually occurred, and is not a fantasy, dream, plan or some other (experience-distant) mental construction, such as a general event. Thus, recollective experience effectively says 'this mental representation is a memory of an event experienced by the self'. Note that it does not follow from this that recollective experience always indicates a true memory – 'true' that is in the sense that the recalled experience actually occurred – but when recollective experience is present the probability is high that the remembered event was one that had been previously experienced (Conway *et al.*, 1996; Roediger and McDermott, 1995).

3.3 The working self

Constructing an autobiographical memory is a complex form of cognition and has several effects on processing generally. One of the main effects is that the entire cognitive system enters what Tulving (1983) called **retrieval mode**. In retrieval mode attention, or part thereof, is directed inwards towards internal representations of knowledge, and conscious awareness becomes dominated by these representations. As a memory is formed the rememberer's awareness becomes emotionally influenced by recollective experience and a powerful sense of the self in the past arises. The division of attention that then occurs gives rise to an attenuation of all other cognitive processes and, because of this, recall of AMs could, potentially, be highly dysfunctional in that current processing sequences would be disrupted. In extreme cases, such as in the involuntary and intrusive recall of prior trauma that is symptomatic of PTSD, autobiographical recall may be pathologically disruptive to everyday functioning (as in memory 5 at the beginning of this chapter). The point being that constructing a specific and detailed AM is a major cognitive occurrence with consequences for all other types of processing. Memory construction has therefore to be controlled and according to Conway and Pleydell-Pearce (2000) this is one of the main functions of the working self (see also Markus and Ruvolo, 1989).

3.3.1 Goals and the working self

The working self is conceived as a complex hierarchy of interconnected goals, all of which are in varying states of activation, but only some of which can enter consciousness. The working self may also contain representations of at least some goal-related knowledge, e.g. lifetime periods, life schema and life story or stories, as well as currently active models of the self. It is through the working self goal structure that episodic memories are formed and autobiographical knowledge is abstracted from experience. Thus, goal-related experience is prioritized in terms of encoding, consolidation, accessibility and construction into specific, if transitory, autobiographical memories. Strong evidence exists showing that overall goal orientation of particular personality types acts to raise the accessibility of goal-related autobiographical knowledge and so facilitate their recall. This work has its origin in a seminal paper by Markus (1977) who found that people with a strong personality trait relating to the dependent–independent dimension showed preferential access to memories of experiences in which they had behaved in dependent or independent ways. In contrast, individuals within whom the dependent–independent dimension was weak did not have this memory bias.

These types of self-memory congruency effects have since been observed in several studies and most especially in the work of McAdams into power, intimacy and generativity (McAdams, 1982, 1985, 2001; McAdams *et al.*, 1997). McAdams (1982), using the Thematic Apperception Test, TAT (Murray, 1938, 1943), in order to assess non-conscious aspects of personality (McClelland *et al.*, 1989), categorized individuals (on the basis of their TAT responses) into those with a strong intimacy motivation or, in contrast, with a distinctive power motivation. Content analysis of subsequently free-recalled memories of 'peak' and other experiences found that the intimacy motivation group recalled peak experiences with a preponderance of intimacy themes compared to individuals who scored lower on this motivation, who in turn showed no memory bias. Similarly, the power motivation group recalled peak experiences with strong themes of power and satisfaction. Interestingly, neither group showed biases in memories for more mundane, less emotional, less self-defining memories. These striking biases in memory availability by dominant motive type suggest that the goal structure of the working self makes highly available those aspects of the knowledge base that relate most directly to currently active goals. In more recent work McAdams *et al.* (1997) have examined the influence of the Eriksonian notion of 'generativity' on the life stories of middle-aged adults (Erikson, 1950). Generativity refers to nurturing and caring for those things, products and people that have the potential to outlast the self. Those individuals who were judged high in generativity, i.e. who had a 'commitment' life story, were found to recall a preponderance of events highly related to aspects of generativity. In contrast, those participants who were not identified as holding a commitment story showed no such bias.

Work by Woike and her colleagues has further established the connection between personality and memory (Woike, 1995; Woike *et al.*, 1999). In the tradition of personality research deriving from Murray (1938) and McClelland (e.g. McClelland *et al.*, 1989), Woike identified implicit and explicit motives in a group of people who then recorded memorable events over a period of 60 days. According to McClelland *et al.* (1989), implicit motives are evident in preferences for certain types of affective experience such as 'doing well' for achievement and 'feeling close' for intimacy whereas explicit motives are present in social values and aspects of the self that can be introspected. A corollary of this view is that affective experiences should give rise to memories associated with implicit motives. Explicit motives, on the other hand, should lead to memories of less affective, routine experiences, more closely associated with self-description than with measures of implicit motives (i.e. TAT performance). This was exactly Woike's finding in both a diary study and in a laboratory-based autobiographical memory retrieval implicit/explicit motive priming experiment. In a subsequent study Woike *et al.* (1999) investigated groups of individuals classified as 'agentic' (concerned with personal power, achievement and independence) or as 'communion' (concerned with relationships, interdependence and others). Agentic personality types are considered to structure knowledge in terms of 'differentiation' (the emphasis is on differences, separateness and independence) whereas communal individuals, in contrast, structure knowledge in terms of 'integration' (the emphasis is on similarity, congruity and interdependence). Across a series of studies, people with agentic self-focus were found to consistently recall emotional memories of events that involved issues of agency (mastery, humiliation) with their content structured in terms of differentiation. People with communal self-focus recalled emotion memories featuring others, often significant others, in acts of love and friendship, with the memory content structured in terms of integration. These findings clearly implicate the self (particularly the focus of the self) in determining recall and lend further weight to the suggestion that the working self influences access to sets of goal-related memories. (Reflecting on the content of your own memories how would you classify yourself – agentic? communal? Neither clearly one nor the other?)

In an intriguing study Pillemer *et al.* (1996; also Pillemer, 1998) investigated memory for specific educational episodes (memory 4, at the beginning of this chapter). The initial impetus for this work was the observation that autobiographies often contain accounts of highly specific events that were 'turning points' (**self-defining moments**) for the individual and that usually involved the adoption of a superordinate life goal that then determined much of the individual's later activities. Pillemer *et al.* (1996) found that students and alumni were frequently able to report, in detail, highly vivid memories of interactions with professors and other teachers that had profoundly influenced their academic interests and, sometimes, the whole of their lives. These were often events in which superordinate long-term goals were adopted by the individual, e.g. to become a chemist, a writer, etc. Consider the following account by a postgraduate mature student of her first undergraduate Shakespeare class:

> I was fascinated by the easy way the professor roamed through Shake-speare, by just the amount of knowledge he had. He seemed to know everything. In fact, after class, I asked him if he could identify a quote I had found about fencing, 'Keep up your bright swords, for the dew will rust them.' Immediately he said 'Othello, Act 1 Scene 2, I believe.' Which turned out to be exactly right. I wanted to know a body of literature that well. I'm still working on it.
>
> *(Pillemer* et al.*, 1996, p.330)*

Of course, not all self-defining moments are positive and Pillemer *et al.* (1996, and Pillemer, 1998), in the only questionnaire study of these types of memories to date, list several other memories of more negative educational experiences that led to a subject being dropped, negatively conceived as 'difficult' or 'boring', and, in some cases, the emergence of negative conceptions of self as a poor or incompetent learner.

Singer and Salovey (1993) provide one of the main statements on the relation between goals and memories. A major finding in their study was that memories associated with feelings of happiness and pride were strongly linked with goal attainment and the smooth running of personal plans (see also Sheldon and Elliot, 1999). In contrast, memories associated with feelings of sadness and anger were linked to the progressive failure to achieve goals. Singer and Salovey (1993) proposed that each individual had a set of **self-defining memories** that contained critical knowledge of progress on the attainment of long-term goals. Such goals, e.g. attaining independence, intimacy, mastery and so on, may have been adopted as solutions to dominant self-discrepancies arising from childhood experiences (Strauman, 1996). Related to this, Thorne (1995) found that the content of memories freely recalled across the lifespan by 20-year-olds conformed to what she called 'developmental truths'. Thus, memories from childhood very frequently referred to situations in which the child wanted help, approval and love, usually from the parents, whereas memories from late adolescence and early adulthood referred to events in which the rememberer wanted reciprocal love, was assertive or helped another.

The notion of a 'working self' consisting of an active complex goal hierarchy is a useful way in which to understand the pattern of findings from the study of personality and autobiographical memory. The evidence points to a particular role for the working self, and that is to modulate access to knowledge in long-term memory and to control what new knowledge enters the knowledge base, i.e. which episodic memories are rehearsed and so become integrated with long-term knowledge structures. Note that none of this control need take place consciously, and the nature of the active working self's control structures may make some long-term knowledge highly accessible, e.g. self-congruent knowledge, whereas other knowledge may be inhibited, e.g. self-incongruent knowledge. In terms of encoding, working self goal structures may non-consciously direct attention and influence post-encoding processing, i.e. rehearsal, and in this way determine what is retained (Ross, 1989).

3.4 Constructing autobiographical memories

It has long been known that autobiographical memories can be intentionally constructed or, alternatively, may come to mind without the formation of any specific intention to recall a memory, i.e. to enter retrieval mode. We refer to the former type of construction as *generative retrieval* and the latter type as *direct retrieval*.

Generative retrieval occurs when remembering is intentional and the knowledge base is iteratively sampled as a memory is effortfully constructed. During this protracted process an initial cue is used to probe the knowledge base and accessed knowledge is evaluated against a retrieval model generated by the working self. If the constraints of the retrieval model are satisfied then a memory is formed, and the knowledge activated in the knowledge base (by the cue) together with associated goals of the working self form the autobiographical memory in that episode of remembering. Usually this process takes several or more cycles of access, evaluation and cue elaboration, as a stable pattern of activated knowledge that meets the constraints of the retrieval model gradually emerges. For example, in attempting to construct an AM to a cue such as 'cinema', a rememberer might elaborate the cue into the question 'when did I go to the cinema a lot?' This cue might lead to access of the lifetime period 'when I was a student'. Lifetime period knowledge can then be used to access general events, which in turn access episodic memories, and in this way a specific and task-relevant AM is constructed. Perhaps you were aware of this process when recalling memories to the cues 'chair', 'illness' and 'summer' in Activity 7.2? Figure 7.3 lists two protocols collected from people recalling memories to cue words while saying aloud what was going through their minds. Perhaps you were aware of similar types of knowledge coming to mind when you recalled your memories? Figure 7.4 provides a diagrammatic illustration of generative and direct retrieval.

Although the process of generative retrieval may seem laborious and is certainly effortful (retrieval times to word cues usually average between five and eight seconds), it nevertheless may operate with high efficiency when the system is in retrieval mode and multiple memories are to be recalled. Such circumstances would arise in a conversation with another person about a shared experience or in a discourse in which accounts of autobiographical memories form a part, e.g. in strategic self-disclosure, etc. Generally, however, recalling specific AMs is disruptive to other forms of cognition and, perhaps because of this, only occurs fluently under special conditions (intention to remember and retrieval mode). Indeed, the potential for disruption is great as autobiographical knowledge is highly cue-sensitive, and patterns of activation across autobiographical knowledge structures in long-term memory continually arise and dissipate in response to external and internal cues. These patterns dissipate over the components of general

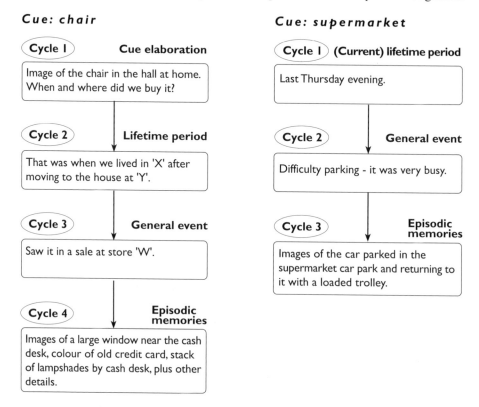

Cue: chair

Cycle 1   Cue elaboration

Image of the chair in the hall at home. When and where did we buy it?

Cycle 2   Lifetime period

That was when we lived in 'X' after moving to the house at 'Y'.

Cycle 3   General event

Saw it in a sale at store 'W'.

Cycle 4   Episodic memories

Images of a large window near the cash desk, colour of old credit card, stack of lampshades by cash desk, plus other details.

Cue: supermarket

Cycle 1 (Current) lifetime period

Last Thursday evening.

Cycle 2   General event

Difficulty parking - it was very busy.

Cycle 3   Episodic memories

Images of the car parked in the supermarket car park and returning to it with a loaded trolley.

Figure 7.3 Two protocols collected while rememberers related what came to mind when recalling memories to cue words

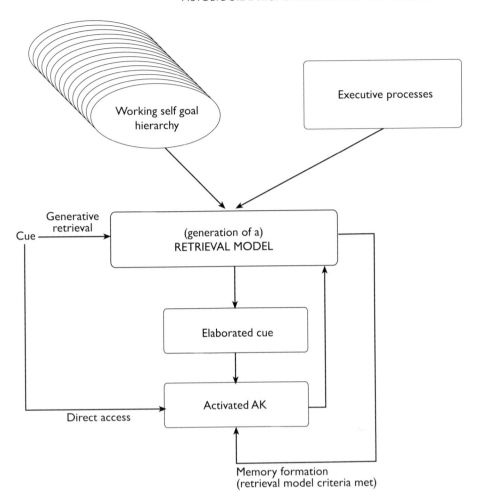

Figure 7.4   Direct and generative retrieval

event and lifetime period knowledge structures (see Figure 7.2) but rarely spontaneously settle down into stable patterns that activate episodic memories. Nevertheless, when a cue activates a general event and associated episodic memories, a specific autobiographical memory can, apparently effortlessly and spontaneously, be formed: in other words **direct retrieval** occurs. In direct retrieval a cue causes a pattern of activation in autobiographical knowledge (AK) that stabilizes as a specific autobiographical memory and bypasses the stages of generative retrieval (repeated autobiographical knowledge access, evaluation and cue elaboration) (see Box 7.1 overleaf). Automatic awareness of the autobiographical memory does not necessarily follow and the working self can prevent (inhibit) a fully formed autobiographical memory from entering awareness (becoming linked to working self goal structures and initiating retrieval mode) if, for example, this would disrupt other processing that had a higher priority, i.e. for attaining a higher-priority goal. One example of direct retrieval that enters awareness has been mentioned earlier, that is when patients with PTSD experience intrusive memories of a trauma that are involuntary triggered by cues linked to that event.

┌─ 7.1 ──────────────────────────────────── Research study ─┐

Haque and Conway's autobiographical memory 'probe' experiments

An experiment by Haque and Conway (2001) illustrates how both types of retrieval occur when people recall specific autobiographical memories to a range of cue words naming common activities, locations and emotions. In this experiment the cue words were displayed on a computer screen and participants attempted to recall a memory to each cue individually.

In order to 'probe' the process of memory construction a signal was displayed two seconds, five seconds or 30 seconds after the cue word was on-screen. In response to the signal the participant had to report as exactly as they could the current contents of consciousness.

The reports were then classified for the predominant type of knowledge they contained, i.e. lifetime period, general event, specific memory or 'nothing in mind'. Table 7.2 (below) shows the number and percentage of each type of report at each of the probe intervals. From Table 7.2 it can be seen that similar numbers of reports at the two-second probe contain either autobiographical knowledge (lifetime periods and general events) or specific autobiographical memories.

Autobiographical knowledge indicates the operation of the generative retrieval process (a memory has not yet been formed) whereas the report of specific autobiographical memories at this very short probe indicates direct retrieval. Thus both types of retrieval can occur in the same individual. As can also be seen from Table 7.2, the incidence of reports of autobiographical knowledge at the longer probe times sharply decreases, although note the persistence of some general event knowledge, while the formation of specific memories strongly increases. As might be expected, as the retrieval time lengthens so the generative process runs its course and specific autobiographical memories were formed.

Table 7.2 Distribution of protocols by protocol type and probe time in experiment 1 from Haque and Conway (2001)

Protocol type	Time of probe		
	Two seconds	Five seconds	Thirty seconds
Lifetime period	30 (70%)	10 (23%)	3 (6%)
General event	18 (32%)	23 (41%)	15 (27%)
Specific memory	33 (19%)	59 (35%)	79 (46%)
Nothing in mind	19 (63%)	8 (27%)	3 (10%)

The generation of autobiographical memories is complex. Which is, perhaps, not so surprising given the central nature of this type of memory to self. The basic idea is, however, relatively simple: a control process (the working self) modulates access to the autobiographical knowledge base (autobiographical knowledge and episodic memories). In the case of a cue that directly maps onto episodic memories, as part of a general event and a lifetime period, a stable pattern of activation is formed and a specific autobiographical memory can then become linked to working self goals, at which point a memory enters conscious awareness. If the cue does not correspond directly to prestored knowledge then it needs to be elaborated and the autobiographical knowledge base will be iteratively sampled as outputs (activated knowledge) are evaluated and the cue elaborated, i.e. cue specificity is increased. In this way the generative retrieval process successively elaborates the cue and, in so doing, it channels activation into autobiographical memory knowledge structures until a stable pattern of activation is formed that satisfies working self constraints, i.e. that the memory should be about topic 'X' and should have features 'Y' for it to be accepted as a memory. Once this occurs a specific autobiographical memory is formed and can enter conscious awareness. This constructive process, despite being effortful and attention-demanding, works fluently in everyday cognition. It occurs outside conscious awareness, although some of the products of generative retrieval can be consciously experienced, e.g. cue elaboration and activated long-term knowledge.

Summary of Section 3

- Autobiographical remembering of a specific episode is *constructive* in nature. It brings together autobiographical knowledge (general events and lifetime periods), generic images and episodic memories.
- Recently Conway (2001) suggests a reconceptualization of 'episodic memory'. Accordingly, episodic memory is thought to consist of 'experience-near', highly specific, sensory–perceptual details of recent experiences. Only those episodic memories that then go on to be linked to long-term memory will be available later to support the formation of subsequent autobiographical memories.
- One role of the working self is to control the process of autobiographical memory construction. This is because constructing an autobiographical memory is a major cognitive occurrence, and has consequences for all other types of processing. The working self can be thought of as a complex goal hierarchy, modulating access to knowledge in long-term memory, and controlling knowledge that can enter the knowledge base. Episodic memories are then interpreted in terms of the self.
- The process of memory construction itself can be either intentional (generative retrieval) or unintentional (direct retrieval).

4   Autobiographical memory in distress

As mentioned earlier (see memory 5, at the beginning of this chapter) probably the most outstanding form of direct retrieval occurs in the clinical disorder, PTSD, in which memories for traumatic experiences figure prominently (Brewin and Holmes, 2003, provide a recent review). In PTSD a range of symptoms are present but one that is most marked is that of persistent intrusive thoughts and memories. Consider the case of John (see overleaf).

Case study

NB John is not the real name of this patient. Details of the case have been changed in order to protect anonymity.

'John' was seen for an emergency appointment with a psychiatrist due to his recent suicidal thoughts. The psychiatrist noted that three months previously he had seen a friend fall to his death from a building, but would not talk about it. He was then referred for assessment with a clinical psychologist. At the first meeting he appeared distracted, jumpy and low in mood. He had stopped work three months previously and spent all day at home. He did not like to leave his house, although felt safer going out in the dark. He could not listen to music. He reported feeling very tired as he frequently had nightmares. He also described being overwhelmed by mental images of his friend's death, which he tried hard to push away from his mind. He had periods where he felt unreal and cut off from other people.

Although autobiographical remembering often involves an effortful and constructive process, in an individual like John it seems almost impossible to prevent memories of the trauma coming spontaneously to mind. It is as though these were directly retrieved despite the clear disruption they caused. Such direct retrieval of scenes from highly negative experiences is perhaps not so uncommon. Think back to a traumatic experience that you may have had, such as a car crash. Did it ever haunt you afterwards, with vivid images of the experience just 'popping' into mind? Or have you ever been to see a horror film and then found the next day that images of the worst scenes intrude into your mind? People with PTSD like John, and like the man who provided memory 5 (at the beginning of the chapter) during therapy for PTSD relating to his road traffic accident, may have numerous intrusive memories of a trauma in a single day. Often these cause destabilizing emotions like intense anxiety, guilt, fear, and often all of these occur when a trauma image intrudes uncontrollably into consciousness. Memory intrusions in PTSD are highly disruptive to other cognitive processes, they hijack attention and ongoing experience, and in so doing make even the most routine tasks difficult. The sufferer is constantly being thrown into 'retrieval mode' and this diverts attentional resources away from other goal-driven processes. It is perhaps one of the reasons that John withdrew from work and daily life: the goals of everyday cognition were just too difficult for him to attain while his attentional capacity was taken up with intrusive thoughts and memories.

PTSD is made up of several components (American Psychiatric Association, 1994): the traumatic event; response at the time of trauma; and subsequent psychological symptoms.

4.1   Traumatic event

First of all, the patient needs to report having experienced a 'traumatic event'. This is typically a situation in which the individual experienced or witnessed actual or threatened death, or serious injury to self or others. Examples include natural disasters, sexual assault, road traffic accidents, physical attack and torture. Trauma in this context does not include the everyday use of the word trauma, such as having a 'traumatic day' at work. In John's case, the trauma was seeing his friend fall down the centre shaft of a stairwell in a block of flats, to his death.

4.2   Response at the time of trauma

It is not only the experience of a trauma that contributes to a diagnosis of PTSD. The person's reaction to the trauma is also critical. For example, soldiers fighting in an army or doctors performing surgery are exposed to death or serious injury routinely. While many people in such occupations do at some stage become traumatized, many do not. In comparison to the number of people who have experienced 'a trauma', community studies have estimated variable rates of PTSD occurring within the general population ranging from 1 per cent to 14 per cent (American Psychiatric Association, 1994). Clearly, not everyone who has a trauma goes on to develop PTSD. Thus, the second component of PTSD is that the person's response to the trauma involved intense fear, hopelessness or horror (American Psychiatric Association, 1994). For example, if there were two people in a car that crashed into the side of a bus, narrowly missing a head-on collision, one person might think 'I'm going to die' and be intensely afraid. The other person might feel only mild fear and conclude 'Phew! I'm so lucky this isn't worse'. Only the first person would display a symptom of PTSD and, most probably, only this person would go on to develop the full range of PTSD symptoms. In other words the traumatic event has to be experienced as stressful in a major way and possibly the neurobiological stress response of a major release of glucocorticoids must also occur if PTSD is to follow.

While the American Psychiatric Association's definition focuses on reactions of intense fear, hopelessness and horror, other intense emotions are also frequently experienced at the time of trauma such as anger or shame (Grey et al., 2001). Conway and Pleydell-Pearce (2000) suggest that the perception of extreme danger and or imminent death poses a fundamental challenge to the goal system of the working self. This is because the prospect of imminent death or extensive injury (physical or psychological) falls outside the range of plans, goals and self-images that constitute the working self. Thus, the trauma experience cannot be easily processed by the working self as it threatens the entire goal system, and because of this the experience cannot readily be integrated with autobiographical memory knowledge structures in long-term memory. On the other hand if the working self were to survive such trauma it would be highly useful from a survival perspective to retain a detailed record of what occurred. Thus, the tension is between either not encoding the (life) threatening experience (traumatic amnesia) or keeping a good record of it just in case one survives (a vivid, or 'flashbulb', memory). In fact, what is frequently observed in PTSD is, initially at least, a fragmentary often jumbled memory containing highly vivid details that are unordered with respect to their original order of experience, and often interspersed with extensive 'gaps' (islands of amnesia). Just the sort of compromise we might expect when the working self is caught in the double bind of encoding and not encoding. Conway and Pleydell-Pearce (2000) suggest that in some cases the working self responds by encoding aspects of the traumatic experience in terms of all the then active working self goals (rather than by integrating the new knowledge into the autobiographical knowledge base). The net effect of this is that (episodic) memories of some selective moments of the trauma memories appear to be 'burned' into memory (see Brewin *et al.*, 1996, and Ehlers and Clark, 2000, for other models of PTSD).

In John's trauma, he was on the stairs several floors below his friend when he slipped, so could not see him initially. John's first reaction was intense fear that the banging sound meant impending danger. Then he experienced intense horror as he saw his friend fall past. He therefore meets the 'emotional response' criteria for PTSD. At the time John also felt intensely unreal, as if he was watching the event happen to him from outside of his body. He felt as if time had slowed down and that he was watching the event in slow motion. This phenomenon is known as detachment or dissociation (American Psychiatric Association, 1994), and is a common reaction during trauma. At the time of trauma, the feelings of unreality John experienced can be thought of as protecting the working self from the destabilizing psychological impact of the trauma (van der Kolk *et al.*, 1996). That is, through mentally distancing himself from the situation he may have protected the working self from being overwhelmed with emotion. Interestingly, it is also worth noting that while dissociation may be protective at the time of trauma it is also a strong predictor of developing PTSD (Shalev *et al.*, 1996).

4.3   Subsequent psychological symptoms

PTSD includes various psychological symptoms displayed by the patient. The symptoms present in three groups:

4.3.1   Re-experiencing symptoms including intrusive memories

'Re-experiencing' a trauma includes having recurrent and intrusive recollections of the event (known collectively as 'intrusions'), recurrent distressing dreams, having 'flashbacks' that involve suddenly acting or feeling as if the event were happening again, as well as intense physiological reactivity and psychological distress to reminders of the event. Ehlers *et al.* (2004) provide many case study examples of intrusive flashback memories; one of their examples neatly illustrates just how powerful these traumatic episodic memories can be in hijacking the entire cognitive system:

> A patient who thought that he was going to die during an assault and would never see his children again, was not able to access the fact that he actually survived and saw his children again when he remembered this particularly distressing point of the assault. And when the intrusion occurred he would again be overwhelmed with sadness.
>
> *(Ehlers* et al.*, 2004)*

It should be noted that these sensory–perceptual–affective details are just the sort of autobiographical knowledge contained in recently formed episodic memories in the model outlined earlier. Indeed, it is central to the PTSD illness that the re-experience is mediated by episodic memories of the traumatic event itself. And this stands in sharp contrast to other psychological disorders that may also feature intrusive imagery of an *imagined* traumatic event (as in some cases of psychosis, e.g. of being cut in two by a man wielding a large sword; Morrison *et al.*, 2002) or of a catastrophic future event (as in obsessive compulsive disorder, e.g. violently attacking elderly parents with an axe; de Silva, 1986). Thus, John, for example, was plagued by countless episodic images of his trauma, and mentioning the incident in his assessment interview caused him to re-experience them. He had five specific images that intruded. These were:

- a banging noise

- seeing his friend fall past him

- the bottom of a helicopter ambulance

- the exterior of the block of flats

- himself swearing at another friend.

These episodic images contained sensory and emotional experience from the time of encoding that included mood states at the time of trauma (for John, fear and horror) and feelings of unreality.

4.3.2 Avoidance symptoms

Various reminders of the trauma trigger the re-experiencing of traumatic memories. In the exercise you did earlier you saw how cue words facilitate retrieval of detailed episodic memories. However, the key point about both generative and direct retrieval is that at some stage during retrieval a cue has to be present that can access the *content* of the sought-for knowledge (Tulving and Thompson, 1973). In PTSD, there may however be many cues for the trauma knowledge (especially if this is represented in memory in terms of goals active at the time of experience) and these have a tendency to generalize to other stimuli with shared features. For example, for a person raped by a bearded man, all men with beards may trigger re-experiencing symptoms, i.e. memory intrusions. Even more generally for someone who had a road traffic accident with a red car, the colour red, even on postboxes or clothes, may trigger intrusive memories of the crash. These generalizations are made non-consciously and at first it may not be evident why an intrusive memory comes to mind. Ehlers *et al.* (2004) give the following example: 'A rape victim noticed that she was feeling extremely anxious while talking to a female friend in a restaurant and subsequently realized that the feeling was probably triggered by the presence of a man on another table who bore some physical similarity with the rapist' (Ehlers *et al.*, 2004).

PTSD sufferers rapidly learn what triggers their re-experiencing intrusive memories and, once learned, such potent cues are avoided, which can sometimes lead to dysfunctional behaviour, e.g. avoiding all red objects of a certain size, leaving a restaurant abruptly. **Avoidance** is then the second cluster of PTSD symptoms. John, for example, stopped playing all music as any rhythmic beat caused him to re-experience the 'banging' image and distress. He stopped going out during the day as the sight of tall buildings also brought back powerful intrusions. He also avoided talking about the trauma, which made it difficult in therapy initially. Although avoidance may feel helpful in the short term, in the longer term avoidance of reminders of a trauma will not enable someone with PTSD to recover. Avoidance forms part of the vicious cycle which maintains the disorder (Ehlers and Clark, 2000).

4.3.3   Amnesia as avoidance

A further form of avoidance is involuntary in nature and takes the form of amnesia for the trauma, or parts of the trauma. This may occur because the working self inhibits knowledge that was nonetheless encoded: often in therapy some memory returns to PTSD patients suggesting that it was in fact inhibited rather than not encoded. On the other hand the overwhelming of the working self by negative emotions may render encoding through this structure ineffective. The result is an amnesia more like that seen in anterograde amnesia following brain damage. This could also occur because the stress response causes a temporary increase in glucocorticoids and while levels of this neurohormone are raised the MTL (medial temporal lobe) is temporarily disabled. At his therapy assessment John was not able to recall his memory of the time between seeing his friend fall past him at the top of the stairwell, and then when he was standing outside the building in a crowd. He said it felt like a 'gap' and, unlike the rest of his trauma, he was unable to recall it even with effort. Some patients can report having no awareness for hours after a trauma, and arriving in a place miles away with no idea of how they have got there – a dysfunctional and distressing consequence of **psychogenic** or **functional** amnesia (so termed to distinguish it from **organic amnesia** but, of course, all amnesia presumably has a physiological correlate).

4.3.4   Hyperarousal symptoms

Hyperarousal may feel like being in a constant state of 'red alert' for potential danger. People with PTSD have an exaggerated startle response in that even small, unexpected noises make them jump. John repeatedly flinched throughout his assessment interview, for example if he heard a sound in the corridor outside. Other symptoms of hyperarousal are impaired concentration and irritability. Some patients are no longer able to concentrate on simple activities such as reading a newspaper or cooking. Impaired concentration links with features of autobiographical memory discussed earlier; that is, the process of retrieval of specific events (such as intrusions) is disruptive to other cognitive processes. John found it difficult to read the psychological assessment questionnaires and even to sustain attention when watching television.

4.4   Impact of symptoms

The final component of PTSD is the duration and impact of the disorder. To meet the diagnostic criteria the person must have had the cluster of PTSD symptoms for at least one month. This is because after a trauma most people typically have trauma symptoms, such as intrusive memories, for a short time. The impact criterion is standard to most mental disorders; that is, that the symptoms have caused significant and persistent distress for the person, for example in their occupation or socially. John had stopped working and also avoided all his friends. Indeed he was so distressed by his symptoms and the impact they had had on his life that he had begun to contemplate committing suicide.

In summary, then, to receive a diagnosis of PTSD, a patient must have experienced a traumatic event and responded to it with fear, helplessness or horror. The patient must persistently re-experience the trauma, avoid stimuli associated with it and have symptoms of increased arousal such as an exaggerated startle response. The trauma in John's case of PTSD was witnessing the violent death of a friend. John showed the full range of PTSD symptoms, especially intense intrusive memories, and these had a profound negative impact on his quality of life. Now we have gone through the diagnosis, go back and read the case vignette at the start of this section. Can you see how the symptoms John presented at assessment make sense?

4.5   The nature of intrusive trauma memories

Re-experiencing trauma in the form of intrusive memories is the hallmark symptom of PTSD, and because of it PTSD is one of the major psychopathological disorders of autobiographical memory. Phenomenologically, intrusive trauma memories have several distinctive features that relate to our understanding of normal non-traumatized autobiographical remembering. For instance, intrusive memories are image-based and they very often take the form of visual sensory–perceptual snapshots or 'film clips' (Ehlers and Steil, 1995). Just the sort of mental representation characterized earlier as sensory–perceptual–affective experience-near 'episodic' memories. Notably this contrasts with mental experiences associated with other anxiety disorders such as ruminative thoughts and worries, which often present in verbal form. The intrusive trauma images, although typically visual, may also incorporate sounds and smells and, sometimes, bodily sensations (Ehlers et al., 2002). For example, a woman who was raped in the dark, encoded memory in non-visual sensory modalities, and during treatment reported suddenly experiencing physical pain and smells. John's images were a mixture of visual and auditory images. The memories also contain the emotion experienced at the time of trauma, such as fear, shame or disgust (Grey et al., 2002) or feelings of unreality. As his friend fell past him, John felt unreal and saw the scene as if he were outside of his own body looking down on himself. He therefore experienced most of his intrusive images as if he was 'out-of-body' and often felt unreal. Also, intrusive memories can include verbal cognition from the time of trauma, typically catastrophic thoughts such as 'I'm going to die' (Holmes et al., 2005).

Trauma memories have a quality of 'nowness' or 'live feel' (cf. Brown and Kulik, 1977). In normal autobiographical remembering the recall of specific events is accompanied by visual images and recollective experience, but in PTSD intrusive memories can be so compelling that the trauma feels as if it is in reality happening again. That is to say that the recollective experience component, the sense of the self in the past, appears to be overwhelmed or blocked by the intensity of re-experience: the PTSD sufferer does not have a sense or feeling of the self in the past; instead they are *actually* in that past moment. One woman with PTSD, for example, had a traumatic experience involving gun shots. Whenever she heard a sudden bang, such as a balloon pop at a children's birthday party, she would feel as if it was happening again and throw herself to the floor in protection. This type of experience is an example of a 'flashback'. Such cue-driven direct recall of overwhelming re-experienced memories is unusual in normal autobiographical remembering. Nevertheless, the same mechanisms may be operating: namely a cue accesses the content of a sensory–perceptual–affective episodic memory and this becomes rapidly available to attention and consciousness. Without the working self to effectively intervene in direct retrieval the memory will capture attention and dominate consciousness. Perhaps this would occur much more frequently in normal recall if control processes did not act to prevent patterns of activation, which constantly arise and dissipate in the knowledge base, coming to mind. Additionally, if episodic memories were more integrated with the autobiographical knowledge base it seems likely that they would not come to mind with such a feeling of 'nowness' and instead be recollectively experienced as a part of an extended and integral past. Indeed one of the goals of successful treatment of PTSD is to reach a point at which, when a patient recalls a trauma memory, it is experienced more like a normal autobiographical memory, as a part of the past and less as a part of the 'now' (Ehlers and Clark, 2000). In other words, the aim is to restore recollective experience.

Another point of departure between normal and trauma memories is that, unlike usual autobiographical remembering, the intrusive memories of trauma in people with PTSD often seem to be exact copies of what was experienced at the time of trauma. Moreover, the intrusions are usually highly consistent, being the same each time they come to mind. Such impressive consistency suggests that the same mental representation (episodic) memory is accessed each time an intrusion occurs. However, the veridicality of trauma images is a contentious issue and these may not always be based on experience. Holmes *et al.* (2005) found that, of a sample of patients with PTSD, approximately 2 per cent of different intrusive images were reported by participants as not actually being of their trauma experience. While this indicates that participants believed that most of their intrusions were of the event, it is possible that objectively they may not have been. Images, for instance, can be associated with beliefs that do not accurately reflect what in reality happened. Hackmann *et al.* (2004) report the case of a woman who, after a house fire, experienced repeated intrusions of curtains burning. These led her to believe that her daughter was burning alive. However, she also had another intrusion of when she saw her daughter's body in the morgue, which was unburned. The daughter had in fact died of smoke inhalation. The patient was, however, unable to connect the different information in the two images. Possibly these contradictory, highly vivid trauma images reflect unresolved affective conflicts in the patient.

Incidents of distortion and false images in trauma memories do then occur (Ehlers *et al.*, 2004; Conway *et al.*, 2004) and they pose an interesting question, namely: if a memory of a trauma is created in part to preserve a detailed record of what occurred when one survived a trauma, how can it contain distortions and errors? The question has not yet been addressed by the appropriate research but we might speculatively consider the role of the working self in generating phantasies that protect the self from deeply undermining cognition. Whatever eventually turns out to be the explanation it is clear that distortion in PTSD images requires just as much an explanation as do accurate flashbacks.

Trauma images are like 'highlights' picked out in a trailer for a film, except that they can occur one by one rather than as a sequence and often do not appear to coalesce in any obvious way and instead present as fragmented and disorganized

(Foa *et al.*, 1995). Earlier it was reported that John had five distinct images of his trauma and these too appeared unorganized and fragmented. Interestingly, most PTSD patients spontaneously report between three and five trauma images (Hackmann *et al.*, 2004) suggesting that there may be some consistency in accessing trauma memories. More generally, however, one of the fascinating questions about trauma memories is why are there intrusive images of some moments but not others? Researchers have begun to address this question by investigating 'hotspots' in trauma memories (Richards and Lovell, 1999; Ehlers and Clark, 2000). These are elicited by asking the patient 'What are the worst parts of your trauma when you describe it?' These worst moments correspond to the moments that intrude. Grey *et al.* (2001) found that hotspot images are associated with a wide range of 'peak' emotions. They consist of the sensory–perceptual information encoded at that point in time, as well as the cognition linked to the specific emotion. For example, a patient had an extremely fear-filled image of the sound of impact during a crash and the sensation of being flung forwards, accompanied by the cognition 'I'm going to die'. Hotspots that return as intrusive memories may then relate to moments during the experience of trauma when the working self was most intensely challenged and, clearly, repetitively and intrusively recalling such moments must act to destabilize the self.

Summary of Section 4

- Direct retrieval in an extreme, disruptive and distressing form is illustrated by the intrusive memories of trauma (e.g. flashbacks) experienced by people with post-traumatic stress disorder (PTSD).
- The features of PTSD include the traumatic episode itself, the person's experience at encoding, symptoms of re-experiencing the trauma in memory, avoidance and amnesia, and hyperarousal. The case study considered the clinical features from an autobiographical memory perspective.

5   Conclusion: what are autobiographical memories for?

A distinction is often drawn between 'correspondence' and 'coherence' models of memory. Correspondence models take as fundamental the accuracy of memory and its capacity, i.e. how much can be accurately remembered. Coherence models, in contrast, are not greatly concerned with accuracy and, instead, view the coherence of knowledge as being the fundamental principle guiding retention and remembering. The model of autobiographical memory described in this chapter draws on both these concepts and has as a central tenet what might be called adaptive coherence. Adaptive coherence always entails some degree of correspondence. Thus, episodic memories are summary records of short time-slices of experience and, to the extent that the experience accurately represented reality, then episodic memories are accurate records of the world. However, what is retained is filtered through the goal structure of the working self and integrated with pre-existing, long-term memory knowledge structures and is, accordingly, highly selective. Furthermore, what is retained is not simply stored in some sort of passive way, like books on a library shelf, but rather is contextualized by autobiographical knowledge and brought into association with other autobiographical knowledge, at varying levels of specificity, when constructed as a memory. Episodic memories are then *interpreted* in terms of the self. And this brings us to the closing question of this chapter: what are autobiographical memories for? As we have seen, autobiographical knowledge and constructed memories serve many functions, as must be the case for such a central form of cognition, although ultimately autobiographical memory can be characterized as having one overriding function – it links, indeed it binds, the self to reality.

Now that you have read this chapter you can reinforce and extend your learning by reading an original journal article associated with it, available online from the DD303 website. Remember, these are original journal articles, so the style is different from this textbook, and don't be too concerned if you can't follow every detail.

Further reading

For reviews of autobiographical memory research see:

Conway, M.A. and Pleydell-Pearce, C.W. (2000) 'The construction of autobiographical memories in the self memory system', *Psychological Review*, vol.107, no.2, pp.261–88.

McAdams, D.P. (2001) 'The psychology of life stories', *Review of General Psychology*, vol.5, no.2, pp.100–22.

For reviews of the major theories of PTSD and treatment see:

Brewin, C.R. and Holmes, E.A. (2003) 'Psychological theories of posttraumatic stress disorder', *Clinical Psychology Review*, vol.23, no.3, pp.339–76.

Foa, E.B., Keane, T.M. and Friedman, M.J. (eds) (2000) *Effective Treatments for PTSD*, New York, Guilford Press.

References

American Psychiatric Association (1994) *Diagnostic and Statistical Manual of Mental Disorders: DSM-IV* (4th edn), Washington, DC, American Psychiatric Association.

Baddeley, A.D. (1986) *Working Memory*, Oxford, Clarendon Press.

Baddeley, A.D. (2000) 'The episodic buffer: a new component of working memory?', *Trends in Cognitive Sciences*, vol.4, no.11, pp.417–23.

Beike, D.R. and Landoll, S.L. (2000) 'Striving for a consistent life story: cognitive reactions to autobiographical memories', *Social Cognition*, vol.18, no.3, pp.292–318.

Bluck, S. and Habermas, T. (2000) 'The life story schema', *Motivation and Emotion*, vol.24, no.2, pp.121–47.

Brewer, W.F. (1986) 'What is autobiographical memory?' in Rubin, D.C. (ed.) *Autobiographical Memory*, Cambridge, Cambridge University Press.

Brewer, W.F. (1988) 'Memory for randomly sampled autobiographical events' in Neisser, U. and Winograd, E. (eds) *Remembering Reconsidered: Ecological and Traditional Approaches to the Study of Memory*, New York, Cambridge University Press.

Brewer, W.F. (1996) 'What is recollective memory?' in Rubin, D.C. (ed.) *Remembering Our Past. Studies in Autobiographical Memory*, Cambridge, Cambridge University Press.

Brewin, C.R., Dalgleish, T. and Joseph, S. (1996) 'A dual representation theory of posttraumatic stress disorder', *Psychological Review*, vol.103, no.4, pp.670–86.

Brewin, C.R. and Holmes, E.A. (2003) 'Psychological theories of posttraumatic stress disorder', *Clinical Psychology Review*, vol.23, no.3, pp.339–76.

Brown, N.R. and Schopflocher, D. (1998) 'Event cueing, event clusters, and the temporal distribution of autobiographical memories', *Applied Cognitive Psychology*, vol.12, no.4, pp.305–19.

Brown, R. and Kulik, J. (1977) 'Flashbulb memories', *Cognition*, vol.5, no.1, pp.73–99.

Conway, M.A. (1996) 'Autobiographical memories and autobiographical knowledge' in Rubin, D.C. (ed.) *Remembering Our Past: Studies in Autobiographical Memory*, Cambridge, Cambridge University Press.

Conway, M.A. (2001) 'Sensory perceptual episodic memory and its context: autobiographical memory', *Philosophical Transactions of the Royal Society – Series B – Biological Sciences*, vol.356, no.1413, pp.1375–84.

Conway, M.A., Collins, A.F., Gathercole, S.E. and Anderson, S.J. (1996) 'Recollections of true and false autobiographical memories', *Journal of Experimental Psychology: General*, vol.125, no.1, pp.69–95.

Conway, M.A., Meares, K. and Standart, S. (2004) 'Images and goals', *Memory*, vol.12, pp.525–31.

Conway, M.A. and Pleydell-Pearce, C.W. (2000) 'The construction of autobiographical memories in the self memory system', *Psychological Review*, vol.107, no.2, pp.261–88.

Conway, M.A. and Rubin, D.C. (1993) 'The structure of autobiographical memory' in Collins, A.E., Gathercole, S.E., Conway, M.A. and Morris, P.E.M. (eds) *Theories of Memory*, Hove, Lawrence Erlbaum Associates.

de Silva, P. (1986) 'Obsessional compulsive imagery', *Behaviour Research and Therapy*, vol.24, no.3, pp.333–50.

Dritschel, B., Williams, J.M.G., Baddeley, A.D. and Nimmo-Smith, I. (1992) 'Autobiographical fluency: a method for the study of personal memory', *Memory and Cognition*, vol.20, pp.133–40.

Ehlers, A. and Clark, D.M. (2000) 'A cognitive model of posttraumatic stress disorder', *Behaviour Research and Therapy*, vol.38, no.4, pp.319–45.

Ehlers, A., Hackmann, A. and Michael, T. (2004) 'Intrusive re-experiencing in post-traumatic stress disorder: phenomenology, theory and therapy', *Memory*, vol.12, pp.403–15.

Ehlers, A., Hackmann, A., Steil, R., Clohessy, S., Wenninger, K. and Winter, H. (2002) 'The nature of intrusive memories after trauma: the warning signal hypothesis', *Behaviour Research and Therapy*, vol.40, no.9, pp.995–1002.

Ehlers, A. and Steil, R. (1995) 'Maintenance of intrusive memories in posttraumatic stress disorder: a cognitive approach', *Behavioural and Cognitive Psychotherapy*, vol.23, no.3, pp.217–49.

Erikson, E.H. (1950) *Childhood and Society*, New York, W.W. Norton and Company.

Erikson, E.H. and Erikson, J.M. (1982/1997) *The Life Cycle Completed*, New York, W.W. Norton & Co.

Fitzgerald, J.M. (1988) 'Vivid memories and the reminiscence phenomenon: the role of a self narrative', *Human Development*, vol.31, pp.261–73.

Fitzgerald, J.M. (1996) 'Intersecting meanings of reminiscence in adult development and aging' in Rubin, D.C. (ed.) *Remembering Our Past: Studies in Autobiographical Memory*, Cambridge, Cambridge University Press.

Fitzgerald, J.M. and Lawrence, R. (1984) 'Autobiographical memory across the life-span', *Journal of Gerontology*, vol.39, no.6, pp.692–8.

Fivush, R., Hammond, C. and Reese, E. (1996) 'Remembering, recounting, and reminiscing: the development of autobiographical memory in social context' in Rubin, D.C. (ed.) *Remembering Our Past: Studies in Autobiographical Memory*, Cambridge, Cambridge University Press.

Foa, E.B., Molnar, C. and Cashman, L. (1995) 'Change in rape narratives during exposure therapy for posttraumatic stress disorder', *Journal of Traumatic Stress*, vol.8, no.4, pp.675–90.

Franklin, H.C. and Holding, D.H. (1977) 'Personal memories at different ages', *Quarterly Journal of Experimental Psychology*, vol.29, pp.527–32.

Freud, S. (1955, first published 1899) 'Screen memories' in Strachey, J. (ed. and trans.) *The Standard Edition of the Complete Psychological Works of Sigmund Freud Volume 3*, London, Hogarth Press.

Fromholt, P. and Larsen, S.F. (1991) 'Autobiographical memory in normal aging and primary degenerative dementia (dementia of the Alzheimer type)', *Journal of Gerontology: Psychological Sciences*, vol.46, pp.85–91.

Fromholt, P. and Larsen, S.F. (1992) 'Autobiographical memory and life-history narratives in aging and dementia (Alzheimer type)' in Conway, M.A., Rubin, D.C., Spinnler, H. and Wagenaar, W. (eds) *Theoretical Perspectives on Autobiographical Memory*, Utrecht, Kluwer Academic Publishers.

Gardiner, J.M. and Richardson-Klavehn, A. (2000) 'Remembering and knowing' in Tulving, E. and Craik, F.I.M. (eds) *Handbook of Memory*, Oxford, Oxford University Press.

Grey, N., Holmes, E. and Brewin, C. (2001) 'It's not only fear: peri-traumatic emotional "hot spots" in posttraumatic stress disorder', *Behavioural and Cognitive Psychotherapy*, vol.29, no.3, pp.367–72.

Grey, N., Young, K. and Holmes, E. (2002) 'Cognitive restructuring within reliving: a treatment for peri-traumatic emotional "hot spots" in posttraumatic stress disorder', *Behavioural and Cognitive Psychotherapy*, vol.30, no.1, pp.37–56.

Hackmann, A., Ehlers, A., Speckens, A. and Clark, D.M. (2004) 'Characteristics and content of intrusive memories in PTSD and their changes with treatment', *Journal of Traumatic Stress*, vol.17, no.3, pp.231–40.

Haque, S. and Conway, M.A. (2001) 'Probing the process of autobiographical memory retrieval', *European Journal of Cognitive Psychology*, vol.13, no.3, pp.1–19.

Hollway, W. and Jefferson, T. (2000) 'Doing qualitative research differently', *Free Association, Narrative and the Interview Method*, London, Sage.

Holmes, A. and Conway, M.A. (1999) 'Generation identity and the reminiscence bump: memories for public and private events', *Journal of Adult Development*, vol.6, pp.21–34.

Holmes, E.A., Grey, N. and Young, K.A.D. (2005) 'Intrusive images and "hotspots" of trauma memories in posttraumatic stress disorder: an exploratory investigation of emotions and cognitive themes', *Journal of Behavior Therapy and Experimental Psychiatry*, vol.36, pp.3–17.

Howe, M.L. and Courage, M.L. (1997) 'The emergence and early development of autobiographical memory', *Psychological Review*, vol.104, pp.499–523.

Johnson-Laird, P.N. (1983) *Mental Models*, Cambridge, MA, Harvard University Press.

Larsen, S.F. (1998) 'What is it like to remember? On phenomenal qualities of memory' in Thompson, C.P., Herrmann, D.J., Bruce, D., Reed, J.D., Payne, D.G. and Toglia, M.P. (eds) *Autobiographical Memory: Theoretical and Applied Perspectives,* Mahwah, NJ, Erlbaum.

Markus, H. (1977) 'Self-schemata and processing information about the self', *Journal of Personality and Social Psychology*, vol.35, no.2, pp.63–78.

Markus, H. and Ruvolo, A. (1989) 'Possible selves: personalized representations of goals' in Pervin, L.A. (ed.) *Goal Concepts in Personality and Social Psychology*, Hillsdale, NJ, Lawrence Erlbaum Associates.

McAdams, D.P. (1982) 'Experiences of intimacy and power: relationships between social motives and autobiographical memory', *Journal of Personality and Social Psychology*, vol.42, no.2, pp.292–302.

McAdams, D.P. (1985) *Power, Intimacy, and the Life Story: Personological Inquiries into Identity*, New York, Guilford Press.

McAdams, D.P. (2001) 'The psychology of life stories', *Review of General Psychology*, vol.5, no.2, pp.100–22.

McAdams, D.P., Diamond, A., de Audin, E. and Mansfield (1997) 'Stories of commitment: the psychosocial construction of generative lives', *Journal of Personality and Social Psychology*, vol.72, no.3, pp.678–94.

McAdams, D.P., Reynolds, J., Lewis, M.L., Patten, A. and Bowman, P.T. (2001) 'When bad things turn good and good things turn bad: sequences of redemption and contamination in life narrative, and their relation to psychosocial adaptation in midlife adults and in students', *Personality and Social Psychology Bulletin*, vol.27, pp.472–83.

McClelland, D.C., Koestner, R. and Weinberger, J. (1989) 'How do self-attributed and implicit motives differ?', *Psychological Review*, vol.96, no.4, pp.690–702.

Morrison, A.P., Beck, A.T., Glentworth, D., Dunn, H., Reid, G., Larkin, W. and Williams, S. (2002) 'Imagery and psychotic symptoms: a preliminary investigation', *Behaviour Research and Therapy*, vol.40, pp.1063–72.

Murray, H.A. (1938) *Explorations in Personality*, New York, Oxford University Press.

Murray, H.A. (1943) *The Thematic Apperception Test: Manual*, Cambridge, MA, Harvard University Press.

Pillemer, D.B. (1998) *Momentous Events, Vivid Memories*, Cambridge, MA, Harvard University Press.

Pillemer, D.B., Picariello, M.L., Law, A.B. and Reichman, J.S. (1996) 'Memories of college: the importance of specific educational episodes' in Rubin, D.C. (ed.) *Remembering Our Past: Studies in Autobiographical Memory*, Cambridge, Cambridge University Press.

Pillemer, D.B. and White, S.H. (1989) 'Childhood events recalled by children and adults' in Reese, H.W. (ed.) *Advances in Child Development and Behaviour Volume 21*, San Diego, CA, Academic Press.

Richards, D. and Lovell, K. (1999) 'Behavioural and cognitive interventions in the treatment of PTSD' in Yule, W. (ed.) *Post-traumatic Stress Disorders: Concepts and Therapy*, Chichester, Wiley.

Robinson, J.A. (1992) 'First experience memories: contexts and function in personal histories' in Conway, M.A., Rubin, D.C., Spinnler, H. and Wagenaar, W. (eds) *Theoretical Perspectives on Autobiographical Memory*, Dordrecht, The Netherlands, Kluwer Academic Publishers.

Roediger, H.L., III and McDermott, K.B. (1995) 'Creating false memories: remembering words not presented in lists', *Journal of Experimental Psychology: Learning, Memory, and Cognition*, vol.21, pp.803–14.

Ross, M. (1989) 'Relation of implicit theories to the construction of personal histories', *Psychological Review*, vol.96, pp.341–57.

Rubin, D.C. (2002) 'Autobiographical memory across the lifespan' in Graf, P. and Ohta, N. (eds) *Lifespan Development of Human Memory*, Cambridge, MA, MIT Press.

Rubin, D.C. and Greenberg, D.L. (1998) 'Visual-memory-deficit amnesia: a distinct amnesic presentation and etiology', *Proceedings of the National Academy of Sciences*, vol.95, pp.1–4.

Rubin, D.C., Rahhal, T.A. and Poon, L.W. (1998) 'Things learned in early adulthood are remembered best', *Memory and Cognition*, vol.26, pp.3–19.

Rubin, D.C. and Schulkind, M.D. (1997) 'The distribution of autobiographical memories across the lifespan', *Memory and Cognition*, vol.25, pp.859–66.

Rubin, D.C., Wetzler, S.E. and Nebes, R.D. (1986) 'Autobiographical memory across the adult lifespan' in Rubin, D.C. (ed.) *Autobiographical Memory*, New York, Cambridge University Press.

Schank, R.C. and Abelson, R.P. (1977) *Scripts, Plans, Goals, and Understanding*, Hillsdale, NJ, Erlbaum.

Schuman, H., Belli, R.F. and Bischoping, K. (1997) 'The generational basis of historical knowledge' in Jodelet, D., Pennebaker, J. and Paez, D. (eds) *Political Events and Collective Memories*, London, Routledge.

Sehulster, J.R. (1996) 'In my era: evidence for the perception of a special period in the past', *Memory*, vol.4, pp.145–58.

Shalev, A.T., Peri, T., Canetti, L. and Schreiber, S. (1996) 'Predictors of PTSD in injured trauma survivors: a prospective study', *American Journal of Psychiatry*, vol.153, no.2, pp.219–25.

Sheldon, K.M. and Elliot, A.J. (1999) 'Goal striving, need satisfaction, and longitudinal well-being: the self-concordance model', *Journal of Personality and Social Psychology*, vol.76, no.3, pp.482–97.

Singer, J.A. and Salovey, P. (1993) *The Remembered Self*, New York, The Free Press.

Strauman, T.J. (1996) 'Stability within the self: a longitudinal study of the structural implications of self-discrepancy theory', *Journal of Personality and Social Psychology*, vol.71, no.6, pp.1142–53.

Thorne, A. (1995) 'Developmental truths in memories of childhood and adolescence', *Journal of Personality*, vol.63, no.2, pp.138–63.

Tulving, E. (1972) 'Episodic and semantic memory' in Tulving, E. and Donaldson, W. (eds) *Organization of Memory*, New York, Academic Press.

Tulving, E. (1983) *Elements of Episodic Memory*, Oxford, Clarendon Press.

Tulving, E. and Thompson, D.M. (1973) 'Encoding specificity and retrieval process in episodic memory', *Psychological Review*, vol.80, pp.352–73.

van der Kolk, B.A., van der Hart, O. and Marmar, C.S. (1996) 'Dissociation and information processing in posttraumatic stress disorder' in van der Kolk, B.A., McFarlane, A.C. and Weisaeth, L. (eds) *Traumatic Stress*, New York, Guilford Press.

Wheeler, M.A., Stuss, D.T. and Tulving, E. (1997) 'Towards a theory of episodic memory: the frontal lobes and autonoetic consciousness', *Psychological Bulletin*, vol.121, pp.351–4.

Woike, B. (1995) 'Most-memorable experiences: evidence for a link between implicit and explicit motives and social cognitive processes in everyday life', *Journal of Personality and Social Psychology*, vol.68, no.6, pp.1081–91.

Woike, B., Gershkovich, I., Piorkowski, R. and Polo, M. (1999) 'The role of motives in the content and structure of autobiographical memory', *Journal of Personality and Social Psychology*, vol.76, no.4, pp.600–12.

PART 3

CONCEPTS AND LANGUAGE

Introduction

In Part 1, we saw how cognitive psychology seeks to explain cognition in terms of information processing by developing and refining accounts that are expressed in terms of representations, which carry information, and computations, which transform the representations in various ways. In Part 2, we examined memory and different accounts of working memory, long-term memory and autobiographical memory.

In Part 3, we turn our attention to three related areas of cognition: language, categorization and thought.

We tend to think of language as a medium via which thoughts may be expressed, and to consider language and thinking as inherently human capabilities. Categorization, our ability to group things together into discrete categories bearing labels such as fruit, vegetables, tables and chairs, can be examined in different ways. It can be analysed from a perceptual point of view – how particular visual or auditory features, for example, can influence how we categorize the scenes that we perceive – and also from a linguistic viewpoint – how our categorization is influenced by the information we receive via language and also by the words we have available. In placing language, categorization and thought in Part 3, we have chosen to emphasize the many links between these areas. We also hope to draw attention to some of the links to other parts of the book too, such as those between categorization and perception, and between thinking and problem solving. Indeed, categorization or semantic classification can be seen as the next stage on from perceptual classification, the focus of Chapter 4.

Gareth Gaskell's Chapter 8 addresses some of the ideas that are later developed in Chapter 9, but seeks to explain something that superficially appears very different – how we comprehend both spoken and written language. The chapters in Part 1, and Chapter 9 to some extent, are concerned with how we perceive and pick up information concerning our environment, and how we use this information to infer the presence and nature of objects, and the categories to which they belong. Chapters 8 and 10 mark a concern with the social world, with how we communicate about our world to others. As Gareth Gaskell states in opening his chapter, understanding our ability to use language is key to understanding what differentiates humans from other animals, and key to understanding human cognition. What it is to be human is addressed in Chapter 10.

Chapter 8 draws our attention to many aspects of language processing that we normally take for granted. In comprehending spoken language, we have to infer which words are present in a stream of speech, an ability we learn as children. We also have to learn to make use of our knowledge of the speech sounds used in our particular language(s). These processes are easily taken for granted, and researchers have had to coin new terms and posit new theoretical structures, such as the mental lexicon, in order to make sense of the comprehension process. Researchers have assumed that different kinds of knowledge are brought to bear at different stages of comprehension. Models of the process that incorporate new theoretical structures and different kinds of knowledge have been constructed (e.g. the cohort model) and experiments conducted to evaluate them. Indeed, and in contrast with Chapter 9,

Chapter 8 focuses mainly on processing accounts and how well they explain experimental data. Also in contrast with Chapter 9, some of the processing accounts are sufficiently well specified that they have been developed as computational models. TRACE, for example, is a connectionist model, as is IAC, a model similar to one you saw in Chapter 4. That researchers have been able to develop such models successfully is a testament to how advanced our understanding is of the cognitive processes of language comprehension.

Nevertheless, running through Chapter 8, and in common with Chapter 9, is a concern with the extent to which we require general knowledge for processing language, and the time point at which this knowledge is brought to bear. The bottom-up (and autonomous) view is that, for example, semantic knowledge is only called upon late on in processing, and only then to adjudicate between interpretations of the incoming input. The top-down (and interactive) view is that such knowledge may operate early, and influence which interpretations are pursued. This important debate, ranging over phenomena such as spoken and written word recognition, ambiguity resolution and sentence comprehension, is as important as it is unresolved.

In Chapter 9, Nick Braisby outlines several different theoretical approaches to categorization. Despite being a fundamental ability, categorization appears to elude a comprehensive treatment. The first two theories outlined, classical and prototype theories, imply that concepts, our mental representations of categories, can be neatly demarcated one from another, and each understood in terms of sets of features. According to both theories we place items into a category if they possess a criterial number of these features. Such theories are knowledge-lean; that is, they assume first that it is possible to demarcate category-relevant knowledge, and second that only this knowledge is relevant to determining categorization.

However, both of these theories suffer a number of problems. The alternative theories discussed in the chapter assume that categorization is knowledge-rich; that is, it involves broader knowledge structures – lay theories about domains are implicated by the 'theory' theory of concepts, and beliefs about what constitute essential properties are implied by psychological essentialism.

As broader knowledge structures get invoked to explain categorization, however, you will see that it becomes harder to state theories precisely, and the discussion of theories in the chapter reflects this. Whereas classical and prototype theories are outlined with some precision, so that one can imagine detailed accounts of the process of categorization being given, 'theory'-based and essentialist theories are hard to define, and it is unclear whether an information-processing account could be developed at present.

Because of the difficulty in developing precise accounts of representations of categories and the processes constituting categorization, researchers have been led to revisit some of the simplifying assumptions previously made in this literature. Perhaps, for example, there might be different kinds of categorization for different kinds of category, or for different kinds of categorizer. In some sense, researchers are considering again what categorization really is. In the terminology of Marr's levels that we saw in Chapter 1, in spite of its fundamental importance, researchers are still seeking agreement over a level 1 account of categorization. Only then might we hope to develop precise level 2 accounts.

In Chapter 10, Alison Green considers a range of different perspectives on language and thought. A good starting point is to examine ideas on how language and thought have evolved, and whether or not these capabilities confer an evolutionary advantage upon us. Research at the interface with archaeology, anthropology and linguistics reveals fascinating advances in our understanding of the minds of our forebears. The excitement of working in such a rapidly developing field has to be weighed against the possibility that some avenues may prove to be dead ends, and it is important to acknowledge that our understanding of the evolution of language and thought may look rather different in a few years' time.

While Chapter 8 deals with the language system, Chapter 10 examines the interface between language and thought. Does thought depend on language, does language depend on thought, or is there a complex interdependency between the two? One intriguing issue that arises here centres on whether or not we possess a 'language of thought'. The 'language of thought' thesis underpins some of the ideas presented in Chapter 9, and centres on what is given, or innate, a question that philosophers have considered over the centuries. Nativism in its strongest form asserts that some capabilities are innate, and Chapter 10 examines this position with regard to both language and thought. Whilst it is clear that some things must be given, as we see in Chapter 10, specifying in detail what those things might be is a vexing task. Chapter 10 examines 'belief' as a propositional attitude, an example of a mental stance which might indicate that the individual has a 'theory of mind'. A 'theory of mind' appears to be a uniquely human attribute.

Contrasting with the nativist approach to language is that of the radical pragmatists. Radical pragmatics examines the extent to which meaning is context-dependent. We see that while researchers have taken very different stances to language, they are in fact asking rather different questions. Chomsky's recent emphasis is on language as a 'perfect' system and the minimal requirements for such a system, while Sperber has focused on language in use.

Finally, Chapter 10 reviews the linguistic determinism thesis, which postulates that language determines the kinds of thoughts we might have. In evaluating the evidence for this, we develop an understanding of what is required to adequately test the classic Whorfian hypothesis. Some have adopted the more conservative linguistic relativism position, arguing that language influences rather than determines thought. Chapter 10 examines the evidence and shows just how difficult a task it is to unambiguously describe the nature of the relationship between language and thought.

What do these three chapters reveal about the cognitive approach? Perhaps most notable in these chapters is the breadth of the cognitive approach. Researchers tackle very diverse questions – from what knowledge we have of categories to the question of how language and thought interface – but do so from a common perspective, that of seeking to posit mental representations, which carry information, and computational processes that transform them.

The chapters also invite us to think about the success and future of the cognitive approach. Chapter 8 shows how cognitive psychology has been successful in generating detailed processing models of language comprehension. Chapters 9 and 10 show a different kind of success: though researchers have yet to answer some of the basic questions about categorization, language and thought, the cognitive approach has helped them to generate different theoretical frameworks and empirical means of examining them. That is, the success of the approach can be measured not only in terms of the success of proposed models, but also in terms of the generation of new research questions. These new research questions point to promising collaborations at the interface with different disciplines.

To summarize, the three chapters in this part reveal a reciprocity between the precision with which theories and models may be specified and the extent to which a cognitive process appears to be knowledge-rich, the extent to which it seems to draw on general knowledge. The more general knowledge a process draws upon, the harder it is for researchers to develop precise models. It appears that precision – one of the hallmarks of a scientific account – can be achieved only when the knowledge that influences a cognitive process can be isolated or separated from other kinds of knowledge and demarcated in distinct processing modules. The question as to the modularity of cognition is one to which we shall return again and again.

Language processing   Chapter 8

Gareth Gaskell

1   Introduction

What are the qualities of human beings that differentiate us from other species? You can probably think of many characteristics, but pretty high on most people's lists would be the ability to produce and understand language. Linguistic abilities underpin all manner of social interactions – from simple acts such as buying a bus ticket or greeting a friend, right up to constructing and refining political and legal systems. Like many aspects of cognition, the ability to use language develops apparently effortlessly in the early years of life, and can be applied rapidly and automatically.

This chapter looks under the surface of the language system, in order to understand the unconscious operations that take place during language processing. Our focus is on the basic mechanisms required for language understanding. For example, understanding a simple spoken sentence involves a whole string of abilities: the perceptual system must be able to identify speech sounds, locate word boundaries in sentences, recognize words, access their meanings, and then integrate the word meanings into a coherent whole, respecting the grammatical role each word plays. Each of these abilities has been extensively researched, with numerous models of how information is processed being proposed and tested, and this chapter provides an overview of our current understanding in these cases. As you will see, there often remains considerable disagreement about some quite fundamental properties of the language system. Nonetheless, there has also been substantial progress in terms of identifying some of the features required of the language system for it to work the way it does.

The structure of this chapter roughly follows the time course of processing in language perception. Section 2 builds on some of the ideas about recognition introduced in Chapter 4, but looks specifically at the processes that result in the identification of spoken and written words. Models of these processes generally assume that word recognition involves access to a **mental lexicon** – something that was briefly introduced in Chapter 5 in the context of lexical concepts – which stores relevant information relating to the words we know (e.g. what they mean). Section 3 deals with the contents of the mental lexicon, and how this information might be organized. Finally, Section 4 looks at the process of sentence comprehension beyond the mental lexicon. It deals with how listeners use their knowledge of the grammar of a language to construct the meaning of a sentence. In each section some of the influential models of language processing are discussed, along with key experimental studies that help us to evaluate and refine these models.

2   Word recognition

Adult speakers of English tend to know somewhere between 50,000 and 100,000 words. Most common words are easy to describe and use, suggesting their meanings are clearly accessible. Less common words are perhaps represented more vaguely, with some words difficult to define out of context, but nonetheless generating a feeling of familiarity. For example, you might be reasonably confident that *tarantella* is a word and have good knowledge of how it should be pronounced, but you might still be unable to give a good definition of what it is (a fast whirling dance, once believed to be a cure for a tarantula bite!).

So quite a lot of information is stored in the mental lexicon about word meanings and pronunciations. The goal of word recognition is to access this information as quickly as possible. We shall look at how this process occurs in two different sensory modalities: auditory and visual. This may at first seem repetitious, but there are some important differences between the two modalities that, at this level of the language system, lead to quite different models of recognition processes. Before you read through the sections on word recognition, you may wish to remind yourself of the broader issues involved in recognition, as described in Chapter 4.

2.1   Spoken word recognition

Speech is the primary medium of language. Widespread literacy has emerged only in some cultures, and only in the last century or two, meaning that reading is, in evolutionary terms, a new ability. Speech in contrast is something that almost all humans acquire, and has been around long enough for some aspects of spoken language to be thought of as innate. Speech is also primary in the sense that we learn to understand and produce speech before we learn to read and write. For these reasons, we will firstly look at how spoken word recognition operates, and then go on to examine the visual modality.

2.1.1   Segmenting the speech stream

ACTIVITY 8.1

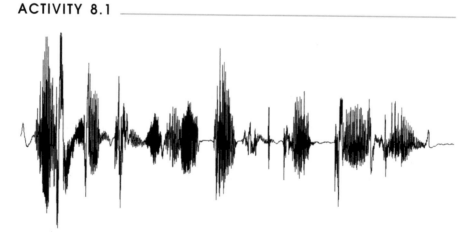

Figure 8.1   A speech waveform

The waveform in Figure 8.1 depicts a typical sound wave that might enter the ear when you hear someone speak. Try to work out from the sound wave how many words have been spoken, and pencil in a mark where you think each word boundary lies.

COMMENT

When you have noted down your estimates, compare them with the actual boundaries marked at the end of the chapter. How did you decide on likely word boundaries, and was this method a useful one? Most people assume that silent gaps between words are likely boundary markers, but they can be misleading. Some word boundaries do not involve silence because the surrounding **phonemes** are **coarticulated**, meaning that they blend together. A phoneme is the speech equivalent of a letter (they are normally annotated with surrounding slash marks), so, for example, /k/ and /ə/ are the first two phonemes in *confess*. Coarticulation refers to the fact that you have to prepare for upcoming phonemes well before they are produced, and these preparations lead to changes in the phonemes currently being pronounced. For example, the /d/ phoneme in 'do' and 'dah' sounds slightly different because of the following vowel. In addition, some silent gaps do not mark word boundaries: they are just points where the airways are closed in the course of uttering a word. For example, when you say the word 'spoken' your lips close briefly in order to produce the sudden release of air in the phoneme /p/. This results in a short period of silence between the /s/ and the /p/.

Our conscious experience of spoken words is in some ways similar to our experience of text on a page: words are perceived as coherent and discrete events, so we generally don't experience any difficulty in finding the dividing line between two words. However, the truth of the matter is that the speech waveform has no simple equivalent of the white space between printed words. Instead, as Activity 8.1 shows, silent gaps are unreliable as indicators of spoken word boundaries. Yet somehow the language system must be able to divide the speech stream up, so that the words contained in it can be recognized and understood. How then does this word **segmentation** process operate?

Models of segmentation can generally be divided into two types: (1) **pre-lexical** models and (2) **lexical** models. Pre-lexical models rely on characteristics of the speech stream that might mark a likely word boundary, whereas in lexical models segmentation is guided by knowledge of *how words sound*. The first model is pretty straightforward: the only issue at stake is what type of characteristic or cue can be extracted from the speech waveform as a useful indicator of a word boundary. We have already seen that silent gaps are not sufficient, but nonetheless silence can be useful, particularly if it lasts quite a long time.

Another important pre-lexical cue comes from the *rhythm* of speech. All languages have some unit of temporal regularity, and this provides the basic rhythm when an utterance is produced. In English, this unit is known as a **metrical foot**, and consists of a strong (stressed) syllable, followed optionally by one or more weak (unstressed) syllables (as you can see from Figure 8.2). Strong syllables are

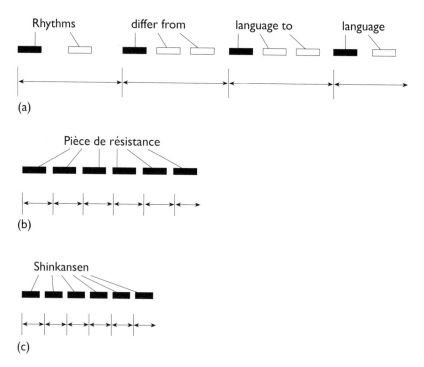

Figure 8.2   Examples of language rhythms. In English (a) the basic unit of rhythm is the strong syllable (the filled boxes). These stressed syllables are roughly equally spaced out in time when you produce a sentence, no matter how many weak syllables (unfilled boxes) there are between the strong syllables. Each group of strong and weak syllables is known as a 'foot', so when you say the sentence in (a), it may feel like you are speaking more quickly towards the end of the sentence because you need to fit in more weak syllables to maintain the gaps between the strong syllables. In French (b), the syllable is the unit of rhythm and so all syllables are roughly equally spaced in time. The rhythmic unit in Japanese (c) can be even smaller than a syllable. For example, *shinkansen* ('bullet train') contains six units of rhythm (including three single consonants), but only three syllables

reasonably clear landmarks in the speech stream, and most words that have a meaning (such as *bacon* or *throw*) rather than a grammatical role (e.g. *it*, *of*) begin with a strong syllable (Cutler and Carter, 1987). So, a segmentation strategy that predicts a word boundary before each strong syllable would seem like a valuable one for English speakers.

Cutler and Norris (1988) provided evidence supporting this idea: they played pairs of nonsense syllables to listeners, and asked them to monitor for any familiar word embedded in the speech (this is known as the **wordspotting** task – think trainspotting but duller). For example, in the sequence 'mintayve', which consists of two strong syllables, there is the embedded word 'mint'. Cutler and Norris argued that for a sequence like this listeners should identify the two strong syllable onsets (the /m/ and the /t/), and search for any words they know beginning at those points. This segmentation would obscure recognition of the word 'mint', because it spans a hypothesized word boundary (i.e. they would tend to hear two units: 'min' and 'tayve'). On the other hand, a sequence like 'mintesh' (where the second weak syllable contains a reduced 'uh' vowel) would tend to be segmented as a single unit, and so spotting the word 'mint' should be relatively easy. Their prediction turned out to be correct, suggesting that listeners make use of the rhythm of English in order to identify likely word boundaries. In languages where different rhythmic units dominate, such as French (syllables) or Japanese (subsyllabic units), similar sensitivities have been demonstrated (see Cutler and Otake, 2002), suggesting that early in life people 'tune into' their native language and optimize their segmentation strategy accordingly.

These (and other) pre-lexical cues are clearly valuable for identifying likely word boundaries in a sentence of utterances. However, none of the models that rely on pre-lexical cues can claim complete accuracy in boundary identification. This means that there will be cases where a boundary is incorrectly predicted, and other cases where a real boundary is missed. For example, a word like *confess* begins with a weak syllable, and so its onset would be missed by a pre-lexical segmentation strategy based on strong syllables. It seems that there must be some other mechanism available for cases like this. This is where lexical models can offer more insight: lexical segmentation models rely on our knowledge of particular words' **phonological representation** (what they sound like) to guide segmentation. The simplest version of this kind of strategy would involve recognizing each word in an utterance sequentially, and so predicting a new word at the boundary of the existing word (e.g. Marslen-Wilson and Welsh, 1978). For example, think about how the sentence 'Confess tomorrow or die!' might be segmented. If you can recognize the first word quickly (before it finishes), then you can use the knowledge that this word ends in /s/ to predict a word boundary as soon as the /s/ is encountered. You can then start again on word recognition with the speech following the /s/ (*tomorrow*). The problem here though is that most words are much shorter than *confess* and *tomorrow*, and cannot be recognized within the time-span of their acoustic waveforms, meaning that a lot of backtracking would be required to locate word boundaries using this method (think about trying to segment the sentence 'Own up now or die' using the same strategy).

We shall return to this issue in Section 2.1.3, when we evaluate the TRACE model of spoken-word recognition (McClelland and Elman, 1986), which provides a more powerful lexical segmentation mechanism. Although there is plenty of evidence supporting pre-lexical mechanisms, it remains likely that lexical competition operates alongside them to provide a more robust system for dividing up the speech stream.

Learning to segment speech

The cross-linguistic differences between segmentation mechanisms highlight the fact that the ability to segment speech is one that must be learnt during the course of language development. French and English babies aren't innately specified with different segmentation mechanisms; instead these develop as a consequence of exposure to language. Saffran *et al.* (1996) provided an impressive demonstration of how statistical information can aid the development of both segmentation and vocabulary acquisition.

They devised an artificial language made up of three-syllable words such as *dapiku* or *golatu*, and then used a computer to synthesize a long continuous stream of speech containing these 'words'. Their intention was to produce a sequence in their artificial language that contained absolutely no acoustic or rhythmic cues to the location of word boundaries. If people only make use of acoustic and rhythmic segmentation cues then the speech they hear should appear as unsegmented nonsense. However, if they can make use of statistical information about *co-occurrence* of syllables, then they may start to pick out the words of the language. In other words, they might start to notice that the syllables *da*, *pi* and *ku* quite often occur in sequence.

Using what is known as a 'head-turning' procedure, 8-month-old infants were tested on their perception of this kind of speech. The infants were presented with words from the artificial language on one loudspeaker and jumbled syllables (e.g. *pikugo*) on another. The idea was that if the infants found the words from the language familiar, they might spend more time listening to the novel sequences (and turn their heads towards the associated loudspeaker). Using this technique, Saffran *et al.* (1996) found that the infants *did* begin to pick out the words from the stream of syllables after just two minutes of the speech. This ability to learn the statistical properties of patterns is quite universal – it operates for adults and children as well as babies, and works just as well for non-speech stimuli such as tones or shapes (Saffran *et al.*, 1999). Therefore, speech segmentation may make use of a wide-ranging **implicit learning** ability, which may even be shared by other primates, such as tamarin monkeys (Hauser *et al.*, 2001).

2.1.2 Parallel activation

A spoken word typically lasts about half a second. In many ways it might simplify matters if the recognition process began only once the whole of a word had been heard. However, for the language system, this would be valuable time wasted. Instead, speech is continually evaluated and re-evaluated against numerous potential candidates for the identity of each word: this is known as **parallel activation**. A great advantage of this method of assessment is that it can lead to determination of a word's identity well before the end of the word is heard.

The mechanism sketched above is most clearly exemplified by the cohort model of Marslen-Wilson and colleagues (Marslen-Wilson and Welsh, 1978; Marslen-Wilson, 1987). This model assumes that as the beginning of a word is encountered, the **word-initial cohort** (a set of words that match the speech so far) is activated. For example, if the beginning of the word were 'cuh' (as in *confess*), then the word-initial cohort would include words like *canoe, cocoon, karate* and so on, because these words all match the speech so far. Then, as more of the word was heard, the recognition process simply becomes one of whittling down the set of potential candidates. For example, 'conf...' would rule out all the words above, but not *confess, confetti* or *confide*. At some point in this process (the **uniqueness point**) the candidate set should be reduced to a single word. According to the cohort model, the recognition process is then complete. As mentioned above, the recognition point in this kind of model can be well before the end of the word, meaning that valuable time is saved in interpreting the speaker's message.

However, even this conception of the process doesn't reflect the full fluency of word recognition. So far, we haven't discussed the *goal* of the recognition process – accessing our stored knowledge about a word. One might assume that this occurs at the recognition point of a word. However, it seems that access to meaning can occur substantially earlier. Marslen-Wilson (1987) demonstrated this using **cross-modal priming**. This technique – which is used to examine the extent to which the meaning of a spoken word has been retrieved – involves hearing a spoken **prime** word, followed swiftly by a visual **target** word. Participants were given the task of deciding whether the target was a word or not as quickly as possible. Semantic similarity between a prime–target pair such as 'confess' and *sin* leads to faster responses to the target (compared with an unrelated control pair, such as 'tennis' and *sin*). This implies that, on reaching the end of the word, the meaning of 'confess' has been activated. The question that Marslen-Wilson addressed was whether the meaning would be activated at an earlier point, before the uniqueness point had been reached. He found that when something like 'confe...' was used as a prime, responses to the target word *sin* were still facilitated. The same spoken fragment would also facilitate responses to the target *wedding*, which was semantically related to an alternative cohort member, *confetti*. This suggests that the meanings of both *confess* and *confetti* are briefly accessed while the word *confess* is being heard.

You might want to reflect on what this result means in terms of how we recognize spoken words. It suggests that when we hear a word, we don't just activate the meaning of that word, we also activate, very briefly, the meanings of other words that begin with the same phonemes. Meanings of likely candidates are activated before the perceptual system can identify the word being heard, which ensures that the relevant meaning has been retrieved by the time the word is identified.

Parallel activation of multiple meanings is an important property of the language recognition system. The alternative – a serial search, which would be a bit like looking through a dictionary for a word meaning – is unlikely to be as efficient (particularly for words near the end of the list). However, it is worth questioning the extent of parallel activation. For example, could it be the case that there is no limit to the number of meanings that can be activated briefly? And can these multiple meanings be accessed without any interference between them? Gaskell and Marslen-Wilson (2002) argued that meaning activation is limited, again on the basis of cross-modal priming data. They showed that if many meanings are activated at the same time, the resultant priming effect is relatively weak compared with the amount of priming found when just one or two meanings are compatible with the speech input. It appears to be the case that activating more than one meaning can only occur partially, so the gradual reduction of the cohort set of matching words is accompanied by a gradual isolation and amplification of the relevant meaning. Nonetheless, an overriding characteristic of the speech perception system is to access *too much* information rather than too little. This maximizes the chances of having accessed the correct meaning as soon as enough information has been perceived to identify the particular word.

2.1.3 Lexical competition

Marslen-Wilson's cohort model was important because it incorporated parallel evaluation of multiple lexical candidates, and emphasized the swiftness and efficiency of the recognition process. Later models used a slightly different characterization, and relied on the activation and competition metaphor (introduced in Chapter 4 in the discussion of the IAC model of face recognition). In these models, each word in the lexicon is associated with an **activation level** during word recognition, which reflects the strength of evidence in favour of that particular word. The cohort model in its original form (Marslen-Wilson and Welsh, 1978) can be thought of as a dichotomous activation model: words are either members of the cohort (equivalent to an activation level of 1) or they aren't (activation level 0). The advantage of more general models of lexical competition such as TRACE (McClelland and Elman, 1986) is that they can use continuously varying activation levels to reflect the strengths of hypotheses more generally. This is useful in cases where a number of words are consistent with the speech input so far, but the information in the speech stream matches some words better than others. If activation levels are on a continuous scale, then this inequality can be reflected in the activations assigned to word candidates.

The TRACE model is a connectionist model that assumes three levels of representation: the **phonetic feature** level (phonetic features are basically bits of phonemes), the phoneme level and the word level (containing a node for each word the listener knows). The idea of the model is that the speech stream is represented as changing patterns of activation at the phonetic feature level. These nodes feed into a phoneme recognition level, where a phonemic representation of speech is constructed. A word node has connections from all the phonemes within that word. For example, the *confess* node would have connections feeding into it from the /k/, /ə/, /n/, /f/, /ɛ/ and /s/ phoneme nodes. If the phoneme nodes for that word became activated, activation would then spread to the *confess* word node, resulting in strong activation for that word. The net result is that word-node activations reflect the degree to which each word matches the incoming speech.

A second mechanism provides a way of selecting between active words. Nodes at the word level in TRACE are connected by inhibitory links. When any word node becomes activated, it starts to inhibit all other word nodes (i.e. by decreasing their activation) with the strength of inhibition depending on the degree to which that node is activated. This competitive element tends to amplify differences in word activations, so that it becomes clear which words are actually in the speech stream and which are just *similar to* the words in the speech stream. So if the spoken word was *confess*, then the node for *confetti* would become strongly activated as well, because all phonemes in the input apart from the final one fit the representation of *confetti*. However, the *confess* node would be activated to a slightly greater extent because all phonemes in the input are consistent. Both these word nodes would be strongly inhibited by the other, but the greater **bottom-up support** (i.e. greater consistency with the incoming signal) for *confess* would ensure that the *confess* node would eventually win the competition, remaining activated when the *confetti* node had been strongly inhibited.

This 'winner-takes-all' activation and competition approach is common to many models both within language (we shall see another example in Section 2.2) and across cognition (e.g. face recognition). These commonalities across different areas of cognition are valuable, as they provide a way of extracting more general principles of cognitive processing from specific examples. In the case of speech, lexical competition provides a simple mechanism for deciding which words best match the speech input. As we saw in Section 2.1.1, it also provides a subsidiary means of segmenting the speech stream into words. This is because it is not just words which have the same onset, such as *confess* and *confetti*, that compete, but also words that simply overlap to some extent, such as *confess* and *fester* (see Figure 8.3). These words have a syllable in common (i.e. the second syllable of confess and the first syllable of fester). If this syllable is perceived, then both of these words will become activated, but through lexical competition only one will remain active. The segmentation problem can then be viewed as having been solved *implicitly* in the

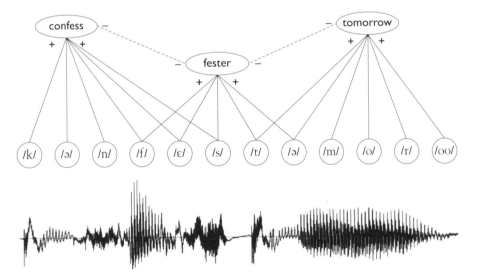

Figure 8.3   Illustration of lexical competition in the TRACE model. The speech stream activates a set of phonetic feature nodes (not shown), which then activate the corresponding phoneme nodes. Word nodes at the lexical level are linked up to the relevant phoneme nodes with positive links (solid lines). In this case, the speech is actually 'confess tomorrow'. This sequence actually fits three words completely: *confess*, *fester* and *tomorrow*. These word nodes have inhibitory connections between them that vary in strength depending on their degree of overlap. So there is no inhibitory link between the *confess* and *tomorrow* nodes, but the *fester* node has inhibitory links to both *confess* and *tomorrow* (broken lines). The combined inhibition of the fester node from the other nodes has the effect of suppressing its activation, leaving only *confess* and *tomorrow* as active lexical candidates. The competitive links between words in TRACE allow word recognition to be carried out, and also provide a mechanism for word boundary identification (there must be a boundary between the /s/ of confess and the /t/ of tomorrow)

activation of the word nodes. For example, if *confess* wins the competition then there must be a word boundary at the end of the syllable '*fess*', but if fester wins the competition then the boundary must be at the start of '*fess*'.

This general version of lexical competition is supported by a wordspotting experiment by McQueen *et al.* (1994). They looked at the time taken to spot a word like *mess* in two different types of embedding sequence. In a sequence like 'duhmess' the first two syllables match a longer word: *domestic*. If lexical competition operates for all overlapping words (see Figure 8.3), then the inhibitory link from the *domestic* node should make it difficult to spot *mess*. McQueen *et al.* found that detection rates were indeed lower and slower in this case, as compared to a case like 'nuhmess', in which a longer competitor does not exist. Lexical competition appears to be a rather neat way of performing two essential processes (word identification and segmentation) at the same time. Word identification performed in this way has the added bonus of providing a partial solution to the segmentation problem.

2.2   Visual word recognition

In this section we focus on the special qualities of word recognition in the visual domain, looking at how the recognition process operates, how visual and auditory processes are linked, and how eye movements are linked to the recognition system. Compared to speech, text might be thought of as an unproblematic medium. After all, it is relatively easy to spot where words begin and end, and text isn't transient in the way that speech is – if you misperceive a word on the page, you can simply go back to that word and try again. However, the availability of textual information also raises specific issues that must be addressed by models of visual word recognition. For example, because textual information is freely available over an extended period of time, we need to understand how the recognition system determines where the eyes should fixate, and for how long.

2.2.1   Models of visual word recognition

We have already seen how TRACE models *spoken* word recognition in terms of activation and competition in a multi-level connectionist network. TRACE was in fact a variant of an earlier model of visual word recognition proposed by McClelland and Rumelhart (1981). The visual model is often known as the IAC (interactive activation and competition) model, and shares many properties with the IAC model of face recognition you met in Chapter 4. The model contains three levels of nodes, representing activation of (1) visual features, (2) letters and (3) words. Like TRACE, it is the inhibitory units within a level that provide a competitive activation system. Visual input is represented by activation at the **featural** level, and facilitatory and inhibitory links between levels of representation allow activation to build up at the higher levels. In this way, visual word recognition can be modelled as an interactive competition process.

An important property of many of these competition networks is that as well as allowing activation to flow up through the system (i.e. from features through letters to words), during the course of recognition they also allow activation to flow in the other direction (from words downwards). This is another example of the concept of top-down processing that was introduced in Chapter 3. For example, if the word node for *slim* became activated, the activation would feed back through facilitatory links to the constituent letter nodes (i.e. 's', 'l', 'i' and 'm'). At first glance, these feedback links appear redundant, because the letter nodes are going to be activated in any case by bottom-up sensory information. But their value becomes apparent in cases where the bottom-up information is degraded in some way. For example, suppose that the first letter of *slim* was obscured slightly, so that the 's' letter node was only weakly activated by the visual input. In this case, the *slim* word node would still be activated by the three unambiguous letters, and would in turn increase the activation of the 's' letter node. The result would be correct recognition of the obscured letter, despite the weakness of the sensory evidence.

This kind of top-down influence can be useful in explaining **lexical effects** on lower-level processing. A classic finding in word recognition (known as the 'word superiority effect', or WSE) is that letter detection is easier when the letter forms part of a word (e.g. the letter 'i' is easier to detect in *slim* than in *spim*). This can be attributed to the influence of the word node for *slim* providing a secondary source of activation for recognition of 'i', whereas there is no secondary source for a non-word like *spim*. So the top-down feedback connections in the IAC model provide a neat explanation of why we often find lexical influences on recognition of sublexical units like letters.

However, Grainger and Jacobs (1994) demonstrated that a variant of the IAC model could also explain the WSE without any top-down feedback. They proposed that responses to the letter-detection task were based on two different levels of representation: a letter-detection response could be based on activation of letter nodes *or* word nodes. The idea here was that one of the pieces of information about a word stored in the mental lexicon is a description of the written form of the word. So if a word node reaches a critical level then the spelling of that word should be activated, triggering a response. The upshot was that the incorporation of a second basis for responses using lexical information allowed the WSE to be accommodated in a model that only used bottom-up flow of activation.

The experimental finding of WSE remains a robust and important phenomenon, but the research of Grainger and Jacobs shows that there is more than one way of explaining the effect. Whether or not top-down processing is needed is one of the most contentious questions in the area of word recognition (both auditory and visual) and other areas of perception, and it remains a hotly debated topic amongst cognitive psychologists (e.g. Norris *et al.*, 2000, and associated commentaries).

2.2.2 Mappings between spelling and sound

So far we have treated the question of how words are recognized separately for spoken and written words. This section looks at how these two modalities interact, and what this tells us about the language system. There is an obvious need for interaction in order to spell a word that you have just heard, or read aloud in a written sentence. But there are more subtle reasons for suspecting that there are links between the **orthography** of a word (its spelling) and its **phonology** (its sound). Some of the data we shall now look at suggest that visual word recognition relies strongly on spoken word representations and processes.

ACTIVITY 8.2

Think about what processes might operate when you read aloud the following words: *bell, stick, pint, yacht, colonel.* How does a reader convert the orthographic (or written) form to a phonological one in order to pronounce the words, and where is the phonological information stored? Would the same processes operate when you read the following non-words: *dobe, leck, brane, noyz?*

COMMENT

Researchers often refer to two different ways of reading words aloud (what we could call 'retrieving their phonology'). The division is much like the division between phonics and whole-word methods of teaching children to read. **Assembled phonology** (like phonics) means generating a pronunciation based on a set of mappings between letters and sounds for your language. For example the 'b' in *bell* corresponds to the /b/ phoneme, and there are similar conversion rules for 'e' and 'll'. This works well for words such as *bell* and *stick*, because they follow these conversion rules (i.e. they are regular items), and also for non-words like *dobe* and *leck*. But what about *pint, yacht* and *colonel?* A simple sounding out of these irregular words would lead to the wrong pronunciation (e.g. *pint* might be pronounced to rhyme with *hint*), suggesting that an alternative mechanism is available. This is often known as **addressed phonology**, and (like whole-word methods of teaching reading) relies on some kind of stored pronunciation of the whole word in the mental lexicon. *Brane* and *noyz* are unusual because their pronunciation coincides with the pronunciations of real words (i.e. *brain* and *noise*). These **pseudohomophones** (non-words that can be pronounced to sound like words) are generally only found in rock lyrics and some rather fiendish language experiments (see below).

As described in Activity 8.2, reading aloud is often portrayed in terms of two separate mechanisms: assembled and addressed phonology. The separate mechanisms are explicitly represented in dual-route models of reading such as the DRC model of Coltheart *et al.* (2001). DRC (see Figure 8.4) is a complex and powerful model, and builds on more than 100 years of theorizing about multiple routes in reading processes. For current purposes, the critical feature of the model is that it contains a 'rule-based' route to pronunciation via a grapheme–phoneme rule system (assembled phonology; see right-hand side of Figure 8.4), plus a 'lexical' route that requires retrieval of a stored pronunciation (addressed phonology; see left-hand side of Figure 8.4). Looking at the speed with which written words can be named often assesses the degree to which these routes are involved in reading. A typical finding is that regular words are named faster than irregular words (e.g. *pint*), but that this advantage is only present for **low-frequency** words (i.e. words that occur relatively rarely in the language). This can be explained by dual-route models in terms of a race between the two routes. Regular words can be named via either the lexical or the rule-based route to pronunciation, whereas irregular words can only make use of the lexical route. On the whole, naming speeds are faster when two routes are available (naming a regular word can be based on the output of whichever route delivers the pronunciation first), than when only one route is available (irregular words).

For low-frequency words, the advantage of two routes over one for regular words results in them being named more quickly. For high-frequency words, it is assumed that the lexical route operates very quickly regardless of regularity, and so the influence of the additional rule-based route is minimal.

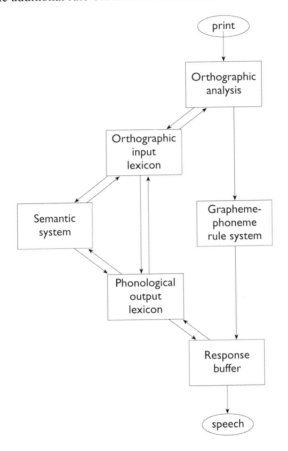

Figure 8.4 DRC model

Source: Coltheart *et al.*, 2001, Figure 6

Regularity is not the only variable that determines the speed with which a word can be named. Glushko (1979) showed that the properties of **neighbouring** words – words that have similar spellings, *not* words that are in neighbouring locations – are also critical. For example, people are quick to name a word like *wade*, because it is a regular word, but also because all neighbouring words with the same final letters have a consistent pronunciation (e.g. *made, jade, spade*). On the other hand, although wave is also a regular word, its neighbours are inconsistent in terms of pronunciation (e.g. *have* and *slave* don't rhyme). This inconsistency results in slower naming. Simple dual-route models, which apply the same rules to regular items irrespective of their neighbours, could not easily explain consistency effects, and an alternative conception of the spelling-sound mapping arose partly as a response. Seidenberg and McClelland (1989) proposed that a single connectionist network could provide a basis for modelling naming of both regular and irregular items, while accounting for effects of neighbouring items, as in Glushko's consistency effect.

There is an obvious need for phonology to be accessed in reading aloud, because speaking requires a phonological representation. But does phonology also have a role to play when a reader simply has to identify and understand written words? Van Orden (1987) showed that phonological representations are involved in silent reading even when they are detrimental to performance. Van Orden asked participants to decide whether visually presented words were members of particular categories, such as whether a *rose* is a flower. Critically, participants found it difficult to reject **homophones** to a category member, such as *rows*. In these cases participants would frequently make an incorrect response, suggesting that they were activating the pronunciation of the homophone, and this was creating confusion. A similar effect was found when the critical items were pseudohomophones (e.g. *roze*).

Other demonstrations have consolidated the idea that spoken word representations are heavily involved in visual word recognition in many different languages. This may seem rather bizarre – surely word recognition based on visual features would be simpler and quicker? But we need to remember that speech perception is to some extent an innate ability, and we learn to understand spoken language very early in life. So when we begin to read, we already have a perfectly tuned recognition system for speech. It therefore makes sense for the visual recognition system to 'latch onto' the spoken system in order to ease the learning process. A major issue, however, relates to whether and how the phonological system can be bypassed later in life as reading becomes more skilled (Frost, 1998).

2.2.3   Eye movements in reading

Speech perception is a relatively passive process, in that the listener doesn't need to perform any overt action in order to listen to a conversation. Reading a book or newspaper, however, is more active, because the reader controls the speed of uptake of information, and must direct their eyes in order to take in new information. Eye movements turn out to be enormously useful in revealing how the language system operates.

As discussed in Chapter 3, eye movements may feel quite smooth and continuous introspectively, but they really consist of **saccades** (jerky movements), followed by **fixations** (more-or-less-stationary periods) during which visual information is processed. Eye-tracking techniques can monitor the movements of the eyes during reading, and relate them to the location of the reader's gaze (see Box 8.2). Figure 8.5 illustrates the fixations involved in the processing of a typical sentence. Each numbered circle corresponds to the gaze location for a single fixation. Fixations typically last about 200 ms, but their durations are strongly dependent on the linguistic processing involved. For example, fixation duration is strongly dependent on the frequency of a word's usage in the language (Rayner and Duffy, 1986). This, along with many other effects, suggests that fixations are a measure of some kind of processing difficulty, and so they can reveal influential variables in reading.

8.2 — Methods

Eye tracking

Eye-tracking techniques generally rely on the fact that various parts of the eye such as the lens and the cornea reflect light. If a light source (usually infrared) is directed at the eye from a given angle, the angle of the reflection can be used to determine the orientation of the eye, and consequently the direction of gaze. Precise measurements can be made if the eye-tracking system combines measurements from more than one surface within the eye.

In studies of reading, the position of the head is often fixed using a chinrest and headrest and the participant is presented with text on a computer screen. Given that the head position is fixed and the distance from the screen is known, the reader's *gaze* location relative to the text can be calculated from the gaze-angle measurements. This results in a set of timed fixations to the text, as illustrated in Figure 8.5.

It is clear how eye-tracking studies would be beneficial for understanding how we read. However, a less obvious use of eye tracking is in the study of *spoken* language. Here, the participant is presented with a spoken sentence in the context of some visual scene, and the eye movements of the listener are monitored. For example, if a participant is sitting in front of a table with some candy and a candle on it, and is asked to pick up the candy, it is revealing to find out at what point people look at the candle, and correlate this with the amount of speech information they have received at that point (Tanenhaus *et al.*, 1995). In this kind of situation (see Section 4.4 for another example of this method), the participant needs to be able to move their head freely. To allow for this, a slightly different type of tracker is used, consisting of an eye tracker mounted on the head plus a second system for determining head position.

As Figure 8.5 illustrates, our eyes don't simply move from one word to the next as reading proceeds. Some words are skipped altogether, whereas others require multiple fixations. In a significant proportion of cases, readers perform regressive saccades (i.e. they move backwards through the text), as marked by the grey circle in Figure 8.5. Short **function words** (grammatical words like *we* and *on*) are much more likely to be skipped than **content words** (words that convey meaning, like *sentence* and *look*), and regressions can often tell us about cases where a word has been misinterpreted, due to some ambiguity (Starr and Rayner, 2001).

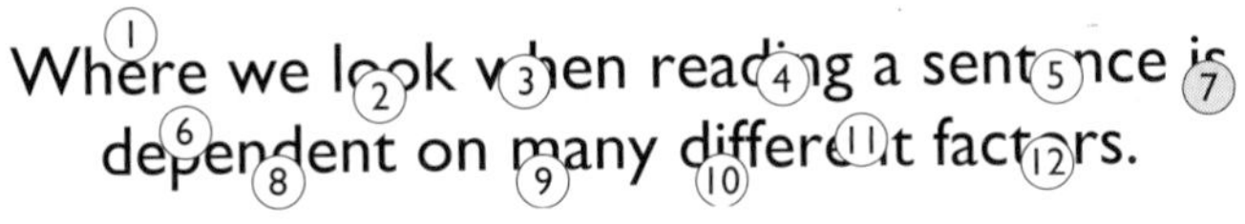

Where we look when reading a sentence is
dependent on many different factors.

Figure 8.5   Example of typical eye movements during reading

Eye-movement data are also valuable in terms of understanding where we fixate *within* a word. O'Regan and Jacobs (1992) showed that words are identified most quickly if they are fixated at a point in the word known as the **optimal viewing position**, or OVP. The OVP is generally near the middle of a word, but can be slightly left of centre in the case of longer words. The fact that fixations work best if they are near the middle of the word makes sense, given that visual acuity is best in the **foveal** (central) region of the retina (try fixating on the edge of this page and reading the text!). This slight but consistent bias in favour of left of centre is more intriguing. Shillcock *et al.* (2000) argued that this bias reflects a balancing of the informativeness of the parts of the word to the left and right of the fixation point. The OVP should be left of centre for longer words because there is greater redundancy towards the end of most of these words. For the word *cognition*, for example, it would be easier to guess what the word is from the first five letters (*cogni*) than the last five (*ition*). Shillcock *et al.* also found that for some shorter words such as *it*, the theoretical OVP was outside the word, either to the left or the right, perhaps explaining why shorter words are often not fixated when reading.

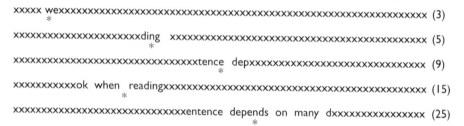

Figure 8.6   Example stimuli in a moving window experiment (e.g. McConkie and Rayner, 1975). The numbers in parentheses are the window sizes in characters. In a typical experiment the participant sits in front of a computer screen, with an eye-tracking system monitoring her gaze. Wherever the participant directs her gaze along a line of *xs* the computer displays around that point small 'windows' of unobscured text. All text outside this window is obscured by *xs* (in some experiments the gaps between words were preserved). The asterisk below each example marks the fixation point, and would not be seen by a participant (participants can fixate where they like). In this case the sentence is 'Where we look when reading a sentence depends on many different factors'

How much textual information can be utilized when a reader makes a fixation? The foveal region of the retina has the greatest acuity, but it spans a limited angle. It is possible that information can also be gained from the **parafoveal** region, which is wider but has reduced acuity. Rayner and colleagues have carried out a number of ingenious experiments aimed at assessing the perceptual span of readers. In one experiment they applied a moving window to text shown on a computer screen so that only a certain number of letters to the left and right of the current fixation point could be read (see Figure 8.6). Whenever the participant shifted their gaze, the window shifted accordingly. They found that if the window is small, reading is a slow and painful process, but for larger windows participants are barely aware of the text beyond the window that is masked.

The idea behind this technique is that the experimenter can gradually increase the window size until a point is reached at which reading speed and comprehension are normal. At this point one can be confident that the text beyond the window range is not used for normal reading. The results suggest that the perceptual span for English readers is quite limited: about 15 characters to the right of fixation and 3 characters to the left. The asymmetry is due to the left-to-right nature of reading in English – there is more useful information to be gained in text following the fixation position than the text preceding the fixation (which has normally already been read). In a right-to-left language like Hebrew the asymmetry is swapped, showing that the perceptual span in reading is shaped by the requirements of the written language.

Summary of Section 2

- In speech, finding out where words begin and end is a non-trivial problem. Models of word segmentation rely on either features of the speech stream or knowledge about how words sound.
- Word recognition relies on parallel assessment of multiple options, and competition between word candidates.
- Models of word recognition differ in the extent to which top-down processing is required.
- Visual word recognition relies to a considerable extent on speech codes.
- Studying eye movements during reading reveals what aspects of visual word recognition cause difficulties.

3   The mental lexicon

In Section 2, word recognition was largely viewed as an identification procedure. That is to say, we assumed that the mental lexicon stores representations of what words sound and look like, and that when we hear or see a word there is a recognition process that compares the input with stored representations. However, identification is just the first step towards understanding a word – what we *really* need to know is what a word means. In this section we shall move beyond identification, and look more closely at how word meanings are accessed during the recognition process. We shall look at the **semantic content** (how word meanings are stored) and the **semantic organization** (how word meanings are related) of the mental lexicon. Before we do this, we shall also take a brief look at quite a difficult area of language processing known as **morphology**.

3.1   Morphology

Morphology deals with the size of units in the mental lexicon. It's often taken for granted that the basic unit of the mental lexicon is the word, but in fact many words can be broken down into **morphemes** (the smallest meaningful unit within a word) when they are perceived. This implies that the morpheme is the true basic unit. This is particularly the case for languages such as Turkish in which words tend to be rather long, cumbersome units, and a lexicon based on morphemes would be more economical (fewer entries) and more flexible.

Most people are aware that words can be divided up into meaningful units, and that these units follow some grammatical rules. For example, we know that plurals in English are generally derived by adding an 's' to the singular form, as in *cats* or *dogs*. In its spoken form, the rule is slightly more complex: speakers add on /s/, /z/ or /iz/, depending on the final phoneme of the singular form (think about how you would say the plural forms *cats*, *dogs* and *pieces*). This kind of relatively minor modification of a word (for example, marking pluralization or tense) is known as an **inflectional change**, and is covered by a branch of morphology known as **inflectional morphology**. More major modifications are possible as well, in which the grammatical class of a word may change. For example, the suffix -*ness* can change an adjective to a noun (as in *happiness* or *weakness*). Similarly, the suffix -*ly* can change an adjective into an adverb. These modifications form part of **derivational morphology**.

The examples of morphological change given above are particularly straightforward. All involve regular changes in which the meaning of the word is predictable from the meanings of the morphemes. But things are not always so simple. For example, according to the regular pluralization rule, the plural form of *mouse* should be *mouses* not *mice*. *Mice* is an example of an irregular plural form, and similar irregularities exist in many types of morphological change. Similarly, the meanings of the morphemes making up a word may not always determine the meaning of the whole word. It's easy to spot the relationship in meaning between *govern* and *government*, but not between *depart* and *department*, yet both pairs have (at least supposedly) the same morphological relationship.

The descriptions given here are linguistic ones, but do they have any relevance to cognitive psychology? In other words, do the regularities that exist between families of words have any effect on the organization of the mental lexicon? It is quite possible that our recognition system is set up to recognize words, regardless of their substructure. This **full-listing** approach would mean that recognizing a word made up of many morphemes such as *disenchantment* is essentially the same process as recognizing a single-morpheme word such as *cat*. The opposite extreme – often known as the affix-stripping or **decompositional** approach (Taft and Forster, 1975) – is that words are chopped up into morphemes as they are perceived, and the morpheme is the basic unit of representation in the lexicon.

One way of looking at whether the lexicon is organized in terms of morphemes is to test whether we can add morphemes on to unknown words. A classic demonstration of this kind of generalization is Berko's 'wug test' (1958), in which children were encouraged to generate the plural form of novel words. For example, a child might see a drawing of a toy and be told that it was a *wug*. The child would then see two of these toys and be prompted to say what they were. Children found it easy to generate the correct inflected form (*wugs*), suggesting that they had learnt some kind of pluralization rule, and that the 's' can operate as an independent morpheme. The pluralization suffix is a particularly common one, but other morphemes such as -*ment*, as in *government*, or *en*-, as in *enact*, are more rare. This factor may affect the way different morphemes are represented in the lexicon. It may be that common morphemes such as the plural morpheme are stored as separate units, but less common units have no separate representation.

Marslen-Wilson *et al.* (1994) used the priming methodology to examine whether morphemic units exist in the mental lexicon. Their reasoning was that if words are broken down into morphemes then we should be able to get strong priming effects between words containing the same morpheme. They found that priming of this type depended on some shared meaning between the two words. So hearing *cruelty* resulted in faster processing of *cruel* because they have similar meanings, but hearing *casualty* did not prime responses to *casual*, presumably because there was no clear link between the meanings of the two words.

These results suggest that extreme positions such as full-listing or full decomposition are untenable. Factors such as the transparency of the semantic link between morphemes and words determine the extent to which morphemes are represented in the mental lexicon. So it may make more sense to have a pragmatic view of morphological processing, in which morphological decomposition only occurs if there is some clear benefit to be had. Different morphemes within a language may be treated in different ways, and there may also be differences between languages in terms of the extent to which the mental lexicon relies on morphemes.

3.2 Accessing word meanings

Chapter 9 will introduce you to the notion of lexical concepts – a class of concepts specific to words. In this section we shall relate the ideas underlying concepts and categories to the operation of the semantic system. We shall examine the kinds of information that become available once a word has been recognized, and also look at the problem of how to select the appropriate meaning in cases where a word is ambiguous.

3.2.1 Semantic representations

Once a word has been recognized the relevant information about that word must be accessed, so that the word, and ultimately the sentence, can be understood. Most models of language perception start to get slightly hazy at this point, because while word forms are quite concrete and easy to define, their meanings are rather less tangible, and may vary quite strongly from person to person.

Two theories of how word meanings might be represented have gained popularity since the 1970s, both of which have links to the kinds of ideas discussed in Section 2.2 with respect to interactive activation models. Spreading activation models (e.g. Collins and Loftus, 1975) assume that words can be represented by units or nodes, as in the TRACE and IAC models of word recognition. The difference here is that links between nodes in spreading activation networks represent semantic relationships between words. Collins and Loftus's original model in 1975 used different kinds of links for different kinds of semantic relationship. For example, the network could encode the fact that a canary is a bird, by linking the nodes for *canary* and *bird* with an 'is a' link, or that a canary has wings using a 'has' connection. Other models didn't use labelled links but simply connected together words that were similar in meaning. The application to word recognition would be that once a word has been recognized (for example by activating the correct node in the IAC model), activation would spread to the semantic network, and then along links to related words, thus generating a set of known facts about that word, and activating a set of semantically related words.

The alternative **featural** theory of semantic representation assumes that word meanings are represented as a set of **semantic features** or properties (a bit like some of the theories of concepts explored in Chapter 9). The idea here is that the mental lexicon contains a large set of features, and that each word representation consists of a subset of these features. For example, the features relevant for the word canary might include ('has wings', 'can fly', 'is a bird' and so on). The feature model has also been incorporated into connectionist models of recognition, allowing the linkage of recognition models and semantic representations. In this case, the activation of a written or spoken representation would lead to a pattern of activation on a set of semantic nodes, with each node representing a semantic feature (e.g. Masson, 1995).

These two approaches are highly underspecified, and could potentially accommodate many different patterns of data. Despite this, you might find it useful when you read through the experimental findings listed below to think about how the findings might be accommodated by featural and spreading activation theories. Most studies of semantic representations of words have addressed what kinds of information can be accessed and when. Clearly, all kinds of information about a word could be stored in the mental lexicon, but the information required to understand a sentence must be readily available in a fraction of a second, and this time constraint may have some consequences for what types of information are stored.

The most popular tool for investigating the types of semantic information stored in the mental lexicon is semantic priming. For example, an experiment might use pairs of semantically related words, such as *bread* and *butter*, with participants asked to perform some kind of speeded task such as lexical decision (is it a word or not?) or naming (say the word aloud) to the second item of the pair. In this case, the assumption is that if responses are facilitated (i.e. quicker) when there is a semantic relationship between the words, then that semantic relationship must be represented in the mental lexicon (in a spreading activation model there might be a link between the words).

So what kinds of relationship between words can support semantic priming? Perhaps the most robust effect involves pairs of **associated** words (words that seem to go together naturally). **Association strength** is often measured by asking people to say or write down the word that first comes into their heads when they read a target word. So if you were asked to provide an associate for the word *cheddar* you would probably say *cheese*. According to the University of South Florida norms (Nelson *et al.*, 1998), that's what more than 90 per cent of respondents say (curiously, a further 3 per cent of their respondents said *Swiss*!). In any case, the fact that presenting one word results in facilitated processing of an associated word suggests that associative links between words are represented in the lexicon in some way.

The problem with this conclusion is that the types of relationship found for associated word pairs are quite variable, ranging from near synonyms (words that have very similar meanings, such as *portion* and *part*) to antonyms (words that have opposite meanings, such as *gain* and *lose*), to words that just crop up in the same context (e.g. *law* and *break*). For this reason, researchers have often tried to look for semantic priming in cases where words have only weak associations, but still retain some specific semantic link (e.g. *horse* and *sheep*). The data here are more equivocal, which suggests that non-associative links might be weaker in some way, or rely on a different mechanism compared with associative links.

Nonetheless, Lucas (2000) reviewed a large set of semantic priming experiments and reached the conclusion that non-associative semantic priming effects were robust, with perhaps the strongest evidence for links in the lexicon between members of the same category (e.g. *horse–pig*) and instrument–action pairs such as *broom* and *sweep*.

Kellenbach *et al.* (2000) looked at whether words might be linked in terms of the visual or perceptual properties of the objects they represented. For example, *button* and *coin* both refer to flat, round objects. This kind of priming had been observed weakly in some studies, but not others. However, Kellenbach *et al.* (2000) used two measures of priming: the first was the standard reaction time test, and the second was based on brain activity using the ERP technique (see Box 8.3 in Section 3.2.2). They found no effect in the reaction time test, but nonetheless a robust effect on the brain response to the target word, suggesting that even in this case, where the semantic link was too subtle to be detected by conventional techniques, a priming relationship still existed. So it seems that the semantic information that becomes available when a word is perceived is far from minimal. Instead, many different aspects of meaning are accessed. Current research says little about how these different aspects of meaning are organized and accessed, but even at this stage it seems that associative, pure semantic and perceptual knowledge might be accessed in different ways.

3.2.2 Semantic ambiguity

In many cases, the operation of activating a word's meaning in the mental lexicon is made more difficult because the word is ambiguous in some way. For example, what does the word *bank* mean to you? You may immediately think of a high-street bank, but then later realize that *bank* could mean the side of a river as well. This is because *bank* is a homonym: a word that has multiple unrelated meanings. There are also more subtle possibilities: the first meaning of bank is most commonly applied to the place you keep your money. But a blood bank, while clearly related, is a somewhat different concept, as is the bank at a casino. So *bank* is a polysemous word, as well as a homonym, because it has multiple related senses. Further ambiguity is caused by the fact that bank could be a verb (transitive or intransitive) or a noun, but we shall leave this **syntactic ambiguity** to the next section. Homonyms are thankfully reasonably rare (roughly 7 per cent of common English words according to Rodd *et al.*, 2002), but the vast majority of words have multiple senses, which means that we really need to deal with ambiguity effectively if we are going to understand language.

Normally, the sentential context of an ambiguous word will provide some valuable clues to allow the relevant meaning of the word to be selected. So the question that researchers have focused on is *how* sentential context influences meaning selection in cases of ambiguity. Two opposing views have emerged since the 1980s (you may note similarities between the debate here and the debate on top-down and bottom-up processing discussed in Section 2.2). According to the **autonomous** view, all meanings of an ambiguous word are first accessed, and then the contextually compatible meaning is selected from these alternatives. The **interactive** view has a stronger role for sentential context, in that it may in some cases rule out inappropriate meanings before they are fully accessed. So these two viewpoints differ in terms of whether there is a short period of time in which meanings of words are accessed regardless of sentential context.

Using cross-modal semantic priming, Swinney (1979) found evidence for autonomous activation of ambiguous word meanings. In his experiment, participants heard homonyms like 'bugs' embedded in sentential contexts, and were asked to make a lexical decision to a visual target related to one of the meanings of the prime or an unrelated control word (see Figure 8.7).

UNBIASED CONTEXT

Hear: 'Rumour had it that, for years, the government building had been plagued with problems. The man was not surprised when he found several bugs in the corner of his room'

See: ANT / SPY / SEW

BIASED CONTEXT

Hear: 'Rumour had it that, for years, the government building had been plagued with problems. The man was not surprised when he found several spiders, roaches and other bugs in the corner of his room'

See: ANT / SPY / SEW

Figure 8.7 Example trial in Swinney's (1979) priming experiment. In the unbiased context, both meanings of bugs are plausible (relating to insects and relating to spying). The activation of each meaning is assessed using the reaction time to a related word (ant or spy), compared with a control unrelated word (sew). In the biased context, only the insect meaning is plausible by the time the homonym is heard

Swinney found that whether or not the sentence context was biased towards one meaning of the homonym, both related targets were primed. This implies that both meanings of the ambiguous word were accessed, despite the fact that in the biased condition only one meaning was compatible with the sentential context. When the experiment was repeated with the targets presented roughly one second later, only the contextually appropriate meaning appeared to be activated. So Swinney's data suggested that there is a short window of up to a second in which the meanings of ambiguous words are accessed without regard to sentential context, supporting the autonomous model.

Variants of Swinney's experiment have been run many times, and once again there is some inconsistency in the pattern of priming. In some cases it seems that only one meaning is activated if the homonym has one particularly common meaning and the sentential context is strongly constraining towards that meaning (Tabossi and Zardon, 1993). Lucas (1999) has also shown that studies demonstrating exhaustive access of ambiguous word meanings often still show *more* priming for the contextually appropriate meaning than the inappropriate one. Therefore it seems that at least some interactive processing is likely in accessing word meanings, although sentential context may only rule out inappropriate meanings in specific circumstances.

8.3 ──────────────────────────────── **Methods**

Event-related potential (ERP) studies of semantic processing

The ERP methodology relies on the fact that brain activity creates an electromagnetic field that can be measured by a set of electrodes placed on the scalp. Typically, the recording of activity is synchronized with the presentation of a stimulus, and many recordings using different stimuli must be averaged to generate an interpretable waveform. The resultant ERP waveform often contains a set of characteristic peaks at different delays.

A negative peak occurring roughly 400 ms after the stimulus has been presented (known as the N400) has been identified with the integration of semantic information into sentential context. A typical finding is that the size of the N400 peak associated with a word in sentential context is inversely related to how easily that word fits into the context (Kutas and Hillyard, 1980). So the N400 peak associated with the word *spoon* might be small in the sentence 'James ate the cereal with a dessert spoon', but large in the sentence 'James caught the salmon using a fishing spoon'. This sensitivity to semantic congruency makes the ERP technique an excellent one for examining issues such as lexical ambiguity resolution.

Van Petten and Kutas (1987) compared ERP and standard priming methods of assessing the effects of sentential context on meaning activation for ambiguous words such as *bank*. They showed that even when standard priming techniques detected no influence of sentential context the ERP waveforms for the ambiguous words were subtly different, suggesting that sentential context was influencing the processing of these words, and strengthening the case for an interactive account of lexical ambiguity resolution.

Summary of Section 3

- The mental lexicon stores the meanings of words. Although the subject is contentious, it seems that some words are broken down into smaller units called morphemes.
- A wide variety of information about the meaning of a word becomes available when a word is recognized, including associative knowledge, pure semantic information and perceptual features.
- For words with more than one meaning, the sentential context of the meaning can help select the relevant meaning. This process is to some extent interactive.

4   Sentence comprehension

So far, language perception has largely been described in terms of recognition processes. Up to the level of the lexicon, the job of the perceptual system is simply to allow recognition of familiar sequences (words or morphemes) and retrieve stored knowledge relating to these items. When we discussed morphology, there was a little more **productivity** involved. That is, people can recognize and make use of novel morphological variants of familiar morphemes. So, for example, even if the word *polysemous* were new to you when it was mentioned in the previous section, you would probably find it quite easy to define its morphological relative, *polysemy*. However, when we get to the level of the sentence, the character of language perception changes abruptly. Sentences are almost always new, in that the same permutation of words has often never been encountered before. If perception at this level were still simply a recognition process, then we would completely fail to understand all but the most simple or common sentences. The solution to this problem is to treat sentence processing not as a pure recognition process but as a *constructive* process. When we read or hear a sentence, we take the individual components – the words – and combine them to produce something that may be quite novel to us, but hopefully bears some relationship to the message the speaker or writer intended. You might think of this process in terms of building up a mental model of the information being communicated (see Chapter 13 on reasoning). Accordingly, the listener or reader takes each word and deduces its grammatical or syntactic role in the current sentence. Termed **parsing**, this process is the focus of the final section in this chapter.

4.1 Syntax

ACTIVITY 8.3

Please read the following passages and sentences and think about whether they seem grammatical to you. Give each one a rating from 1 to 10, where grammatical-sounding passages get high marks.

1   The most beautiful thing we can experience is the mysterious. It is the source of all true art and all science. He to whom this emotion is a stranger, who can no longer pause to wonder and stand rapt in awe, is as good as dead: his eyes are closed.

2   Her five-year mission: to explore strange, new worlds; to seek out new life and new civilizations; to boldly go where no man has gone before.

3   Please cup, gimme cup.

4   Colourless green ideas sleep furiously.

5   In become words sentence the rather have jumbled this.

COMMENT

People have quite reliable intuitions about the grammaticality of sentences, despite often being unable to define exactly what makes a sentence grammatical. You probably gave the first two passages fairly high ratings. Passage 1 is a quotation from Albert Einstein, and applies quite well to the study of syntax: mysterious but potentially very revealing! Passage 2 may be familiar as the opening line of the *Star Trek* series. You might be tempted to mark this down as being less grammatical, because it contains a famous example of a split infinitive: 'to boldly go'. However, this kind of (most likely mistaken) grammatical rule is not what cognitive psychologists are typically interested in: we do not wish to dictate what the best or most eloquent way of speaking is, we simply wish to understand how people really speak. In these terms splitting the infinitive is a perfectly acceptable and grammatical form of language. Sentence 3 is not grammatical by most definitions, but if a two-year-old said it to you, you would understand what they meant quite easily. Sentence 4 is in some ways the opposite of Sentence 3, in that it seems grammatical, yet meaningless. It was made famous by Noam Chomsky as an example of how syntax and semantics can be dissociable. Finally, Sentence 5 is clearly ungrammatical and pretty hard to extract any meaning from. After a while you may be able to work out that the sentence is a scrambled version of 'The words in this sentence have become rather jumbled'. It demonstrates just how important it is for us to have some mutually agreed conventions for word order, and this is precisely what syntax is!

Before embarking on a review of the models and data relevant to sentence processing, it is worth having a quick look at linguistic views of language structure. The constraints of our vocal and auditory systems dictate that words are uttered one by one in a serial fashion. However, according to many syntactic theories, this serial transmission obscures what is actually a hierarchical structure. Figure 8.8 illustrates the kind of syntactic structure that might be assigned to a simple sentence like 'The girl spotted the yacht'.

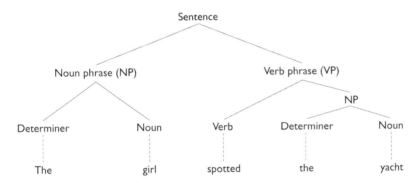

Figure 8.8   A simple phrase structure tree

In this hierarchical analysis, each word is assigned a syntactic role in the sentence. The broken lines mark the links between each word and its role. These constituents are then grouped into phrases according to **phrase structure** rules, which are grammatical rules of English that indicate how phrases can combine. At the highest level the phrases combine to form a sentence. The analysis of sentences using **phrase structure grammar** offers a purely linguistic description, but we can see how it might apply to human language processing. On the perceptual side, we might think parsing should involve taking each word in a sentence, fleshing out its grammatical role and building a phrase structure tree that fits the sentence. This would not in itself recover the meaning of the sentence, but it would assist in this process, by facilitating the **thematic role assignment** for the sentence (i.e. identifying the fact that the girl is the doer, identifying spotting as the activity she is doing, and that the yacht is what she is doing it to!).

Parsing is made more difficult by the fact that, as mentioned earlier, many words can be used in different grammatical roles. For example, the word *spotted* is used as a verb in Figure 8.8, but can be used as an adjective, as in a *spotted dress*. Equally, the noun *yacht* can be used as a verb, as in *to yacht around the world*. In the example sentence these alternative roles can be ruled out, because they would not form a grammatically coherent sentence in their alternative roles, but in many cases full sentences can be interpreted in different grammatically well-formed ways. Altmann (1998) gives the example of the sentence 'Time flies like an arrow', which has more than 50 grammatically permissible interpretations. For example, *time* appears to be acting as a noun but it could also be used as a verb, as in to 'time an egg'. Similarly, *flies* is most obviously a verb, but it could act as a plural noun – someone could time some flies! Semantically, such an interpretation may make little sense, but it could still be grammatical – just like Chomsky's famous example (Sentence 4 in Activity 8.3). In these cases we need to make use of more than just syntactic knowledge to resolve the ambiguity. The next section discusses how different models of parsing cope with ambiguities of this type. All models assume that we need to make use of multiple sources of information but they differ in terms of the priority of the different information types.

4.2 Models of parsing

We found in Section 2.1 that the language system makes good use of the short time it takes to say a word. As speech enters the perceptual system, the cohort of potential candidates is whittled down, ensuring minimal delay in retrieving a word's meaning. One can ask the same question at the sentence level: does parsing assign a syntactic structure only at major syntactic boundaries (or even at the end of a sentence), or does it do so **incrementally**, refining the set of plausible syntactic structures every time a new word is recognized? It will not surprise you to learn that current models of sentence processing assume that parsing is incremental, and again this makes sense in terms of maximizing the availability of information for responding to the sentence. There are numerous demonstrations of incremental processing, employing a wide range of methods – an early example is the study of Tyler and Marslen-Wilson (1977). They made use of ambiguous phrases such as *landing planes*. With a preceding context such as 'If you walk too near the runway, ...' the natural interpretation of *landing* is as an adjective (e.g. 'landing planes are dangerous' would be a suitable continuation), whereas following 'If you've been trained as a pilot, ...' the interpretation is more likely to be as a verb (e.g. 'landing planes is easy'). Tyler and Marslen-Wilson wanted to know whether listeners showed a contextual bias in their parsing of the ambiguous phrase. If parsing is delayed until a syntactic boundary is reached, then there should be no effect of preceding context on listeners' expectations about whether the word following *landing planes* was either *is* or *are*. They gauged listeners' expectations by presenting spoken fragments such as 'If you've been trained as a pilot, landing planes ...' to participants and asking them to name a visual target word (either *is* or *are* in this case). They found that the speed of a naming response depended on the preceding context of the ambiguous phrase. Appropriate continuations were named quickly, compared with inappropriate ones. This is incompatible with the 'delayed parsing' hypothesis, because such a model predicts no effect of appropriateness. Instead it fits in with the idea that a plausible parse of a sentence is built up incrementally, and this influences expectations about upcoming words.

One of the most influential models of parsing, often known as the garden path model (Frazier, 1979), assumes that parsing is incremental, so each word is allocated a syntactic role as soon as it is perceived. In cases where more than one syntactic structure is compatible with the sentence so far, the parser makes a decision about which alternative to pursue based on syntactic information alone. The 'garden path' element comes in because the model predicts that there will be cases where the parse chosen at a point of ambiguity is incorrect (so the listener is 'led down the garden path'). Later in the sentence this incorrect selection will become clear, causing some backtracking as an alternative interpretation is attempted. The idea of pursuing some hypothesis and then reaching a dead-end requiring reanalysis fits in with people's intuitions about how they interpret some sentences. A famous example of 'garden pathing' is the sentence: 'The horse raced past the barn fell' (Bever, 1970). As you read this sentence, you may have had problems integrating the final word. Some people think that maybe there is an 'and' missing between *barn* and *fell*, or that there is a comma missing between *past* and *the*. But there is an alternative interpretation, which is a reduced version of 'The horse that was raced past the barn fell'. According to the garden path model, this alternative is not chosen when the word *raced* is first perceived, leading to trouble with interpretation later in the sentence.

The garden path model makes use of a set of guiding principles that specify which parse should be selected in the case of syntactic ambiguities, and these principles involve only syntactic information. The details of these principles are not essential – it is more important to keep in mind that the garden path model assumes a *serial* parser that maintains only one potential parse of a sentence at a time, and has an *autonomous* component, in that the initial evaluation of a word's role in a sentence is based only on syntactic factors. In direct contrast, constraint-based models (e.g. MacDonald *et al.*, 1994) assume that parsing is *parallel* and *interactive*. So rather than maintaining a single syntactic analysis, these models allow more than one potential parse of a sentence to be evaluated at the same time (just as the cohort model of word recognition evaluates numerous candidates for word identification). Constraint-based models are thought of as interactive because they eliminate the autonomous stage of parsing assumed by the garden path model. Instead, other factors, such as frequency and semantic plausibility, can influence parsing immediately.

MacDonald *et al.*'s model also increases the involvement of the lexicon in the parsing process, by assuming that some information about how a word can combine with other words is stored in the lexicon. By this kind of account, parsing becomes a bit like fitting the pieces of a jigsaw together. Each piece contains information about a word, including the kinds of syntactic context the word could fit into, and parsing involves fitting all the pieces together so that the words form a coherent sentence.

The two models described here are by no means the only models of parsing that researchers currently consider, but they do mark out the kinds of properties that generate debate in this area, and they highlight the kinds of questions that we need to investigate through experimentation. First and foremost among these, we need to try to address the question of whether parsing is autonomous, or whether it makes use of non-syntactic sources of information stored in the lexicon.

4.3   Is parsing autonomous?

As we have seen, the garden path model makes the strong prediction that the initial syntactic analysis of a word is unaffected by factors such as the meaning of the preceding context, or the meaning of the words. In essence, the model puts all aspects of semantics aside until a word has been assigned a syntactic role. Initial data on the resolution of syntactic ambiguity showed garden path effects fully consistent with the autonomous approach of Frazier's model. In addition, some experiments designed specifically to look for semantic influences on syntactic ambiguity resolution found none. Ferreira and Clifton (1986) investigated how readers interpret verbs in phrases such as 'The defendant examined ...'. Before you read on, think about how you might continue this sentence fragment. There are two common roles that 'examined' can play in this context. It could simply be the main verb of the sentence, as in 'The defendant examined his hands'. But it could also form part of what is known as a **reduced relative** clause. A relative clause might be 'The defendant that was examined by the lawyer ...', and the reduced form would simply be the same but with 'that was' eliminated. The garden path model states that the preferred structure when *examined* is encountered is the more straightforward main verb interpretation. So if the sentence continuation is in fact a reduced relative structure, the Frazier model predicts a garden path effect when the true structure of the sentence becomes clear. So when a reader encounters 'The defendant examined by the lawyer turned out to be unreliable' they should show evidence of processing difficulty. This is exactly what Ferreira and Clifton found, using the eye-tracking methodology – people tended to fixate on the region just after the ambiguity, suggesting that they were having trouble incorporating the new information into their initially selected parse of the sentence.

The critical question here was whether the meaning of the word preceding the ambiguous verb could affect the garden path effect. So Ferreira and Clifton compared sentences like the one above to sentences like 'The evidence examined by the lawyer turned out to be unreliable'. In this case *evidence* is inanimate, which reduces the plausibility of the main verb interpretation (i.e. it seems unlikely that the evidence would examine anything). Despite the semantic bias towards the alternative reading, the garden path effect remained (i.e. fixation times remained long). On the surface, this seems like sound support for the autonomy assumed by the garden path model.

However, Trueswell *et al.* (1994) noticed that some of the contexts used by Ferreira and Clifton were less constraining than the example above. It is difficult to imagine a situation in which evidence could examine something, but Trueswell *et al.* argued that this was not the case for about half the materials used in the original experiment (e.g. 'the car towed ...' where *car* is inanimate, but still quite a plausible candidate for something that tows). They ran another eye-tracking experiment using a similar design, but with more constraining semantic contexts, and found that these contexts could lessen or even eliminate the garden path effect. The results of this and other similar studies are important because they show that, in some circumstances, the parsing system can be strongly affected by the semantic plausibility of the various parses of the system. The garden path model could perhaps be saved if the autonomous parsing component is assumed to last only a short time, and that other factors come into place soon afterwards, but this greatly weakens the predictive power of the model, because it becomes harder to distinguish from models which allow semantic factors to play a stronger role. But it is worth remembering that Frazier's syntactic constraints are not rendered immaterial by the finding that parsing is influenced by semantic plausibility. Instead, syntactic constraints appear to operate in *combination* with other constraints, with the ultimate goal being to weigh up the likelihood of different parses of a sentence in cases of ambiguity.

4.4 Constraints on parsing

It seems that the parsing system can be influenced by quite a number of different factors when it encounters an ambiguity. When a sentence is spoken, there is often useful information in the rhythm of the sentence. Think about how you might say the sentence 'Jane hit the man with the hammer' in the cases where (a) the man has a hammer or (b) Jane has a hammer. One way to distinguish between these two possibilities is by changing your speech rate mid-sentence, so that different sets of words are grouped together. Of course these changes will be exaggerated when the speaker is aware of the potential ambiguity, but even in normal speech, the speaker can reduce ambiguity with changes in pitch and timing, and the listener can make use of this information (Warren, 1996). At a very different level, information about how often words are used in different syntactic structures can also influence the parsing process. This factor can be seen at work in the earlier example from Bever (1970), 'The horse raced past the barn fell'. One of the reasons this sentence causes so many problems is because the verb race is rarely used as a **past participle** (i.e. as in 'the horse that was raced ...'). Not all verbs have this strong bias, so for example *released* has the opposite bias – it is more likely to be used as a past participle (e.g. 'The hostage was released') than as a past tense of a main verb (e.g. 'The government released a press statement'). Trueswell (1996) showed that this lexical frequency factor also influenced the way in which sentences are parsed. People seem to be able to keep track of the ways in which words are used in different sentences, and apply this knowledge in cases of ambiguity.

Perhaps the most striking example of a contextual influence on syntactic processing is based on the use of visual information. Tanenhaus *et al.* (1995) wanted to know whether the visual context of a sentence would affect the interpretation of syntactic ambiguities. In order to do this, they sat participants at a table on which some objects like apples and towels were placed, and gave them instructions to move the objects such as 'Put the apple on the towel in the box'. The participants wore head-mounted eye trackers so that the experimenters could monitor eye movements as the sentences were heard (see Box 8.2 in Section 2.2.3). The sentences had a temporary syntactic ambiguity, which in the case of the example here involves the phrase 'on the towel'. We know from studies like Ferreira and Clifton (1986) that when people hear 'Put the apple on the towel ...' they tend to interpret 'on the towel' as the desired destination of the apple. But the continuation '... in the box' should force a reassessment of the sentence (i.e. the sentence is a reduced form of 'Put the apple that's on the towel in the box'). We have seen that various sentential factors such as semantic plausibility can reduce or eliminate this garden path effect, but what about external, environmental context? Tanenhaus *et al.* (1995) gave the participants instructions in two types of external context (see Figure 8.9). In one case (see Figure 8.9(a)), there was an apple on a towel, another towel and a box. This context supports the initial interpretation of 'on the towel' as referring to the destination, so people tended to look at the apple and then the empty towel, and only looked at the true intended destination once the disambiguating speech ('in the box') was heard. However, when the scene also included a second apple on a napkin (see Figure 8.9(b)) participants' eye movements were quite different. Now when they heard 'on the towel', they rarely looked at the empty towel, because they interpreted 'on the towel' as distinguishing information between the two apples (one was on a towel and one on a napkin). In other words, the environmental situation provided a source of information that could eliminate the garden path effect.

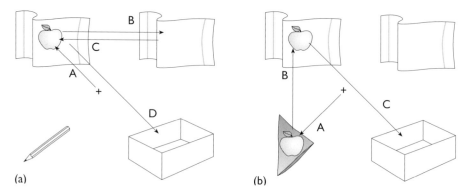

(a)   (b)

Figure 8.9 Two visual contexts from Tanenhaus et al. (1995) showing the typical sequence of eye movements in response to the ambiguous instruction 'Put the apple on the towel in the box'. Eye fixations began at the central cross, and continued in the sequence indicated by the capital letters

Source: based on Tanenhaus et al., 1995, Figures 1 and 2

Summary of Section 4

- Understanding a sentence requires a parsing process in which each word is assigned a grammatical role.
- The garden path model assumes that the parser operates autonomously, without any influence of non-syntactic factors.
- Recent studies of syntactic ambiguity resolution suggest that a variety of different constraints can influence parsing, including even the environment of the listener.

5   Conclusion

This chapter has provided a brief account of some of the main components of the language system, particularly with reference to recognizing words and under-standing sentences. We have seen that many of the processes involved can be modelled in terms of competition between multiple candidates, implying that the language system is busy evaluating countless hypotheses about an utterance at numerous levels, at any moment in time. Thankfully we remain blissfully unaware of these operations, with only a pretty terse 'executive summary' of the process available to conscious awareness.

Another recurring theme has involved the extent to which components of the system operate independently of each other. There is a long way to go in this debate, but the current state of play seems to be one in which there is a surprising level of linkage between subsystems. So reading a word engages processes and representations related to speech perception, and the way in which you process a spoken sentence can be influenced by the real-world context in which you hear it. This interconnectedness may well reflect two aspects of language processing: the complexity of language, and the speed with which we need to communicate. In terms of language development, it makes a lot of sense to reuse existing mechanisms when we are trying to add a new mechanism such as the mechanism for reading. In terms of adult language processing, it makes sense to call on as much useful information as possible to minimize the time it takes to comprehend a sentence.

Now that you have read this chapter you can reinforce and extend your learning by reading an original journal article associated with it, available online from the DD303 website. Remember, these are original journal articles, so the style is different from this textbook, and don't be too concerned if you can't follow every detail.

Answer to Activity 8.1

The approximate word boundary positions are marked in Figure 8.10, along with the words themselves. Some gaps in the speech (low amplitude signal) are aligned with word boundaries (e.g. between *quite* and *carefully*, marked ✓), whereas others are not (e.g. within *spoken*, marked ✗). In general, short periods of silence are poor indicators of word boundaries, meaning that we have to find better ways to segment speech.

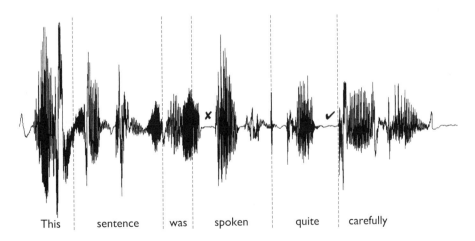

This   sentence   was   spoken   quite   carefully

Figure 8.10   Typical word boundaries in a fluent sentence

Further reading

Altmann, G.T.M. (2001) 'The mechanics of language: psycholinguistics in review', *British Journal of Psychology*, vol.92, pp.129–70.

Harley, T. (2001) *The Psychology of Language: From Data to Theory*, Hove, Psychology Press.

References

Altmann, G.T.M. (1998) 'Ambiguity in sentence processing', *Trends in Cognitive Sciences*, vol.2, no.4, pp.146–52.

Berko, J. (1958) 'The child's learning of English morphology', *Word*, vol.14, no.2, pp.150–77.

Bever, T.G. (1970) 'The cognitive basis for linguistic structures', in Hayes, J. (ed.) *Cognition and the Development of Language*, New York, Wiley.

Collins, A.M. and Loftus, E.F. (1975) 'A spreading-activation theory of semantic processing', *Psychological Review*, vol.82, no.6, pp.407–28.

Coltheart, M., Rastle, K., Perry, C., Langdon, R. and Ziegler, J. (2001) 'DRC: a dual route cascaded model of visual word recognition and reading aloud', *Psychological Review*, vol.108, no.1, pp.204–56.

Cutler, A. and Carter, D.M. (1987) 'The predominance of strong initial syllables in the English vocabulary', *Computer Speech and Language*, vol.2, no.2, pp.133–42.

Cutler, A. and Norris, D. (1988) 'The role of strong syllables in segmentation for lexical access', *Journal of Experimental Psychology: Human Perception and Performance*, vol.14, no.1, pp.113–21.

Cutler, A. and Otake, T. (2002) 'Rhythmic categories in spoken-word recognition', *Journal of Memory and Language*, vol.46, no.2, pp.296–322.

Ferreira, F. and Clifton, C. (1986) 'The independence of syntactic processing', *Journal of Memory and Language*, vol.25, no.3, pp.348–68.

Frazier, L. (1979) *On Comprehending Sentences: Syntactic Parsing Strategies*, Bloomington, IN, Indiana University Linguistics Club.

Frost, R. (1998) 'Toward a strong phonological theory of visual word recognition: true issues and false trails', *Psychological Bulletin*, vol.123, no.1, pp.71–99.

Gaskell, M.G. and Marslen-Wilson, W.D. (2002) 'Representation and competition in the perception of spoken words', *Cognitive Psychology*, vol.45, no.2, pp.220–66.

Glushko, R.J. (1979) 'The organization and activation of orthographic knowledge in reading aloud', *Journal of Experimental Psychology: Human Perception and Performance*, vol.5, no.4, pp.674–91.

Grainger, J. and Jacobs, A.M. (1994) 'A dual read-out model of word context effects in letter perception – further investigations of the word superiority effect', *Journal of Experimental Psychology: Human Perception and Performance*, vol.20, no.6, pp.1158–76.

Hauser, M.D., Newport, E.L. and Aslin, R.N. (2001) 'Segmentation of the speech stream in a non-human primate: statistical learning in cotton-top tamarins', *Cognition*, vol.78, no.3, pp.B53–64.

Kellenbach, M.L., Wijers, A.A. and Mulder, G. (2000) 'Visual semantic features are activated during the processing of concrete words: event-related potential evidence for perceptual semantic priming', *Cognitive Brain Research*, vol.10, nos.1–2, pp.67–75.

Kutas, M. and Hillyard, S.A. (1980) 'Reading senseless sentences: brain potentials reflect semantic incongruity', *Science*, vol.207, no.4427, pp.203–5.

Lucas, M. (1999) 'Context effects in lexical access: a meta-analysis', *Memory and Cognition*, vol.27, no.3, pp.385–98.

Lucas, M. (2000) 'Semantic priming without association: a meta-analytic review', *Psychonomic Bulletin and Review*, vol.7, no.4, pp.618–30.

MacDonald, M.C., Pearlmutter, N.J. and Seidenberg, M.S. (1994) 'Lexical nature of syntactic ambiguity resolution', *Psychological Review*, vol.101, no.4, pp.676–703.

Marslen-Wilson, W.D. (1987) 'Functional parallelism in spoken word recognition', *Cognition*, vol.25, no.1, pp.71–102.

Marslen-Wilson, W.D. and Welsh, A. (1978) 'Processing interactions and lexical access during word recognition in continuous speech', *Cognitive Psychology*, vol.10, no.1, pp.29–63.

Marslen-Wilson, W.D., Tyler, L.K., Waksler, R. and Older, L. (1994) 'Morphology and meaning in the English mental lexicon', *Psychological Review*, vol.101, no.1, pp.3–33.

Masson, M.E.J. (1995) 'A distributed memory model of semantic priming', *Journal of Experimental Psychology: Learning, Memory and Cognition*, vol.21, no.1, pp.3–23.

McClelland, J.L. and Elman, J.L. (1986) 'The TRACE model of speech perception', *Cognitive Psychology*, vol.18, no.1, pp.1–86.

McClelland, J.L. and Rumelhart, D.E. (1981) 'An interactive activation model of context effects in letter perception. Part 1: an account of basic findings', *Psychological Review*, vol.88, no.3, pp.375–407.

McConkie, G.W. and Rayner, K. (1975) 'The span of the effective stimulus during a fixation in reading', *Perception and Psychophysics*, vol.17, no.6, pp.578–86.

McQueen, J.M., Norris, D. and Cutler, A. (1994) 'Competition in spoken word recognition – spotting words in other words', *Journal of Experimental Psychology: Learning Memory and Cognition*, vol.20, no.3, pp.621–38.

Nelson, D.L., McEvoy, C.L. and Schreiber, T.A. (1998) *The University of South Florida Word Association, Rhyme, and Word Fragment Norm* [online]. Available from http://w3.usf.edu/FreeAssociation (accessed 19 January 2004).

Norris, D., McQueen, J.M. and Cutler, A. (2000) 'Merging information in speech recognition: feedback is never necessary', *Behavioral and Brain Sciences*, vol.23, no.3, pp.299–370.

O'Regan, J.K. and Jacobs, A.M. (1992) 'Optimal viewing position effect in word recognition – a challenge to current theory', *Journal of Experimental Psychology: Human Perception and Performance*, vol.18, no.1, pp.185–97.

Rayner, K. and Duffy, S.A. (1986) 'Lexical complexity and fixation times in reading – effects of word-frequency, verb complexity, and lexical ambiguity', *Memory and Cognition*, vol.14, no.3, pp.191–201.

Rodd, J., Gaskell, G. and Marslen-Wilson, W. (2002) 'Making sense of semantic ambiguity: semantic competition in lexical access', *Journal of Memory and Language*, vol.46, no.2, pp.245–66.

Saffran, J.R., Aslin, R.N. and Newport, E.L. (1996) 'Statistical learning by 8-month-old infants', *Science*, vol.274, no.5294, pp.1926–8.

Saffran, J.R., Johnson, E.K., Aslin, R.N. and Newport, E.L. (1999) 'Statistical learning of tone sequences by human infants and adults', *Cognition*, vol.70, no.1, pp.27–52.

Seidenberg, M.S. and McClelland, J.L. (1989) 'A distributed, developmental model of word recognition and naming', *Psychological Review*, vol.96, no.3, pp.523–68.

Shillcock, R., Ellison, T.M. and Monaghan, P. (2000) 'Eye-fixation behavior, lexical storage, and visual word recognition in a split processing model', *Psychological Review*, vol.107, no.4, pp.824–51.

Starr, M. and Rayner, K. (2001) 'Eye movements during reading: some current controversies', *Trends in Cognitive Sciences*, vol.5, no.4, pp.156–63.

Swinney, D.A. (1979) 'Lexical access during sentence comprehension: (re)consideration of context effects', *Journal of Verbal Learning and Verbal Behavior*, vol.18, no.5, pp.645–59.

Tabossi, P. and Zardon, F. (1993) 'Processing ambiguous words in context', *Journal of Memory and Language*, vol.32, no.3, pp.359–72.

Taft, M. and Forster, K.I. (1975) 'Lexical storage and retrieval of prefixed words', *Journal of Verbal Learning and Verbal Behavior*, vol.14, no.6, pp.638–47.

Tanenhaus, M.K., Spivey-Knowlton, M.J., Eberhard, K.M. and Sedivy, J.C. (1995) 'Integration of visual and linguistic information in spoken language comprehension', *Science*, vol.268, no.5217, pp.1632–4.

Trueswell, J.C. (1996) 'The role of lexical frequency in syntactic ambiguity resolution', *Journal of Memory and Language*, vol.35, no.4, pp.566–85.

Trueswell, J.C., Tanenhaus, M.K. and Garnsey, S.M. (1994) 'Semantic influences on parsing – use of thematic role information in syntactic ambiguity resolution', *Journal of Memory and Language*, vol.33, no.3, pp.285–318.

Tyler, L.K. and Marslen-Wilson, W.D. (1977) 'The on-line effects of semantic context on syntactic processing', *Journal of Verbal Learning and Verbal Behavior*, vol.16, no.6, pp.683–92.

Van Orden, G.C. (1987) 'A rows is a rose – spelling, sound, and reading', *Memory and Cognition*, vol.15, no.3, pp.181–98.

Van Petten, C. and Kutas, M. (1987) 'Ambiguous words in context – an event-related potential analysis of the time course of meaning activation', *Journal of Memory and Language*, vol.26, no.2, pp.188–208.

Warren, P. (1996) 'Prosody and parsing: an introduction', *Language and Cognitive Processes*, vol.11, nos.1–2, pp.1–16.

Concepts

Nick Braisby

1   Introduction

In the UK some years ago a television channel screened a programme that involved contestants guessing the identity of unusual antique artefacts. The contestants were allowed to hold the objects, and discuss their ideas as to what they might be. But the objects were chosen so that it was not at all obvious what they were used for, nor what they were called. In the parlance of cognitive psychology, soon to be explained, they were selected because they were difficult to categorize – they were objects for which the contestants could not readily find an appropriate concept. You can get an idea of the difficulty faced by these contestants from Activity 9.1.

ACTIVITY 9.1

Figure 9.1 shows some obscure artefacts that may be found in the kitchen. Try to guess what these objects are – answers are given at the end of the chapter.

Figure 9.1   Three (more or less) obscure objects that may be found in the kitchen

Normally we categorize things effortlessly. Looking around me now I can't see a single object that I can't label or categorize – I don't have to think hard to identify the appropriate concept for each and every one. But how do we do this? For, as Activity 9.1 shows, as did the television programme, categorizing something, finding the right concept, can be difficult. In fact, as we shall see, even effortless categorizations are ultimately difficult to explain. The first step is to work out what concepts are.

1.1   Concepts, categories and words

Dictionaries say that the word 'concept' has different senses. There is a non-technical sense, one that relates loosely to ideas and thoughts. So, for example, we might say that a manager has created a new marketing 'concept', meaning he or she has introduced a new idea for promoting a product. However, it is the psychological or philosophical sense that is of interest here. According to this, **concepts** are general ideas formed in the mind: 'general' meaning that concepts apply to every one of a class of things (usually described as a category). For example, my concept of 'cat' must be a general idea of cats – an idea of what cats are in general, that is, an idea about all cats, not just my pet cat Rosie curled up on the sofa.

Already this raises two important issues. First, concepts are related to **categories**. Our talk of concepts normally presupposes the existence of a corresponding category. The philosopher of science, Franz Brentano (1838–1917), argued that a mental state has two components – a mental act, internal to the mind, and a mental content (the thing that the mental act is about) that is *external* to the mind. The mental state of representing a concept has this dual aspect. In thinking 'Rosie is a cat' I perform an activity (thinking) and my thought has a content that is external to the mind – the thought is about Rosie and her relation to the category of (domestic) cats. So, although concepts are internal to the mind, the categories that concepts are about are external. Indeed, researchers often adopt the terminological distinction that the word 'concept' refers to something in the mind and 'category' refers to those things in the world which a concept is about.

Second, concepts and categories are linked to words. I used words to communicate the idea that thoughts (such as Rosie is a cat) contain concepts, and that concepts are about categories. Words like 'cat' help you to work out what concept I have in mind (the concept 'cat'). However, it would be too simplistic to suggest that words always pick out concepts straightforwardly. Ambiguous words link to more than one concept – 'chest' relates both to the concept of a body part (torso) and to the concept of furniture (as in chest of drawers). In addition, most words are polysemous – they have many distinct but closely related senses. 'Cat' can refer to the category of domestic cats, but also to big cats and to all felines. Concepts, unlike words, do not have multiple senses, since they are general ideas about particular categories. So, we probably have several concepts that all link to the word 'cat' – a concept of 'domestic cat', a concept of 'feline' and so on. Mapping the precise relationships between concepts and words is not at all easy, so for much of this chapter I will assume, as most researchers do for practical reasons, that words pick out concepts in a straightforward manner. Towards the end of the chapter, though, I will try to show some of the complexity of this relationship.

Having considered some preliminaries, we can now turn to the kind of evidence psychologists have used to infer the nature of concepts.

1.2 Categorization

Bruner *et al.* (1956, p.1) suggested that 'to categorize is to render discriminably different things equivalent, to group objects and events and people around us into classes, and to respond to them in terms of their class membership rather than their uniqueness'. According to this definition, concepts are at work whenever people show similarities in behaviour toward different objects and whenever they show differences in behaviour toward different objects. If, for example, you pat two different dogs, you behave similarly towards them, in spite of their differences. On these definitions you do so because you treat them as instances of the category 'dog'. Likewise, patting a dog but not a house plant signals that you treat these as members of different categories.

Even though concepts may be at work almost all of the time, our focus will be on a restricted range of behaviours that involve giving fairly explicit and often linguistic judgements about category membership. This kind of categorization behaviour (henceforth, 'categorization') has provided the primary evidence as to the nature of concepts.

Categorization behaviour could be more broadly construed however. Potter and Wetherell (1987) and Edwards and Potter (1992) show how attention to natural discourse reveals many subtleties in how people choose which category words to use, and how they then use them in particular contexts. This 'discursive' approach can show how categorization is affected by social influences, such as the social status of the people discoursing, and how using category words serves broader goals than merely that of reporting one's beliefs about category membership. Though this line of work reveals important aspects of categorization, cognitive psychologists are interested in what we can learn about categorization processes in general; that is, in what might be common to different instances of categorization in different contexts.

Categorization behaviour also need not be so closely tied to language. Indeed, many researchers attribute concepts to non-linguistic animals. Sappington and Goldman (1994) investigated the abilities of Arabian horses to learn to discriminate patterns. They claimed that horses that learned to discriminate triangles from other shapes had actually acquired a concept – in this case, the concept of 'triangularity' – as opposed to merely having learned the particular triangular patterns to which they had been exposed. Again, though, this chapter focuses on what we know of human cognitive achievements, and hence on the nature of human concepts.

My bracketing-off of these two issues does not solely reflect a pragmatic desire to get on with discussing the matters of most relevance to cognitive psychology, but also the contentious nature of these issues. For instance, some cognitive scientists have argued that the idea that animals might possess concepts is not actually coherent (Chater and Heyes, 1994). Similarly, others have argued against a strong discursive position, according to which categories are socially constructed (e.g. Pinker, 1997; Fodor, 1998).

So, accepting that judgements of category membership are the principal indices of categorization, we can now turn to some of the techniques psychologists have used to elicit these. One method is the **sorting** task. In this task, participants are shown an array of different items (sometimes words printed on cards) and asked to sort them into groups. Ross and Murphy (1999) used this technique to examine how people categorize foods. They found, for example, that people sometimes put eggs in the same group as bacon and cereal (suggesting a category of breakfast foods), whereas at other times they put eggs together with butter and milk (suggesting a category of dairy products). The groups into which items are categorized are taken to reflect corresponding concepts. The fact that eggs are sometimes put into different groups is consistent with Barsalou's (1983) findings (and also with the discursive view) that categorization depends upon people's goals or purposes. So, for example, when asked to say what falls into the category 'things to take with you in case of fire' people would mention items that would not normally be found together in the same category (e.g. loved ones, pets and family heirlooms).

If the sorting task seems abstract and artificial, go into your kitchen and look at how the different foods and gadgets are organized. You will probably find items grouped into categories – herbs and spices in one place, for example, fruit in another, vegetables in yet another. I group foods together even in my supermarket carrier bags – usually into nothing more complicated than frozen, chilled and room temperature – when the person at the checkout gives me enough time to do so! So, placing members of a category together is really an everyday activity that the sorting task taps into in a measurable and controlled way.

ACTIVITY 9.2

Think of the properties that dogs have. You might think dogs 'bark', 'have four legs', 'run after sticks', 'pant' and so on. Now consider the concept of 'cat'. Take two minutes to write down some of the properties cats have. Don't dwell on any particular property: just write down whatever comes to mind. If you get to 10 properties, stop.

COMMENT

Simple though this task seems, it gets hard to think of new properties after a while. Psychologists use this **property-listing** (or **attribute-listing**) technique to investigate people's concepts, obtaining results from many participants for each category. They then compare the lists from different people and generate a further list of the most frequently mentioned properties. This gives an indication of the information incorporated in people's concepts, and the frequency of mention indicates how central each property is to the concept.

The sorting task and property-listing technique highlight a third aspect of concepts – they are invoked to explain categorization behaviour. We behave differently with cats and dogs, because cats and dogs belong to different categories, and so our concepts of cats and dogs must differ. The differences (and similarities) between cats and dogs are reflected in our concepts, and it is these concepts that are involved in producing our behaviour.

1.3 The wider story of concepts

Perhaps because concepts are implicated in so much of our behaviour, their role often goes unnoticed. However, there have been times when concepts have been the explicit focus of discussion. Umberto Eco (1999) discusses the example of the platypus. In 1798 a stuffed platypus was sent to the British Museum. Initially, it was considered so strange that it was thought to be a hoax, with its beak artificially grafted onto its body. For the next eighty years the question of how the platypus should be categorized was hotly debated. Finally, in 1884, it was declared to be a type of mammal, called a 'monotreme', which both lays eggs and suckles its young, and this categorization has stuck (though, of course, as you will see in Section 2.1.4, it is conceivable that even this categorization might again come into question).

This case of scientific 'discovery' reminds us that all of our concepts have a past. Even such basic concepts as 'human', 'table' and 'food' have a rich, though perhaps not fully discoverable, history. But the example of the platypus shows that categorization can be a very complex process. Even though everyday categorizations seem effortless and routine, it took the best scientific minds nearly 90 years to decide how the platypus should be categorized.

Box 9.1 offers another example of where categorization has been more explicitly discussed; legal and moral cases provide others. In the UK, for example, the law applies differently to adults and children. So, it is important to be able to categorize everyone as either a child or an adult. Yet, it is too difficult to identify a precise age for the boundary between children and adults, and so parliaments have to decide, arbitrarily, where it should lie.

9.1

Categorization and diagnosis

Clinicians need to categorize conditions and diseases in order to treat their patients. Though we usually call this diagnosis, it is really a form of categorization – clinicians consider the various properties or symptoms that a patient manifests, and attempt to categorize or diagnose the underlying condition. For example, diagnosing or categorizing chronic fatigue, or ME, is notoriously difficult. Macintyre (1998) suggests diagnosis should be based on major criteria – chronic unexplained fatigue that is debilitating, and which is not due to exertion, nor substantially alleviated by rest. She also suggests that at least four out of eight minor criteria should be present (e.g. sore throat, muscle pain).

Categorization can also be seen in the *Diagnostic and Statistical Manual of Mental Disorders* (American Psychiatric Association, 1994), which gives criteria for diagnosing different mental illnesses. For example, a diagnosis of schizophrenia should be made on the basis of characteristic symptoms, social or occupational dysfunction, duration and so on. Although the manual lists five characteristic symptoms (e.g. delusions, hallucinations, disorganized speech, grossly disorganized or catatonic behaviour), it indicates that a diagnosis of schizophrenia may be made when only two are present.

You will see later that both of these kinds of diagnosis, which require only a certain number of a longer list of symptoms to be present, relate to a particular theoretical approach to concepts. Though our discussion of concepts is rooted in laboratory-based studies, it is just a short step to matters of practical import.

Fascinating though these examples are, the rest of the chapter concentrates on more everyday categorizations. Researchers have tended to adopt a methodological strategy of explaining the simpler cases first, in the hope that explanations can then be developed for more complex cases. As you will see, even everyday categorizations are surprisingly difficult to explain.

1.4   Concepts and cognition

In Chapter 4, you saw that the word 'recognition' labels different kinds of process. The authors focused on what was called 'perceptual classification' and you may have wondered about the subsequent stage labelled 'semantic classification'. Well, semantic classification is what concepts are all about. So, the use of concepts to classify – for example, using the concept of 'cat' to classify or categorize my pet cat Rosie – can be viewed as a further kind of recognition.

Concepts can also be seen as the basic units of semantic memory. While episodic memory stores memories of particular episodes, such as what happened on your last birthday, semantic memory is our long-term memory for facts about the world such as 'cats are animals'. The episodic–semantic distinction, which you initially met in

Chapter 2, was discussed in more detail in Chapter 6. For our purposes, we simply note that elements of semantic memory such as 'cats are animals' express relationships between concepts (between 'cat' and 'animal' in this case).

We have already mentioned the relationship between concepts and words, but many researchers assume a more explicit link. It is thought that some concepts, called **lexical concepts** (i.e. concepts for which there is a single word), represent our understandings of the meanings of words and are stored in something called the mental lexicon (see Chapter 8). For example, our concept of 'cat' would represent what we believe the word 'cat' means. The process of understanding language therefore partly involves retrieving lexical concepts from the mental lexicon. Of course, this is a complex process: there may be several lexical concepts corresponding to a single word like 'cat', so we would also have to identify which lexical concept is most appropriate. These and other complexities were developed in Chapter 8.

Concepts also play a role in reasoning. Your list from Activity 9.2 indicates some of the information in your concept of 'cat'. You may have written things like 'meows', 'likes fish', 'mammal' and so on. You might not have written 'has a heart' but this is a property of cats too. Now suppose someone asked you whether Rosie has a heart. My guess is that you would say she does. But this is curious, because I have told you only that Rosie is a cat. How have you managed to draw the inference that she has a heart? The answer, of course, is that your concept of 'cat' indicates that cats are mammals, and your concept of 'mammal' indicates that mammals have hearts. From these concepts you can infer that cats, like Rosie, have hearts. Such inferences might not always be valid of course – though I don't doubt Rosie has a heart, for all I know, maybe, miraculously, she has some complex artificial pump instead. The complexities of reasoning, of drawing inferences, are the topic of Chapter 11.

Because concepts allow us to make inferences, they simplify the task of remembering information. If you want to remember the properties of Rosie, you would do well simply to remember that she is a cat. If she were unusual (such as having a piece of her ear missing), you might have to remember that information too. But you do not need to remember explicitly that Rosie meows, or that she has a heart, because you can draw these inferences simply by knowing she is a cat. Suffice it to say that our ability to store concepts in semantic memory, together with our ability to reason and draw inferences, simplifies the task of remembering information. Here, concepts, reasoning and memory all act together.

Summary of Section 1

- Concepts are ideas in the mind that are about categories in the world.
- Words tend to pick out concepts, though the exact relationship between them is complex.
- The principal evidence for concepts comes from categorization behaviour, which involves people making judgements concerning category membership.
- Concepts play a wide role in cognition, being involved in recognition, language, reasoning and semantic memory, to name but a few.

2   Explaining categorization

How do we decide that some items belong to the same category and other items belong to different categories? What is it about different cats, for example, that makes us think they are all 'cats' and not 'dogs'?

2.1   Similarity I: the classical view of concepts

According to the **classical** view of concepts, which has its roots in the philosophical writings of Aristotle (Sutcliffe, 1993), things belong to categories because they possess certain properties in common. There are two aspects to this idea. First, if something is a member of a category, then it must possess the properties common to the category's members. Second, if something possesses the properties common to a category's members, then it too must be a member of the category. The first aspect asserts that possession of the common properties is necessary for category membership; the second indicates that possession of the common properties is sufficient for category membership. The classical view, then, is that there are both *necessary* and *sufficient* conditions on category membership. Another way of expressing this is to say that the classical view is that concepts provide **definitions** of their corresponding category.

In this view, categorization is explained in terms of a comparison of any putative instance with the conditions that define the category. If the instance matches the concept on each and every condition, then it falls within the category – it is a member of the category. If it fails to match on any condition, then the instance falls outside the category – it is a non-member. Let's consider an example – the category of bachelors. The classical view contends that the category can be defined, that there are properties that are both necessary and sufficient for membership. Might this be true? Dictionaries tell us that bachelors are unmarried, adult males. Perhaps these properties are necessary and sufficient for bachelorhood. If they are, then any person who is a bachelor must also be unmarried, adult and male. Conversely, any person who is unmarried, adult and male must be a bachelor. And this seems right: it doesn't seem possible to imagine a bachelor who is married, say. Nor does it seem possible to imagine someone who is unmarried, adult and male who isn't a bachelor.

ACTIVITY 9.3 ⎯⎯⎯⎯⎯⎯⎯⎯⎯⎯⎯⎯⎯⎯⎯⎯⎯⎯

Consider the categories sparrow, gold, chair, introvert, red and even number. Can you provide definitions for them? Take a few minutes to list the properties for each that you think are important for category membership. Don't worry if you find this difficult: just write down what comes to mind. If you can't think of anything, pass on to the next category. When you have finished try to answer the following questions. First, do you think each of these properties is necessary for category membership (i.e. must every member of the category possess the property)? Second, are the properties for each category, when taken together, sufficient for membership in the category (i.e. must anything that possesses these properties necessarily be a member of the category)?

COMMENT

Most people find this kind of activity difficult. In spite of the classical view, it is surprisingly difficult to think of watertight definitions – you might have succeeded for 'even number' but perhaps not for the other categories. We will consider this again in Section 2.1.4.

The classical view was supported by some early, empirical investigations (e.g. Hull, 1920; Bruner *et al.*, 1956) that showed people categorized instances according to whether they possessed the necessary and sufficient conditions of the category. However, despite being sporadically defended (e.g. Sutcliffe, 1993), there have been numerous criticisms. The first concerns the phenomenon known as 'typicality'.

2.1.1   Typicality

Since the classical view contends that all members of a category must satisfy the same definition, it follows that they should all be equally good members of that category. However, psychologists have found systematic inequalities between category members. Rosch (1973) elicited participants' ratings of the typicality or 'goodness-of-exemplar' (sometimes referred to as GOE) of particular instances of a category – the method is often known as a **typicality ratings** method. Rosch's instructions give a sense of what is involved.

> Think of dogs. You all have some notion of what a 'real dog', a 'doggy dog' is. To me a retriever or a German shepherd is a very doggy dog while a Pekinese is a less doggy dog. Notice that this kind of judgement has nothing to do with how well you like the thing ... You may prefer to own a Pekinese without thinking that it is the breed that best represents what people mean by dogginess.
>
> *(Rosch, 1973, pp.131–2)*

ACTIVITY 9.4

Now that you have read Rosch's instructions, write down the following words on the left-hand side of a sheet of paper, putting each word on a new line: pineapple, olive, apple, fig, plum and strawberry. Then, to the right of each word, write down the number (between 1 and 7) that best reflects how well the word fits your idea or image of the category 'fruit'. A '1' means the object is a very good example of your idea of what the category is, a '7' means the object fits very poorly with your idea or image of the category (or is not a member at all).

COMMENT

When you have written down your answers, compare your ratings with those of Rosch shown in the first column of Table 9.1 (see over next page). How might you explain these ratings? Many people feel that their ratings reflect how familiar they are with particular instances, or how frequently those instances are encountered.

You might think that in a society where figs were more commonplace than apples, for example, the typicality of these items would be reversed. In a series of studies, Barsalou (1985) investigated the influences of familiarity and frequency on typicality. Contrary to what one might think, he found that typicality did not correlate with familiarity, and only correlated with frequency to a limited extent. So, it seems that even if penguins were much more common in our lives than they are, and we were all much more familiar with them, we would still think of them as atypical birds!

Rosch's results for four different categories are shown in Table 9.1 (overleaf). She took these ratings to be indicative of the internal structure of categories, and this conclusion was supported by other empirical work. For instance, Rips *et al.* (1973) and Rosch (1975) examined the relationship between typicality and the time it takes participants to verify sentences that express categorization judgements. The method is often known as **category** or **sentence verification**. For example, the sentences might be 'a robin is a bird' (typical instance) and 'a penguin is a bird' (atypical instance). Participants were asked to respond either 'Yes' (meaning they thought the sentence was true) or 'No' (meaning they thought it was false) as quickly as possible. The results showed that for highly typical sentences people were much quicker to verify the sentence (i.e. the sentence 'a robin is a bird' was verified more quickly than the sentence 'a penguin is a bird').

Further support for the idea that categories have internal structure came from Rosch and Mervis (1975). They used the property- or attribute-listing method, the method you tried in Activity 9.2. They asked their participants to generate lists of properties for a series of category instances, for example, robin and penguin for the category bird. The results showed that less typical instances shared properties with fewer category members, while more typical instances shared properties with many other instances. For example, robins have properties – flying, eating worms, building nests – that are shared with many other birds. Penguins have properties – swimming, not flying – that are shared with relatively few other birds.

Using methods such as these, Rosch, Mervis and others provided impressive evidence that categories have what we might think of as a rich **internal structure**. A definition serves to demarcate members of a category from non-members, but even things inside the category are highly structured. Both penguins and robins would satisfy the definition of a bird, but there are important systematic differences between them that are reflected in the cognitive processes governing categorization. And this seems contrary to the classical view's suggestion that all category members must equally satisfy a category's definition. How can categories have highly typical and atypical members if the classical view is correct? And how strongly does such evidence count against the classical view?

Though the classical view makes strong claims about the membership of categories – membership should be all-or-none – it says nothing about their internal structure. So, the findings of rich internal structure do not show the classical view to be wrong, unless, of course, internal structure reflects category membership. If a penguin were not only a less typical bird than a robin, but also less of a

Table 9.1   Rosch's (1973) typicality ratings for various instances of four categories

Fruit		Vegetable		Sport		Vehicle	
Apple	1.3	Carrot	1.1	Football	1.2	Car	1.0
Plum	2.3	Asparagus	1.3	Hockey	1.8	Scooter	2.5
Pineapple	2.3	Celery	1.7	Gymnastics	2.6	Boat	2.7
Strawberry	2.3	Onion	2.7	Wrestling	3.0	Tricycle	3.5
Fig	4.7	Parsley	3.8	Archery	3.9	Skis	5.7
Olive	6.2	Pickle	4.4	Weight-lifting	4.7	Horse	5.9

category member than a robin, then ratings of typicality might reflect a graded notion of category membership in which categories have some clear members, some clear non-members and a range of cases in between. Then, category membership, quite palpably, would not be all-or-none. On the other hand, if typicality does not reflect graded membership, it may be compatible with the classical view. However, typicality effects do expose an inadequacy in the classical view, even if they do not contradict its basic tenets. It is not at all obvious how the classical view might explain typicality effects; at the very least, it would need supplementing.

2.1.2 Borderline cases

If membership in a category is 'all-or-none', as the classical view suggests, then there should be no borderline cases: an item either satisfies the definition of a category or it doesn't. Intuition alone tells us there are items whose category membership is unclear. Colour categories, for example, have no obvious boundary. It seems impossible to draw a line on the colour spectrum, say, between red and orange. For where does a red shade fade into orange? Rather, in between these two categories, there seem to be shades that are neither unequivocally red nor unequivocally orange, hence our use of phrases such as 'a reddy-orange'.

McCloskey and Glucksberg (1978) provided evidence that confirmed this intuition for a whole range of categories. They used a method of asking for **categorization judgements**. They asked their participants to respond either 'Yes' or 'No' to questions of category membership (such as 'Is a robin a bird?'). Participants were also asked to rate the same instances for typicality. McCloskey and Glucksberg then considered the level of agreement that participants showed in their categorization judgements, both across individuals and within the same individuals over two times of testing. They found that participants readily agreed on highly typical and atypical items, yet disagreed over time and across individuals for some items of intermediate typicality. For example, people rated 'chair' as a highly typical item of 'furniture', and were consistent amongst themselves, and over time, in judging a chair to be an item of furniture. Similarly, with highly atypical items such as a ceiling, they were consistent in judging this not to be an example of furniture. With items of intermediate typicality, such as bookends, they were much less consistent. Some people judged these to be items of furniture, others did not; and some people changed their judgements across the two times of testing. McCloskey and Glucksberg thus gave empirical weight to the intuition that many categories have borderline cases.

How telling is this evidence? The classical view certainly implies that categories should have no borderline cases. However, it is at least possible that some of the instances that appear borderline are not genuinely indeterminate, unlike the case of colour categories. It might be that patterns of disagreement reveal a lack of knowledge. For example, you may not know whether a tomato is a fruit or a vegetable. Perhaps sometimes you will say it is a fruit, other times you might say it is a vegetable. But, if you consult a dictionary, you will be told that it is a fruit, even though it is usually used as a vegetable (e.g. in sauces). So, it is possible that an instance definitely belongs to one or other category (i.e. is not borderline), but uncertainty makes the item appear borderline. Another possibility is that inconsistency reflects perspective dependence. It might be, for example, that you know that a tomato is technically a fruit, but your categorization judgement is influenced by the fact that it is used mostly as a vegetable. So, you might agree, in a culinary context, that a tomato is a vegetable, but disagree in the context of a biology lesson.

Though these remain logical possibilities, it is not obvious that McCloskey and Glucksberg's examples actually did involve uncertainty or perspective dependence. Though people disagreed about whether bookends count as furniture, it seems implausible that they did not have enough information or were adopting different perspectives. So, in the absence of alternative explanations, the compelling evidence for borderline cases seems to undermine the classical view.

2.1.3 Intransitivity of categorization

A further source of difficulties for the classical view has been the observation of intransitivity in categorization judgements. Transitivity is observed with many relationships: the relation 'taller than' is transitive because if 'A is taller than B' and 'B is taller than C', then it simply follows that 'A is taller than C'. The relationship is 'transitive' because the last statement follows from the first two.

Is categorization transitive? That is, if As are members of category B, and Bs are members of category C, does it follow that As are also members of category C? According to the classical view it does (and perhaps your intuition agrees). As you have seen, the classical view holds that membership in a category is all or none – if an instance falls into a category, it does so unequivocally. So, if rabbits are mammals then, according to the classical view, they possess the defining features of mammals, and so are mammals unequivocally. Likewise, if mammals are animals, then they possess the defining features of animals, and so are animals unequivocally. There can be no exceptions. So it should just follow, unequivocally, that rabbits must also be animals.

Hampton (1982), however, showed that people's categorization judgements are not in general consistent with transitivity. For example, he found that participants would agree that 'car seats are a kind of chair' and that 'chairs are a kind of furniture' but not agree that 'car seats are a kind of furniture'. Similarly, people might agree that

Big Ben is a clock and that clocks are furniture, but not that Big Ben is an item of furniture. The fact that people strongly reject the transitive inference in these cases represents a real problem for the classical view.

2.1.4 The lack of definitions

In developing his account of language games, Wittgenstein (1953) considered the idea, as implied by the classical view, that there are common properties to all instances of the category of game:

> Consider for example the proceedings that we call 'games'. I mean board-games, card-games, ball-games, Olympic games, and so on. What is common to them all? – Don't say: 'There *must* be something common, or they would not be called "games"' – but *look and see* whether there is anything common to all. – For if you look at them you will not see something that is common to *all*, but similarities, relationships, and a whole series of them at that. ...
>
> I can think of no better expression to characterize these similarities than 'family resemblances'; for the various resemblances between members of a family: build, features, colour of eyes, gait, temperament, etc. etc. overlap and criss-cross in the same way. – And I shall say: 'games' form a family.
>
> *(Wittgenstein, 1953, paras 66–7)*

If Wittgenstein is right, then the classical view is simply mistaken. Whereas it contends that categories have common properties, Wittgenstein's position is that most categories are like 'game' – when you look closely for common properties, you find none. Recall Activity 9.3: there you tried to offer definitions of categories such as red, and introvert. Most people find this task difficult, except perhaps for 'even number', where there is a rule that defines category membership. Wittgenstein suggests that most categories are really indefinable. Indeed, his position makes sense of a striking anomaly: despite the classical view having a long history, people have identified very few examples of categories that can be defined. Most researchers are forced to fall back on one of a very few examples – my choice of 'bachelor' is particularly hackneyed! I couldn't use another example, such as 'tree', 'river', 'chair' or 'ship', because no-one has identified watertight definitions for these categories.

Nonetheless, Wittgenstein has not proved that natural categories cannot be defined, and so it is possible that someone might yet provide definitions. But the philosophers Kripke (1972) and Putnam (1975) undermined even that idea. They considered what would happen if something that was taken to be 'definitional' was later found to be wrong. Consider the concept of 'cat'. Most people would say that cats are mammals, that they have fur and meow, and so on. Are these necessary properties of the category? Well, perhaps there are some cats that don't meow, some that don't have fur, but surely all cats are mammals – almost by definition one might say. Putnam considered the implications of discovering that all cats are really robots controlled from Mars (i.e. not mammals at all). This is a thought experiment, of course, so don't worry that the scenario is improbable, or even impossible. The critical issue is what would be the implications of such a discovery. In particular, would the things that we had previously called cats still be cats? What do you think? If you had a pet cat, would it still be a 'cat' after this discovery? Kripke and Putnam believe that it would – those things we called cats before the discovery are still cats afterwards (i.e. the robots controlled from Mars are still cats). But since robots aren't mammals, 'being a mammal' could not be a defining feature of cats, even though we previously thought it was! The conclusion that Kripke and Putnam draw is that we might be shown to be wrong about virtually any property that we happen to believe is true (or even defining) of a category.

This is how Pinker puts it:

> What is the definition of *lion*? You might say 'a large, ferocious cat that lives in Africa'. ... Suppose scientists discovered that lions weren't innately ferocious ... Suppose it turned out that they were not even cats ... you would probably feel that these ... were still really lions, even if not a word of the definition survived. Lions just don't *have* definitions.
>
> *(Pinker, 1997, p.323, original emphasis)*

There are less fanciful examples that convey the same point. As you saw in Section 1.3, people thought the platypus bizarrely combined the features of birds (a bill), amphibians (swimming) and mammals (fur). Suppose that some people came to believe, erroneously, that the platypus really was a strange kind of bird. What Kripke and Putnam argue is that in a case like this, no matter how strongly held the belief, it could never be definitional for these people that a platypus is a bird. If it were, then as soon as it was determined that the platypus was a mammal after all, by the very same definition it would no longer be a platypus. The arguments of Kripke and Putnam hinge on the intuition that the platypus will still be a 'platypus' no matter what we come to believe, and no matter how wrong those beliefs ultimately turn out. If so, then our beliefs about natural categories never really amount to definitions and the classical view must be mistaken.

2.2   Similarity II: prototype theories of concepts

The combined weight of evidence calling into question the classical view led researchers to consider alternatives. Observations of typicality effects suggested to some that concepts are organized around a measure of the central tendency of a category, known as the **prototype**. Sometimes the prototype may correspond to an actual instance, but in general it is like a 'best' category member, formed by statistically aggregating over examples of the category one encounters. Rosch, for instance, believed that it is a feature of the natural world that certain attributes or properties tend to correlate or cluster together, and it is these natural clusters of correlated attributes that prototypes describe. For example, the prototype for 'bird' might describe the cluster of properties such as having feathers, wings, a beak and an ability to fly. These properties cluster together in a way that feathers, lips, gills and an ability to swing through tree branches do not. Whether or not an instance is a category member then depends upon how similar it is to the prototype: an instance falls within the category if it achieves a certain criterion of similarity. If an instance is too dissimilar, it mismatches on too many properties, then it falls outside the category.

This account is a little like the classical view: both are committed to the idea that similarity explains categorization. For classical theory, instances fall within a category if they match each and every element of the category's definition, and outside the category if they mismatch on any one. The critical difference is that for prototype theories an instance may fall within a category even if it mismatches on a number of properties. Though it might not seem dramatic, a simple illustration shows how significant a move this really is. Suppose a category is characterized by five properties (call them A, B, C, D and E). Now suppose that there is a criterion for membership in the category such that an instance can mismatch on up to, but no more than, two of these five properties. Then there are a number of logical possibilities for category membership, as shown in Table 9.2.

Table 9.2 Different kinds of instances (1 to 4) for a category with five characteristic properties. A tick implies an instance matches on a particular property; a cross implies a mismatch

Instances	Properties				
	A	B	C	D	E
1	✓	✓	✓	✓	✓
2	✓	✓	✓	✓	✗
3	✓	✗	✓	✗	✓
4	✗	✓	✗	✓	✓

Instance 1 possesses all the characteristic properties of the category. No instance could match on more properties, and so we could think of this as a highly typical, perhaps even a prototypical, instance. Instance 2 mismatches on one property and so is less typical. Instances 3 and 4 mismatch on two properties and are less typical again. What Table 9.2 shows is that this category could not be given a simple definition in terms of the five properties: for each property A to E there is an instance of the category that does not possess that property. Hence, not one of A to E is a *necessary* property. So, although prototype theories could be thought of as having merely relaxed the classical view's criteria for category membership, the upshot is prototype theory might be able to explain category membership for the many categories that resist definition. (Note the similarities between Table 9.2 and the discussion of diagnosis in Box 9.1 – can you see how the criteria proposed for diagnosing schizophrenia and ME treat these as prototype concepts?)

Prototype theories have been formulated in different ways. Smith *et al.*'s (1988) formalization captures many of the qualities found in different versions. Table 9.3 gives their illustration of a prototype representation for 'apple'.

Table 9.3 highlights some of the differences between prototype theories and the classical view. First, there are multiple possible values for each attribute, capturing the fact that no one value is necessary for category membership – for example,

Table 9.3   Prototype representation for apple

Diagnosticity	Attribute	Value	Weight
1	COLOUR	red	25
		green	5
		brown	
		...	...
.5	SHAPE	round	15
		square	1
		cylindrical	5
		...	...
.25	TEXTURE	smooth	25
		rough	5
		bumpy	5
		...	...

Source: adapted from Smith et al., 1988

apples are typically, but not necessarily, red. Second, diagnosticities indicate the extent to which each attribute is important for deciding category membership. Third, the values are weighted and these weights indicate the extent to which each value contributes to typicality; the highest weighted values are those of the prototype. Categorization depends upon achieving a criterion similarity with the representation of the concept, one that depends on matching properties as before, but now diagnosticities and weights enter into the computation as well (though we don't need to go into detail). Prototype theories can readily explain the typicality effects discovered by Rosch and her co-workers.

1   Instances that differ in typicality are assumed to differ in terms of the weighting of values on which they match the concept. For example, in Table 9.3, a difference in typicality between red and brown apples is reflected in a difference in the weighting for red and brown.

2   Sentences such as 'a robin is a bird' are likely to be verified more quickly than 'a penguin is a bird' because, for high-typicality instances, the criterial similarity required for verifying the sentence is likely to be achieved after matching just a few properties. This is because most attributes that match will have higher-weighted values, and so any criterion for category membership will be reached quickly. For low-typicality instances like penguin, many attributes will mismatch or will have low weighted values, and so more matches will have to be made before the criterion is reached.

3   Typicality is likely to correlate with how widely category members share attributes. This follows from the fact that the diagnosticities of attributes and weights of values themselves reflect the statistical distribution of those attributes and values. The more widely shared a value is, the greater is its weight. In Table 9.3, for example, 'round shape' receives a high weight

indicating that many (many) more apples are round than square. Since high typicality instances tend to match on high-weighted values; it follows that they will also possess properties that are widely shared.

However, despite prototype theory being able to accommodate many of the findings that undermined the classical view, difficulties have emerged, as we shall now see.

2.2.1 The meaning of typicality effects

Armstrong *et al.* (1983) considered whether typicality effects occur for concepts that appear to be definitional. Their examples of definitional concepts included 'female', 'plane geometric figure', 'odd number' and 'even number' (as in Activity 9.3). Armstrong *et al.* believed that category membership for these concepts is determined not by similarity to a prototype, but by a definition: whether a number is even depends on whether dividing it by 2 yields an integer. Curiously, however, they found a range of robust typicality effects (as in Table 9.4), implying that even these apparently definitional concepts have an internal structure; these effects were also found using the sentence verification task.

Table 9.4   Typicality ratings for instances of well-defined categories

Even number	Typicality rating	Female	Typicality rating
4	1.1	mother	1.7
8	1.5	housewife	2.4
10	1.7	princess	3.0
18	2.6	waitress	3.2
34	3.4	policewoman	3.9
106	3.9	comedienne	4.5
Odd number	**Typicality rating**	**Plane geometry figure**	**Typicality rating**
3	1.6	square	1.3
7	1.9	triangle	1.5
23	2.4	rectangle	1.9
57	2.6	circle	2.1
501	3.5	trapezoid	3.1
447	3.7	ellipse	3.4

Source: Armstrong *et al.*, 1983

At first glance Armstrong *et al.*'s data could be taken to imply that even concepts such as odd number are not really definitional after all, but organized around a prototype. However, Armstrong *et al.* didn't regard this as a serious possibility. Instead, they argued that the existence of typicality effects should not be taken as conclusive evidence that category membership is determined by similarity to a prototype. They proposed instead a dual-process model, in which concepts possess a 'core' that is used when we judge category membership and a set of identification procedures that we use to identify instances of a category on particular occasions (often rapidly). Armstrong *et al.* suggested that the classical view might explain the concept's core, while prototype theory explains identification procedures. Unfortunately, inasmuch as this proposal involves both theoretical approaches, it appears to inherit some of the problems faced by each.

2.2.2   The context sensitivity of typicality effects

Another difficulty for prototype theory is the observation that typicality effects change with context. If, as Rosch thought, prototypes reflect natural correlations or clusters of properties, one would expect the prototype to be stable.

However, Roth and Shoben (1983) showed that typicality effects are changed by linguistic context. For example, their participants rated the typicality of different farm animals with respect to the category 'animal'. Participants were first presented with a context sentence that emphasized a particular activity; for example, 'Bertha enjoyed riding the animal' or 'Bertha enjoyed milking the animal'. The context sentence was then followed by a sentence frame such as 'The ___ quite liked it too'. Participants were asked to rate the typicality of a list of animal words that would complete the sentence frame. Importantly, the list contained words such as 'horse' and 'cow' that fitted well with one context sentence but not with others – though both words were judged to be possible completions of the sentences. Roth and Shoben found that when the context sentence referred to milking, cows were considered to be more typical animals than horses. However, when the context referred to riding, horses were considered more typical animals than cows. (You might notice similarities with the discussion of priming in Chapter 2.)

Medin and Shoben (1988) also found that typicality judgements change with context. They asked their participants to rate various kinds of spoon for typicality in the category 'spoon'. Participants rated metal spoons as more typical than wooden spoons, and small spoons as more typical than large spoons. Therefore, one might expect that small metal spoons would be most typical of all and that large wooden spoons would be least typical, with small wooden and large metal spoons intermediate. However, while Medin and Shoben found that small metal spoons were more typical than large metal spoons, they found that large wooden spoons were more typical than small wooden spoons. So, the contribution to typicality made by the values 'large' and 'small' depended on whether one was thinking about metal spoons or wooden spoons.

Prototype theories cannot easily explain such demonstrations of the instability of typicality. First, the very idea of instability seems to be at odds with Rosch's claim that prototypes correspond to stable clusters of correlated properties that reflect the structure of the natural world. Second, in connection with Table 9.3, Roth and Shoben's results suggest that the weightings of values and/or diagnosticities of attributes are themselves changeable. However, it is unclear what mechanism could be responsible for such changes. Third, Medin and Shoben's results suggest that the contributions to typicality of different properties (e.g. size and material made from) are mutually dependent. Yet the representation in Table 9.3 assumes that the attributes and values are independent of one another.

2.2.3 Complex concepts

As noted in Section 1.4, it is commonplace to assume that concepts express our understandings of the meanings of words. So, the concept 'red' is assumed to express what we understand as the meaning of the word 'red'; the concept 'car' is thought to provide the meaning of the word 'car'. But this immediately raises the question: what kind of concept provides the meaning of the phrase 'red car'?

Researchers have tried to explain the meanings of phrases and larger linguistic units in terms of complex concepts; that is, combinations of lexical concepts. The meaning of the phrase 'red car' would then be explained in terms of the combination of the constituent lexical concepts: 'red' and 'car'. How could concepts combine to yield the meaning of such a phrase?

If concepts are structured around prototypes, then perhaps they could combine through combining their prototypes. The difficulty, however, is that no-one really knows how this might be done. Though many suggestions have been made, they all appear to fail for one reason or other. For example, one suggestion has been that the prototype for 'red car' is formed from the prototype for 'red' and the prototype for 'car' (the prototypical red car would therefore be a prototypical car that was prototypically red).

While this seems a sensible suggestion, and appears to give the right interpretation for 'red car', this could not work in general. Following the same reasoning, the prototypical 'pet fish' ought to be a prototypical fish that is also prototypically pet-like – perhaps something like a cuddly salmon. The real prototypical 'pet fish' of course is more like a goldfish – neither a prototypical pet nor a prototypical fish. More problematic still for combining prototypes, the prototypical 'stone lion' ought to be something like a real lion made of stone, that is, an impossible object. How could the prototypes for 'stone' (perhaps granite or limestone) and 'lion' (a real lion) combine to give the right interpretation (i.e. a stone statue of a lion)? If you feel these examples are a little whimsical, take a look at newspaper headlines as these often use phrases with a similar structure. For example, it isn't easy to see how the meaning of 'killer firework' could be explained by the combination of the constituent prototypes: a prototypical killer might be a sadistic criminal, or perhaps a virulent disease; a prototypical firework might be a rocket. How would these prototypes combine to yield the required interpretation? Complex concepts continue to present real difficulties for most theories of concepts (cf. Fodor, 1998).

2.3 Common-sense theories: the theory-based view

Both classical and prototype theories explain categorization in terms of similarity using quite simple feature sets. But the problems these theories have encountered have led researchers first to question the importance of similarity and second to propose that categorization involves much larger knowledge structures, called theories (or common-sense theories to distinguish them from scientific ones). The approach has become known as the concepts as theory view or the 'theory' theory of concepts.

Before we turn to the 'theory' theory we should note, however, that similarity-based accounts have achieved considerable success and remain popular. Hampton (1998) conveys some sense of this. Using McCloskey and Glucksberg's (1978) data (they collected both typicality ratings and categorization judgements as you saw in Section 2.1.2), he examined whether the probability of an item being judged a category member could be predicted from its typicality (reflecting its similarity to a prototype).

Focusing on just the borderline cases, Hampton showed that typicality was a very good predictor, explaining somewhere between 46 per cent and 96 per cent of the variance in categorization probability. So, regardless of the difficulties facing similarity-based accounts, similarity (as measured by typicality) seems to be a good indicator of categorization. Nonetheless, Hampton found other predictors of categorization probability (though none was as good a predictor as typicality). These included lack of familiarity; the extent to which an instance was judged 'only technically speaking a member' of a category (e.g. a dolphin is technically speaking a mammal, but superficially appears more similar to fish); and the extent to which participants judged an instance was 'technically speaking not a member' (e.g. a bat is technically speaking not a bird despite superficially appearing more similar to birds than to mammals). That these last two factors were predictors suggests that categorization draws upon deeper, more theoretical, knowledge than just similarity alone.

We now turn to some of the reasons why, in spite of these successes, many researchers have become dissatisfied with the notion of similarity.

2.3.1   Problems with similarity

The philosopher Nelson Goodman identified a number of problems with similarity; indeed, he described it as 'a pretender, an impostor, a quack' (Goodman, 1972, p.437). One concern is with whether similarity genuinely helps us to explain categorization. After all, in prototype theories, saying that an instance is similar to the prototype means that the two share some properties in common. But note that this further explication removes the notion of similarity: 'is similar to' becomes translated as 'shares properties with'. So, what explains categorization is not similarity *per se* but the sharing of properties.

However, a further problem arises since there is no obvious limit to the number of properties any two objects may share. Murphy and Medin (1985, p.292) ask us to consider the similarity of plums and lawnmowers: 'You might say these have little in common, but of course both weigh less than 10,000 kg (and less than 10,001 kg), both did not exist 10,000,000 years ago (and 10,000,001 years ago), both cannot hear well, both can be dropped, both take up space, and so on.' It seems that, depending on what counts as a *relevant* property, plums and lawnmowers could either be seen as very dissimilar, or very similar. So, for similarity, explicated in terms of shared properties, to provide meaningful explanations of categorization, we need to know what counts as a property. We need some way of declaring 'lack of hearing ability' as irrelevant in comparing plums and lawnmowers, for example. For Murphy and Medin (1985), observations such as these suggest that similarity is shorthand for something else that explains why categories hang together, or cohere.

2.3.2   The role of common-sense theories

In opposition to similarity-based views, Murphy and Medin argued that concepts are explanation-based, that there is some explanatory principle or theory that unites the category. They offer the example of someone at a party who jumps into a swimming pool fully clothed. You might categorize this person as being intoxicated, but a similarity-based view cannot explain this because your concept of 'intoxicated' is unlikely to include the property 'jumps into swimming pools fully clothed'. So how might we explain the categorization? Murphy and Medin argue that categorizing the person as 'intoxicated' plays a role in explaining their behaviour, that is, in explaining why they jumped into the swimming pool.

Might this explanatory basis be found in categorization more generally? If so, then categorizing a robin as a bird ought to provide some kind of explanation of the robin's properties, analogous to the case of the intoxicated swimmer. Such a categorization does appear to provide a (partial) explanation: knowing that a robin is a bird helps explain why it has feathers and a beak. The explanation is partial, since we could go on to ask why birds have beaks and feathers, but it is an explanation nonetheless. After all, were we to discover that a robin is not a bird, we would want to know why it has feathers and a beak. Without the categorization we would be in need of an explanation.

We noted in Section 2.2.2 that similarity-based approaches cannot easily explain the non-independence of attributes. For Murphy and Medin, relationships between attributes are evidence that our concepts are embedded in larger and broader knowledge structures. Sometimes these structures have been labelled 'common-sense theories', sometimes merely 'background knowledge'. But if such knowledge structures are at work in categorization, why might people have previously concluded that concepts are similarity-based? Murphy and Medin speculate that many categorization judgements become automatized, particularly when members of the same category have relatively consistent perceptual properties. Under these conditions, the role of our underlying theories becomes obscured, and so we may (erroneously) conclude that categorization is determined by similarity. However, even in these cases, when novel instances emerge (such as robot cats), or where there is disagreement (with borderlines perhaps), we turn to our underlying theories.

What evidence is there that categorization is determined by theories as opposed to similarity? Rips (1989) asked his participants to consider triads of objects. Two objects belonged to distinct categories (e.g. a pizza and a US quarter) and were chosen so that participants' largest estimate of the size of one category (the quarter) was smaller than their smallest estimate of the other (the pizza). Rips then asked his participants to consider a third object, telling them only that it was of intermediate size (i.e. larger than the largest estimated size of a quarter and smaller than the smallest estimated size of a pizza). He asked which of the two other categories this third object was more likely to belong to, and which of the two it was most similar to. The two judgements dissociated: that is, participants judged the object more likely to be a pizza, but more similar to a quarter.

Other dissociations between categorization and similarity have been demonstrated (e.g. Rips and Collins, 1993; Roberson et al., 1999). Kroska and Goldstone (1996) showed their participants scenarios that described a putative emotion. Each scenario constituted a set of phrases so that one phrase was central to one emotion and other phrases were characteristic of a different emotion. For example, one scenario included the phrases 'Threat of harm or death', 'Being accepted, belonging' and 'Experiencing highly pleasurable stimuli or sensations'. The first of these phrases was considered central to the emotion category 'fear'. The remaining two phrases were considered characteristic of the emotion category 'joy'. Kroska and Goldstone found that their participants tended to categorize this scenario as an instance of fear (i.e. a member of the category 'fear') but they also judged it to be more similar to an instance of joy. That is, judgements of category membership were influenced by properties considered central to a category, while judgements of similarity were influenced by characteristic properties. Again, these findings show that judgements of category membership can dissociate from judgements of similarity.

It seems that there are deeper reasons for people's categorizations – in the quarter example, perhaps they realized that pizzas can, in principle, be any size, whereas their common-sense theories of coins tell them they are produced to a regulation standard (see Box 9.2 for developmental evidence).

9.2

Categorization in development

Support for the idea that knowledge of deeper, causal principles is at work in categorization has come from work looking at children's categorization. Keil (1989), for instance, used both discovery and transformation procedures to examine how children weigh appearance and theoretical properties. For example, in a discovery, children might be told of a novel hybrid animal that looked and behaved just like a zebra. However, they would be told also that it had been discovered that this animal had the insides of a horse and was the offspring of two horses. Younger children (around 4 years of age) tended to say the animal was a zebra, whereas older children (around 7 years) tended to judge the animal to be a horse. Therefore, younger children seemed to be influenced more by the superficial characteristics of the animal (e.g. appearance), and older children more by its biologically relevant properties (e.g. lineage).

Similar results were found using a transformation procedure. Children were told of a raccoon that underwent a series of transformations so that it ended up looking and behaving like a skunk. For example, it might have skunk-like stripes dyed on its fur, and have a surgical implant so that it could emit foul-smelling liquid. Again, younger children seemed dominated by appearance-based properties; they judged that the raccoon was now a skunk. The older children, in contrast, judged that the animal was still a raccoon.

Keil has referred to this age-related change in children's categorization as the 'characteristic-to-defining shift' since he thought the younger children were influenced by properties (i.e. appearances) that were only characteristic of the category, while the older children were beginning to deploy something like the beginnings of a biological theory, and were paying attention to properties that were more defining. However, as Murphy (2002) points out, it is probably not the case that the younger and older children have qualitatively distinct styles of categorization. It is more likely that the younger children simply do not know enough about biological categories to work out which properties are characteristic, and which are defining.

2.3.3 Difficulties with the 'theory' theory

The 'theory' theory has proved an important and useful way of thinking about concepts. It has, for instance, reminded researchers of difficulties with the notion of similarity, and it has proved to be a useful peg on which to hang a range of disparate findings whose common theme is that categorization is influenced by deeper, causal knowledge of categories, as well as by knowledge of their superficial properties.

However, there are a number of difficulties with the 'theory' theory. Some of the findings taken to support the 'theory' theory are really demonstrations that similarity does not always explain categorization and this does not necessarily imply that theories are what is needed. Moreover, it is not clear what is meant by 'theory'. Whereas similarity-based views could be made relatively precise (see Table 9.3 for instance), formalizing 'theory' theories seems much more difficult. Some researchers have tried to pin down what is meant by a common-sense theory via a comparison with scientific theories (cf. Gopnik, 1996). However, other researchers believe such a comparison undermines the idea that common-sense theories are theories at all (cf. Gellatly, 1997). For example, Murphy (2000) argues that the background knowledge that influences concepts is too simplistic and mundane to be likened to a scientific theory. Indeed, he eschews the term 'theory' in favour of the more neutral 'knowledge'.

A further difficulty with the 'theory' theory is that it is hard to imagine how combining theories could explain complex concepts. Scientific theories are notoriously difficult to combine. Indeed, for decades, theoretical physicists have struggled to combine theories of electricity, magnetism and gravity into one unified theory. So how can theories be combined so effortlessly in understanding phrases like 'red car' when they are so difficult to combine in general? Even if we talk of combining knowledge rather than theories, we are still left with the difficult problem of working out which knowledge gets combined and the mechanism by which this is done.

Given these problems, it is ironic that the theory-based view is motivated in part by difficulties with the notion of similarity. Arguably, it has supplanted this with the equally mysterious notion of a 'theory'.

2.4 Psychological essentialism

Psychological essentialism is one attempt at formulating more precisely the view that categorization is influenced by deeper, explanatory principles. Medin (1989) and Medin and Ortony (1989) suggested that people believe that, and act as though, category members have certain essential properties in common. That is, people categorize things according to their beliefs about essential properties. They may also believe that the essential properties constrain a category's more superficial properties. For example, the essential properties of birds might be thought to involve their genetic make-up, properties that would constrain their appearance and behaviour.

Essential properties can be characterized as properties such that if an object did not possess them, it would not be that object. The essential properties of birds are properties that all birds necessarily possess; if something doesn't possess them, then it isn't a bird. Essential properties may seem rather like the defining properties of the classical view. However, there is one critical difference. According to psychological essentialism most people will not know what a category's essential properties are, but will still believe that the category has some. We might speculate as to what the essential properties are – perhaps for biological categories they would be genetic properties – but, in general, our beliefs will be vague and may turn out to be incorrect. So psychological essentialism proposes that people's concepts may contain a 'place-holder' for an essence – and the place-holder may even be empty, reflecting a lack of knowledge as to what the essential properties might be.

Of course not everyone's place-holder need be empty. Indeed, it is usually thought that discovering essential properties is a job for science. A metallurgist or chemist, perhaps, might uncover the essential properties of gold, just as a biologist might for birds. So, experts may have their place-holders partially or completely filled – they may know (or think they know) the essential properties. But these beliefs may turn out to be in error too, so the place-holder is presumably capable of revision. We can illustrate psychological essentialism with the platypus example of Section 2.1.4. Soon after its discovery, lay-people presumably came to believe that the platypus had a certain essence, but had no idea what this might be (their essence 'place-holder' was empty). Experts at the time might have filled their essence place-holder in different ways: some thought the platypus was essentially an amphibian; others that it was a mammal. But the contents of these place-holders changed as more was learnt. Finally, the experts settled on the view that the platypus was mammalian, and as lay-people adopted this view they filled out their essence place-holder accordingly.

Psychological essentialism is consistent with much of the evidence supporting the 'theory' theory. Much evidence supporting psychological essentialism specifically has come from studies of the development of categorization (see Box 9.2). For instance, Gelman and Wellman (1991) found that even 4- and 5-year-old children believe the insides of objects to be more important than their outsides in determining category membership. For example, they asked children whether a dog would still be a dog if its outsides were removed, and also if its insides were removed. Children thought that instances would remain in the category if the outsides were removed, but not if their insides were removed. According to Gelman and Wellman, children are being essentialist since they believe that something internal, something hidden and 'inner', is causally responsible for category membership.

However, psychological essentialism has not gone unchallenged. Malt (1994) examined the concept of water. If people believe H_2O to be the essence of water, then their categorization of liquids as water should be strongly influenced by the proportion of H_2O those liquids contain. However, Malt found that people's categorizations were strongly influenced by the source of the water, its location and its function. Indeed, pond water was thought to be 'water' but was judged to contain only 78.8 per cent H_2O; tears were judged not to be 'water' but to contain 88.6 per cent H_2O. So the belief in the presence or absence of H_2O was not the only factor in deciding membership in the category 'water'.

In Section 2.1.4, we considered the arguments of the philosophers Kripke (1972) and Putnam (1975). For example, Putnam argued that even if we discovered that all cats are robots controlled from Mars, they would still be cats. What we didn't note there is that they used thought experiments such as this to support essentialism. Braisby *et al.* (1996) subjected these to an empirical test. They asked participants to give categorization judgements in thought experiments such as Putnam's robot cat. In one condition they were told:

> You have a female pet cat named Tibby. For many years people have assumed cats to be mammals. However, scientists have recently discovered that they are all, in fact, robots controlled from Mars. Upon close examination, you discover that Tibby too is a robot, just as the scientists suggest.

Participants were then asked to indicate whether they thought that a series of statements were true or false. These included statements expressing essentialist intuitions (e.g. 'Tibby is a cat, though we were wrong about her being a mammal.') and statements that expressed the contrary intuition (e.g. 'Tibby is not a cat, though she is a robot controlled from Mars.'). Only about half of the participants thought that these essentialist statements were true, and the contrary ones false. Moreover, many participants seemed to give contradictory judgements: they either judged both statements to be true, or judged both to be false. Braisby *et al.* argued that these findings did not support essentialism, but implied that concepts change their content according to context and perspective (cf. Braisby and Franks, 1997).

There has also been mixed evidence concerning the role that expert opinion plays in categorization. Malt (1990) presented people with objects that they were told appeared 'halfway' between two categories (e.g. a tree halfway between an oak and a maple) and asked them to indicate how they would solve the dilemma of categorizing the object. She offered her participants three options. They could 'ask an expert', 'call it whichever you want' or indicate that they could 'tell which it is' if they could only think about it long enough. For pairs of natural categories such as 'robin–sparrow' and 'trout–bass', 75 per cent of participants suggested they would ask an expert, whereas for pairs of artefact categories, such as 'boat–ship', 63 per cent of participants suggested it was possible to 'call it whichever you want'. This evidence suggests that people may be psychologically essentialist for natural categories, at least to some degree, because they recognize that experts may be in a better position to judge categorization when lay-people cannot. However, the data overall are not conclusive. Braisby (2001) examined the extent to which people modify their categorization judgements for genetically modified biological categories when told the opinions of experts. For example, his participants might be asked to consider a genetically modified salmon, and were told either that expert biologists had judged that it was a salmon or that they had judged that it was not. He found that only around half of the participants changed their categorization judgements to conform to the judgements of the biologists. Moreover, around a quarter of participants would change their categorization judgements to conform to those of shoppers (i.e. a group presumed not to be expert with respect to the category's essential properties). Braisby argued that only around a quarter of participants were modifying their categorization judgements because of the biologists' expertise with the relevant essential properties, and so the majority of responses did not provide evidence for psychological essentialism. Indeed, participants seemed to base their judgements on non-essential properties such as appearance and function (as well as genetic make-up).

Lastly, it should be noted that much of the evidence cited in support of psychological essentialism (e.g. Gelman and Wellman, 1991) only indirectly relates to beliefs in essential properties. Gelman and Wellman, for example, found that children thought that removing the outsides from something like a dog did not alter its category membership, but removing its insides did. However, for these data to support essentialism, a further inference is required, one that relates insides to essences. In a similar vein, Strevens (2000) actually argues that the notion of essence or essential properties is not required to explain empirical data such as these. Of course, psychological essentialists have responded to some of these criticisms so it seems fair to say that the arguments are not yet settled. However, some of the criticisms of other theories may also apply to psychological essentialism – how might it help us understand complex concepts, for example?

Summary of Section 2

- The classical view, that concepts are definitions of categories, is undermined by arguments that many categories cannot be defined, and cannot readily explain typicality effects, borderline cases and intransitivity.
- The prototype view, that categorization is determined by similarity to the prototype, explains most typicality effects. However, it cannot readily explain the context sensitivity of typicality, nor how prototypes might combine in complex concepts. There is a residual question as to whether the existence of typicality effects implies a prototype organization.
- The theory-based view helps explain the non-independence of attributes in concepts, and dissociations between categorization and similarity. It also avoids some of the criticisms aimed at similarity. However, it is not clear how theories might combine in complex concepts, and the notion of a theory is very under-specified.
- Psychological essentialism apparently explains findings that even young children believe inner, hidden properties are causally responsible for category membership. However, it is not clear whether the notion of essence is required to explain data such as these. Moreover, the idea that people categorize according to essential properties has received mixed empirical support, as has the notion that people might defer to expert categorizations.

3   Where next?

In this chapter we have canvassed some of the principal approaches that have been taken in developing a theory of concepts. In some respects, it seems as if the study of concepts is the study of theories that do not work for one reason or other. The classical view falters because we cannot identify necessary and sufficient conditions for category membership for all but a very few concepts. Prototype theory has difficulties explaining context sensitivity and complex concepts. Ultimately, both suffer for their use of the notion of similarity, which seems unable to explain categorization fully. Theory-based notions of concepts are imprecise and cannot obviously explain complex concepts. Lastly, psychological essentialism has received mixed empirical support, and much of the empirical evidence only indirectly relates to the notion of essences.

However, such a picture of the psychology of concepts is unnecessarily gloomy. Indeed, it turns out that we have probably learned more about the phenomena of categorization even as various theories have been found wanting. And, of course, adherents of those theories continue to introduce modifications in order to explain recalcitrant data. Nonetheless, our discussion of the different theoretical approaches raises (at least) two questions. What sense can we make of so many different theoretical treatments, when none is without problems? And where might researchers next turn their attention if there is, as yet, no common theoretical framework? As I shall try to suggest, one way of answering these questions is to consider to what extent categorization is a unitary phenomenon.

3.1   Is all categorization the same?

Perhaps the different theoretical treatments of concepts reflect the fact that categorization is not one single process. Maybe people categorize items in different ways in different circumstances. Indeed, discursive psychologists, whose approach we earlier bracketed off, might argue that categorization depends essentially on context, and that there is nothing common to all the cases that we call categorization. Were context to have such an unbridled influence we might expect categorization to appear unsystematic. Yet, much of the evidence presented in this chapter points to the opposite – we have examined a wide range of empirical data that are highly robust.

One way of reconciling the idea that people categorize things differently on different occasions with the idea that categorization is nonetheless systematic is to suggest that there are (a determinate number of) different kinds of categorization. Moreover, it is conceivable that these could be usefully framed by the different theories of concepts. For example, perhaps the classical view gives a useful account of categorization in cases where we need to provide or appeal to definitions. In law, for instance, often we need to reach an agreement or adopt a convention as to whether something belongs to a category (e.g. whether a 16-year-old is a child or an adult). Similarly, prototype theory may usefully explain categorization in circumstances where we need to categorize something rapidly, or perhaps under uncertainty, maybe when we are in a position to take into account only an object's superficial properties. Likewise, theory-based views may describe categorization when we are seeking a more reflective and considered judgement, perhaps when we are using categorization in order to explain something. And essentialism may usefully explain how we categorize when we wish to be consistent with expertise and a scientific knowledge of the world.

Speculative though this is, Smith and Sloman (1994) have provided evidence that suggests there may be some truth to this possibility. They sought to replicate the dissociation between similarity and categorization judgements obtained by Rips (1989) and described in Section 2.3.2. Rips found that people judged an object intermediate in size between a quarter and a pizza to be more similar to a quarter, but more likely to be a pizza. Smith and Sloman obtained the same dissociation only when participants were required to think aloud whilst making their decisions and so articulate reasons for their judgements (that is, they provided a concurrent verbal protocol; see Chapter 11). Smith and Sloman interpret this finding as pointing to two modes of categorization: (1) a similarity-based mode of categorization, and (2) a rule-based mode. The implication is that people will either focus on similarity or on underlying rules and structure depending on how the categorization task is presented. When in similarity-based mode, categorization seems to conform to similarity-based accounts, such as prototype theories. When in rule-based mode, categorization seems to be more theory- or explanation-based. Though this does not show that there are as many different ways of categorizing as there are theories of concepts, it does suggest that categorization may not be a single process. It is a possibility, therefore, that some of the different accounts of concepts may be implicitly concerned with different kinds of purpose in categorization, and ultimately with different kinds of categorization.

In a similar vein we can rethink the phenomena that are taken as evidence of the nature of concepts. Earlier we noted that concepts and words bear a complex relationship to one another, but much of the evidence we have so far reviewed has tended to equate the use of category words with categorization. However, while our use of category labels is certainly influenced by our beliefs about categorization, it is also influenced by language more generally. Indeed, we can label something with a category word yet not believe that it belongs to the category – describing a statue of a lion as a 'lion', for example, does not indicate that we think the statue really is a lion. Malt *et al.* (1999) showed how the same is true for how we label containers, such as 'box', 'bottle' and 'jar'. They found that whether an item was called a 'bottle' depended not so much on how similar it was to a prototypical bottle, but whether there was something similar that was also called a 'bottle'. In this way, for example, a shampoo container might get called a shampoo 'bottle' despite bearing little similarity to a prototypical bottle. So, whether we apply a category label (e.g. bottle) to an object depends in part on how that label has been used historically and only in part on whether we think that the object really belongs to the labelled category (i.e. on whether the object really is a bottle).

3.2   Are all concepts the same?

Another possibility that we should consider is the extent to which different types of category require a different theoretical treatment. Already you might have noticed how each theory seems to work most convincingly for a slightly different set of examples. In Activity 9.3 you tried to list the properties of a range of different categories: sparrow, gold, chair, introvert, red and even number. Did you feel then that these categories were very different from one another? If so, we can perhaps make sense of this intuition.

Some categories like even number seem amenable to definition. For these **well-defined** categories, the classical view appears to give a good explanation of category membership, though it does not obviously explain how some even numbers are considered more typical than others. Perhaps this would require something like Armstrong *et al.*'s dual-process account, and involve its attendant difficulties (see Section 2.2.1). Nonetheless, it may be that a modified classical view would provide a good explanation of these kinds of category.

In a similar vein, prototype theories seem to work well for **fuzzy** categories – like red in Activity 9.3 – categories that seem to have genuine borderline cases. For these, similarity to a prototype might provide the best explanation of category membership, since there is no prospect of defining these categories, nor do people in general seem to have relevant common-sense theories (e.g. a theory of the deeper causal principles by which red things come to appear red). Perhaps categories like chair are fuzzy in the same way.

Theory-based and essentialist approaches are likely to be most successful for categories for which people have common-sense theories. Perhaps unsurprisingly, these include many categories for which scientific theories have also been developed; for example, sparrow and gold, from Activity 9.3. These are categories where it is relevant to develop a deeper, explanatory knowledge of the causal principles underlying the category. Interestingly, it has been argued that essentialism may also help to explain people's concepts of social categories; for instance, introvert in Activity 9.3 (Haslam *et al.*, 2000).

Of course, this is no more than a possibility, and it may be that a single theoretical approach will be devised that can accommodate all of the different kinds of category we have considered. Even if people accepted that different categories require different theoretical treatments, it would still be important to find some way of relating the different theories so we could understand in what sense they were all theories of concepts.

3.3   Are all categorizers the same?

Consonant with the above considerations, we might also consider whether all categorizers are the same. Medin *et al.* (1997) recruited participants from three occupational groups with correspondingly different experience and knowledge of trees: maintenance workers, landscapers and taxonomists. They then asked them to sort the names of 48 different kinds of tree into whatever groups made sense. The taxonomists tended to reproduce a scientific way of sorting the trees; the maintenance workers produced a similar sorting, although they gave more emphasis to superficial characteristics (such as whether trees were broad-leaved). They also tended to include a 'weed tree' group that was not present in the taxonomists' sorts, and which included trees that cause particular maintenance problems. The landscapers didn't reproduce a scientific taxonomy, but justified their sorts in terms of factors such as landscape utility, size and aesthetic value. Lynch *et al.* (2000) also showed how the typicality ratings of the same kinds of tree expert differed from those of novices. Typicality for the expert group reflected similarity to ideals, so trees judged to be best examples of the category were not of average or prototypical height, but of extreme height; in contrast, the ratings of the novices were largely influenced by familiarity.

Studies such as these suggest that different people do not necessarily categorize things in the same way. The goals that a person has as well as the extent of their knowledge may influence the way they categorize and, by extension, be reflected in their concepts.

Summary of Section 3

It is possible that the failings of one or all of the approaches to concepts may be due to any combination of the following:

- Categorization may not be a single process; and different kinds of categorization may lend themselves to different theoretical treatments.
- Different types of category have different properties and so may require different theoretical treatments.
- Different groups of people may categorize things in different ways, according to their goals and the nature of their knowledge, and so may fit the claims of different theories.

4   Conclusion

Overall, it seems that category knowledge is multi-layered, encompassing knowledge of the causal properties relevant to a category, knowledge relevant to explaining category membership and the properties of instances, knowledge of function, and knowledge of superficial properties useful for identification and judgements about appearance. It also seems that we are capable of calling on different kinds of category knowledge on different occasions and for different purposes. While these observations are not inconsistent with a single theoretical treatment of concepts, they nonetheless raise the prospect that competing theories provide good explanations of somewhat different sets of phenomena, and so are not directly in contradiction. However the theoretical debates may or may not be resolved, I hope this chapter has convinced you of the importance of concepts to an understanding of cognition. Though categorization presents substantial challenges for researchers, these are challenges for all cognitive psychologists. Only once they have been met are we likely to be able to develop a good understanding of the mind. (None of which is likely to trouble Rosie.)

Figure 9.2   Rosie (untroubled)

Now that you have read this chapter you can reinforce and extend your learning by reading an original journal article associated with it, available online from the DD303 website. Remember, these are original journal articles, so the style is different from this textbook, and don't be too concerned if you can't follow every detail.

Answer to Activity 9.1

Here are the identities of the objects shown in Figure 9.1 (from left to right): olive stoner; asparagus peeler; pickle picker, ideal for retrieving the very last pickled onion or gherkin from a jar.

Further reading

Inevitably in a chapter of this length, I have omitted some important issues. Most notably, I have not touched on the exemplar view of concepts, the literature on category learning, or the issue of basic level concepts. For these, I would strongly recommend Greg Murphy's excellent book. For a philosophically inspired selection of psychological and philosophical works, see Laurence and Margolis.

Laurence, S. and Margolis, E. (1999) (eds) *Concepts: Core Readings*, Cambridge, MA, MIT Press.

Murphy, G.L. (2002) *The Big Book of Concepts*, Cambridge, MA, MIT Press.

References

American Psychiatric Association (1994) *Diagnostic and Statistical Manual of Mental Disorders: DSM-IV* (4th edn), Washington, DC, American Psychiatric Association.

Armstrong, S.L., Gleitman, L. and Gleitman, H. (1983) 'What some concepts might not be', *Cognition*, vol.13, pp.263–308.

Barsalou, L.W. (1983) 'Ad hoc categories', *Memory and Cognition*, vol.11, pp.211–27.

Barsalou, L.W. (1985) 'Ideals, central tendency, and frequency of instantiation as determinants of graded structure in categories', *Journal of Experimental Psychology: Learning, Memory and Cognition*, vol.11, pp.629–54.

Braisby, N.R. (2001) 'Deference in categorization: evidence for essentialism?', in Moore, J.D. and Stenning, K. (eds) *Proceedings of the Twenty-third Annual Conference of the Cognitive Science Society,* Mahwah, NJ, Lawrence Erlbaum.

Braisby, N.R. and Franks, B. (1997) 'What does word use tell us about conceptual content?', *Psychology of Language and Communication*, vol.1, no.2, pp.5–16.

Braisby, N.R., Franks, B. and Hampton, J.A. (1996) 'Essentialism, word use and concepts', *Cognition*, vol.59, pp.247–74.

Bruner, J.S., Goodnow, J.J. and Austin, G.A. (1956) *A Study of Thinking*, New York, John Wiley.

Chater, N. and Heyes, C.M. (1994) 'Animal concepts: content and discontent', *Mind and Language*, vol.9, pp.209–46.

Eco, U. (1999) *Kant and the Platypus: Essays on Language and Cognition*, London, Secker & Warburg.

Edwards, D. and Potter, J. (1992) *Discursive Psychology*, London, Sage.

Fodor, J.A. (1998) *Concepts: Where Cognitive Science Went Wrong*, Oxford, Clarendon Press.

Gellatly, A.R.H. (1997) 'Why the young child has neither a theory of mind nor a theory of anything else', *Human Development*, vol.40, pp.1–19.

Gelman, S. and Wellman, H. (1991) 'Insides and essences: early understandings of the non-obvious', *Cognition*, vol.38, pp.213–44.

Goodman, N. (1972) 'Seven strictures on similarity', in Goodman, N. (ed.) *Problems and Projects*, Indianapolis, IN, Bobbs-Merrill.

Gopnik, A. (1996) 'The scientist as child', *Philosophy of Science*, vol.63, pp.485–514.

Hampton, J.A. (1982) 'A demonstration of intransitivity in natural categories', *Cognition*, vol.12, pp.151–64.

Hampton, J.A. (1998) 'Similarity-based categorization and fuzziness of natural categories', *Cognition*, vol.65, pp.137–65.

Haslam, N., Rothschild, L. and Ernst, D. (2000) 'Essentialist beliefs about social categories', *British Journal of Social Psychology*, vol.39, pp.113–27.

Hull, C.L. (1920) 'Quantitative aspects of the evolution of concepts', *Psychological Monographs*, vol.28.

Keil, F. (1989) *Concepts, Kinds and Cognitive Development*, Cambridge, MA, MIT Press.

Kripke, S.A. (1972) 'Naming and necessity', in Davidson, D. and Harman, G. (eds) *Semantics of Natural Languages*, Dordrecht, Reidel.

Kroska, A. and Goldstone, R.L. (1996) 'Dissociations in the similarity and categorization of emotions', *Cognition and Emotion*, vol.10, no.1, pp.27–45.

Lynch, E.B., Coley, J.D. and Medin, D.L. (2000) 'Tall is typical: central tendency, ideal dimensions and graded category structure among tree experts and novices', *Memory and Cognition*, vol.28, no.1, pp.41–50.

Macintyre, A. (1998) *ME: Chronic Fatigue Syndrome: A Practical Guide*, London, Thorsons.

Malt, B.C. (1990) 'Features and beliefs in the mental representation of categories', *Journal of Memory and Language*, vol.29, pp.289–315.

Malt, B.C. (1994) 'Water is not H_2O', *Cognitive Psychology*, vol.27, pp.41–70.

Malt, B.C., Sloman, S.A., Gennari, S., Shi, M. and Wang, Y. (1999) 'Knowing versus naming: similarity and the linguistic categorization of artefacts', *Journal of Memory and Language*, vol.40, pp.230–62.

McCloskey, M. and Glucksberg, S. (1978) 'Natural categories: well-defined or fuzzy sets?', *Memory and Cognition*, vol.6, pp.462–72.

Medin, D.L. (1989) 'Concepts and conceptual structure', *American Psychologist*, vol.44, no.12, pp.1469–81.

Medin, D.L., Lynch, E.B., Coley, J.D. and Atran, S. (1997) 'Categorization and reasoning among tree experts: do all roads lead to Rome?', *Cognitive Psychology*, vol.32, pp.49–96.

Medin, D.L. and Ortony, A. (1989) 'Psychological essentialism', in Vosniadou, S. and Ortony, A. (eds) *Similarity and Analogical Reasoning*, Cambridge, Cambridge University Press.

Medin, D.L. and Shoben, E.J. (1988) 'Context and structure in conceptual combination', *Cognitive Psychology*, vol.20, pp.158–90.

Murphy, G.L. (2000) 'Explanatory concepts', in Keil, F.C. and Wilson, R.A. (eds) *Explanation and Cognition*, Cambridge, MA, MIT Press.

Murphy, G.L. (2002) *The Big Book of Concepts*, Cambridge, MA, MIT Press.

Murphy, G.L. and Medin, D.L. (1985) 'The role of theories in conceptual coherence', *Psychological Review*, vol.92, pp.289–316.

Pinker, S. (1997) *How the Mind Works*, London, Penguin Books.

Potter, J. and Wetherell, M. (1987) *Discourse and Social Psychology*, London, Sage.

Putnam, H. (1975) 'The meaning of "meaning"', in *Mind, Language and Reality*, vol.2, *Philosophical Papers*, Cambridge, Cambridge University Press.

Rips, L.J. (1989) 'Similarity, typicality and categorization', in Vosniadou, S. and Ortony, A. (eds) *Similarity and Analogical Reasoning*, Cambridge, Cambridge University Press.

Rips, L.J., Shoben, E.J. and Smith, E.E. (1973) 'Semantic distance and the verification of semantic relations', *Journal of Verbal Learning and Verbal Behaviour*, vol.12, pp.1–20.

Rips, L.J. and Collins, A. (1993) 'Categories and resemblance', *Journal of Experimental Psychology: General*, vol.122, pp.468–86.

Roberson, D., Davidoff, J. and Braisby, N. (1999) 'Similarity and categorization: neuropsychological evidence for a dissociation in explicit categorization tasks', *Cognition*, vol.71, pp.1–42.

Rosch, E.H. (1973) 'On the internal structure of perceptual and semantic categories', in Moore, T.E. (ed.) *Cognitive Development and the Acquisition of Language*, New York, Academic Press.

Rosch, E.H. (1975) 'Cognitive representations of semantic categories', *Journal of Experimental Psychology: General*, vol.104, pp.192–233.

Rosch, E.H. and Mervis, C.B. (1975) 'Family resemblances: studies in the internal structure of categories', *Cognitive Psychology*, vol.7, pp.573–605.

Ross, B.H. and Murphy, G.L. (1999) 'Food for thought: cross-classification and category organization in a complex real-world domain', *Cognitive Psychology*, vol.38, pp.495–553.

Roth, E.M. and Shoben, E.J. (1983) 'The effect of context on the structure of categories', *Cognitive Psychology*, vol.15, pp.346–78.

Sappington, B.F. and Goldman, L. (1994) 'Discrimination learning and concept formation in the Arabian horse', *Journal of Animal Science*, vol.72, no.12, pp.3080–7.

Smith, E.E., Osherson, D.N., Rips, L.J. and Keane, M. (1988) 'Combining prototypes: a selective modification model', *Cognitive Science*, vol.12, pp.485–527.

Smith, E.E. and Sloman, S.A. (1994) 'Similarity- versus rule-based categorization', *Memory and Cognition*, vol.22, no.4, pp.377–86.

Strevens, M. (2000) 'The essentialist aspect of naive theories', *Cognition*, no.74, pp.149–75.

Sutcliffe, J.P. (1993) 'In defence of the "classical view": a realist account of class and concept', in van Mechelen, J., Hampton, J.A., Michalski, R. and Theuns, P. (eds) *Categories and Concepts: Theoretical Views and Inductive Data Analysis*, London, Academic Press.

Wittgenstein, L. (1953) *Philosophical Investigations* (trans. by G.E.M. Anscombe), Oxford, Basil Blackwell.

Language and thought

Chapter 10

Alison J. K. Green

1 Introduction

Do androids dream of electric sheep? This curious question is the title of the classic novel, written by Philip K. Dick and first published in 1968. The novel was subsequently the basis for Ridley Scott's cult movie *Blade Runner* (1982). The novel tackles several themes, one of which is what it is to be human. For example, the main character in the movie, Deckard, is himself unsure as to whether he is human or android; his android lover, Rachael, is unaware that she is not human. How can we know that we are human, and what does it mean to know? As we shall see, the title of the novel is interesting too, in that the individual words and their connotations are signposts to some of the most interesting phenomena in language and thought. Thus, this chapter will focus on human nature, on language and thinking as aspects of what it is to be human, and on relationships between language and thinking.

ACTIVITY 10.1

How many windows are there in your home?

Once you have arrived at an answer, reflect on how you went about this task.

COMMENT

In carrying out this simple exercise, you may have found yourself taking an imaginary walk around your home, noting each window as you passed it. This may have been a vivid process, during which the image of each window appeared clearly, or perhaps it was less detailed, and you noted the windows rapidly as you encountered each part of the house. Now, in reflecting on how you went about this exercise, the chances are you will have engaged in inner speaking, talking to yourself about how you went about counting the windows. Non-verbal thoughts, such as images of windows and rooms, can be transformed into verbalizable ones. This is something we practise when we introspect on how we went about a task. Psychologists have formalized this process in the method known as **verbal protocol analysis**. In this chapter we expand on language as a means for expressing thoughts, and say more about verbal protocol analysis in Chapter 11.

In writing this chapter, I am aware that I am using language to convey thoughts. It seems reasonable to propose that in so doing, my thoughts (many of which I will experience as something akin to inner speech) are expressed in my writing, and language is therefore a vehicle for communicating thoughts, in this case via writing. But is this all that it is, and am I merely thinking for writing? We shall explore this idea later in the chapter. Of course, I can indulge my interest in language in various ways too, by using certain expressions and by noting those that to me seem interesting. For example, an item that recently caught my eye was introduced with the caption:

> Dog eating biscuits with human hands.
>
> *(Virgin Media News, 2010)*

This statement invites at least two equally bizarre and implausible interpretations, neither of which is readily acceptable. One reading of the caption conjures up the idea of a type of biscuit that eats dogs and also happens to have human hands, while another possibility is that of a dog that possesses human hands and happens to be eating biscuits. Both are obviously fantastical constructions.

I can certainly entertain thoughts about the ways in which language might appear to enrich my thinking. Can we go so far as to say, though, that the language we speak influences, or even determines, our thinking? This is the essence of what has come to be known as the Whorfian hypothesis, after Benjamin Lee Whorf. Whorf's (1956) **linguistic determinism hypothesis** has recently been rigorously re-examined, as we shall see in Section 5.

There are a number of alternative positions that contrast with the view that language influences thought. Piaget (1923) holds a **constructivist** position, in which cognition is seen to lay the basis for other capabilities, of which language is just one. Some **nativists** assert that language is independent of thought; this position is most frequently associated these days with the work of Chomsky (2006). The position of the nativists is in stark contrast to that of the **empiricists**, for whom experience determines who we are and what we become. Finally, **radical pragmatists**, such as Sperber (1985), do away with the issue of whether or not word meanings are innate by denying that they exist in any fixed sense at all. Instead, radical pragmatics looks at language in context.

Language and thought are two capabilities we possess that are significant in understanding what it is that makes us human. Culture is another facet of human experience that also bears on this question. In this chapter, we explore language, thought and culture, and the ways in which they interrelate. We shall look at some research on the evolution of language and thought, and we shall consider some of the key debates around linguistic determinism, nativism and radical pragmatics.

1.1 Some definitions

We begin with some definitions of culture, language and thought. The following were taken from the *Compact Oxford English Dictionary*:

Culture

- **noun 1** the arts and other manifestations of human intellectual achievement regarded collectively. **2** a refined understanding or appreciation of this. **3** the customs, institutions, and achievements of a particular nation, people, or group. **4** the cultivation of plants, breeding of animals, or production of cells or tissues. **5** a preparation of cells grown in an artificial medium containing nutrients.

- **verb** maintain (tissue cells, bacteria, etc.) in conditions suitable for growth.

Language

- **noun 1** the method of human communication, either spoken or written, consisting of the use of words in a structured and conventional way. **2** the system of communication used by a particular community or country. **3** the phraseology and vocabulary of a particular group: legal language. **4** the manner or style of a piece of writing or speech. **5** computing a system of symbols and rules for writing programs or algorithms.

Thought[1]

- **noun 1** an idea or opinion produced by thinking or occurring suddenly in the mind. **2** the action or process of thinking. **3** (**one's thoughts**) one's mind or attention. **4** an act of considering or remembering. **5** careful consideration or attention: *I haven't given it much thought.* **6** (**thought of**) an intention, hope, or idea of: *they had no thought of surrender.* **7** the formation of opinions, especially as a philosophy or system of ideas, or the opinions so formed.

Thought[2]

- past and past participle of THINK.

We can see that 'culture' has several meanings. The one that we are interested in here is that centred on culture as a uniquely human product of our nature, individual and collective. We can view the act of thinking as an activity that gives rise to culture, and one that is influenced by, and situated within, culture. And finally language plays a role in communicating within our culture, whilst also giving rise to our culture. We examine the distinction between language and communication in Section 2.1.

ACTIVITY 10.2

Imagine you are searching on Google for particular items, perhaps a must-have present that is out of stock in the shops, a hard-to-find vintage toy or an engine part for your beloved Austin 7. Make a note of the search terms you would use. Try to think of three or four search terms.

Now, consider a different situation, in which you are working on an assignment for work. You need to look up some terms to find out what they mean. Generate three or four words or terms you need defined and write these down.

COMMENT

Compare the two categories of search terms you have produced. Is there a pattern? You may have found that in one list you have used predominantly plurals, whereas in the other list you have used the singular.

Internet search engines have access to a massive volume of information on how people search for information and what they then do. It seems that people who are interested in finding out about something will search for the singular, for example 'particle accelerator', whereas someone interested in buying an item is more likely to search for the plural term, for example 'pond liners' or 'memory foam mattresses'. The singular term is generic and likely to yield definitions and explanations, whereas the plural is referential and will yield exemplars.

1.2 Preliminary ideas on language and thought

First, we examine some ideas on language and thinking, many of which have been considered by philosophers. Philosophers have made many important and distinctive contributions to our understanding of language and thought, not least by carefully explicating what we mean when we refer to 'language', 'thought' and 'culture'. It is the careful examination of terms that enables us to then ask the right questions.

Language has traditionally been considered a uniquely human capability, and the creative nature of human language has been acknowledged for centuries. Indeed, this characterization of language as a means for freely expressing thoughts bears on classic philosophical debates on the nature of the interaction between mind and body, and on other epistemological debates between philosophers who might loosely be considered nativists or empiricists. Early empiricists, such as David Hume and John Locke, tended towards the position that experiences shape who we are and how we think. For Hume, there is no direct apprehension of cause and effect, for example. We simply detect associations and patterns, and learn to expect event B if it tends to be preceded by event A. This detection of mere association is vaguely reminiscent of later behaviourist ideas. Immanuel Kant, on the other hand, appreciated the inadequacies of extreme nativism and extreme empiricism (positions that we explore in more detail in Sections 3 and 5), and argued against rationalist notions of innate knowledge. He understood the nativist perspective, in that he acknowledged that some things must be innate and we must 'know' objects in certain a priori ways, but that need not entail the knowledge itself being innate. He also recognized that we do not passively learn associations between perceived events and objects; we organize our experiences in terms of fundamental and innate concepts of causality, logic, number, space, substance and time. For Kant, then, the newborn mind is equipped with an innate framework for acquiring and storing information, an idea that was more fully explicated later by Piaget (1923).

With the advent of a more experimental psychology in the late nineteenth century came new approaches to tackling issues in psychology. Wilhelm Wundt pioneered the technique of **introspection**, a method for analysing conscious experience into its component sensations. Introspection is often mistakenly considered a very rudimentary form of reflecting on perception and sensation. In fact, it was for its time a sophisticated method geared towards understanding elemental aspects of experience, and Wundt's contribution to psychology is justly recognized to this day. It is worth noting that introspection is sometimes inappropriately contrasted with verbal protocol analysis, a different method that is explicitly geared towards the examination of thoughts. Wundt's North American contemporary, William James, eloquently summarized and reflected the European experimental tradition. He also questioned the notion that our conscious thoughts could be reduced to atomic units and saw volition as 'a psychic or moral fact pure and simple' that is 'absolutely completed when the stable state of the idea is there' (James, 1892, p.449). As we see in Box 10.1, some went so far as to deny the very essence of thinking.

10.1 ─────────────────────── **Research study**

Thinking as 'subvocal speech'

Watson and the behaviourists discounted thinking as little more than subvocal speech, though this position quickly became untenable. Watson had to retreat to the implausible claim that all thinking really was reducible to 'implicit language responses' that were too small to be detected by equipment available at the time. However, the futility of this stance was finally driven home by the infamous curare experiment of Smith *et al.* (1947). This remarkable study set out to explore whether or not curare, which was then routinely used to paralyse animals, had any effects on the brain. Smith himself was the apparently willing participant, and he received an astonishing dose of curare that was 2.5 times the amount required to achieve respiratory paralysis. After around 30 minutes, 'respiratory embarrass-ment' was reported to have occurred, and his breathing was then supported (though the curare continued to be administered). All this took place while the patient was conscious. The experiment demonstrated that thought occurred even when the vocal apparatus was temporarily paralysed.

From this point on, the behaviourist position on thinking was clearly untenable, and arguably it could be said that ignoring thought reflected a fundamental misunderstanding of what it is to be human. In short, behaviourism had not been asking the right set of questions.

Davidson (2001) argues that to be a thinker, one needs to be capable of both believing and appreciating that beliefs can be held in error. Triangulation for Davidson is a process through which one agent takes another agent's statement to be erroneous, such as a child referring to a donkey as a 'pony' in front of his mother. Both agents are looking at the donkey, one referring to it as a 'pony' in the belief that it is a 'pony', the other knowing it to be a donkey, and knowing also that the child's reference to it as a 'pony' is incorrect and that the child's belief is therefore wrong. The capacity for erroneous representation, for apprehending that an object has been falsely labelled, is present quite early on. Koenig and Echols (2003) noted that 16-month-old infants behaved differently towards a speaker who labelled an object falsely than when she labelled it correctly. Does this mean that reasoning about the beliefs and intentions of another is independent of language? We discuss attribution of belief and the role of language in the context of **theory of mind** later in the chapter.

Some of the many important and interesting questions are:

- What have we inherited and what do we acquire?

- Is language a prerequisite for thought, or is thought required for language?

- Is the meaning of our linguistic expressions determinate or is it relative to a context?

We shall examine these questions as the chapter progresses. Next, we return to Philip K. Dick's intriguing tale to help us consider what language and thinking are, and to consider why we might have evolved such facilities.

Summary of Section 1

- Ideas on language, thought and their interrelationships extend back many centuries.
- Key questions centre on what is innate and what is acquired.

2   Some fundamentals of language and thought

So, do androids dream of electric sheep? The question begins with a verb (and contains another verb, which we shall return to later in this chapter), and not just any verb, but the verb 'do', which captures for many of us the essence of our schoolbook knowledge of verbs as 'doing' words. All languages (written, spoken and gestural) consist of several components, one of which is **syntax**. Syntax is a series of mechanisms for arranging words into meaningful sentences. One crucial and very interesting aspect of syntax is that sentences are built around verbs. Pinker (2007) gives a fascinating account of the relationship between verb constructions and human nature, highlighting commonalities amongst verbs that suggest a '**language of thought**', a position most closely associated with Fodor (1975), and about which we shall learn more in Section 3.1. In learning a language, children demonstrate that they are somehow encoding and using the incredible range of input they encounter. When my young daughter generated the response, 'I'm not very talented for that, Mummy' in response to me asking her if she would like to eat a particular item, she was not repeating something she had heard. In confusing 'talented' with 'keen', words which both have connotations of 'positively lends itself', she was demonstrating for me the remarkable process of language acquisition, and something of its inherent systematicity. Pinker notes that the ideas that seem to underpin verbs most frequently are those of space, time, causation, possession and intentions. In a sense, then, these common threads suggest that something akin to a language of thought, closely aligned with natural language, underpins our thinking.

'Androids' and 'sheep' are of course nouns and nouns are 'naming' words. Do nouns simply label concepts we already possess? We are familiar with a category of animal that is a 'sheep', and whilst we know that sheep are not electrical entities, we can readily bring to mind the notion of 'electric sheep'. Does this mean that the concept was already there in the first place, along with thousands of other, as yet undiscovered, concepts for things such as the black daffodil or affluent time?

ACTIVITY 10.3 ⎯⎯⎯⎯⎯⎯⎯⎯⎯⎯⎯⎯⎯⎯⎯⎯⎯⎯⎯⎯⎯⎯⎯⎯

'No means no.'

Generate some more examples like this. What do they tell us? Are the common words serving the same function?

COMMENT

What is interesting about this example is that the first instance of 'no' is quite evidently not the same as the second instance of 'no', and this tautological statement has a simple literalism that belies the poetic richness of the underlying cultural structure. The first 'no' serves as the subject of the sentence, the second 'no' functions in the predicate to show the essential quality of 'no', which is that it is unambiguously negative.

⎯⎯⎯⎯⎯⎯⎯⎯⎯⎯⎯⎯⎯⎯⎯⎯⎯⎯⎯⎯⎯⎯⎯⎯⎯⎯⎯⎯⎯⎯⎯⎯⎯⎯

Language is a good deal more than mere **communication**, as we shall see in the next section.

2.1   Language and communication

Chapter 8 focuses on our ability to produce and understand language – capabilities we take for granted and understand as uniquely human. While both animals and humans communicate, it is generally accepted and understood that only humans spontaneously use language to communicate. Thus, while many animals communicate, and do so in a variety of ways, human communication has certain properties that mark it as qualitatively distinct from animal communication. Aitchison (2007) has proposed 10 features that characterize human language:

- use of the vocal–auditory channel
- arbitrariness
- semanticity
- cultural transmission
- spontaneous usage
- turn taking
- duality
- displacement
- structure dependence
- creativity.

Of course, it could be said that animal communication has at least some of these attributes too, in which case human and animal communication could be said to be similar. However, Aitchison suggests that semanticity, displacement, structure dependence and creativity may be held to be unique to human language.

2.1.1   Semanticity

Humans use words to stand for, or represent, objects and actions. Thus, when I use the word 'kakariki', I actually mean one of my pet parakeets, and when I choose to use the word 'dash' instead of 'walk', I do so to indicate that I am moving in a hurried way. Animals, on the other hand, use sounds and signals to convey information about a situation. For example, blackbirds give a recognizable call when danger is present. However, the call does not represent the danger (e.g. a cat) – it merely communicates that there is danger.

2.1.2   Displacement

Displacement, or using language to refer to events and objects far removed in time and place, is common in human communication. Elements of this may be found in animal communication (e.g. the oft-cited 'waggle dance' of the worker bee; Von Frisch, 1967). Recent research on episodic memory in scrub jays and other corvids (Clayton and Russell, 2009) indicates that these birds are capable of food-caching behaviour, and that they show evidence of remembering what, where and when in relation to caching episodes. Food caching, then, is an activity that one might argue has the potential at least to inform displacement-like communication in animals, and indeed benefit those species capable of so doing. However, the incidence and extent of such displacement amidst animals is so limited that it would be inappropriate to consider displacement a common feature of animal communication. What is interesting, though, is that precursors to episodic memory may be seen in animals and in children.

2.1.3   Structure dependence

Human language is structure-dependent. Chomsky (2006) gives a variety of examples to illustrate this. We apply operations to strings of words in a systematic way, and these operations depend upon the 'deep structure' inherent in the string of words. Chomsky's **transformational grammar** was one attempt to specify a set of transformational rules, or operations, that mediate between the deep structure and surface structure of a sentence or utterance. Thus, we generally cannot apply rules that are structurally independent to sequences of words whilst preserving the meaning of those words. Consider the examples in Table 10.1.

Table 10.1

I am writing a new book	Am I writing a new book?
Avatar has failed to win a Best Film Oscar	Has *Avatar* failed to win a Best Film Oscar?
In 2015 there will be a total solar eclipse	2015 in there will be a total solar eclipse
The Jerusalem artichoke is a member of the sunflower family	Jerusalem the artichoke is a member of the sunflower family

Inverting the first two words of the statements produces grammatically correct interrogatives in the first and second examples, but clearly does not in the third and fourth examples. Any rules there might be have to take into account the underlying structure and meaning of a statement.

2.1.4   Creative use of language

Our everyday use of language is inherently creative. Having learned a language, we can both comprehend and generate innumerable novel grammatical expressions. The facility with which this happens seems uniquely human. There is scant evidence for creative communication in the animal world.

So, we can see that language and communication are not the same thing. Animal communication has elements in common with human language, and the extent of the correspondence varies between species. This raises questions as to how and why we developed language, and thought. Is language a function of evolution, its precursors existing amongst animals, or does it instead mark a qualitative and species-specific gear change, more akin to revolution?

2.2   Evolution of language and thought

There is a wealth of research on the evolution of language and mind, much of it truly interdisciplinary in approach and scope. This area is highly active, with new ideas and perspectives emerging rapidly, and it will be interesting to see which of the many potentially fruitful lines of inquiry endure. We touch on some of the most recent and

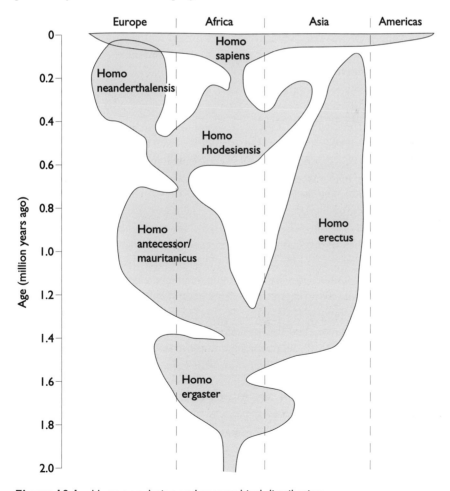

Figure 10.1   Human evolution and geographical distribution

Source: Reed *et al.*, 2004, Figure 5

exciting ideas in this section. Figure 10.1 depicts the evolutionary tree for humans and other hominids. We see from this that when *Homo sapiens* evolved from *Homo rhodesiensis*, *Homo erectus* and then *Homo neanderthalensis* disappeared rather swiftly. Two interesting observations, to which we shall return, are that *Homo sapiens* quickly populated the globe and that *Homo sapiens* and *Homo neanderthalensis* populated Europe contemporaneously.

Pinker and Bloom (1990) have argued that syntax may have evolved in response to the same kinds of adaptive processes as those that gave rise to the vertebrate eye, for example. Language, then, is not an 'evolutionary spandrel',[1] but could have arisen in a non-random way, albeit over a relatively short period of time (each small step towards a language capability conferring an advantage to the individual making that step). Contrary to Chomsky, who has suggested that language is indeed an evolutionary spandrel – universal grammar conferring no discernible evolutionary advantage – Pinker and Bloom make the reasonable point that grammar is useful because it enables the communicator to be precise, and precision potentially confers an advantage.

For instance, imagine considering that 'she walked over to the colleague who shouted' is essentially the same as 'she walked over to the colleague and shouted'. The two statements are very similar, but they differ dramatically in meaning, and that difference hinges on just one word. Having an inbuilt tendency towards precision not only reduces the chance of things going wrong when language learning starts, but may also increase the effectiveness with which we interact with others and our environments.

2.2.1 The faculty of language

Hauser *et al.* (2002) make a useful yet controversial distinction between a faculty of language in the broad sense, and a faculty of language in a narrow sense. The former includes a sensory-motor system, a conceptual–intentional system and mechanisms that support recursion. The latter, however, includes only a recursive component (to which we return later) and it is this they argue that is uniquely human. Evidence drawn from the disciplines of anthropology, biology, psychology and neuroscience suggests that the characteristics of a broadly conceived faculty of language may be found in varying degrees among non-human animals. Thus, rather than language being a unique product of evolution, Hauser *et al.* argue that some elements of our linguistic capabilities are actually by-products or consequences of existing neural organization, not all of which are unique to humans. For example, we have a well-developed capacity for vocal imitation, and this is shared with other species, such as dolphins, parrots and songbirds. The evidence for such vocal imitation amongst monkeys and apes is very scant indeed. One interpretation of this is that our imitative capabilities evolved relatively recently. So, in accounting for the evolution of our language capabilities from the point at which first gorillas and then chimpanzees split from the evolutionary line that culminates in *Homo sapiens* (the only surviving species from the genus *Homo*) approximately 6 million years (6 Ma) ago, the important questions to

---

[1] A fortunate accident that came about through chance mutation (or perhaps as a by-product of humans developing a large and complex brain) rather than by design.

address are: what have we inherited relatively unchanged; which components have been modified; and which elements have emerged over time? Hauser *et al.* argue that while recursion may be the uniquely human characteristic of our faculty of language in its narrow sense, we are as yet unclear on whether recursion per se exists in non-human animals.

What is recursion and why is it seen to be fundamental to language? Recursion enables us to embed complex clauses, though it also supports many other things we might do. For example, many puzzle problems require the discovery and application of a recursive strategy for solution (see the Tower of Hanoi problem in Section 2.2 of Chapter 11). Coolidge and Wynn (2007) go further, and argue that recursion is the basis for subjunctive thinking. Thus, recursion enables us to entertain 'What if?' thoughts, and to engage in counterfactual thinking.

As Figure 10.1 shows, at the point at which *Homo sapiens* evolved from *Homo rhodesiensis*, around 250,000 years (250 Ka) ago, there were already two other species of the genus *Homo, Homo neanderthalensis* and *Homo erectus*. Both species declined, leaving only *Homo sapiens*. The emergence of *Homo sapiens* also coincided with 'The Great Leap Forward' around 50,000 years ago, a phase during which the rate of development of human culture accelerated, and different populations diversified, something that had not previously been noted in earlier species of hominids. This begs questions as to what gave rise to this advancement. One way to approach this is to speculate on the differences between *Homo neanderthalensis* and *Homo sapiens*, as differences may have contributed to the extinction of the former. Given the foregoing, if recursion is fundamental to language, then what might have been the cognitive capabilities of the Neanderthal mind?

2.2.2   The Neanderthal mind

Wynn and Coolidge (2004), working in the new field of cognitive archaeology, focus on possible differences in cognitive capabilities between Neanderthals and humans. They argue that there must have been a fundamental neurological difference between the two species. In a fascinating and speculative article, Wynn and Coolidge infer aspects of the Neanderthal mind and personality, arguing that a key, but small, difference in working memory capacity could be the key distinguishing factor. The palaeoanthropological record indicates that during the period in which Neanderthals coexisted with humans, the technological skills of the two groups were similar, and both groups were essentially hunter–gatherers. However, there is little evidence for acculturation – Neanderthals did not truly adopt the cultural practices of humans, nor did humans adopt the Neanderthal practices. This suggests that the two societies coexisted for thousands of years, while remaining separate.[2] Biological evidence suggests that whatever the difference was that impeded Neanderthal acculturation, it must have been small, since the brain size and morphology of the two species were

---

[2] A recent examination of modern human DNA carried out by Jeffrey Long, an anthropologist at the University of New Mexico, suggests that both *Homo neanderthalensis* and *Homo heidelbergensis* may have interbred with *Homo sapiens*. This raises the intriguing possibility that some of us may carry Neanderthal DNA (Nature News, 20 April 2010).

comparable. Had there been a dramatic difference in intelligence, for example, then humans would have outperformed the Neanderthals, which could have accelerated their demise.

Assuming, then, there was not a fundamental, neurological reorganization that led to the human brain, could a difference in working memory capacity be the small but significant difference between humans and Neanderthals? Wynn and Coolidge draw on the archaeological record to infer the capabilities of the Neanderthal mind. The Palaeolithic period is associated with a method of stone-knapping referred to as the Levallois reduction technique. The stone-age flint-knappers prepared a stone core which they then used over a period of time to manufacture chipped stone artefacts of predetermined size and shape. What is particularly interesting about this technique is that it is a skilled strategy, requiring specification of a goal, a plan of execution, the monitoring of progress towards that goal and adjustment of the plan where necessary. In short, Levallois reduction may be seen as an example of expert problem solving. While the technique is not without controversy, researchers have attempted to understand the Levallois method by refitting cores (i.e. trying to piece together the sequence of flake removal), careful examination of artefacts and experimental replication.

Cognitive archaeologists (e.g. Schlanger, 1996) now argue that the Levallois technique is not the mere execution of a preset programme (which could succeed or fail); rather, it is a structured and goal-oriented method reflecting the generative interplay between the mental and material activities of the ancient flint-knapper. If Levallois reduction is indeed expert problem solving, then understanding it helps us to understand the Neanderthal mind. Levallois knapping required knowledge and motor skill, or dexterity. The knowledge required would have been declarative knowledge of the qualities of the raw materials, desired edge angles and so on. Declarative knowledge on its own is insufficient, though, as archaeologists who understand flint-knapping cannot actually produce a Levallois flake. Procedural *savoir faire* is needed to do that. The Neanderthal Levallois knappers may have been adept at deploying their expert knowledge from a long-term working memory.

The notion of **long-term working memory** (L-TWM) has been developed by Ericsson and Kintsch (1995) to understand the advantage of experts for remembering information within their domain of expertise. This remarkable ability to recall information at a glance is domain-specific, and so does not indicate that experts possess superior memory ability (see Chapter 11 for a fuller account of expertise). Thus, both Neanderthals and our human ancestors may have been equally adept in utilizing L-TWM, but what might be the consequences for the Neanderthal of a reduced working memory capacity? Modern neuropsychological evidence from studies of patients with reduced working memory capacity (e.g. Duncan *et al.*, 1996) indicates that Neanderthals may have had difficulties adapting to novel conditions and generating flexible new behaviours to fit situations outside their domains of expertise. This is consistent with the lack of evidence for Neanderthals moving outside Europe.

Beyond this, though, language amongst Neanderthals could also have been compromised by a reduced-capacity working memory. Coolidge and Wynn (2007) suggest that the syntactical complexity that characterizes modern human languages would have been beyond the reach of the Neanderthal mind, and utterances would therefore necessarily have been briefer and simpler in structure. Limited phonological storage capacity would have ruled out the possibility of complex embedded clauses and other manifestations of recursion in cognition. Sentences would have been limited in terms of the amount of information they could convey, and of course Neanderthal recipients of verbal communication would have had limited capabilities to comprehend language.

Cognitive archaeologists are also asking new questions about the possible ways in which the environment might influence cognition, and this is exemplified in ideas about the 'brain–artefact interface' (Malafouris, 2010). Magnetic resonance imaging scans of London taxi drivers and a control group of participants (Maguire *et al.*, 2000) revealed differences in hippocampal volume between the two groups,[3] and these differences were correlated with the number of years spent as a taxi driver. The results are not due to those with greater hippocampal volume simply choosing to become taxi drivers. So, the evidence suggests that practice and experience effect structural changes in the brain. Malafouris argues that we must consider the role of artefacts, such as the clay token system used for counting, in understanding the impact of culture on the brain. For example, clay tokens may have been used to support exact numerical reasoning at a time when symbols and numerical words to denote number did not exist. Malafouris suggests that engaging with these physical tokens may have facilitated structural changes in the brain and a 'recycling' of existing systems for more specific purposes. The ideas echo those of Zhang and Norman (1994), in Chapter 11, and their observations of the facilitating effects on problem solving of externally represented elements. Research examining the extent of neural plasticity is very recent and it would be premature to draw too many firm conclusions at this stage. However, the observations that brains interact with artefacts and that there is a degree of reciprocity between culture and brain seem to be fruitful ones.

If a difference in working memory was indeed a factor that ultimately led to the replacement of Neanderthals by modern humans, then we might also want to speculate on other characteristics of the Neanderthal mind and personality. Although the facts of Neanderthal creativity are disputed,[4] the evidence points to relatively low levels of creativity. Whilst both *Homo sapiens* and Neanderthals may have experienced dreams, it seems unlikely that the Neanderthal mind, constrained by a limited working memory, would have experienced, reflected upon or talked about bizarre dreams about fantastical creatures, such as electric sheep. Recursion, described by Hauser *et al.* (2002) earlier, could indeed be the fundamental property that enables subjunctive 'What if?' thinking to take place.

---

[3] The hippocampus is an area of the brain involved in memory, and particularly spatial memory (O'Keefe and Nadel, 1978).

[4] A recent item from BBC News (9 January 2010) reports findings of a study by Joao Zilhao suggesting that Neanderthals may have adorned their bodies with shell jewellery and body paint.

ACTIVITY 10.4

'What if?'

Imagine a Bank Holiday weekend is approaching and one of your tasks is to replace your child's junior bed with a full-size single loft bed. The current bed and the chest of drawers fit perfectly along one wall, and all walls measure the same length. However, the new bed is longer than the old one and so the chest of drawers has to go somewhere else. There is a long radiator along the second wall and a window so it cannot go there. There is a fitted wardrobe along the third wall, and that cannot be moved. The fourth wall has the doorway and a bookcase. Spend a minute or two imagining how you might solve the problem so that all the furniture fits in the room.

COMMENT

This is essentially a problem-solving activity in which various possible solutions have to be envisaged and evaluated to see if they will work. Physically moving each item and trying out the various options is possible, but a lot of hard work. One approach to solving the problem is to measure everything and then mentally work out what can go where, bearing in mind the constraints at each point, and which item is where. Nothing can be omitted. This kind of problem solving can be effortful and demanding of working memory resources.

A solution? An insight might suggest that you locate the chest of drawers *underneath* the new bed! We return to insight in Chapter 11.

Summary of Section 2

In this section, we have briefly examined some evolutionary arguments about the emergence of human language and thought.

- Language and communication are two distinct activities.
- It is likely that the precursors to human language include at least some species-independent capacities, as well as some species-dependent capacities.
- A relatively small enhancement to working memory capacity could have supported recursion in *Homo sapiens*, which in turn enabled linguistic and other cognitive advances to be made.
- Cognitive archaeologists and neuroscientists are also exploring the impact of culture, and whether this can effect structural changes in the brain.

3   Nativism and thought

In Chapter 9, we examined the nature of **concepts** and how we categorize. But how do we acquire concepts, and what influences the nature of the categories we acquire and use? We saw there that people vary in how they categorize, and the variations are attributable in part to knowledge, experience and goals. Here, we take a step further and examine ideas and research on the origins of concepts.

As stated earlier, we are taught at an early age that nouns are 'naming' words. The basic epistemological conundrum is this: how can we ever think about certain concepts or ideas for the very first time without first having some sort of prior notion of the concept or entity in question? The question allows us to consider one of the interfaces between language and thought. There is little doubt that we are born with certain mechanisms and capabilities, and so to that extent there is a sense in which at least some things must be innate. The debate, which has engaged some of the most prominent researchers and theorists in linguistics, philosophy and psychology, centres on what is innate and what is acquired.

3.1 Extreme nativism

Extreme nativism is a position that advocates that the facility in question has a significant innate component. In the context of thought, Fodor (1975) is a key exponent of the idea that there are innate concepts. Piaget's constructivist position is different. Language is seen to be a cognitive process, just like many others, though the process of cognitive development is essentially pre-programmed, and it is in that sense that Piaget is considered here. We examine both positions in the following sections.

3.2 Piaget and epistemology

Piaget (1923) has argued that language depends on thought for its development, and therefore his position is one in which cognition provides the basis upon which language develops. For Piaget, then, language is an emergent property of more generalized intellectual functioning. Language is one of a number of functions with the capacity for representation, and in that sense it is no different from pretend play or dreaming. Even the highly structured nature of language itself is not held to be unique, and is viewed as comparable to the structure inherent in actions, such as the notion of a schema for grasping a rattle. The assertion that language depends on cognitive development rests on four different strands of evidence:

- Thinking in infants precedes the emergence of language.

- Language, deferred imitation, symbolic play, evocative memory and mental imagery all appear simultaneously, suggesting that language and other capabilities emerge as a result of cognitive development.

- A third strand of evidence derives from the apparent fact that language does not affect reasoning capabilities in middle childhood.

- Finally, the nature of speech in early childhood is taken to indicate that the communicative function of speech emerges as a consequence of cognitive development.

If, as Piaget argued, cognitive development is necessary for the emergence of language and other capabilities, then blind children, who experience impoverished sensory input, should be retarded in language development relative to seeing children. However, this is generally not so. While there are some differences in the types of words blind and seeing children acquire,[5] the rate and point at which the earliest words are acquired do not appear to differ (Bigelow, 1987; Nelson, 1973). One difficulty with a straightforward rejection of Piaget's theory is that parents of children who are hearing- or sight-impaired may compensate for the impairment. As Messer (2000) argues, it then becomes difficult to categorically state that language development would not have been compromised had parents or guardians not adapted in some way.

In a similar vein, if a certain level of cognitive development is required to support language, then Piaget's notion of 'object permanence', which is attained at around 18 months of age, should necessarily precede the acquisition of concepts of objects and names. Xu (2002) found that, if anything, the opposite may be true. Making available to young children two easily distinguishable labels for two different objects actually enhanced the ability of 9-month-old children to distinguish the two objects. A single label alone, or two distinct tones, did not bring about the same facilitating effect.

The evidence then for impairment in cognitive processing causing impairments in syntactic processing is very scant indeed. Evidence from blind children does indicate that there are differences between blind and seeing children, but these are the kind of differences one would expect, such as blind children referring less often to objects that cannot be touched or perceived in some way (such as the moon and stars). However, a further possibility is that Piaget was wrong to assume that impoverished sensory input would retard cognitive development. If Piaget was wrong, then research on linguistic development among blind children (and indeed among deaf children) may tell us nothing at all about whether or not language depends upon thought for its development.

So, the evidence reported here shows just how difficult it is to establish a causal relationship between language and thought. Even if we did reject the notion that language depends upon thought for its development, we shall see in the next section that this would not necessarily mean that nativism as a whole is flawed.

3.3   Fodor and the 'language of thought'

Fodor (1975) is generally considered a proponent of extreme nativism. In this instance, we consider him as an advocate of a position that holds that all concepts are innate and that we possess a **language of thought**. Chomsky (2006), as we shall see later, is a staunch proponent of the view that the syntax of language is innate and universal, and while Chomsky has expounded at length a view of the faculty of language, the sense in which he uses the term module or faculty is quite distinct from Fodor's use of these terms. However, Fodor and Chomsky have views that are complementary in some respects. The doctrine of language of thought has two main emphases, the first centring on the content of concepts and the second on the structure of propositions.

---

[5] Unsurprisingly, there tend to be fewer object words amongst the first words that blind children acquire (Bigelow, 1987).

3.3.1 Are concepts indefinable?

Fodor (1983) has argued that some aspects of cognition are **modular**, each module being 'informationally encapsulated'. By this he means specialized for a particular type of representational input, and delivering a module-specific output. Language, then, is one such module. However, he argues against a more widespread 'massive modularity' of the mind itself, and states that the 'central system', comprising thinking, reasoning, consciousness and world knowledge, is non-modular. Of course, if there are specialized modules, then the issue of how information is transferred between modules arises, and Fodor deals with this by proposing 'interface modules', which must either transform information from one code to another, or somehow merge information into a form readable by both modules.

While Fodor's modularity is beyond the scope of this chapter, the general notion of modularity has a long history, and traces of it are found in the early ideas on phrenology – the idea that mental faculties could be associated with physical areas of the brain. This 'vertical', domain-specific view of the mind contrasts with a more 'horizontal' view of the mind, in which mental processes are the product of interactions between domain-independent faculties.

Whatever the organization of the mind, there is a fundamental problem in explaining the acquisition of concepts. Concept acquisition is in some respects a good example of a classic 'chicken and egg' problem. Empiricists might argue that to acquire and understand a new concept, children must engage in inductive generalization. By this is meant that the child must go through a process of hypothesis testing and confirmation over a range of instances to establish whether or not something is an exemplar of a given concept. But to do this, the child must already possess or have represented those very features that define the concept. Fodor believes that what takes place is better seen as 'belief fixation' than learning. Concepts are not learned; they are innately given. Russell (2004) explains the process thus:

1 Concept learning boils down to inductive extrapolation by hypothesis formation and confirmation.
2 The child will have hypotheses of the kind 'X is a chair iff it is a portable seat for one',[6] 'X is a bucket iff it is a portable seat for one'.
3 The environment will inform the child about the truth or falsity of these hypotheses.
4 Where do these hypotheses come from? Ultimately, it must be from the child.
5 If they are innately present then they must be in a representational format of some kind.
6 As the format must comprise elements standing for sets of data it must be symbolic.
7 So there must be an innate language of thought.

(Russell, 2004, p.17)

---

[6] Here, iff means 'if and only if'.

Logically, some things must be innately given. A child cannot ever learn the meaning of the word 'cat', for example, unless she or he has the means for representing the constituents of cat (furry, small, moves on four legs), all of which may be further decomposed until the point at which an end is reached. The end is for Fodor the language of thought, which is akin to a computer's machine code. We do not actually see or directly interact with the machine code, but it is the machine code nonetheless which underpins the functioning of the computer.

So, if all concepts are innately given, then what of concepts for complex or modern entities like the iPad or the notion of 'fandom'? How could these possibly be innate? Certain concepts must be innate, such as the ability to represent colour, shape and sound and to differentiate colours, for example. So, one possibility is that complex concepts may be decomposed into their simpler, elemental components. 'Sister' is both female and sibling, for example, so 'sister' may be decomposed into these two (arguably) simpler units. One would assume that it should be harder to work with complex concepts than with simpler concepts, but intuitively we find this not to be so. Fodor *et al.* (1980) have argued that concepts are not simply definitions, that a complex concept is no harder to use than a simple concept, and that neither is readily definable. A cat, for example, is small and furry and walks on four legs, but so do rabbits and hamsters. The word 'rabbit' does considerably more than offer a label for something small and furry. For Fodor, then, Gertrude Stein's famous line 'A rose is a rose is a rose' means just that.[7] Concepts seem to defy definition (for a recap on issues in understanding concepts and categories, refer back to Chapter 9). If Fodor is right, then language learning somehow proceeds on the basis of trying to correctly associate a word with one of many innately given concepts, a process that would seem inordinately complicated if many thousands of concepts are already present.

3.3.2 The structure of propositions

The second aspect of the doctrine of language of thought is complex. A starting point is the assumption that we must conceive of thinking as the process through which individuals take up a particular mental stance towards a given mental state. The stance then may be to think, believe, hope, expect and so on, whilst the state is imbued with causal power and has a constituent structure, in some sense – syntax. The ideas here are more complex than merely stating that thoughts express intentions. For example, whilst writing, I am hoping that Monica will arrive soon to collect my daughter. The thought does more than just capture my expectation that my daughter will soon be picked up. Language of thought argues that just as the intentional object of the thought (what I am thinking about) is complex, so too is the mental state that gives rise to the thought itself.

A theory of thinking must account for the nature of thinking. In thinking, we move from thought to thought. Thinking has the same kind of creative and productive potential as language, and just as linguistic capacities seem to be systematic, so too do cognitive capabilities.

If we do indeed have a language of thought, how does it account for transitions between thoughts? It would seem implausible to suppose that, given that sentences

---

[7] The line is from Gertrude Stein's (1913) poem, 'Sacred Emily'.

express thoughts, thoughts may be unstructured when we know that sentences are indeed structured. So, if language of thought has mental syntax, then there must be rules governing transitions from thought to thought. If a sentence is only partially heard, we are able to formulate a thought about that fragment. For example, 'Yesterday, Susan saw ...' may be represented such that the missing second noun phrase (the event or thing or person that Susan saw) is present. Reorganizing the structure of the thought may then give rise to a question, 'Who did Susan see?' or 'What did Susan see?' The restructuring of the constituent components is reflected in the response. We have, in essence, seamlessly moved from one thought to another, related thought.

Thinking, like language, is phenomenally productive. We each think and comprehend new thoughts every moment of our lives, and we generate and understand new sentences at a similar rate. How is this achieved? Fodor's argument seems to be that both thought and natural language have certain properties in common, and that in the case of language this property derives from natural languages having combinatorial semantics. So, thought must also have combinatorial semantics. Russell (2004) neatly points out that an argument of this form is in fact a good example of the logical fallacy of **affirming the consequent** (see Section 2.3 of Chapter 13 for a fuller explanation of this). The fallacy is clearer to see in the following example:

If p then q	If almonds drop from my tree and pollute my pond then my fish will die
q	My fish have died
therefore p	Therefore, almonds fell from my tree and polluted my pond

Does this mean that language of thought is simply wrong, and that something other than combinatorial semantics underpins thinking? Fodor (1987) ably defends his position, arguing that he is making an inference as to the best explanation, and seeking the best explanation is a perfectly legitimate endeavour. Thus, advances will be made by choosing appropriate hypotheses and testing these. For now, language of thought is a viable hypothesis.

Related to the preceding point is the assertion that thoughts have constituent structure, just as natural languages do. As Fodor points out, in our native language we can readily comprehend and generate a sentence of the form, 'John loves the girl', and we can just as easily entertain the corresponding thought, 'The girl loves John'. However, a non-native speaker of English with only a limited vocabulary might comprehend only the first sentence, and be unable to generate or comprehend the second idea. The example is an interesting one, in that it demonstrates that if we can understand the utterance that John loves the girl, then we can understand the thought that John loves the girl, and understanding that particular thought means that it is also possible to entertain and understand the thought that the girl loves John. Whether or not we believe that the girl loves John is a separate matter, and the notion of belief as one of a set of propositional attitudes is one we turn to in the next section.

3.3.3 Propositional attitudes

A propositional **attitude** is a mental stance, our sense of knowing that, believing, expecting, hoping, worrying and so on. Closely related to the notion of propositional attitudes is 'theory of mind', the ability to understand another person's behaviour in terms of propositional attitude ascriptions. Much of this research has centred on the **false-belief task**, a classic example of which is presented in Box 10.2. If an individual or animal appreciates that another has a false belief, then it may be stated that the former has a 'theory of mind'.

10.2   **Research study**

The false-belief task

Wimmer and Perner (1983) explored the development of propositional attitudes in children using two sketches involving a character, Maxi, and his mother. They constructed a number of scenarios to examine the ways in which children aged 3–9 years understood the wrong belief of another. In the scenario we shall describe here, children observed Maxi in a room in which there were two cupboards, one blue and one green. They watched Maxi put some chocolate into the blue cupboard and then leave the room. While Maxi was out of the room, the children then saw his mother come along, remove the chocolate from the blue cupboard, take a piece off and then place it in a different location, this time in the green cupboard. Maxi then returned and the experimenter asked the children, 'Where will Maxi look for the chocolate?' Since Maxi has not seen the chocolate being moved, children have to assume that Maxi will still believe that the object is at the original location and in the blue cupboard. This is of course the kind of response we would expect an adult to make, knowing that Maxi does not know that the chocolate has been moved from one location to another.

Results showed that none of the 3- to 4-year-olds, 57 per cent of the 4- to 6-year-olds and 86 per cent of the 6- to 9-year-olds pointed correctly to the blue cupboard. Wimmer and Perner were able to show that the failure to correctly identify where Maxi would look for the chocolate was not due to forgetting, because most children when asked were able to point correctly to the initial location in which Maxi had placed the chocolate. Wimmer and Perner interpreted these results as indicating that it is only at around 4 years of age that children appreciate that another individual may hold a false belief when that person lacks some crucial information. In short, a theory of mind develops.

There have been a number of interpretations of why it is that children as young as 3 years of age tend to fail the false-belief task, predicting that the character will search for the object in its present location as opposed to the location the protagonist believes it to be in.

First, we need to examine at closer quarters the notion of **belief**, and distinguish belief from **knowledge**. For example, I know that London is the capital of England, and this fact represents a reality, a piece of information that was acquired many years ago. Is knowledge then just a belief that is true and something that the individual has grounds to believe to be true? Russell (2007) shows that the thesis that knowledge is merely 'justified true belief' is not tenable. For Russell, a theory of mind is a theory of how facts are reasons for acting and believing. One interpretation of the young child's failure of the false-belief test appeals to the child's inability to suppress her own knowledge (that the location of the object has now changed), and this inability to suppress the pre-potent response is therefore an explanation in terms of executive function. If this were the case, then asking the child to explain why Maxi goes to the wrong box should not be problematic, yet Wimmer and Mayringer (1998) show that young children find explanation questions of this sort just as difficult as the standard prediction questions. Furthermore, even allowing for immaturity in executive capabilities, why would children imagine that they should inhibit a given response? Young children seem to have a deficit in appreciating that not seeing entails not knowing – they fail to appreciate that Maxi not experiencing the change of location of chocolate means that he does not know of the change. Why should there be a discontinuity, then, between appreciating the connection between seeing and knowing, and yet not appreciating that not seeing entails not knowing? Russell argues that the former connection is innately given, while the latter requires an additional inferential step, which has to be learned.

Could it be that young children fail the false-belief task because they lack the linguistic competence to do so? De Villiers and de Villiers (2003) point to evidence from studies of deaf children and argue that there is support for the hypothesis that deaf children with delayed language experience delays in understanding and reasoning about mental states. There is further evidence relevant to de Villiers and de Villiers's contention that language plays an important role in the development of false belief. Clements and Perner (1994) constructed a clever non-verbal version of the false-belief task, centred on a mouse looking for cheese, which is moved, and measured eye gaze as well as verbal responses. They recruited young children and grouped them into the following age groups:

- 2 years 5 months to 2 years 10 months

- 2 years 11 months to 3 years 2 months

- 3 years 3 months to 3 years 7 months

- 3 years 8 months to 3 years 11 months

- 4 years to 4 years 6 months.

The key condition here was one in which the children could not see Sam the mouse until he popped up from one of two mouseholes, either location A, where he had left the cheese (and would imagine it still to be), or location B, where the cheese actually is. In the control condition, Sam the mouse saw the cheese being moved. What is striking about these results is that from around 2 years 11 months, children correctly looked longer at the mousehole they expected the mouse to emerge from, given its false belief that the cheese would be in the unchanged location, and that the looking behaviour of young children deviated markedly from the eye gaze patterns in all but the oldest of the children. This suggests, then, that children have implicit knowledge of the mouse's false belief yet they do not articulate this until some time later. However, these results do not rule out the possibility that language is simply important to false-belief reasoning rather than a prerequisite. The distinction is subtle, but theoretically important.

While there is evidence that both young children and some animals may demonstrate awareness of the intentions, desires and fears of another, these need to be distinguished from the case of a creature understanding that another has a false *belief.* Research on false belief has proceeded rapidly in recent years, and it is an arena within which some of the most interesting questions are being asked.

Is there evidence that non-human primates appreciate that another agent may have a false belief? Call and Tomasello (1999) constructed a non-verbal version of the false-belief task and compared the performance of young children on both the non-verbal and the standard verbal versions of the task. They found that performance on both tasks correlated substantially, and performance improved with age, suggesting that their non-verbal task had validity as a test of false belief. Call and Tomasello then presented the non-verbal version of the false-belief task described earlier to a group of great apes, none of whom was able to pass the test. Hare and Tomasello (2004) used a variant on the object-choice task to investigate the use of pointing to inform others amongst chimpanzees. In the standard object-choice task, one human 'hider' first hides some food for an ape in one of a choice of containers. Another human 'helper' then assists the ape in finding the food by tilting the container and showing the ape the food therein. Next, the hiding procedure is repeated, and this time the 'helper' indicates the location of the food to the ape by either staring at the container or pointing to it. Typically, apes perform at chance level in choosing the right container, even though their eyes can follow the gaze or pointing of the helper. They appear not to understand what the gazing and pointing gestures actually mean, and cannot see them as the collaborative, helpful gestures that they are.

Both humans and non-human primates have the motor capacity to point, yet apes do not appear to use pointing to inform and to share information, and do not appear to understand that others may use gesture to help or to inform. What is fascinating is that in a competitive version of the task, Hare and Tomasello found that apes behaved differently. When the human reached unsuccessfully for the container that held food, the apes responded by retrieving the correct container and finding the food. How do we account for these different responses to a rather similar situation? Hare and Tomasello argue that the standard version of the object-choice task is a collaborative task, in which the ape must understand the collaborative intention of another and the humans' desire to enable the ape to profit from the communicative gesture. This appears to be beyond the social–cognitive competence of the ape. However, in the situation where the human attempts to grasp the bucket, the ape can simply infer that the human's behaviour must indicate that the bucket contains something worth having.

Human infants point from around 14 months of age and perform well above chance on the object-choice task, demonstrating that they do understand the collaborative nature of pointing (Behne *et al.*, 2005). Moll and Tomasello (2007) suggest that the difference between infants and apes could be that apes do not possess a 'joint attentional frame' within which gestures may have both individualistic and shared meaning. Thus, Moll and Tomasello make a strong case for the role of cooperation and culture in the shaping of a Vygotskian human social intelligence and our powerful capacity for perspective taking. The evolution of human social intelligence is beyond the scope of this chapter, but it seems possible that our uniquely human capacity for perspectival cognitive representations arose not through competition but through the evolution of collaborative capabilities, similar to those described by Vygotsky (1978).

Summary of Section 3

- While it seems unlikely that the strong nativist Piagetian position that language depends on thought is tenable, this does not validate Chomsky's independence thesis.
- Fodor's proposal that we are born with something of the order of 50,000 concepts is certainly radical, but it is flawed in many ways.
- The notion of a language of thought, however, is appealing and accounts for transitions between thoughts, and from thoughts to language.
- The false-belief task has been used as a test of theory of mind, and having a theory of mind is one inherently human capacity.

4 Language: nativism and radical pragmatics

If language of thought has mental syntax, with rules governing the transitions from thought to thought, is it also true that language itself has a definable structure? We know that language has syntax, but to what extent does language have a fundamental 'design specification'?

Chomsky, as we saw earlier, has long been an exponent of the position that a **universal grammar** underpins language, and that there is an innate basis to language acquisition. At the other extreme, we find radical pragmatics, an approach that rejects the notion that words have fixed meanings. Instead, meaning is fluid and dependent upon context. We shall first look briefly at language acquisition, and then we will consider the case for a universal grammar. Finally, we will briefly consider the pragmatist approach and the study of language in use.

4.1 Linguistic universals

The problem for the young child learning language is that although language directed towards the child may be somewhat simplified (Dockrell and Messer, 1999), the child must assimilate and make sense of complex information without formal tuition and with cognitive capabilities that are not yet fully mature. If there is some kind of mismatch between input and capacities to process that input, yet we are able to easily acquire a language, then one possibility is that language is an innate capability. The hypothesis is both intuitively appealing and plausible. To explore this hypothesis, we need to consider evidence from a variety of sources. First, we look at the ordering of subject, verb and object in languages used around the world.

While many languages are spoken around the world, the distribution of the different possibilities for word order is not random. English is a subject–verb–object (SVO) language, in that sentences and utterances tend to take the form, 'Susan spoke to Margaret'. Japanese, on the other hand, is an SOV language. The number of possible permutations of SVO orderings is 3!, ($3 \times 2 \times 1$), or 6.

Table 10.2 Distribution of word order permutations

Subject	Object	Verb	45%
Subject	Verb	Object	42%
Verb	Subject	Object	9%
Verb	Object	Subject	3%
Object	Verb	Subject	1%
Object	Subject	Verb	0%[1]

Source: Baker, 2001

[1] Baker (2001) reports one example of a very rare OSV language spoken by the Warao tribe, who live in the Orinoco delta of Venezuela.

You will see from Table 10.2 that the distribution of the different possible word order permutations is not random (a chi-square 'goodness of fit' test would yield a highly significant result). Why should this be so? One possibility is that the prevalence of SOV and SVO languages reflects an innate component of language. Another possibility is that word order reflects an innate aspect of cognition. Learning a language may be a matter of linking words with innate concepts, such as 'what' and 'where'. A third possibility is that some possible word orders are actually rather hard to acquire (in terms of information processing and syntactic effort) and so we have developed a tendency to favour languages that are easier to comprehend and use. Finally, language development always takes place in an environment, and environmental factors may predispose us towards noting more important features of our environments. It is therefore hard to conclude firmly that linguistic universals are innate, though few doubt their existence.

4.2 Language: structure and parameters

Chomsky (1965), a staunch rationalist, originally proposed that language development is guided by an innate language acquisition device. According to this model, language is a separate, independent faculty. This initial, standard theory distinguished between an utterance's 'surface structure' and its 'deep structure'. Later, in the 1980s, the model evolved into the principles and parameters theory. Here, the task for the child is to learn the grammar of a language, a task akin to learning the rules or parameters that apply in language comprehension and use. Thus, a child does not have to learn each word in a piecemeal fashion, but instead has to abstract the rules governing language use. The process may be seen as analogous to fine-tuning an early wireless to get the best reception. Initially, the sound quality for any given station is poor and crackly, but careful tuning improves reception and sound quality. If language acquisition is learning how to 'tune' innate linguistic capabilities then language acquisition among deaf children is an interesting case. We can formulate and test the following hypothesis. If language development is independent of cognition and drives cognitive development, then we should observe differences in cognitive development between hearing-impaired and non-hearing-impaired children.

We know that deaf children may learn sign language, and will spontaneously use gestures in ever more sophisticated ways in the absence of direct instruction (Mohay, 1982). We also know that the developmental trajectory of sign language amongst children follows that of normal spoken language (Meier, 1991). Thus, research tends to indicate that deafness does not impede linguistic development amongst children, a conclusion that is sometimes interpreted inappropriately as support for Chomsky's independence hypothesis. However, it is hard to see what the parallels for verbal language parameters might be within the various sign languages. Furthermore, if language development is merely about learning the rules for parameter setting, then the feats of bilingual children, who learn two languages simultaneously, are hard to explain. If two sets of parameters need to be learned, then language development should at least be retarded. However, studies show this not to be so (see Messer, 2000 for a review).

4.3   A design for language?

The principles and parameters theory gave way to Chomsky's (1995) minimalist programme. The latter has been seen as a radical departure from the principles and parameters theory – so much so that in 1997 the *Guardian* newspaper is reputed to have reported that Chomsky had abandoned his old theory in favour of a new one. Russell (2004) argues eloquently that rather than marking the abandonment of its predecessor, the minimalist programme instead represents a shift in emphasis by Chomsky to a more bottom-up, biologically driven approach to linguistic theory, elements of which we see in some of Chomsky's collaborative research (e.g. Hauser *et al.*, 2002). The central tenet of the minimalist programme is the notion of an 'optimal design' for language. In recent years, it has come to be associated with biolinguistics, the interdisciplinary study of the faculty of language.

In focusing on the question of how well designed language is for the purposes of being useful, Chomsky has to contend with two seemingly conflicting tensions. These centre on the notion that syntax may be the product of some small mutation that brought about the faculty of language. However, if syntax is an autonomous system, it is unbelievably well suited to the task to which it is almost incidentally assigned – language and the expression of thoughts. Could this be accidental? (One of the appealing aspects of pragmatism, which we discuss in the next section, is that this uncomfortable problem tends to be swept to one side.) Language has to interface not only with conceptual–intentional (or thought) systems – raising questions about the interface between linguistic code and language of thought code – but also with articulatory and perceptual systems. If language emerged in some ad hoc way, then its fitness for purpose is remarkable.

Central to Chomsky's minimalist programme thesis is the notion of language as innate and modular, and language as a 'perfect' system. Language interacts with other systems, and it is autonomous. The notion of perfection depends on there being no redundancy in the system, so that any clear and coherent thought can readily find an accurate and appropriate verbal expression (and note that this does not require such expressions to be unambiguous). Syntactic autonomy, then, would seem to be at odds with any notion of language as merely negotiated meaning amongst a group of individuals. We turn to the pragmatist approach to language in the next section.

4.4 Radical pragmatics

Radical pragmatics deviates markedly from notions of words having a fixed, underlying conceptual structure. The pragmatist approach examines language in use, and one strand of research focuses on the examination of the multiple meanings of words (polysemy and homonymy) and the different meanings that phrases may take, depending on context.

Homonyms are examples of words that may take many different meanings, while polysemous words are those that have a number of distinct, but related senses.

ACTIVITY 10.5

Try to generate some examples of homonyms and polysemous words.

COMMENT

You probably found this harder than you might have expected. A good example of a homonym is 'culture', and no doubt you generated many others. However, polysemous examples that make the point might be 'fast car', which is fast in a subtly different way to a 'fast woman'. 'Black grapes' are black in a subtly different way to 'black olives', which in turn have a blackness that is not the same as that of a 'black tulip'.

If the meaning of a colour word can vary from context to context, depending on the object to which it refers, does this render meaningless the efforts of conceptual semantics?

Radical pragmatics emerged partly as a response to difficulties with conceptual semantics, but it also represents a separate branch of language philosophy that centres on language use, as opposed to language as a formal system. Grice (1989) is frequently credited with making a distinction between the literal meaning of a sentence and the speaker's intended meaning. In so doing, he introduced the notion of **implicature** into understanding language. Once the notion of the speaker or author's intent is introduced, then by implication we have to consider that individual's competence.

Arguably one interesting facet of pragmatics is the assertion that a model that assumes that an utterance expresses exactly what the speaker intended in the manner intended, and that the meaning of an utterance is received as intended, is perhaps overly simplistic. For example, consider the following exchange between two individuals who are not very well disposed towards each other:

First person: Hi, I heard you had entered the London Marathon. Hope you do well!

Second person: I bet you do.

The response of the second person here is not the benign acknowledgement of good wishes, but instead a rather cynical rejection of the literal meaning of the desire expressed. Sperber and Wilson (1981) use ironical examples to demonstrate that in conversation we can elect to reject the literal meaning of a statement and instead appreciate its figurative meaning. However, does this mean that the meaning of a word is not fixed until it is used in a context? The precision of our language in use does not support this. Verbs are used in very specific ways, and we instantly recognize the 'clunkiness' of grammatically correct but atypical constructions:

> She shuddered into the room.
> The kitten scratched up the tree.

We can make sense of these utterances, but they jar in a way that suggests an intolerance of this kind of verbal abuse. Pinker (2007) draws on a wealth of examples to illustrate the precise manner in which verbs signify meaning. There are many ways to describe the process by which a vessel comes to contain a liquid. If I ask someone to pour me a glass of orange juice, I am likely to attend to the pouring of the juice into a glass. If I ask for my glass to be filled, I am more likely to focus on the amount of juice going into my glass, and the point at which I have enough.

One area in which these ideas are actively pursued is that of **authorship**. There is a substantial body of work on authorship and text. A 'text' is a body of language, and may be a single word or an entire book, and may be written or spoken. A written text is not simply a sequence of words with a single, unambiguous meaning, but a multidimensional space in which there are many components.

The text has an author, who intends to convey an idea to the reader. The 'reader' includes the actual reader of the text (in this case, you) and the author's representation and understanding of who the reader may be. The text itself is more than the simple transmission of information, because words have been selected and the skill of the author in doing this to convey meaning may vary. In writing this chapter, 'I' am writing to my perception of 'you'. My perception of who you are influences the way in which I write and the words I choose to use. We can depict the process using the model in Figure 10.2, adapted from Rimmon-Kenan (1983).

Real author → Implied author → (Narrator) → (Narratee) → Implied reader → Real reader

Figure 10.2

The 'real author' is the person writing the text (me), while the 'real reader' is the actual person reading the text (you). The 'implied author' is a construct, a product of the text and the readers' perceptions of the text.[8] The 'implied reader' is the author's construction of who the reader might be, and this construction clearly shapes the way in which a text is produced, though some reject that the author's identity plays any part in the true meaning of a text.[9] The two narrative roles pertain to the 'voice' of a text, the narratee being the agent addressed by the narrator. These different roles and constructs become apparent when we look carefully at texts and notice when the author takes a break from storytelling and starts to have a chat with the reader.

---

[8] Unsurprisingly, implied authors are often perceived to be smarter and wittier than their living embodiments!

[9] Barthes (1977) famously wrote on the 'death of the author', arguing for a shift in emphasis towards language and what is stated in a text, and away from the author. Curiously, there are echoes of this in Edwin Boring's (1950) essay on 'Great men and scientific progress', in which he criticizes eponymy.

The foregoing, though, does not at all prove the case for pragmatics, rendering Chomsky irrelevant; it merely demonstrates that language has a very interesting social dimension.

Summary of Section 4

- There are commonalities in terms of the underlying structure of different languages.
- Chomsky argues that these linguistic universals are innate.
- Interdisciplinary research looking at language as a 'perfect' system is interesting and Chomsky's ideas need rigorous testing.
- The pragmatist approach addresses and raises questions about how meaning is constructed, and this need not entail a rejection of syntactic autonomy, the cornerstone of the minimalist programme.

5 Linguistic determinism

Contrasting with the nativist position (and also with the independence thesis, which sees language as independent of thought) is an alternative approach that focuses on the extent to which language influences, or even determines, thought. This approach is closely associated with the Sapir–Whorf hypothesis (or alternatively the Whorfian hypothesis). Whorf, then a fire prevention officer and a graduate in chemical engineering, pursued his interest in anthropology and linguistics in his spare time, under the guidance of his mentor, Edward Sapir.

The strong form of the Whorfian hypothesis, **linguistic determinism**, asserts that the language we speak causally influences the thoughts we can have, though it is apparent in Whorf's (1956) writing that he also considered that language is itself subject to deeper, unconscious processes. In this sense, then, it is not clear whether Whorf intended the stark and perhaps naively 'strong' version of the hypothesis that bears his name. Since the work was published some 15 years after his death, Whorf did not have the opportunity to disambiguate or elaborate on these ideas, though he was at least spared the waspish criticism that has emerged over the years, as scholars have taken to task the most common and unfortunate misrepresentation of his position as centring simply on how many words for 'snow' Eskimos apparently have.[10] The weaker position, referred to as **linguistic relativism**, asserts that language influences thought, and this claim is considerably less controversial than the determinism thesis. To truly demonstrate linguistic determinism, evidence of the following kind is needed:

1   Evidence that speakers of one language cannot think or entertain thoughts that come naturally to speakers of another language.

---

[10] See Pullum (1989) for a witty comment on the way in which a misunderstood point became urban legend.

2   The difference in thinking would have to involve higher cognitive processes, so that one group of speakers would be left at an impasse, unable to proceed. The difference would therefore have to be more than simply failing to comprehend a particular word or concept in another language.

3   Finally, the difference in thinking would have to be demonstrably caused by language, and not merely reflected in language or a cultural artefact.

5.1   Does language influence the way in which we 'see' the world?

Many of the early claims for evidence of Whorf's (1956) hypothesis derived from early studies on colour perception and naming. Brown and Lenneberg's (1954) study of colour acknowledged that while individuals the world over may have the same cognitive capabilities for perceiving colour, the ways in which we think about and categorize colour may vary. In this sense, then, their study was a test of the hypothesis that language (as evidenced in colour categories used) may influence thought. They found a positive correlation between recognition of a given colour from an array and the 'codability' of a colour. 'Codability' was a function of five different measures: the variable designed to give a measure of speed of naming of a colour; inter- and intra-rater agreement on the name of the colour in question; and also the nature of the label used to name the colour (was one colour term used, as in 'blue' for example, or was the colour term a sequence of words, such as 'pale violet–mauve'?). Whilst theirs is an interesting paper technically, Brown and Lenneberg acknowledge that the main results of the study indicate associations between variables, rather than any causal link between language and thought. An interesting footnote to their study acknowledges that:

> While this seems a fair statement of Whorf's usual views, he occasionally took a somewhat more conservative position.
>
> *(Brown and Lenneberg, 1954, p.454)*

It seems clear, then, that different versions of the Whorfian hypothesis have been maintained and tested. In the following sections, we examine three ways in which the hypothesis that language influences thought have been tested. Researchers have considered this question in the domains of syntax and semantics, colour perception, object naming, spatial knowledge and thinking for speaking.

5.2   Does language influence colour perception?

Colour has for some time been a domain of interest for researchers interested in the Whorfian hypothesis. Colour has properties of brightness, hue and saturation that may be manipulated experimentally, and we know that the number of colour terms used linguistically to denote colours varies between two and 12 from culture to culture. For example, the Dani people of New Guinea use just two colour terms, to denote the neighbouring 'cool' (blues and greens) and 'warm' (yellows, oranges and reds) categories, whereas English speakers use around 11 basic colour terms. These cultural variations are long-lived and thus provide a fertile forum in which to examine the possibility that entrenched differences between cultures in the use of colour terms might influence non-linguistic processes involved in colour perception.

Heider and Olivier (1972) tested this hypothesis amongst English-speaking Americans and the Dani of Indonesian New Guinea. They compared the ways in which both groups named colour chips and their subsequent memory for the colours, measured by performance in selecting the appropriate colour chip from an array of similarly coloured chips. The naming task yielded the predicted results, in that the Dani speakers tended to use the two colour terms with which they were familiar while the English speakers used the 11 colour terms with which they were familiar. Performance on the memory task, however, did not differ between the two groups, and this was cited as strong evidence against the Whorfian hypothesis. It seemed that colour perception was not subject to any malleable influences of language. Later studies, though, have yielded results that are conflicting and hard to interpret.

Roberson *et al.* (2000) carried out a replication of the Heider and Olivier study, comparing the colour perception of the Berinmo people of Papua New Guinea with that of English speakers. The Berinmo people use five colour terms to denote the colours of the spectrum; greens and blues are represented in one category, while other greens, yellows and oranges are represented in another category. The colour green, then, is split between categories, unlike the Dani and English colour categories. Roberson *et al.*'s findings on the key memory measures differ from those reported by Heider and Olivier, claiming evidence for an effect of language on colour perception.

However, in an evaluation of these studies, Munnich and Landau (2003) make an intriguing observation. In both studies, individuals verbally rehearsed the colours seen during the interval for the memory task. So, speakers with more colour terms at their disposal would immediately have an advantage, in that the availability of more colour terms would aid the task of distinguishing colours. Thus, it is difficult to rule out the possibility that linguistic representations mediated performance and so it is impossible to conclude that language influenced non-linguistic thinking. A stronger test of the Whorfian hypothesis, then, needs explicitly to rule out the possibility of linguistic encoding.

5.3   Does language influence spatial cognition?

The possible influence of language on thought has been investigated in the context of spatial cognition and non-linguistic tasks. Speakers of different languages encode spatial layout and orientation using different terms. English and Dutch speakers refer to right and left in the context of object-centred frames of reference, and use the compass points of north, south, east and west for a geographic frame of reference. South American Mayans who speak the language Tzeltal use an absolute system for all such relationships: thus a person may be said to be south of another person, just as a town may be said to be east of another town, or a piece of fruit on a table west of another piece of fruit on the same table. Brown and Levinson (1993) were interested in the possibility that these different frames of reference might influence the encoding of spatial relationships in non-linguistic tasks. They asked Tzeltal and Dutch speakers to view an array of objects placed on a table, and then to turn 180 degrees and either reconstruct the original array or choose one that matched it from a selection. The point of the rotation was to reverse the relative frame of reference (left becomes right and vice versa) whilst preserving the absolute frame of reference (north is always north). Reconstructions and selections of arrays would indicate whether the relative or absolute frame of reference had been used. Findings from the study were very clear. Tzeltal speakers showed a preference for an absolute frame of reference, preserving the north–south order of objects that had been presented in the original arrays. However, Dutch speakers appeared to prefer the relative frame of reference, reversing the absolute order of objects.

On the face of it, then, these results appear to offer incontrovertible support for the Whorfian hypothesis that language can shape the way in which we see the world, and importantly these data were obtained using a non-linguistic task. Li and Gleitman (2002), however, have replicated some of these studies and have shown that changing the environment in which the spatial tasks occur can change the frame of reference used. In one study, Li and Gleitman carried out the spatial frame of reference task in a room that was either devoid of other objects with blinds drawn over a window, or that contained other objects and had the blinds pulled back, so that a view of the outside could be seen. In the minimal environment, participants tended to use a relative frame of reference, whereas in the more natural, information-rich environment, participants tended to use an absolute frame of reference. The key point is that participants were all English speakers. Li and Gleitman were therefore able to conclude that the environment is a far more salient determinant of the frame of reference used than is the language the individual speaks. It is of course possible that language did in some way mediate in the spatial frame of reference tasks, and so both Brown and Levinson's data and Li and Gleitman's results are susceptible to the criticism that participants may have verbally encoded the locations of items within the array that was later reconstructed. However, the fact that English speakers changed their frame of reference shows that whatever the effects of linguistic mediation in this task, environmental cues appear to have a far more significant impact on the frame of reference chosen.

Boroditsky (2001) investigated the possibility that the linguistic spatial and temporal metaphors we use may influence thinking. This is potentially an interesting line of investigation, since the use of metaphor is pervasive in thinking and problem solving. To test this hypothesis, she contrasted the response times of native English and native Mandarin speakers, who had learned to speak English also from around 6 years of age, on a verification task. Native English speakers tend to use expressions such as, 'I'm really looking forward to tomorrow' and 'We'll have to put back the date of the next meeting'. Boroditsky argues that these are predominantly horizontal metaphors,[11] and they are commonly used in other languages. Mandarin speakers, on the other hand, also use vertical metaphors to refer to events in time. Thus, 'Tony Blair is up from Gordon Brown' would mean that Tony Blair was prime minister ahead of Gordon Brown. Boroditsky argued that if these long-entrenched linguistic conventions influence thought, then evidence for this may be obtained in a verification task requiring temporal and spatial judgments. To do this, native English and Mandarin speakers viewed scenes containing objects that were arranged along either the vertical dimension or the horizontal dimension. They were then asked to

---

[11] Readers will no doubt be able to bring to bear examples in English of the influence of the vertical dimension. For example, English speakers may refer to something being 'passed down the generations' or an event 'coming up'.

verify statements presented in English about temporal relationships. English speakers were quicker to verify statements after horizontal priming while Mandarin speakers exhibited faster response times after vertical priming. Boroditsky argued that Mandarin speakers' natural way of thinking using the vertical dimension influenced response times, even though testing took place in English. This appeared to be evidence for language influencing thought. Boroditsky is clear in her paper that the strong Whorfian view is not tenable, though she does make a case for the influence of language on thought being most likely in the case of learning relations (which are usually encoded by verbs and spatial propositions) than in learning-object concepts. The former require extensive experience with language whereas the latter may be more readily discerned and individuated through perceptual experiences.

While Boroditsky's conclusions are compelling, her findings have not been replicated. January and Kako (2007) were unable to replicate Boroditsky's results in six attempts to repeat her study. They vigorously refute her findings while also criticizing her method and interpretation. One of January and Kako's interesting findings was obtained from a study they carried out using native English speakers who were taught over a series of 90 trials to use the vertical metaphor to refer to temporal relations (e.g. Bill Clinton was president below Ronald Reagan). These participants then completed the same experimental procedure that Boroditsky (2001) had described. Remarkably, their response times on the verification task suggested a switch to a vertical metaphor, in that there appeared to be an effect of vertical priming. These results are very hard to reconcile with the position that long-held linguistic conventions influence how we think. If 90 exposures to a new way of thinking can apparently effect a change in how native English speakers thought about temporal relations, then why was a similar reversal not apparent in the Boroditsky study amongst the native Mandarin speakers who had been using English as their second language for many years?

5.4   Linguistic relativism

While there is scant evidence for language directly influencing thought via the ways in which we perceive the world, we can still examine the possibility that language augments our higher-order cognitive capabilities, such as those required for reasoning and problem solving. Here, we shall consider whether labelling objects may help us to reason about those objects, and whether the very act of speaking causes us to think about what we want to say. In other words, do we think before we speak, and do we literally put our thoughts down on paper?

Rattermann and Gentner (1998) examined the possibility that relational reasoning might be enhanced if children were taught to use relational labels. In so doing, they sought to test the hypothesis that language may influence cognitive development. They carried out a series of experiments to explore the relational reasoning performance of children aged 3, 4 and 5 years, comparing this to the performance of a group of 3-year-olds who were taught to use relational labels (e.g. big, little, tiny) to denote monotonic change in size. The task required the children to work out under which object in their array a sticker might be found. Children viewed two simple but non-identical arrays of objects (arranged in order of size), one placed in front of them and the other in front of the experimenter (see Figure 10.3).

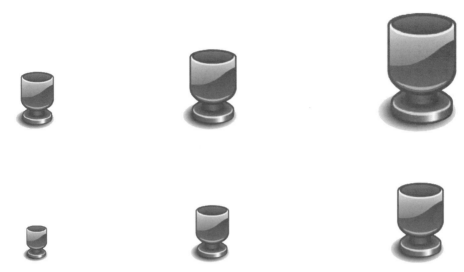

Figure 10.3   An example of the kind of array used by Rattermann and Gentner (1998)

The child was told that the sticker could be found by looking 'in the same place' in their array. So, if the experimenter placed a sticker under the second largest object located in the middle of her array, the correct place for the child to look in her corresponding array would be in the middle location. To select the correct object, the child has to ignore size matches between the arrays and instead select on the basis of location within the array. The task is relatively easy for young children when the objects are similar and varying only in size, but when different objects are used within the arrays (such as a cup, a toy car and a toy house), the task is much harder. With similar objects, 3- and 4-year-olds performed at well above the chance level of 33 per cent, and were correct on roughly two-thirds of trials. The 5-year-olds showed close to 100 per cent accuracy. With the more complex objects, though, the 3- and 4-year-olds performed at roughly chance level, while the 5-year-olds' performance dropped to around 67 per cent. However, the 3-year-olds taught to use relational labels performed as well as the 5-year-olds on the similar-object task (achieving 89 per cent accuracy) and achieved 79 per cent accuracy on the more complex object task. These findings suggest that the additional information afforded by the labels enhanced the relational reasoning performance of young children. It is not yet clear whether these benefits endure, or transfer to related tasks.

Slobin (1987, 2003) points out that language influences thought when we are thinking with the intent to use language. In a move away from an arguably sterile and stale search for ways in which language might determine thought, where the focus has been on tasks that do not involve language, Slobin has pointed out that much of our thinking is for specific purposes, and these purposes include speaking, writing and translation. In a sense, Slobin is absolutely right, in that having thought about a topic with a view to talking about it, we select from a set of words available to us when we wish to express those thoughts. For example, Slobin (2003) reviews research that indicates that speakers of different languages may describe manner of motion in more or less rich ways in novels. He notes that some languages, such as English and Russian, pay considerable attention to manner of motion ('he moved quietly along the corridor') while other languages, such as Spanish and Turkish, use fewer descriptors of motion in written text. The difference is interesting, but what does it actually tell us about thinking? We cannot conclude from differences in cultural conventions in writing about movement that there are cultural variations in how we actually think about movement.

Summary of Section 5

- The evidence for the hypothesis of strong linguistic determinism is very scant indeed. We could almost go so far as to suggest the question is inappropriate.
- There is, however, evidence that language influences thought.

6 Conclusion

This chapter set out to describe just some of the work that has been carried out on two of the most fascinating aspects of human nature. The philosophical underpinnings of this work are crucial, as nowhere do rationalists, empiricists and pragmatists clash more than at the interface between language and thinking.

Research at the interfaces between cognitive psychology, archaeology, anthropology and neuroscience is forging ahead, and new ideas are being generated, contested and revised at a rapid pace. This is yielding remarkable insights into the possible cognitive capabilities of our forebears and our Neanderthal relatives. Would a Neanderthal have possessed a theory of mind, for example? Did a small difference in working memory capacity result in *Homo sapiens* out-competing Neanderthals?

We have reviewed and evaluated rationalist, empiricist and pragmatic accounts of language and thinking. The accumulated evidence suggests a complex interdependence between language and thought, though this conclusion is sterile unless viewed within a context. So, research on theory of mind, for example, shows that while very young children may be able to correctly visually anticipate the behaviour of another with a false belief, this anticipation is not paralleled in their verbal behaviour. These sorts of discrepancies raise questions about how language and thinking interface and Fodor's language of thought offers a viable framework within which to address such questions.

Further reading

A useful text that further develops some interdisciplinary themes in language and thought is the still relevant volume edited by Carruthers and Boucher. Others may prefer the wonderfully articulate and stimulating approach of Steven Pinker, whose website alone is well worth visiting: http://pinker.wjh.harvard.edu/index.html.

Carruthers, P. and Boucher, S. (1998) *Language and Thought: Interdisciplinary Themes*, Cambridge, Cambridge University Press.

Pinker, S. (2008) *The Seven Words You Can't Say On Television*, London, Penguin Books.

References

Aitchison, J. (2007) *The Articulate Mammal* (5th edn), Oxford, Blackwell.

Baker, M. (2001) *The Atoms of Language: The Mind's Hidden Rules of Grammar*, New York, Basic Books.

Barthes, R. (1977) 'The death of the author', in Barthes, R. *Image–Music–Text*, London, Fontana Press.

BBC News (9 January 2010) http://www.news.bbc.co.uk (Accessed 29 April 2010).

Behne, T., Carpenter, M. and Tomasello, M. (2005) 'One-year olds comprehend the communicative intentions behind gestures in a hiding game', *Developmental Science*, vol.8, pp.492–9.

Bigelow, A. (1987) 'Early words of blind children', *Journal of Child Language*, vol.14, pp.47–56.

Boring, E.G. (1950) 'Great men and scientific progress', *Proceedings of the American Philosophical Society*, vol.94, pp.339–51.

Boroditsky, L. (2001) 'Does language shape thought? Mandarin and English speakers' conceptions of time', *Cognitive Psychology*, vol.43, pp.1–22.

Brown, P. and Levinson, S.C. (1993) 'Linguistic and nonlinguistic coding of spatial arrays: explorations in Mayan cognition', *Working Paper 24*, Nijmegen, Max Planck Institute for Psycholinguistics, Cognitive Anthropology Research Group.

Brown, R.W. and Lenneberg, E.H. (1954) 'A study in language and cognition', *Journal of Abnormal and Social Psychology*, vol.49, pp.454–62.

Call, J. and Tomasello, M. (1999) 'A nonverbal false belief task: the performance of children and great apes', *Child Development*, vol.70, pp.381–95.

Chomsky, N. (1965) *Aspects of the Theory of Syntax*, Cambridge, MA, MIT Press.

Chomsky, N. (1995) *The Minimalist Program*, Cambridge, MA, MIT Press.

Chomsky, N. (2006) *Language and Mind* (3rd edn), Cambridge, Cambridge University Press.

Clayton, N.S. and Russell, J. (2009) 'Looking for episodic memory in animals and young children: prospects for a new minimalism', *Neuropsychologia*, vol.47, pp.2330–40.

Clements, W.A. and Perner, J. (1994) 'Implicit understanding of belief', *Cognitive Development*, vol.9, pp.377–95.

Coolidge, F.L. and Wynn, T. (2007) 'The working memory account of Neanderthal cognition. How phonological storage capacity may be related to recursion and the pragmatics of modern speech', *Journal of Human Evolution*, vol.52, pp.707–10.

Davidson, D. (2001) 'Externalisms', in Kotstko, P., Pagin, P. and Segal, G. (eds) *Interpreting Davidson*, Stanford, CA, CSLI Publications.

De Villiers, J.G. and de Villiers, P.A. (2003) 'Language for thought: coming to understand false beliefs', in Gentner, D. and Goldin-Meadow, S. (eds) *Language in Mind*, Cambridge, MA, MIT Press.

Dick, Philip K. (1968) *Do Androids Dream of Electric Sheep?*, New York, Doubleday.

Dockrell, J. and Messer, D.J. (1999) *Children's Language and Communication Difficulties. Understanding, Identification and Intervention*, London, Cassell.

Duncan, J., Emslie, H., Williams, P., Johnson, R. and Freer, C. (1996) 'Intelligence and the frontal lobe: the organization of goal-directed behavior', *Cognitive Psychology*, vol.30, pp.257–303.

Ericsson, K.A. and Kintsch, W. (1995) 'Long-term working memory', *Psychological Review*, vol.102, pp.211–45.

Fodor, J.A. (1975) *The Language of Thought*, New York, Crowell.

Fodor, J.A. (1983) *The Modularity of Mind: An Essay in Faculty Psychology*, Cambridge, MA, MIT Press.

Fodor, J.A. (1987) *Psychosemantics*, Cambridge, MA, MIT Press.

Fodor, J.A., Garrett, M.F., Walker, E.C.T. and Parkes, C.H. (1980) 'Against definitions', *Cognition*, vol.8, pp.263–367.

Grice, H.P. (1989) *Studies in the Way of Words*, Cambridge, MA, Harvard University Press.

Hare, B. and Tomasello, M. (2004) 'Chimpanzees are more skillful in competitive than in cooperative cognitive tasks', *Animal Behavior*, vol.68, pp.571–81.

Hauser, M.D., Chomsky, N. and Tecumseh Fitch, W. (2002) 'The faculty of language: what is it, who has it, and how did it evolve?', *Science*, vol.298, pp.1569–79.

Heider, E. and Olivier, D. (1972) 'The structure of the color space in naming and memory for two languages', *Cognitive Psychology*, vol.3, pp.337–54.

James, W. (1892) *Text Book of Psychology*, London, Macmillan.

January, D. and Kako E. (2007) 'Re-evaluating evidence for linguistic relativity: reply to Boroditsky (2001)', *Cognition*, vol.104, pp.417–26.

Koenig, M.A. and Echols, C.H. (2003) 'Infants' understanding of false-labelling events: the referential role of words and the speaker's use of them', *Cognition*, vol.87, pp.179–208.

Li, P. and Gleitman, L. (2002) 'Turning the tables: language and spatial reasoning', *Cognition*, vol.83, pp.265–94.

Maguire, E.A., Gadian, D.G. and Johnsrude, I.S. (2000) 'Navigation-related structural change in the hippocampi of taxi drivers', *Proceedings of the National Academy of Sciences*, vol.97, pp.4398–403.

Malafouris, L. (2010) 'The brain–artefact interface (BAI): a challenge for archaeology and cultural neuroscience', *Social Cognitive and Affective Neuroscience Advance Access*, 19 January.

Meier, R.P. (1991) 'Language acquisition by deaf children', *American Scientist*, vol.79, pp.60–70.

Messer, D.J. (2000) 'State of the art: language acquisition', *The Psychologist*, vol.13, pp.138–43.

Mohay, H. (1982) 'A preliminary description of the communication systems evolved by two deaf children in the absence of a sign language model', *Sign Language Studies*, vol.34, pp.73–90.

Moll, H. and Tomasello, T. (2007) 'Co-operation and human cognition: the Vygotskian intelligence hypothesis', *Philosophical Transactions of the Royal Society B*, DOI: 10.1098/rstb.2006.2000.

Munnich, E. and Landau, B. (2003) 'The effects of spatial language on spatial representation: setting some boundaries', in Gentner, D. and Goldin-Meadow, S. (eds) *Language in Mind*, Cambridge, MA, MIT Press.

Nature News (20 April 2010) http://www.nature.com/news (Accessed 27April 2010).

Nelson, K. (1973) 'Structure and strategy in learning to talk', *Monographs of the Society for Research in Child Development*, 38 (serial no. 149).

O'Keefe, J. and Nadel, L. (1978) *The Hippocampus as a Cognitive Map*, Oxford, Oxford University Press.

Piaget, J. (1923) *The Language and Thought of the Child* (trans. M. Gabain, 1955), Cleveland, OH, Meridian.

Pinker, S. (2007) *The Stuff of Thought*, London, Penguin.

Pinker, S. and Bloom, P. (1990) 'Natural language and natural selection', *Behavioural and Brain Sciences*, vol.13, pp.707–84.

Pullum, G.K. (1989) 'The great Eskimo vocabulary hoax', *Natural Language and Linguistic Theory*, vol.7, pp.275–81.

Rattermann, M.J. and Gentner, D. (1998) 'More evidence for a relational shift in the development of analogy: children's performance on a causal-mapping task', *Cognitive Development*, vol.13, pp.453–78.

Reed, D.L., Smith, V.S., Hammond, S.L., Rogers, A.R. and Clayton, D.H. (2004) 'Genetic analysis of lice supports direct contact between modern and archaic humans', *PLoS Biology*, vol.2, DOI: 10.1371/journal.pbio.0020340.

Rimmon-Kenan, S. (1983) *Narrative Fiction: Contemporary Poetics*, London, Routledge.

Roberson, D., Davies, I. and Davidoff, J. (2000) 'Colour categories are not universal: replications and new evidence from a Stone-Age culture', *Journal of Experimental Psychology: General*, vol.129, pp.369–98.

Russell, J. (2004) *What is Language Development?*, Oxford, Oxford University Press.

Russell, J. (2007) 'Controlling core knowledge: conditions for the ascription of intentional states to self and others by children', *Synthese*, vol.159, pp.167–96.

Schlanger, N. (1996) 'Understanding Levallois: lithic technology and cognitive archaeology', *Cambridge Archaeological Journal*, vol.6, pp.231–54.

Slobin, D.I. (1987) 'Thinking for speaking', *Proceedings of the Thirteenth Annual Meeting of the Berkeley Linguistics Society*, pp.435–44.

Slobin, D.I. (2003) 'Language and thought online: cognitive consequences of linguistic relativity', in Gentner, D. and Goldin-Meadow, S. (eds) *Language in Mind: Advances in the Study of Language and Thought*, Cambridge, MA, MIT Press.

Smith, S.M., Brown, H.O., Toman, J.E.P. and Goodman, L.S. (1947) 'The lack of cerebral effects of d-tubocuarine', *Anesthesiology*, vol.8, pp.1–14.

Sperber, D. (1985) 'Anthropology and psychology: towards an epidemiology of representations', *Man*, vol.20, pp.73–89.

Sperber, D. and Wilson, D. (1981) 'Irony and the use–mention distinction', in Cole, P. (ed.) *Radical Pragmatics*, New York, Academic Press.

Virgin Media News (2010) http://www.virginmedia.co.uk (Accessed 2 March 2010).

Von Frisch, K. (1967) *The Dance Language and Orientation of Bees*, Cambridge, MA, Harvard University Press.

Vygotsky, L.S. (1978) *Mind in Society: The Development of Higher Psychological Processes*, Cambridge, MA, Harvard University Press.

Whorf, B. (1956) *Language, Thought and Reality: Selected Writings of Benjamin Lee Whorf* (ed. J. B. Carroll), Cambridge, MA, MIT Press.

Wimmer, H. and Mayringer, H. (1998) 'False belief understanding in young children: explanations do not develop before predictions', *International Journal of Behavioural Development*, vol.22, pp.403–22.

Wimmer, H. and Perner, J. (1983) 'Beliefs about beliefs: representation and constraining function of wrong beliefs in young children's understanding of deception', *Cognition*, vol.13, pp.103–28.

Wynn, T. and Coolidge, F.L. (2004) 'The expert Neanderthal mind', *Journal of Human Evolution*, vol.46, pp.467–87.

Xu, F. (2002) 'The role of language in acquiring object kind concepts in infancy', *Cognition*, vol.85, pp.223–50.

Zhang, J. and Norman, D.A. (1994) 'Representations in distributed cognitive tasks', *Cognitive Science*, vol.18, pp.87–122.

PART 4
THINKING

Introduction

In Part 4, the focus shifts to what have been termed thinking processes. Specifically, the chapters address three distinct kinds of thinking that arise in different kinds of task – in general terms, these are tasks that require us to solve problems (Chapter 11), come to judgements and make decisions (Chapter 12) and to reason and draw conclusions (Chapter 13).

In Chapter 11, Alison Green and Ken Gilhooly address human problem solving. You might think that problem solving is a somewhat artificial activity, inspired by abstract and contrived problems such as crossword puzzles, or the Rubik's cube. But problem solving in cognitive psychology is intended to encompass a wide range of activities in which we need to identify the solution to a current problem. Everyday problems range from the easy, such as how to make a cup of tea in someone else's kitchen, to the complex, such as how to achieve career success. Everyday problems are not always easily defined – think of the different problems that need solving in order to achieve a successful career – and so psychologists have often relied on more formally specified problems, of which the authors of Chapter 11 provide numerous examples.

Historically, cognitive psychology has tended to avoid the study of individual differences because it aims to understand cognitive processes in general. However, in Chapter 5 of Part 2, we saw how the study of individual differences can help us to evaluate theories of cognition and, conversely, how the theories can help us to understand the nature of the individual differences. In Chapter 11, the importance of individual differences is emphasized again. First, the authors note that some individuals are novices in solving certain classes of problem and some are expert. In playing chess, for example, some individuals achieve grand master status whereas others, while knowing the rules of the game, are considerably less skilled. The problem-solving approaches of these groups differ in important ways, and so it is not true to say that people in general tackle chess problems in the same way. Second, as the authors also point out, experts themselves differ from one another in relevant ways – that is, they do not form a homogeneous group – and novices also differ from one another.

Certain aspects of the study of problem solving that are raised in Chapter 11 become themes for the whole of Part 4. One is that cognitive psychologists place at least as much emphasis on the study of errors in problem solving as they do on cases of success. Indeed, as we shall see, errors provide important information concerning underlying cognitive processes, and this theme is continued in Chapters 12 and 13.

Another theme established in Chapter 11 is the importance of establishing a framework within which phenomena can be analysed and understood, and which in turn can be used to derive new research questions. In Chapter 11, Alison Green and Ken Gilhooly introduce the notion of a 'state–space' and show how this notion can help us to understand problems and to analyse human performance when attempting to solve them.

In Chapter 12, Peter Ayton introduces the topics of judgement and decision making. How do we form judgements and make decisions, and how best should we understand and analyse these cognitive activities? One thing the author makes clear from the outset is that it is possible to develop different kinds of theory, depending on the starting point and purpose of the theorist. A theory could, for example, emphasise how judgement and decision-making processes *ought* to proceed, and use this as a basis for analysing human performance. Alternatively, a theorist could take as their starting point an understanding of how people *actually* make decisions, including poor ones. That there are these two approaches – normative and descriptive – continues the theme, established in Chapter 11, of the importance of researchers establishing an appropriate explanatory framework. In essence, the chapter can be seen as an extended discussion of whether two particular normative approaches provide an adequate understanding of human judgement and decision making.

In the first part of Chapter 12, Peter Ayton discusses the normative theory of subjective expected utility, and its use as a vehicle for understanding human decision making. As you will see, this theory requires us to express the likelihood of particular outcomes as mathematical probabilities, though you may be relieved to know that the key mathematical ideas are relatively simple. Probabilities are also required to understand a normative approach to judgement under uncertainty, which involves the application of Bayes' theorem.

While the normative approaches rely on mathematical formulations of how judgement and decision making ought to proceed, the majority of the chapter discusses evidence that human performance actually departs from these mathematical standards – that human performance is characterized by apparent errors. The chapter compares such normative theories with descriptive accounts of actual human performance – prospect theory and the heuristics and biases approach. Although these accounts are seen ultimately to be more successful, the normative approaches nonetheless play an important role in helping researchers to develop a more appropriate explanatory framework. In particular, observations that human performance deviates systematically from mathematical standards have provided researchers with extremely valuable information.

The particular descriptive approaches discussed in the chapter are not without their problems however. One important line of criticism comes from an approach that considers the adaptive function, in evolutionary terms, of decision-making processes. Some researchers have argued that such processes would have evolved to be 'fast and frugal', and the chapter cites evidence in favour of this view.

Some of these concerns can also be found in Chapter 13. In this chapter, Mike Oaksford shows how research into reasoning also started from a formal framework for understanding how people ought to reason – that of logic. The first part of Chapter 13 outlines the nature of logic, and in particular the forms of reasoning that are taken to be logically valid, and those taken to be logically invalid. As with the normative approaches discussed in Chapter 12, logic provides a valuable framework for trying to understand human reasoning. It has also helped researchers to establish the core phenomena of reasoning, and to develop paradigms to investigate these.

As with Chapter 12, a key observation also running throughout Chapter 13 is that human reasoning systematically departs from the normative standards established by logic. Predicting and understanding these logical errors has thus become an important benchmark for theories of human reasoning. A number of such theories have been developed, and the chapter focuses mostly on three approaches – mental logic, mental models and the probabilistic approach. Each of these approaches is evaluated against evidence that has accrued from the use of two key paradigms or tasks – conditional inference, and the Wason selection task – and we see again the use of expected utilities and also Bayes' theorem.

Specifically in connection with a version of the Wason selection task, the chapter also discusses a fourth approach to reasoning. This approach emphasizes the importance of theories of reasoning positing processes that can be seen to have an evolutionarily adaptive function. Mike Oaksford also discusses the relationship between logical reasoning and IQ, showing once again the importance of individual differences.

As suggested above, there are a number of themes running throughout the three chapters of this Part 4. One theme that has not been mentioned so far is rationality. Errors, or departures from a logical or mathematical standard, could be taken as signs of the intrinsic irrationality of human thought. After all, so the argument goes, if human beings are rational they ought to solve problems, make judgements and decisions, and reason according to certain standards, often assumed to be provided by formal models, such as mathematics and logic. Departures from these mathematical and logical standards then would be signs of irrationality. However, although these three chapters do not take rationality as their central focus, the establishment of theories of actual human performance provide grounds for understanding rationality differently. In connection with Chapter 12, for example, perhaps it would be rational to use heuristics and biases to come to a judgement, or, related to Chapter 13, perhaps it would be rational to rely on a probabilistic method for tackling a task, even if this sometimes generates logical 'errors'.

Finally, one thing you may notice about the three chapters in this part is that there is very little mention of computer modelling, neuropsychology or neuroimaging. Although this inevitably reflects to a degree the practical limits imposed by writing a chapter to a certain length, it also reflects a particular emphasis common to the three chapters with trying to develop an appropriate explanatory framework. If you recall the discussion of Marr's levels of explanation in Chapter 1, it is as if cognitive psychologists studying thinking are still trying to establish what is computed when we reason, or make decisions, or solve problems. Consistent with this is the fact that some researchers are appealing to evolution to help provide an explanatory framework. The suggestion that researchers are still grappling with difficult questions at Marr's computational level provides one way of understanding the emphasis on formal approaches – such as state–spaces in Chapter 11, probability in Chapter 12 and logic in Chapter 13. Such formal approaches provide an idealized model of what needs to be computed, i.e. Marr's level 1 (idealized because we observe systematic departures from this in actual human thinking). The combination of these models and observations of systematic human 'error' provides researchers with an effective means for analysing human thinking. As research develops further, and detailed questions subsequently arise concerning the actual processes by which thinking is achieved, neuropsychological, neuroimaging and computer-modelling work is likely to become much more relevant.

Problem solving   Chapter 11

Alison J. K. Green and Ken Gilhooly

1   Introduction

Problem solving is an essential, familiar and pervasive part of everyday life. Examples are all around us. Consider an infant trying to fit shapes into the appropriate holes of a shape-sorting toy, or a child trying to count out the correct sum of money to buy a new CD, or perhaps an adult weighing up the pros and cons of a job offer. While we shall be looking here at examples of human problem solving, problem solving occurs in animal life too. Naturally occurring instances include tool use and searching for food. Problem solving in all its manifestations is an activity that structures everyday life in meaningful ways.

By studying the myriad ways in which we solve problems, we hope to learn how problems are solved effectively, and to understand what goes wrong when they are not. Why should we be interested in finding out about *unsuccessful* problem solving? An interesting aspect of failure involves investigating the errors that people make, in order to understand why a particular error occurred and to try to prevent it from happening again. Some errors are made with little cost (for example, sprinkling coffee instead of sugar over cornflakes at breakfast), but other errors can be quite catastrophic (for example, an oil-laden vessel running aground near a shoreline wildlife reserve). Diagnosing errors and redesigning tasks to guard against critical errors are important applications for problem-solving research. We discuss others later on in the chapter.

Where does problem solving 'sit' in relation to other areas of psychology? Problem solving is an activity that draws together the various different components of cognition. For instance, linguistic skills are used to read about a political problem and engage in a debate about it. Visual perception is necessary for understanding a graphically presented engineering problem and for drawing a solution. We use memory to recover any prior knowledge we might have that could be relevant to solving a new problem, and attention plays a role in all problem solving.

Problem solving takes place over time, interleaving a range of cognitive processes and drawing upon pieces of knowledge, which are represented in various ways. The notion of 'representation' is central to cognitive psychology. We shall ask you to assume that information used in problem solving comes to be internally represented.

Because problem solving occurs over time, we need to study not just the cognitive processes and mental representations involved in problem solving, but also the ways in which these processes and representations interact with others. Problem solving then, like reasoning, judgement and decision making, is an activity that necessarily draws upon a range of cognitive processes.

In fact, problem solving often involves reasoning, judgement and decision making. For instance, a general practitioner gathering information about a sick patient's symptoms may deduce from the description the patient gives that the problem is a bacterial, rather than a viral, infection. The doctor may then make a judgement about the severity of the infection, before making a decision on an antibiotic to prescribe.

In this chapter, we examine the ways in which individuals approach a variety of problem types, ranging from simple, puzzle problems to more complex, real-world problems. Everyday problems can be complex and challenging, with constraints in operation that mean that the solution we choose or find may not be an ideal one. As individuals we can, if we are reasonably adept, persistent or just plain lucky, solve many of the problems that come our way. Quite often, though, our initial attempts fail and we have to turn to another source to help solve the problem – a manual, for instance, in the case of a tricky computer installation problem, or perhaps someone knowledgeable in the problem area if all else fails.

While some problems may be viewed as unwelcome obstacles, to be avoided where possible, there are occasions where we keenly seek out problems to occupy our time. An expert mathematician, for instance, may spend hours identifying a problem, primarily for the pleasure derived in exploring and solving it. Similarly, 'make-over' television programmes can be very entertaining as viewers watch an undecorated room or a derelict garden transformed by the experts in a matter of days into something quite different. Some of us undoubtedly while away the hours working on tricky crossword puzzles, computer games or trying to make (or repair) something at home.

Our aim in this chapter is to present an overview of research on problem solving. In doing this, we have had to be selective, and have elected to present work that we believe has been both influential and interesting to try to give you a flavour of what has been going on in the field. As you read on, you will learn that how people represent problems is a principal determinant of problem-solving success. Much of the research we shall examine addresses the question of which factors influence the construction of a problem representation.

We aim to show you how ideas about problem solving have developed and changed. You will learn that early work on problem solving was often confined to puzzle problems and that, later on, researchers became interested in more complex domains, where knowledge and experience are central to successful problem solving. The issues we shall explore centre on the nature of problem solving, and the relationships between problem solving, learning, experience and creativity. The kinds of questions we shall be asking include:

1   What are the different forms of problem-solving activity?

2   How do we solve different sorts of problems?

3   Why is representation important?

First, we shall try to define a 'problem' and then look at conceptions of problems and problem solving.

1.1 What is a 'problem'?

Before reading on, try the following activity.

ACTIVITY 11.1 ⎯⎯⎯⎯⎯⎯⎯⎯⎯⎯⎯⎯⎯⎯⎯⎯⎯⎯⎯⎯⎯

What do you think are the defining attributes of problems? You will probably draw upon some examples from your own experience to help you. You might like to think back to Chapter 9 to help you think of problems in terms of properties, categories and so on. Make a list of all the attributes you can think of, and then try to construct a sentence or two, defining problems. Try not to spend more than a couple of minutes on this.

COMMENT

The answer to the question, 'What is a problem?' is not at all easy, as the exercise shows. You may find that you want to vary your definition, depending upon the type of problem you have in mind. You may find that you cannot come up with a definition at all, or that you came up with several and cannot choose between them. Of course, if it is difficult to define what we mean by a 'problem', then it becomes even more difficult to construct models and theories of problem-solving behaviour, and to compare and contrast such models and theories. Clear definitions are therefore important at the outset.

Consider the following examples of problems that a given individual might come across, some more commonplace than others:

1   Who can I ask to babysit the children so that I can go out next Thursday evening?

2   How can I make sure that the stone I have just played in my game of Go[1] 'lives'?

3   Is there a way I can arrange some paper pattern pieces on my dress material so that all the pieces fit and I don't have to buy any more material?

The problem in the first example is finding a babysitter, which could involve searching through an address book, recovering some names from memory or calling round on a friend and asking for a favour. If these fail to produce a name, then other options include carrying out a more extensive search. A bit of inspired guesswork might lead to an internet babysitting site, and locating a babysitter to solve the problem. Notice that there are several ways to satisfactorily solve this problem, and that the possible solutions vary in degree of novelty. The availability of a possible solution method may well vary too, depending upon the context (is there time to explore different possible solutions to the problem?), social setting (is there a network of likely babysitters to call upon?) and culture (is it acceptable to use an internet babysitting agency?).

---

[1] The aim in Go is to use stones (one player takes black stones, the other white) to surround territory on a board. A stone (or stones) 'lives' if it cannot be surrounded, and therefore removed, from the board. Territory is 'won' if stones of one colour completely surround stones of the other colour, and the winner is the player who surrounds the most territory.

The problem in the second example centres on the ancient Korean game of Go. Here, the problem seems more to do with experience, knowledge and skill, although motivation (does playing badly matter?), personality and emotion (are there personal costs in playing badly?) and cultural factors (different cultures have different conventions for Go) may well be involved too. Again, there are different solutions available, in that a number of different moves may achieve the goal of ensuring the 'survival' of the stone in question.

The final problem is different again, because it involves perception in 'seeing' how to lay all the pieces out, together with some creative or lateral thinking in optimizing layout so that all the pieces do indeed fit correctly. There may be one or more possible ways to arrange the pieces and solve the problem, one of which may be better (for example, in ensuring that cut pieces of fabric fit together in a way that matches up a pattern at seams).

These examples show that while problems do share some common character-istics (see the discussion of concepts in Chapter 9), it is also true that different problems are affected by different factors, both internal (for example, motivation and personality) and external (for example, social and cultural factors).

Duncker (1945, p.1) offered a concise definition of a problem that captures something of the essence of our everyday experience of problems. He wrote that: 'a problem exists when a living organism has a goal but does not know how this goal is to be reached'. The definition is still serviceable today because it conveys the notion of a 'gap' between a current state and a goal or desired state. If there are no obstacles preventing the individual from moving from the current state to the desired state, then there cannot be said to be a problem. Problems, then, consist of three components: a starting state, a goal state and a set of available actions to move from the starting state to the goal. According to this type of definition, what constitutes a problem for one individual may not be a problem for another. For instance, a moderate Go player might have some difficulty ensuring that a newly placed stone survives in her current game if her opponent is a much stronger player than her. The stronger opponent however will almost certainly have considerably less difficulty in making his stones live.

So far, we have tried to present some defining characteristics of problems. Before we move on to discuss research on problem solving, we want to draw your attention to one of the principal methods used in problem-solving research: protocol analysis.

1.2   Protocol analysis in problem-solving research

Cognitive scientists make extensive use of a method known as 'protocol analysis'. At the core of the approach is the view that information represented in working memory may be verbalized, either directly if in verbal form, or through transformation if in non-verbal form. Information retained in long-term memory must first be transferred to working memory before it can be reported. Thus, the 'protocol' of protocol analysis is a verbal account of information that is heeded as a task is carried out. The protocol that results from thinking aloud is assumed to preserve the order in which information has been heeded. Using careful instructions, and with a little practice, most people can 'think aloud', either while working on a task, or immediately after completing a task.

Protocol analysis depends upon fundamental assumptions, the most basic of which are that cognition is information processing, that information is stored in different memory stores, and that recently acquired information is retained in working memory.

The method has many uses, particularly in helping to identify differences between individuals in terms of information heeded, and processes and strategies used, as a task is carried out. Let us suppose that our research question centres on investigating cognitive processes in arithmetic, and that we have asked two individuals to think aloud while calculating the sum of $63 + 37$. Both give the answer '100'. Did both arrive at the answer in the same way? One way of addressing this question is to compare the verbal reports produced:

> First individual: 'OK, what is the sum of 63 plus 37? Easy – that's 100.'
> Second individual: 'What is the sum of 63 plus 37? 60 plus 30 ... 60, 70, 80, 90. 3 plus 7 is 10. 90 plus 10 is 100. It's 100.'

The first individual simply reads out the problem statement and then reports the answer. There is little evidence of any problem solving here, and the answer appears to be readily available – it is as if the individual is retrieving a number fact. The second individual also begins by reading the problem statement, but then goes about the problem rather differently. The protocol suggests that her strategy is a 'counting on' strategy, starting with 60, then counting on 30, giving 90. She then adds the units 3 and 7, giving 10, and finally adds 10 to 90 to give the answer. The example shows that different people can arrive at the same answer, but use different methods. It also shows that protocol analysis can reveal useful information about strategies underlying behaviour.

Protocol analysis is a very useful tool for identifying different strategies people use in problem solving – strategies that may not be obvious from problem solutions alone. Of course, there are situations where protocol analysis is not a suitable approach (for example, where the requirement to think aloud might actually change the way in which the task is carried out).

It is important to recognize that thinking aloud is not the direct externalization of our cognitive processes. Rather, mental processes may be inferred through the careful analysis of verbal protocols. We illustrate an application of protocol analysis in Box 11.1.

11.1 — Methods

Protocol analysis applied to medical diagnosis

Medical diagnosis is a complex skill, requiring the clinician to bring to bear his or her knowledge and skill in accurately diagnosing a given patient's disorder. Expert clinicians have acquired both biomedical and clinical knowledge. Biomedical knowledge includes knowledge of anatomy, biochemistry and physiology, while clinical knowledge is often expressed in terms of associations between symptoms, or clinical findings, and disease categories. There has been some debate over the extent to which expert clinicians use biomedical knowledge in making diagnoses. Lesgold et al. (1998) found that expert clinicians made extensive use of biomedical knowledge, whereas Boshuizen and Schmidt (1992) found they made very little use.

Gilhooly et al. (1997) hypothesized that when experts can use contextual information (e.g. patient's age, gender and lifestyle habits) to aid a diagnosis, their use of biomedical knowledge may be suppressed. Gilhooly et al. tested this hypothesis through their analysis of think-aloud protocols produced by clinicians varying in skill level. They asked a group of clinicians to interpret electrocardiogram (ECG) trace information. The ECG is regularly used to assess the electrical activity of the heart, and to help identify abnormal patterns of activity that might indicate an underlying problem. Skill is required to interpret an ECG trace, and to use this in making an accurate diagnosis, which then becomes the basis for a patient's treatment regime.

Gilhooly et al. asked groups of registrars (the 'experts'), house officers (the 'intermediates') and third-year medical students (the 'novices') to think aloud while they studied and diagnosed eight different ECG traces, presented with no context information. They then analysed the protocols, examining them for evidence of biomedical and clinical knowledge. For example, uses of key terms such as 'polarization', 'activation' or 'conducting' were categorized as biomedical references. Uses of words such as 'chronic' or 'hypertension' were classified as clinical references. Clinicians also described the ECG traces directly in their protocols, giving a third category of words. In this way, the protocols produced by the clinicians were segmented into much smaller chunks, corresponding to clinical or biomedical inferences, or trace descriptions.

Reassuringly, the more experienced and skilled the clinicians were, the more accurate their diagnoses. The results of the protocol analysis showed that more skilled clinicians made more extensive use of their biomedical knowledge than less skilled clinicians, particularly in evaluating possible diagnoses. They also made more use of their clinical knowledge than the less skilled clinicians.

What does this study tell us? First, it resolves the apparently discrepant findings in the literature. Increased use of biomedical knowledge *is* associated with expertise, when clinicians are not able to use shortcuts to aid a diagnosis. Second, the study shows that protocol analysis can be a very useful tool in helping us to understand problem solving in real-world situations. Verbal protocols can give valuable insights into knowledge and processes involved in problem solving.

Summary of Section 1

- Problems involve a start state, a goal state and a set of actions or operators that may be applied to move from one state to the next until the goal is achieved.
- Protocol analysis is a key method in problem-solving research.

2 'Simple' problem solving

In this section we discuss themes and issues in research on what might loosely be termed 'simple' problem solving, although, as you will see, the problems used are not always simple to solve. So-called 'simple' problems, which do not require extensive background knowledge, are sometimes known as 'puzzles' and have often been used in research as most participants can attempt such problems within a reasonably short time. The issue of representation, and the various ways in which manipulations of problems affect representation, and in turn, problem-solving performance, is very much at the centre of this branch of problem-solving research.

2.1 The Gestalt legacy

Simple problem solving began to be studied intensively from the 1910s by a group of German psychologists known as the **Gestaltists**. The hallmarks of the Gestalt approach were the phenomenon of insight, and the view that the whole is greater than the sum of its parts. Insight has famously been labelled the 'aha!' phenomenon, in that sudden restructuring or re-representings of a problem can sometimes lead to a solution.

The Gestalt school particularly emphasized the role of **insight** in problem solving. An example can be found in the story of young Gauss (Hall, 1970) who later went on to become a prominent mathematician (well known for deriving the formula for the normal distribution curve). As a young schoolchild, Gauss surprised his teacher by very quickly producing the correct answer to the sum of all the numbers from 1 to 100. He gave the answer (5050) not by very fast mental arithmetic but by noticing a pattern in the number sequence, viz., that the numbers form pairs (1+100 =101, 2+99 =101, 3 + 98 = 101 ... and so on). There are 50 pairs and each pair sums to 101: hence the answer is 5050. In this example then a good structuring, or representation, of the problem helps considerably.

The processes of restructuring were investigated further by Duncker (1945) who asked participants to think aloud as they tackled problems that required insight to solve. An example is the X-ray problem (see Figure 11.1 below). Participants were shown a diagram and told that it represented a patient with a tumour in the centre of his body. The problem was how to use an X-ray apparatus to destroy the tumour without destroying the surrounding healthy tissue. Participants usually tried alternative restructurings of the problem in terms of subgoals that could lead to solutions. Thus, the major goal could be achieved if a subgoal of avoiding damage to healthy tissue could be achieved. The most common solutions involved a subgoal of lowering intensity of rays on their way through the healthy tissue. This subgoal led to the solution of using a number of weaker rays, which then converged on the tumour at lethal intensity, thereby destroying the tumour. (An alternative solution involved using a lens to focus a broad band of weak rays on the tumour so that lethal intensity was reached only at the focal point.)

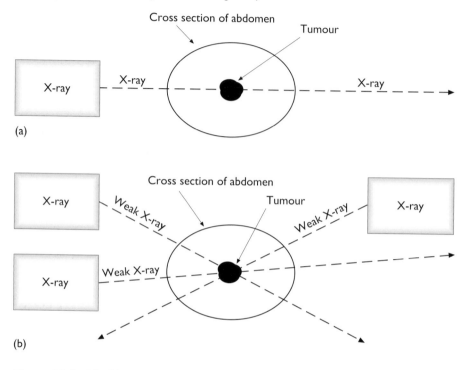

Figure 11.1   The X-ray problem

The Gestalt psychologists also investigated cases where insight was generally not achieved because participants were trapped by misleading representations that prevented solution. So-called **'set'** effects arise when learned or habitual ways of tackling a problem prevent the solver from identifying better and simpler methods, or when unwarranted assumptions are made.

Set can be induced by experience with a series of similar problems. Luchins and Luchins (1959) studied problem sets in a series of experiments using water jar problems (presented as a pencil-and-paper exercise). In these tasks participants were asked to say how one could get exactly a specified amount of water using jars of fixed capacity and an unlimited source of water. For example:

> Given three jars (A, B and C) of capacities 18, 43 and 10 units respectively, how could you obtain exactly 5 units of water?

The solution may be expressed as B – A – 2C. After a series of problems with that same general solution, participants had great difficulty with the following problem:

> Given three jars (A, B and C) of capacities 28, 76 and 3 units respectively, how could you obtain exactly 25 units of water?

In fact, the solution to this problem is quite simple (i.e. A – C) but when this problem is presented after a series of problems involving the long solution (B – A – 2C) many participants used the inefficient method and either failed to solve the problem, or took considerably longer to use the A – C method than did a control group of participants.

Figure 11.2 illustrates the 9-dot problem, often used to investigate this particular type of set effect. This problem is another example of the set effect, this time produced by the *layout* of the task. Try the following activity.

ACTIVITY 11.2

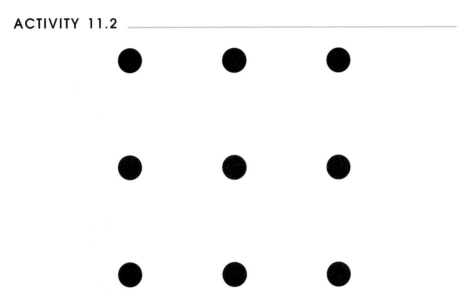

Figure 11.2   The 9-dot problem

Starting from any point, draw four straight lines (without lifting the pen from the page) so that each of the nine dots has at least one line running through it.

COMMENT

Most participants interpret the instructions as meaning that they must stay within the square shape of the dots; however, a solution is not possible without breaking this set and going outside the square. Figure 11.3 shows a solution.

A related block to effective problem solving known as **'functional fixity'** (also identified by work in the Gestalt tradition) tends to be observed when an object has to be used in a *new way*. Duncker (1945) carried out the classic study of functional fixity using the 'box' (or 'candle' problem). In this task, participants were presented with tacks, matches, three small boxes and three candles. The problem was to mount the candles side by side on a door, so that they could burn safely. For one group of participants the boxes were empty but for the other group (experimental group) the boxes were used as containers and held matches, tacks and candles. The solution is to use the boxes not as containers but as platforms and fix them to the door using the tacks. It was found that the solving rate was much higher in the control group than in the experimental group. Duncker explained this result in terms of a failure to

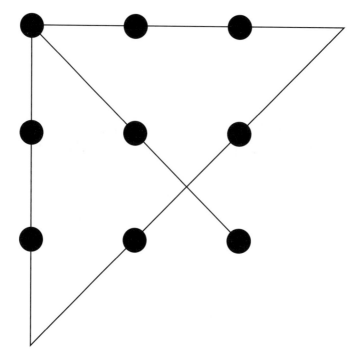

Figure 11.3   A solution to the 9-dot problem

perceive the possible platform function of the boxes when they were presented as containers. Functional fixity has been independently demonstrated and explored further in a number of later studies (e.g. Adamson and Taylor, 1954; Glucksberg and Danks, 1968). The phenomenon appears to be a robust one and is a likely source of difficulty in real-life problem solving.

There are many real-world examples of functional fixity effects. An interesting early example is the history of the steam engine. In 1775, the first Watt steam engine was used to pump water from a colliery, thus solving the problem of flooding. Before steam engines, either buckets or inefficient suction pumps had been used. It was some years before it was appreciated that steam engines could be used for locomotion as well as pumping water.

These early studies demonstrate the importance of representation and its impact upon problem solving. Later research, as we shall see in the next section, went on to examine representational effects in a wider range of problems in more depth.

2.2   Representation in puzzle problem solving

The 'representational effect' has been acknowledged for some time in problem-solving research. Simon and Hayes (1976) constructed several versions of the Tower of Hanoi problem (see Figure 11.4 below), which involves discs of varying sizes arranged on three pegs. The goal is to move the three discs from one peg (e.g. peg A) to another peg (e.g. peg C) using a sequence of legal moves. Typical constraints for this problem are that a larger disc can never be placed on top of a smaller disc (see below, though, for a variation on this rule) and only one disc may be moved at a time.

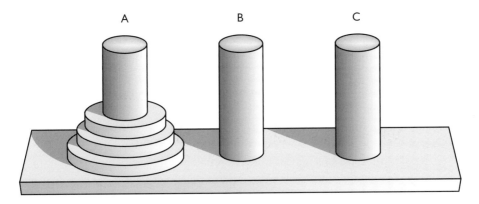

Figure 11.4   The three-disc version of the Tower of Hanoi problem

'State–space' diagrams present a given problem's state at each move juncture. Problem structures can be mapped out and compared using state–space diagrams. (The state–space diagram for the Tower of Hanoi is quite complex. See Figure 11.5, though, for another example of a state–space diagram, drawn to illustrate the structure of the simpler 'hobbits and orcs' problem, previously known as the 'missionaries and cannibals' problem.)

Problems that share the same underlying structure (i.e. have identical state–space diagrams) are said to be **isomorphic**. Simon and Hayes contrasted two structurally similar versions of a 'monster' problem. Their 'monster' problem was itself isomorphic to the Tower of Hanoi problem. In the 'move' version, differently sized monsters transferred globes of different sizes to each other according to a set of rules. In the 'change' version, monsters differing in size each held a globe, which had to be changed in size to conform to particular rules. Despite being isomorphs, the 'change' problem was considerably harder to solve than the 'move' problem. People seemed to construct rather different representations of the two problems; the representation constructed for the 'move' problem entailed simpler processing operations than that constructed for the 'change' problem.

Zhang and Norman (1994) developed a theory to account for representational effects with these sorts of problems. They designed a number of isomorphic versions of the basic Tower of Hanoi problem, and explored ways in which different rules influenced problem difficulty. Their theoretical framework distinguishes between **'internal'** and **'external'** representations. Internal problem representations entail a processing and representational burden, because the information needed to solve the problem has to be encoded and maintained in some form. Internal rules then are rules that need to be memorized, such as:

1   Only one disc may be transferred at a time.

2   A smaller disc may never be placed on top of a larger disc (notice that this is the reverse of the usual rule for this problem).

External rules differ, however, in that they are not stated explicitly in the instructions, but are implied or necessitated by the problem itself. For instance, a form of the Tower of Hanoi where discs are replaced by cups of different sizes, filled with coffee, involves an external version of Rule 2 above (a smaller cup would fall into the larger cup, spilling coffee). The environment then can provide constraints, so some rules need not be internalized. Size and location are properties that need not be internally represented, since differences in size and location are readily perceived. However, dimensional information may be represented internally. For instance, if colour is used to represent some task-relevant information, then the relationships between colours and information may have to be learned.

External representations appear to make problem solving easier, although they also change the nature of the task. We return to this point later in Section 5 in our examination of the relationship between problem solving and learning.

Some problem representations have attributes that may hamper (or facilitate) problem solving. Once a problem has been encoded and represented, problem solving may be described as a search through a set of possible moves (or 'problem space').

2.3 The information-processing approach: problem solving as search

Solving a problem may require us to find a suitable sequence of actions drawn from a small set of actions (for instance, moving a series of coloured tiles around a small board until they form a particular pattern or picture). Alternatively, solving some problems may entail selecting or discovering a single action from a large set, for example, using one object that can meet the goal from all objects known to the solver. Within the information-processing approach, problem solving is generally seen as a **search** process.

The initiator of problem solving is a current goal, that is, a representation of a state that is desired but not currently true. Therefore, goals direct the course of thinking by guiding retrieval of goal-relevant material and aiding in the assessment of directions of search as promising or not. Search may proceed in a **forwards** direction from the starting state by generating possible actions, evaluating the results of those actions and then choosing for further exploration those with best outcomes when assessed against the goal. Search may also proceed **backwards** from the goal by using a **problem reduction** or **means–ends** approach, which breaks down the overall goal into subgoals that should be easier to achieve.

For example, the problem of booking a trip to New York from London might be broken down (or 'reduced') into subgoals that could include 'buying a ticket' and 'getting our passports updated'. 'Buying a ticket' can be broken down further into subgoals such as 'finding an airline' and 'deciding on travel dates' (which in turn can be broken down further still to 'check availability of seats'). The initial goal of getting to New York cannot be achieved until all the steps, and their required conditions, have been identified. The problem is solved by working 'backwards' from the goal, starting with the first subgoal for which the conditions may be met (e.g. establishing that there are seats available for the date on which we want to travel and selecting these), and then completing other subgoals until the major goal is achieved and the trip is booked.

A number of studies of search in problem solving have used the Tower of London task (which is similar to the Tower of Hanoi). The problem has a number of variants but basically requires participants to first plan out how to move a set of coloured same-sized discs arranged over three pegs from a starting pattern to a target pattern by moving only one disc at a time. Search processes are assumed to involve the holding of goals and intermediate results in the limited-capacity working memory (see Chapter 5).

Gilhooly *et al.* (1999) studied individuals thinking aloud while solving the Tower of London problem. Their results suggest that working memory limitations tend to shape search patterns so that typically one action is selected from those available at each step. Search builds up a limited length of sequence before returning to the start state and re-exploring. (This process of searching depth first to a certain limit, then backing up and systematically searching all branches of the search tree to the depth limit is known as 'progressive deepening'.) Gilhooly *et al.* found that the general strategy used was means–ends analysis, which generated a search pattern focused on reducing differences between the current state and the goal state. Means–ends analysis has been generally found to be the typical approach in the related Tower of Hanoi problem (Luger, 1976).

Similar results, indicating very focused mental search, have also arisen from studies of the hobbits and orcs task (Thomas, 1974; Simon and Reed, 1976) and the water jars task (Atwood and Polson, 1976). The state–space diagram for the hobbits and orcs task (Figure 11.5) appears in Box 11.2 (overleaf).

Means–ends analysis typically involves reducing differences between the current state and the goal state, and so moves that bring the solver closer to the goal tend to be preferred. Thomas (1974) found that participants solving the hobbits and orcs problem found the transition from State 110 to State 221 (see Figure 11.5) especially problematic. The move involves bringing back one hobbit and one orc, which seems at odds with the general strategy of moving closer and closer towards the goal.

The water jars problem has also been used to examine search in problem solving. The problem requires participants to find a way of moving water between jars of given capacities from a starting state in which the largest is full to a goal state in which the water is distributed in a particular way over the three jars.

Response data from both the hobbits and orcs and the water jugs problems suggest a model in which solvers look ahead, evaluating a few possible steps at each point in terms of whether they appear to lead to new states closer to the goal or not. For example, at State 331, in Figure 11.5, a solver could look ahead to the next move and evaluate two possibilities, which would move them either to State 220 or State 310. Solvers appear to prefer moves that seem to take them closer to the goal, repeating the entire procedure until the goal is reached (Jeffries *et al.*, 1977). The preference for new states is a heuristic to avoid looping (or revisiting old states in a particular sequence, or cycle), as it is all too easy in these tasks to go round in circles! Avoiding loops is also important in the Tower of London task and Davies (2000) found that participants did not simply rely on

── 11.2 ──

The hobbits and orcs task

The hobbits and orcs task requires participants to find a way of transporting three hobbits and three orcs safely across a river in a boat. The boat can only hold two creatures at a time and on either side of the river the orcs must never outnumber the hobbits at any time.

In this state–space diagram (see Figure 11.5), each box represents a single state of the task. The number of hobbits (H) and orcs (O) on the left- and right-hand side of each box indicate the number of hobbits and orcs on the left and right banks of the river at any given time. Each state is labelled with a three-digit number, with the first digit representing the number of hobbits, the second the number of orcs and the third the number of boats all on the left bank of the river. So, for example, State 331 (near top left) indicates the start of the problem, with three hobbits, three orcs and the boat all on the left bank of the river. State 000 (top right) is the solution state, with all six creatures and the boat transported to the opposite side.

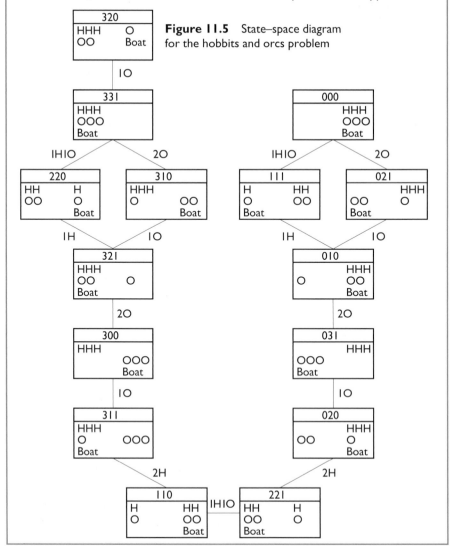

Figure 11.5   State–space diagram for the hobbits and orcs problem

memory to judge whether a state had been encountered previously but would seek to infer whether it could have been a precursor of the present state. If the state in question could not have been a precursor then it was safe to assume that it was new.

2.4   Information-processing approaches to insight

Sometimes, a change of representation may be required in order to solve problems that initially induce unhelpful ways of representing the problem. As we discussed earlier, the Gestalt school in the 1920s and 1930s regarded such restructuring as the basis of insight into difficult problems. Though the Gestalt approach was criticized for a lack of clarity in explaining how restructuring took place, Ohlsson (1992) offered some suggestions as to how restructuring might occur.

Ohlsson (1992) proposed that when working on a problem people generate possible actions or **operators** from long-term memory, which are cued by the problem representation. Applying the operators to the current problem state leads to a new problem state, which in turn elicits further possible operators. In this way, a problem with a useful initial representation may be solved as eventually a state is reached from which cued operators lead to the goal. However, if the initial representation is misleading, then a state will be reached in which no new useful operators can be retrieved. Subjectively, we experience this state, labelled an **impasse**, as a mental 'blank'; we cannot think of anything new to try. Ohlsson suggests that impasses can be overcome by changing the problem representation so that new operators can be cued, retrieved and tried out. Specifically, Ohlsson proposed three ways in which the problem representation could be changed or re-structured and these are (1) **elaboration**, (2) **re-encoding** and (3) **constraint relaxation**.

Elaboration involves adding information to the representation by observing previously unnoticed features. For example, to use the matchbox tray in solving the 'candle' problem (Duncker, 1945), discussed earlier, the solver has to notice the possible use of the tray as a platform.

Re-encoding involves changing the encoding rather than simply adding new information. For example, how could a man have legally married 20 women in one month in a country where polygamy is illegal and none of the women have died or been divorced? To solve this, we have to change the encoding of 'married' from the man becoming husband to each woman to the man causing others to become married to each other, for example, the man in question could be a minister who is entitled to perform marriage ceremonies.

Constraint relaxation involves making the goal requirements less restrictive than initially assumed. For example, one source of difficulty in the 9-dot problem is the tendency to over-restrict the goal so that the four lines are kept within the square array of dots; removing (or relaxing) this constraint is necessary for a solution. Chronicle et al. (2001) found that another major source of difficulty with the 9-dot problem is that people tend to apply a heuristic search process for lines that cancel as many dots as possible; such a search process generates three lines within the square and the failure of the approach would only be realized with an extended look-ahead. Chronicle et al. argue that Ohlsson's re-encoding (where the problem representation is altered) is required: hence, the general failure of attempts to facilitate performance by giving hints about the need to move outside the square.

A further demonstration of the role of constraint relaxation comes from studies by Knoblich *et al.* (1999) of matchstick algebra problems. Examples of these types of problem are as follows: make the equations below, involving Roman numerals, true by moving a single stick (see Figure 11.6).

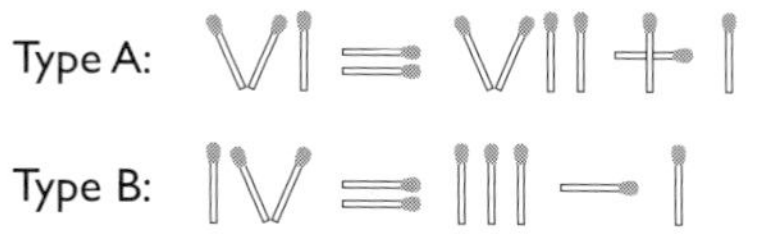

Type A: $VI = VII + I$

Type B: $IV = III - I$

Figure 11.6 Matchstick algebra problem

There are large differences in solution times and rates for these types of problems, with Type A being easier than Type B. In the Type A example, the rightmost stick from the 'VII' is moved to the right of 'VI'. This gives 'VII = VI + I', which is true. In the Type B problem, the operators '=' and '−' are changed by moving one of the horizontal sticks from the '=' and placing it over the '−' to make the true equation 'IV − III = I'. Knoblich *et al.* argue that it is harder to break the constraint on changing operators than on changing number values.

Summary of Section 2

- Problem solving begins with a problem representation.
- The information-processing approach analyses problem solving in terms of search within the space of possibilities arising from a particular way of representing the problem.
- Manipulating instructions and the appearance of problems appears to influence the nature of the problem representation constructed, which in turn can affect the ease with which the problem may be solved.
- Some representations of supposedly 'simple' problems render the problems extremely difficult to solve.

3   Analogical problem solving

As we saw in the previous section, some problems we encounter are novel and difficult to solve even when they require a minimum of background knowledge and experience. However, we often encounter problems that are rather similar to problems we have tackled previously. Even if a solution to a new problem is not known, we may know and be reminded of the solution to similar problems and be able to use that known solution to suggest a solution to the new problem. That is, we may be guided to solution by the use of an analogy.

3.1   Analogies in problem solving

Spellman and Holyoak (1992) found that experimental participants readily accepted analogies of the kind often used in discussions of international politics. For example, when Saddam Hussein attacked Kuwait in 1990, many commentators likened him to Adolf Hitler and George Bush Snr to Winston Churchill. Similarly, some regarded the 'Domino' theory – the US government's belief that if one Asian country fell to communism then others would quickly follow – as compelling justification for the war on Vietnam.

In science, analogies have often been used to develop understanding. For example, the heart has been seen as analogous to a water pump and atomic structure as similar to that of the solar system. In cognitive psychology, we hope that analogies between human and computer information processing will likewise prove useful.

Studies of analogy use in problem solving have often used Duncker's X-ray problem, which you met in Section 2, as the target problem. You may remember that the problem was to use rays to destroy a tumour in the centre of a body without destroying healthy tissue. The solution was to converge a number of weak rays on the tumour, which would then have a cumulative effect at that point. Gick and Holyoak (1980) gave their participants an analogous (or 'base') story about a general seeking to take a castle who had to divide his forces into small groups who then attacked the castle simultaneously on all sides. Participants were then given the X-ray problem, with and without a hint. The hint indicated that solvers should try to use the story to solve the X-ray problem. A control group did not receive the analogue before tackling the X-ray problem. Rate of solving was low for participants who had not been given the analogue, somewhat higher when the analogue alone had been given and markedly higher for the analogue followed by a hint.

Later studies (Holyoak and Koh, 1987; Keane, 1988) indicated that the closer the base story is in surface features to the target problem, the more transfer is likely. For example, Keane found that a very close analogy of a surgeon treating a brain tumour by radiation was much more often retrieved and used in tackling the X-ray problem, even after a week's delay, than was the more remotely analogous story of the general dividing his forces.

Anolli *et al.* (2001) found that retrieval of a remote analogy was ineffective in itself without provision of a hint that the analogy contained a useful clue to solution. In a series of seven studies little benefit in terms of solving was found for simply reminding participants of the analogous story without a hint to use the story. However, retrieval plus a hint was very effective.

Dunbar (2001) has noted that there is an *analogical paradox*; the paradox is that in real life use of abstract analogies that depend on deep structural similarities is common, while in laboratory studies participants tend to use superficial features and have difficulty with deeper forms of analogy. Blanchette and Dunbar (2000) found that participants who were asked to produce analogies that could be used in arguments about whether or not drastic cuts should be made in public spending during a budgetary crisis readily produced deep analogies that drew on a range of content areas having little superficial resemblance to political matters. Blanchette and Dunbar proposed that generating analogies requires participants to use structural rather than superficial features; also, the subject matter of the naturalistic analogy studies has been familiar and understood in some depth. In typical laboratory studies, the material is not highly familiar and there is little pressure to encode the base story in a deep way. A possible interpretation of Anolli *et al.*'s (2001) results (namely, target problem solution is increased by reminding of the base story plus a hint that the analogy contained a useful clue to solution) is that the hint encouraged a deeper structural representation of the base story, which in turn facilitates application of the analogy.

3.2   How do analogies work?

The first detailed theory of how people apply analogies in problem solving was the 'structure-mapping' theory (Gentner, 1983; Gentner and Markman, 1997; Gentner *et al.*, 2001). According to this theory, there is a process of **analogical mapping** whereby a **structural alignment** is established between the representations of the base and the target. That is to say, explicit correspondences are established between the represented elements and relationships in the two situations. As an example, consider the solar system analogy of the atom. Typically, the solar system would be represented as having two types of object (the sun and the planets) and these exhibit various properties and relationships (e.g. sun is more massive than planets; planets orbit the sun). The analogy would align the sun with the nucleus of the atom and the planets with electrons. Aspects of the solar system model that do not map are omitted (e.g. no equivalent of moons in the atom). Higher-order relationships also guide the alignment process. Thus, there is a higher-order relationship such that less massive objects orbit more massive objects; this guides the inference from the solar system analogy that the electrons revolve around the nucleus. Falkenhaimer *et al.* (1986) have successfully implemented the detailed model as a computer model known as the 'structure mapping engine' (SME).

Gentner and Gentner (1983) showed that different base analogies were common for understanding electrical flow. These influenced how well people solved different problems regarding electrical flow through circuits with batteries and resistors arranged in parallel or in series. The main analogies were electricity as a flow of fluid through pipes or as a flow of crowds through passageways. Example differences between the two analogical mappings are that in the fluid analogy electrical resistance would be mapped to pipe width while in the crowd analogy resistance is mapped to gates in the passageway. People who used the fluid analogy performed better on battery problems; people who used crowd analogies were better on resistor problems. People pre-trained on both the analogies also showed similar results. A number of models similar to the structure mapping theory have been proposed including the 'analogical constraint mapping engine' (ACME) (Holyoak and Thagard, 1989) and the 'incremental analogy machine' (IAM) (Keane, 1994).

Summary of Section 3

- Research on analogical problem solving illustrates a paradox: we often cannot help but be reminded of problems similar to one we presently face. However, we often fail to see the crucial relationships between a current problem and one we have previously encountered.
- Representation seems to be at the core of the paradox.

4 'Complex' problem solving

While research on the ways in which we solve puzzles and analogies has mapped out the terrain to a certain extent, it should be apparent that understanding how people solve the relatively 'knowledge-lean' problems we have looked at so far is only a part of the picture. Many problems require a considerable amount of knowledge if they are to be solved successfully. This section focuses on 'complex' problem solving, or problem solving that requires an extensive knowledge base. Does knowledge of a domain affect problem representation, and hence the likelihood with which a problem will be solved? Do problem representations change as knowledge is acquired and as skill develops? Can we characterize the development of skill in problem solving? Researchers have turned their attention to how experts and novices solve problems in their attempts to try to answer these questions.

While it may seem obvious that experts know more than novices, until relatively recently the layperson's view of the expert might well have encapsulated the view that experts owe their skill to superior mental capacities, rather than to a vast body of specialist knowledge. The shift in emphasis began with some ground-breaking research on chess skill. We shall examine this work in some detail, because much of the later research on expert and novice problem solving developed from the early chess studies, and because findings obtained in later studies tend to echo those of the chess experiments described below.

First, some words on terminology. Researchers have examined both **adversary** and **non-adversary** problem solving. Chess play is an example of adversarial problem solving, because the game of chess involves an opponent. Code breaking, de-bugging computer programs and medical diagnosis are examples of non-adversarial problem domains. Those engaged in adversary problem solving then must consider not only their own possible actions, but also those of an opponent.

4.1   The role of knowledge in expert problem solving

4.1.1   Early chess studies

De Groot (1946/1965) carried out a series of now classic studies of chess players. These were extremely significant and heralded the start of a new emphasis on knowledge in skilled problem solving. Information processing had taken centre stage as the dominant paradigm and many researchers busied themselves with the construction of models of cognitive processors and processes. Up until then, it had been implicitly, if not explicitly, assumed that skilled problem solvers must have superior information-processing capabilities. De Groot tested this assumption in a novel way.

De Groot asked five grand masters (the highest skill level attainable in chess) and five skilled players to think aloud as they studied a chessboard and chose a move. If information-processing capacities are a key determinant of expertise, then we would expect to find the grand master players, with their superior capacities, searching further ahead and conducting broader searches for candidate moves. The evidence from the think-aloud protocols however was surprising and revealed no reliable quantitative differences at all between the grand masters and the highly skilled players. The only difference that did emerge between the two groups was unremarkable – the grand masters ultimately chose better moves.

De Groot also employed what is known as a 'recall–reconstruction' paradigm (see Box 11.3). He showed chess players chessboards with pieces arranged from actual games. The boards were presented to players for 2–15 seconds, and then removed. He then asked the chess players to reconstruct the board positions from memory. The chess masters could reconstruct the boards almost without error (91 per cent of pieces correctly replaced), whereas the poorer players averaged only 41 per cent correct. Skill level then was linked to the amount of information remembered about the chessboard positions.

Chase and Simon (1973b) devised a second task, where players had to reconstruct a chessboard while the board they had to correctly match was still in view. Although this may seem an odd task, the point was to find out how many pieces were placed on the target board after each glance, what those pieces were, and how much time elapsed between placing pieces on the board. Chase and Simon found that the strongest chess players replaced more chess pieces on the board following each glance, replaced pieces more quickly and tended to replace pieces together that bore some meaningful relationship to each other than did the weaker players. These findings suggested that experts not only possess more knowledge about their domain of expertise, but that their knowledge is organized in more meaningful and readily accessible ways.

These early studies of chess skill showed that skill depended at least in part on the acquisition of domain knowledge, and stimulated a vast amount of research on the nature of expert problem solving and the relationship between knowledge and skill. We summarize some of the key studies below. These studies sought to characterize the empirical phenomena associated with skill in problem solving, phenomena that theories of skill acquisition and problem solving would ultimately have to accommodate and explain.

─ 11.3 ──────────────────────────── Research study ─

The recall–reconstruction paradigm in chess

Chase and Simon (1973a) extended the basic chessboard recall–reconstruction paradigm, originally used by Lemmens and Jongman in an unpublished study of 1964. In one study, Chase and Simon presented boards with between 20 and 22 chess pieces arranged on them to three chess players (a master, a Class A [highly skilled] player and a novice). Some of the boards were presented with chess pieces arranged as they might be in a real game (see Figure 11.7), while others were presented with the chess pieces arranged at random.

Figure 11.7 A chessboard position from a real game

Source: adapted from Chase and Simon, 1973a

Players were given five seconds to study each board. The board was then covered up, and each player was asked to reconstruct on another board the position just seen. Results from the first memory trial showed that the master player was much better (16 pieces replaced correctly) at accurately replacing the chess pieces than both the Class A player (8 pieces replaced correctly) and the novice player (only 4 pieces replaced correctly). The skilled players' advantage only held for chessboards with pieces placed in plausible, real-game positions. When the different players were asked to reconstruct the random boards from memory, all players performed equally poorly, correctly replacing only a small proportion of pieces. This suggested a connection between memory for meaningful patterns and problem-solving skill.

4.1.2   Experts work forwards

Larkin *et al.* (1980) were interested in possible strategic differences between experts and novices. Experts know more than novices, but do they also use qualitatively different problem-solving strategies to novices? They asked expert and novice physicists to solve a range of physics problems. Using protocol analysis, they found that experts tended to use a **working forwards** strategy, beginning with information given in the problem statement and using that to derive a solution. Novices, on the other hand, used a **working backwards** strategy (means–ends analysis), starting with the goal, or quantity to be solved, and working backwards from that to the given information, until they were able to solve one part of the problem. Novices then typically retraced their steps, working forwards until the problem was solved.

Why do experts and novices use different problem-solving strategies? It appears that experts use their domain knowledge to generate a good problem representation, which supports the use of a working forwards strategy. In the absence of detailed knowledge about the relationships between variables relevant to the problem, novices seem to have no option but to fall back on means–ends analysis, or even trial and error learning.

4.1.3   Experts have better problem representations

Chi *et al.* (1982) tackled the issue of problem representation and categorization by experts and novices. Experts know more and they use distinct problem-solving strategies. Is expert problem solving also supported by more effective ways of representing and categorizing problems? Chi *et al.* asked expert and novice physicists to think aloud as they categorized physics problems on the basis of similarities in terms of how the problems might be solved. Unusually, then, participants did not actually have to solve the problems.

The two skill groups did not differ on quantitative measures, such as number of categories or time to categorize. This showed that novices were not limited in their capacity to discriminate problems. However, there were clear qualitative differences in the nature of the categories into which problems were sorted. Novices referred to objects and key words contained in the problem (such as 'levers' and 'pulleys'), and appeared to use these irrelevant 'surface structure' details as a basis for categorization. Experts, on the other hand, referred to the physics principles and laws (the 'deep structure') that were needed to solve the problems in their justifications. Problems that could be solved by reference to the same principle or law were perceived by the experts to be similar and were grouped together. Novices tended to group together problems that were similar in 'surface structure', while experts sorted problems on the basis of similarity in 'deep structure'. It seems then that experts are aware of commonalities between problems in terms of how they might be solved.

Schoenfeld and Herrmann (1982) carried out a rather similar study, looking at mathematical problem categorization among mathematics professors and novices. Their participants read through the set of problems and then grouped together those problems they considered to be mathematically similar. The study confirmed the findings of Chi *et al.* (1982), with novices sorting the problems on the basis of superficial details, or surface structure, and the professors sorting problems on the basis of similarities in solution methods, or deep structure. (You will notice some similarities here with the discussion in Chapter 9 of how different groups of people categorized trees.)

Chi *et al.* found in their study that experts were able to perceive an appropriate solution method within 45 seconds. This suggests that knowledge useful for a particular problem is accessed, or becomes available, when a problem is categorized as a specific type. These categories may correspond to problem schemata or 'packets' of knowledge that can be used to solve a particular type of problem.

4.1.4   Experts become expert through extensive practice

It is often said that 'practice makes perfect'. In the context of problem solving, researchers noticed many years ago that performance improves with practice in a very systematic and predictable fashion. What is particularly interesting is the observation that, regardless of what is being learned, performance improves with practice in a highly predictable way. The relationship, known as the 'power law of practice', has been known for a long time, though there is an ongoing debate as to whether practice learning data are best fit by a power function, or some other function. The relationship shows up in Snoddy's (1926) study of mirror-tracing of visual mazes. It appears in perceptual tasks such as Kolers' (1975) studies on mirror-reading (where text is transformed), in pattern recognition (Neisser *et al.*, 1963), and in tasks from the domain of human–computer interaction (e.g. Card *et al.*, 1983).

Practice then seems to be a factor in the development of skill. The improvement in performance with practice applies over a wide range of activities that are better described as 'tasks' and which include problem-solving tasks, as well as other kinds of tasks (for example, juggling and search tasks). Why does performance improve with practice? Three main classes of explanation have been proposed:

1   Individual task components are executed more efficiently.

2   Sequences of task components are executed more efficiently.

3   Qualitative changes occur in representations of task structure.

The first two explanations argue that performance improves with practice because the piecemeal recovery of declarative knowledge into working memory is reduced, and because we learn to run off sequences of procedures in ever greater units or chunks. The third explanation asserts that performance improves because the nature of the task changes, either because the task is restructured or because we shift from algorithm-based to memory-based processing (an example of the latter is Logan's [1988] 'instance' theory of automaticity).

How much practice is needed to achieve excellence? Ericsson *et al.* (1993) have given ten years as a ballpark figure for attaining high levels of performance in a variety of areas (e.g. chess, mathematics and violin playing). In a review of the literature on practice and performance, Ericsson (1991) has suggested that it takes at least ten years to reach the international level of performance in sports, the arts and sciences. Simon and Chase (1973) estimated that it took some 3,000 hours' practice to become an expert and around 30,000 hours to become a chess master. The preparation period may often commence at an early age, possibly because it takes so long to acquire the necessary knowledge. While it clearly takes a long time to attain very high levels of performance, it is nevertheless possible to train subjects to improve on their previous best performance. Ericsson and Harris (1990) trained an individual who was not a chess player over a period of 50 hours to recognize chess positions almost as accurately as some chess masters.

However, as Ericsson and Polson (1988) found, practice itself is not a guarantee of superior performance. In their study, the waiter most skilled in remembering orders used more effective encoding strategies and achieved much better performance than his equally experienced counterparts, who did not use the same optimal encoding strategies to remember dinner orders. This means that something else must mediate between practice and performance.

What appears to be critically important is not how much practice individuals have, but what they actually do while they are practising the skill. If it takes a very long time to become expert, then clearly we need to document what individuals do over a longer time scale than is usually considered. We return to this point in Section 5.2 when we explore individual differences in problem-solving performance.

4.2   A modal model of expertise?

The early chess studies triggered a vast amount of research that used what became known as the 'expert–novice' paradigm. The model of chess expertise that emerged became known as the 'pattern recognition hypothesis', because it assumed that skilled performance depended upon the ability to access previously learned patterns, such as configurations of chess pieces on a board, from long-term memory.

The general idea that performance depends upon a large body of highly structured domain-relevant knowledge and skill has been borrowed by researchers examining skill-related differences in non-adversarial domains such as physics (Chi *et al.*, 1982), mathematical problem solving (Schoenfeld and Herrmann, 1982), computer programming (McKeithen *et al.*, 1981) and political science problem solving (Voss *et al.*, 1983). Results consistently showed a link between expertise and knowledge, suggesting that a 'modal model' of expertise was emerging, whereby expertise depends upon the acquisition and organization in long-term memory of domain-relevant knowledge and skill.

Although supported by the data, these initial observations about expertise seem descriptive and lack explanatory power. Sternberg (1995) is but one researcher to have commented upon this. Over-use of the paradigm appeared to constrain the nature of the findings to a series of observations about experts 'knowing more' than novices. Accounting for these findings was nonetheless a challenge for theories of skill acquisition, but many researchers recognized that there was more to expertise than the gradual accumulation of domain-specific knowledge.

As we shall see in the next section, when researchers began to explore different questions about the nature of expertise and about skill acquisition, some findings emerged that challenged the prevailing view of expertise while at the same time yielding valuable insights into the relationship between memory and skill, and the development of expertise itself.

Summary of Section 4

- On memory tests for information from their domain of expertise, experts remember more than novices.
- Experts are superior to novices in knowledge rather than in basic capacities.
- Experts use a working forwards strategy, while novices tend to work backwards.
- Experts construct better problem representations than novices.
- Experts become expert through extensive practice.

5   Prospects for problem-solving research

In this section, we focus on research that points to some limitations of the general model of expertise outlined above, and we go on to discuss some of the directions research in problem solving has been taking.

5.1   Does expertise transfer?

It is perhaps ironic that early indications that all was not well with the modal model of expertise came from research on chess skill, which had originally played such a large part in stimulating research on expert and novice problem solving.

5.1.1   Chess skill and memory

The classic chess recall–reconstruction experiments (as discussed in Box 11.3 above) showed that the master chess players' memory advantage held only for meaningful chess positions, suggesting that memory determines chess skill. However, subsequent studies of expert chess play question this conclusion and suggest that memory cannot be the sole determinant of skill (Holding, 1985).

For instance, Holding and Reynolds (1982) sought to determine whether skill differences could be shown in the absence of differences in memory. They asked players differing in their skill ratings to memorize random positions. Next, players were asked to select the best continuation moves. Skill level was unrelated to recall of random positions, replicating the findings of de Groot (1965). However, the interesting finding is that the number of best moves chosen correlated positively with playing strength. Therefore, differences in memory for chess patterns cannot account for the finding that better players chose more good moves from random starting states. This suggests that, for highly skilled chess players at least, something other than memory for highly familiar configurations of chess pieces may be implicated in chess skill. An additional factor is likely to be the ability to evaluate a given position.

Holding (1979) set out to examine the relationship between skill level and evaluation among chess players. He presented fifty players varying in skill level (from Class A players, the strongest, to Class E players, the weakest) with a set of test positions and asked them to indicate which side had the advantage, and to rate the strength of the advantage. The results confirmed that the ability to evaluate chess positions is an important dimension of chess skill. Stronger players were more often right about the outcomes of the games from which the test positions were taken. Also, the subjects were asked to suggest what they thought was the best move in each position. The average number of times that the players' move choices corresponded with the grand master move in the actual games varied systematically with rating class (A: 3.6; B: 3.0; C: 2.9; D: 2.3; and E: 1.6). Therefore, the higher-rated players made more good moves and fewer evaluation errors.

5.1.2   The role of general and specific methods

Schraagen (1993) carried out a more detailed examination of the problem-solving performance of different groups of experts and novices. Most studies of expertise have shown that experts draw upon a large body of domain knowledge when asked to solve a problem from their domain of expertise. Anderson's (1983) ACT* theory predicts that when domain knowledge is lacking, experts should fall back on general strategies, or 'weak methods'. Schraagen asked his participants to design an experiment in the area of sensory psychology. He compared the reasoning of domain experts (psychologists with around 10 years' experience in designing experiments in the area of sensory psychology) with 'design' experts (psychologists with around 10 years' experience in designing psychology experiments in general). The problem facing subjects was to design an experiment to investigate what people taste when they drink a given brand of cola. While domain knowledge was important (the domain experts generated better solutions), the form of the design experts' reasoning was comparable to that of the domain experts. When knowledge is lacking, it seems that there may be skills of intermediate generality that do transfer. These findings are at odds with theoretical frameworks that argue for the domain specificity of expertise.

Schunn and Anderson (1999) carried out a similar study to examine whether expert scientists from different domains shared some skills. They asked domain experts (psychologists skilled in designing memory experiments), task experts (psychologists skilled in areas other than memory research) and undergraduate students studying different courses to think aloud while designing an experiment to investigate an unexplained aspect of memory. Analysis of protocols and performance data showed that the domain experts designed the best experiments. Domain experts and task experts differed in terms of domain-specific skills, while task experts and undergraduates differed on domain-general skills. Through the analysis of verbal protocols, the researchers were able to identify a much larger set of domain-general skills that are important in scientific reasoning.

5.2   Individual differences

The expert–novice paradigm contrasts the performance of experts and novices solving the same set of problems drawn from a given domain. Although the problems used are likely to be non-trivial to the novices, they scarcely present a problem in any meaningful sense to the experts. This is necessarily so because if the problems were truly challenging for the experts, novices would not be able to even begin to solve them. However, if the experts have not really been taxed with a 'problem', have we learned anything at all about expert problem solving? The expert–novice paradigm also tends to imply that novices know nothing, or know little of relevance. As we shall see, novices do not approach novel problems with 'empty heads'. They bring to bear whatever knowledge and strategies they are able to and, in doing so, it is clear that some novices are better learners than others. We shall now examine the extent to which implicit assumptions about the homogeneity of both novice and expert groups are reasonable.

5.2.1   Are all learners the same?

Novices have tended to be described in terms of what they do not have, or do not do. A more positive approach is to examine what novices *can* do, and ways in which they differ. In so doing, this work shifts the emphasis from problem-solving performance to learning and the acquisition of skill in problem solving. Models and theories of problem-solving performance must not only account for differences between skilled and less-skilled individuals, they must also explain how skill is acquired.

Some interesting work has examined differences between good and poor learners, and this has shed some light on what might mediate between practice and performance. Many of us will have noticed that people tend to differ in rate of learning. While it is an over-simplification to suggest that novices start with a blank slate, most novices begin from a position of not having much of the skill in question. If knowledge relevant to the skill does not mediate or support their performance early on, then what does?

Thorndyke and Stasz (1980) examined learning strategies differentiating good from poor learners of map information. Good learners used more efficient techniques for encoding spatial information, more accurately determined what they knew and what they had yet to learn, and were better able to focus their attention on map elements they had not yet learned. Green and Gilhooly (1990) conducted a similar experiment, studying novices learning to use a statistical package on a mainframe computer. Good learners tended to adopt an exploratory approach to learning, made better use of worked examples from handouts and evaluated their learning. Slower learners tended to over-use worked examples, generated and tested more erroneous hypotheses and seemed to either ignore, or fail to use, error feedback. Both these studies suggest that good learners make effective use of **metacognitive** processes and strategies.

Chi *et al.* (1989) and Chi *et al.* (1994) have been especially interested in the role played by explanation in learning and, in particular, whether novices may be distinguished by the extent to which they generate explanations while solving problems. In their studies, they equated students for background knowledge (of physics and biology) and then analysed the think-aloud protocols students produced as they studied the problems. In one study, good learners seemed to spontaneously self-explain more than poor learners. Good learners used the examples they had studied to check their solutions whereas poor learners used the examples to help them to find solutions. Chi *et al.* (1994) showed that prompting students to self-explain as they studied led to better problem solving than simply asking students to study the materials. Renkl (1997) showed that the self-explaining effect is not simply due to some students spending longer studying. In a study that controlled for time-on-task, Renkl found that quality of self-explanations reliably predicted learning success. Generating self-explanations then, whether spontaneously or in response to a prompt to do so, seems to serve an elaborating role in early learning, aiding understanding and schema development. Schema development is of course central to skill development.

5.2.2   Can we enhance the rate of skill acquisition?

Sweller and his colleagues (Sweller, 1988; Sweller *et al.*, 1983) have demonstrated that schema acquisition can be retarded by the use of means–ends analysis. Paradoxically, the very strategy that novices appear to rely on in early learning (recall Section 4.1.2, and the study by Larkin *et al.*, 1980) has been shown to inhibit knowledge acquisition. Sweller *et al.* hypothesized that an emphasis on a goal (which occurs with the means–ends analysis strategy) might overload the system, leaving few resources available for inducing relevant schematic knowledge. They tested this hypothesis by de-emphasizing the goal in a set of kinematics (a branch of physics) problems given to one group of novices. For example, one problem ended in the following way: 'In 18 sec a racing car can start from rest and travel 305.1 m. Calculate the value of as many variables as you can.'

A second group of novices received the same problems, but the final sentence was altered to include a specific goal:

'In 18 sec a racing car can start from rest and travel 305.1 m. What speed will it reach?'

Participants who were given the no-goal problems switched more swiftly to a working forwards strategy than did novices who were given the goal problems. One interpretation of these findings is that the presence of a goal biases individuals towards the use of a means–ends strategy, which imposes high processing demands. This would have the effect of reducing the available resources for acquiring knowledge about the relationships among principles. De-emphasizing the goal then could work by reducing working memory load, thereby freeing resources. This would facilitate schema acquisition, thereby enhancing learning.

There is an alternative explanation for the facilitating effect of reduced goal specificity on learning. Vollmeyer *et al.* (1996) examined the effects of goal specificity and systematicity of learning strategy in learning and transfer within a complex dynamic system. Their findings were consistent with Sweller's claim that general problem-solving methods might enable a person to attain a specific goal, but do not promote learning of the overall structure of a problem space. Burns and Vollmeyer (2002) have taken this work further, and have shown that non-specific goals seem to aid learning by encouraging more hypothesis testing. Their work shows that it seems to be hypothesis testing, rather than the reduction in goal specificity, that encourages learning.

There may be another dimension to the effects of goal specificity on learning and problem solving. Green (2002) argued that reducing goal specificity also has the effect of altering the way in which a problem comes to be represented. In her experiment, it was the nature of the problem representation that was crucial to performance, rather than the reduction in goal specificity. Green also points out that it is important to distinguish learning from problem solving. Instructions that led to swift learning seemed to result in poor problem solving, while instructions that seemed to lead to slower learning paid off later on by giving rise to better problem solving. Different instructions influence the nature of the task or problem representation, and this in turn affects both learning and problem-solving performance. This echoes the point we made earlier with regard to the impact of internal and external representations upon learning and problem solving.

Some recent studies by Haider and Frensch (1996, 1999a and b) have focused on ways in which we learn to ignore task-irrelevant information, and process only task-relevant information. Haider and Frensch have shown that as we become more skilled, we typically learn to ignore redundant information. Not all individuals behave in the same way though. In one of their studies, they found that some individuals fail to reduce the amount of information heeded, even after extended practice. Green and Wright (2003) have extended these findings, examining what happens when two information sources associated with one event are presented. When individuals have a choice of information sources relevant to the task, they tend to prefer to use the first encountered source. Information reduction then serves to reduce processing of task-irrelevant, as well as duplicated (but possibly task-relevant) information. The assumption that we come to process less information is at odds with some theories of skill acquisition like ACT* and ACT-R.

The studies we have discussed in this section provide some clues as to how individuals learn to solve problems more effectively. What is apparent is that learners do not all behave in the same way. Certain learning procedures and strategies facilitate knowledge acquisition, and there is evidence that problem representation again plays a key role.

Novices seem to differ from each other then, and their rates of learning can vary. Do experts form a homogeneous group? We examine this question now.

5.2.3 Do experts differ?

It is sometimes tacitly assumed that experts form a homogeneous group, with considerable overlap among experts in what they know. If this is the case, then we may safely generalize from studies of experts, and talk about 'typical' expert problem-solving behaviour. However, it is likely that the assumption of homogeneity is at best an over-simplification. Draper (1984) carried out a study of expertise in UNIX (a computer operating system that uses brief commands, often in the form of consonant strings, e.g. 'LS' [lists all the files in the current directory]). He found that UNIX users share some knowledge of UNIX commands, but mostly they use different commands from each other. Further, the size of their vocabulary of commands varies greatly from individual to individual. If it was simply the case that experts knew more than novices, then we might expect the expert user's vocabulary of UNIX commands to subsume the novice user's vocabulary. Draper's results show that this is not the case. In fact, there is very little overlap between the novice and the expert users' vocabularies. Novices do not all use the same commands as each other, and neither do experts. Draper argues that UNIX experts are better seen as specialists with a subset of UNIX commands.

What have we learned from such studies? First, we see that 'experts' differ among themselves. This point was also made by Charness (1991), in his examination of chess skill, who found that chess masters do not know the full range of opening variations (there are some 50,000), middle-game combinations (around 1,817) and endgames (some 8,500). Indeed, it is questionable whether they could actually learn the full set. Instead, chess masters specialize in a subset of each of the three classes. Second, we can see that there are different kinds of expertise. The physics expert, for example, is an expert in a domain where knowledge of the principles themselves is sufficient to solve most of the problems that may be encountered. The chess master and the UNIX expert exercise their skill in a domain where it is virtually impossible to learn all there is to know. There is not a body of 'principles' as such that are logically sufficient to solve most problems.

Chess, computer programming and physics are, nonetheless, well-defined domains. In the case of chess in particular, certain problem states can become highly familiar, and stronger players can capitalize upon their ability to recognize good problem states. Sometimes, though, recognition hinders the construction of optimal representations.

Summary of Section 5

- Neither experts nor novices form a homogeneous group.
- Skill in problem solving involves more than just the accumulation of knowledge.
- Problem-solving skill may be enhanced in a number of ways.

6   Conclusion

Nearly a century of research on problem solving has yielded some impressive findings. Important phenomena, such as insight and fixation, which have long taxed researchers are now amenable to more rigorous, systematic investigation thanks to methodological and theoretical advances, not to mention the advent of cognitive modelling. We now have a better understanding of analogical reasoning, helping us to appreciate how analogical reasoning occurs and why it sometimes fails. Advances have been made in understanding how we become skilled in solving problems from a wide range of complex domains, which have in turn led to a better understanding of expertise and learning.

We do not yet have a theory of problem solving; nor do we have a theory of learning, but progress is being made. Underpinning research on problem solving though is a recurring theme, and it is this: representation is fundamental to problem solving, just as it is fundamental to many other areas of psychology. Problem representation is likely to be influenced by many variables, some of which we have only begun to explore. We hope we have stimulated your interest in this area of psychology sufficiently that you will see the potential for problem-solving research in terms of its wider application, as well as its theoretical significance.

Now that you have read this chapter you can reinforce and extend your learning by reading an original journal article associated with it, available online from the DD303 website. Remember, these are original journal articles, so the style is different from this textbook, and don't be too concerned if you can't follow every detail.

Further reading

Chronicle, E.P., MacGregor, J.N. and Ormerod, T.C. (2004) 'What makes an insight problem? The roles of heuristics, goal conception and solution recoding in knowledge-lean problems', *Journal of Experimental Psychology: Learning, Memory and Cognition*, vol.30, pp.14–27.

Anderson, J.R. (2002) 'Spanning seven orders of magnitude: a challenge for cognitive modeling', *Cognitive Science*, vol.26, pp.85–112.

Ericsson, K.A. and Kintsch, W. (1995) 'Long-term working memory', *Psychological Review*, vol.102, no.2, pp.211–45.

References

Adamson, R.E. and Taylor, D.W. (1954) 'Functional fixedness as related to elapsed time and set', *Journal of Experimental Psychology*, vol.47, pp.122–6.

Anderson, J.R. (1983) *The Architecture of Cognition*, Cambridge, MA, Harvard.

Anolli, L., Antonietti, A., Crisafulli, L. and Cantoia, M. (2001) 'Accessing source information in analogical problem-solving', *Quarterly Journal of Experimental Psychology*, vol.54A, pp.237–61.

Atwood, M.E. and Polson, P.G. (1976) 'A process model for water jug problems', *Cognitive Psychology*, vol.8, pp.191–216.

Blanchette, I. and Dunbar, K. (2000) 'How analogies are generated: the roles of structural and superficial similarity', *Memory and Cognition*, vol.28, pp.108–24.

Boshuizen, H.P.A. and Schmidt, H.G. (1992) 'On the role of biomedical knowledge in clinical reasoning by experts, intermediates and novices', *Cognitive Science*, vol.16, pp.153–84.

Burns, B.D. and Vollmeyer, R. (2002) 'Goal specificity effects on hypothesis testing in problem solving', *Quarterly Journal of Experimental Psychology*, vol.55A, no.1, pp.241–61.

Card, S.K., Moran, T.P. and Newell, A. (1983) *The Psychology of Human–Computer Interaction*, Hillsdale, NJ, Erlbaum.

Charness, N. (1991) 'Expertise in chess: the balance between knowledge and search' in Ericsson, K.A. and Smith, J. (eds) *Towards a General Theory of Expertise: Prospects and Limits*, Cambridge, MA, Cambridge University Press.

Chase, W.G. and Simon, H.A. (1973a) 'The mind's eye in chess' in Chase, W.G. (ed.) *Visual Information Processing*, New York, Academic Press.

Chase, W.G. and Simon, H.A. (1973b) 'Perception in chess', *Cognitive Psychology*, vol.4, pp.55–81.

Chi, M.T.H., Bassok, M., Lewis, M.W., Reimann, P. and Glaser, R. (1989) 'Self-explanations: how students study and use examples in learning to solve problems', *Cognitive Science*, vol.13, pp.145–82.

Chi, M.T.H., Glaser, R. and Rees, E. (1982) 'Expertise in problem solving' in Sternberg, R.J. (ed.) *Advances in the Psychology of Human Intelligence*, Hillsdale, NJ, Erlbaum.

Chi, M.T.H., de Leeuw, N., Chiu, M-H. and LaVancher, C. (1994) 'Eliciting self-explanations improves understanding', *Cognitive Science*, vol.18, no.3, pp.439–77.

Chronicle, E.P., Ormerod, T.C. and MacGregor, J.N. (2001) 'When insight just won't come: the failure of visual cues in the nine-dot problem', *Quarterly Journal of Experimental Psychology*, vol.54A, no.3, pp.903–19.

De Groot, A.D. (1965) *Thought and Choice in Chess* (original edition in Dutch, 1946), The Hague, Mouton.

Davies, S.P. (2000) 'Move evaluation as a predictor and moderator of success in solutions to well-structured problems', *Quarterly Journal of Experimental Psychology*, vol.53A, no.4, pp.186–201.

Draper, S.W. (1984) 'The nature of expertise in UNIX' in Diaper, D., Gilmore, D., Cockton, G. and Shackel, B. (eds) *Proceedings of Interact*, Amsterdam, Elsevier, pp.465–71.

Dunbar, K. (2001) 'The analogical paradox: why analogy is so easy in naturalistic settings, yet so difficult in the psychology laboratory' in Gentner, D., Holyoak, K.J. and Kokinov, B. (eds) *Analogy: Perspectives from Cognitive Science*, Cambridge, MA, MIT Press.

Duncker, K. (1945) 'On problem solving', *Psychological Monographs*, 58, whole, no.270, pp.1–113.

Ericsson, K.A. (1991) 'Prospects and limits of the empirical study of expertise: an introduction' in Ericsson, K.A. and Smith, J. (eds) *Towards a General Theory of Expertise: Prospects and Limits*, Cambridge, MA, Cambridge University Press.

Ericsson, K.A. and Harris, M. (1990) 'Expert chess memory without chess knowledge. A training study' Poster presentation at the 31st Meeting of the Psychonomics Society, New Orleans.

Ericsson, K.A., Krampe, R.T. and Tesch-Rohmer, C. (1993) 'The role of deliberate practice', *Psychological Review*, vol.100, no.3, pp.363–406.

Ericsson, K.A. and Polson, P.G. (1988) 'Memory for restaurant orders' in Chi, M.T.H., Glaser, R. and Farr, M. (eds) *The Nature of Expertise*, Hillsdale, NJ, Erlbaum.

Falkenhainer, B., Forbus, K.D. and Gentner, D. (1986) 'The structure-mapping engine', *Proceedings of the Meeting of the American Association for Artificial Intelligence*, pp.272–7.

Gentner, D. (1983) 'Structure-mapping: a theoretical framework for analogy', *Cognitive Science*, vol.7, pp.155–70.

Gentner, D., Bowdle, B., Wolff, P. and Boronat, C. (2001) 'Metaphor is like analogy' in Gentner, D., Holyoak, K.J. and Kokinov, B.N. (eds) *The Analogical Mind: Perspectives from Cognitive Science*, Cambridge, MA, MIT Press, pp.199–253.

Gentner, D. and Gentner, D.R. (1983) 'Flowing waters or teeming crowds: mental models of electricity' in Gentner, D. and Stevens, A.L. (eds) *Mental Models*, Hillsdale, NJ, Lawrence Erlbaum Associates, pp.99–129. (Reprinted in Brosnan, M.J. (ed.) *Cognitive Functions: Classic Readings in Representation and Reasoning*, Eltham, London, Greenwich University Press.)

Gentner, D. and Markman, A.B. (1997) 'Structure mapping in analogy and similarity', *American Psychologist*, vol.52, no.1, pp.45–56.

Gick, M.L. and Holyoak, K.J. (1980) 'Analogical problem solving', *Cognitive Psychology*, vol.12, pp.306–55.

Gilhooly, K.J., McGeorge, P., Hunter, J., Rawles, J.M., Kirby, I.K., Green, C. and Wynn, V. (1997) 'Biomedical knowledge in diagnostic thinking: the case of electrocardiogram (ECG) interpretation', *European Journal of Cognitive Psychology*, vol.9, no.2, pp.199–223.

Gilhooly, K.J., Phillips, L.H., Wynn, V., Logie, R.H. and Della Sala, S. (1999) 'Planning processes and age in the 5 disk Tower of London task', *Thinking and Reasoning*, vol.5, no.4, pp.339–61.

Glucksberg, S. and Danks, J.H. (1968) 'Effects of discriminative labels', *Journal of Verbal Learning and Verbal Behaviour*, vol.7, pp.72–6.

Green, A.J.K. (2002) 'Learning procedures and goal specificity in learning and problem solving tasks', *European Journal of Cognitive Psychology*, vol.14, no.1, pp.105–26.

Green, A.J.K. and Gilhooly, K.J. (1990) 'Individual differences and effective learning procedures: the case of statistical computing', *International Journal of Man–Machine Studies*, vol.33, pp.97–119.

Green, A.J.K. and Wright, M.J. (2003) 'Reduction of task-relevant information in skill acquisition', *European Journal of Cognitive Psychology*, vol.15, no.2, pp.267–90.

Haider, H. and Frensch, P.A. (1996) 'The role of information reduction in skill acquisition', *Cognitive Psychology*, vol.30, no.3, pp.304–37.

Haider, H. and Frensch, P.A. (1999a) 'Eye movement during skill acquisition: more evidence for the information reduction hypothesis', *Journal of Experimental Psychology: Learning, Memory, and Cognition*, vol.25, no.1, pp.172–90.

Haider, H. and Frensch, P.A. (1999b) 'Information reduction during skill acquisition: the influence of task instruction', *Journal of Experimental Psychology: Applied*, vol.5, no.2, pp.129–51.

Hall, T. (1970) *Carl Friedrich Gauss: A Biography* (trans. by A. Froderberg), Cambridge, MA, MIT Press.

Holding, D.H. (1979) 'The evaluation of chess positions', *Simulation and Games*, vol.10, pp.207–21.

Holding, D.H. (1985) *The Psychology of Chess Skill*, Hillsdale, NJ, Erlbaum.

Holding, D.H. and Reynolds, R.I. (1982) 'Recall or evaluation of chess positions as determinants of chess skill', *Memory and Cognition*, vol.10, pp.237–42.

Holyoak, K.J. and Koh, K. (1987) 'Surface and structural similarity in analogical transfer', *Memory and Cognition*, vol.15, pp.332–40.

Holyoak, K.J. and Thagard, P. (1989) 'A computational model of analogical problem solving' in Vosniadou, S. and Ortony, A. (eds) *Similarity and Analogical Reasoning*, Cambridge, MA, Cambridge University Press, pp.242–66.

Jeffries, R., Polson, P.G., Razran, L. and Atwood, M.E. (1977) 'A process model for missionaries–cannibals and other river crossing problems', *Cognitive Psychology*, vol.9, pp.412–20.

Keane, M. (1988) *Analogical Problem Solving*, Chichester, Ellis Horwood.

Keane, M.T. (1994) 'Constraints on analogical mapping: a comparison of three models', *Cognitive Science*, vol.18, no.3, pp.387–438.

Knoblich, G., Ohlsson, S., Haider, H. and Rhenius, D. (1999) 'Constraint relaxation and chunk decomposition in insight problem solving', *Journal of Experimental Psychology: Learning, Memory and Cognition*, vol.25, no.6, pp.1543–55.

Kolers, P.A. (1975) 'Memorial consequences of automatized encoding', *Journal of Experimental Psychology: Human Learning and Memory*, vol.1, pp.689–701.

Larkin, J., McDermott, J., Simon, D.P. and Simon, H.A. (1980) 'Models of competence in solving physics problems', *Cognitive Science*, vol.4, pp.317–45.

Lesgold, A.M., Rubinson, H., Feltovich, P.J., Glaser, R., Klopfer, D. and Wang, Y. (1998) 'Expertise in a complex skill: diagnosing X-ray pictures' in Chi, M.T.H., Glaser, R. and Farr, M. (eds) *The Nature of Expertise*, Hillsdale, NJ, Erlbaum, pp.311–42.

Logan, G.D. (1988) 'Toward an instance theory of automatization', *Psychological Review*, vol.95, pp.492–527.

Luchins, A.S. and Luchins, E.H. (1959) *Rigidity of Behaviour*, Eugene, OR, University of Oregon Press.

Luger, G.F. (1976) 'The use of state–space to record the behavioural effects of subproblems and symmetries on the Tower of Hanoi problem', *International Journal of Man–Machine Studies*, vol.8, pp.411–21.

McKeithen, K.B., Reitman, J.S., Rueter, H.H. and Hirtle, S.C. (1981) 'Knowledge organization and skill differences in computer programmers', *Cognitive Psychology*, vol.13, pp.307–25.

Neisser, U., Novick, R. and Lazar, R. (1963) 'Searching for ten targets simultaneously', *Perceptual and Motor Skills*, vol.17, pp.955–61.

Ohlsson, S. (1992) 'Information processing explanations of insight and related phenomena' in Keane, M.T. and Gilhooly, K.J. (eds) *Advances in the Psychology of Thinking*, London, Harvester Wheatsheaf.

Renkl, A. (1997) 'Learning from worked-out examples: a study of individual differences', *Cognitive Science*, vol.21, no.1, pp.1–29.

Schoenfeld, A.H. and Herrmann, D.J. (1982) 'Problem perception and knowledge structure in expert and novice mathematical problem solvers', *Journal of Experimental Psychology: Learning, Memory and Cognition*, vol.8, no.5, pp.484–94.

Schraagen, J.M. (1993) 'How experts solve a novel problem in experimental design', *Cognitive Science*, vol.17, no.2, pp.285–309.

Schunn, C.D. and Anderson, J.R. (1999) 'The generality/specificity of expertise in scientific reasoning', *Cognitive Science*, vol.23, no.3, pp.337–70.

Simon, H.A. and Chase, W.G. (1973) 'Skill in chess', *American Scientist*, vol.61, pp.394–403.

Simon, H.A. and Hayes, J.R. (1976) 'The understanding process: problem isomorphs', *Cognitive Psychology*, vol.8, pp.165–90.

Simon, H.A. and Reed, S.K. (1976) 'Modelling strategy shifts on a problem solving task', *Cognitive Psychology*, vol.8, pp.86–97.

Snoddy, G.S. (1926) 'Learning and stability', *Journal of Applied Psychology*, vol.10, pp.1–36.

Spellman, B.A. and Holyoak, K.J. (1992) 'If Saddam is Hitler then who is George Bush? Analogical mapping between systems of social roles', *Journal of Personality and Social Psychology*, vol.62, pp.913–33.

Sternberg, R.J. (1995) 'Expertise in complex problem solving' in Frensch, P.A. and Funke, J. (eds) *Complex Problem Solving*, Hillsdale, NJ, Erlbaum.

Sweller, J. (1988) 'Cognitive load during problem solving: effects on learning', *Cognitive Science*, vol.12, no.2, pp.257–85.

Sweller, J., Mawer, R.F. and Ward, M.R. (1983) 'Development of expertise in mathematical problem solving', *Journal of Experimental Psychology: General*, vol.112, no.4, pp.639–61.

Thomas, J.C., Jr (1974) 'An analysis of behaviour in the hobbits–orcs problem', *Cognitive Psychology*, vol.6, pp.257–69.

Thorndyke, P.W. and Stasz, C. (1980) 'Individual differences in procedures for knowledge acquisition from maps', *Cognitive Psychology*, vol.12, pp.137–75.

Vollmeyer, R., Burns, B.D. and Holyoak, K.J. (1996) 'The impact of goal specificity on strategy use and the acquisition of problem structure', *Cognitive Science*, vol.20, pp.75–100.

Voss, J.F., Greene, T.R., Post, T.A. and Penner, B.C. (1983) 'Problem solving skill in the social sciences' in Bower, G. (ed.) *The Psychology of Learning and Motivation*, vol.17, New York, Academic Press.

Zhang, J. and Norman, D.A. (1994) 'Representations in distributed cognitive tasks', *Cognitive Science*, vol.18, no.1, pp.87–122.

Judgement and decision making

Chapter 12

Peter Ayton

1 Introduction

How do people make judgements and decisions? The question has become a steadily increasing preoccupation of cognitive psychology. Plainly, making decisions is a fundamental and everyday human and animal (and, perhaps, machine) activity. Yet, until the 1950s psychologists had hardly given the question any serious thought. Doubtless, this had something to do with the dominance of the behaviourist school of thought throughout the first half of the twentieth century. The behaviourists assumed that human behaviour could be explained entirely in terms of reflexes, stimulus–response associations and the effects of reinforcers upon them. Accordingly, they shunned the study of mental processes and entirely excluded 'mental' terms like desires and goals. As a historical consequence, the foundations of decision research, and hence its contemporary shape, have been strongly influenced by thinking from disciplines *outside* psychology – specifically from mathematics and economics.

This influence from outside psychology left its mark – mathematicians and economists have different concerns to psychologists. The question posed and pursued by thinkers from outside psychology was not how *do* people actually make decisions but how, ideally, *should* decisions be made? What are *good* judgements and decisions and how should we recognize them? As we will see, *behavioural* judgement and decision research – the investigation of *how* people make decisions – has been strongly influenced by a fundamental underlying premise: that the objective of decision making should be to make the 'best' choice, and that the best choice can, by some method, be computed.

Judgement and decision making are sometimes distinguished on the basis that *judgements are what underlie decisions*. Judgements can be estimates of some objective quantity – how far away is this object? How dangerous is that hobby? Decisions typically reflect judgements of the qualities of options – but also the preferences of the decision maker.

Of course, real people are not idealized decision-making machines or supercomputers; they do not have unlimited time, knowledge and computational power but a rather limited information-processing capacity. Accordingly, not infrequently, people make mistakes – for example, they may overlook or forget important considerations; they also get bored, suffer anxiety and may not always be sure quite what they want or are trying to achieve. As a consequence, what people do is not always quite the same as what they themselves would agree that they *should* do.

1.1 Theories of decision making

Psychologists are of course interested in understanding what people actually do, but this has very often been studied in comparison to what it has been assumed they *should* do. As a result, there are two types of theory of decision making – the 'ought' and the 'is' – commonly referred to as **normative** and **descriptive** theories respectively. Normative theories define the supposed ideal decision while descriptive theories attempt to characterize how people actually make decisions.

The very existence of this dichotomy suggests that perhaps human decision making is faulty. Indeed, debating whether or not people are essentially rational or irrational decision makers has long been a preoccupation of researchers in this field (cf. Cohen, 1981), just as the rationality of thought has been a key concern for researchers studying human reasoning (as you will see in Chapter 13). However, noting a disparity between the ideal and the actual should not, in itself, cause us to leap to the conclusion that there is something *fundamentally* wrong with the way people make judgements and decisions. In other areas of cognitive psychology, such a step would be seen as clearly absurd; for instance, human memory is manifestly fallible and yet we do not conclude from this that people's memories are inherently inadequate for the purpose of living their lives.

While persistent errors of judgement or choice could be taken to indicate a fundamental irrationality, researchers in judgement and decision making have tended to adopt a similar position to researchers working in vision. Vision scientists, for instance, do not conclude from the robustness of the Müller-Lyer illusion (see Section 1, Chapter 3) that people are generally poor at inferring object lengths – let alone that visual perception is fundamentally incompetent. Nevertheless, as we will see, people do make judgements and decisions that are inconsistent with normative theory.

1.2 Supporting decision making

If people don't behave as normative theories prescribe, what can be done about it? What should people do to make better choices? What instruction, modes of thinking or decision aids can help real people to make better decisions? A third strand of research straddling the normative and descriptive – the **prescriptive** approach – investigates how to help people make better decisions. One prescriptive approach is decision analysis. Decision analysis is the attempt to help people to make better decisions that conform to normative theory. However, decision analysis is more than just that: helping people to understand and explicate their own objectives and values, search for options and evidence and appreciate their implications is not a straightforward matter. Decision analysis uses a number of techniques, including decision trees (which you will meet in Section 2.1), to help people decompose complex decisions into more manageable components, elicit values and beliefs for the elements and apply normative principles to their reintegration.

Summary of Section 1

- Judgements underlie decisions.
- Researchers distinguish between actual (descriptive) and ideal (normative) decision making.
- Decision analysis can support people in making better decisions – a prescriptive approach.

2   Normative theory of choice under risk

In many situations where we must make a choice, we will be uncertain about whether the possible outcomes will turn out to be good or not so good. Consequently, risk is an inescapable fact of life. Some sorts of risky decisions are easy to imagine: a person may have to consider whether to continue living with a debilitating health condition or risk surgery that might help but could leave them worse off. Investment decisions often involve contemplating whether to put money in a safe investment with a small return or a riskier investment that might yield a lot of money but could lose everything. Decisions of this sort can be analysed as **gambles**. Gambling is the dominant metaphor in decision research as gambles involve *uncertainty* about what will happen.

The most extensively applied normative model of risky choice is called **subjective expected utility** theory (SEU). This theory is an extension by Savage (1954) of the 'expected utility' theory published by von Neumann and Morgenstern (1944) in their book *Theory of Games and Economic Behavior*. Von Neumann and Morgenstern's analysis was applied to games of chance with known or computable probabilities. Savage's extension of the theory allowed for what he called 'personal probabilities' – commonly referred to nowadays as 'subjective probabilities'. Savage's generalization of the theory allows it to be applied to decision situations where no objective mathematical probabilities are available and where judgements may be no more than expressed beliefs about likelihoods.

For example: imagine contemplating an invitation to a picnic. Suppose you have to write an essay over the weekend in question but do not want to miss out on anything really good. On the other hand, you wouldn't want to waste time at a boring or horrible picnic. You may be unsure whether it will rain or not; whether Tarquin (an individual about whom you have very strong views) will be present or not; and there could be any number of other factors that would affect the value of accepting the invitation. So how should you decide?

According to standard normative theory, a rational decision maker should trade off the value of all the possible outcomes by the likelihood of obtaining them. Just as the value of a lottery ticket will vary according to both the value of the prizes *and* the chances of winning them, so, according to the normative theory of choice, do choice options. What is the value of an idyllic or dreadful picnic? What is the value of any of the alternative activities you could indulge in? How likely is it to rain or that Tarquin will be there? All the relevant elements must be quantified and combined to compute the optimal decision. How this is done is illustrated in the next section where the technique of decision analysis is described.

2.1   Prescriptive application of normative theory: decision analysis

Decision analysis is a technology based on SEU that was developed in the 1960s to improve decision making (cf. Raiffa, 1968; Schlaifer, 1969). Decision analysts use normative theory to represent decision problems so that, ideally at least, the normatively correct decision can be computed. In the classic decision analytic framework (von Winterfeldt and Edwards, 1986) numerical probabilities are assigned to all the different events identified in a **decision tree**. The decision tree is simply a means of representing or modelling the decision. The best alternative is then selected by combining the probabilities and the utilities corresponding to the possible outcomes associated with each of the possible alternatives.

Figure 12.1 shows a simple decision tree for our student trying to decide whether to go on a picnic or stay at home and write an essay. The tree portrays two possible actions or events – picnic or essay – and three possible future events (weather conditions) that would affect the value or utility of the resulting six identifiable outcomes. Of course, there could be many more options (students' weekend options involve more than essays and picnics) and possible future conditions (there may well be more than the weather to consider). The utilities, as in this case, will often reflect subjective evaluations of the quality of the outcomes – though for business or

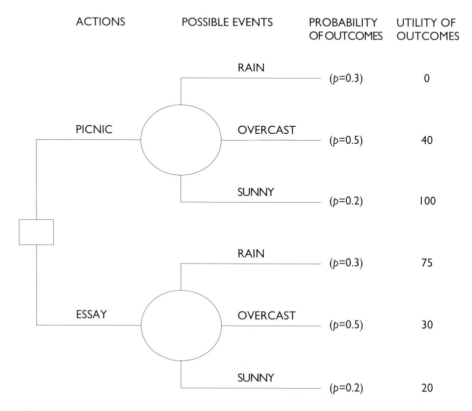

ACTIONS	POSSIBLE EVENTS	PROBABILITY OF OUTCOMES	UTILITY OF OUTCOMES
	RAIN	(p=0.3)	0
PICNIC	OVERCAST	(p=0.5)	40
	SUNNY	(p=0.2)	100
	RAIN	(p=0.3)	75
ESSAY	OVERCAST	(p=0.5)	30
	SUNNY	(p=0.2)	20

Figure 12.1   Decision tree for deciding whether to go on a picnic or write an essay

financial decisions it might reflect monetary profits. Here, the scale for utility is arbitrary – let's suppose the student was asked to rate each of the six possible outcomes on a 0–100 scale assigning 0 to the worst outcome, 100 to the best and scaling the others relative to those. A picnic in the sun is rated the best outcome and a picnic in the rain the worst. Writing an essay at home is affected by the weather, albeit differently, because, as any student knows, a sunny day is the worst time to have to stay in and work – especially if you know your friends are out having fun. These figures might not reflect your own utilities for these outcomes – utility is personal. You might revel in rainy picnics – if so, your utilities for this decision would be quite different.

We also need likelihoods for the three different weather conditions. In some countries weather forecasters routinely broadcast these, but as long as they accurately reflect our real beliefs, we could use our own judgements. Decision theory can only tell you how to decide given your beliefs about the utility and likelihood of the relevant events. With these data, we can now compute the expected utility of the two actions identified in the tree. The expected utility of each *outcome* is defined as the probability or likelihood of that outcome (P) multiplied by its utility (U). The expected utility of an *action* is the sum of such expected utilities for each of the possible *outcomes*. So, the expected utility of the picnic *action* is the sum of the expected utilities for the rainy picnic, the overcast picnic and the sunny picnic:

$$SEU(picnic) = \sum P \times U = P(rainy\ picnic) \times U(rainy\ picnic)$$
$$+ P(overcast\ picnic) \times U(overcast\ picnic)$$
$$+ P(sunny\ picnic) \times U(sunny\ picnic)$$
$$= 0.3 \times 0 + 0.5 \times 40 + 0.2 \times 100$$
$$= 40$$

That is, by multiplying the utility of each outcome by the likelihood of obtaining it, we can calculate that the expected utility for the picnic is 40. Similarly, we can calculate that the expected utility for the essay is 41.5. Because the expected utility of the essay is greater than that for the picnic *this* student should write the essay.

The difference between 41.5 and 40 may seem rather close, but remember that the numerical scales are arbitrary. In practice, a decision analyst using this procedure as part of the *prescriptive* approach to assist decision making would go back and check that reasonable variations in the values entered in the tree do not alter the decision. If they do, then the user must be sure that the numbers genuinely reflect their beliefs and values.

ACTIVITY 12.1

Try to produce a decision tree for two activities you might consider doing. For example, you might want to compare going to a party with going to the cinema. Your enjoyment of a party may depend on who else is going, and where the party is. Going to the cinema may be fun if you can see a film you particularly want to see, or may be just an opportunity to while away some time if you are indifferent to the films on show. Think about which you would choose to do. Now try computing the expected utility for the two actions. Which action does the analysis suggest you *should* choose? Are they the same and, if not, why do you think they differ?

COMMENT

The calculations illustrate how the expected utility theory defines a normative decision, but why follow this procedure? The assumption is that you might not make such a good decision by relying on unaided intuition. The decision tree can help you to clarify the relevant events and the structure of the decision while the computations based on your stated values will follow the normative theory. Alas, there is no normative technique for eliciting the correct structure of decisions from individuals. However, in decision-analytic practice decision trees are used more to facilitate thought rather than to definitively represent complex decisions; a realistic portrayal of all relevant act–event combinations might result in a complicated mess.

Since its initial inception, the role of decision analysis has changed (Phillips, 1989). Nowadays, decision analysts view decision trees as tools to aid thinking, not as providing solutions (von Winterfeldt and Edwards, 1986). The theory of **requisite decision modelling** (Phillips, 1984) claims that models of decisions need only be sufficient in structure and content to resolve the issues at hand. A good model captures the essential elements of a decision situation for the purposes of the decisions to be made. An iterative procedure is followed involving constructing the model, analysis, model refinement and subsequent reanalysis. At the point when no additional intuitions emerge from further analysis, the model is said to be *requisite*. The claim is that this procedure helps to develop a shared understanding and fosters commitment to the way forward. Note that these are social purposes. The technical computations of a decision analysis are less than half the story of improving decision making. Constructing representations of decisions and eliciting values are not achieved by mechanical operations; they often involve deep thought – or what some (cf. Watson and Buede, 1987) call 'soul searching'. Perhaps the greatest virtue of decision analysis is that it obliges decision makers to make explicit all the bases of a decision.

In the next section, we shall examine some of the principles underlying SEU, and consider the extent to which SEU accurately describes human decision making.

2.2 Axioms underlying subjective expected utility theory

Mathematicians such as von Neumann and Savage established that SEU is implied by the acceptance of certain principles or axioms: **comparability**, **transitivity**, **dominance**, **independence** and **invariance**. According to SEU, if a decision maker violates one or more of these axioms, then their choices will not maximize expected utility and so will not be normative. The axioms therefore define a kind of coherence to our choices and give them internal consistency. We shall look at them in more detail now:

- Comparability (or completeness)

  If you have to evaluate two alternatives A and B you must be able to say whether you:

  1   prefer A to B or

  2   prefer B to A or

  3   are indifferent between A and B.

- Transitivity

  If you prefer A to B and B to C then you must prefer A to C. That is, choices should be capable of being ordered.

- Dominance

  An option is dominant and must be preferred if, when compared to another option, it is better in at least one respect and at least as good or better in every other respect. *Dominated* options must never be preferred.

- Independence

  If there is some outcome that is unaffected by, or independent of, your choice then this outcome should not affect your choice.

- Invariance

  Different representations of the same choice problem should result in the same choices. That is, the preference for options should be independent of how they are described.

2.3   Violations of the axioms

Although the axioms might strike you as uncontentious and straightforward, they can be questioned. For example, the comparability axiom is threatened by claims that people may not be indifferent just because they are unable to say which of two states they prefer. Curiously, even the original architects of the theory admitted that it might not always be a reasonable assumption:

> We have conceded that one may doubt whether a person can always decide which of two alternatives ... he prefers. If the general comparability assumption is not made, a mathematical theory ... is still possible.
>
> *(von Neumann and Morgenstern, 1944, pp.19–20)*

The axioms also seem to vary somewhat in their intuitive appeal; while independence and transitivity might not be obvious requirements for rational choice, dominance and invariance appear essential. Nonetheless, psychologists have shown that, under certain conditions, systematic violations of each of the axioms can be observed in people's choices (Tversky and Kahneman, 1986). Since violations of the axioms imply that people are not choosing according to the normative theory, we could conclude one of two things: either that there is something wrong with the choices or that there is something wrong with the normative theory (or perhaps both) – in any case, as we shall now see, SEU does not provide a good description of actual human choices.

2.3.1 Violations of transitivity

Observed violations of the transitivity axiom have generally led to the conclusion that people's choices are not ideal. For example, Tversky (1969) asked people to state their preferences between pairs of college applicants rated on three dimensions – intelligence, emotional stability and social facility (as in Table 12.1).

Table 12.1 Ratings of five applicants on three dimensions

Applicant	Intelligence	Emotional stability	Social facility
A	69	84	75
B	72	78	65
C	75	72	55
D	78	66	45
E	81	60	35

Now try Activity 12.2.

ACTIVITY 12.2

Consider the following pairs of applicants in Table 12.1: A–B, B–C, C–D, D–E and E–A. For each pair, write down which of the two applicants you would prefer given their ratings. Do note, however, that you should weight intelligence more highly than either of the other dimensions.

COMMENT

Tversky's subjects were presented with all possible pairs of applicants (together with some others), one pair at a time, and were similarly told to weight intelligence more than the other two dimensions. Subjects typically preferred A to B; B to C; C to D; and D to E. However, violations of transitivity were demonstrated by the typical simultaneous preference for E over A. Did your own preferences coincide with these? If not, try to work out why Tversky's subjects might have adopted the preferences they did.

If people reliably mapped all the dimension scores of each option onto a common currency of utility, then *systematic* violations of transitivity would not occur – so demonstrations of intransitive preference are revealing about the nature of the choice process. For Tversky (1969, p.46), this was key: 'The main interest in the present results lies not so much in the fact that transitivity can be violated but rather in what these violations reveal about the choice mechanism.' Tversky suggested ways in which decision making might be rendered less cognitively demanding by applying decision rules that simplify the task. He offered two hypotheses about the choice process: (1) people compare the alternatives on each dimension in turn, rather than *evaluating* each option on all dimensions before comparing overall evaluations, and (2) that people ignore dimensions on which the alternatives – even if discriminable – are rated similarly.

For example, when comparing successive pairs in the chain such as A and B on intelligence, subjects may decide that the difference between them is negligible – and so, in the interests of simplifying the decision, ignore it altogether. However, small differences add up – at the ends of the chain the difference in intelligence between A and E is too big to ignore – hence, the observed pattern of intransitivity. Note that this explanation (that people try to simplify decisions by ignoring information) assumes that people have limited information-processing capacity.

In relation to SEU, intransitivity is an irrational pattern of choice but it may be reassuring to note that it is not a uniquely human condition. For instance, in an experiment where bees chose between artificial flowers that offered varying amounts of nectar with varying degrees of accessibility, Shafir (1994) found that they violated transitivity in their foraging preferences for flowers. As bees have been successfully foraging for millions of years it is tempting to assume that perhaps the costs – intransitive preferences cannot maximize expected utility – are outweighed by the gains – presumably, reduced information processing.

When confronted with evidence of intransitivity in their choices, people typically immediately concede that there is some inconsistency and are usually willing to change their choices to preserve transitivity. Hence, they seem to endorse the normative status of the axiom even though their violations show that transitivity is not descriptive of human choice.

2.3.2   Violations of the independence axiom

Violations of the independence axiom are more problematic, and have proved a serious challenge to both the normative and descriptive status of SEU. The first challenge came from the French economist and Nobel laureate Maurice Allais who published a paper in 1953 describing what is now called the **Allais paradox** (Allais, 1953, 1979).

Allais observed that people are reluctant to exchange a certain prospect of something wonderful (e.g. receiving $1,000,000) for a not quite certain prospect of something even more wonderful (e.g. 99 per cent chance of receiving $5,000,000). The paradox occurs because if both the above prospects are reduced in likelihood by a similar amount (so that neither offers certainty) people *are* usually willing to exchange a smidgen of likelihood for a substantial increase in benefit. Box 12.1 shows how this is a problem for SEU.

Allais made it perfectly clear that he considered that the intuitions which produced the paradox *should* overrule the independence axiom, that is, the normative theory was not valid. He even claimed: 'It is quite disappointing to have to exert so much effort to prove the illusory character of a formulation whose oversimplification is evident to anyone with a little psychological intuition' (Allais and Hagen, 1979, p.105). Others, including Savage, who, embarrassingly, initially succumbed to the paradox in his own choices, felt differently and argued that the intuitions underlying the choices were wrong and that the theory was normatively correct.

12.1

The Allais paradox

Table 12.2   The Allais paradox as a choice of lotteries: each lottery involves 100 tickets. The table shows the number of tickets that win anything from $0 to $5,000,000

| | | Lottery ticket numbers (1–100) | | |
		1	2–11	12–100
Situation 1	Choice A	$1,000,000	$1,000,000	$1,000,000
	Choice B	$0	$5,000,000	$1,000,000
Situation 2	Choice C	$1,000,000	$1,000,000	$0
	Choice D	$0	$5,000,000	$0

Table 12.2 shows two separate situations where you can choose to take part in one of two lotteries and draw one ticket from the lottery you choose. In Situation 1 you can choose between lotteries A and B. If you are like most people you would choose A, as this guarantees $1,000,000. B could deliver $5,000,000 but there is a small chance of ending up with nothing at all.

However, when faced with the choice in Situation 2, between C and D, most people prefer D – now they are willing to face a very slight increase in the prospect of getting nothing at all in order to have a chance of winning $5,000,000.

To see how this violates the independence axiom, simply cover up the last column – now the two situations appear identical. As the contents of the last column are identical ($1,000,000) for A and B in Situation 1, and also for C and D ($0) in Situation 2, then, according to the axiom, the information in this column should not influence your choice. So, if you prefer A to B, you should also prefer C to D.

When made aware that they are violating the independence axiom, people sometimes alter their choices to conform to it (Keller, 1985) but sometimes – even after a thorough explanation of its virtues – they don't (Slovic and Tversky, 1974). Slovic and Tversky suggested that people may alter their choices to concur with the axiom – not through appreciating the merits of so doing – but because they might be intimidated by the suggestion that not doing so would be irrational. Their paper concludes with a delightful imaginary debate between Savage and Allais wherein Savage insists that people only reject the axiom when they do not understand it, while Allais (who plausibly claimed to both understand and reject the axiom) asks how Savage could distinguish between failure to understand the axiom and enlightened rejection of it. The debate highlights an irresolvable conflict between two different intuitions – those that support the axiom and those that support the pattern of choices in the Allais paradox. Ultimately, rather like the Ten Commandments (which are also often violated), the normative status of SEU and its axioms is not in any sense a demonstrable truth – they only appeal (or not) as principles to live by.

Summary of Section 2

- SEU provides a normative theory of decision making under uncertainty.
- Decision analysis offers a prescription for making decisions using SEU.
- Conforming to SEU is equivalent to adhering to certain axioms.
- Human decision making has been shown to violate these axioms, implying that it is not adequately described by SEU.

3   Findings from behavioural decision research

Most decision researchers accept the normative status of SEU but also consider that it does not describe human decision making. Some thirty years after the emergence of SEU, Slovic *et al.* (1977, p.9) reviewed the psychological literature and commented: '... during the past 5 years, the proponents of SEU have been greatly outnumbered by its critics'. Edwards (1992) polled an all-star cast of leading decision theorists at a conference. They unanimously endorsed traditional SEU as the appropriate normative model but unanimously agreed that people don't behave as the model requires. Nonetheless, and perhaps in spite of the survival of SEU as a normative theory (albeit on the basis of opinion polls), Allais was awarded the Nobel Prize for Economics in 1988.

Violations of the axioms of SEU imply that it does not provide a valid description of human decision making. There is now a considerable mass of empirical evidence indicating that SEU does not predict human decisions either. One piece of evidence comes from Edwards (1955), who offered experimental subjects choices between bets of equal expected value such as the choice between Gambles A and B in Figure 12.2 below. If you accept Gamble A, it will give a 0.6 probability (or 60 per cent chance) of winning £2.00, and a 0.4 chance of £4.00; Gamble B gives a 0.2 probability of winning £14.00 and a 0.8 probability of winning nothing.

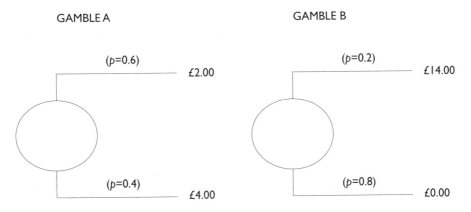

Figure 12.2   Two simple gambles of equal expected value

If we assume that the amounts of money are in direct proportion to people's utility for each outcome, then we can calculate the expected utility (EU) for the bets:

$$EU(Gamble\ A) = (0.6 \times £2) + (0.4 \times £4) = 2.8$$

$$EU(Gamble\ B) = (0.2 \times £14) + (0.8 \times £0) = 2.8$$

In a series of experiments, Edwards found that most people have definite preferences between bets of equal expected value. Compared to a good chance of winning a small amount they preferred a long shot of winning a large amount – provided there was no chance of losing very much. People strongly avoided gambles that involved even a low probability of losing a lot. Edwards concluded that SEU was not a guide for their choices between gambles. Later, Lichtenstein *et al.* (1969) found that expected value is irrelevant even when the concept was carefully explained to respondents.

3.1   The 'preference reversal phenomenon'

Far worse was to come for SEU however when the **preference reversal phenomenon** was discovered. Slovic and Lichtenstein (1968) had noticed that ratings of a gamble's attractiveness, as well as choices between pairs of gambles, were strongly influenced by the *probability* of winning and losing. Yet when asked how much they would be willing to pay in order to take the gamble, or the smallest amount they would be willing to sell the gamble for, people were more heavily influenced by the *amounts* that could be won or lost. Lichtenstein and Slovic (1973) realized that if there was a different basis for *choosing* than for *valuing* it should be possible to construct pairs of gambles so that people would prefer A to B but pay more for B than A. They were able to demonstrate this effect in a series of studies – including one conducted with real gambles in a Las Vegas casino. Typically, one bet would have a high probability of winning a modest amount (called the '*p* bet') while the other would offer a lower probability of winning a higher amount (called the '$ bet'):

> *p* bet: 11/12 *chance of winning* 12 *chips*
>
> 1/12 *chance of winning* 24 *chips*
>
> $ bet: 2/12 *chance of winning* 79 *chips*
>
> 10/12 *chance of losing* 5 *chips*

These two gambles were chosen equally often by the casino subjects; however, the $ bet received a higher selling price about 88 per cent of the time. Among those choosing the *p* bet, 87 per cent gave a higher selling price to the $ bet. So, people value the $ bet more highly than the *p* bet, but don't prefer the $ bet any more than the *p* bet. From a rational perspective this is a hopeless pattern of behaviour.

The finding, replicated numerous times since (Slovic, 1995), clearly poses a major threat to the SEU view of rational choice. Two economists, Grether and Plott (1979, p.623), realizing that: 'it suggests that no optimisation principle of any sort lies behind even the simplest of human choices', conducted a series of studies 'designed to discredit the psychologists' works as applied to economics'. However, even after controlling for all the economic explanations of the phenomenon that they could find – including that the experiment be conducted by economists rather than psychologists ('Psychologists have the reputation for deceiving subjects', p.629) – the reversals persisted.

3.2   Causes of anomalies in choice

Why do preference reversals occur? Slovic (1995) summarized the evidence in favour of a 'scale compatibility hypothesis'. The idea is that the weight of an option attribute in judgement or choice is influenced by its compatibility with the response mode. As economic value is expressed in terms of money, subjects find it easier to use the monetary aspect of the gamble to set the *value* of the gamble. However, when asked which gamble they *prefer* subjects have no similarly compelling reason to weight the monetary aspect of the gamble to determine their choice. You should note that this explanation does not depend on the presence of risk or uncertainty and indeed Tversky *et al.* (1990) have demonstrated preference reversals for options where no risk is present.

3.2.1   The 'prominence effect'

To account for another aspect of preference reversals, Tversky *et al.* (1988) identified a specific instance of the compatibility effect, which they termed the **prominence effect**. Slovic (1975) had observed that, after earlier adjusting the pay-offs of two gambles so as to make them equally valuable, people did not randomly choose between them but typically chose the gamble with the higher likelihood of winning. Tversky *et al.* (1988) suggested that the more prominent (or important) attribute would weigh more heavily in making a choice than in a matching task (as explained below). For example, in one problem, respondents were asked to imagine two programmes being considered by a transport ministry for dealing with traffic accidents in a country where 600 people are killed every year. Both programmes were described in terms of their annual costs and the expected annual number of casualties that would result if each was introduced. For the choice task, people were asked to choose between the following two options:

Choice task		
Option A	570 casualties	Cost $12 million
Option B	500 casualties	Cost $55 million

Of those who took part in the experiment, 67 per cent preferred B to A – note that this implies that the difference in casualties (70) is more important than the difference in costs ($43 million).

Other respondents performed a matching task, where they had to fill in the missing value so as to make the two programmes equally attractive:

Matching task		
Option A	570 casualties	Cost $12 million
Option B	500 casualties	Cost $?

The typical matching value was less than $55 million – indeed, only 4 per cent of respondents gave a value higher than $55 million.

Plainly, the trade-off between attributes is different with matching than with choice. Why? Tversky *et al.* argued that *choice* invites more *qualitative* reasoning – people select the option that is superior on the most important attribute (lives saved). This is cognitively simpler, easier to justify and resolves the conflict between the two attributes – albeit by effectively ignoring it. Matching however entails a more quantitative assessment. The matching task cannot be performed at all without paying attention to the values of both attributes and their relative importance.

Real-world choices often resemble matching or choice tasks. For example, you might ask yourself what is the most you are prepared to pay when shopping for a particular item (as in the matching task), or you could ask yourself whether you are willing to pay the advertised price for the item (as in the choice task). The evidence suggests that the decisions will tend to diverge. Similar effects may well affect budget setting and resource allocation decisions. Comparing budget allocation (matching) with budget cutting (choice) the prominence hypothesis suggests that, when forced to choose what items to cut from a hospital budget, health provision (the most important attribute) may fare better than (say) staff pay.

3.2.2 Choosing and rejecting options

Shafir (1993) has shown that choosing one of two items is not the complement of rejecting one of the two items. Sometimes when deciding between two options, people both select and reject the same option. When we are trying to select an option we tend to focus on positive features and when we are looking for reasons to reject an item we tend to focus on negative. Thus, items that have obvious positive features will be selected over items that do not. Similarly, items that have obvious negative features will be rejected before items that do not. It seems that rather than rank order options, as mandated by SEU, people look for *reasons* for their decisions. This has led to the proposal of a **reason-based theory of choice** (Shafir *et al.*, 1993) according to which reasons for choosing are more influential when we choose rather than reject, and reasons for rejecting are more influential when we reject rather than choose.

Failure to resolve conflict in choices can also be revealing of reasoning. The economist, Thomas Schelling, tells of an occasion when he went to buy an encyclopaedia for his children (cf. Shafir *et al.*, 1993). At the bookshop he was presented with two attractive encyclopaedias and, finding it difficult to choose between them, went home with neither – despite feeling that he would have happily bought either if it had been the only one available. Unresolved conflict can cause people to defer choosing because they lack a clear reason to select either option.

3.2.3 The 'evaluability principle'

Difficulty in interpreting value is addressed in a study conducted by Hsee (1998) who has developed the notion of **evaluability** to explain a type of preference reversal that occurs when items are evaluated separately or jointly. For example, if shopping for a piano in a musical instrument shop you might compare several pianos. At an auction or second-hand shop, however, you might have to consider a single piano.

Hsee argues that attributes vary in how easy or difficult they are to evaluate, and that their evaluability varies according to whether options are considered in isolation or in relation to other options. In one experiment Hsee asked people to assume they were music students looking for a used music dictionary. In the joint-evaluation condition, participants were shown two dictionaries, A and B (see Table 12.3), and asked how much they would be willing to pay for each. Willingness to pay was higher for Dictionary B ($27) than A ($19), presumably because of its greater number of entries. However, in the single-evaluation condition when one group of participants evaluated only A and another group evaluated only B, the mean willingness to pay was higher for A ($24) than B ($20).

Table 12.3   Attributes of two dictionaries in Hsee's (1998) study

	Year of publication	Number of entries	Any defects?
Dictionary A	1993	10,000	No, it's like new
Dictionary B	1993	20,000	Yes, the cover is torn; otherwise it's like new

Hsee explains this reversal by means of the **evaluability principle**. He argues that, without a direct comparison, the 'number of entries' attribute is hard to evaluate because the evaluator does not have a precise notion of *how good* or *how bad* 10,000 (or 20,000) entries is. However, the 'defects' attribute is evaluable because it translates easily into a precise good/bad response – most people find a defective dictionary unattractive and a like-new one attractive – and thus it carries more weight in the independent evaluation. Under joint evaluation, however, the buyer can see that B is far superior on the more important attribute, number of entries. Thus, the 'number of entries' attribute becomes *evaluable* through the comparison process.

Summary of Section 3

- Preference reversals illustrate that SEU fails to predict aspects of human decision making.
- The prominence and evaluability of attributes, and whether a task involves choosing or rejecting, have been shown to influence people's choices, effects not predicted by SEU.

4   Prospect theory

One important general conclusion that follows from these demonstrations of anomalies in choice is that people don't have a set of pre-existing stable values, that is, preferences, that they simply apply to choice situations. What is evident is that decisions change because the underlying bases of decisions change according to the demands of the decision task and the nature and context of the information presented. The unstable nature of preferences raises difficult – perhaps even unsolvable – questions regarding people's preferences. If different procedures for eliciting preferences elicit different choices, then how can preferences be defined and how should they be measured?

Kahneman and Tversky (1979) have proposed a descriptive model for decision making under risk, called **prospect theory**, which explains many of the phenomena that cannot be accounted for by SEU. Unlike SEU, prospect theory does not define ideal choices. It is a descriptive, not a normative, theory intended to account for human choices. Prospect theory is essentially an adapted version of SEU, which is modified so as to account for the observed discrepancies with SEU. Prospect theory identifies two phases to the choice process:

1   In the editing phase, the decision problem is represented; 'negligible' components may be discarded and a reference point is used to enable decision outcomes to be construed as 'gains' or 'losses'.

2   In the second phase, attitudes towards risks involving gains and losses are used to evaluate the identified prospects.

Prospect theory proposes that people evaluate decision outcomes in terms of gains or losses from a neutral reference point. Figure 12.3 shows how people are thought to value gains and losses. The horizontal axis to the right of the origin shows objective gains ($); as they increase the subjective value of the gains (v ($)) also increases but with a diminishing slope. This illustrates the fact that, for example, the psychological difference between $0 and $10 is greater than that between $100 and $110. Notice there is a similar effect for losses – the slope to the left of the origin shows that losses also diminish in a similar fashion. As the slope is not uniform, your *attitude* to risks varies as a function of where you see yourself on the curve. For contemplating gains (to the right of the origin) decisions will tend to be *risk averse* – most people decline to risk a gain of $10 for a 50 per cent chance of winning $20. By contrast, with losses, to the left of the origin, decisions tend to be *risk seeking* – in order to avoid a sure loss of $10 most people would be tempted to risk a 50 per cent chance of losing $20.

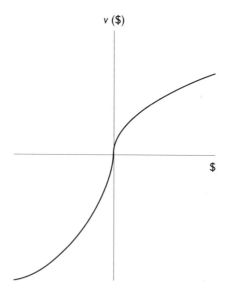

Figure 12.3   The value function in prospect theory showing the subjective value of a gain or loss as a function of the actual or objective amount of gain or loss

4.1 Prospect theory and 'loss aversion'

Another critical feature of the value function is that the curve is steeper for losses than for gains. This models the observation of **loss aversion** – that people feel losses more than they do gains of equivalent value. Famously, the economist Paul Samuelson once offered a bet to an economist colleague. They would flip a coin and if the colleague won he would get $200; if he lost he would have to pay Samuelson $100. The colleague, claiming he would feel the $100 loss more than the $200 gain, turned the bet down but mentioned that if Samuelson would play the bet 100 times he would play. (You might have noticed that this pair of preferences is paradoxical with respect to SEU – anyone declining one gamble should not accept any number of plays of the same gamble; Samuelson, 1963.)

Another attitude applied in the evaluation phase is that probability is distorted. Probabilities (p) are replaced by decision weights ($\pi(p)$). Note that this distortion does not apply to the judgement or estimation of probability but to the probability that results from judgement or even one supplied to the decision maker. Figure 12.4 shows that low probabilities (except zero, which is given zero weight) are over-weighted. Note the lower end of the curve is above the diagonal dashed line. Moderate and high probabilities (except certainty, which is given the correct weight of 1) are under-weighted: note the upper end of the curve is below the diagonal dashed line.

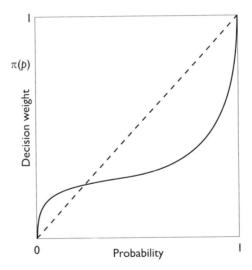

Figure 12.4 The weighting function in prospect theory showing the weighted probability $\pi(p)$ given to probabilities p varying between 0 and 1

The weighting function of prospect theory accounts for the behaviour observed in the Allais paradox. Because people weight probabilities just below certainty far less than they should, they correspondingly give certainty a *relatively* very high value: 100 per cent certainty is weighted a great deal more than 99 per cent. Moreover, very small probabilities are over-weighted – referring back to Allais we can see that people would worry disproportionately about the 1 per cent chance of not winning.

4.2 'Framing' effects

Kahneman and Tversky have reported numerous experiments demonstrating phenomena not anticipated by SEU but predicted by prospect theory. For example, the idea that gains and losses are determined by application of a reference point predicts **framing effects**. Tversky and Kahneman (1981) asked respondents to imagine that the USA was preparing for the outbreak of an unusual disease expected to kill 600 people. Two alternative programmes had been proposed to combat the disease.

- If Programme A is adopted, 200 people will be saved.

- If Programme B is adopted, there is a one-third probability that 600 people will be saved and a two-thirds chance that no people will be saved.

You should note that the options are described in terms of gains – the number of lives that might be saved. Of the respondents, 72 per cent chose Programme A and 28 per cent chose Programme B – definitely saving 200 lives is seen as more attractive than a one-third chance of saving 600 lives. For gains, as we saw in Figure 12.3, people are risk averse – as a result, gains that are certain are more attractive than a gamble of equal expected value.

A second group of respondents was presented with a different description of the two programmes.

- If Programme C is adopted, 400 people will die.

- If Programme D is adopted, there is a one-third probability that nobody will die and a two-thirds chance that 600 people will die.

In this case, only 22 per cent of respondents chose Programme C while 78 per cent chose Programme D. Of course, Programmes C and D are identical to Programmes A and B except that now the outcomes are 'framed' in terms of the numbers of lives that might be lost. Framed as a loss, the same risky option becomes more popular than the riskless option (a clear violation of the invariance axiom that you met earlier). The reversal of preference can be explained by the change of the reference point in conjunction with the shape of the value function. With gains, the reference point is defined by what will happen if nothing is done: 600 dead. Programme A looks attractive as it definitely saves 200 while Programme B risks a two-thirds chance of saving nobody. The relative overweighting of certainty will also contribute to the relative attractiveness of the sure gain of Programme A. In the domain of loss, the reference point is defined by the present: nobody has yet died. Programme D is more attractive as 600 deaths are not substantially worse than 400, and it offers a chance that nobody will die.

Summary of Section 4

- Prospect theory can account for an enormous range of observed anomalies in choice both in laboratory experiments and in field data representing real-life decisions.
- People feel losses more than they do gains of equivalent value.
- Framing of options influences preference patterns.

5   Judgement under uncertainty

As I noted earlier, judgement and choice can be distinguished on the basis that judgements are what underlie choices. To compute the ideal choice, the normative theory requires inputs of value and likelihood, which typically will be judgements by decision makers. Plainly, evaluating likelihood is a crucial prerequisite for effective decision making under uncertainty. For this reason, research on judgement of likelihood has a particular significance.

5.1   Judging probabilities and Bayes' theorem

In the 1960s, Ward Edwards and his colleagues conducted a number of studies using what were called the **book bag** and **poker chip paradigms**. A typical experiment would involve two opaque bags. Each bag contained 100 coloured poker chips in different but stated proportions of red to blue. Suppose Bag A contains seventy red and thirty blue chips while Bag B contains thirty red and seventy blue chips. The experimenter first chooses one bag at random and then draws a series of chips from it. After each draw, the poker chip is replaced and the bag well shaken before the next chip is drawn. The subjects' task is to say how confident they are – in probability terms – that the chosen bag is A, containing predominantly red chips, or B, containing predominantly blue chips.

Bayes' theorem can be used to calculate how the objective probabilities change after each piece of new information, and so can be used to evaluate human performance (see Box 12.2). Where the two competing hypotheses are that the bag is A and the bag is B, and the information is the drawing of a red chip, Bayes' theorem gives the following equality:

$$\frac{p(A \mid RED)}{p(B \mid RED)} = \frac{p(RED \mid A)}{p(RED \mid B)} \times \frac{p(A)}{p(B)}$$

where $p(A|RED)$ stands for the probability that the bag is A, given that a red chip has been drawn.

Prior to drawing any chips the probability that the bag is A and that the bag is B are both 0.5; if we draw one red chip the likelihood of this is 0.7 for Bag A and 0.3 for Bag B. We can substitute these values into Bayes' theorem:

$$\frac{p(A \mid RED)}{p(B \mid RED)} = \frac{0.7}{0.3} \times \frac{0.5}{0.5}$$

$$\frac{p(A \mid RED)}{p(B \mid RED)} = \frac{0.35}{0.15}$$

Therefore, the odds for Bag A over Bag B after drawing one red chip are 0.35:0.15 or, converting these into percentage probabilities, 70 per cent for Bag A and 30 per cent for Bag B. Bayes' theorem can then be used after each subsequent drawing of a chip to calculate how these probabilities should change.

Thus, for example, following the drawing of the red chip and prior to drawing a second chip our new prior odds ratio is $\frac{7}{0.3}$. If we replaced the red chip and shook the bag so the probabilities of drawing a red and blue chip remained as before, the impact

┌───┐

12.2 ─────────────────────────────────────── **Research study** ─┐

Using Bayes' theorem

So, how good are people at judging probabilities? In order to work this out, we can try using an objective standard to which we can compare human performance. One early benchmark used for this purpose was Bayes' theorem (which you will also meet in Chapter 13), a mathematical formula used for combining probabilities; it is of interest to decision makers as it can be used as a normative theory for how degrees of belief in a hypothesis might be revised in the light of new information.

Bayes' theorem states that the odds of a hypothesis being correct in the light of new information (**posterior odds**) is the product of two elements: (1) the **prior odds** (the initial odds) of the hypothesis being correct *before* the information is observed multiplied by (2) the **likelihood ratio** – the ratio of the probabilities that, given the information, the hypothesis is correct (H) or incorrect ($\overline{H}$).

$$\frac{p(H \mid D)}{p(\overline{H} \mid D)} = \frac{p(D \mid H)}{p(D \mid \overline{H})} \times \frac{p(H)}{p(\overline{H})} \quad (H = \text{hypothesis}; \ D = \text{datum})$$

You should note that $p(H \mid D)$ stands for the probability that the hypothesis is true, given that the datum or information D is true (read the vertical line as 'given'). Then, reading the formula from left to right, the three terms are:

1   The posterior odds ratio of H and $\overline{H}$ (not H) being true given D.

2   The likelihood ratio, representing the information value of D (the datum or information).

3   The prior odds of H and $\overline{H}$ (not H) being true before D is known.

If the probability of observing D when H is true is different from the probability of observing D when H is not true, then the information is diagnostic and the posterior odds will be different to the prior odds. The equation can be applied to any pair of competing hypotheses (A and B) by replacing H and $\overline{H}$ with A and B.

└───┘

of drawing a second chip would now be applied to our new prior ratio to compute another posterior odds ratio. If it was yet another red chip, belief in Bag A would be $\frac{0.7}{0.3} \times \frac{0.7}{0.3} = \frac{0.49}{0.09}$ – roughly 85%:15% – even more favourable for Bag A. If the second chip was blue, the information for each bag would be equivocal – our new posterior odds ratio would be $\frac{0.7}{0.3} \times \frac{0.3}{0.7} = \frac{0.21}{0.21}$ – 50:50 odds that it is Bag A or Bag B.

A crucial aspect of the logic of these studies is that the experimenter is able to compare the subjective probabilities estimated by subjects with the objective probabilities calculated using Bayes' theorem. All of the information required as inputs to Bayes' theorem is explicit and unambiguous. Ironically, though, this underplays the importance of the *subjectivity* probabilities. Because the experimenters assumed that they could objectively compute *the* correct answer, they reasoned that the subjective probabilities should be the same for all subjects faced with the same evidence. Calculating the objective probabilities and using them as a comparison then was absolutely necessary in order to be able to assess the accuracy of people's judgements. However, it also indicates the artificiality of this kind of task, and is at the root of the difficulties that were to emerge with interpreting subjects' behaviour.

5.2   Does Bayes' theorem describe human judgement?

The experiments conducted with the procedure discussed above produced ample evidence that human judgement under these conditions is not well described by Bayes' theorem. Although subjects' revisions of their probability judgements were proportional to the values calculated from Bayes' theorem, they did not revise their opinions sufficiently in the light of the evidence – a phenomenon that was labelled **conservatism**. The clear suggestion was that human judgement was poor, although there was some debate as to the precise reason for this. Perhaps it was due to a failure to understand the impact of the evidence or to an inability to combine the probability estimates according to Bayes' theorem.

Aside from the theoretical interest in these possibilities, there were practical implications of this debate. If people are good at assessing probabilities but poor at combining them (as Edwards [1968] suggested) then perhaps they could be helped; a relatively simple remedy would be to design a support system that took the human assessments and combined them using Bayes' theorem. However, if people were poor at assessing the component probabilities, then there wouldn't be much point in devising systems to help them combine these. 'Garbage in – garbage out' was a popular aphorism for summarizing this possibility.

However, before any firm conclusions were reached as to the cause of conservatism, the research exploring the phenomenon fizzled out. Two reasons for this can be identified. One cause (which we will consider in Sections 5.3 and 5.4) was the emergence of research into heuristics and biases and, in particular, the discovery of what Kahneman and Tversky (1973) called base-rate neglect. Before this development, however, growing disquiet was being voiced about the validity of book bag and poker chip experiments for assessing judgement.

Several studies had shown that quite subtle differences in the way that the tasks were presented to subjects resulted in considerable variability in the amount of conservatism. For example, the **diagnosticity** of the data seemed an important variable. Diagnosticity of information means how much impact it has on opinion revision. Diagnosticity is indicated by the likelihood ratio. Imagine, instead of our two bags with a 70/30 split in the proportions of blue and red poker chips, the bags contained 51 chips of one colour and 49 of the other. Clearly, two consecutive draws of a red chip would not be very diagnostic as to which of the two bags was being sampled. Phillips and Edwards' (1966) experiments showed that the more diagnostic the information, the more conservative was the subject. But when the information was very weakly diagnostic, as in this particular example, human probability revision, far from being conservative, was too extreme.

Another important factor was how the information was presented. Presenting information all at once or one bit at a time is irrelevant according to Bayes' theorem but Peterson *et al.* (1965) found that presenting one item of information at a time, eliciting revisions after each item, produced less conservatism than giving the same information all in one go. Pitz *et al.* (1967) described this as an **inertia effect**: if an initial sequence of information favoured one of the hypotheses under evaluation, subjects tended not to reduce their belief when confronted with later conflicting information.

DuCharme and Peterson (1968) investigated probability revision in a situation they considered nearer to real life than the standard paradigm. Most experiments, they complained, usually restricted information to one of two discrete possibilities (red or blue chip). In the real world, information leading to revision of opinion does not have discrete values but varies along a continuum. They gave their subjects the task of deciding which population was being sampled from – males or females – on the basis of the information given by randomly sampling heights from one of the populations. Using this task, DuCharme and Peterson found conservatism reduced to half the level found in the more artificial tasks. They concluded that this was due to their subjects' greater familiarity with the height distributions underlying their task.

Winkler and Murphy (1973) expressed further doubt concerning the validity of the conclusions from the book bag and poker chip paradigms. They argued that the standard task differed in several crucial aspects from the real world:

1   The pieces of evidence usually presented to subjects are conditionally independent. That is, knowing one piece of information does not change the likelihood of the other: producing one red chip from a bag, and then replacing it, does not affect the likelihood of drawing another red chip. However, in real-world situations this assumption often does not make sense. For example, someone trying to discriminate hostile from friendly aircraft might spot an aircraft flying a non-standard route that fails to respond to radio signals. Flying off course and failing to respond are not independent – both could be caused by equipment failure. So, after observing one we should be less influenced by the other.

    Winkler and Murphy argued that in many real-world situations lack of conditional independence of the information renders much of it redundant. In the standard tasks, subjects may have treated the information as if it was conditionally dependent and so one possible explanation for conservatism is that subjects are behaving much as they would do in familiar situations that involve redundant information sources.

2   In most experiments, the contents of the bags are fixed but in reality our hypotheses are not always constant; indeed, evidence may cause us to change the set of hypotheses under consideration.

3   In reality, information may be somewhat unreliable and therefore less diagnostic than the perfectly reliable colours of the poker chips.

4   Typical experiments offer very diagnostic evidence – clearly favouring one hypothesis – whereas in reality evidence is very often weakly diagnostic. Again the result of generalizing from experience may be the appearance of conservatism. You will recall Phillips and Edwards' (1966) discovery that probability revision was too extreme with very weakly diagnostic evidence.

Winkler and Murphy concluded that 'conservatism may be an artifact caused by dissimilarities between the laboratory and the real world'.

5.3   Heuristics and biases

From the early 1970s Kahneman and Tversky provided a plethora of demonstrations of human judgemental error and linked these to the operation of a set of **mental heuristics** – mental rules of thumb – that they proposed the mind uses to simplify the process of judgement. These foibles, they argued, indicated that the underlying processes of judgement were not normative (e.g. did not compute probabilities using Bayes' theorem) but instead used simpler rules that were easier for the brain to implement quickly.

The logic of their empirical research was to infer the characteristics of the mental processes underlying judgement by studying persistent biases – those not due to inattention or fatigue. The idea, spelled out in Kahneman *et al.* (1982), is that, due to limited mental processing capacity, strategies of simplification are required to reduce the complexity of judgement tasks and render them tractable by the kind of mind that people have. Accordingly, the principal reason for interest in judgemental biases was not merely that subjects made errors but that the errors revealed how people made use of relatively simple but error-prone heuristics for making judgements.

5.3.1   The 'representativeness' heuristic

The **representativeness** heuristic is used to determine how likely it is that an event is a member of a category by considering how similar or typical the event is to the category (remember the similarity-based approach to categorization discussed in Chapter 9?). For example, people may judge the likelihood that a given individual is a librarian by the extent to which the individual resembles a 'typical' librarian. This may seem a reasonable strategy but it neglects consideration of the relative prevalence of librarians in society as a whole: the so-called **base rate**. We have seen that Bayes' theorem prescribes that prior likelihood is an important component when assessing the impact of new information. So, when given information about an individual, the chances that he or she is a member of a profession will still be influenced by the prior likelihood – or base rate – for that profession. Knowing that someone regularly works in the British Library might increase your belief that they are a famous writer, but it is still more likely that she or he is a librarian because there are more of them than famous writers. Tversky and Kahneman found that when base rates of different categories varied, judgements of the occupations of described people were correspondingly biased – due to base-rate neglect. People using the representativeness heuristic for forecasting were employing a form of stereotyping in which similarity dominated other cues as a basis for judgement.

In Kahneman and Tversky's (1973) experiments demonstrating neglect of base rates, subjects were found to ignore information concerning the prior probabilities of the hypotheses – the polar opposite of conservatism. For example, in one study subjects were presented with this brief personal description of an individual called Jack:

> Jack is a 45-year-old man. He is married and has four children. He is generally conservative, careful and ambitious. He shows no interest in political and social issues and spends most of his free time on his many hobbies which include home carpentry, sailing and mathematical puzzles.

Half the subjects were told that the description had been drawn from a sample of seventy engineers and thirty lawyers while the other half were told that the description was drawn from a sample of thirty engineers and seventy lawyers. So, the base rate, or prevalence of engineers, for the two groups was 70 per cent and 30 per cent respectively. However, when asked to estimate the probability that Jack was an engineer, the mean estimates of the two groups were only very slightly different (50 per cent vs 55 per cent). On the basis of such results, Kahneman and Tversky concluded that prior probabilities are largely ignored when individuating information is made available.

Kahneman and Tversky then gave a description designed to be totally uninformative about the profession of the individual:

> Dick is a 30-year-old man. He is married with no children. A man of high ability and high motivation, he promises to be quite successful in his field. He is well liked by his colleagues.

When contemplating this description, subjects given markedly different base rates produced identical median estimates of 50 per cent. Kahneman and Tversky concluded that base rates were properly utilized when no specific information was given, but that base rates were neglected when even worthless information was provided (as in this example).

Tversky and Kahneman (1983) also invoked judgement by representativeness to explain the **conjunction fallacy** whereby a conjunction of two events is judged to be more likely than one of those events alone. The fallacy violates a simple principle of probability: the probability of a conjunction A and B can never exceed either the probability of A or the probability of B. Nevertheless, subjects who read a description of a woman called Linda who had a history of interest in liberal causes thought it more likely that she was a feminist bank clerk (i.e. a conjunction – Linda is a feminist *and* a bank clerk) than just a bank clerk, thereby violating the conjunction rule. Of course, though all feminist bank clerks are bank clerks, feminist bank clerks are more *representative* of people interested in liberal causes than bank clerks in general. So, while valid probabilities respect the conjunction rule, judgements of representativeness may not.

5.3.2 The 'availability' heuristic

The **availability** heuristic is invoked when people estimate likelihood or relative frequency by the ease with which instances can be brought to mind. Instances of frequent events are typically easier to recall than instances of less frequent events so availability will often be a valid cue for estimates of likelihood. However, availability is affected by factors other than likelihood. For example, recent events and emotionally salient events are easier to recollect. It is a common experience that the perceived riskiness of air travel arises in the immediate wake of an air disaster.

Judgements made on the basis of availability then are vulnerable to bias whenever availability and likelihood are uncorrelated.

5.3.3   The 'anchor and adjust' heuristic

The **anchor and adjust** heuristic is used when people make estimates by starting from an initial value and then adjust it to arrive at their final estimate. The claim is that adjustment is typically insufficient. For instance, one experimental task required subjects to estimate various quantities stated in percentages (e.g. the percentage of African countries in the UN). Subjects communicated their answers by using a spinner wheel showing numbers between 0 and 100. For each question, the wheel was spun and then subjects were first asked whether the true answer was above or below this arbitrary value. They then gave their estimate of the actual value. Perversely, people's estimates were found to correlate with the initial (entirely random) starting point (cf. Wilson *et al.*, 1996).

5.4   Evaluating the heuristics and biases account

The heuristics and biases research provided a methodology, a vivid explanatory framework and a strong suggestion that judgement is not as good as it might be. Kahneman and Tversky (1982) made clear that the main goal of their research was to understand the processes that produce both valid and invalid judgements. However, it soon became apparent that 'although errors of judgement are but a method by which some cognitive processes are studied, the method has become a significant part of the message' (Kahneman and Tversky, 1982, p.494). So how should we regard human judgement?

There has been an enormous amount of discussion of Tversky and Kahneman's findings and claims. Researchers in the heuristics and biases tradition have generated shock and astonishment that people seem so bad at judging probability despite the fact that we all live in an uncertain world. Not surprisingly, these claims have been challenged. Some question whether the demonstrations of biases in judgement apply to experts operating in their domain of expertise or merely to student samples. Another argument is that the experimental tasks set to subjects provide a misleading perspective of their competence. A third argument is that the standards for the assessment of judgement are inappropriate.

Consideration of a prominent critique of Tversky and Kahneman's argument is given below.

5.4.1   Representativeness and base-rate neglect

Following Tversky and Kahneman's original demonstration of base-rate neglect, research established that base rates might be attended to more (though usually not sufficiently) if they were perceived as relevant (Bar-Hillel, 1980), had a causal role (Kahneman and Tversky, 1982) or were 'vivid' rather than 'pallid' (Nisbett and Ross, 1980). However, Gigerenzer *et al.* (1988) argued that the variations in base-rate neglect have nothing to do with any of these factors *per se*, but arise because different problems may to varying degrees encourage the subject to represent the problem as a Bayesian revision problem. Just because the experimenter assumes that she has defined a probability problem does not imply that the subject will see it in the same way. In particular, subjects may have reasons not to take the base rate asserted by the experimenter as their subjective prior probability. In Kahneman and Tversky's original experiments the descriptions were not actually randomly sampled (as the subjects were told) but especially selected to be 'representative' of the professions. To the extent that subjects suspected this was the case then they would be entitled to ignore the offered base rate.

Gigerenzer *et al.* (1988) let their subjects experience the sampling themselves. Their subjects examined ten pieces of paper each marked lawyer or engineer in proportion to the base rates. Subjects then drew one of the pieces of paper from an urn and unfolded it so they could read a description of an individual without being able to see the mark defining it as being of a lawyer or engineer. In these circumstances, subjects used the base rates in a proper fashion – base-rate neglect 'disappeared'. However in a replication where base rates were asserted, rather than sampled, Kahneman and Tversky's base-rate neglect was replicated.

Kahneman and Tversky (1996) have argued that a fair summary of the research would be that explicitly presented base rates are generally under-weighted but not ignored. They also pointed out that, in Gigerenzer *et al.*'s (1988) experiment, subjects who sampled the information themselves still produced judgements that deviated from the Bayesian solution in the direction predicted by representativeness. Evidently then representativeness is useful for predicting judgements. However, to the extent that base rates are not entirely ignored (Koehler, 1995), the heuristic rationale for representativeness is limited. You will recall that the original explanation for base-rate neglect was the operation of a simple heuristic that reduced the need for integration of information. If judgements in these experiments reflect use of base rates – albeit to a limited extent – it is hard to account for findings by the operation of a simplifying representativeness heuristic.

5.4.2 Frequency and the conjunction fallacy

Tversky and Kahneman (1983) reported evidence that violations of the conjunction rule largely disappeared when subjects were requested to assess the relative **frequency** of events rather than the probability of a single event. Thus, instead of being asked about the likelihood for a particular individual, subjects were requested to assess how many people in a survey of 100 adult males had had heart attacks and then were asked to assess the number who were both over 55 years old *and* had had heart attacks. Only 25 per cent of subjects violated the conjunction rule by giving higher values to the latter than to the former. When asked about likelihoods for single events, however, it is typically the vast majority of subjects who violate the rule. This difference in performance between frequency and single-event versions of the conjunction problem has been replicated several times since (cf. Gigerenzer, 1994).

Gigerenzer (1994) has suggested that people are naturally adapted to reasoning with information in the form of frequencies and that because of this the conjunction fallacy 'disappears' if reasoning is based on frequencies. This suggests that the difficulties that people experience in solving probability problems can be reduced if the problems require subjects to assess relative frequency for a class of events rather than the probability of a single event. Thus, it is possible that if judgements were elicited with frequency formats there would be no biases. Kahneman and Tversky (1996) disagree and argue that the frequency format serves to provide subjects with a powerful cue to the relation of inclusion between sets that are explicitly compared, or evaluated in immediate succession. When the structure of the conjunction is made more apparent, then subjects who appreciate the constraint supplied by the rule will be less likely to violate it. According to their account, salient cues to set inclusion – not the frequency information *per se* – prompted subjects to adjust their judgement.

To test this explanation, Kahneman and Tversky (1996) reported a new variation of the conjunction problem experiment where subjects made judgements of frequencies but the cues to set inclusion were removed. They presented subjects with the description of Linda and then asked their subjects to suppose that there were 1,000 women who fit the description. They then asked one group of subjects to estimate how many of them would be bank tellers; a second, independent group of subjects were asked how many were bank tellers and active feminists; a third group made evaluations for both categories. As predicted, those subjects who evaluated both categories mostly conformed to the conjunction rule. However, in a between-groups comparison of the other two groups, the estimates for 'bank tellers and active feminists' were found to be significantly higher than the estimates for bank tellers. Kahneman and Tversky argue that these results show that subjects use the representativeness heuristic to generate their judgements and then edit their responses to respect class inclusion where they detect cues to that relation. Thus, they concluded that the key variable controlling adherence to the conjunction rule is not the relative frequency format *per se* but the opportunity to detect the relation of class inclusion.

Other authors have investigated the impact of frequency information (Evans *et al.*, 2000; Girotto and Gonzales, 2002) and concluded that it is not the frequency information *per se* but the perceived relations between the entities that is affected by different versions of the problem, though this is rejected by Hoffrage *et al.* (2002). We need to understand more of the reasons underlying the limiting conditions of cognitive biases – how it is that seemingly inconsequential changes in the format of information can so radically alter the quality of judgement. Biases that can apparently be cured so simply cannot plausibly be held to reveal fundamental and immutable characteristics of judgement processes. We shall now consider the history of one well-known cognitive bias: overconfidence.

5.5 Overconfidence

In the 1970s and 1980s a considerable amount of evidence was marshalled for the view that people suffer from an overconfidence bias. Typical laboratory studies of calibration ask subjects to answer a question such as:

'Which is further south?'   (a) Rome, or

(b) New York

Subjects are required to indicate the answer that they think is correct and then state how confident they are on a probability scale ranging from 50 per cent to 100 per cent (the minimum is 50 per cent since one of the answers is always correct and 50 per cent is the probability of guessing correctly). To be well calibrated, an assessed probability should correspond with the number of correct judgements over a number of assessments. For example, if you assign a probability of 70 per cent to each of ten predictions then you should get seven of those predictions correct. Typically, however, people tend to give **overconfident** responses – their average confidence is higher than their proportion of correct answers. McClelland and Bolger (1994) and Harvey (1997) give comprehensive reviews of this aspect of probabilistic judgement.

Overconfidence has been recorded in the judgements of experts. For example, Christensen-Szalanski and Bushyhead (1981) explored the validity of the probabilities given by physicians to diagnoses of pneumonia. They found that the probabilities were poorly calibrated and very overconfident; the proportion of patients who turned out to have pneumonia was far less than the probability statements implied. Wagenaar and Keren (1986) found overconfidence in lawyers' predictions of the outcome of court trials in which they represented one side. As they point out, it is inconceivable that the lawyers do not pay attention to the outcomes of trials in which they have participated, so why don't they learn to make well-calibrated judgements?

Could the circumstances in which some experts operate impede the proper monitoring of feedback necessary for the development of well-calibrated judgements? A consideration of the reports of well-calibrated experts supports this notion; they all appear to be cases where some explicit unambiguous quantification of uncertainty is routinely made and the outcome feedback is prompt and unambiguous. Doctors and lawyers don't routinely quantify their uncertainty, and may have to wait months to discover the outcomes of their judgements, the truth of which may never be revealed.

The most commonly cited example of well-calibrated judgements is weather forecasters' estimates of the likelihood of rainfall (Murphy and Winkler, 1984) but there are others. Keren (1987) found highly experienced tournament bridge players (but not experienced non-tournament players) made well-calibrated forecasts of the likelihood that their bids would be made, and Phillips (1987) reports well-calibrated forecasts of horse races by bookmakers. In each of these three cases, the judgements made by the experts are precise numerical statements and the outcome feedback is unambiguous and received promptly and so can be easily compared with the initial forecast. Under these circumstances, experts are unlikely to be insensitive to the experience of being surprised; there is very little scope for neglecting, or denying, any mismatch between forecast and outcome.

Following the ideas of Brunswik (1943, 1955) – that cognition is well adapted to people's natural environments – some judgement researchers have argued that overconfidence is an artifact of artificial experimental tasks and the non-representative sampling of stimulus materials. Gigerenzer et al. (1991) and Juslin (1994) claim that overconfidence is observed because the typical general knowledge quizzes used in most experiments contain a disproportionate number of misleading items. For example, most people judge wrongly that Rome is south of New York. These authors found that when knowledge items are randomly sampled the overconfidence phenomenon disappears. Gigerenzer et al. (1991) presented their subjects with randomly selected pairs of German cities. When asked to select the biggest and indicate their confidence, overconfidence was not observed.

Erev et al. (1994) spotted another misleading source of evidence of over-confidence. They explained that overconfidence might, to some degree, reflect an underlying random component of judgement. When any two variables are not perfectly correlated – and confidence and accuracy aren't *perfectly* correlated – there will be a regression effect. For example, the heights of fathers and their sons are positively – but not perfectly – correlated. Consequently, a sample of the (adult) sons of extremely tall fathers will, on average, be shorter than their fathers *and at the same time* a sample of the fathers of extremely tall (adult) sons will, on average, be shorter than their sons. Thus, depending on how you sampled – either looking at very tall sons or very tall fathers – could lead you to two opposite conclusions about the direction of a (non-existent) difference between the populations.

So could it really be that all the evidence for overconfidence is merely an illusion created by inappropriate sampling of test items and regression effects? Budescu *et al.* (1997) attempted to measure and control for the regression effects caused by random variation in judgements by presenting the same items (random pairs of large American cities) on several occasions to their subjects. They found that the vast majority of the individuals in their study (87 per cent) were biased towards overconfidence even after the effects of random error in their judgements had been taken into account. As they also used a representative sample of items, both the artifactual sources of overconfidence should have been eliminated.

Juslin *et al.* (2000) report a meta-analysis comparing 35 studies, where the items for judgement were randomly selected from a defined domain, with 95 studies where items were selected non-randomly by experimenters. While overconfidence was evident for selected items, it was close to zero for randomly sampled items, which suggests that overconfidence is not simply a ubiquitous cognitive bias. This analysis suggests that the appearance of overconfidence may be an illusion – not one experienced by experimental subjects, but one inadvertently created and suffered by researchers, and so not a cognitive bias in their respondents.

Summary of Section 5

- There have been many demonstrations of human judgemental error, linking errors to the operation of various heuristics and biases.
- There is evidence that many of these reported biases disappear when the wording of the problems is changed. Whether this reflects sensitivity to particular cues or adaptivity to frequency information formats is the subject of debate.

6   Fast and frugal theories of decision making

Another approach to judgement and choice that has recently emerged tests the efficacy of heuristics on information occurring 'in the wild' rather than on specially contrived laboratory problems. Gigerenzer and Goldstein (1996) comparatively evaluated the performance of a set of different decision strategies. Instead of focusing on violations of normative rules, they produced a measure of the efficacy of simple mental strategies for judgement by measuring the number of correct inferences that different strategies made. The class of simple models that Gigerenzer and Goldstein tested were what they called **fast and frugal** heuristics: 'frugal' because these heuristics used just one piece of information in order to make decisions; 'fast' because they didn't attempt any sort of integration of different bits of information prescribed by such normative procedures as SEU or Bayes' theorem. By the standards of classical rationality enshrined in normative rules, the mental strategies that Gigerenzer and Goldstein considered look very primitive. Indeed, they were quite explicit about the fact that the simple heuristics that they tested violate basic axioms such as transitivity. Nevertheless, the proof of the pudding is in the eating; as we have seen, people and bees violate transitivity and yet manage to get by.

The inspiration for this exercise was Simon's (1956) idea of **bounded rationality**. Simon emphasized that, due to its limited capacity, human information processing would be obliged to use **satisficing** methods for problem solving (satisficing is an old Northumbrian word meaning to satisfy). Simon used it to describe decision procedures that, while not optimal, reflect the constraints supplied by human information-processing capacity and the opportunities provided by the structure of the environment. Most research on human judgement has focused on the non-optimal nature of simple human information-processing strategies – the importance of the environment structure in determining performance has been overlooked. Nevertheless, we have seen how evidence for both conservatism and overconfidence was undermined by considering how mental strategies might exploit the way information is structured in the natural environment. But could judgement strategies that violate normative rules and utilize just one piece of information possibly be of effective service?

In their study, Gigerenzer and Goldstein used the properties of a set of German cities as information on which to base decisions as to which city was the biggest. Commonly known correlates of city size such as whether it is the state capital, has a university, a football club in the top division or an inter-city rail station were the cues that the heuristics could use. One heuristic that Gigerenzer and Goldstein tested they called 'Take the Best' – so called as it simply worked through the cues in order of their predictive validity until one was found that discriminated between two cities and then responded accordingly. Thus, if the two cities under consideration could not be discriminated on the basis of the most diagnostic cue (e.g. whether it is the state capital or not) the search through memory continues. The search for discriminatory cue values proceeds in order of their relative diagnosticity until a cue is found that discriminates the two cities (e.g. one has an inter-city rail station and the other does not), whereupon information retrieval is stopped and the judgement made according to this single cue.

Gigerenzer and Goldstein compared simple heuristics such as 'Take the Best' with other decision rules that integrate multiple bits of information (such as multiple regression). They modelled the effect of limited knowledge by simulating six classes of subjects who knew varying proportions of the cue values associated with the cities. Surprisingly, they found that 'Take the Best' did as well as any of the other algorithms and considerably better than some. As it only uses one piece of information it would be much faster than any process that retrieves multiple bits of information and attempts integration of the information. The result is important for demonstrating that, although adherence to normative rules may be sufficient for good judgement, it is not necessary.

Further demonstrations of the efficacy of fast and frugal heuristics have studied binary decisions in a wide range of types of knowledge environment (e.g. which professor has the highest salary? Which US city has more homeless people?). These studies extended the application beyond choice to value estimation, categorization and memory (Gigerenzer *et al.*, 1999). Goldstein and Gigerenzer (2002) asked American and German students which is bigger: San Antonio or San Diego? While 62 per cent of the Americans correctly named San Diego, 100 per cent of the German students were correct. The Germans were applying a **recognition heuristic** – if you recognize one and not the other, pick the city you have heard of. As you usually hear about the bigger cities of foreign countries before the smaller ones this will be a pretty good cue. Because the Americans had heard of both cities they couldn't apply this cue and had to rely on other, apparently less valid, cues. In the same way, for city-size decisions, American students were slightly more accurate about German cities than American cities. Ignorance can even sometimes be helpful because simple mental heuristics *can* exploit the structure of information in the environment to make good inferences. As a consequence of such results, we might question the present pre-eminent status of normative rules for defining rationality and for serving as a benchmark for assessing human judgement.

Summary of Section 6

- Human decision making may employ fast and frugal heuristics – simple rules that yield quick decisions yet which can be highly accurate in certain natural environments.

7   Conclusion

The idea that people don't decide as they should was appreciated by psychologists very early on. In a seminal paper, which effectively introduced the study of decision making to psychology, Edwards (1954, p.382) wrote: 'It is easy for a psychologist to point out that an economic man ... is very unlike a real man.' Yet for economists this disparity is less clear. As Lopes (a psychologist) put it: 'Economics considers itself a normative science, the very term an oxymoron of ought and is' (1994, p.222). Psychologists and economists think rather differently about the behavioural research exploring decision making (cf. Hertwig and Ortmann, 2001; Lopes, 1994). To psychologists, it is evident that people cannot conceivably represent all the relevant information that normative models require for judgement and decision: 'Who could design a brain that could perform the way this model mandates? Every single one of us would have to know and understand everything completely, and at once' (Daniel Kahneman quoted by Bernstein, 1996).

While it may be a tad optimistic to presume that the social sciences are on the verge of reconciliation and consensus on this subject, psychology has, since the

1950s, made enormous progress in establishing that actual human decision making cannot be satisfactorily characterized in the idealized way mathematics and economics have assumed. Moreover, alternative descriptive theories that account for the discrepancies are emerging. Perhaps the best recent piece of evidence for that claim is that a psychologist – Daniel Kahneman – shared the 2002 Nobel Prize for Economics 'for having integrated insights from psychological research into economic science, especially concerning human judgement and decision making under uncertainty' (Nobel citation, 2002).

Does the rejection of normative theory as a model for human judgement and choice imply that judgement and choice must be poor or even 'irrational'? No. Although the evidence that people do not perform ideally is clear, any reasonable standards of rationality must surely accept that the computational requirements of normative models are beyond the capacity of a human brain: nevertheless, such bounded rationality (cf. Simon, 1956) does not imply irrationality.

In my (admittedly fallible) judgement the issues surrounding the nature and evaluation of human judgement and decision making are profound and will not be resolved easily or in the near future. To make further progress, we need studies that do more than merely knock down the straw man defined by normative models. Among the many questions that arise, two broad issues can be framed: first, how is it that we are as competent as we evidently are? Second, what can we do about how incompetent we evidently are? Quite how it is that people perform as effectively as they do by applying non-normative mental strategies to the limited information that they can process – and how we might learn to improve our decision making – remains to be explored and explained.

Now that you have read this chapter you can reinforce and extend your learning by reading an original journal article associated with it, available online from the DD303 website. Remember, these are original journal articles, so the style is different from this textbook, and don't be too concerned if you can't follow every detail.

Further reading

Gigerenzer, G. and Selten, R. (eds) (2001) *Bounded Rationality: The Adaptive Toolbox*, Cambridge, MA, MIT Press.

Kahneman, D. and Tversky, A. (eds) (2000) *Choices, Values and Frames*, Cambridge, Cambridge University Press.

Koehler, D. and Harvey, N. (eds) (2004) *Blackwell Handbook of Judgment and Decision Making*, Oxford, Blackwell Publishing.

References

Allais, M. (1953) 'Le comportement de l'homme rationnel devant le risque, critique des posulats et axioms de l'école Américaine', *Econometrica*, vol.21, pp.503–46.

Allais, M. (1979) 'The foundations of a positive theory of choice involving risk and a criticism of the postulates and axioms of the American school' in Allais, M. and Hagen, O. (eds) *Expected Utility Hypothesis and the Allais Paradox*, Dordrecht, Reidel.

Allais, M. and Hagen, O. (eds) (1979) *op. cit.*, Dordrecht, Reidel.

Bar-Hillel, M. (1980) 'The base-rate fallacy in probability judgements', *Acta Psychologica*, vol.44, pp.211–33.

Bernstein, P.L. (1996) *Against the Gods: The Remarkable Story of Risk*, New York, Wiley.

Brunswik, E. (1943) 'Organismic achievement and environmental probability', *Psychological Review*, vol.50, pp.255–72.

Brunswik, E. (1955) 'Representative design and probabilistic theory in a functional psychology', *Psychological Review*, vol.62, pp.193–217.

Budescu, D., Wallsten, T.S. and Au, W.T. (1997) 'On the importance of random error in the study of probabilistic judgement: Part II: Applying the stochastic judgement model to detect systematic trends', *Journal of Behavioral Decision Making*, vol.10, pp.173–88.

Christensen-Szalanski, J.J.J. and Bushyhead, J.B. (1981) 'Physicians' use of probabilistic information in a real clinical setting', *Journal of Experimental Psychology, Human Perception and Performance*, vol.7, pp.928–35.

Cohen, L.J. (1981) 'Can human irrationality be experimentally demonstrated?', *Behavioral and Brain Sciences*, vol.4, pp.317–70.

DuCharme, W.M. and Peterson, C.R. (1968) 'Intuitive inference about normally distributed populations', *Journal of Experimental Psychology*, vol.78, pp.269–75.

Edwards, W. (1954) 'The theory of decision making', *Psychological Bulletin*, vol.41, pp.380–417.

Edwards, W. (1955) 'The prediction of decisions among bets', *Journal of Experimental Psychology*, vol.50, pp.201–14.

Edwards, W. (1968) 'Conservatism in human information processing' in Kleinmuntz, B. (ed.) *Formal Representation of Human Judgment*, New York, Wiley.

Edwards, W. (1992) 'Toward the demise of economic man and woman: bottom lines from Santa Cruz' in Edwards, W. (ed.) *Utility Theories: Measurements and Applications*, Dordrecht, Kluwer.

Erev, I., Wallsten, T.S. and Budescu, D.V. (1994) 'Simultaneous over-and underconfidence: the role of error in judgement processes', *Psychological Review*, vol.101, pp.519–28.

Evans, J. St B.T., Handley, S.J., Perham, N., Over, D.E. and Thompson, V.A. (2000) 'Frequency versus probability formats in statistical word problems', *Cognition*, vol.77, pp.197–213.

Gigerenzer, G. (1994) 'Why the distinction between single event probabilities and frequencies is important for psychology and vice-versa' in Wright, G. and Ayton, P. (eds) *Subjective Probability*, Chichester, Wiley.

Gigerenzer, G., Hell, W. and Blank, H. (1988) 'Presentation and content: the use of base rates as a continuous variable', *Journal of Experimental Psychology: Human Perception and Performance*, vol.14, pp.513–25.

Gigerenzer, G., Hoffrage, U. and Kleinbölting, H. (1991) 'Probabilistic mental models: a Brunswikian theory of confidence', *Psychological Review*, vol.98, pp.506–28.

Gigerenzer, G. and Goldstein, D.G. (1996) 'Reasoning the fast and frugal way: models of bounded rationality', *Psychological Review*, vol.103, pp.650–69.

Gigerenzer, G., Todd, P.M. and The ABC Research Group (1999) *Simple Heuristics that Make us Smart*, Oxford, Oxford University Press.

Girotto, V. and Gonzales, M. (2002) 'Chances and frequencies in probabilistic reasoning: rejoinder to Hoffrage, Gigerenzer, Krauss, and Martignon', *Cognition*, vol.84, pp.353–9.

Goldstein, D.G. and Gigerenzer, G. (2002) 'Models of ecological rationality: the recognition heuristic', *Psychological Review*, vol.109, pp.75–90.

Grether, D.M. and Plott, C.R. (1979) 'Economic theory of choice and the preference reversal phenomenon', *American Economic Review*, vol.69, pp.623–38.

Harvey, N. (1997) 'Confidence in judgement', *Trends in Cognitive Sciences*, 1, pp.78–82.

Hertwig, R. and Ortmann, A. (2001) 'Experimental practices in economics: a methodological challenge for psychologists?', *Behavioral and Brain Sciences*, vol.24, p.383.

Hoffrage, U., Gigerenzer, G., Krauss, S. and Martignon, L. (2002) 'Representation facilitates reasoning: what natural frequencies are and what they are not', *Cognition*, vol.84, pp.343–52.

Hsee, C.K. (1998) 'Less is better; when low-value options are valued more highly than high-value options', *Journal of Behavioral Decision Making*, vol.11, pp.107–21.

Juslin, P. (1994) 'The overconfidence phenomenon as a consequence of informal experimenter-guided selection of almanac items', *Organizational Behavior and Human Decision Processes*, vol.57, pp.226–46.

Juslin, P., Winman, A. and Olsson, H. (2000) 'Naive empiricism and dogmatism in confidence research: a critical examination of the hard–easy effect', *Psychological Review*, vol.107, pp.384–96.

Kahneman, D., Slovic, P. and Tversky, A. (eds) (1982) *Judgement under Uncertainty: Heuristics and Biases*, Cambridge, Cambridge University Press.

Kahneman, D. and Tversky, A. (1972) 'Subjective probability: a judgement of representativeness', *Cognitive Psychology*, vol.3, pp.430–54.

Kahneman, D. and Tversky, A. (1973) 'On the psychology of prediction', *Psychological Review*, vol.80, pp.237–51.

Kahneman, D. and Tversky, A. (1979) 'Prospect theory: an analysis of decision making under risk', *Econometrica*, vol.47, pp.263–91.

Kahneman, D. and Tversky, A. (1982) 'On the study of statistical intuitions' in Kahneman, D., Slovic, P. and Tversky, A. (eds) (1982) *op. cit.*

Kahneman, D. and Tversky, A. (1996) 'On the reality of cognitive illusions: a reply to Gigerenzer's critique', *Psychological Review*, vol.103, pp.582–91.

Keller, L.R. (1985) 'The effects of problem representation on the sure-thing and substitution principles', *Management Science*, vol.31, pp.738–51.

Keren, G.B. (1987) 'Facing uncertainty in the game of bridge: a calibration study', *Organizational Behavior and Human Decision Processes*, vol.39, pp.98–114.

Koehler, J.J. (1995) 'The base-rate fallacy reconsidered – descriptive, normative, and methodological challenges', *Behavioral and Brain Sciences*, vol.19, pp.1–55.

Lichtenstein, S. and Slovic, P. (1973) 'Response-induced reversals of preference in gambling: an extended replication in Las Vegas', *Journal of Experimental Psychology*, vol.101, pp.16–20.

Lichtenstein, S., Slovic, P. and Zink, D. (1969) 'Effect of instruction in expected value on optimality of gambling decisions', *Journal of Experimental Psychology*, vol.79, pp.236–40.

Lopes, L.L. (1994) 'Psychology and economics: perspectives on risk, cooperation, and the marketplace', *Annual Review of Psychology*, vol.45, pp.197–227.

McClelland, A.G.R. and Bolger, F. (1994) 'The calibration of subjective probabilities: theories and models 1980–1994' in Wright, G. and Ayton, P. (eds) *Subjective Probability*, New York, Wiley.

Murphy, A.H. and Winkler, R.L. (1984) 'Probability forecasting in meteorology', *Journal of the American Statistical Association*, vol.79, pp.489–500.

Nisbett, R. and Ross, L. (1980) *Human Inference: Strategies and Shortcomings*, Englewood Cliffs, NJ, Prentice Hall.

Nobel Foundation (2004) *The Bank of Sweden Prize in Economic Sciences in Memory of Alfred Nobel*, http://www.nobel.se/economics/laureates/2002/index.html (accessed 27 July 2004).

Peterson, C.R., Schneider, R.J. and Miller, A.J. (1965) 'Sample size and the revision of subjective probability', *Journal of Experimental Psychology*, vol.69, pp.522–7.

Phillips, L.D. (1984) 'A theory of requisite decision-models', *Acta Psychologica*, vol.56, pp.29–48.

Phillips, L.D. (1987) 'On the adequacy of judgmental probability forecasts' in Wright, G. and Ayton, P. (eds) *Judgemental Forecasting*, Chichester, Wiley.

Phillips, L.D. (1989) 'Decision analysis in the 1990s' in Shahini, A. and Stainton, R. (eds) *Tutorial Papers in Operational Research 1989*, Birmingham, Operational Research Society.

Phillips, L.D. and Edwards, W. (1966) 'Conservatism in simple probability inference tasks', *Journal of Experimental Psychology*, vol.72, pp.346–57.

Pitz, G.F., Downing, L. and Rheinold, H. (1967) 'Sequential effects in the revision of subjective probabilities', *Canadian Journal of Psychology*, vol.21, pp.381–93.

Raiffa, H. (1968) *Decision Analysis*, Reading, MA, Addison Wesley.

Samuelson, P.A. (1963) 'Risk and uncertainty: a fallacy of large numbers', *Scientia*, vol.98, pp.108–13.

Savage, L. (1954) *The Foundations of Statistics*, New York, Wiley.

Schlaifer, R. (1969) *Analysis of Decisions under Uncertainty*, New York, McGraw Hill.

Shafir, E. (1993) 'Choosing versus rejecting: why some options are both better and worse than others', *Memory and Cognition*, vol.21, pp.546–56.

Shafir, E., Simonson, I. and Tversky, A. (1993) 'Reason-based choice', *Cognition*, vol.49, pp.11–36.

Shafir, S. (1994) 'Intransitivity of preferences in honeybees: support for "comparative" evaluation of foraging options', *Animal Behaviour*, vol.48, pp.55–67.

Simon, H.A. (1956) 'Rational choice and the structure of the environment', *Psychological Review*, vol.63, pp.129–38.

Slovic, P. (1975) 'Choice between equally valued alternatives', *Journal of Experimental Psychology: Human Perception and Performance*, vol.1, pp.280–7.

Slovic, P. (1995) 'The construction of preference', *American Psychologist*, vol.50, pp.364–71.

Slovic, P., Fischhoff, B. and Lichtenstein, S. (1977) 'Behavioral decision theory', *Annual Review of Psychology*, vol.28, pp.1–39.

Slovic, P. and Lichtenstein, S. (1968) 'Relative importance of probabilities and payoffs in risk taking', *Journal of Experimental Psychology Monograph*, vol.78, pp.1–18.

Slovic, P. and Tversky, A. (1974) 'Who accepts Savage's axiom?', *Behavioral Science*, vol.19, pp.368–73.

Tversky, A. (1969) 'Intransitivity of preferences', *Psychological Review*, vol.76, pp.31–48.

Tversky, A. and Kahneman, D. (1974) 'Judgement under uncertainty: heuristics and biases', *Science*, vol.185, pp.1124–31.

Tversky, A. and Kahneman, D. (1981) 'The framing of decisions and the psychology of choice', *Science*, vol.211, pp.453–8.

Tversky, A. and Kahneman, D. (1983) 'Extensional versus intuitive reasoning: the conjunction fallacy in probability judgement', *Psychological Review*, vol.90, pp.293–315.

Tversky, A. and Kahneman, D. (1986) 'Rational choice and the framing of decisions', *Journal of Business*, vol.59, S251–S278.

Tversky, A., Sattath, S. and Slovic, P. (1988) 'Contingent weighting in judgement and choice', *Psychological Review*, vol.95, pp.371–84.

Tversky, A., Slovic, P. and Kahneman, D. (1990) 'The causes of preference reversal', *American Economic Review*, vol.80, pp.204–17.

von Neumann, J. and Morgenstern, O. (1944) *Theory of Games and Economic Behavior*, Princeton, NJ, Princeton University Press.

von Winterfeldt, D. and Edwards, W. (1986) *Decision Analysis and Behavioral Research*, Cambridge, Cambridge University Press.

Wagenaar, W.A. and Keren, G.B. (1986) 'Does the expert know? The reliability of predictions and confidence ratings of experts' in Hollnagel, E., Mancini, G. and Woods, D.D. (eds) *Intelligent Decision Support in Process Environments*, Berlin, Springer-Verlag.

Watson, S.R. and Buede, D.M. (1987) *Decision Synthesis: The Principles and Practice of Decision Analysis*, Cambridge, Cambridge University Press.

Wilson, T.D., Houston, C.E., Etling, K.M. and Brekke, N. (1996) 'A new look at anchoring effects: basic anchoring and its antecedents', *Journal of Experimental Psychology: General*, vol.125, pp.387–402.

Winkler, R.L. and Murphy, A.M. (1973) 'Experiments in the laboratory and the real world', *Organizational Behavior and Human Performance*, vol.20, pp.252–70.

Reasoning

Chapter 13

Mike Oaksford

1 Introduction

Suppose a friend tells you that

> 1 | *If John finds out, then he will be furious.*

and you discover later that

> 2 | *John found out.*

If you then conclude that

> 3 | *John was furious.*

you will have engaged in **reasoning** – that is, you will have inferred a **conclusion** (3) from some initial information or **premises** (1) and (2).

Reasoning has been studied since the time of the ancient Greeks. Aristotle suggested that reasoning is one of the abilities that marks us off from the other animals, implying that only humans are able to reason and only humans have minds that are capable of rational thought.

1.1 Reasoning and logic

Aristotle also developed the first system of **logic**: he produced a set of rules by which to judge whether certain passages of reasoning, like the one above, were valid; that is, for telling whether the conclusion (3) really does follow from the premises (1) and (2). This is one of the sources of a strong line adopted by some researchers in this area: reasoning is the process of applying logical laws.

This strong line also emerges in the foundations of modern logic – for instance, in Boole's *The Laws of Thought* (1854). In that book, Boole described a set of rules that determine how we can draw inferences from statements like *if ... then* (as in Example 1). The book's title clearly reveals that the author's intention was to describe the laws that govern human reasoning.

More recently, Piaget placed the ability to reason according to logical rules at the pinnacle of his **stage theory** of cognitive development, that is, at the formal operational stage (Inhelder and Piaget, 1958). One of our main concerns in this chapter will be to determine whether logic provides a good model of human reasoning. This does not mean that we should expect people to reason perfectly logically. Although we may all be *capable* of reasoning logically, perfect performance may, for example, take up too much memory. In which case, we might expect some errors to emerge and, as we will see, such errors have been observed.

Another theme that will emerge is whether logic is appropriate to describe real human reasoning at all. The full title of Boole's (1854) book was *An Investigation of the Laws of Thought On Which Are Founded the Mathematical Theories of Logic and Probabilities*. Almost one half of the book was devoted to probability theory, which Boole thought may provide a better theory of everyday reasoning. As we will see, some researchers do not view people's reasoning behaviour as *error prone but logical*. Rather, they view it as relatively *error free but probabilistic*. This difference emerges as a result of assigning differing meanings to the important words that figure in a passage of reasoning. In this chapter, we will concentrate heavily on the construction *if ... then*. According to some researchers, *if ... then* should be interpreted logically, in terms of the conditions under which it is true or false. For example, (1) is false if John does not get furious when he finds out; otherwise, it is true. Other researchers view (1) as describing a causal relation between two events, so that John finding out causes him to get furious. From this view, (1) should be interpreted probabilistically, in terms of the strength of the evidence one might have for believing that John will get furious given that he finds out. Of course, different people may know different things about John, which may lead them to different evaluations of the probability that he gets furious when he finds out. This could lead to individual differences in reasoning, and as we will see in Section 6.2, such differences have also been observed.

A further theme of this chapter arises from the fact that the experimental work on human reasoning shows that, according to logic, people do make many errors. If being logical is what we mean by being rational then these results may have some serious consequences. For example, in law people can only be held responsible for their actions if they can rationally evaluate the consequences of those actions. But if people are not rational, then how can society hold them responsible for what they do? Moreover, where is the boundary between sanity and insanity to be drawn? A sane person is one who responds rationally to the world and to other people. But if most normal adults are irrational, then who is sane and who is insane? In evaluating psychological theories in this area, it will therefore be important for us to pay close attention to what they have to say about human rationality.

The first issue we address is the sheer ubiquity of human reasoning. Reasoning, like doing the crossword, may seem like an activity we rarely – if ever – engage in. However, most of our common-sense psychological explanations of each other's behaviour assume that we are reasoning all the time.

1.2 Reasoning in everyday life

People are so dependent on reasoning processes that they tend to go unnoticed. Nonetheless, it is easy to show that a great deal of human behavior depends on reasoning processes. Suppose you see your neighbour arriving home. She passes her garage and sees that her partner's car is on the drive. When she reaches the door, instead of taking out her key and opening the door as she has done every night for the last twenty years, she rings the doorbell. Why your neighbour broke her habitual pattern of behaviour can be explained in an instant:

She saw that the car was there. She *knows* that, for it to be there, someone must have driven it from town where her partner dropped her off in the morning. Because she *knows* that only her partner has the keys, she *infers* that her partner drove it. She further *infers* that if the car is on the drive then her partner is in the house and hence he can open the door when she rings the bell. Consequently, rather than take out her key, she rings the doorbell.

Two pieces of information are already given. The first comes from prior knowledge: *if the car was there someone drove it.* The second comes directly from perception, that is, *the car was there.* These two pieces of information are combined in an inference to yield new information: someone drove the car. We can depict the inference as follows.

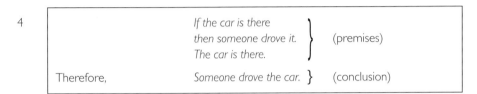

The given information can be regarded as the premises and the new information the conclusion of a passage of reasoning. The subsequent steps that lead your neighbour to the final conclusion that she should ring the doorbell can all be characterized in the same way. So it would seem that even the most mundane passage of human behaviour involves complex reasoning processes that require using given information (premises) to infer new information (conclusions).

So, how do we know when we can draw a conclusion from a set of premises? Suppose we had replaced the conclusion in example (4) above with the statement 'Her partner had a cream tea'. This would be new information too, but the conclusion does not seem to be valid – it does not seem to be related to the premises in the right kind of way. Simply believing the premises in (4) does not compel you to believe this conclusion. Trying to describe the relationship between premises and valid conclusions is the core of characterizing *logical or deductive* reasoning. The idea, as with Aristotle and Boole, is to provide rules that indicate when a conclusion does or does not follow from a set of premises. This is the subject of Section 2.

Summary of Section 1

- Human reasoning and rationality have been understood, contrastively, in terms of the use of logic or probability.
- Human reasoning, involving the drawing of new information (conclusions) from given information (premises), is ubiquitous.

2   Deductive reasoning and logic

Logic provides an account of the relationship between the premises and the conclusion of a deductive argument. First, we shall look at the structure of a logical argument.

2.1   Logical connectives

Logic starts from the idea that sentences are made up of two very general building blocks. First, there are **descriptive clauses** or sentences that say something true or false about the world, for example, 'John has a runny nose' or 'John has a cold'. Second, there are **structure-building words** that allow us to combine sentences to produce more complex sentences, for instance, 'John has a runny nose *and* John has a cold', '*if* John has a runny nose, *then* he has a cold'. Along with *and* and *if ... then*, other structure-building words include *or* and *not*. Collectively, these words are called **connectives** because they connect two simpler sentences together.

The most important of these is *if ... then*, which forms, schematically, sentences of the form *if p then q*, which are called **conditionals**. The *p* clause is called the **antecedent** and the *q* clause is called the **consequent**.

2.2   When are arguments logically valid?

In a **logically valid** argument, the truth of the premises guarantees the truth of the conclusion. Let us assume that sentences are simply true or false depending on whether what they say really is the case. So the sentence 'John has a runny nose' is true if and only if John has a runny nose; otherwise, it is false. How do we determine whether complex sentences made using the connectives are true or false? Well, *not* is particularly simple because all it does is reverse the truth value of a proposition. So, if 'John has a runny nose' is true then 'John does not have a runny nose' must be false. Conversely, if 'John has a runny nose' is false then 'John does not have a runny nose' must be true.

What about the other connectives? You should note that the other three connectives all connect two sentences, for example, 'John has a runny nose *and* John has a cold'. Each sentence making up this complex sentence could be either true or false. Thus, there are four possibilities. If *p* = 'John has a runny nose' and *q* = 'John has a cold', then

- either *p* is true and *q* is true
- or *p* is true and *q* is false
- or *p* is false and *q* is true
- or *p* is false and *q* is false.

In only one of these possibilities would we intuitively say that the complex sentence 'John has a runny nose *and* John has a cold' is true, that is, when *p* is true and *q* is true; otherwise, this complex sentence is false. So we can regard the connective *and* as mapping pairs of truth values on to a truth value. When both *p* and *q* are true, then *p and q* is true; for all other pairs, it is false. We can show this mapping in what is called a 'truth table' (see Table 13.1).

Table 13.1 Truth tables for the logical connectives *not*, *and*, and *if ... then*. The second and third columns show the four possible combinations of truth values for sentences *p* and *q*. Each is assumed to be either true or false. The four columns to the right show for each connective the truth value of the complex sentence formed from the connective and the sentences *p* and *q*

	Sentences		**not**	**and**	**if ... then**
			____	**Connectives**	____
Possibility	*p*	*q*	**not** *p*	**not** *q*	*p* **and** *q*	**if** *p* **then** *q*
A	true	true	false	false	true	true
B	true	false	false	true	false	false
C	false	true	true	false	false	true
D	false	false	true	true	false	true

Now try Activity 13.1

ACTIVITY 13.1 ————————————————————————

Use Table 13.1 to see whether you agree with the truth tables for *not* and for *and*. Choose any two simple sentences (i.e. ones not already containing a connective such as *or*, *if ... then*, or *and*). Let *p* stand for one of the sentences and *q* for the other. Then consider the four possibilities A to D in turn (e.g. in A, *p* is true and *q* is true). That is, imagine your two sentences are either true or false, according to each possibility. Then for each possibility try to work out what you would say about the truth of the two sentences (1) *not p* and (2) *p and q*.

——

Truth tables such as those in Table 13.1 illustrate what we have said about the relation between the premises and conclusion of a deductive argument. We said that if you believe the premises of a deductive argument, then somehow you are compelled to believe the conclusion. This means, for example, that if it is (always) true that 'if John has a runny nose then he has a cold' and it is true that 'John has a runny nose', then it has to be true that 'John has a cold'. Table 13.1 shows this. Again, let *p* = 'John has a runny nose' and *q* = 'John has a cold'. If we look at Table 13.1, then we see that whenever *if p then q* and *p* are true (i.e. possibility A), *q* is also true. So if both premises *if p then q* (the conditional) and *p* (the antecedent) are true, then the conclusion *q* (the consequent) must be true – there are no other possibilities! We describe this by saying that the inference, or the drawing of this conclusion, is logically valid. This particular form of inference is also referred to as **modus ponens** (**MP**) and can be depicted as follows:

5	Modus ponens (MP)	
	Inference in schematic form	Example
	If p then q	If John has a runny nose, then he has a cold
	p	John has a runny nose
∴	q	Therefore, John has a cold

Another logically valid inference is **modus tollens (MT)**, illustrated below.

6	Modus tollens (MT)	
	Inference in schematic form	Example
	If p then q	If John has a runny nose, then he has a cold
	Not q	John does not have a cold
∴	Not p	Therefore, John does not have a runny nose

We can similarly show that this inference is logically valid using Table 13.1. Of course, *not q* is true when *q* is false. Now, *if p then q* and *not q* are both true only in the last line of the truth table (possibility D). However, in possibility D, *p* is false, and so *not p* is true. So, if the two premises are true, then *not p* must be true also, as again there are no other possibilities. So if the conditional is true and John does not have a cold, then John cannot have a runny nose.

2.3 Logically invalid inferences

Two logically invalid inference patterns have been investigated in the psychology of reasoning: **affirming the consequent (AC)** and **denying the antecedent (DA)**:

7	Affirming the consequent (AC)	
	Inference in schematic form	Example
	If p then q	If John has a runny nose, then he has a cold
	q	John has a cold
∴	p	Therefore, John has a runny nose

8	Denying the antecedent (DA)	
	Inference in schematic form	Example
	If p then q	If John has a runny nose, then he has a cold
	Not p	John does not have a runny nose
∴	Not q	Therefore, John does not have a cold

Remember, both of these forms of inference are *not* logically valid, even though you may feel that they appear to make some sense. To see why they are not logically valid, try Activity 13.2.

ACTIVITY 13.2

Using Table 13.1, try to work out why AC and DA are not logically valid. Remember how we saw that MP and MT are valid. First, we worked out in which of the four possibilities A to D both premises were true at the same time. Second, we considered whether the conclusion was always true in those possibilities. For logically invalid inferences, there should be a possibility in which both premises are true but the conclusion is false. Which possibilities show AC and DA to be logically invalid? Answers are given at the end of the chapter.

2.4   Form and meaning in logic

We can now illustrate a critical distinction in logic between *form* and *meaning*. Examples (5) and (6) above show the *form* of the logically valid inferences MP and MT. We know they are logically valid because of Table 13.1. The table encodes the *meanings* of the connectives. It tells us that if the premises are true then the conclusion must be true (which, as you saw above, is the definition of logical validity). However, to draw the MP or MT inference we do not need to make reference to the truth table, that is, to the meaning of the conditional.

To draw the inference in (4), for example, all you need do is match this example to the *formal rule* in (5). (4) is simply a particular instantiation of (5). Using (5) we can automatically make the logically valid inference, simply because of the *form* of the argument, without worrying about what it means. This distinction between *form* and *meaning* is central to two of the theories of reasoning we look at later on. One theory – **mental logic** – argues that we have formal inference rules, like (5), in our heads, so that drawing inferences relies only on *form*. The other, **mental models**, argues that we do something much more like considering Table 13.1, so that drawing inferences relies on the *meaning* of the connectives.

Summary of Section 2

- Logic provides rules, based on the truth or falsity of propositions, to determine whether an inference is valid.
- A (logically) valid inference is one in which the conclusion is always true whenever the premises are true.
- There are two ways of establishing the validity of an inference: semantic, using truth tables, and formal, using rules of inference (e.g. (5) and (6)).

3 Psychological theories of reasoning

There are a wide variety of theoretical approaches to the psychology of human reasoning. In Section 3, the main theoretical approaches are discussed: mental logic, mental models and the probabilistic approach. These are all *general* theories of reasoning in that they are intended to apply to most reasoning tasks.

3.1 Mental logic

The **mental logic** group of theories (there are several different versions of the basic account [Braine and O'Brien, 1998; Rips, 1994]) are also known as **formal rule** theories. As the name suggests, these accounts are close in spirit to Piaget's view that adult human thought is the operation of formal logic (Inhelder and Piaget, 1958). The idea behind these theories is that people possess a system of formal mental logic that contains inference rules such as (5) above. However, people's failure to reason logically all of the time can then be explained by assuming that they do not possess all the formal logical rules that are licensed by the truth tables in Table 13.1. Without a particular rule, some inferences will be more difficult to make than others.

3.2 Mental models

Mental models theory (Johnson-Laird, 1983; Johnson-Laird and Byrne, 1991) shares the intuition with mental logic that people are in principle capable of logical reasoning. However, rather than applying formal rules, mental models theory argues that people reason over pictorial representations of what sentences *mean*. These representations concern the different *possibilities* that a logical expression may allow (just as each row in Table 13.1 concerns a different possibility).

One way of thinking about the connectives is that they exclude different possibilities. For example, if *if p then q* is true then there are only three possibilities (A, C and D in Table 13.1) – it would not be possible for *p* to be true and *q* false (B). So, to interpret the sentence *if p then q* people may need to hold in mind three possibilities – that is, they may need a mental model that represents each possibility. However, given the limited capacity of working memory (as you saw in Chapter 5), people may not be able to represent all of these possibilities at once. Rather, there may be a preferred initial representation or interpretation. This idea is the core of the mental models theory. In this account each possibility is referred to as a 'mental model'. How people manipulate these mental models explains their reasoning performance.

3.3 The probabilistic approach

According to the probabilistic approach, logic simply does not provide the right framework for understanding people's everyday inferences (Oaksford and Chater, 1994, 1998). For example, perversely, according to logic, a good reason to believe that *if John has a runny nose then he has a cold* is that you do *not* believe that *John has a runny nose*. This is because, according to logic, a conditional is true whenever its antecedent is false (see possibilities C and D in Table 13.1). But *not* believing that *John has a runny nose* is not sufficient grounds for believing the conditional. What appears to be required is the belief that John's having a runny nose makes it very likely that he has a cold. This involves assessing the *conditional probability* that

John has a cold given that he has a runny nose. So if you have noticed John having a runny nose on say 100 occasions, 95 of which involved him having a cold, then the relevant conditional probability is 0.95. We can write this as follows:

P(*John has a cold*|*John has a runny nose*) = 0.95 (| *should be read as 'given'*)

This implies that belief in the conditional is a matter of degree, rather than the (completely) true or (completely) false implied by logic. This was recently confirmed by Evans *et al.* (2003). If all you know is that John has a runny nose, then your degree of belief in this rule indicates that there is a 95 per cent chance that he has a cold. According to the probabilistic approach, most inferences are *uncertain* because the conditional rules on which they are based describe the real world in which logical certainty is a rare commodity. This account of reasoning performance therefore suggests replacing logic with probability theory as the framework for understanding inferences people should make.

The contrast between the first two general theories of reasoning and the last is important because the concept of what it is to be rational fundamentally changes. In the first two theories, rationality is still defined as logical reasoning, and errors (or apparent departures from rationality) are explained in terms of performance limitations such as the limited nature of short-term memory. In contrast, according to the probabilistic approach, probability theory replaces logic as the criterion of what is rational, and rationality is defined in terms of probabilistic reasoning.

However, assessing theories in any area of science depends first and foremost on the ability to explain data. In Sections 4 and 5 we look at some of the experimental results from the two principal reasoning tasks that have been used to assess human reasoning: conditional inference and Wason's selection task.

Summary of Section 3

- Mental logic theories assume people use formal rules of inference but errors may arise because they do not possess all of the possible rules.
- Mental models theory assumes people represent the true possibilities licensed by connectives. Failing to represent all of these possibilities may then lead to errors.
- The probabilistic approach assumes people are not drawing logical, deductive inferences but endorse inferences based on their assessment and evaluation of appropriate conditional probabilities.

4   Conditional inference

In a **conditional inference** task (Evans, 1977; Taplin, 1971) participants are presented with a conditional sentence (the conditional premise) and various facts relating either to the antecedent or consequent of the sentence (the categorical premise). In our example, the conditional premise would be *if John has a runny nose, he has a cold*. Different categorical premises would then relate to different schemes of inference: for example, *John has a runny nose* relates to the MP inference, *John does not have a cold* relates to MT, *John has a cold* to AC and *John does not have a runny nose* to DA. Participants are asked to indicate what conclusion follows from these two premises, that is, the categorical and the conditional premises. Logic dictates that inferences should be made for the logically valid schemes of inference MP and MT, and withheld for the logically invalid inferences AC and DA. We now review the main findings on conditional inference. For each finding we then discuss how the main theories explain the results.

4.1   The abstract conditional inference task

Typically, these reasoning tasks are conducted using abstract alphanumeric stimuli – letters and numbers – in order to try and rule out any effects of prior knowledge and so to investigate reasoning 'in the raw', that is, to investigate the basic operating characteristics of the cognitive system.

In the abstract conditional inference task participants are told to assume that, for example, the premises, *if there is an A then there is a 2* and *there is an A*, are true and are asked whether they can conclude that *there is a 2* (as MP indicates). Schroyens and Schaeken (2003) summarized 65 of these experiments, and their results are shown in Table 13.2.

Table 13.2 Proportion of participants endorsing inferences in the abstract conditional inference task

Inference type	Proportion of participants endorsing inference (%)
MP	97
MT	72
AC	63
DA	55

Source: adapted from Schroyens and Schaeken, 2003

Comparing the mean values in Table 13.2 pair-wise, all six comparisons reveal highly significant differences. So, MP is endorsed more than MT, which is endorsed more than AC, which is endorsed more than DA. This pattern is not consistent with logic, according to which participants should endorse MP and MT fully and equally, and not endorse other inferences.

4.1.1 Mental logic

Mental logicians (e.g. Rips, 1994) explain the difference in the extent to which people endorse MP and MT by proposing that people possess the MP inference rule (5) but do not possess the MT inference rule (6). In order to draw the MT inference, much more complex reasoning would be needed, as outlined below in (9).

Reconsider the example of MT given in (6).

9	*If John has a runny nose, then he has a cold*
	John does not have a cold
	Therefore, John does not have a runny nose

To reach the conclusion, Rips (1994) argues that people assume the contrary is true, that is, they assume that *John has a runny nose*, and then find that a contradiction results. If *John has a runny nose* is true then, using MP, it can be combined with the conditional premise to yield the conclusion *John has a cold*. But this conclusion contradicts the actual categorical premise *John does not have a cold*. Since the assumption results in a contradiction, the original assumption must be false, that is, *John has a runny nose* must be false and so *John does not have a runny nose* must be true! This way of drawing the MT inference is called ***reductio ad absurdum*** or RAA. The complexity of this inference is then thought to explain why the MT inference is drawn less often than MP.

Indeed, this strategy may also explain the results for DA and AC (Rips, 1994). Conditionals in natural language can be ambiguous and may sometimes be interpreted as **bi-conditionals**. Table 13.3 gives a truth table for a bi-conditional, sometimes expressed as *if and only if ... then ...*

Table 13.3 A truth table for the bi-conditional *if and only if ... then ...* Note how the bi-conditional *if and only if p then q* is true only when both *if p then q* and *if q then p* are true

			Connectives		
			If ... then ...		If and only if ... then ...
	Sentences		Complex sentences		
Possibility	*p*	*q*	If *p* then *q*	If *q* then *p*	If and only if *p* then *q*
A	true	true	true	true	true
B	true	false	false	true	false
C	false	true	true	false	false
D	false	false	true	true	true

As Table 13.3 shows, the bi-conditional *if and only if John has a runny nose, then he has a cold* is true whenever both the standard conditional *if John has a runny nose, then he has a cold* and the converse conditional *if John has a cold, then he has a runny nose* are true. This means that if people interpret *if John has a runny nose, then he has a cold* as a bi-conditional, then they should draw the logically valid MP and MT inferences on both the standard conditional (*if p then q*) and also on the converse conditional (*if q then p*). However, note that MP and MT on the converse conditional are equivalent to AC and DA on the standard conditional: that is MP on *if John has a cold, then he has a runny nose* is equivalent to AC on *if John has a runny nose, then he has a cold*; similarly, for MT and DA. Consequently, those participants who interpret the rule as a bi-conditional should endorse both DA and AC. However, since AC is equivalent to the easier MP on the converse conditional, and DA to the more difficult MT, they should endorse AC more than DA. This corresponds well to the pattern of endorsements observed in Schroyens and Schaeken's (2003) summary of the data. So, according to mental logic theory, people's performance on this task is rational because it is actually logical: it is just that (1) some logical inferences are harder than others given the logical rules we possess and (2) some people misinterpret the conditional as a bi-conditional.

4.1.2 Mental models

Table 13.4(a) shows the **initial mental model** representation for the conditional *if p then q*. It represents the possibility in which *p* is true and *q* is true (like possibility A in Table 13.3). The three dots (or ellipsis) indicate that there may be other relevant mental models or possibilities that are not currently being considered. These other possibilities are available, perhaps temporarily held in some short-term memory store, but are not explicitly represented. The square brackets indicate that *p* cannot be paired with any other term. In particular, this captures the fact that *p* cannot be paired with *not q*, because this is the possibility that the conditional excludes (possibility B in Table 13.1). Table 13.4(c) shows the initial mental model for the bi-conditional *if and only if p then q*. Both *p* and *q* are now in square brackets because neither can be paired with anything else: this rules out the *p, not q* (possibility B) and the *not p, q* (C) possibilities.

Table 13.4 Initial mental models for the conditional (a) and bi-conditional (c), and fleshed-out versions of these (b) and (d) respectively. The three dots (ellipsis) indicate that there may be other relevant mental models not explicitly represented. The square brackets indicate that an item cannot be paired with any other term. The inferences that can be drawn from each model are abbreviated at the bottom of the table

Conditional *if p then q*		Bi-conditional *if and only if p then q*	
Initial model	Fleshed-out model	Initial model	Fleshed-out model
[p] q	[p] q	[p] [q]	[p] [q]
...	not p q	...	not p not q
	not p not q		
(a)	(b)	(c)	(d)
MP	MP MT	MP AC	MP DA AC MT

Table 13.4(b) shows the **fleshed-out mental model** for the conditional, where the other possibilities not excluded by the initial interpretation in Table 13.4(a) are now explicitly represented. Table 13.4(d) similarly shows a fleshed-out mental model for the bi-conditional. Now try Activity 13.3.

ACTIVITY 13.3

For each of the inferences MP, MT, AC and DA, using the mental models shown in Table 13.4, try to work out why each inference can be made (or not as the case may be) in each model. You should find that the process is very like checking the truth table in Activity 13.1.

COMMENT

Suppose participants adopt the initial conditional interpretation in Table 13.4(a). While the categorical premise of both MP (p) and AC (q) would match the model, q could be paired with something other than p. So, given the categorical premise q, no conclusion can be drawn. However, p can only be paired with q (that is what the square brackets mean) so, given the categorical premise p, participants can conclude q. That is, they will only be able to draw the MP inference.

Participants that adopt the fleshed-out conditional interpretation in Table 13.4(b) can make both the MT and MP inferences. Although all categorical premises now match the model, only p and *not q* are constrained in their pairings. From p we can conclude q (MP) since p is only paired with q, and from *not q* we can conclude *not p* (MT) since *not q* is only paired with *not p*.

Participants who adopt the initial bi-conditional interpretation in Table 13.4(c) can make the MP inference and the AC inference. MP goes through for the same reason as for the initial conditional interpretation. AC goes through because now q can only be paired with p.

Participants that adopt the fleshed-out bi-conditional interpretation in Table 13.4(d) can draw all inferences. This is because the categorical premise of all inferences finds a match in the model and each is uniquely paired with only a single item.

The fact that mental models only represent the true possibilities, together with the distinction between initial and fleshed-out mental models, is the primary means by which mental models theory explains the data on conditional inference. The explanation depends on assuming different subsets of participants adopt these four different mental models. Table 13.4 shows that MP can be endorsed in all representations, DA can only be endorsed in one, and AC and MT can both be endorsed in two. So if equal numbers of participants adopted each representation, then MP would be endorsed more than both AC and MT, which would be endorsed in equal proportion, and all would be endorsed more than DA. That participants actually endorse MT more than AC can be explained by assuming that more participants flesh out the conditional interpretation in Table 13.4(b) than adopt the initial bi-conditional interpretation in Table 13.4(c).

4.1.3 Probabilistic approach

According to the probabilistic approach people draw inferences according to how probable they think the conclusion is given the premises (Oaksford and Chater, 2003a; Oaksford *et al.*, 2000). MP is straightforward. Given the conditional premise, *if John has a runny nose, then he has a cold*, this inference will be drawn in proportion to the conditional probability that *John has a cold* given that *he has a runny nose*, a probability that we can write as *P(cold|runny nose)*. So for example, given the categorical premise, *John has a runny nose* (and no other information) the best bet as to the probability that *John has a cold* is the proportion of times that John has a cold when he has a runny nose. In our example above, we supposed this to be 0.95. Given that the consequent is highly likely given the antecedent, we can assume it is equally highly likely that people will endorse this inference. Calculating probabilities for the remaining inferences requires the assumption that people possess information about the probability of John having a runny nose (*P(runny nose)*) and the probability that he has a cold (*P(cold)*). Consider the AC inference in which you are told that *John has a cold* and are asked whether you would endorse the conclusion that *John has a runny nose*. What you are interested in is the probability that *John has a runny nose* given *John has a cold* (*P(runny nose|cold)*), i.e. the converse of MP. Probability theory allows us to calculate this probability using a form of Bayes' theorem (note that Chapter 12 used a somewhat different form):

$$P(runny\ nose|cold) = \frac{P(cold|runny\ nose)P(runny\ nose)}{P(cold|runny\ nose)P(runny\ nose) + P(cold|not\ runny\ nose)P(not\ runny\ nose)}$$

We know that *P(cold|runny nose)* = 0.95. Suppose that John rarely has a runny nose and so over the year he has only a 5 per cent chance of having one, so *P(runny nose)* = 0.05 and therefore *P(not runny nose)* = 0.95. What about *P(cold|not runny nose)*, that is, the probability of *John having a cold* given *he does not have a runny nose*? This is likely to be quite low but not 0. Let us set this to 0.03. *P(runny nose|cold)* can then be calculated using the equation above and comes to 0.61. This then would be the probability of drawing the AC inference. Probabilities can be derived in a similar way for DA and MT.

To assess how well this account can explain the standard abstract results, the equations predicting the probabilities with which each inference should be drawn can be fitted to the data. This means that the values of *P(cold|runny nose)*, *P(runny nose)* and *P(cold)*, which we chose freely in the above example, are chosen to provide the best possible predictions for the frequencies with which each inference is endorsed. The probabilistic account provides a close fit to the abstract data, predicting the following frequencies for each inference (actual frequencies in brackets): MP = 0.88 (0.97), DA = 0.51 (0.55), AC = 0.68 (0.63), MT = 0.77 (0.72) (Oaksford and Chater, 2003a). Note that fitting an account to the data in this way is not unique to the probabilistic approach. The numbers of participants adopting the conditional or bi-conditional interpretation and the numbers fleshing out or drawing RAA inferences are all free to vary and must be fixed from the data, just as probabilities are in the probabilistic approach.

4.2   Everyday reasoning and the suppression effect

A general property of everyday inferences is that they can be defeated (Oaksford and Chater, 1998). For example, if you infer that *John has a cold* because *he has a runny nose*, but then discover that *he has hay fever*, your inference is defeated. Because such inferences can be defeated in this way they are called **defeasible inferences**. Take another example: we generally believe that *birds fly*, which can be expressed as the conditional *if something is a bird, then it flies*. So we might conclude that *Tweety can fly* on learning that *Tweety is a bird*. However, if we then discover the new information that *Tweety is an ostrich*, then this inference is defeated. It thus seems that many of the inferences we draw in everyday life may be non-deductive, that is, the truth of the conclusion is not guaranteed by the truth of the premises.

There have been many experiments investigating these aspects of everyday reasoning. They show that the inferences, MP and MT, and the fallacies, DA and AC, can be **suppressed** by providing information about possible defeaters. For example, if you are told that *if the key is turned then the car starts* and that *the key is turned*, you are likely to endorse the MP inference to the conclusion that *the car starts*. However, if you are also told that *the petrol tank is empty*, you are less likely to endorse this conclusion because the car will *not* start if the petrol tank is empty. An empty petrol tank provides an *exception* to the rule. This exception would also mean that you are less likely to endorse MT. If you knew that *the car didn't start* you may not infer that *the key was not turned* because the empty petrol tank may be the cause of the car not starting. These exceptions have been called 'additional antecedents' (Byrne, 1989).

Other information can suppress DA and AC. For example, if you are told that *if the key is turned then the car starts* and that *the key is not turned*, you might be tempted to endorse the DA inference to the conclusion that *the car does not start*. However, if you are also told that *the car was hot-wired*, you may be less likely to endorse this conclusion (because the car may start even though the key was not turned because it has been hot-wired). This condition would also mean that you are less likely to endorse AC. If you knew that *the car started* you may not infer that *the key was turned* because the car starting may have been caused by being hot-wired. These conditions have been called 'alternative antecedents' (Byrne, 1989).

Byrne (1989) demonstrated all these effects by providing participants with explicit rules containing this additional information, as in (10) and (11) below.

10	Additional antecedents (MP)
	If the key is turned the car starts
	If there is fuel in the tank the car starts
	The key is turned
	The car starts?

11

Alternative antecedents (AC)
If the key is turned the car starts
If it is hot-wired the car starts
The car starts
The key was turned?

The results of Byrne's (1989) experiment 1 are shown in Figure 13.1 below. The simple condition did not include any additional or alternative antecedents and reflects the standard pattern of results (see Table 13.2). Figure 13.1 shows clearly that providing participants with information concerning alternative antecedents suppresses DA and AC but not MP or MT, whereas information concerning additional antecedents suppresses MP and MT but not DA or AC.

Similar effects have been demonstrated *without* presenting additional or alternative antecedents explicitly (Cummins *et al.*, 1991; Cummins, 1995). Thus, people seem to automatically retrieve this information from memory to influence their reasoning performance. A range of causal conditionals, like those we have looked at, were pre-tested for the number of additional or alternative antecedents participants could bring to mind. It was shown that the effects of additional or alternative antecedents were *graded*, that is, the more additional or alternative antecedents a rule allowed the greater the suppression effects observed. As we will see, this result does not sit well with theories that regard these effects as *all or nothing*. In experiments where participants *rated* how likely an inference was to go through on a scale of 1–7 (Cummins *et al.*, 1991; Cummins, 1995) ***all or nothing***

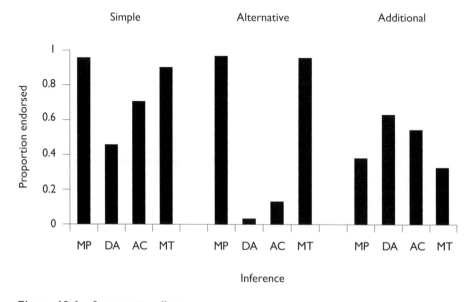

Figure 13.1   Suppression effects
Source: Byrne, 1989, Table 1

behaviour suggests the data should be made up of different proportions of two types of individual: those who give only ratings of 1, meaning they 'do not endorse' the conclusion, and those who give only ratings of 7, meaning they do 'endorse' the conclusion. However, in experiments like these, around 50 per cent of each participant's responses are *intermediate* values (i.e. not ratings of 1 or 7) (Oaksford *et al.*, 2000, experiment 3), which is not consistent with all or nothing behaviour.

4.2.1 Mental logic

In Byrne's (1989) experiments (see (10) and (11) above) participants were provided with two conditional rules with the same consequents. So for additional antecedents, (10), the key needs to be turned and there needs to be fuel in the tank for the car to start. However, for alternative antecedents (11) either turning the key *or* hot-wiring will start the car. This means that people may represent these premises as single rules with complex antecedents.

10′ | If the key is turned and there is fuel in the tank, then the car starts

11′ | If the key is turned or it is hot-wired, then the car starts

Let us look at the MP and MT inferences for (10′).

- MP inference: the categorical premise *the key is turned* does not satisfy the antecedent, which is only true if *the key is turned* and *there is fuel in the tank* (see Table 13.1). Consequently, logically this single categorical premise does not license the conclusion that *the car starts* and so the MP inference cannot be drawn.

- MT inference: from the categorical premise *the car does not start*, by MT, one can conclude that the complex sentence *the key is turned and there is fuel in the tank* is false. Logically, one cannot infer that *the key was not turned* because there could be no fuel in the tank, and so the MT inference should not be drawn. Similar reasoning applies to (11′) for the DA and the AC inferences.

ACTIVITY 13.4

For (11′) see if you can work out why DA and AC should be suppressed. A clue for the DA inference is that *not (the key is turned or the car is hot-wired)* is equivalent to *the key is not turned* and *the car is not hot-wired*. Table 13.5 gives the truth table for *or*.

Table 13.5 A truth table for *or*

Possibility	Sentences		Connective or Complex sentence
	p	*q*	*p* or *q*
A	true	true	true
B	true	false	true
C	false	true	true
D	false	false	false

Although mental logic can offer explanations for suppression effects, it nevertheless suggests that reasoning behavior should be all or nothing – that conclusions should either be endorsed or not. This is hard to reconcile with Cummins' (1995) data, which revealed graded effects. One possible response is to suggest that mental logic provides a good explanation of deductive inference but that graded effects tap non-deductive inference (Rips, 2001, 2002b) (see Section 6.1.1).

4.2.2 Mental models

The mental models explanation of the suppression effects depends on the availability of counter-examples. Just as for the mental logic approach, mental models theory (Byrne *et al.*, 1999) suggests that people represent information about additional antecedents using *and*, and they represent information about alternative antecedents using *or*. This yields initial mental models representations for (10′) and (11′) as shown in the top part of Table 13.6.

Table 13.6 Mental models representations for (10′) and (11′)

Additional antecedents			Alternative antecedents		
If the key is turned and there is fuel in the tank then the car starts			*If the key is turned or it is hot-wired then the car starts*		
turn	fuel	starts	turn		starts
				hot-wired	starts
	...			...	
turn	not (fuel)	not (starts)	not (turn)	hot-wired	starts
	(10′)			(11′)	

For (10′) a fully fleshed-out version of the mental model for *and* will include the case where the key is turned but the car does not start because there is no fuel. For (11′) a fully fleshed-out version of the mental model for *or* will include the case where the key is not turned but the car starts because it was hot-wired. These models are shown after the ellipsis. This particular example shows why these counter-examples need to be available.

We have deliberately picked an example that appeals to your prior knowledge of cars and the factors that determine whether they start or not. This is called the **principle of pragmatic modulation** (Johnson-Laird and Byrne, 2002). That is, general knowledge in long-term memory can modulate the interpretation of conditionals, in this case making certain counter-examples much easier to access and represent.

Mental models also suggests that suppression effects should be all or nothing. However, some researchers working within the mental models framework (Quinn and Markovits, 2002; Schroyens and Schaeken, 2003) have suggested that mental models should be supplemented with a validating search procedure. A conclusion is suggested by the mental model, and then long-term memory is searched to see if there is a counter-example. These might influence reasoning either in an all or nothing way (Quinn and Markovits, 2002) or in a graded, probabilistic way (Schroyens and Schaeken, 2003). Opting for this explanation of suppression effects means that people can no longer be thought of as performing strictly logical inferences. If people take a conditional to be true then, logically speaking, there can be no need to search for counter-examples – people should only search long-term memory for counter-examples if they are not strictly taking the conditional to be true.

4.2.3   Probabilistic approach

Suppression effects in conditional inference are explained in terms of the effects of additional and alternative antecedents on the appropriate conditional probabilities (Oaksford and Chater, 2003c). Suppose you were asked to estimate the probability of a car starting given you have turned the key. You might base your estimate on the proportion of times cars have started when you have turned the key. Suppose you are now provided with an *additional antecedent*, or you retrieve one from memory – perhaps the possibility that the petrol tank is empty. Now estimate again the probability of the car starting given you have turned the key. As an empty petrol tank will prevent the car from starting, presumably this probability will now be smaller than in your first estimate, when all you were told was that the key was turned. That is, your estimate of the probability that the car starts is suppressed. In the suppression experiments people are not provided with the information in this way. Rather, they are given reminders about general preventative factors, like empty fuel tanks. According to the probabilistic approach, this has the effect of reducing people's estimates of the conditional probability of the car starting given you turn the key, $P(car\ starts|key\ turned)$. Thus, information about additional antecedents suppresses MP and MT inferences.

Explaining suppression effects for alternative antecedents follows a similar pattern. Alternative antecedents emphasize that, for example, it is possible to start cars without turning the key, for instance, by hot-wiring. They therefore suggest that the probability of the car starting given you don't turn the key, $P(car\ starts|key\ not\ turned)$, is higher than you first thought. This has to reduce the probability of the car not starting given that you do not turn the key, $P(car\ does\ not\ start|key\ not\ turned)$. This is simply because these probabilities must sum to 1, so that $P(car\ starts|key\ not\ turned) + P(car\ does\ not\ start|key\ not\ turned) = 1$. So, if one goes up, the other must come down. The probability of the car not starting given that you do not turn the key is the probability that you must assess to determine whether to draw the DA inference. This is why alternative antecedents suppress the DA and AC inferences according to the probabilistic approach.

Summary of Section 4

- Both the standard abstract task and suppression experiments yield results that appear inconsistent with logic.
- Mental logic explains these by assuming that people use a more complex inference to perform MT, and that some adopt a bi-conditional interpretation. Additional and alternative antecedents are represented in terms of complex antecedents (using the connectives *and* and *or*).
- Mental models theory assumes some people adopt the bi-conditional interpretation and that some do not flesh out initial semantic representations. Suppression effects are explained by the principle of pragmatic modulation.
- The probabilistic approach suggests that people reason by judging the probabilities and conditional probabilities of events. Suppression effects arise because additional and alternative antecedents modulate these probabilities.
- Graded effects, which can be explained by the probabilistic approach, have led some mental logicians to argue for a distinction between deductive and non-deductive inference and some mental models theorists to introduce a probabilistic component.

5 Wason's selection task

Wason's selection task is probably the most used task in the psychology of reasoning (Wason, 1968). We look first at the original *abstract* form of the task and then at how each theory explains the data.

5.1 The abstract selection task

In this version of the task people assess whether evidence is relevant to the truth or falsity of a conditional rule (Wason, 1968). In the abstract version, the rule concerns cards that have a number on one side and a letter on the other (see Figure 13.2). A typical rule is *if there is an A on one side* (call this *p*), *then there is a 2 on the other side* (*q*).

Four cards are placed before the participant, so that just one side is visible, showing an *A* (*p* card), a *K* (*not p* card), a *2* (*q* card) and a *7* (*not q* card) (Figure 13.2). Participants are told that each card has a letter on one side and a number on the other. They are then asked to pick those cards they must turn over to test whether the rule *if there is an A on one side then there is a 2 on the other side* is true or false. It was shown in Table 13.1 that sentences like *if p then q* are only false when the antecedent, *p*, is true (there is an *A* on one side) and the consequent, *q*, is false (there is not a *2* on the other side). Consequently, according to logic, only a card with an *A* on one side but without a *2* on the other side makes this rule false. There are only two cards that could possibly be of this type: the *A* card could have a number other than *2* on the other side, and the *7* card could have an *A* on the other side. So, logically, people should select the *A* and the *7* cards to turn over, as these are the only cards that could falsify the rule, but not the *K* or the *2* cards.

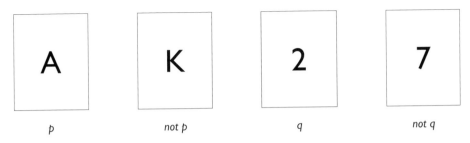

Figure 13.2 The four cards in the abstract version of Wason's selection task. For convenience, the cards have been annotated according to their match to *if p then q* (these annotations are not seen by participants)

However, these selections are rarely observed in the experimental results, as you will see in Table 13.7. That is, as few as 4 per cent of participants make the response predicted by logic. Participants typically select cards that could confirm the rule, that is, the *p* and *q* cards. However, according to logic, the choice of the *q* card is irrational, and is an example of so-called **confirmation bias**. That is, people appear to be trying to find cards that have an *A (p)* on one side and a *2 (q)* on the other side. Consequently, if we judge whether people are rational by a logical standard then these results seem to indicate that people are irrational.

Table 13.7 Typical results in the Wason selection task

Cards selected	Proportion of participants selecting cards (%)
p and *q* cards	46
p card only	33
p, *q* and *not q* cards	7
p and *not q* cards	4
other card combinations	10

Source: Johnson-Laird and Wason, 1970, Table 1

The degree of people's apparent irrationality was illustrated further by work on the **matching effect**. Evans and Lynch (1973) used rules that also contained negations, for example, *if there is an A on one side then there is* **not** *a 2 on the other side*. Participants continued to select the *A* and the *2* card. For this rule these are now the logical responses because a card that does *not* have *not 2* on it must have a *2* on it, so *A* and *2* now correspond to the *p* and *not q* cards. However, if they were showing confirmation bias they should now select the *A* and the *7* card. Selecting the *A* and the *2* card for both the standard and the negated rules seems only consistent with **matching bias**. That is, participants are not engaging rationally in the task at all but are simply choosing cards that match the letters and numbers mentioned in the rule.

5.1.1 Mental logic

The mental logic approach to the selection task is identical to that taken for the conditional inference task. The account then relies on the following identities: MP = *p* card, DA = *not p* card, AC = *q* card and MT = *not q* card. That is, the card sides that participants see are taken to be the categorical premises in conditional inferences. So, for example, given the rule *if A then 2*, deciding to turn the *A* card (*p*) is equivalent to drawing an MP inference to predict that there is a *2* on the other side. Suppose participants misinterpret the rule as a bi-conditional, so they also believe that *if 2 then A*. Given this interpretation, deciding to turn the *not A* card is like drawing the logically valid MT inference to predict that there is a *not 2* on the other side (which is equivalent to the logically invalid DA on the original rule as stated).

You should note that this account predicts that the proportion of people selecting the cards in the selection task should mirror the proportion of participants endorsing the corresponding conditional inferences. But this is not observed. In the selection task, the *q* card is endorsed more than the *not q* card, yet in the conditional inference task the MT inference is endorsed more than AC.

One reason for this discrepancy between the results on the two tasks may be the way in which the categorical premises are presented in the selection task. Take MT. In the conditional inference task, people see *if A then 2, not 2*, therefore, *not A* and are asked to judge the appropriateness of the conclusion. However, in the selection task, they are told *if A then 2*, are shown a card with *7* on one side, and are given no explicit conclusion. The point is that they have to infer that *7* is an instance of the category of numbers that are *not 2*. Presenting a negated premise in this way has been labelled an **implicit negation** (Evans *et al.*, 1996) and this is always the method used in the selection task. When implicit negations are used in the conditional inference task the typical pattern for the *if A then 2* rule becomes very close to the corresponding pattern of card selections in the selection task, given the identities above (as you will see in Table 13.8).

Table 13.8 Proportion of participants endorsing inferences in the abstract conditional inference task with implicit negations

Inference type	Proportion of participants endorsing inference (%)
MP	95
MT	58
AC	79
DA	38

Source: Evans and Handley, 1999, Table 5

This account may also explain the matching effect. If, for example, *not 2* is shown on the cards, rather than *7*, then the matching effect goes away (Evans *et al.*, 1996). So the matching effect may be a result of having to process implicit negations, rather than an inherent illogicality. In sum, it would appear that people may indeed be drawing conditional inferences in the selection task using the upturned face as the categorical premise.

5.1.2 Mental models

Mental models theory also explains the selection task results in a similar way to the conditional inference task. However, now people consider each possibility for whether there could be something on the other side of the card that bears on the truth or falsity of the rule. The frequencies of card selections depend on the proportions of participants adopting the different interpretations. We examine the card that should be turned for each interpretation by looking at Table 13.9 (which is a copy of Table 13.4).

Table 13.9 Initial mental models for the conditional (a) and bi-conditional (c), and fleshed-out versions of these (b) and (d) respectively. The three dots (or ellipsis) indicate that there may be other relevant mental models not explicitly represented. The square brackets indicate that an item cannot be paired with any other term. The inferences that can be drawn from each model are abbreviated at the bottom of the table

Conditional *if p then q*		Bi-conditional *if and only if p then q*	
Initial model	Fleshed-out model	Initial model	Fleshed-out model
[p] q	[p] q	[p] [q]	[p] [q]
...	not p q	...	not p not q
	not p not q		
(a)	(b)	(c)	(d)
MP	MP MT	MP AC	MP DA AC MT

If the conditional interpretation is adopted but it is not fleshed out (Table 13.9(a)) then people will only turn the *A* (*p*) card. This is because the mental model indicates that a *p* card (*A*) must be paired with a *q* (*2*). So, if a card has a *2* on the other side it suggests the rule is true but if it has a *7* (*not q*) on the other it falsifies the rule. The *2* card, however, will be consistent with the rule being true whatever is on its other side.

If the conditional interpretation is adopted and fleshed out ((b) in Table 13.9) then people will turn the *A* (*p*) and the *7* (*not q*) cards. The reason for the selection of the *A* (*p*) card is the same as in (a). The *7* (*not q*) card is now selected because it is represented as having to be paired with a *not p* and so if it has an *A* (*p*) on the other side it falsifies the rule.

ACTIVITY 13.5

See if you can work out which cards should be selected for the bi-conditional interpretations and why. In each of Tables 13.9(c) and 13.9(d) look to see which pairs must go together in each model. A clue is given by the identities between card selections and conditional inferences in the mental logic section.

The matching effect is given exactly the same explanation in mental models theory as in mental logic. That is, it is a product of having to process implicit negations (Evans and Handley, 1999; Johnson-Laird and Byrne, 2002).

5.1.3 Probabilistic approach

The probabilistic approach suggests that selecting the *p* and the *q* card, far from being irrational, is in fact the *optimal* response. The general idea is quite simple, although the mathematics can be a bit off-putting (Oaksford and Chater, 1994, 1996,

2003b). For the adventurous, a worked example is provided in Box 13.1, though don't worry if this is too off-putting – the ideas behind the calculations are explained here. The central idea in the selection task is that people are looking for the most informative evidence to help them decide whether a rule is true or false. For example, people might have to decide whether John's having a runny nose is more often associated with having a cold than one would expect by chance. If it is, then there is a predictive relationship such that his having a runny nose allows you to predict that he has a cold – they are *dependent*. If there is no such relationship, then they are *independent*.

To determine which cards are more informative, information is quantified as *bits* of information. People are initially assumed to be maximally uncertain about the relationship between runny noses and colds. That is, the two possible hypotheses – that (1) they are dependent and (2) that they independent – are given an even or equal chance (0.5) of being true or false. This means that people's uncertainty is the highest it can be at 1 bit. Turning cards to reveal data can reduce this uncertainty. So, for example, turning the *runny nose* (*p*) card to find that *John did not have a cold* (*not q*) on this occasion should reduce my uncertainty about which hypothesis is true. I should now feel more certain that for John runny noses and colds are independent (see Box 13.1). This reduction in my uncertainty is called **information gain**. However, participants in the selection task don't actually turn the cards over – they merely state which they would turn over! So what gets calculated is *expected information gain*. This is the reduction in uncertainty averaged over the two possibilities, that is, the other side of the *runny nose* card could reveal that John had a cold or that he did not, on this occasion.

Expected information gain can be calculated for each card (Box 13.1 shows the calculation for just the *p* card [*runny nose*]). Calculating the relevant probabilities of what is on the other side for each card involves the same three probabilities as in the conditional inference task. That is, the probability that John has a runny nose, $P(r)$, the probability that he has a cold, $P(c)$, and the probability that he has a cold given he has a runny nose, $P(c|r)$. If $P(r)$ and $P(c)$ are both low (as in Box 13.1, that is, 0.2 and 0.3 respectively), which is called the **rarity assumption**, then the expected information gain for the *q* card (*John has a cold*) is higher than for the *not q* card (*John does not have a cold*). Therefore, this model explains the standard finding in the abstract task as a *rational* consequence of trying to identify the most informative data.

We can perhaps see why this happens intuitively using an alternative example of a rule: *if a pan drops in the kitchen, then it makes a clanging noise*. According to logic, testing this hypothesis exhaustively (i.e. in the real world, rather than the restricted circumstances of the selection task) would involve investigating every instance of not hearing a clanging noise, to see whether a pan has dropped noiselessly. This clearly makes no sense because hearing a clanging noise is a very rare event.

13.1

Calculating expected information gain

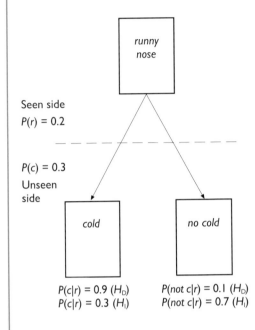

H_D Dependence hypothesis: *if runny nose then cold* $P(c|r) = 0.9$

H_I Independence hypothesis: no relationship $P(c|r) = P(c) = 0.3$

Assume *runny nose* card is turned to reveal *no cold*, this is the datum, D.

Belief before turning the card:
$P(H_D) = P(H_I) = 0.5$

Uncertainty before: $I(H_I) =$

$$\sum P(H_i)\log_2\left(\frac{1}{P(H_i)}\right) = 1 \text{ bit}$$

Uncertainty after: $I(H_i|D) =$

$$\sum P(H_i|D)\log_2\left(\frac{1}{P(H_i|D)}\right)$$

Seen side
$P(r) = 0.2$

$P(c) = 0.3$
Unseen side

cold

no cold

$P(c|r) = 0.9$ (H_D)
$P(c|r) = 0.3$ (H_I)

$P(\text{not } c|r) = 0.1$ (H_D)
$P(\text{not } c|r) = 0.7$ (H_I)

$$P(H_D|D) = \frac{P(D|H_D)P(H_D)}{\sum P(D|H_i)P(H_i)} = \frac{0.1 \times 0.5}{0.1 \times 0.5 + 0.7 \times 0.5} = 0.125, \text{ and so } P(H_I|D) = 0.875,$$

i.e. highly probable H_I is true.

Therefore, uncertainty after $= 0.125\log_2(1/0.125) + 0.875\log_2(1/0.875) = 0.544$ bits.

Amount by which uncertainty has reduced, or *information gain*, $= I(H_i) - I(H_D|D) = 1 - 0.544 = 0.456$ bits. However, the card is never turned. So the *expected* uncertainty after turning the card is calculated. By similar means we can calculate the uncertainty after finding *cold* $= 0.811$. Expected uncertainty $= 0.5 \times (0.9 + 0.3) \times 0.811 + 0.5 \times (0.1 + 0.7)$ $\times 0.544 = 0.704$.

Therefore, the expected reduction in uncertainty, or *expected information gain*, after turning the *runny nose* card $= 1 - 0.704 = 0.296$ bits.

This probabilistic account also explains the matching effect as a rational consequence of manipulating probabilities (Oaksford and Chater, 1994, 2003b). The probability that John does not have a cold is greater than the probability that he does: most people are cold free most of the time. So, apart from being implausible, a rule like *if John has a runny nose, he does not have a cold* introduces a high probability event in the consequent. It turns out that if either the antecedent or consequent has a high probability, then the expected information gain for the *not q* card is higher than for the *q* card. So people should select the *John has a cold* (the *not q*) card for this rule as well, which is the matching effect.

5.2   The deontic selection task

Deontic reasoning is reasoning about what you should or should not do. Research in this area has recently engendered the most controversy in reasoning research. This is largely because of the strong claim made by evolutionary psychology that this research reveals the effects of various innate cognitive modules. In this section we will therefore also consider this approach to human reasoning.

Some early work on the selection task seemed to show that logic-like performance was observed when *real-world* materials, as opposed to abstract materials, were used (Wason and Shapiro, 1971). People seemed to select the more logical *p* and *not q* cards for rules like (12) and (13) below:

12	If Johnny travels to Manchester, then he takes the train.

13	If you use a second class stamp, then you must leave the envelope unsealed.

However, it was found that rules like (12) only sometimes led to logical responses whereas rules like (13) (and [14] below), for which participants were told to imagine that they were immigration officials at the airport and the cards represented immigration forms, reliably produced logic-like performance (Cheng and Holyoak, 1985).

14	If you are entering the country, then you must have a cholera inoculation.

(12), and all of the conditionals we have considered prior to this section, are called **indicative conditionals** – they describe the world or how someone behaves in it. (13) and (14) are **deontic conditionals** – they are prescriptive and state how people *should* or *should not* behave. This marks an important distinction (Manktelow and Over, 1987) for only deontic conditionals appear to produce logic-like performance reliably. Now logic indicates how the truth of a conditional depends on the truth of its antecedent and consequent, but note that the selection task for a deontic conditional cannot be solved using standard logic. Whereas finding out that Johnny travelled to Manchester by car brings into question the truth of (12), finding out someone entered the country without a cholera inoculation does *not* question the *truth* of (14). (14) can remain in force regardless of the number of people found violating it. So, for deontic conditionals, correctly selecting the *p* and *not q* cards now has nothing to do with the *truth* of the rule, and so nothing to do with logic.

This point came sharply into focus when researchers began to investigate the factors that affect reasoning with deontic conditionals. The rule illustrated by example (14) is an *obligation* rule, that is, it describes the preconditions (having an inoculation against cholera) that you are *obliged* to satisfy to carry out an action, that is, entering the country. These deontic rules can also be framed as **permission rules** (Cosmides, 1989) as in (14′).

14′	*If you have a cholera inoculation, then you may enter the country.*

This rule now describes an action you are *permitted* to carry out if you satisfy the pre-condition of having a cholera inoculation.

There are two potentially important differences between examples (14′) and (14). First, in (14′) the precondition is now in the antecedent of the rule and the action is in the consequent. Second, in (14′) *must* has changed to *may*, reflecting the fact that one is allowed, but not obliged, to enter the country on having a cholera inoculation. The first difference has an important implication. An immigration official needs to identify people who break immigration laws – people trying to enter the country without a cholera inoculation – regardless of whether the rule is expressed as in (14′) or (14). For (14), as we have seen, this corresponds to selecting the *p* and *not q* cards. However, in (14′) these antecedents and consequents are swapped around. Now, entering the country becomes the logical consequent *q*, and having a cholera inoculation the logical antecedent *p*. So, if participants are looking for potential law breakers, as they are asked to do in this task, then they should select the *not p* and *q* cards. Cosmides (1989) observed exactly this behaviour. This pattern of responses would appear to have nothing to do with the logic of the conditional. Other manipulations have revealed similar performance (Manktelow and Over, 1991).

In sum, the deontic selection task seems to reveal the conditions under which people can reason logically. However, the factors that affect deontic reasoning, that is, the nature of the rules, *obligation vs permission*, show that it is not *logical* reasoning that is facilitated. This is because the *not p* and *q* card selection cannot be predicted from logic, although it makes perfect sense for the rules introduced in the deontic selection task. We now look at how these findings have been interpreted by the different psychological theories of reasoning.

5.2.1 Mental logic

Mental logicians have not explicitly addressed the deontic selection task. However, philosophers and mathematicians have formulated logical theories to account for the meanings of words such as *must* and *may*, which feature in deontic conditionals. So, in principle, mental logic might be extended to account for these inferences in the future (Manktelow and Over, 1987).

5.2.2 Mental models

In its basic principles the mental models account of the deontic selection task is continuous with the explanation provided for the standard selection task and indeed for all reasoning. People represent possibilities and identify counter-examples. The crucial distinction for explaining the deontic selection task is that what is deontically possible or permissible does not correspond to what is factually possible (Johnson-Laird and Byrne, 2002). So for example, if it is true that *if I turn the key then the car starts* then the three mental models as in Table 13.9(b) would represent factual possibilities (the model in which the key is turned but the car does not start is not possible).

However, for (14), all four truth table cases are factually possible – even the case where someone enters the country without a cholera inoculation. The deontic rule does not say that this does *not* happen, it says it *should* not happen, that is, it is factually possible but deontically impermissible. This means that the representation of (14) is as follows (see Figure 13.3):

Factual possibilities		Deontic possibilities	
factually possible	*Entering*	*Cholera inoculation*	deontically possible
factually possible	*Not entering*	*Cholera inoculation*	deontically possible
factually possible	*Not entering*	*No cholera inoculation*	deontically possible
factually possible	*Entering*	*No cholera inoculation*	deontically impossible

Figure 13.3   Factual and deontic possibilities represented in a fleshed-out mental model for the rule *if you are entering the country, then you must have a cholera inoculation*

That is, people explicitly label or mentally tag the different possibilities indicating whether they are permissible (deontically possible) or impermissible (deontically impossible). Exactly the same mental representation is formed of example (14'), *if you have a cholera inoculation, then you may enter the country*. So, in both cases people are looking for cases that are deontically impossible. This explains why people select logically different cases – for (14) they select *p* and *not q* and for (14') they select *not p* and *q*. Even though they are logically different, these choices represent the same deontic case (Johnson-Laird and Byrne, 2002).

5.2.3 The probabilistic approach

The probabilistic approach to the deontic selection task (Oaksford and Chater, 1994) adopts a decision-theoretic framework first proposed by Manktelow and Over (1987, 1991). In decision theory (as you saw in Chapter 12) people are deemed to make choices that help to maximize *expected utility*, where utilities are the values people place on various outcomes. In the deontic selection task, the instructions ask people to place a high value on instances of unfairness – for instance, where someone enters the country without having had a cholera inoculation.

Suppose you are to enforce (14). Your goal is to find people entering the country who do not have a cholera inoculation. You might assign a high positive utility to this case; but the remaining possibilities are uninteresting and so are assigned a small (possibly negative) utility. Suppose also that you have no prior knowledge of the likelihood of people having had a cholera inoculation or of them trying to enter the country (so all possibilities are equally likely). Then Oaksford and Chater's (1994) formal model can be illustrated by annotating utilities and probabilities to a mental model (Johnson-Laird *et al.*, 1999) (see Table 13.10).

Table 13.10 A mental model for the rule *if you are entering the country, then you must have a cholera inoculation* annotated with utilities and probabilities for each case

		Utilities	**Probabilities**
Entering	Cholera inoculation	−0.1	0.25
Not entering	Cholera inoculation	−0.1	0.25
Not entering	No cholera inoculation	−0.1	0.25
Entering	No cholera inoculation	5	0.25

Given these assumptions it turns out that the cards with greatest expected utilities are the *entering* (*p*) and *no cholera inoculation* (*not q*) cards and so, according to the principle of maximizing expected utility, you should therefore pick the *p* and *not q* cards. (Box 13.2 shows how these expected utilities are calculated.)

13.2 ——————————————————————————— Methods

Calculating expected utilities

Given the utilities and probabilities in Table 13.10, it is possible to calculate expected utility associated with turning each card. For example, for the card marked *entering* we need to consider two probabilities: the probability that this person has had a cholera inoculation and the probability that they have not. The first, the probability of the person having had an inoculation given they are trying to enter the country, is 0.5, that is, the probability of entering with an inoculation (0.25) divided by the probability of entering the country (0.5). A similar calculation gives the same value (0.5) for the second probability, that the person does not have an inoculation given they are trying to enter. These probabilities (*P*) are then multiplied by the corresponding utilities (*U*) and summed to provide the expected utility (*EU*) associated with turning the card. So:

EU(entering) = *P(cholera inoculation* | *entering*) × *U(entering, cholera inoculation)*
        + *P(no cholera inoculation* | *entering*) × *U(entering, no cholera inoculation)*

and therefore:

EU(entering) = 0.5 × −0.1 + 0.5 × 5 = 2.45

Similar calculations can be carried out for each card:

EU(not entering) = 0.5 × −0.1 + 0.5 × −0.1 = −0.1

EU(cholera inoculation) = 0.5 × −0.1 + 0.5 × −0.1 = −0.1

EU(no cholera inoculation) = 0.5 × 5 + 0.5 × −0.1 = 2.45

This decision-theoretic account makes the same predictions as mental models theory. However, it also suggests that people's deontic reasoning should be sensitive to manipulations of utility and probability and there is evidence that seems to support this suggestion (Kirby, 1994; Manktelow *et al.*, 1995).

5.2.4 Evolutionary psychology

Evolutionary psychology sees many cognitive mechanisms as innately specified, having adapted under evolutionary pressures to cope with problems confronted by early humans. Evolutionary psychologists have also argued that deontic reasoning might be under the control of innately specified cognitive modules (Cosmides, 1989; Fiddick *et al.*, 2000).

Many of the effects observed in the deontic selection task can be explained by assuming that there is a cognitive module for social contracts that govern the operation of social exchanges (Cosmides, 1989; Fiddick *et al.*, 2000). A social exchange involves satisfying a requirement in order to receive a benefit from another individual or a group. This can be expressed as a social contract, either in the form of an obligation rule (15) or a permission rule (16).

15	*If you accept the benefit then you must satisfy the requirement.*

16	*If you satisfy the requirement then you are entitled to the benefit.*

The cognitive module specialized for reasoning about social contracts would be largely insensitive to the logic of the conditionals used to describe them. What is important for survival out on the savannah is not whether the rule is *true* but whether you get *cheated*. Consequently, you should look out for people who take the benefit but do not fulfil the requirement. For (14), this corresponds to someone entering the country without having had a cholera inoculation. Consequently, this account can explain the results on the standard deontic selection task.

What distinguishes this account from other explanations? The point of invoking cognitive modules is that their processing is automatic and will tend to override any domain-general reasoning processes. Moreover, they are domain-specific, and so (15) and (16) should only apply to situations where there is a clear *benefit–requirement* relationship. Cosmides (1989) constructed two task versions using rules like (17).

17	*If a student is to be assigned to Grover High School, then that student must live in Grover city.*

In one version of the task participants were told that going to Grover High (the *p* case) was a benefit compared to going to Hanover High (the *not p* case). In another version, this information was not included, so although the obligation to live in Grover city was stated, there was no suggestion that going to Grover High was a benefit. Far more people selected the *p* and *not q* cards when the benefit was mentioned explicitly than when it was not. Consequently, it would appear that the obligation rule form is not sufficient to produce the *p* and *not q* response – the *p* and *q* cases must be understood as benefit and requirement respectively.

Further experiments appeared to show that people have an automatic understanding of social exchange situations in the absence of any explicit rules (Fiddick *et al.*, 2000). In one condition, participants were given the rule *if you give me some potatoes, then I will give you some corn*. In another condition, participants were told to imagine they were a farmer who walks into the neighbouring village and meets someone who says *I want some potatoes* to which they respond *I want some corn*. Participants are then given four cards corresponding to four people marked:

you gave this person potatoes, you gave this person nothing, this person gave you corn, and this person gave you nothing. Participants are asked to check whether any of the people represented by the cards have cheated them. Both groups performed equally well. Now this could be because people interpret the rule-less version as involving the rule. However, Fiddick *et al.* (2000) observed that people could translate the rule-less scenario into any one of four different underlying rules, any one of which would be consistent with a social exchange, but only one of which could produce the observed results. Consequently, it would seem that reliable deontic selection task performance requires the appropriate *benefits* and *require-ments* to be specified but is independent of the use of a conditional rule. So, an explanation of these tasks does not seem to involve the logic of the conditional. (However, this interpretation has been the subject of intense debate, e.g. Sperber and Girotto, 2002.)

Summary of Section 5

- There are two major reasoning paradigms that use the Wason selection task.
    - The standard abstract task and the matching effect.
    - The deontic selection task.
- *Mental logic* suggests that people use the card face they can see to draw conditional inferences, though it has not been extended to the deontic task.
- *Mental models* suggest that people check their mental models for cases relevant to the abstract rule and, for deontic cases, tag the factual possibilities according to their deontic possibility.
- *The probabilistic approach* suggests that people select cards that carry most information about the relationship expressed in the conditional and, in the deontic task, select cards that have greatest expected utility.

6   Conclusion

We have seen how the principal theories of reasoning account for the most researched experimental tasks. The ability to explain these results is one main criterion by which to judge these theories. As we saw, they all fared reasonably well. In this final section, we continue evaluating these different theories, in particular for what they have to say about the issue of human rationality. We also take the opportunity to introduce some further evidence that might decide between these theories. In evaluating theories, there are two possible approaches we might consider, **competitive** and **integrative**.

In a competitive approach, each theory is regarded as in competition to be the one true theory of reasoning. The idea is that the proponents of each theory fight their own corner, attempting to find the killer argument or experiment that will support their theory and falsify all the others. This approach tends to lead to acrimonious exchanges in the literature. However, rarely is any argument or evidence regarded as fatal. Indeed, in this and in many other areas of psychology, such wrangles usually end up in some kind of compromise position where it is conceded that each theory probably has its own merits and proper domain of application. Consequently, the final position arrived at is often an *integration* of theoretical positions. In this light, we first look at the relative merits of each theory before closing this chapter by looking to integrative approaches.

6.1　Theoretical evaluation

In this section we look at each theory and examine further evidence to distinguish between these theories where it exists. However, this evaluation falls short of plumping for one theory over another.

6.1.1　Mental logic

Mental logic theories have several advantages:

- They are formally very well specified, so theoreticians can prove mathematically what these theories predict.

- They preserve a full logical conception of what it is to reason rationally.

However, they also have some disadvantages:

- It is unclear how mental logic can apply to a range of data (for example, the graded phenomena observed in the suppression experiments). Consequently, the range of coverage of the theory is quite narrow.

Recently, this has led some mental logicians (Rips, 2001, 2002a and b) to propose a sharp distinction between *non-deductive* and *deductive* reasoning. The former are evaluated in terms of how probable the premises make the conclusion, which Rips calls *inductive strength*. People may be able to evaluate arguments for both *inductive strength* and *deductive validity*. This last issue points to a possible integration whereby mental logic deals with clear-cut cases of deductive reasoning and other theories, perhaps the probabilistic approach, deal with the rest.

6.1.2　Mental models

Features in favour of mental models include:

- The range of coverage of the data. For many phenomena in human reasoning mental models provide the only existing account. While mental logic may have the advantage of depth, mental models have the advantage of breadth.

- More reasoning researchers work in this framework than in any other.

However, as with mental logic there are problems:

- Pragmatic modulation does not seem consistent with graded effects. If people take a conditional to be true then, logically speaking, there can be no need to search for counter-examples.

There are also some more general issues:

- The attempt to provide the 'crucial experiment' that clearly falsifies mental logic while supporting mental models has largely been unsuccessful (though some recent work could be argued to play this role, e.g. Johnson-Laird and Savary, 1999).

It is difficult to gauge what mental models theory says about human rationality. Although initially motivated by the logical meanings associated with the structure-building words, mental models theory has been extended well beyond the scope of standard logic. Within the scope of standard logical inference, mental models theory can be seen as preserving human rationality because it *approximates* logical reasoning. However, beyond the scope of standard logical inference, mental models theorists rarely show that their theories approximate any logical or mathematical theory of reasoning. Consequently, in these domains it is difficult to tell whether the theory preserves human rationality or not. This is where the mental logic theory and the probabilistic approach agree – both attempt to preserve human rationality by showing that most reasoning behaviour approximates to either logic or probability theory.

The cognitive neuroscience of reasoning may also address the issue of whether people reason with a language-based mental logic or more imagery-based mental models. For example, in a recent neuroimaging study of people performing conditional inference and other reasoning tasks (Goel *et al.*, 1998), it was found that activation was primarily restricted to the left hemisphere language centres, rather than the right hemisphere imagery systems. Results like this seem to argue for a mental logic approach. However, such data are far from conclusive but it is certainly an interesting future direction for reasoning research.

6.1.3 Probabilistic approach

The general advantages of the probabilistic approach are:

- Much more of human reasoning behaviour can be seen as rational but account must be taken of people's prior knowledge of the environment, for example, the rarity assumption.

- Predictions can be derived for how manipulating probabilities and utilities should affect reasoning performance and these have generally been confirmed.

The disadvantages of the probabilistic approach are:

- The coverage of the probabilistic approach is small compared to the mental models approach.

- The theory only provides an account of how the cognitive system should behave given certain inputs. It does not provide an account of the cognitive representations and processes involved that some feel is the proper level of psychological explanation.

It is important to bear in mind that this theory suggests that the standard of rationality should change. Rather than judge human reasoning by logical standards, it should be judged by a probabilistic standard. When it is, a lot more of people's behaviour can be viewed as rational than the early experiments on human reasoning led us to expect.

6.1.4 Evolutionary psychology

It is difficult to judge the evolutionary psychology approach by the same standards as the other theories because even compared to the mental logic and probabilistic approaches its scope is extremely limited. However, within the domain of deontic reasoning there is some further neuropsychological evidence that may be relevant. The evolutionary approach suggests that people have two innate cognitive modules, one for social contracts and one for reasoning about *hazard management*. The latter involves reasoning about rules like, *if you clear up blood, you must wear rubber gloves* (Manktelow and Over, 1991). The rule indicates the precautions you should take if you encounter a hazardous situation. According to the domain-general theories, such rules are dealt with by the same mechanisms that deal with social contract rules. However, there is recent evidence of a neuropsychological patient with brain damage, who shows an impaired ability to reason about social contracts but an intact ability to reason about hazard management rules (Stone *et al.*, 2002). This seems to suggest that this patient has an intact innate hazard management module but a damaged innate social contract module. However, unless a patient is found with the opposite deficit, that is, impaired hazard management reasoning and intact social contract reasoning, these results remain inconclusive.

6.2 Integration, dual processes and individual differences

Attempts to integrate theories of reasoning centre on dual-process theories that have a long pedigree in reasoning research (Evans, 1984; Evans and Over, 1996; Stanovich and West, 2000). These theories suggest a two-way partition in reasoning abilities. As we have already suggested, this is similar to some mental logic theorists who have invoked the distinction between deductive and non-deductive reasoning (Rips, 2002b). Typically, these theories suggest that we do have a, perhaps limited, ability for explicit logical reasoning that may be embodied in mental logic or in mental models. However, a lot of reasoning goes on implicitly and is independent of these logical processes. More recently the distinction has been drawn between two types of rationality (Evans and Over, 1996). People are rational in one sense when their reasoning conforms to a normative standard like logic. They are rational in another sense when they reason in order to achieve their goals in the world, regardless of whether their reasoning conforms to a normative standard. Different mental processes are involved in these forms of reasoning.

One recent source of evidence for this approach is the study of individual differences (Stanovich and West, 2000). For example, it has been shown that the ability to make the logically correct response on the selection task is associated with IQ (Stanovich and West, 1998). It would appear that participants with a high IQ are capable of interpreting this task logically (and choosing the *p* and *not q* cards). However, when you consider just the remaining participants, then IQ seems to correlate with the non-logical but standard *p* and *q* card response (Newstead *et al.*, 2004). This evidence seems to argue for a dual-process theory. Perhaps people possess automatic unconscious reasoning mechanisms that operate in accordance with probabilistic standards of reasoning (explaining the *p* and *q* cards' selection). However, those with higher IQs may be capable of ignoring the prior knowledge that is required to determine the relevant probabilities, and can then reason logically about the task.

Such integrative approaches are also consistent with the trend among some mental model theorists to add probabilistic components to the core theory (Schroyens and Schaeken, 2003). The critical question then becomes the balance of reasoning processes. That high IQ is apparently associated with logical responses suggests that perhaps most human reasoning is carried out by unconscious, probabilistic or inductive processes. However, the jury is still very far from delivering a verdict on this question. Nonetheless, the emergence of integrative approaches should be seen as a positive sign. This is because it opens up the area of human reasoning to more interesting possibilities, other than that my theory is right and yours is wrong!

Now that you have read this chapter you can reinforce and extend your learning by reading an original journal article associated with it, available online from the DD303 website. Remember, these are original journal articles, so the style is different from this textbook, and don't be too concerned if you can't follow every detail.

Answer to Activity 13.2

Possibility C shows AC to be an invalid form of inference. In this, both *if p then q* and *q* are true, but *p* is false. Possibility C also shows DA to be invalid: though *if p then q* and *not p* are true, *not q* is false.

Further reading

Braine, M.D.S. and O'Brien, D.P. (eds) (1998) *Mental Logic*, Mahwah, NJ, Lawrence Erlbaum Associates.

Johnson-Laird, P.N. and Byrne, R.M.J. (1991) *Deduction*, Mahwah, NJ, Lawrence Erlbaum Associates.

Oaksford, M. and Chater, N. (1998) *Rationality in an Uncertain World*, Hove, Psychology Press.

Manktelow, K.I. (1999) *Reasoning and Thinking*, Hove, Psychology Press.

References

Boole, G. (1854) *An Investigation of the Laws of Thought On Which are Founded the Mathematical Theories of Logic and Probabilities*, Cambridge, Macmillan and Co.

Braine, M.D.S. and O'Brien, D.P. (eds) (1998) *Mental Logic*, Mahwah, NJ, Lawrence Erlbaum Associates.

Byrne, R.M.J. (1989) 'Suppressing valid inferences with conditionals', *Cognition*, vol.31, pp.1–21.

Byrne, R.M.J., Espino, O. and Santamaria, C. (1999) 'Counter-examples and the suppression of inferences', *Journal of Memory and Language*, vol.40, pp.347–73.

Cheng, P.W. and Holyoak, K.J. (1985) 'Pragmatic reasoning schemas', *Cognitive Psychology*, vol.17, pp.391–416.

Cosmides, L. (1989) 'The logic of social exchange: has natural selection shaped how humans reason? Studies with the Wason selection task', *Cognition*, vol.31, pp.187–276.

Cummins, D.D., Lubart, T., Alksnis, O. and Rist, R. (1991) 'Conditional reasoning and causation', *Memory and Cognition*, vol.19, pp.274–82.

Cummins, D.D. (1995) 'Naive theories and causal deduction', *Memory and Cognition*, vol.23, no.5, pp.646–58.

Evans, J. St B.T. (1977) 'Linguistic factors in reasoning', *Quarterly Journal of Experimental Psychology*, vol.29, pp.297–306.

Evans, J. St B.T. (1984) 'Heuristic and analytic processes in reasoning', *British Journal of Psychology*, vol.75, pp.451–68.

Evans, J. St B.T., Clibbens, J. and Rood, B. (1996) 'The role of implicit and explicit negation in conditional reasoning bias', *Journal of Memory and Language*, vol.35, no.3, pp.392–409.

Evans, J. St B.T. and Handley, S.J. (1999) 'The role of negation in conditional inference', *Quarterly Journal of Experimental Psychology: Human Experimental Psychology*, vol.52A, no.3, pp.739–69.

Evans. J. St B.T. and Lynch, J.S. (1973) 'Matching bias in the selection task', *British Journal of Psychology*, vol.64, pp.391–7.

Evans, J.B. St B.T. and Over, D.E. (1996) *Rationality and Reasoning*, Hove, Psychology Press.

Evans, J.B. St B.T., Handley, S.J. and Over, P.E. (2003) 'Conditionals and conditional probability', *Journal of Experimental Psychology: Learning, Memory and Cognition*, vol.29, pp.321–35.

Fiddick, L., Cosmides, L. and Tooby, J. (2000) 'No interpretation without representation: the role of domain-specific representations and inferences in the Wason selection task', *Cognition*, vol.77, no.1, pp.1–79.

Goel, V., Gold, B., Kapur, S. and Houle, S. (1998) 'Neuroanatomical correlates of human reasoning', *Neuropsychologia*, vol.29, pp.901–9.

Inhelder, B. and Piaget, J. (1958) *The Growth of Logical Reasoning*, New York, Basic Books.

Johnson-Laird, P.N., Legrenzi, P., Girotto, V., Legrenzi, M.S. and Caverni, J.P. (1999) 'Naive probability: a mental model theory of extensional reasoning', *Psychological Review*, vol.106, no.1, pp.62–88.

Johnson-Laird, P.N. and Savary, F. (1999) 'Illusory inferences: a novel class of erroneous deductions', *Cognition*, vol.71, no.3, pp.191–229.

Johnson-Laird, P.N. and Wason, P.C. (1970) 'Insight into a logical relation', *Quarterly Journal of Experimental Psychology*, vol.22, no.1, pp.49–61.

Johnson-Laird, P.N. (1983) *Mental Models*, Cambridge, Cambridge University Press.

Johnson-Laird, P.N. and Byrne, R.M.J. (eds) (1991) *Deduction*, Hillsdale, NJ, Erlbaum.

Johnson-Laird, P.N. and Byrne, R.M.J. (2002) 'Conditionals: a theory of meaning, pragmatics, and inference', *Psychological Review*, vol.109, no.4, pp.646–78.

Kirby, K.N. (1994) 'Probabilities and utilities of fictional outcomes in Wason's four card selection task', *Cognition*, vol.51, pp.1–28.

Manktelow, K.I. and Over, D.E. (1987) 'Reasoning and rationality', *Mind and Language*, vol.2, pp.199–219.

Manktelow, K.I. and Over, D.E. (1991) 'Social roles and utilities in reasoning with deontic conditionals', *Cognition*, vol.39, pp.85–105.

Manktelow, K.I., Sutherland, E.J. and Over, D.E. (1995) 'Probabilistic factors in deontic reasoning', *Thinking and Reasoning*, vol.1, pp.201–20.

Newstead, S.E., Handley, S.J., Harley, C., Wright, H. and Farrelly, D. (2004) 'Individual difference in deductive reasoning', *Quarterly Journal of Experimental Psychology*, vol.57, pp.33–60.

Oaksford, M. and Chater, N. (1994) 'A rational analysis of the selection task as optimal data selection', *Psychological Review*, vol.101, pp.608–31.

Oaksford, M. and Chater, N. (1996) 'Rational explanation of the selection task', *Psychological Review*, vol.103, pp.381–91.

Oaksford, M. and Chater, N. (1998) *Rationality in an Uncertain World: Essays on the Cognitive Science of Human Reasoning*, Hove, Psychology Press.

Oaksford, M. and Chater, N. (2003a) 'Computational levels and conditional inference: reply to Schroyens and Schaeken', *Journal of Experimental Psychology: Learning, Memory, and Cognition*, vol.29, no.1, pp.150–6.

Oaksford, M. and Chater, N. (2003b) 'Optimal data selection: revision, review and re-evaluation', *Psychonomic Bulletin and Review*, vol.10, pp.289–318.

Oaksford, M. and Chater, N. (2003c) 'Probabilities and pragmatics in conditional inference: suppression and order effects' in Hardman, D. and Macchi, L. (eds) *Thinking: Psychological Perspectives on Reasoning, Judgment and Decision Making*, London, John Wiley and Sons, pp.95–122.

Oaksford, M., Chater, N. and Larkin, J. (2000) 'Probabilities and polarity biases in conditional inference', *Journal of Experimental Psychology: Learning, Memory, and Cognition*, vol.26, no.4, pp.883–99.

Quinn, S. and Markovits, H. (2002) 'Conditional reasoning with causal premises: evidence for a retrieval model', *Thinking and Reasoning*, vol.8, no.3, pp.179–91.

Rips, L.J. (1994) *The Psychology of Proof*, Cambridge, MA, MIT Press.

Rips, L.J. (2001) 'Two kinds of reasoning', *Psychological Science*, vol.121, no.2, pp.129–34.

Rips, L.J. (2002a) 'Reasoning imperialism' in Elio, R. (ed.) *Common Sense, Reasoning and Rationality*, New York, Oxford University Press, pp.215–35.

Rips, L.J. (2002b) 'Reasoning' in Pashler, H. and Medin, D. (eds) *Steven's Handbook of Experimental Psychology, Memory and Cognitive Processes*, 3rd edn, vol.2, New York, John Wiley and Sons, pp.363–411.

Schroyens, W. and Schaeken, W. (2003) 'A critique of Oaksford, Chater, and Larkin's (2000) conditional probability model of conditional reasoning', *Journal of Experimental Psychology: Learning, Memory, and Cognition*, vol.29, no.1, pp.140–9.

Sperber, D. and Girotto, V. (2002) 'Use or misuse of the selection task?: rejoinder to Fiddick, Cosmides, and Tooby', *Cognition*, vol.85, no.3, pp.277–90.

Stanovich, K.E. and West, R.F. (1998) 'Cognitive ability and variation in selection task performance', *Thinking and Reasoning*, vol.4, no.3, pp.193–230.

Stanovich, K.E. and West, R.F. (2000) 'Individual differences in reasoning: implications for the rationality debate?', *Behavioral and Brain Sciences*, vol.23, no.5, pp.645–64.

Stone, V.E., Cosmides, L., Tooby, J., Kroll, N. and Knight, R.T. (2002) 'Selective impairment of reasoning about social exchange in a patient with bilateral limbic system damage', *Proceedings of the National Academy of Sciences*, vol.99, no.17, pp.11531–6.

Taplin, J.E. (1971) 'Reasoning with conditional sentences', *Journal of Verbal Learning and Verbal Behaviour*, no.10, pp.219–25.

Wason, P.C. (1968) 'Reasoning about a rule', *Quarterly Journal of Experimental Psychology*, vol.20, pp.273–81.

Wason, P.C. and Shapiro, D. (1971) 'Natural and contrived experience in a reasoning problem', *Quarterly Journal of Experimental Psychology*, vol.23, pp.63–71.

PART 5

CHALLENGES FOR COGNITIVE PSYCHOLOGY

Introduction

What have you learnt so far from this textbook? Hopefully, a great deal about cognitive psychology – what it is, what methods it uses, what topics it tackles and what questions it asks. So, now you may be asking, what does it all mean? And how does it relate to real life? Applying cognitive theories and models isn't just difficult for you as students; it's one of the biggest challenges that face cognitive researchers. Why is it such a challenge? Well, it's a challenge for a number of reasons. First, you will have seen that individual aspects of cognition (e.g. attention, memory, etc.) have been presented in separate chapters. This is because the processes involved are extremely complex. Indeed, researchers can spend their whole working life examining just one area of cognitive psychology! So, the complex nature of cognition is our first challenge. Second, we know that cognitive processes don't operate independently. We can process information in different ways at the same time. So how do these processes interact? And what do they interact with? We aren't just robotic cognitive processers. Yes, we are thinkers, problem solvers and language users, but we are also conscious, emotional, social beings. So how can we apply what we know about cognitive processes to a wider context? Well, this poses one of the biggest challenges to cognitive psychology.

In Chapter 14, Jenny Yiend and Bundy Mackintosh examine the complex relationship between cognition and emotion. This chapter defines different aspects of emotion processing: physiological responses, behavioural responses (social) and emotional feelings. It then goes on to examine research that has demonstrated the interaction between cognition and emotion, for example the impact of mood on memory. Emotional feelings are what most people think of when reflecting on their conscious experiences. In fact, it's impossible to think of consciousness without thinking about feelings. Emotion and consciousness also interact with every other area of cognitive processing. For example, we can shift our conscious awareness from one task to another (attentional processing) depending on both meaning (emotion) and physical attributes (sound). We also consciously experience meaning and emotion in text. While there are obvious interactions, what does it actually mean to be conscious? Jackie Andrade tackles this in Chapter 15 by outlining the philosophical approaches and placing consciousness within the realm of cognitive psychology. Jackie then examines research on implicit learning (learning without conscious awareness) and modularity before providing an analysis of what the function of consciousness might be. The final chapter (Chapter 16) places cognitive psychology within a wider societal context. By using the topics of memory and the law and intelligence, Hayley Ness illustrates not only how cognitive theories and research have been applied in differing contexts, but also how cognition interacts with other areas of psychology such as social and developmental psychology. It is hoped that by the end of this section, you will have a greater understanding of cognition in context, be able to make links between different areas of psychology and generate exciting new research questions of your own.

Chapter 14

Cognition and emotion

Jenny Yiend and Bundy Mackintosh

1 Introduction

This chapter is concerned not just with cognition but with how emotions influence, and are influenced by, cognitive processes. Emotions are such a familiar and fundamental aspect of everyday life that it is often this very ability to experience and express emotion that is seen as a crucial distinction between the behaviour of humans and (possibly imaginary) high-functioning computers or robots. As you have seen in previous chapters, it is possible for a computer to solve successfully many difficult tasks and so mimic human achievements. However, one very salient distinction between the performance of computer and human is that the computer won't show pleasure when reaching its goal nor frustration if it fails, let alone empathy with its human operator. We shall consider whether this is really an advance later in the chapter.

When emotions seem such an important part of our lives, it might come as a surprise that despite the rapid development of psychology as a discrete scientific discipline since the mid 1800s, the study of emotion has largely taken a back seat. Why should this be so? One reason is undoubtedly the behaviourist legacy. Behaviourists such as John B. Watson (1878–1958) and Burrhus Frederick Skinner (1904–1990) recognized the need for scientific rigour and objective, verifiable measurement and were therefore exclusively concerned with the overt behaviours displayed by an organism – those which could be directly observed and measured. For behaviourists, reference to unseen mental processes was taboo. Their emphasis on objectivity and empiricism continues to be an important influence in cognitive psychology today. This historical bias for a long time deterred study of emotion, in which the main component – feelings – can only be accessed through introspection. Undoubtedly, another factor has been the attitude towards emotions often expressed in Western European societies among others. At least since Plato (375 BC) emotions have been viewed as impediments to rational thought. Darwin thought of them as childish or immature responses, a residual hangover from our evolutionary past that no longer had useful functions for the mature adult. However, the study of emotion and how it interacts with cognition has enjoyed a resurgence of interest. This is largely because of the development of objective, quantifiable ways of measuring the concomitants of emotion, such as psychophysiological techniques, brain imaging and a shift in attitude towards the importance and function of emotions in everyday life.

ACTIVITY 14.1

Stop for a moment and reflect on one recent episode when you experienced emotion and try to jot down three or more aspects that characterized this occasion as being emotional.

COMMENT

This is often a hard task, since one common feature of emotional situations is that it is sometimes difficult to put into words what is happening! However, you may have noted your feelings and perhaps what or whom you considered was the cause of the emotion. Did you include a description of how you behaved or a change in body sensations?

One example could go something like this (note the different elements of this description):

> One day when I was alone at home a special delivery van stopped at our house looking for an address nearby. I stepped outside to point out directions, the front door blew in the wind and locked behind me. 'No problem', I thought, and went to the usual hiding place to retrieve the spare key. It was missing. Now I felt anger, frustration and regret. Why wasn't the key in its usual place? I blamed others for not replacing it. Why had I been so stupid to let the door slam? I swore and banged my fist. I went back to the door and rattled the handle. I was taking deep breaths and felt my heart beating fast with annoyance. I paced rapidly up and down whilst I tried to work out what to do next ...

1.1 Components of emotion

From the example above it is clear that there are different aspects to any emotional response. Traditionally, psychologists have identified at least three characteristics that are embodied within an emotional episode. These are:

- behaviours
- bodily responses (physiology)
- feelings.

1.1.1 Emotional behaviour and expression

Many of the behaviours associated with emotion will be familiar to you. Some simple examples include laughing when you are happy; withdrawing from something you find disgusting; becoming agitated and raising your voice when you are angry, and quiet, withdrawn and slow when you are sad. Facial expressions that are characteristic of different emotions are also examples of behavioural responses. As these are all observable phenomena, they can be easier to study empirically than internal feelings. However, they cannot generally be used to infer emotions directly since, unlike most of the bodily (physiological) responses associated with emotion, emotional expressions can be brought under some degree of control. You can suppress your smile; make a special effort to appear cheerful when sad; feign interest in order to be polite; and curb your angry behaviour if it might jeopardize your well-being. More problematic for research, various cultures and social groups differ in their code of conduct with respect to emotional expressions. For example, in some cultures, such as in many Arabian countries, public grieving involves overt crying, moaning and beating of the chest which are seen as appropriate expressions of respect for the dead in assembled company, whereas in others, for instance in Japan, a polite smile and tight emotional control are expected.

Unlike the very individual feeling of emotion and internal bodily response to emotion, emotional behaviour, including emotion expressions, is visible to others; that is, it can communicate (albeit imperfectly) the individual's emotional status. In any form of communication, understanding the mechanism fully requires researching both the recognition and the production of the appropriate signals (as discussed in Chapter 8). So far, much more research effort has been directed towards recognition rather than production of behavioural correlates of emotion. Facial expressions, rather than other emotion behaviour such as 'body language', have attracted most research attention.

1.1.2 Bodily responses

The bodily responses associated with emotions are the physiological reactions such as sweating when you feel anxious, or your heart racing when you feel agitated or excited. These reactions have been refined during evolution and are vital to survival. For example, if a lion attacks then there must be little delay before escape ('flight'), or maybe aggression ('fight'), begins. Typically an animal's body will respond to this kind of threat by diverting the blood flow away from less vital regions, such as the gut (digesting lunch suddenly is less important than ensuring you don't become someone else's). The extra blood, and therefore energy, is supplied to the major muscle blocks and the brain (rapid processing of information is needed or energy could be wasted running in the wrong direction). The contents of the blood are altered, boosting 'fuel' in the form of blood glucose, and cholesterol, and increasing clotting agent (which serves to stem blood loss in case of wounds), and so on. This physiological reaction stands us in good stead when physical action is required to ensure survival.

Many of these bodily responses are controlled by the **autonomic nervous system (ANS)** (see Figure 14.1 overleaf), a network of nerve fibres throughout the body that transmits signals to the various organs, muscles and glands. The ANS is divided into two sections. The **sympathetic ANS** produces effects associated with arousal. These include secretion of the hormone adrenalin from a gland near the kidneys. Adrenalin release initiates and enhances sympathetic activity leading to changes such as accelerating heart rate, vasoconstriction (constriction of the blood vessels), increased respiration (breathing) rate and depth, and reduced gastro-intestinal (gut) activity. The intricate pattern of changes in hormone levels, breathing, redirection of blood flow and pressure and changes in its constituents, and the many other changes occurring under stress all prepare the body for physical exertion (the 'flight or fight' response described above). This is a physiological pattern fine-tuned by evolution and shared by other mammals, with only relatively minor details differing between species. In contrast, the **parasympathetic ANS** tends to dominate during periods of rest, having broadly opposing effects on the body.

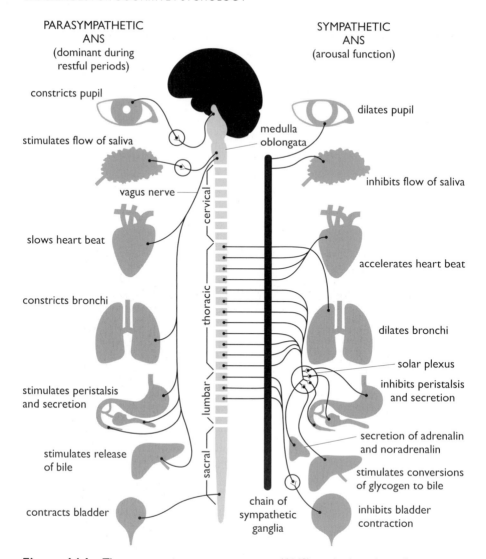

Figure 14.1 The autonomic nervous system (ANS) and physiological responses associated with emotions, showing sympathetic and parasympathetic sections

Source: Reber, 1995, p.76

Box 14.1 discusses techniques for measuring physiological responses and so for investigating this component of emotion.

14.1 ———————————————————————————————— Methods

Measuring emotion using psychophysiology

Most emotional states tend to lead to increased arousal and therefore produce corresponding physiological signs. Psychologists have been able to devise ways of measuring this physiological change precisely. For example, by applying a tiny electrical current across the fingers we can measure the electrical resistance of the skin. This changes according to minute differences in the amount of sweat

---

produced and so provides a physiological measure known as either GSR (galvanic skin response) or SC (skin conductance), that correlates with changes in arousal (recall the use of GSR responses to detect the influence of 'shocked' words in the non-attended messages discussed in Chapter 2, Section 1.3). The measurement of changes in GSR has also been used as a 'lie detector' picking up individuals' emotional response arising during deception. Heart rate, another psychophysiological measure, is usually measured as 'beats per minute' using a simple transducer which converts the movement produced by the pulse into electrical energy. Other common measures include cortisol levels in the blood (related to adrenalin production), electromyography (EMG: muscle tension and activity, usually recorded from the face), respiration rate and surface skin temperature (related to dilation or constriction of the blood vessels).

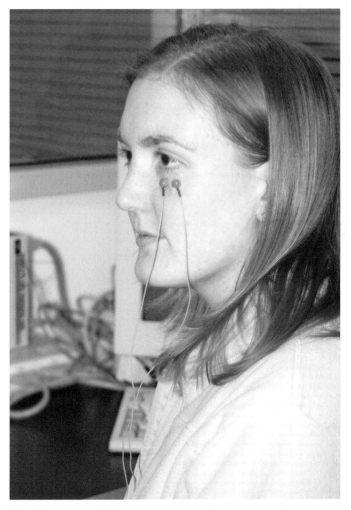

Figure 14.2   Measuring EMG: electrodes are shown under the eye and measure 'startle' or 'blink' magnitude, which is the muscle contraction produced when you blink or are surprised, for example in response to a sudden loud noise

1.1.3 Feeling emotions

Feelings are private and subjective. They are, by definition, states of experiential awareness. Around the world, humans can usually report a wide range of different states or feelings, from anger to fear to love, which can be recognized and understood by those around them. Within psychology the feeling component of emotion is inextricably bound up with notions of conscious awareness and the subjective self (see Chapters 7 and 15). Emotion researchers are often interested in whether the stimuli or tasks that they use elicit positive or negative feelings, and if so to what degree. They certainly acknowledge that feelings co-occur with the other markers of emotion, but otherwise cognitive psychologists have concentrated less on feeling states than on exploration of the cognitive processing associated with emotions and emotional information.

ACTIVITY 14.2

Thinking back to what you've learned so far about cognition, would you say that emotions may also have a cognitive component as well as the components we have just discussed (behaviour, bodily responses, feelings)? If so, we would be able to study the cognitive side of emotions using the techniques and paradigms familiar to cognitive scientists.

COMMENT

Looking only at the three components of emotion discussed above, you might well answer 'no' with regard to bodily responses and feelings. The behavioural component of emotions includes face perception, which will be familiar from Chapter 4, though in emotion research it is the emotional expression not identity that is of interest. However, as we proceed you will see that many of the tools developed by cognitive scientists can be widely adapted to the study of emotions. Not only do cognitive processes interact with emotions, but many psychologists believe that they are an integral part of producing the emotions themselves.

One issue that researchers face when trying to study any of the components of emotion described above is how to elicit realistic effects in the laboratory. In real life, emotions are usually stronger than those seen in the laboratory, so we have to be cautious when generalizing from the results of any given study. There are at least two reasons why it is difficult to study the behaviours, physiology and feelings associated with *strong* emotions:

1   It is sometimes unethical to induce strong emotions, for example strongly negative ones, in a laboratory setting.

2   Strong emotions are hard to elicit in a predictable fashion and take a while to die down, making laboratory study impractical.

For these reasons, you will find throughout this chapter that the study of cognition and emotion is largely confined to consideration of relatively mild emotional states and the processing of mildly emotional information. However, the information gained from such work provides useful insights about possible cognitive processing when emotion is more extreme.

Summary of Section 1

- Although the study of emotions from a cognitive point of view has historically been neglected, the advent of new techniques and new ideas as to the significance and function of emotions has brought a resurgence of interest in the study of emotion and how it interacts with cognition.

- There are thought to be three main components of emotions:
  - emotional behaviour and expression (e.g. emotional facial expressions)
  - bodily responses (e.g. galvanic skin response)
  - feelings.

2   Different emotions

You should now have some idea of what is meant by the term 'emotion' in psychology. Next we shall consider how one might classify and explain the huge variety of different emotions that individuals typically report. Psychologists usually take one of two approaches to dealing with the task of accounting for different emotional experiences. Some refer to a set of **basic emotions**, while others take a **dimensional** view.

2.1   Basic emotions

One approach has been to assume that underlying the richness of emotion experience there are a small number of discrete emotions – ones considered to be the most fundamental or important. This idea is analogous to the processing of colour by the visual system, where the whole range and subtlety of our colour experience is achieved through stimulation of just three different types of cones in the retina. Likewise, it is argued that different combinations of 'basic emotions' can produce all the other emotions. For example, a mixture of joy and acceptance produces friendliness according to Plutchik, a prominent basic emotions theorist.

There are several distinct challenges to the notion of basic emotions: one is to provide evidence for the existence of a small number of discrete emotion states; another is to decide how many emotions should be called basic and which ones they are. The idea of basic emotions has considerable general support but few agree exactly on the appropriate number and type of emotions that should be included. This point is illustrated by Table 14.1 (overleaf).

Despite these widely differing views there are five emotions, sometimes called **the Big Five**, that appear to represent a broad consensus among basic emotions psychologists. These are anger, fear, sadness, disgust and happiness. One of the most influential psychologists from this tradition, Paul Ekman, building on research described by Darwin in *The Expression of the Emotions in Man and Animals* (1998, first published in 1872), has collected a formidable body of information from cross-cultural studies to support the fundamental status and importance of these five emotions. He was impressed by the observation that wherever he travelled people

Table 14.1   Basic emotion theorists and the emotions they propose

Emotion theorist	Fundamental emotion
Arnold	Anger, aversion, courage, dejection, desire, despair, fear, hate, hope, love, sadness
Ekman, Friesen and Ellsworth	Anger, disgust, fear, joy, sadness, surprise
Frijda	Desire, happiness, interest, surprise, wonder, sorrow
Gray	Rage and terror, anxiety, joy
Izard	Anger, contempt, disgust, distress, fear, guilt, interest, joy, shame, surprise
James	Fear, grief, love, rage
McDougall	Anger, disgust, elation, fear, subjection, tender-emotion, wonder
Mowrer	Pain, pleasure
Oatley and Johnson-Laird	Anger, disgust, anxiety, happiness, sadness
Panksepp	Expectancy, fear, rage, panic
Plutchik	Acceptance, anger, anticipation, disgust, joy, fear, sadness, surprise
Tomkins	Anger, interest, contempt, disgust, distress, fear, joy, shame, surprise
Watson	Fear, love, rage
Weiner and Graham	Happiness, sadness

Source: Power and Dalgleish, 1997

displayed broadly similar emotions, and that he had no difficulty in interpreting them despite language barriers. For more systematic research his main method was to show pictures of facial expressions, such as those in Figure 14.3(a), and determine whether peoples from different cultures consistently select the same emotion label to describe each one.

Figure 14.3(b) shows some typical results for six emotions – the Big Five plus surprise. Although there is some variation, particularly within isolated non-literate cultures, there is always agreement above what would be expected if people were just guessing (the 'chance' level, shown by the white bars). Ekman also provided evidence for basic emotions in the production as well as in the recognition of expressions. He visited a visually isolated non-literate group in New Guinea (people who had not previously met or seen pictures of anyone from outside their own cultural group) and asked them to show him what their face would look like if they were sad, happy and so on. He then took videos of their expressions and played them back to American students, who had to decide which emotion was being displayed by the New Guineans. The American judges had no problem in identifying the different emotions according to the (translated) labels to which the New Guineans had been responding, which further supports the notion of pancultural or universal emotions (Ekman *et al.*, 1969; Ekman, 1999, provides a review of all his work).

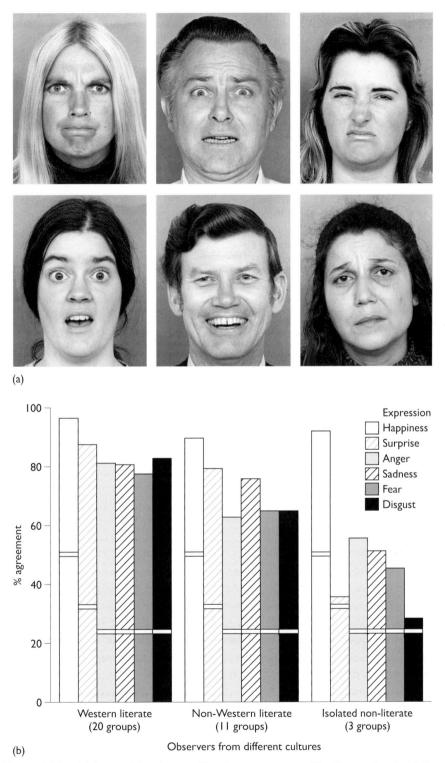

(a)

(b) Observers from different cultures

Figure 14.3 (a) Some of the photos of facial expressions used by Ekman, showing (left to right) anger, fear, disgust, surprise, happiness and sadness; (b) results from cross-cultural studies showing differences in recognizing facial expressions of six emotions

Source: (a) Ekman and Friesen, 2003; (b) Rosenzweig et al., 1999, Figure 15.3, p.414

In support of the basic emotions approach, Ekman provides extensive evidence from cross-cultural work such as ratings of spontaneous displays of emotion across different cultures. More convincingly, he has used objective measurements of facial behaviour (how much different parts of the face move) and compared these across cultures and countries – for instance, by testing participants from Japan and the USA (Ekman, 1973). His studies have also extended to infants from different cultures (Ekman and Oster, 1979). You may wonder why Ekman chose to look particularly at infants' facial expressions rather than adults'. If a characteristic or ability is present in infants, who have had little opportunity to be influenced by their culture or upbringing, then that is additional evidence for that characteristic being largely genetic rather than learned. The spontaneous facial expressions of blind children (Medicus *et al.*, 1994; Eibl Eibesfeldt, 1988) also support the idea that there may be basic emotions, and further that they may have biological rather than social origins. Other theorists such as Plutchik and Frijda (Plutchik and Landau, 1973; Frijda, 2001; Frijda and Tcherkassof, 1997) rely not only on facial expressions but on whole body movements – what is often called 'body language'.

Ekman's assumption about the inheritance of emotion is shared by many others promoting the notion of basic emotions. For these researchers it follows that such emotions arise from subcortical brain mechanisms that we still share with many other species (e.g. Panksepp, 1989; Panksepp *et al.*, 1991; LeDoux, 1989). Debate is still active concerning whether and which emotions are basic, or whether it is clusters of related emotions that should be considered together. However, many believe that the development of the brain systems underlying something approximating to the basic emotions seems to have arisen far back in our evolutionary past before the separation of mammals, reptiles and birds. Box 14.2 discusses how technology for imaging the brain has begun to shed light on the relationship between specific emotions and particular brain structures.

14.2 ———————————————————————— **Methods**

Imaging emotions in the brain

Although techniques for imaging the structure of the brain (taking pictures without the need to make any actual physical intrusion) have been used in medicine for several decades, the ability to study changes in activation associated with brain function is a more recent and rapidly growing technique. Two common techniques are PET (positron emission tomography) and fMRI (functional magnetic resonance imaging). PET involves injecting the participant with very slightly radioactive water, which then travels around the body including the brain, emitting its radiation as it goes. Participants perform an experiment usually designed to test particular hypotheses about which brain areas are involved in the task(s) concerned. Because the most active areas of the brain will draw the most blood, these areas will also be emitting the most radioactivity. This is measured using special gamma ray (the energy component of radioactivity) detecting equipment, and thanks to complex software can be translated into brain images, which look similar to those shown in colour Plates 6 and 7. fMRI also produces similar looking images of brain activation involved in a task – but using a different method. A strong magnetic field is applied across the brain that aligns certain particles in the blood (called 'de-oxygenated haemoglobin' molecules) in the same direction (similar to the way iron filings line up towards a magnet). When this field is removed these particles 'precess', or move back again, and in doing so each particle emits a discrete 'package' of energy, which is detected by specialist equipment. The more active an area of the brain is, the more of these particles it has and consequently the more energy is emitted during precession.

Brain-imaging techniques such as those described above are revealing some very interesting results about emotions. For example, many studies have now shown that a structure called the amygdala is involved in the processing of all types of emotion and is particularly strongly activated in response to fear stimuli. Similarly, two areas are implicated in recognizing disgust: the insula, an area of cortex (the convoluted outer layer of the brain) and the basal ganglia (an evolutionarily old area in the brain stem). This has been corroborated by data from a patient who has damage to these areas and is particularly poor at recognizing disgust in others (Calder *et al.*, 2000).

Colour Plate 6 shows the areas of the brain where different studies have reported activation resulting from either the processing of fearful faces (green squares) or learning about fear (red circles). The image on the left is a horizontal 'slice' through the brain, with the eyes at the top end and the back of the head at the bottom. The image on the right is the same sort of slice, but taken higher up, more towards the top of the head. There is a tendency for the activation triggered by processing fearful faces to involve the left amygdala, whereas learning about fear seems to produce more bilateral activation.

Colour Plate 7 shows the areas where studies have found brain responses to disgust. As with Plate 6, the two images depict different slices through the brain. The insula activations are shown in purple, and basal ganglia activations in red. The basal ganglia signals are mainly in the right hemisphere, whereas the insula signals are more evenly distributed across the two hemispheres.

Another feature of these new brain-imaging techniques is that as well as the cognitive processing of emotion described above, they can give us an objective measure of the 'feelings' side of emotion (see Section 1.1.3). As we said earlier, feelings have been notoriously hard to study in psychology because the only way to measure them was to rely on people's subjective self-reports of their own internal state – the much-scorned 'introspection'. Now, though, we can investigate how brain activity changes according to the strength and nature of our feelings and this is a possibility that is only just starting to be exploited.

2.2 Verbal labels

The fact that very similar verbal labels are used across widely differing languages and cultures is sometimes used as evidence in support of the existence of a discrete set of basic emotions corresponding to those labels. Scherer and colleagues (e.g. Scherer and Wallbott, 1994 a and b; Wallbott and Scherer, 1988, first published

1986) have compared verbal labels for emotions in 37 countries and were able to translate the English terms for the seven emotions studied (anger, fear, sadness, joy, disgust, shame and guilt) into each of the other languages. If all languages include words to describe the so-called basic emotions, and these emotions can be recognized across all cultures, however remote or different from each other, then that gives reason for believing in the universality of the concepts for the basic emotions. What about all the other emotion words: where do they fit into the idea of basic emotions? Scherer and others introduce the idea of 'modal emotions'; that is, the idea that a number of these other emotion words may cluster together under a common 'theme', and that the specific clustering of emotion words betrays the underlying emotion concepts of the individual (recall discussions about concepts in Chapter 9). To complicate matters, different languages and cultures do seem to differ in the number and categorization of their emotion terms. It is not surprising to find that the range of situations that trigger emotions varies across cultures, but, in addition, different emotions are either elaborated or downgraded in emphasis. There appears to be a set of universals – for instance, loss of a loved one leading to sadness, and attack to fear or anger – as well as a multitude of cultural specifics, such as whether looking directly at a woman's face evokes sensations of polite interaction, flattery or insult. Whilst debate continues about whether there are a small number of basic emotions and whether these are necessarily inherited, it is clear that there are many cultural differences in emotions. Thus, there are cross-cultural differences in:

- the number and type of complex emotions
- the triggers for many emotions
- the socially acceptable rules for which emotions should be displayed in certain contexts.

2.3 The dimensional approach

The concept of 'basic emotions' is not without challenge. Theorists such as Ortony and Turner (1990) have asked why, if basic emotions are so basic, there is so much disagreement about which count as basic, with some contenders (e.g. interest and desire) sometimes not even being considered as emotions at all. An alternative dimensional approach, as the name implies, assumes that the full range of emotional experience can be explained by identifying a few key dimensions. If there are only two key dimensions, then all emotions could be identified as being located in a two-dimensional space specifying the relative contribution provided by each of the two dimensions. An example of this approach is shown in Figure 14.4.

The 'affect grid' in Figure 14.4 is taken from work by Peter Lang and colleagues, who concentrate on studying our physiological responses to emotional material. There are two dimensions, **arousal** and **valence** (valence refers to the positive/pleasant or negative/unpleasant qualities of something). The figure shows people's ratings of how 'aroused' and how 'positive or negative' they feel about a variety of different pictures. Other, separate dimensions, such as 'dominance' have also been proposed, producing a more complex three-dimensional space (dominance reflects a quality related to how dominated vs in control the participant feels when considering

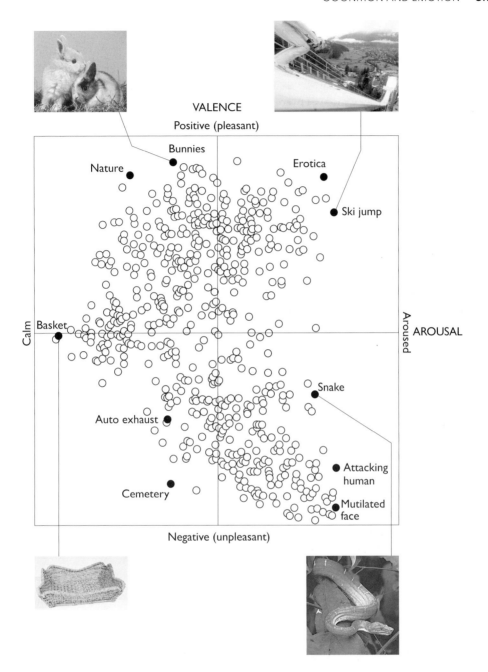

Figure 14.4 The affect grid and example pictures (the ratings on the grid are for pictures similar to those shown)

Source: Dawson *et al.*, 1999, Figure 8.2, p.161

this emotion or emotional information). This approach circumvents some of the problems associated with basic emotions. It has the advantage of suggesting how the different emotions relate to one another and makes it easy to understand how different languages could have developed different words to describe subtly different mixes of emotion experience. However, some emotions appear to combine attributes that the dimensional model assumes should be at opposite ends of a single continuum. For instance, nostalgia seems to combine attributes of positive valence (the positive value of past experiences) with negative valence (sadness or regret at their passing); and the excitement of extreme sports or roller-coaster rides combines pleasure (positive valence) with fear (negative valence) to create the characteristic exhilaration and excitement. Furthermore, it is still necessary to determine the dimensions, and how many should be used, and to decide how these relate (if at all) to the evidence suggesting the existence of basic emotions.

ACTIVITY 14.3

You might like to consider how you would map the different discrete emotions onto the affect grid. Where would you place sadness, contentment, fear and excitement, for example?

COMMENT

You have probably opted for bottom left, top left, bottom right and top right for sadness, contentment, fear and excitement respectively. Sadness, for example, could be considered as fairly unpleasant with little excitement or energy. But notice too that the grid allows for a lot more variation between items. You may also notice that the distribution has a 'C' shape to it. It appears that there are plenty of things that we consider to be neutral (neither pleasant nor unpleasant) and not particularly arousing, but very few arousing neutral items! Putting it another way, if something is arousing we tend to find it either really good or really bad (or as already noted, maybe both together).

Summary of Section 2

- Some psychologists classify different emotions by identifying discrete or basic emotions.
- The Big Five basic emotions are widely recognized by many psychologists and there is reasonable evidence to support this classification.
- The use of similar verbal labels, and production and recognition of emotional expressions across different cultures, further supports the notion of basic emotions.
- An alternative approach is to use a small number of continuously varying dimensions to describe the range of emotional experience.

3   The function of emotions

Emotions and emotional responses to events could surely not have evolved unless they served a useful purpose, but what purpose or purposes might these be?

ACTIVITY 14.4

Can you think of any aspect of emotions already touched upon in this chapter that might bestow a useful advantage on animals (including humans)?

COMMENT

Think (or look) back to Section 1.1.2 on physiological responses to emotion. You will recall that, in response to a frightening event, rapid physiological changes take place that prepare the body for 'fight or flight'. Undoubtedly the rapid mobilization of the body's resources in this way provides a potentially life-saving advantage.

3.1   Emotions alter goals

One influential modern theory of the function of emotions is that of Oatley and Johnson-Laird (1987). They have proposed an evolutionary account of emotions that suggests the role of emotion is to signal that ongoing behaviour should be interrupted to take account of a conflicting goal. They argue that humans have many different motivations and goals. Events will happen that require setting or resetting of priorities amongst these goals, such as giving up the goal of planting next summer's food crop in favour of running away from an attacking lion. For example, sadness caused by bereavement is not maladaptive, but in their framework is seen as having the function of initiating readjustment of life goals that included the lost one. When the relationship was close, this period of reassessing or reforming goals could be lengthy.

Table 14.2   Summary of emotions and their associated goals according to Oatley and Johnson-Laird

Emotion	Juncture of current plan	Behaviour/response
Happiness	Subgoals being achieved	Continue with plan, modifying as necessary
Sadness	Failure of major plan or loss of active goal	Do nothing/search for new plan
Anxiety	Self-preservation goal threatened	Stop, attend vigilantly to environment and/or escape
Anger	Active plan frustrated	Try harder, and/or aggress
Disgust	Gustatory goal frustrated	Reject substance and/or withdraw

Source: Oatley and Jenkins, 1996, Table 9.1, p.256

Central to Oatley and Johnson-Laird's theory is the notion of cognitive readjustment to emotional events. However, the exact mechanisms are not spelled out. Unlike the physiological changes that we discuss next, the mechanism behind changes in cognitive processing in response to emotions is much less well understood. Later in the chapter (Sections 4.2 and 4.3) we touch on some aspects of attentional deployment and memory in emotion, but there is still a considerable shortfall in our understanding of how internal emotional status influences cognition and how processing of emotional information is prioritized and influences cognitive function.

3.2 Emotions mobilize physiological resources

It is relatively easy to see how the physiological changes involved in emotions are part and parcel of the need to readjust goals, sometimes with great rapidity. It is vital that if your life is threatened, then your body is ready to respond in the best possible way to ensure your survival. In Section 1.1.2 we described some of the bodily responses associated with emotions such as fear and gave an example of how these assist in ensuring survival. The physiological reactions described there stand us in good stead when physical action is required. Often in modern life, however, an emotional threat requires not increased physical exertion but less. One example is the threat of a pending examination, which requires long hours sitting still at a desk to revise rather than any physical exertion of the body. Similarly, most of us have experienced the fear of a near accident while driving, but all our bodies actually need to do to avoid the danger is perform minimal, albeit rapid, movements of the hands on the steering wheel and the feet on the brakes.

Does this mean that many emotional reactions, especially fear responses, no longer have useful functions? No. There are still many occasions when rapid physical responses avert death or injury. Even before an exam, when you won't be fighting or fleeing (even if you feel you'd like to), the increased adrenalin and physiological arousal will provide an energizing effect that can improve performance, if maintained at an optimal level. However, too much anxiety impairs performance as the anxiety itself interferes with cognitive function and the physiological reaction makes it hard to relax and sit still. At the other end of the spectrum, not enough arousal – in other words boredom or disinterest – also impairs performance.

This finding, expressed formally by Yerkes and Dodson (1908), is known as the **Yerkes–Dodson law**, and is shown in Figure 14.5. Notice too that, for an easier task, higher levels of arousal are needed to attain the optimal level of performance compared with a hard task. The Yerkes–Dodson law seems reasonable and suggests that appropriate levels of emotion can indeed be useful – both too much and too little emotional arousal can put an organism at a disadvantage.

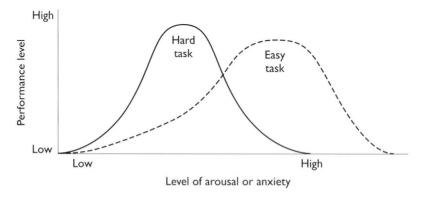

Figure 14.5 Yerkes–Dodson law

Source: Eysenck and Keane, 1996, Figure 18.8, p.454

3.3   Emotional expressions as communication

What function might emotional expressions fulfil and can we see evidence of them in other animals? Charles Darwin formalized the evolutionary view of the emotions in one of his later works entitled *The Expression of the Emotions in Man and Animals* (1998, first published in 1872). As well as acknowledging the more obvious evolutionary advantage of physiological changes during emotions (such as preparation for fight or flight), he highlighted how expressions of emotion serve to communicate the emotional status of an animal to others of their species (so-called conspecifics). However, it has to be said that he felt that emotions and emotion expressions in humans were no longer functional, but merely a relic from our evolutionary past – much as our appendix is seen to be superfluous to digestion. He drew parallels between the expressions of animals and their functions, such as the snarl of a dog communicating a readiness to bite, and the sneer of a human, which presumably has the same origin but no longer sends the same message (normally!).

Figure 14.6   Darwin's comparison between the sneer of a woman and the snarl of a dog

Source: Darwin, 1998, Figures 14 and 22, pp.117 and 246

Darwin might have been partially correct in his feeling that emotion expressions no longer have the function in humans that they do for other animals. We have already considered that display rules for expressions differ from culture to culture. For this difference to occur, then of course we need to control the expression displayed (at least to some extent). This means also that humans are capable of deceiving with their expressions – we can lie about our emotional feelings. Thus, emotional expressions serve multiple functions for humans: they can be honest signals of emotional status, as in other animals, or they can be part of the impression management, polite interaction or social manipulation of the sender.

3.4   Emotions as information

To illustrate the idea of emotions as information let us return to the Capgras delusion first mentioned in Chapter 4 (Section 6, Box 4.2). To remind you of the delusion (or syndrome) we will illustrate it with the case of an individual whom we will call Alan. Alan was in a car accident with his wife. He sustained an injury to his head, and his wife, Christine, was also injured, taken to hospital but later recovered. Alan refused to believe that Christine was still alive. He recognized her face but remained convinced that this was not really her, but a sinister impostor. Remember that in this rare syndrome the sufferer believes that a family member, or someone close, has been replaced by aliens or impostors. In such cases it is believed that although facial recognition is intact, a parallel system for registering the emotional meaning of the face has been damaged. Indeed, when Alan's palms were tested for SC changes (skin conductance – see Box 14.1) when viewing pictures of Christine's face, these responses were absent. SC changes, signalling an emotional response, would normally occur for any of us if viewing either emotional expressions or the face of someone we know. Without them there is no emotional resonance, no sense of affiliation. It would appear that Alan's brain interpreted this lack of physiological feedback as evidence that this was not someone close. However, since the perceptual qualities of the face matched those of his wife, it must be someone who looked just like Christine, an impostor, a frightening and distressing situation for all.

The idea that emotions provide information to guide decision making is fundamental to the theories of Damasio (1996). His views are best explained by describing the task most associated with him, the so-called **gambling task**. You are given four decks of playing cards and asked to select from one and turn the card over. For reasons that are not explained, you are either rewarded or fined as a result of your selection. Your task is to attempt to maximize your winnings. After playing for a while you are likely to find yourself making more selections from two out of the four decks, but you probably won't be able to say exactly why. This task is arranged so that two decks (the 'good decks') give less spectacular wins but also less punishing losses. Choosing from these two over a period of time achieves a modest gain. The other two 'bad decks' sometimes deliver large wins, but also large losses resulting in an overall loss on average. The rule is not hard and fast and so is not generally very obvious as you play. Playing the 'good decks' is the best strategy; you win a little and lose a little, but overall your winnings start to add up. Damasio has developed a theory to explain how people come to operate this strategy successfully, and make other similar decisions in life, when they are acting on hunches rather than full understanding.

According to Damasio, the emotional responses to winning and losing produce physiological changes that he calls **somatic markers**. Over time, through a process of conditioning, the decks come to evoke different physiological responses in the player, essentially representing the accumulated positive emotions of wins together with negative emotions of losses. After extended experience, as the player considers making a selection from each deck the physiological response conditioned to this deck will be initiated and this acts as a marker capable of guiding choice. Damasio suggests that somatic markers represent the 'gut feelings' that we often use to guide our decisions even though we may never become consciously aware of why we have a gut feeling about a particular choice. The function of emotion, for Damasio, is therefore centred around information and future actions.

3.5   What is the function of emotional feelings?

Although we have only touched on the topic, it is relatively easy to propose evolutionary advantages conferred by emotional behaviours and physiological responses to emotions. The same is not true of the function of emotional feelings. Take fear, the example we have used the most. The physiological response to a fearful situation can provide the physical resources to escape danger or stand and fight. Our behaviour, including expressions, functions to communicate our fear to others. But why do we need to experience the unpleasant *feeling* of fear, or anticipated fear (anxiety) when we expect a frightening experience?

Feelings are part of our conscious experience. The functions of consciousness, as you will consider in Chapter 15, are by no means uncontroversial, but one facet that is fairly regularly acknowledged is the notion that consciousness is necessary for performing new tasks or trying to override habits without relying simply on mechanisms of conditioning. This would also apply to learning new responses to an emotional situation such as when soldiers continue to advance into battle despite a strong urge to flee, or in overriding habits such as when suppressing the tendency to respond in anger at a socially inappropriate moment. However, whilst these examples invoke the need for consciousness, they still do not explain the necessity to *feel* the emotions of fear or anger. As the psychology of emotion continues to develop, future theories and research are likely to give us greater insight into the possible function of the feelings associated with emotion.

Summary of Section 3

- Following Darwin, many psychologists believe that emotions have evolutionary functions, including the mobilization of physiological resources, which remain today.
- Oatley and Johnson-Laird maintain that the purpose of emotions is to interrupt current behaviour in order to change priorities and goals in the light of new information.
- Damasio has formulated a somatic marker account of the function of emotions, in which their primary purpose is to provide information, via bodily feedback, which guides future decision making.
- The functions of 'feeling' emotion are still speculative.

4   Emotion influences cognition

4.1   Some important concepts

Before we start to discuss how cognition and emotion interact with each other, there are some important distinctions that you need to become familiar with. The first of these is the distinction between trait and state emotion.

4.1.1 State and trait emotion

State emotion (also called mood or affect) refers to how you feel right now. As you will be aware, this can change from minute to minute, day to day. State emotion is a very transient and variable entity. It is a construct that allows us to acknowledge the fact that momentary feelings may be quite different from the way an individual usually feels. Although state emotions are usually measured by self-report (asking participants to introspect and describe how they feel), they also relate directly to the behaviours and physiology discussed above and can be measured in the same way.

In contrast, **trait emotion** refers to more stable personality characteristics or 'what kind of person' you are. For example, some individuals may be prone to angry outbursts, or have a tendency to worry about things, or be optimistic, always looking on the bright side. Psychologists have directed much effort into trying to capture theoretically these ideas about stable personality characteristics. Thus, traits are theoretical constructs relating to aspects that are more enduring and characteristic of a person, and describe how one person may differ from others. Some common traits that have been proposed and are frequently measured (again by self-report) include: anxiety; depression; social desirability (how much you adapt your behaviour in order to gain the approval of others); anger; impulsivity; and emotional sensitivity.

A trait tends to make a person more prone to experiencing the associated mood state. For example, a high trait anxious individual will tend to feel more anxious for more of the time than a low trait anxious person. This is why certain traits, like anxiety or depression (sadness), are useful to psychologists interested in emotions – they are a more permanent indicator of who tends to have more or less of the relevant state emotion.

4.1.2 Processing vs manifestation of emotion

Another important distinction is between the *manifestation of emotion* itself and *the processing of emotional material*. The manifestation of emotion is exactly what we were discussing in Section 1. Thus, by 'manifestation' we mean both the experience of emotion, the feeling state, and the expression of that experience through bodily changes and behaviours. This is also often known as the 'hot' component to emotion. In contrast the 'cold' component is the processing of emotional material but without emotion being actually experienced. This isn't always an easy distinction to make. It is a bit like the difference between describing an emotional event in a detached way (relating a series of facts) compared with describing it in emotional terms. Obviously the two types of process regularly co-occur – the memory of the facts of an event often brings back the feelings as well – and in this case the manifestation/processing distinction may seem blurred. However, in psychology we often use stimuli such as words or pictures as a way of studying how we process emotional material although these stimuli rarely elicit a strong experience of emotion in participants. It is important to grasp then that studying cognitive processing in emotion can be quite distinct from studying the manifestation of emotion.

You may already have realized that the processing of emotional material is our first example of an interaction between cognition and emotion. In a typical experiment one might present participants with lists of negative emotional words (e.g. cancer, attack, evil) mixed with neutral words (e.g. number, unusual, round) and ask for later recall in a surprise memory test. The emotional aspect in the task is the valence (pleasantness/unpleasantness) of the words, which is the independent variable. The cognitive measure (dependent variable) is how many words of each type are recalled in the memory recall test. You might be interested to know that while most people will remember more positive than negative words (a very common 'positive bias' in emotion processing), individuals with clinical depression tend to remember more of the negative words. Box 14.3 in Section 4.2.1 discusses this further.

As we mentioned above, things can become more complicated when hot and cold emotions occur simultaneously. In the psychology of cognition and emotion we are interested not just in how people process emotional material, but also in how this processing is affected by emotional states and traits. For example, does the processing of sad words change when someone is actually feeling sad at the time? Similarly we might want to know whether people who are vulnerable to anxiety (i.e. high on trait anxiety) process threatening words any differently from those who are not. These more complex questions are what cognition and emotion psychologists are mostly concerned with. Section 4.2 delves deeper into these issues.

4.2 Memory

We start our examination of the interactions between cognition and emotion by considering the ways in which emotional states affect memory for emotional material.

4.2.1 Mood congruent memory

What happens to memory processes when the content of material being encoded matches the mood state of the participant doing that encoding? For example, if you are feeling sad and then happen to watch a sad film, how does this influence your later memory for the film? This scenario could produce an example of **mood congruent memory (MCM)**. Bower and colleagues' classic experiments sparked a great deal of interest in this phenomenon. In a typical example, participants are put in either a happy or sad mood by hypnosis and then read both a happy and a sad story (you may like to consider the ethical implications of doing such a study). Participants are then given a surprise recall test to see how much of each story they recalled. The results are shown in Figure 14.7 overleaf.

As you can see, more was recalled from the story which matched the mood of the participant as they were reading; for example, sad participants recalled more things about the sad story than about the happy one. The phenomenon of mood congruent memory has proved very robust. Also it has sparked a whole field of research into the effects of emotional disorders on cognitive processing, such as the relationship between clinical depression and memory processes.

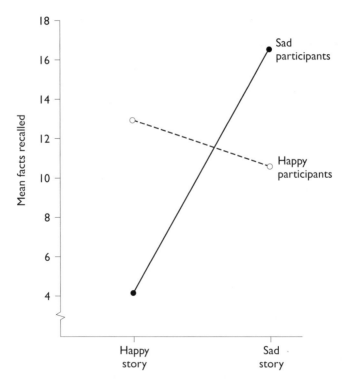

Figure 14.7   Results from Bower's (1981) mood congruent memory experiment

Source: Eysenck and Keane, 1996, Figure 18.4, p.446

ACTIVITY 14.5

You might like to think about what you would predict if you tested a clinically depressed person on memory for negative and neutral information, bearing in mind that one of the hallmarks of clinical depression is chronic low, or sad, mood. After you have considered this, look at Box 14.3.

Interestingly, work on mood congruency has alerted us to the finding that even 'normal' individuals, in no particular mood, seem to have a positive and potentially adaptive bias towards memory for positive information. Some suggest that this helps us to keep a positive outlook on life, in the face of all the problems it throws at us. It is as if we are 'looking at the world through rose-coloured glasses'!

4.2.2   Mood dependent memory

Mood dependent memory (MDM), or mood state dependent recall, is a well-known, but controversial phenomenon. It can be seen as a specific case of the influence of context on memory that was described in Chapter 6. The idea is that your memory for a particular stimulus or event will be better if there is a match between your mood at the time you experienced it and your mood when you try to recall it. For example, imagine you have a heated argument with a friend. Mood dependent memory would suggest that you will remember more of what was actually said if you are in an angry state again than if you are not.

14.3

Clinical depression and memory bias

Typically, individuals with clinical depression and those who are not diagnosed but still report feeling constantly low in mood (subclinical depression) all show mood congruent memory (MCM) effects, sometimes called a 'bias', for negative material. Many different types of experiment have been used to verify this finding, using positive and negative word lists, self-descriptive adjectives, sentences and whole scripts (Matt et al., 1992 offer a meta-analysis). The effect appears to be stronger when participants are aware of the relationship between their mood and the material; and, not surprisingly, when the negative nature of the material is stronger (e.g. 'evil' vs 'bad'). The bias also includes recall of autobiographical memories (see Chapter 7). Although this method might seem inconclusive (maybe depressed people really have had more negative experiences anyway), experiments using mood induction really do suggest that mood affects the valence of the personal memories that are brought to mind.

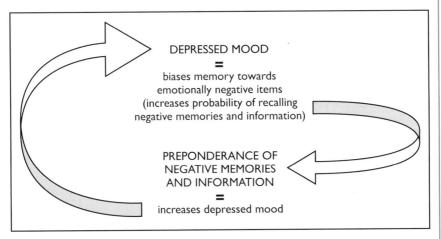

Figure 14.8 It is thought that the mood congruent memory effect contributes to a vicious cycle in which depressed mood enhances the accessibility of negative memories. In turn, having more negative memories in mind is likely to exacerbate depressed mood

Source: based on Teasdale, 1988

These findings are of more than just theoretical interest. It has been suggested that MCM may contribute to keeping someone in a depressed mood and that if we change this cognitive processing bias, then that might help the mood to lift. Teasdale (1988) has developed this idea, as shown in Figure 14.8. The suggestion is that patients' bias towards recalling more negative mood congruent information means that their world will seem more full of negative things than is really the case. This in turn will make them feel even more depressed. You can see that a vicious circle could be set up, where the memory bias contributes to the mood, which enhances the memory bias and so on. Teasdale and others have spent a lifetime of research trying to devise methods of breaking this cycle and coming up with new cognitive treatments for depression, such as a procedure called mindfulness-based cognitive therapy (Segal et al., 2002).

In the laboratory this hypothesis has been tested using the following type of experiment. Participants are put into particular moods (mood induction) by one of several techniques such as hypnosis, listening to appropriate music or reading appropriate passages of text. Then they are asked to learn a list of arbitrary, neutral words while in the induced mood. Participants are later put back into either the same or a different mood and asked to free-recall the words ('remember as many as you can'; no cues or prompts are given). If this second induced mood matches the one they were in when they learned the first list, then recall should be higher.

A classic experiment of this type is that by Bower (1981) who used happy and sad mood induction by hypnosis. Figure 14.9 shows some typical results from their experiment. In this design participants learned two lists of words, list A and list B, one after the other, but only recall for the first list, list A, was tested. As usual, participants were put into either a happy or sad mood before learning took place, one mood for each list. Thus those who learned list A in happy mood then learned list B in sad mood, and vice versa. Then, after both lists had been learned, they were tested on their recall for just the first list. The mood of participants during the test (using a third mood induction) either matched or contrasted with the mood at the time of learning list A. So for some participants mood at recall matched mood at learning (points 1 and 2 in Figure 14.9), whereas for others mood at recall was different from mood at learning (points 3 and 4 in Figure 14.9). You should be able to see from the figure that when learning and test moods were the same, participants were indeed better at remembering list A, compared with participants who tried to recall the same list in a different mood from the one they had learned it.

Perhaps you are wondering what was the point of the second list B? The reason for using two lists was simply that learning list B in a contrasting mood acted as an interference task, which made the experiment more sensitive to the beneficial or detrimental effects of the mood manipulations.

Bower (1981) went on to propose an influential **semantic network** theory to explain these mood and memory effects. The theory is shown in Figure 14.10. Bower suggested that emotions could be represented as nodes in a network, having numerous connections to related semantic items (words, concepts, etc.), other emotion nodes and outputs such as behaviour and autonomic responses. Material such as memories and knowledge is stored in the network and may be connected to some emotion nodes. Nodes become activated by external or internal stimuli and when this happens that activation selectively spreads across the network via the links to other units, a bit like ripples across a pond. Notice that some connections are inhibitory, so that activation of the sadness node, for example, would suppress any activation in the opposite happiness node. When nodes are activated above a certain threshold, then the content of those nodes enters conscious awareness leading to the corresponding feelings and thoughts.

You can perhaps start to see how this theory fits with the results of mood dependent memory experiments. When participants learn a word list in one mood, links are created between the relevant emotion node and the memory representations of those words. Thus when participants try to recall the same words this can be made easier if they are in the same mood thanks to the spreading activation from the

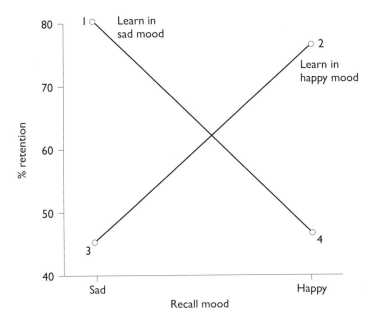

Figure 14.9   Percentage retention of words according to the match between learning mood (happy or sad) and recall mood

Source: based on Bower, 1981, Figure 2, p.132

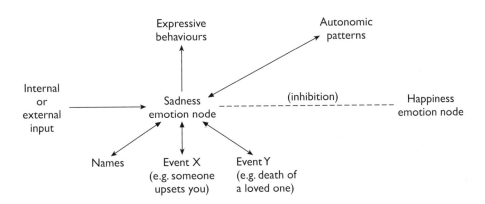

Figure 14.10   An example semantic network theory of emotion

Source: Power and Dalgleish, 1997, Figure 3.2, p.71

associated emotion node. Conversely, in a different mood there will be no advantage from such activation, and indeed it is assumed that inhibition of the word representations from the incongruent emotion node might result.

Since Bower's original experiment there have been many attempts to replicate his finding, but these have met with varied success. It seems that mood dependent memory is not a very robust effect. It is much influenced by factors such as the strength of the mood state that is induced, and the nature of the items to be recalled (e.g. recall using real-life autobiographical events produces better results). However, in a recent review of the work on mood dependent memory Eich and Metcalfe (1989) concluded that the phenomenon itself was genuine, and that the problems lay with the methods used to detect and measure it. There is no doubt that Bower's findings and theory have been remarkably fruitful in their influence on the thinking and direction of emotion research.

Before we move on, it is worth stopping to think what the key difference is between mood dependent memory experiments and those we discussed in Section 4.2.1 under the heading 'Mood congruent memory'. Here we have been concerned merely with the effect of mood on recall, irrespective of what it was that was actually being remembered. With mood congruent effects however there is always a match – or congruity – between the emotional material being recalled and the mood of the individual when encoding that material. Congruity means a match between mood at encoding and material being encoded; dependency refers to a match between mood at encoding and mood at retrieval.

ACTIVITY 14.6

Can you think of examples where congruent or incongruent stimuli (rather than mood states) might influence cognition?

COMMENT

It has regularly been shown that an individual's performance is influenced by whether or not two separate aspects of a situation are matched. For example, in tasks demonstrating the Flanker effect (see Chapter 2, Section 3.3) you may remember that performance depends on how closely matched the targets and the distractors are. The Stroop effect, discussed in Section 4.3 below, is another such example.

4.3   Attention

In the same way that memory for emotional material can be biased in a direction consistent with one's mood, so can attention. A classic example of this is the 'emotional Stroop'.

In the standard Stroop task (Stroop, 1935) (see Chapter 2, Section 3.3, Box 2.2), participants are asked to name out loud, as fast as they can, the colour of the ink in which colour words are written. When the ink colour is different from the meaning of the word itself (e.g. 'blue' written in red ink) participants are slowed down compared with stimuli where the word meaning and ink colour are matched. The effect arises because of the different amounts of interference between congruent ink colour and word meaning compared with a competing or incongruent ink colour and word meaning. The emotional Stroop differs in that, instead of colour words, emotional and neutral words are used, still printed in different colours. Examples of both types of Stroop task are shown in colour Plate 8.

When the emotional Stroop is given, for example, to high trait anxious individuals, then the interference from the anxiety-relevant words is usually greater than that from the neutral words, compared with the same difference when observed in non-anxious individuals. As performance on the Stroop task is generally taken to be a measure of attention towards the word meanings (although the precise mechanisms behind the effect are still not fully understood), then this is an example of an *anxiety-related attentional bias*.

In an attempt to demonstrate more clearly the nature of this attentional bias, MacLeod *et al.* (1986) published a now classic paper using an innovative new method of testing attention allocation. Their design, now known as the **dot probe** or 'attentional probe' task, is shown in Figure 14.11.

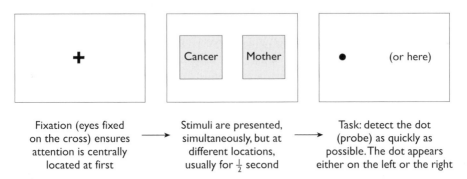

Fixation (eyes fixed → Stimuli are presented, → Task: detect the dot
on the cross) ensures   simultaneously, but at   (probe) as quickly as
attention is centrally   different locations,   possible. The dot appears
located at first   usually for $\frac{1}{2}$ second   either on the left or the right

Figure 14.11   The dot probe task

The task is to respond as rapidly as possible to the presentation of a dot (termed a 'probe' because it is probing where attention is located). This is, therefore, a reaction time (RT) task. On some trials (catch trials) there is no dot, to make sure participants are really looking for it and not just responding as soon as the words disappear. As you can see, before the dot a pair of word stimuli are displayed, one threatening and one neutral. If a participant is consistently faster to find the dot whenever it appears where the threatening item was, then we can reasonably assume that they must have been attending to that item rather than to the neutral item. The original results of MacLeod *et al.* (1986) are shown in Figure 14.12 overleaf.

The figure shows that control (not anxious) participants were just slightly faster when probes appeared in the neutral rather than the threat areas of the display (another example of the normal 'positive bias'). Anxious patients were the other way round – faster for probes appearing where threat words had been than for probes appearing where neutral words had been. This strongly suggested that anxious individuals allocate their attention to threat words rather than to neutral words, whereas controls do not. Thus, consistent with the emotional Stroop results, MacLeod *et al.* found an attentional bias for threat in their anxious patients. These results sparked over a decade of continuing research into this so-called attentional bias for threat. We now know that the bias is seen with many different types of material including words, pictures and faces, but is most prominent when the material matches the current concerns of the individual. For example, snake phobics will show a stronger attentional bias towards pictures of snakes than towards pictures of snarling dogs. This type of bias, with suitable materials, has been shown with patients suffering a variety of anxiety disorders, such as those with phobias, generalized anxiety and post-traumatic stress disorder. It is also apparent, although

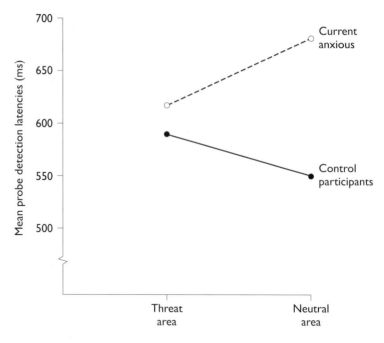

Figure 14.12   Results from MacLeod *et al.* (1986)

Source: Eysenck and Keane, 1996, Figure 18.6, p.450

less reliably so, in non-clinical individuals who have high state anxiety or high trait anxiety, or both.

Look again at Figure 14.8 in Box 14.3, where it is suggested that depression could be exacerbated by a vicious cycle of mood congruent memories contributing to sad mood. Could a similar mechanism be involved in attentional processing? Mathews (1990) proposed that just such a vicious cycle could operate to maintain anxious mood and attention to threat. Imagine that your anxiety makes you pick out and pay more attention to potential threats in the environment. This bias may well make it seem as if your surroundings are full of threats and this would, unsurprisingly, make you feel more anxious, which would perpetuate your attentional bias and so on. You would end up in a hyper-vigilant state, anxious about, and on the look out for, threats of relevance to you. This idea that anxious people are constantly in a vigilant, checking mode is popular in current theorizing about clinical anxiety.

How could you test out whether an attentional bias might cause anxiety or be caused by anxiety (or both), and can anything be done to reverse its effects? Mathews and MacLeod (2002) set themselves such a task by devising methods of directly inducing a positive or negative bias in non-anxious volunteers using specialized training procedures, and then assessing its effects on anxiety levels. Possessing an induced positive bias reduced, whilst a negative bias increased, anxiety levels when exposed to a moderately stressful situation just after training. These results certainly confirm that the attentional bias has a causal effect on anxiety levels, and interestingly that training procedures have been found that directly modify the bias, and can thereby reduce (or increase) anxiety.

Another similarity between attentional bias and the memory biases we discussed in Section 4.2 above is the performance of 'normal', non-anxious controls. As before, it seems that most of us have an adaptive or protective bias in the opposite direction to that of emotionally disordered patients. Look at Figure 14.12 again. Controls are faster in neutral areas than in threat areas, and this has also been found in several subsequent studies. It may be that this represents active avoidance of minor, insignificant threats, such as words and pictures. It would clearly be adaptive to avoid the many distractions of minor threats and single out only serious threats for particular attention.

ACTIVITY 14.7

Can you think of a situation where you paid attention to negative cues in your environment because of a fear that you have? If you haven't noticed this negative bias in yourself, have you ever noticed another, non-negative, attentional bias towards features in the environment?

COMMENT

Anyone who is very afraid of spiders might recognize this characteristic in themselves. Almost invariably they will notice any spider in the surroundings well before their non-phobic companions. Most people have a bias to attend to things that match their special interests. Temporary biases are also common, and can, for instance, occur when you have acquired something new such as when you purchase a new car. For a while you may find yourself noticing many examples of this same model which previously you ignored. This might give you a feel for what it could be like for an anxious individual, although for them it is unpleasant items that just constantly catch their attention without any intention on their part.

Although we have mostly mentioned anxious patients so far, biases favouring attention to threat can also be found in high trait anxious participants, although less reliably. Moreover, these biases tend to be stronger when high state anxious mood and high trait anxiety occur together. Anxious patients tend to have relatively high levels of state anxiety much of the time so it is unsurprising that attentional biases are more robust in this group.

4.4   Semantic interpretation

Semantic interpretation (see Chapter 8) is another cognitive process known to be influenced by emotion. If you see a word such as 'batter', do you think of pancakes or do you think of an assault on an innocent victim? It is surprising how many situations in life can be ambiguous and therefore open to biases of interpretation. In this section we shall consider interpretation of ambiguous linguistic information, but be aware that the same processes apply in many situations. Assessing the nature of the shadow in the path ahead on a dark night, or guessing the meaning of the probing look of the interviewer when you apply for a job, are just two other such examples.

The earliest work on interpretation and emotion used **homophones**. These are words like 'pane' and 'pain' or 'die' and 'dye' which sound the same but have different spellings associated with different meanings. Eysenck *et al.* (1987) asked both high and low trait anxious individuals to write down the homophones as they heard them. All the homophones had both a threatening/unpleasant and a non-threatening or neutral meaning. This simple technique revealed which interpretation had been made, by the spelling which participants chose. They found that the higher the participant's trait anxiety, the more threat spellings they produced. This indicated that trait anxiety was linked to a tendency to assume the negative interpretation of an ambiguous stimulus – i.e. an *interpretative bias*.

However, this method soon fell foul of criticism. For example, it is possible that participants were aware of and had access to both spellings, but just chose to write down the negative one. This matters because, if true it would mean that there was no bias in the actual *interpretation* of the words – both interpretations were made. Instead the bias would be at the stage of making the response, which then says little about the cognitive processing involved in making interpretations.

Later work used an alternative method to avoid this and other problems. For example, in their classic study Richards and French (1992) used **homographs** instead of homophones. These are words which have dual meanings, despite having the same spelling, such as 'batter', 'punch' and 'stalk'. They used these words in a priming experiment involving a lexical decision task (a task described in Chapter 2, Section 1.3). This task involves simply identifying, as rapidly as possible, whether the second of two sequentially presented items is a real word or a meaningless letter string (a non-word). From the participant's point of view the first item that appears is just to be ignored. However, this first word is actually a prime.

As described in Chapter 2, if the prime is related in meaning to the second word, the target (e.g. cat–dog, nurse–doctor), then lexical decisions are expected to be speeded compared to primes and targets which bear no semantic relation (e.g. cat–doctor, nurse–dog).

We can use this logic to infer how participants interpreted the homograph primes. For example, if lexical decisions for trials like batter–assault were faster than for trials like batter–pancake, this would imply that the participant interpreted batter as 'assault' rather than 'pancake'. The results of the Richards and French study, as well as other similar studies, suggest that high anxious participants show a negative bias in interpretation – that is, there is a greater priming effect for target words related to the negative meaning of the homograph than the neutral meaning. For non-anxious participants there is, once again, the familiar positive bias towards the more positive or non-threatening meaning. Further studies have extended this research by using ambiguous sentences or even passages of text, for example:

'The doctor examined little Emily's growth' (her height or her tumour?)

'The two men watched as the chest was opened' (a gruesome operation or an exciting find?)

'Your friend asks you to give a speech at her wedding reception. You prepare some remarks and when the time comes, get to your feet. As you speak, you notice some people in the audience start to laugh' (appreciatively, or rudely?)

The concept of protective processing styles such as these has been described formally in a theory know as **attribution theory**. A common observation is that we attribute good things internally, as something within our control, whereas bad things are attributed externally to others or to circumstances. This reflects a tendency to accept the credit for good outcomes and blame something or someone else for bad outcomes. For example, if you are late for an important meeting or fail your driving test you might say 'I'm terribly sorry but the train times have changed and I couldn't help being late' or 'I had such an unreasonable examiner' or 'My instructor gave me inadequate preparation'; if you are early or on time, or pass your test first time, you might well congratulate yourself for your efficient organization and planning, or excellent driving skills. You may have come across this described elsewhere as the **self-serving attribution bias**.

Although these self-serving biases might seem an irrational way of thinking, the evidence repeatedly supports their existence and, as with other positive biases, they may have protective properties. Moreover, in emotional disorders, particularly in depression or anxiety, we know that this self-serving bias can be lost or even reversed. Such people might think passing the driving test was just luck, or the examiner being lenient, whereas failing was yet more evidence of their own worthlessness and lack of skill. In some situations it can be shown that by lacking the positive bias the depressed person's attribution of their own performance can be more accurate than for non-depressed controls, so-called 'depressive realism'.

ACTIVITY 14.8

When you are next chatting with family or friends, or watching conversations on the television, see if you can identify some of the attributions people make. Does this go along with the attribution theory? Do you notice any examples of the self-serving attribution bias?

It should be noted that, although the various positive biases that we have described are thought to be quite normal, and have protective qualities (such as helping to maintain good mood and a positive self-image), it is equally true that, taken to their limits, they would be maladaptive.

Summary of Section 4

- State emotion refers to the feelings of the moment whereas traits refer to more enduring personality characteristics of an individual.
- The manifestation of emotion is distinct from the processing of emotional material. The former refers to feelings, behaviours and bodily responses. The latter refers to the emotional content of the external stimuli upon which the cognitive system acts.
- The field of cognition and emotion is primarily concerned with the conjunction between state or trait emotions and the processing of emotional material.
- Mood congruent memory (MCM) refers to enhanced memory for material that matches present mood. The phenomenon is particularly apparent in depression and may contribute to the clinical disorder.

- Mood dependent memory (MDM) occurs when recall is enhanced by a match between mood at the time of learning and mood at the time of testing. However, the effect is not very robust. Bower's semantic network theory provides one explanation of MDM and MCM.
- Biases in attention and in semantic interpretation are associated with both trait and state anxiety, and again may contribute to chronic anxiety and clinical anxiety disorders.

5   Does cognition influence emotion?

5.1   A look at some historical answers

Do we laugh *because* we feel happy or is it the laughing itself that *makes* us feel happy? This question has been central to emotion research since its very beginnings back in the 1880s when William James (1843–1910), commonly regarded to be one of the founders of psychology, first considered it. Putting the question another way, is it our experience of the behavioural and bodily responses associated with emotion that make us subjectively feel that emotion? Or do those responses follow on from our subjective experience of emotion?

5.1.1   James–Lange

James's answer to this question in the late nineteenth century was the counter-intuitive one. Namely, he argued that we feel fear *because* we run and we experience happiness as a *result* of laughing: the cognitive and experiential side of emotion was a slave to the physiology of emotion. Carl Lange took a very similar position, and so this view became known as the 'James–Lange' theory (see Figure 14.13(a)). Their observation was that behaviour, most especially in a frightening situation, was initiated too rapidly to have arisen from a *feeling* of fear that was subsequently translated into a conscious decision to act. Rather, they felt that behaviour preceded (conscious) cognition, and more precisely that the experience of emotion depended on the behaviour and bodily reaction that followed an event. More recent studies, such as those of LeDoux (1996) looking at the speed of the startle response to loud noise, indicate that these responses are initiated within a few milliseconds, well before conscious awareness has time to develop. One implication of this way of looking at things is that physiological responses and behaviours must be distinct and occur in unique constellations in order that different emotions actually occur and feel different. Love and fear feel different, according to James, because they result from different physiological signatures.

5.1.2   Cannon–Bard

Walter Cannon and Philip Bard challenged this view in the 1920s precisely because they felt that physiological responses were pretty indistinguishable across most emotions, and indeed that similar physiological patterns (e.g. increased heart rate, sweating and inhibited ingestion) could arise from fever during illness. According to

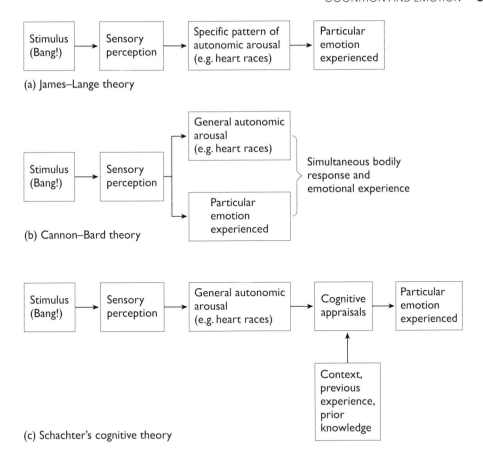

Figure 14.13   Comparing the theories

Source: based on Rosenzweig et al., 1999, Figure 15.1, p.412

them, what distinguishes one emotion from another, given this common physiology, is the pattern of cortical stimulation that arises. For Cannon and Bard, both the autonomic arousal and the subjective experience of a specific emotion could occur simultaneously and were instigated by the higher brain areas such as the cerebral cortex (see Figure 14.13(b)). Thus for Cannon–Bard you don't have to cry (or be suppressing the tendency to do so) to feel sad – there simply has to be an appropriate activation of the thalamus. For the James–Lange theory, preventing crying (and any urge to cry) would prevent sadness.

Both sets of theorists could provide evidence to support their view. The Cannon–Bard camp challenged the view that physiological responses were sufficiently unique to distinguish between the emotions (or indeed between emotion and other causes). They also reasoned that animals and humans with damaged spinal cords, preventing normal physiological responses, nevertheless responded emotionally. In support of the James–Lange theory, emotional response does seem to be blunted in those unfortunate enough to have suffered spinal injury preventing both physiological changes and overt behaviour in response to emotional situations, and this occurs in proportion to the loss of sensation. Emotional feeling is not, however, absent. There must, therefore, be more to emotional feeling than interpreting the sensation of body movement and physiological responses. The debate about the specificity of physiological responses to each emotion, however, still continues. Ekman and colleagues have concluded that there are emotion-specific physiologies for at least anger, fear, disgust and perhaps sadness (Ekman *et al.*, 1983; Levenson *et al.*, 2001). For example, Ekman claims that skin conductance (discussed in Box 14.1) is higher during sadness than the other emotions, and heart rate decelerates during disgust.

However, John Cacioppo, a renowned psychophysiologist, disagrees. Having reviewed all the available data he concluded (Cacioppo *et al.*, 2000) that the evidence for emotion-specific physiology is far more uncertain and suggests that discrete emotions cannot be differentiated by autonomic activity alone. However, he does agree that there may be a consistent distinction between the positive and negative emotions in general. He proposes that negative emotions are associated with greater motivational output than positive and therefore show generally greater levels of autonomic activation.

5.1.3 Schachter–Singer

When cognitive psychology began to take hold in the 1960s, Stanley Schachter and Jerome Singer proposed an alternative to both the earlier James–Lange and Cannon–Bard views. Like James they held that physiological mechanisms were crucial, but like Cannon they also believed that these responses were non-specific and could not distinguish the different emotions. Instead they thought differentiation was achieved by the individual's particular interpretations or attributions about why those bodily responses were occurring. These ambiguous messages from the body were interpreted by taking into account things like the situational context, previous experience of when certain emotions occur, expectations and intellectual knowledge of the world. Physiological arousal may be responsible for feeling emotion but cognitive interpretations, or **cognitive appraisals**, were what distinguished one emotion from another (see Figure 14.13(c)).

The Schachter–Singer theory predicts that it should be possible to change our experience of emotion by changing the cognitive appraisals we make, even if the physiological signs remain the same. To test this they performed a now famous experiment (Schachter and Singer, 1962). Participants were injected with epinephrine (adrenalin), which is a hormone that stimulates activity in the sympathetic nervous system (discussed in Section 1.1.2). Some participants were told that there would be no effect of this injection while others were told that it would make their heart race. The latter group did not report any emotional experience, while the former group did. What does this result say about the James–Lange theory of emotion? The fact that those expecting no effect of injection did actually experience emotion is consistent with James–Lange – the physiology directly led to an emotional experience. However, the other result is inconsistent with that theory. Those able to attribute the bodily sensations to the injection failed to experience emotion. The James–Lange theory makes no allowance for such cognitions to influence emotional experience in this way. It would predict that, despite this knowledge, the physiological arousal should directly give rise to an emotional experience.

In a further aspect of the above experiment, participants were put in a room with a 'stooge' who was party to the experiment and who acted either in an extremely happy or very angry manner. The behaviour of the stooge directly influenced the feelings of those participants who reported experiencing emotion (i.e. those with no foreknowledge of the effects of the injection). Those with the happy stooge reported experiencing happiness, whereas those with the angry stooge reported anger. This demonstrates a strong influence of context on the specific emotion experienced. How does this second finding fit with the James–Lange theory? It is clearly inconsistent with that theory because the same physiological reactions were being experienced differently according to context.

Schachter and Singer used the results of this experiment to support their theory. The non-specific physiological arousal interacted with the social and physical context that participants experienced to determine the precise emotion that was felt. They had succeeded in showing that identical physiological states could be subjectively experienced as different emotions according to how the individual appraised their circumstances. Similarly, subjective emotional experience could be eliminated by telling participants the true source of their bodily sensations. This convincingly showed that cognitive attributions were crucial in whether or not emotions were experienced in their fullest sense.

The Schachter–Singer theory has been criticized. For example, we now know, because we can measure them, that physiological responses associated with different emotions are not in fact identical (and their results have not always been replicated; e.g. Reisenzein, 1983). However, the lasting contribution of this theory was the notion of cognitive appraisal being critically involved in the generation of emotion. The acceptance of this possibility spawned a whole generation of appraisal theorists.

5.1.4 Appraisal theories today

The central idea of appraisal theories is that emotions are elicited and differentiated on the basis of the individual's subjective evaluation of the external situation or event combined with their own physiological state. Although this answers the question of how we differentiate between emotions, it simultaneously raises others. How are these appraisals made – using what yardstick, measuring tool or criteria?

Each different appraisal theory tends to suggest different dimensions that we use when making appraisals. For example, Klaus Scherer proposes specific fixed sets of criteria that we supposedly apply to any situation that comes our way. For example, one criterion is the intrinsic qualities of the event such as how novel or agreeable it is. Another is how significant the event is in terms of our own personal goals or needs. Clearly an event which is neutral in terms of our goals or needs is unlikely to generate emotion. To get an idea of how his criteria can distinguish one emotion from another, look at Table 14.3 overleaf.

Table 14.3 Scherer's appraisal criteria and profiles for different emotions

Stimulus evaluation checks	Anger/rage	Fear/panic	Sadness
Novelty			
• Suddenness	High	High	Low
• Familiarity	Low	Various	Low
• Predictability	Low	Low	Various
Intrinsic pleasantness	Various	Various	Various
Goal significance			
• Concern relevance	Order	Body	Various
• Outcome probability	Very high	High	Very high
• Expectation	Dissonant	Dissonant	Various
• Conduciveness	Obstruct	Obstruct	Obstruct
• Urgency	High	Very high	Low
Coping potential			
• Cause: agent	Other	Other/nature	Various
• Cause: motive	Intent	Various	Chance/neg
• Control	High	Various	Very low
• Power	High	Very low	Very low
• Adjustment	High	Low	Medium
Comparability with standards			
• External	Low	Various	Various
• Internal	Low	Various	Various

Note: 'Various' = different appraisal results are compatible with the respective emotion.

Source: Dalgleish and Power, 1999, Table 30.2, p.639

For example, in the table, items under the fear/panic category suggest that this emotion results from an event (stimulus) that is judged to be 'high' on novelty/ suddenness, 'low' on novelty/predictability; it is of concern to the body's status (goal significance/concern relevance); urgency is high, coping potential/power is very low, and so on. For a number of the appraisals involving fear/panic there can be various options; for instance, under novelty/familiarity it is possible to be afraid of something either familiar or unfamiliar so that this is not a defining feature for that emotion. To give a concrete example, imagine the consequence of a spider emerging from under the sofa for a spider phobic: this is a sudden event; but spiders are familiar (although disliked); they behave unpredictably; their intrinsic pleasantness is 'various', that is, some people find them pleasant (although a spider phobic certainly would not); the ability to cope is perceived as low, and so on. You may feel that it would be impossible to evaluate an event on all these various things *before* feeling the emotion, there surely would not be enough time? This is a fair criticism and one that has been made by opponents of appraisal theory. However, the counter-argument to this is that appraisals do not have to be conscious serial processes; they may well occur in parallel, automatically.

The evidence in support of appraisal theory relies entirely on subjective self-report and for this reason these theories have been heavily criticized. Typically, participants are either asked to remember personal events, or are exposed to experimental manipulations designed to induce an emotion. They are then asked to report, either verbally or using questionnaires, the types of appraisals they engaged in. You may have spotted another problem with this. By definition, participants will not be able to report on any appraisals made unconsciously, and this is a second major criticism of the evidence for appraisal theory. As yet, appraisal theorists have only been able to counter this by stating that no alternative to self-report exists. It will be interesting to see whether appraisal theorists will be able to find ways of accessing automatic evaluations (perhaps using brain-imaging technologies).

5.2   A clash of minds: the cognition/emotion debate

No discussion of cognition and emotion would be complete without considering one famous example of the different approaches psychologists can take. The two main protagonists in the debate were Richard Lazarus and Robert Zajonc (pronounced zy-unce, to rhyme with once).

5.2.1   Zajonc's view

Zajonc disagreed with appraisal theory's contention that emotions are produced by cognitive processes. He challenged the appraisal theorists directly (Zajonc, 1980) making two key assertions:

1   Appraisal is not necessary for emotion to be experienced. Emotions could arise directly without the need for cognitions at all. This is similar to the James–Lange idea in that cognition plays no part in the process of eliciting emotion.

2   The experience of emotion always precedes one's cognitive processing of that emotion. This stronger claim adds to the first by saying that not only is appraisal not necessary, in fact it never occurs before the emotional experience itself. This question of whether emotion precedes cognition, or the other way round, is known as the **primacy debate**.

The following quotation summarizes Zajonc's position very well: 'Affect [meaning mood or state emotion] and cognition are separate and partially independent systems and ... although they ordinarily function conjointly, affect could be generated without a prior cognitive process' (Zajonc, 1984, p.117).

How is this issue of primacy different from William James's question? Do we laugh because we're happy or are we happy because we laugh? James was concerned with the relationship between the conscious feeling of experiencing an emotion and the physiological and behavioural expression of that emotion (see Sections 1.1.1 and 1.1.2). The concept of cognitive appraisal had not yet been articulated. The primacy debate contrasts the cognitive appraisal of an emotion with all its other aspects (feeling, physiology and behaviour).

In support of his argument Zajonc described an experiment which used the famous **mere exposure** effect. Mere exposure refers to the finding that people tend to prefer items to which they have previously been exposed over comparable novel ones. Simple familiarity with something creates a preference for that item. This is presumably one reason for the success of the advertising industry. Zajonc took the mere exposure method and adapted it so that items were presented **subliminally** (below the level of conscious awareness) while participants were engaged in another, primary task. His results revealed that while participants showed no recognition of the subliminal items, they nevertheless gave them higher preference ratings than novel items!

Zajonc argued that these results showed that cognition was not necessary in order to have affective experience. He was assuming, first, that stimuli were not being processed 'cognitively' because they were presented subliminally. Second, he was assuming that preference ratings were tantamount to emotional experience. Both these assumptions have since been challenged. Today the details of non-conscious processing (outside awareness) are controversial, but few would challenge its existence (see Chapter 15). Certainly, it is unlikely that many psychologists now accept Zajonc's implicit assumption that all cognitive processing must be conscious. Likewise equating preference judgements with affect or emotion is probably a step too far. Surely only very limited emotion is involved in rating how much you like something that has no particular meaning or relevance to you?

5.2.2 Lazarus's view

Richard Lazarus, on the other hand, argued that cognitive appraisal was essential for the experience of emotion: 'Cognitive appraisal (of meaning or significance) underlies and is an integral feature of all emotional states' (Lazarus, 1982, p.1021).

In support of his position he undertook several studies. Typically, emotions would be elicited by showing participants anxiety-provoking films. For example, one was a Stone Age circumcision ritual (another showed someone involved in a gruesome industrial accident – it is unlikely that this type of material would obtain ethical approval for use today!). Cognitive appraisal was manipulated by playing one of two soundtracks while participants watched the films. A 'denial' soundtrack included statements indicating that one was a safety film, the people in the films were actors and the ritual in the film was not actually painful. An 'intellectualization' soundtrack emphasized an anthropological perspective and advocated, for example, considering the ritual as a strange native custom. A control condition had no soundtrack. Physiological measures such as GSR (galvanic skin response) and heart rate were taken throughout viewing and suggested that the appraisals produced by the soundtracks did indeed reduce emotional responses significantly compared with the control condition. Although impressive, these results did *not* prove that cognition necessarily precedes affect, but rather that cognitive appraisal *can* convincingly alter emotional response.

5.2.3 A resolution?

Despite the ferocity of their debate about primacy, neither protagonist marshalled sufficient evidence to win the argument. Rather a resolution was reached by both identifying their positions more clearly. Zajonc acknowledged the view that the existence of non-conscious appraisal was a key question, and Lazarus conceded that although appraisal might influence emotion this did not mean it was an essential component. Both agreed that, as Zajonc puts it: 'It is a critical question for cognitive theory and for theories of emotion to determine just what is the minimal information process that is required for emotion. Can untransformed pure sensory input directly generate emotional reactions?' (Zajonc, 1984).

Interestingly, more recent work by Joseph LeDoux (LeDoux, 1989; LeDoux, 1996) has thrown further light on the issue of primacy, suggesting that Zajonc may be right after all. These studies used **lesioned** animals in which specific neural pathways within the animals' brains were deliberately severed by the experimenter. Doing this allows an experimenter to deduce the function of the damaged pathways or regions by giving the animal various tasks to perform and establishing which of these are impaired. You may wish to think about the ethical issues such procedures raise, though we do not have room to consider them here.

Using a variety of tasks manipulating emotions, especially fear, LeDoux has shown that certain brain structures such as the thalamus and the amygdala play different roles in the generation of emotion (see colour Plate 9). Anatomical work has shown that these areas are connected via two routes, as you will see from Figure 14.14. The 'lower' route – so-called because only *evolutionarily old* structures are involved – takes sensory information from the primary sensory areas (the regions of the brain where sensory information arrives first) to the thalamus and then directly to the amygdala. This route bypasses the higher brain structures in the cortex and provides a fast thalamo-amygdala connection involving only one **synapse** (a relay junction between one nerve cell and the next). The 'higher' route – so-called because the *evolutionarily newer* areas such as the cortex are involved – relays information through a more complex route from the thalamus via the sensory cortex to the amygdala.

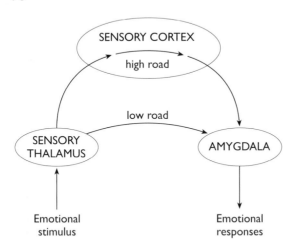

Figure 14.14   The low road and the high road to the amygdala

Source: LeDoux, 1996, Figure 6.13, p.164

LeDoux has shown that learning about new fearful situations or altering existing knowledge about fear requires the higher thalamo-cortical-amygdala route to be intact and functioning. However, once fear responses are well learned, lesions to this higher route do not diminish the response. In such cases the lower thalamo-amygdala route is sufficient. He suggests that the lower route is 'quick and dirty', providing a means of rapid identification of, and initiation of responses to, emotionally significant stimuli without the need for time-consuming higher processing. The higher route, on the other hand, is needed to learn new associations or relearn or extinguish old ones. It is vital in the initial stages of learning about novel fear stimuli, or in the modification of original learning experiences, but when this learning has become automated, the lower, more rapid route seems capable of taking over.

You can see then that this quick and dirty route could be a neuroanatomical substrate (physical basis) for Zajonc's idea of the direct elicitation of emotion without the need for cognition. Maybe the primacy of emotion over cognition was partially right after all. However, the role of the higher route also seems to map onto Lazarus's idea that cognitive processing can precede, or at least influence, emotion. LeDoux suggests that the higher cortical route is necessary to override the quick and dirty route in certain situations – perhaps where the threat turns out not to be so bad, once cognitively processed more fully, or where past knowledge and experience suggest that an emotional reaction would be inappropriate. As is often the case in these debates, both the positions of Lazarus and Zajonc may turn out to be partially correct.

Summary of Section 5

- A question that has always concerned psychologists is whether emotions arise before or after the cognitive processing of the stimuli and situation that elicits them. This is sometimes known as the primacy debate.
- Zajonc argued that emotions do not require prior cognition, whereas Lazarus maintained that cognitive appraisal was an integral part of the production of emotion.
- Recent neuroanatomical and lesion studies suggest that both may have been right after all. LeDoux argues for a 'quick and dirty' neural pathway enabling immediate response to potentially emotional stimuli, without the need for prior cognitive processing. He also proposes a slower cortical route enabling learning and modulation of emotional responses according to the outcome of cognitive appraisals.

6   General summary

In this chapter we began by noting that emotions comprise at least three components: feelings that can only be reported through introspection; behaviours that can be observed; and bodily responses, some of which can be precisely measured using psychophysiological techniques. We discussed two different approaches to classifying emotions: that of dividing emotional experience up into separate 'basic' emotions; and that of using two or more dimensions to describe a continuum of experience. We briefly explored what some of the functions of emotion might be, such as their use for survival, to enhance performance or as information signals to tell us how to behave (the somatic marker hypothesis).

For the rest of the chapter we considered the interaction between emotions and cognition, first by looking at how emotional material is processed differently from non-emotional material. In memory, attention and semantic interpretation we saw how biases in processing usually operate to favour the processing of emotionally significant information. This is a particularly important topic because psychologists believe such biases contribute to emotional disorders such as anxiety and depression. Second, we saw how cognitive appraisals can influence the experience of emotion, and several theoretical variations on this basic idea were described.

Emotion and its interaction with cognition is becoming an increasingly popular area of psychology, helped in part by the availability of new brain-imaging technologies. Armed with the knowledge you have gleaned from this chapter you will be in an excellent position to follow the progress of this exciting area of psychology.

Now that you have read this chapter you can reinforce and extend your learning by reading an original journal article associated with it, available online from the DD303 website. Remember, these are original journal articles, so the style is different from this textbook, and don't be too concerned if you can't follow every detail.

Further reading

Dalgleish, T. and Power, M.J. (1999) *Handbook of Cognition and Emotion*, Chichester, Wiley.

LeDoux, J.E. (1996) *The Emotional Brain*, New York, Simon and Schuster.

Williams, J.M.G., Watts, F.N., MacLeod, C. and Mathews, A. (1997) *Cognitive Psychology and Emotional Disorders* (2nd edn), Chichester, Wiley.

References

Bower, G.H. (1981) 'Mood and memory', *American Psychologist*, vol.36, pp.129–48.

Cacioppo, J.T., Bernston, G.G., Larsen, J.T., Poehlmann, K.M. and Ito, T.A. (2000) 'The psychophysiology of emotion', in Lewis, M. and Haviland-Jones, J.M. (eds) *Handbook of Emotions* (2nd edn), London, Guilford Press.

Calder, A.J., Lawrence, A.D. and Young, A.W. (2001) 'Neuropsychology of fear and loathing', *Nature Reviews Neuroscience*, vol.2, no.5, pp.352–63.

Calder, A.J., Keane, J., Manes, F., Antoun, N. and Young, A.W. (2000) 'Impaired recognition and experience of disgust following brain injury', *Nature Neuroscience*, vol.3, pp.1077–8.

Dalgleish, T. and Power, M.J. (1999) *Handbook of Cognition and Emotion*, Chichester, Wiley.

Damasio, A.R. (1996) 'The somatic marker hypothesis and the possible functions of the prefrontal cortex', *Philosophical Transactions of the Royal Society of London*, Series B, vol.351, pp.1413–20.

Darwin, C. (1998, first published 1872) *The Expression of the Emotions in Man and Animals* (3rd edn), London, Harper Collins.

Dawson, M.E., Schell, A.M. and Bohmelt, A.H. (eds) (1999) *Startle Modification*, Cambridge, Cambridge University Press.

Eibl Eibesfeldt, I. (1988) 'Social interactions in an ethological, cross-cultural perspective', in Poyatos, F. (ed.) *Cross Cultural Perspectives in Nonverbal Communication*, Kirkland, WA, Hogrefe & Huber Publishers.

Eich, E. and Metcalfe, J. (1989) 'Mood dependent memory for internal versus external events', *Journal of Experimental Psychology: Learning, Memory and Cognition*, vol.15, pp.443–55.

Ekman, P. (1973) 'Universal facial expressions in emotion', *Studia Psychologica*, vol.15, pp.140–7.

Ekman, P. (1999) 'Facial expressions', in Dalgleish, T. and Power, M.J. (eds) *Handbook of Cognition and Emotion*, New York, John Wiley & Sons Ltd.

Ekman, P. and Friesen, W.V. (2003) *Unmasking the Face: A Guide to Recognizing Emotions from Facial Clues*, Cambridge, MA, Malor Books.

Ekman, P. and Oster, H. (1979) 'Facial expressions of emotion', *Annual Review of Psychology*, vol.30, pp.527–54.

Ekman, P., Levenson, R.W. and Friesen, W. (1983) 'Autonomic nervous system activity distinguishes among emotions', *Science*, vol.221, pp.1208–10.

Ekman, P., Sorenson, E.R. and Friesen, W.V. (1969) 'Pan-cultural elements in facial displays of emotion', *Science*, vol.164, pp.86–8.

Eysenck, M. and Keane, M.T. (1996) *Cognitive Psychology: A Student's Handbook* (3rd edn), Hove, Psychology Press.

Eysenck, M.W., MacLeod, C. and Mathews, A.M. (1987) 'Cognitive functioning in anxiety', *Psychological Research*, vol.49, pp.189–95.

Frijda, N.H. (2001) 'The self and emotions', in Bosma, H.A. (ed.) *Identity and Emotion: Development through Self Organization, Studies in Emotion and Social Interaction*, New York, Cambridge University Press.

Frijda, N.H. and Tcherkassof, A. (1997) 'Facial expressions as modes of action readiness', in Russell, J.A. and Fernández Dols, J.M. (eds) *The Psychology of Facial Expression, Studies in Emotion and Social Interaction, Second Series*, New York, Cambridge University Press.

Lazarus, R.S. (1982) 'Thoughts on the relations between emotion and cognition', *American Psychologist*, vol.37, pp.1019–24.

LeDoux, J.E. (1989) 'Cognitive–emotional interactions in the brain', *Cognition and Emotion*, vol.3, pp.267–89.

LeDoux, J.E. (1996) *The Emotional Brain*, New York, Simon and Schuster.

Levenson, R.W., Cacioppo, J.T., Davidson, R.J., Lang, P., Ohman, A. and Stemmler, G. (2001) 'Psychophysiology of emotion: a decade and a half later', *Psychophysiology*, vol.38, Supplement S4.

MacLeod, C., Mathews, A. and Tata, P. (1986) 'Attentional bias in emotional disorders', *Journal of Abnormal Psychology*, vol.95, no.1, pp.15–20.

Mathews, A. (1990) 'Why worry? The cognitive function of anxiety', *Behaviour Research and Therapy*, vol.28, no.6, pp.455–68.

Mathews, A. and MacLeod, C. (2002) 'Induced processing biases have causal effects on anxiety', *Cognition and Emotion*, vol.16, no.2, pp.331–54.

Matt, G.E., Vacquez, C. and Campbell, W.K. (1992) 'Mood-congruent recall of affectively toned stimuli: a meta-analytic review', *Clinical Psychological Review*, vol.12, pp.227–55.

Medicus, G., Schleidt, M. and Eibl Eibesfeldt, I. (1994) 'Universelle Zeitkonstante bei Bewegungen taubblinder Kinder' ('Universal time constancy in movements of deaf-blind children'), *Nervenarzt*, vol.65, no.9, pp.598–601.

Oatley, K. and Jenkins, J.M. (1996) *Understanding Emotions*, Oxford, Blackwell Publishers Ltd.

Oatley, K. and Johnson-Laird, P.N. (1987) 'Towards a cognitive theory of emotions', *Cognition and Emotion*, vol.1, pp.29–50.

Ortony, A. and Turner, T.J. (1990) 'What's basic about basic emotions?', *Psychological Review*, vol.97, no.3, pp.315–31.

Panksepp, J. (1989) 'The neurobiology of emotions: of animal brains and human feelings', in Wagner, H. and Manstead, A. (eds) *Handbook of Social Psychophysiology*, *Wiley Handbooks of Psychophysiology*, Oxford, John Wiley and Sons.

Panksepp, J., Sacks, D.S., Crepeau, L.J. and Abbott, B.B. (1991) 'The psycho- and neurobiology of fear systems in the brain', in Denny, M.R. (ed.) *Fear, Avoidance, and Phobias: A Fundamental Analysis*, Hillsdale, NJ, Lawrence Erlbaum Associates Inc.

Plutchik, R. and Landau, H. (1973) 'Perceived dominance and emotional states in small groups', *Psychotherapy: Theory, Research and Practice*, vol.10, pp.341–2.

Power, M.J. and Dalgleish, T. (1997) *Cognition and Emotion: From Order to Disorder*, Hove, Psychology Press.

Reber, A.S. (1995) *The Penguin Dictionary of Psychology* (2nd edn), Harmondsworth, Penguin.

Reisenzein, R. (1983) 'The Schachter theory of emotions: two decades later', *Psychological Bulletin*, vol.94, pp.239–64.

Richards, A. and French, C.C. (1992) 'An anxiety-related bias in semantic activation when processing threat/neutral homographs', *Quarterly Journal of Experimental Psychology*, vol.45, pp.503–25.

Rosenzweig, M.R., Leiman, A.L. and Breedlove, S.M. (1999) *Biological Psychology: An Introduction to Behavioural, Cognitive and Clinical Neuroscience* (2nd edn), Sunderland, MA, Sinauer Associates Inc.

Schachter, S. and Singer, J. (1962) 'Cognitive, social and physiological determinants of emotional state', *Psychological Review*, vol.69, pp.379–99.

Scherer, K.R. and Wallbott, H.G. (1994a) 'Evidence for universality and cultural variation of differential emotion response patterning', *Journal of Personality and Social Psychology*, vol.66, no.2, pp.310–28.

Scherer, K.R. and Wallbott, H.G. (1994b) 'Evidence for universality and cultural variation of differential emotion response patterning: correction', *Journal of Personality and Social Psychology*, vol.67, no.1, p.55.

Segal, Z.V., Williams, J.M.G. and Teasdale, J.D. (2002) *Mindfulness-based Cognitive Therapy for Depression: A New Approach to Preventing Relapse*, New York, Guilford Press.

Stroop, J.R. (1935) 'Studies of interference in serial verbal reactions', *Journal of Experimental Psychology*, vol.18, pp.643–62.

Teasdale, J.D. (1988) 'Cognitive vulnerability to persistent depression', *Cognition and Emotion*, vol.2, no.3, pp.247–74.

Wallbott, H.G. and Scherer, K.R. (1988, first published 1986) 'How universal and specific is emotional experience? Evidence from 27 countries on five continents', in Scherer, K.R. (ed.) *Facets of Emotion: Recent Research*, Hillsdale, NJ, Lawrence Erlbaum Associates Inc. (First published in *Social Science Information* (*Sur les sciences sociales*), vol.25, no.4, pp.763–95.)

Yerkes, R.M. and Dodson, J.D. (1908) 'The relation of strength of stimulus to rapidity of habit-formation', *Journal of Comparative Neurology and Psychology*, vol.18, pp.459–82.

Zajonc, R.B. (1980) 'Feeling and thinking: preferences need no inferences', *American Psychologist*, vol.35, pp.151–75.

Zajonc, R.B. (1984) 'On the primacy of affect', *American Psychologist*, vol.39, pp.117–23.

Consciousness   **Chapter 15**

Jackie Andrade

1   Introduction

Consciousness is probably the most fascinating and challenging subject of psychological research. Although we know that much of human cognition occurs at a subconscious level, most of us feel, rightly or wrongly, that it is our conscious thoughts that form our personalities and inspire our actions. Over centuries, philosophers have provided vocabularies for discussing the human mind, frameworks for investigating consciousness and possible solutions to some of the problems of consciousness. Only more recently have psychologists begun to research consciousness in its own right. Much of this recent research concerns the biological aspects of consciousness. It uses neuroscience techniques such as recording the electrical activity of the brain to discover how brain activity differs when we are conscious, or conscious of something, from when we are unconscious or unconscious of something. However, progress is also being made with cognitive approaches to consciousness. Cognitive psychology is helping to define the functions of consciousness, investigating how conscious processes differ from unconscious processes and suggesting possible evolutionary functions of consciousness. Consciousness research is still a frontier area of psychology. The different explorers still lack agreement about how to explain consciousness, or even how to define the problem, but they are making exciting discoveries.

This chapter aims to explain briefly the historical and philosophical roots of consciousness research, and then to discuss the place of consciousness as a concept in contemporary cognitive psychology. It then considers empirical studies of aspects of consciousness and cognitive accounts of consciousness.

It is difficult to give a coherent account of this topic because, although many areas of cognitive psychology inform our understanding of consciousness, these areas are not well integrated and have not been pulled together into a grand theory of consciousness. Much recent cognitive psychology research in the field of consciousness studies has focused on unconscious cognition (the terms unconscious, non-conscious, and implicit cognition are used interchangeably in much of the literature). Baars (1988) recommends contrasting conscious and unconscious cognition and using the differences between them to infer the functions of consciousness. He calls this procedure 'contrastive analysis'. Many studies do not do this, however, but just focus on trying to demonstrate truly unconscious learning or memory. We shall look at some of these studies to see whether there is convincing evidence that we can remember or learn without being aware of doing so.

Many cognitive psychologists research high-level processes that are apparently dependent on consciousness – for example, visual attention, working memory, mental imagery. As an example of this research, we shall look in Section 2.2 at a relatively old study by Schneider and Shiffrin (1977) that helps show the conditions under which automatic and controlled processes operate. Automatic processes are relatively unconscious, in the sense that we have little awareness of their operation, whereas controlled processes are associated with conscious awareness of what is being processed. The concept of controlled processing appears in the notion of working memory (see Chapter 5), where the central executive controls the operation of the phonological loop and visuo-spatial sketchpad, and in models of action selection, where controlled processing enables us to behave in novel ways rather than acting through habit. We shall discuss working memory and a model of action selection in Section 4 of this chapter when we consider different ways of explaining consciousness.

Dissociations between conscious and unconscious processes might suggest that we have a specific module, or modules, for consciousness. We shall consider how cognitive neuropsychology, the study of the effects of brain injury, can shed light on the issue of where if anywhere consciousness occurs. The main thrust of the chapter though is to explore the functions of consciousness. We shall look briefly at how studies of altered states of consciousness can complement more conventional studies of cognition in suggesting hypotheses about the functions of consciousness. I will argue that although consciousness appears to be associated with particular cognitive processes, for example selective attention, all we really know is that these processes are correlated with conscious awareness of stimuli in the environment or in memory. They are the **cognitive correlates of consciousness**. Discovering these correlates of consciousness does not explain conscious experience – why it feels the way it does to see blue or remember a face or imagine a voice – but it does help us to understand the possible role of consciousness in cognition. This role seems to include integrating selected information from different processing modules and making that information available across the cognitive system so that it can guide our behaviour.

The term 'consciousness' means different things to different people, so we begin by trying to define what it is we want to study.

1.1   Defining consciousness

ACTIVITY 15.1

Before reading further, spend five minutes thinking about what it means to be conscious. Make a list of the special features of consciousness.

COMMENT

Consciousness can be thought of in different ways. There is the state of consciousness, in the sense of being awake and aware of ourselves in our environment, rather than being asleep and more or less oblivious to what is happening around us. Also under this heading come altered states of consciousness brought about by drugs or hypnosis. Then there is consciousness in the sense of awareness of particular sensations or mental events. Thus, while reading this sentence, you may be conscious of someone entering the room or the taste of your coffee, but unconscious of the hardness of your chair or the hum of distant traffic. This sense of consciousness has been termed 'access consciousness'. 'Phenomenal consciousness' refers to the particular qualities of our conscious experiences; what it feels like to taste coffee or hear the sound of footsteps, for example. Finally, there is self-consciousness, our awareness and monitoring of what we are doing, feeling, thinking, etc.

What was on your list of features of consciousness? For many people, one of the most salient aspects of being conscious is that we have a feeling of control over our behaviour and even over our thoughts. We feel we act in a particular way because we decided to act that way, that we have free will. Although it may be difficult to stick to our new year's resolutions, we can modify our behaviour in less ambitious ways. If you get a headache while reading this, you may decide to stop reading – and behave accordingly. Alternatively, you may choose to ignore your headache and attend to the chapter because you wish to finish reading it before going out. Resolving, deciding, choosing, ignoring, pain, attending and wishing are also aspects of our conscious mental life.

Our conscious experience seems fairly continuous. William James (1918, first published in 1890) described it as a 'stream of consciousness'. We have a coherent and persistent awareness of ourselves and our environment, and are unaware of brief or inconsequential changes in our sensory input. For example, you were probably unaware of this page disappearing from view last time you blinked.

Consciousness is not only about our ability to control our behaviour or to know what is going on around us. It is also about feelings and experiences; for example, the smell of spices as you walk past a restaurant, the taste of chocolate, the sensation of jumping into a cold swimming pool or relaxing in a hot bath, the particular feel of looking at something red (rather than something green). Philosophers use the term 'qualia' to describe these qualitative, subjective, experiential aspects of consciousness.

Consciousness has so many different features that, before studying it, we need to know whether it is actually a single thing or several quite different things inappropriately called by the same name. Could a theory of consciousness in principle explain all the different aspects of consciousness that we have discussed so far, or will we need different solutions to different problems of consciousness? This chapter will say little about states of consciousness – being awake rather than asleep for example – although it briefly discusses what altered states of consciousness could reveal about the cognitive correlates of consciousness. It also says nothing about self-consciousness. Rather, it focuses on *consciousness of* particular stimuli or mental events; that is, awareness of particular sights, sounds, memories, ideas, mental images and so on.

Even if we limit our discussion to consciousness *of* things, there are still two aspects of this type of consciousness to consider. There is the consciousness itself, being aware rather than unaware of something, and there is the experience that this consciousness engenders, what it feels like to taste chocolate or perceive green for instance. Block (1995) argues that we should treat these two aspects of consciousness as separate problems. He uses the term **access consciousness** for the problem of how, when we are conscious of something, we are able to name it, remember it, decide whether to pick it up, etc., and **phenomenal consciousness** for the experiential aspects of the problem. The term 'access consciousness' captures the idea that the contents of consciousness are accessible to other cognitive processes; thus we can talk about our memories or remember things we said. Access consciousness describes this cross-talk between different cognitive modules (a module is a set of processes acting together and separately from other sets of processes). Block argues that cognitive psychology only addresses the problem of access consciousness, despite sometimes claiming to solve the problem of phenomenal consciousness as well.

Chalmers (1996) makes a similar distinction. He refers to the problem of how information is shared between modular neural and cognitive systems as the '*easy* problem' of consciousness. Empirical research into vision, memory, attention, decision making and so on addresses the easy problem. The '*hard* problem' of consciousness, according to Chalmers, is to explain how and why the neural or cognitive processes of vision, memory, etc. give us the conscious experiences of seeing colours or enjoying happy recollections. In a similar vein, Levine (1983) argued that there is an 'explanatory gap' between understanding the neural or cognitive basis of consciousness and explaining the phenomenology. There seems to be nothing about neural or cognitive processes that necessitates their being accompanied by particular experiences. Even if we knew everything about the structure and function of the visual system, could that ever be sufficient to explain why it feels the way it does to see red? This chapter discusses the extent to which cognitive psychology has helped advance our understanding of access consciousness.

1.2   Philosophical approaches to consciousness

This section gives a very brief introduction to philosophy of mind, so called because many of the issues pertain to mental processes and states in general, and not merely to conscious processes and states. This section is not intended to be a tutorial on philosophy of mind, just an overview of some of the philosophical issues facing researchers wanting to explain consciousness (in both the access consciousness and phenomenal consciousness senses).

Let's look at the problem of the explanatory gap more closely. Perhaps the reason it is so difficult to relate cognitive and neural brain processes to conscious experience is that they are two entirely different things. Here are three examples of the ways in which they appear to differ:

1   *Phenomenal quality.* Imagine looking at a particularly bright, warm shade of red. How can interactions between neurons or modules in your brain be 'bright' or 'warm' in the way your experience is? If you imagine a hot cup of black coffee, presumably nothing in your brain turns hot or black.

2   *Intentionality.* Philosophers describe conscious states such as desiring, believing and perceiving as 'intentional', meaning they are about things. You can't just desire, you have to desire *something*. It is hard to see how brain states can be about things in the way that mental states are.

3   *Spatial position.* Neurons are physical entities so they take up space. One neuron can be to the left or right of another, but it does not make sense to talk about mental entities such as images or beliefs having spatial positions.

1.2.1   Mind–body dualism

Dualists such as Descartes solve this mind–body problem by arguing that the mind and the brain are entirely different things. The mind consists of an immaterial 'mindstuff' whereas the brain, like the rest of the body, is made of matter – water, protein, lipids, etc. For consciousness researchers, this is a defeatist stance because it means that the mind does not obey natural scientific laws and is not amenable to scientific investigation. There are other strong objections to dualism. Perhaps the most important is that it does not explain how the mind interacts with the brain or body. How can a thought about drinking water make our physical hand move to pick up a glass and take a sip unless the thought is also somehow physical?

1.2.2   Monism

The converse of dualism is monism, the idea that mind and body are essentially the same thing. Philosophers and scientists who assume that consciousness is a property of the physical brain are called materialists. How do materialists deal with the explanatory gap? One way is to take an extreme view known as eliminative materialism. Proponents of this view argue that the apparent explanatory gap arises because we use mentalistic terms such as 'desire' and 'belief' which have no scientific basis. We should eliminate these terms from our scientific vocabulary and concentrate on investigating the underlying neuroscience of consciousness. They compare our current use of mentalistic terms with the use of the term 'phlogiston' (once thought to be a substance that escapes when matter burns), which was abandoned when new theories of natural science emphasized the role of oxygen in combustion. Most materialists do use mentalistic terms but argue that conscious states are brain states and concentrate on investigating their material basis – the chemical and neuronal interactions that underpin consciousness.

Functionalists, the vast majority of whom are also materialists, take a different approach to researching consciousness. Functionalism views mental states as functional or causal states, defined by the ways in which they transform some input (an external stimulus or the product of an earlier cognitive process) into output (information passed to another cognitive module or an overt behaviour). Conscious states are not just epiphenomena – mere by-products of brain processes that have no effect in themselves. Rather, they are the direct causes of our behaviour. Functionalists use the analogy of a computer: the brain is analogous to the hardware of the computer (the silicon chips, wires, etc.) and the mind is analogous to the computer's software. The mind is implemented in ('running in', to use computer jargon) the physical brain, in the way that word-processing software might be implemented in a personal computer. The mind could also be implemented in some other physical system, just as a particular software package could run on different sorts of computers. A logical extension of this position leads us to 'strong artificial intelligence' (strong AI), the argument that, if we could program a computer with the same 'software' as a human, then it would be conscious in the same way as us. A less extreme position, weak AI, assumes that computers can have similar 'mental' properties to humans but that there might be something special about biological entities (e.g. carbon-based sensory systems) that make us conscious in the particular way that we are.

Functionalism lies at the heart of cognitive psychology. It means that cognitive psychologists can focus on investigating mental functions without too much reference to the brain biology that underpins them. Thus cognitive approaches to consciousness focus on explaining the mental processes that cause one conscious state or another, rather than investigating physical brain activity during that conscious state. It is partly a question of finding an appropriate level of explanation for the phenomenon. Just as your success in an exam might best be explained in terms of your level of attention during lectures, the amount of rehearsal time devoted to your notes, etc., rather than in terms of biological memory processes such as long-term potentiation, so might consciousness best be explained in terms of cognitive processes.

1.3 The place of consciousness within cognitive psychology

This section provides a brief reminder of the history of cognitive psychology, to help explain why cognitive psychologists are sometimes ambivalent towards the topic of consciousness, with some using it as a variable in their research but few studying it directly. Early in the history of experimental psychology, Wundt trained 'observers' to use introspection (to 'look into' their minds) to give detailed reports on their mental and emotional responses to stimuli. Introspectionism foundered partly because of the subjective nature of the data it produced. When two observers disagreed, it was not possible for an objective third person to resolve their disagreement by looking into their minds and deciding who was reporting their mental states more accurately, or indeed whether their mental states were the same or different. Other problems for introspectionism included the existence of unconscious, and hence unreportable, processes (e.g. the contribution of unconscious urges to adult behaviour that Freud stressed, and the unconscious processes in vision identified by Helmholtz), and a new emphasis on the functions rather than the structure of mental processes. For example, James (1918) suggested that the function of short-term memory was to keep in consciousness events that have just occurred.

These changes paved the way for a radical shift in the way human behaviour was studied. Behaviourists argued that psychologists should concern themselves with objective data, publicly observable behaviour, rather than subjective introspections. Although behaviourists could investigate what people said about their (mental) experience, speech being a form of behaviour, the emphasis was on studying the relationships between external stimuli and overt, behavioural responses. Consciousness itself was no longer a respectable topic for psychological research.

Cognitive psychology developed gradually from the middle of the twentieth century onwards, stimulated in part by a wartime need to explain the role of human factors in tasks such as radar monitoring and gunnery. It aimed explicitly to explain behaviour in terms of mental activity and thus represented a major shift in attitude towards the mind from behaviourism. Early cognitive theories included components that related to consciousness, such as attention, but they did not tackle the problem of consciousness directly and did not refer to conscious experience. One reason for this shyness of the topic may have been the need to be perceived as rigorously objective and scientific in an era still overshadowed by behaviourism.

Today, consciousness is increasingly considered as a variable in cognition, particularly in learning and memory research where conscious or explicit processing is contrasted with unconscious or implicit processing. Some examples are given in Chapter 6 on encoding and retrieval, as well as in Section 2 of this chapter. In the closely related field of neuropsychology, consciousness is also considered in explanations of conditions such as blindsight. However, there is disagreement about whether the issue is really being tackled. Marcel (1988) argued that 'reference to consciousness in psychological science is demanded, legitimate, and necessary' (p.121). It is demanded because it is what makes our mental life interesting, what seems to make us who we are. According to Marcel, it is legitimate, because the concept of consciousness is no less coherent than other concepts in psychology such as intelligence or personality. It is necessary because we are often implicitly studying consciousness even if we profess to be more interested in some other aspect of cognition. For example, if we ask participants simply to press a button when a light flashes, we are still measuring their conscious experience. If they are not aware of the light flashing, they generally won't respond. (This need not mean, however, that their conscious experience *caused* their response. It could be that the button push and the conscious experience are independent consequences of the nervous system's processing of the light flash.) Despite Marcel's call for more explicit discussion of consciousness in cognitive psychology, Banks (1993) argued that psychologists are still tiptoeing around the issue of consciousness rather as one might tiptoe around to avoid 'waking the insane attic-bound Aunt of a Gothic novel' (p.257). We might mention conscious processes such as attention, mental imagery or explicit memory, but we do not try to explain consciousness itself.

Despite the rise of behaviourism, introspection did not die out completely as a tool for psychological research. For example, 'think aloud' protocols have been used to study memory rehearsal and problem solving (see, for example, Section 1.2 in Chapter 11). However, introspection is becoming more widely used. Some of the studies discussed in the next section rely on participants' reports of whether they were aware of experimental stimuli. Note that the current use of introspection usually only assumes that people have insight into the products of their cognitive processes, not that they can report the processes themselves.

ACTIVITY 15.2

Think of cognitive theories from other chapters. What role does consciousness play in these theories? Do any of the theories help to explain consciousness?

COMMENT

Although many cognitive theories include concepts like attention or working memory, they generally do not specify what processes or qualities make us conscious of some stimuli or cognitive products. For example, are we conscious of information by dint of it being in short-term memory, as James suggested? More recently researchers have argued that we are only fully aware of a subset of representations in working memory (e.g. McElree, 2001). The relationship between consciousness and working memory is discussed in Section 4 of this chapter.

Summary of Section 1

- The term consciousness encompasses the state of being awake, our ability to control our behaviour and be aware of our surroundings, and our mental experiences or 'qualia'.
- There is an explanatory gap between understanding the neural and cognitive functions of the brain and explaining conscious experience.
- Cognitive psychologists view mental states as causal states that affect our behaviour.

2   Empirical research: cognitive studies of consciousness

This section focuses on three areas of cognitive psychology. Each area tackles the problem of consciousness in part by investigating unconscious processes. Although this may seem perverse, it helps us work out what processes are associated only with consciousness and not with unconscious processing. Section 2.1 covers implicit cognition (specifically, implicit memory and learning, where there is no awareness of what is remembered or learned). Research into implicit cognition is important because it can help us to define consciousness better by contrasting it with unconscious processes. It raises the question of what, given the extent of unconscious processing, might be the function of consciousness. Section 2.2 revisits earlier research into automatic and controlled processing. Although not phrased in terms of unconscious and conscious cognition, these studies show us the essential characteristics of conscious processes. They are slow but flexible whereas automatic or unconscious processes are fast and efficient but inflexible. Section 2.3 considers briefly the neuropsychology of consciousness. Studies of conditions such as blindsight help elucidate the function of 'normal' consciousness and raise questions about the functional and physical structure of consciousness. This chapter necessarily misses much of the research in cognitive psychology that relates to consciousness. The areas it does cover are those in which researchers have particularly used their findings to frame questions about consciousness, although even in these areas much research is reported with scant if any mention of what it tells us about consciousness.

2.1   Implicit cognition

2.1.1   Implicit memory

Implicit memory is memory without any accompanying sensation of remembering. It is revealed by changes in performance on specially designed memory tests. For example, if I show you the word 'witness' in the context of an apparently unrelated, non-memory, task and then give you a surprise memory test, you may not recall seeing 'witness' or recognize it as a word from the earlier task. However, if I ask you to say the first word that comes to mind starting 'wit–', your implicit memory for the word will make you more likely to say 'witness' than if you had not just seen that word.

Tests such as this **word-stem completion task** are often referred to as indirect memory tests because they measure memory without directly asking people to decide if they remember the stimuli. Indirect tests are assumed to measure predominantly implicit memory, whereas direct tests measure explicit memory. Note though that no memory test is 'process-pure'; performance on almost any memory test can be influenced by both implicit and explicit memory. For example, if you are asked to think of the first word that comes to mind beginning with 'wit–' and nothing comes to mind, you may try to think back to the earlier task to search for clues, for words that might fit the stem. If you remember that 'witness' was one of the words on the first task, and use that as your response, then you are using your explicit memory and the task is not giving a pure measure of your implicit memory.

Two studies of implicit memory are described below. Further examples are given in Chapter 6, but these two are chosen because they appear to show implicit memory in the absence of explicit memory (with the caveat about the process-impurity of memory tests).

In an early study of implicit memory, Eich (1984) showed that prior presentation of a word in a particular context could bias its subsequent interpretation. Participants in Eich's experiment heard a list of word pairs. One word in each pair was a homophone – that is, it sounded like another word with a different meaning and spelling – for example, PANE (as in 'pane of glass') is a homophone of PAIN (as in 'stomach pain'). The other word in each pair made clear the intended interpretation of the homophone. 'Window-PANE' and 'taxi-FARE' are examples of the word pairs used by Eich. Note that the homophones he used were the less common interpretations, PAIN and FAIR being the more frequently encountered spellings and meanings. Although participants in Eich's study could hear the word pairs, they could not attend to them because their main task was to shadow (repeat) an essay played at the same time. Memory for the homophones was tested in two ways. On the recognition test, participants listened to a list of words and were asked to say whether each word was old (i.e. present in the unattended list of word pairs) or new. This is a direct test of memory because it requires participants to make a judgement about their memory; it is therefore assumed to measure mainly conscious or explicit memory. Participants were unable to recognize the unattended words. For the second memory test, the experimenter read out a list of words and participants were asked to spell them. Their spelling was biased by the previous presentation of the homophones (e.g. they were biased towards spelling P-A-N-E rather than the more common P-A-I-N). This spelling test is an indirect test of memory because it does not require deliberate recollection. These findings therefore suggest that participants had implicit memory for the homophones, but not explicit memory.

Another example of implicit memory in the absence of explicit recollection is the **false fame effect**. Jacoby *et al.* (1989) used a task on which participants had to say whether names belonged to famous people. In the study phase of experiment 2 of their study, participants read aloud a list of 40 non-famous names. In the test phase, 10 of these names were mixed with 10 new non-famous names for a recognition memory test. The remaining 30 names were mixed with 30 new non-famous names and 60 famous names for the fame judgement task. Before the fame judgement task, participants were told that the names they had just read were the names of non-famous people, hence if they recognized any name from the first phase of the experiment they should respond 'non-famous'. The experimenters manipulated the degree of attention paid to the names in the study phase. In the full attention condition, participants were told that the experimenters were interested in their ability to pronounce the names quickly and accurately. In the divided attention condition, they were told to pay as little attention as possible to the pronunciation task, concentrating instead on listening to a stream of spoken digits and spotting runs of three odd numbers. The fame judgement task was sufficiently difficult that participants made a number of false positives, saying that a name was famous when in fact it was not. If participants had encountered a non-famous name earlier in the experiment, they were more likely to judge incorrectly that it was famous if the study phase took place under conditions of divided attention. Divided attention impaired explicit recognition of the names and thus reduced participants' ability to use explicit memory to interpret feelings of familiarity. In the absence of conscious recognition, familiar names were assumed to be famous.

One of the most exciting things about this field of research was the discovery that people with amnesia often performed as well as people with normal memory on the indirect tests of memory. In other words, despite their severely impaired explicit memory, amnesics had almost normal implicit memory. For example, Squire and McKee (1992) replicated the false fame effect in amnesic participants. Amnesics were significantly impaired at recognizing the previously presented names, compared with the control subjects, but they were just as biased towards judging presented non-famous names as famous. Such findings led to new rehabilitation strategies because they showed that amnesics had the potential to learn new information even though they appeared to have no memory. We shall see an example of a new learning strategy that has been used in rehabilitation in Section 3 of this chapter (in Box 15.3 on errorless learning). The dissociation between the effects of brain injury on implicit and explicit memory raises questions about the structure of consciousness. We shall return to these questions in Section 2.3.

Implicit memory phenomena are often referred to as priming. Priming is the improvement in performance caused by previous exposure to the target stimulus or by previous or concurrent exposure to a closely related stimulus. For example, Meyer and Schvaneveldt (1971) showed that participants decided more quickly that pairs of letter strings were two real words when they were related words (e.g. 'doctor' and 'nurse') than unrelated words (e.g. 'doctor' and 'cabbage'). Building on this study, Marcel (1983) showed that participants identified 'doctor' as a real word faster when it was preceded by a very brief presentation of the word 'nurse' than by an unrelated word. The word 'nurse' in this example is called the prime. The idea behind priming is that: (a) activation of an item's representation in memory lingers, so that the representation is still slightly activated next time the item is encountered, making it easier to reactivate even if only a partial cue is presented, such as a word stem; (b) activation spreads to representations of related items, making related representations easier to activate than unrelated, unprimed representations. Priming is also used in a more general sense, to refer to the activation of moods or stereotypes (see Box 15.1 on unconscious influences on behaviour). Demonstrations of priming show that we are not always aware of our knowledge, or of the basis for our behaviour. Priming is often preserved even when brain injury causes impairments to explicit cognition; thus – as with other forms of implicit memory – people with amnesia typically have preserved priming. Box 15.3 on errorless learning (in Section 3) mentions a way of using this preserved priming in rehabilitation. Despite preserved implicit memory, lack of explicit memory has an impact on the more general aspect of consciousness that James (1918) termed our 'stream of consciousness'. Baddeley (1990) cites the example of Clive Wearing, whose amnesia was so severe that he repeatedly noted in his diary that he had just regained consciousness. Memory and consciousness thus appear to be correlated, but the direction of causation is unclear: does normal consciousness require intact memory function or does normal memory function require consciousness? We shall return to this problem of correlational evidence in the conclusion to the chapter.

15.1

Unconscious influences on behaviour

Research in the field of social cognition suggests that priming may considerably influence our behaviour outside the laboratory. Primes may influence our mood and behaviour without us being aware of them. For example, Bargh et al. (1996) asked participants to arrange lists of words to form meaningful sentences. In the experimental group, each word list contained a word related to the concept of old age, for example 'wrinkled', 'ancient'. Participants were surreptitiously timed as they left the laboratory after completing this task. Those in the experimental group, who had been exposed to the 'elderly' primes, left the laboratory more slowly than those in the control group, who were not exposed to those primes. Bargh et al. argued that the primes activated a stereotype of old age and participants behaved in accordance with that stereotype even though they had not noticed the primes.

Neumann and Strack (2000) showed that people's mood can be affected by the mood of others around them, even when they are unaware of their mood change or its cause. When participants listened to text read in a sad voice, they were more likely to rate their own mood as sad but were unaware that their mood had changed as a result of listening to the sad voice.

Lieberman (2000) argues that implicit cognitive processes, such as priming of stereotypes and mood states, underlie the phenomenon commonly known as 'intuition'; that is, our ability to judge social situations and respond appropriately without being aware of the information (other people's moods, etc.) on which we base our judgements.

2.1.2 Implicit learning

Studies of implicit memory show that we can 'remember' things without having any conscious experience of remembering them. A more profound claim has been made by researchers in the field of **implicit learning**, namely that we can learn things without ever being aware of them. If this claim is true, it helps establish some ground rules for our study of consciousness by telling us what is possible without consciousness. Evidence that a lot of learning is possible without consciousness would suggest that consciousness is just an epiphenomenon that plays no causal role in our cognition. We shall therefore look closely at some of the evidence for implicit learning and at some of the methodological problems that face researchers trying to show that participants had no awareness of the material they learned.

One way of demonstrating this unconscious or implicit learning is to present the stimuli to be learned very quickly, too quickly for participants to notice more than just a flash on the screen. This is called subliminal presentation. The study by Marcel (1983) mentioned in Section 2.1.1 has become a controversial classic: a classic because it demonstrated priming even though the presentation of the primes was apparently subliminal; and controversial because of claims that the findings could not be replicated when stricter definitions of 'subliminal' were used. However, subsequent researchers have used subliminal presentation with other test procedures to provide evidence of implicit learning.

Some of this evidence comes from demonstrations of the mere exposure effect, the tendency for people to prefer stimuli they have encountered before even if they were unaware of them during the previous encounter. For example, Kunst-Wilson and Zajonc (1990) presented novel black and white patterns very briefly. Even though participants said they could not see the patterns, because they were presented so briefly, they later tended to select those patterns when presented with pairs of patterns (one presented earlier and one new) and asked to choose the one they preferred. On a recognition test in which participants chose the pattern they remembered seeing earlier from each pair, participants performed at chance, i.e. they were just guessing. So their first, unconscious, encounter with the patterns apparently changed their emotional response to them even though they had no conscious or explicit memory for seeing the patterns before (see also Chapter 14 on cognition and emotion, Section 5.2.1).

As suggested by the controversy over Marcel's (1983) study, there are problems with using subliminal presentation to demonstrate unconscious learning. One problem is ensuring that all stimuli are subliminal for all participants. This is tricky because some stimuli are easier to perceive than others. For example, you can sometimes hear someone say your name even if you don't hear anything else they say because you are attending to another conversation (Moray, 1959). Another limitation is the equipment used to present the stimuli. Early studies used tachistoscopes, boxes that were specially designed to show stimuli for very brief and accurately timed periods. Many researchers now use computers for running their experiments, but computerized presentation times are limited by factors like the screen refresh rate – how quickly the computer redraws the display. A refresh rate of 17 ms means that stimuli can only be presented for multiples of 17 ms. This limitation makes it hard for the experimenter to present a stimulus for long enough to effect some learning but briefly enough to prevent the participant identifying the stimulus.

A solution to these problems is to present stimuli **supraliminally** (for long enough that they can be consciously perceived), but to test learning of some hidden relationship between them. For example, Reber has claimed that people can implicitly learn hidden rules, constituting an **artificial grammar**, that underpin a set of supraliminally presented letter strings. Although they cannot verbalize their knowledge, it allows them to distinguish grammatical from ungrammatical items with above-chance accuracy. Two of Reber's early experiments are discussed below. An example of an artificial grammar is shown in Figure 15.1.

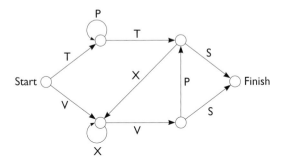

Figure 15.1   The artificial grammar used by Reber (1967). Grammatical letter strings are created by following the arrows through the array from left to right. The curved arrows indicate items that can be repeated

ACTIVITY 15.3

First, trace through the network shown in Figure 15.1 to convince yourself that TPPPTS and VXVPS are grammatical strings whereas VTPS and TPTTTS are ungrammatical. Now try writing down or explaining to a friend the rules of this grammar.

COMMENT

Verbal report is often used as a way of finding out whether participants in implicit learning experiments were aware of the information they learned. The stimuli used in these experiments are typically complex and novel and therefore difficult to describe. You may have struggled to report the rules of Reber's grammar even though you were looking at Figure 15.1 while doing so. The problem of eliciting participants' explicit knowledge through verbal report is addressed later in this section.

Reber (1967) asked participants to learn 28 letter strings or 'sentences' as part of a 'memory experiment'. The sentences were presented in seven sets of four sentences. Each sentence was viewed for 5 seconds, after which the participant tried to write it. After attempting to reproduce the four sentences in a set, the participant was told which sentences they had reproduced correctly and the procedure was repeated until they reached the criterion of reproducing all four sentences correctly on two consecutive trials. The next set of sentences was then presented. For participants in the experimental group, the sentences were formed according to the rules of an artificial grammar. For those in the control group, the sentences contained randomly ordered letters. The results were as follows. Both groups learned the second of the seven sets of sentences in fewer attempts than the first. However, from the third set onwards, the control group continued to make a mean of between eight and 11 errors per set whereas the experimental group continued to improve, making a mean of only three errors on the seventh set. Reber argued that the experimental group acquired knowledge of the grammar that enabled them to learn more efficiently.

A second experiment in Reber's study showed that prior exposure to the grammatical sentences enabled participants to distinguish new grammatical sentences from ungrammatical sentences. Participants learned 20 grammatical sentences in a procedure similar to that described above. They were then tested on 88 trials with new sentences, comprising two presentations each of 22 grammatical sentences (that had not been encountered in the learning phase) and two presentations each of 22 ungrammatical sentences. Participants were told that the sentences they had already learned were grammatical, and were asked to use their knowledge of those sentences to decide if each test sentence was grammatical or ungrammatical. Their decisions were correct on a mean of 79 per cent of trials, well above the mean of 50 per cent expected from chance.

Subsequent studies of artificial grammar learning have used procedures similar to that of this second experiment. Participants learn a set of grammatical strings to a predetermined criterion, and then attempt to distinguish novel grammatical strings from ungrammatical strings. Performance is typically above chance, though not as impressive as in Reber's study, even though participants cannot state the rules they used to decide which were the grammatical items. This apparently implicit learning of the grammar is dissociable from explicit recall of the grammatical strings presented in the learning phase. For example, Knowlton et al. (1992) found that amnesic patients were as good as controls at classifying novel strings as grammatical or ungrammatical, but were poorer at recognizing exemplars that had been encountered in the learning phase.

Nissen and Bullemer (1987) used an alternative procedure for testing implicit learning of hidden regularities between visible stimuli. They gave control and amnesic participants a choice reaction time task in which they had to watch a panel of four lights (ABCD) and, whenever a light came on, to press the key under that light as quickly as possible. Participants were not told that the lights came on in a fixed order (the 10-item sequence DBCACBDCBA was presented repeatedly). Controls and amnesics got faster at this task until the sequence was switched to a random order: at this point, their reaction times increased. The amnesic participants showed no awareness that the lights had come on in a regular sequence. Control participants are also often unaware of the sequence, particularly if they perform the key-pressing task under conditions of divided attention.

A problem with these demonstrations of implicit learning is that we have no way of determining participants' awareness of the key stimuli or relationships while they are doing the task. If we ask them if they are aware of the grammar, for example, then we draw their attention to it and lose the opportunity for demonstrating learning without awareness. So researchers have to ask participants afterwards what they were aware of during the task. This is unsatisfactory, because it relies on people's memory of what they were aware of rather than measuring awareness online. Another problem is that quite a small amount of knowledge may be enough to boost people's performance above the chance level. For instance, they may not know the whole grammar, just that a certain letter can be repeated or come at the start of a letter string. Knowing possible starts for grammatical strings may be sufficient to distinguish a few of the grammatical strings from the ungrammatical strings, resulting in performance that is slightly above baseline. If a test of awareness simply asks 'Were you aware of the grammar?' or 'What was the grammar?', then it will miss the knowledge that actually boosted performance on the grammar test, and that knowledge may well be explicit. Participants may interpret the question as asking for a complete report of the grammar, which they cannot give, and so do not volunteer their knowledge of fragments of the grammar. These problems are discussed by Shanks and St John (1994). They argue that experimenters must use tests of explicit knowledge, or awareness, that meet two criteria before they can claim that learning resulted in truly implicit knowledge. The *information criterion* states that the test of awareness must probe for the sort of information that could support performance on the test of learning (for example, knowledge that a particular letter often comes at the start of a grammatical letter string). The *sensitivity criterion* states that the test of awareness must be sensitive to all the relevant explicit knowledge; it must be just as sensitive as the test of implicit knowledge. Simply asking participants to state the rules of the artificial grammar fails on both counts. It does not prompt them to report fragments of the grammar, thus failing the information criterion, and it does not give them any recall cues, thus failing the sensitivity criterion. The grammar judgement test is more sensitive because it presents the actual grammatical stimuli and these may serve as cues to memory.

Given the difficulty of ensuring lack of awareness of critical stimuli in awake participants, perhaps a better strategy would be to study learning in people who are unconscious. Testing patients receiving anaesthetics offers a way of tackling this issue, though one that presents more difficulties than might at first be imagined. One difficulty is that depth of anaesthesia, or 'degree of unconsciousness', fluctuates during an operation and there is not yet a universally agreed way of measuring this fluctuation or of establishing exactly the depth of anaesthesia at which a person loses consciousness, in the sense of losing all awareness of themselves and their surroundings. Thus a finding that patients can learn information presented during anaesthesia may reflect explicit learning during undetected moments of consciousness, rather than truly unconscious learning. Another difficulty is that the sensitivity of the memory tests has not been established. So, if a study shows no evidence for learning during anaesthesia, this may be due to use of a test that is too insensitive to detect small amounts of preserved learning. Not surprisingly, although many studies have investigated learning during anaesthesia, their findings have been mixed (Andrade, 1995).

Catherine Deeprose and I recently obtained evidence for priming during anaesthesia in a study that overcame some of the problems discussed above (Deeprose *et al.*, 2004). We played words (e.g. 'tractor') to patients during surgery. When the patients came round from the anaesthetic, we asked them to respond to word stems (e.g. 'tra–') with the first word that came to mind. Playing a word during surgery increased the likelihood of patients using that word to complete a word stem on recovery. In other words, they showed some implicit memory for the words even though were anaesthetized while receiving them. We had pilot tested our word-stem completion test to ensure that it was reasonably sensitive and also reasonably uncontaminated by explicit memory (it was relatively unaffected by a manipulation of attention known to affect explicit memory). Thus we gave ourselves a good chance of demonstrating implicit memory for words played during surgery. We minimized the chance of priming occurring during moments of awareness by using an EEG measure of depth of anaesthesia throughout word presentation and testing patients who were unparalysed, because the drugs that are often used to paralyse patients during surgery make it even harder to detect moments of consciousness. We are therefore reasonably confident that we have demonstrated that memories can be primed in someone who is unconscious. The next step is to investigate whether new information can be learned during anaesthesia.

To summarize, there is some evidence for learning without consciousness of what is learned. However, this implicit learning is rather difficult to demonstrate convincingly and is also not very useful, in the sense that we cannot revise, contemplate or tell people about what we have learned implicitly. We cannot select what we learn when learning implicitly, and we cannot retrieve the learned material voluntarily. It would appear that conscious processes (e.g. the active selection, rehearsal and elaboration of information) contribute to much of our everyday learning. Even so, implicit learning may help us to pick up repeated patterns or relationships among stimuli or events, and by doing so help us direct our conscious learning processes towards interesting features of our environment. Implicit memory is easier to demonstrate. When only a small amount of learning has occurred, because of inattention or brain damage for example, the resulting memory may be implicit. We may be unaware of what we have learned because the encoded material does not reach some threshold for consciousness or because it has not been processed by a 'conscious memory module'. This issue of the structure of consciousness is discussed briefly in Section 2.3 on the neuropsychology of consciousness.

2.2   Controlled versus automatic processing

The concept of controlled processing is closely allied to that of conscious processing. As you have seen in the previous section, if we want to demonstrate implicit learning or memory, we have to make it very difficult for participants to process the target material in an active way, for example by distracting their attention from it. This sort of active processing is often known as **controlled processing** (as opposed to automatic processing). The idea of controlled processing is central to concepts such as working memory (discussed in Section 4 as a potential model of consciousness). Controlled cognitive processes typically accompany consciousness – that is, they are cognitive correlates of consciousness. This section therefore describes a classic study by Schneider and Shiffrin (1977) that defined and demonstrated controlled and automatic processes in visual attention.

Schneider and Shiffrin (1977) based their theorizing on Atkinson and Shiffrin's (1968) model of memory (see Chapter 6, Section 2.1), arguing that automatic processes operate on the long-term memory store (an interconnected array of nodes) whereas controlled processes require the limited capacity short-term store, essentially the currently activated nodes of the long-term store. They defined automatic processes as the activation of a sequence of nodes in the long-term store via connections between those nodes that have become relatively permanent through repeated use. Once triggered, automatic processes operate without active control so it is difficult to stop them or change their course. In contrast, activation of a novel sequence of nodes requires attention, which limits our capacity to activating just one novel sequence at a time but gives us control over the activation.

Schneider and Shiffrin demonstrated the difference between these two processing modes using 'target search tasks' that required participants to detect targets as quickly and accurately as possible from arrays of distractors. They manipulated (a) the number of targets participants had to search for; (b) the number of items (targets and distractors combined) on each slide or 'frame'; and (c) the mapping between the set of targets for any series of trials (the 'memory set') and the distractor set. This mapping manipulation was the key to demonstrating automatic and controlled processing modes. In the **consistent mapping** condition, the targets were always selected from the same set of items and the distractors were always selected from a different set so, for example, participants might search for target digits among distractor letters. In the **varied mapping** condition, the targets and distractors were drawn from the same set, so participants might search for letters among letters and a particular letter could be a target on one trial and a distractor on another. Figure 15.2 gives examples of trials in these different conditions.

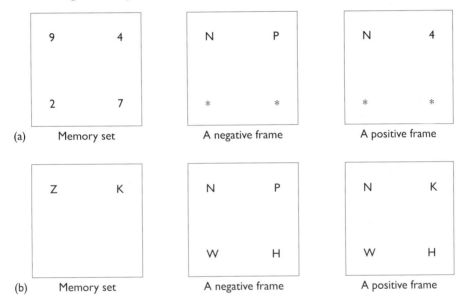

Figure 15.2 Examples of stimuli from Schneider and Shiffrin's (1977) experiments. On a given trial, participants saw and memorized the set of targets for that trial (the 'memory set'). They then saw a sequence of frames. Their task was to detect whether any of the memorized targets appeared in the sequence: (a) shows stimuli from a consistent mapping condition with a memory set size of four and a frame size of two; (b) shows stimuli from a varied mapping condition with a memory set size of two and a frame size of four. The asterisks represent pattern masks in the positions not occupied by targets or distractors

The consistent and varied mapping conditions produced quite different patterns of response times. In the consistent mapping condition, performance was fast and relatively unaffected by memory set size and frame size. In the varied mapping condition, performance was slower and was slowed further still by increasing the number of targets to be searched for and the number of items per frame to be searched. Schneider and Shiffrin argued that the varied mapping condition necessitated a controlled serial search through the array in each frame: hence, the larger the array, the longer the search. In contrast, the consistent mapping condition allowed the items in the arrays to be searched automatically, in parallel, because all we have to do is spot a digit (say) among letters, and we have had many years of practice at recognizing digits. Because we only have to spot a digit, there is no need to maintain the specific identities of the memory set items in short-term memory.

Subsequent researchers have extended Schneider and Shiffrin's description of controlled processes to cover a variety of cognitive processes that are flexible but slow and expensive in terms of cognitive resources. In everyday terms, we use controlled processing when performing novel tasks or wanting to override habitual behaviours. For example, when making black coffee for a friend, we may have to attend to each step of the procedure to stop ourselves adding milk. If talking to our friend at the same time, it is easy to lapse into automatic behaviour and make the 'action slip' of adding milk to their coffee as well as to ours. Automatic processes are typically fast and efficient but inflexible. We are generally unaware of the operation of automatic processes. For example, an experienced tennis player will hit a ball without stopping to think how to do so whereas a novice may have to think about how to hold the racquet, how hard to hit the ball and so on. Automatic processes make little impact on explicit memory, so someone driving a car on 'autopilot' may arrive at their destination safely, but with little memory of the journey. Thus, the concepts of automatic and controlled processing map closely onto the currently more fashionable concepts of unconscious or implicit processing and conscious or explicit processing. But this mapping raises another question: is consciousness something we use to control our behaviour, or do we *become* conscious of our behaviour when we exert control over it?

2.3   The neuropsychology of consciousness

The research presented in the previous sections raises questions about the nature of consciousness. Are we conscious of a stimulus (or of a memory) because it exceeds some threshold of salience or activation, or are we conscious of it because it is processed in a particular way? In other words, is consciousness something that might be associated with very many cognitive processes or is it a feature of particular cognitive modules? Is there even a unitary 'consciousness module'? There are no clear answers to these questions at present, but this section aims to show the potential for neuropsychology to help find answers. While you are reading it, bear in mind that the search for a consciousness module may be futile: Dennett (1991) argues that searching for a place where consciousness happens – a 'Cartesian theatre' – is a mistake based on a misunderstanding of consciousness. We shall meet Dennett again in Section 4.

Studies of altered consciousness following localized brain injury provide a way of assessing whether consciousness is a unitary or modular function. If it is a unitary function, it could be localized in a single 'consciousness area' of the brain, or distributed across a network of interconnected brain regions, or it could be the result of some non-localized process such as synchronized activity across brain regions (see ffytche, 2000). If consciousness is a modular function, then our conscious awareness of colours might be caused by processes localized in quite different brain regions from, say, our conscious awareness of movements or sounds.

At first glance, neuropsychological studies suggest that consciousness is modular because brain injury often causes loss of consciousness of only a subset of sensations and cognitions. For example, people with amnesia are not conscious of information learned since the onset of their amnesia. People with unilateral neglect on the other hand have normal consciousness of their memories but lack consciousness of one side of space. Is it the case then that our consciousness for memories is separate from our consciousness for space, as a modular interpretation would suggest? The answer is not clear. Patients with amnesia may lack consciousness of their memories because they lack critical unconscious processes that feed into a unitary consciousness. Likewise neglect patients may not have suffered damage to a 'consciousness of space' module but rather have deficits in attentional processes that feed into a unitary consciousness.

Zeki and ffytche (1998) studied a blindsight patient known as G.Y. **Blindsight** is a disorder exhibited by some patients with brain damage leading to blindness in part of the visual field. In blindsight, there is a somewhat preserved ability to respond appropriately to visual stimuli in the blind region of the visual field, despite having no sense of seeing them. G.Y.'s blindness is selective, so that he reports having some sort of conscious experience of some visual stimuli in his blind field (e.g. fast-moving stimuli) but denies having any experience of other stimuli (e.g. slow-moving stimuli). Usually, G.Y. can identify a stimulus from a small selection of distractors only if he has some conscious experience of it. Occasionally, however, he can identify stimuli even without any conscious experience; that is, he exhibits blindsight for these stimuli.

Zeki and ffytche (1998) used functional magnetic resonance imaging (fMRI) to compare G.Y.'s brain activity with and without conscious perception of visual stimuli. G.Y. could detect the direction of movement of slow and fast-moving stimuli, but he was usually only conscious of the fast stimuli. The two types of stimuli differentially triggered activity in the motion cortex, the increase in activity being greater with the fast-moving stimuli for which G.Y. reported some conscious experience. Thus, consciousness of visual stimuli appears to be related to the amount of activity in a localized brain area, a brain area specialized for processing that type of stimulus rather than in a general 'consciousness centre'. ffytche (2000) suggests that the increased local activity associated with consciousness may reflect the activity of additional populations of neurons in that brain region or it may reflect more complex processing by neurons that are also active when we are not conscious of the stimulus to which they respond. Note however that although Zeki and ffytche's data support the hypothesis of a modular consciousness, our overall conscious experience – our individual 'stream of consciousness' – may still reflect the aggregation of processing across many brain regions. Consciousness for motion may be dissociable from consciousness for colour, for instance, but these two consciousness modules must somehow be bound together to produce our normal conscious experience of a moving coloured stimulus.

Summary of Section 2

- Studies of priming or implicit memory show that people retain more information than they are aware of remembering.
- Studies of learning without awareness of what is learned have been hotly debated; so-called implicit learning might reflect failure to detect small amounts of awareness. A recent study of learning during anaesthesia suggests that memory priming occurs even when patients are unconscious.
- Schneider and Shiffrin (1977) argued that controlled search processes operate serially and are slow, increasingly so as task demands increase, because they depend on limited-capacity short-term memory systems. Automatic search processes are fast and can operate in parallel because they operate on well-learned pathways in long-term memory. Automatic processing typically happens without awareness, whereas controlled processing is associated with conscious awareness of the task in hand and explicit memory for its products.
- Neuropsychological studies can help determine the structure of consciousness. ffytche (2000) uses a study of blindsight to argue that consciousness is a function of modular brain systems. Alternative arguments are that there is a single 'consciousness module' or that consciousness is a distributed function.

3   What is consciousness for?

3.1   Consciousness and behavioural control

The studies of implicit learning and memory discussed in the previous section suggest that it is possible to learn about a variety of different stimuli without being conscious of them. We appear to 'remember' things without any conscious experience of doing so. If we can do this without consciousness, does consciousness actually serve any function or is it an epiphenomenon, a by-product of brain processes that does not in itself affect the system? This section discusses evidence that consciousness serves a variety of purposes that together make us able to function effectively even in novel environments.

Research into automatic and controlled processes shows that automatic or unconscious processes tend to be fast and efficient but inflexible. Providing there is no competition for sensory systems (e.g. trying to view two complex pictures simultaneously) or response effectors (e.g. trying to write two answers simultaneously), several automatic processes can run concurrently. Controlled or conscious processes, on the other hand, are slower and more demanding of cognitive resources, so it is hard to carry out more than one at a time. Stimuli must therefore be selected for conscious processing. The Cheshire cat illusion, discussed in Activity 15.4 in Section 3.3, illustrates this point. Chapter 2, on attention, discusses how this selection is done. Despite their disadvantages, we need conscious processes when performing new tasks or trying to override habits. This is illustrated by the tendency of people to generate stereotyped responses when distracted from a random generation task, a task that requires frequent strategy shifts to avoid lapsing into stereotyped response patterns. Baddeley *et al.* (1998) asked participants to generate random sequences of digits or key presses. They manipulated the availability of controlled processing resources by asking participants to perform other tasks at the same time (for example, solving problems or retrieving information from long-term memory). In these conditions, faster and more automatic processes generated stereotyped responses such as '1, 2, 3' or parts of familiar telephone numbers. Conscious or controlled processes thus seem to be associated with flexible responding. Box 15.2 on affective priming suggests that conscious processes help us make rational rather than emotional decisions. The research presented in Box 15.3 on errorless learning shows that making mistakes prevents people with amnesia from learning as effectively as they might. With normal memory, consciousness of our memory for past errors may help us adapt our behaviour by learning from our mistakes.

15.2   **Research study**

Affective priming

Zajonc (1980) hypothesized that emotional or affective responses can be triggered by information that undergoes only minimal processing. Cognitive responses require more processing. This is known as the 'affective primacy hypothesis'. Murphy and Zajonc (1993) tested this hypothesis in a series of experiments that compared the influence of subliminal and 'optimal' (i.e. consciously visible or supraliminal) primes on responses to subsequent stimuli.

In the first experiment in their study, Murphy and Zajonc asked 32 participants to rate their liking of Chinese ideographs, on a scale of 1 = 'did not like the ideograph at all' to 5 = 'liked the ideograph quite a bit'. Each ideograph was shown for 2 seconds. There were four types of trial:

- *no-prime controls*, where the ideographs were shown alone

- *irrelevant prime controls*, where a geometric shape preceded each ideograph

- *positive affective prime trials*, where a photograph of a happy face preceded each ideograph

- *negative affective prime trials*, where a photograph of an angry face preceded each ideograph.

For participants in the subliminal prime condition, each slide of a shape or face was presented for just 4 ms, followed immediately by an ideograph that served both as the stimulus to be rated and as a visual mask to prevent the image of the prime lingering in iconic memory. Participants in the optimal prime condition viewed each prime slide for 1,000 ms, followed immediately by the ideograph. A summary of these experimental trials is shown in Figure 15.3.

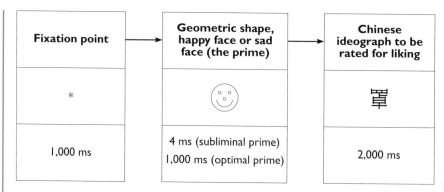

Figure 15.3 Experimental trials used to demonstrate affective priming

The results are shown in Table 15.1. The ideographs were rated as more pleasant when preceded by a subliminal positive prime, compared with the no prime and irrelevant prime control conditions, and more unpleasant when preceded by a subliminal negative prime. In contrast, the visible or 'optimal' primes had no effect on ratings of the ideographs.

Table 15.1 Mean ratings of liking for Chinese ideographs in affective prime, irrelevant prime and no prime conditions

Condition	Subliminal presentation (4 ms)	Optimal presentation (1,000 ms)
Positive prime	3.46	3.02
Negative prime	2.70	3.28
Irrelevant prime	3.06	3.15
No prime	3.06	3.11

In a follow-up experiment, Murphy and Zajonc tested the effects of subliminal and optimal primes on ratings of the size of object represented by each ideograph. This time the relevant primes were small or large shapes and the irrelevant primes were faces with neutral expressions. The results contrasted with those of the experiment described above: the subliminal primes had no effect on ratings of size whereas the large optimal primes led to higher ratings and the small optimal primes to lower ratings.

Conclusion

Murphy and Zajonc (1993) argued that the affective primes altered participants' mood, in the sense that participants had an emotional response to the primes. When participants were aware of their mood change and of its source, they could ignore it when rating the ideographs. However, when they were unaware of it, their affective response to the primes 'spilled over' onto the rating task. For negative primes, the authors referred to this effect as 'free-floating anxiety' – that is, anxiety without awareness of what caused it or what we are anxious about. Consciousness of the primes allowed participants to override their affective response to them when judging the ideographs.

15.3 ——————————————————— Research study

Errorless learning

Baddeley and Wilson (1994) argued that one of the main functions of explicit memory is to help us learn from our mistakes. Without awareness of our errors, past mistakes serve only to prime similar mistakes in the future. They tested their hypothesis by comparing two modes of learning in 32 participants with normal memory (16 young and 16 elderly adults) and 16 participants with amnesia who were assumed to have normal implicit memory combined with impaired explicit memory. Participants with normal memory received one list of 10 words in the errorful learning condition and another list of 10 words in the errorless learning condition. Amnesic participants received five words in each condition, to avoid floor and ceiling effects. The stimulus words were all five letters long and chosen because their two-letter stems could be completed in several ways. For example, the stem QU– could be completed as QUOTE (the stimulus in this case) or QUIET, QUEEN, QUACK, etc. The large number of potential completions maximized the possibility for making errors in the errorful learning condition.

In the errorful learning condition, participants were told that the experimenter was thinking of a five-letter word beginning QU– and asked to guess what the word might be. After making up to four incorrect guesses, the participant was told that the word was QUOTE (or a back-up word if they happened to guess the target straight away) and asked to write it down. This procedure was repeated for the other words in the list, and then again two more times for the entire list.

In the errorless learning condition, participants were told 'I am thinking of a five-letter word beginning with QU and that word is QUOTE please write that down.' The list of target words was presented three times, as in the errorful condition.

These first three trials were termed the pre-training phase. Learning condition was only manipulated during this pre-training phase. The test phase comprised nine further learning trials. On each of these trials, regardless of the initial learning condition, the experimenter provided the first two letters of each word in the list and asked the participant to write down a word starting with those letters from the earlier list. If they could not remember a word from the previous phase, they were asked to say any word that came to mind beginning with those letters. In the case of incorrect responses, the experimenter provided the correct word. Baddeley and Wilson analysed performance in the test phase in terms of the probability of learning – that is, the probability of an item that is not known on one trial becoming learned on the next trial. The learning probabilities for the two learning conditions are illustrated in Figure 15.4 overleaf.

Conclusion

Participants with amnesia benefited considerably more from the errorless learning procedure than the young and elderly participants with normal memory. Without explicit memory for their errors, amnesic participants were unable to correct their mistakes on subsequent trials and so found the learning task particularly difficult when they were encouraged to make errors on the initial, pre-training trials. Errorless learning techniques have been used to teach amnesics useful information such as how to program a personal organizer to remind them of appointments.

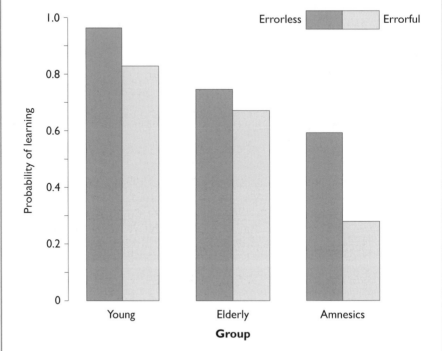

Figure 15.4 Learning probabilities for young, elderly and amnesic participants' learning conditions

Source: Baddeley and Wilson, 1994, Figure 3, p.59

3.2 Cross-talk between cognitive modules

An important feature of consciousness is that it seems to break the modularity of mind. Cognitive psychologists often assume that cognitive processes are modular; that is, that they operate in clusters that function independently from other clusters of processes. Each cluster or 'module' processes a particular sort of information, so there may be one module for comprehending spoken language and another module for recognizing faces. Consciousness involves cross-talk between these otherwise independent modules. If we are conscious of something, we can talk about it, decide to touch it or ignore it, imagine holding or owning it, have beliefs about it. In studies of blindsight, note that patients do not tend to initiate responses towards stimuli. Even though they can respond appropriately to stimuli when encouraged to guess, their residual processing of the stimuli is of little practical use to them. Without the conscious experience of seeing, someone with this condition would not, for example, pick up a glass of water placed in their blind field even if they were thirsty and could point to its location when encouraged to do so. Normally, seeing a glass of water means that we can also drink it or talk about it – consciousness of the visual percept makes it available to action and language modules. In blindsight, although some visual information is processed and influences 'guessing' behaviour, that information is not sufficient to break out of the visual perception module to form a basis for conscious behaviour. Likewise with implicit learning. Although exposure to covert regularities may improve performance on an implicit learning task with similar stimuli, even without awareness of what has been learned, there is limited transfer of this improvement to tasks with different stimuli constructed according to the same rules (e.g. Gomez, 1997). When we are aware of what we have learned, we are better able to apply that learning to novel tasks.

Although cognitive research has helped identify the functions of consciousness, for controlling our behaviour and allowing cross-talk between cognitive modules, it does not explain why these functions are associated with conscious experience. Could it be possible, for a computer, say, to perform these functions without consciousness? Philosophers use the term 'zombie' to refer to the idea of someone exactly like us, with the same cognitive processes as us, the same knowledge, memories, planning abilities, etc., but without consciousness. If this idea makes sense to us (even though zombies are a fiction), then it suggests that the 'hard problem' of consciousness is indeed a very hard problem because there is nothing about our cognitive processes that necessitates the conscious experience that accompanies them (see Chalmers, 1996).

3.3   Altered states of consciousness

The cognitive basis of altered states of consciousness is not well understood. Nonetheless, altered states are interesting because, by providing a contrast, they help us reflect on what 'normal' consciousness is like. Because they are generally dysfunctional states, in the sense that they are not conducive to normal everyday behaviour, they give us clues about the functions of normal conscious states. Altered states are therefore included briefly in this chapter as a discussion point to help you think about the possible functions of consciousness.

Drugs such as ketamine and lysergic acid diethylamide (LSD) cause hallucinations and other perceptual disturbances such as synaesthesia, a condition where stimuli in one sensory modality trigger experiences in another sensory modality (e.g. touching something hard may produce the sensation of seeing green). It appears that these drugs cause a flooding of the sensory system and a breaking down of the modularity of sensory systems. Normal consciousness may therefore involve selecting incoming sensory information to prevent too much information reaching higher-level cognitive processes. Drugs such as alcohol cause loss of inhibition, making us more likely to say things or do things that we would refrain from doing in our normal conscious state. Normal consciousness may therefore involve monitoring and controlling our behaviour.

Hypnosis is a state of deep relaxation that makes people more susceptible to suggestion. There is debate about whether it is truly an altered state of consciousness, or merely a response to the particular combination of relaxation and social pressure to conform to the hypnotist's suggestions. Nonetheless, hypnotized people can perform surprising feats, such as speaking 'forgotten' languages from their childhood or even undergoing minor surgery without painkillers or anaesthetic. One explanation of such feats is that hypnosis reduces our normal tendency to check our mental contents against the outside world. This checking and updating of our mental model of ourselves and our environment is called **reality monitoring**. With reduced reality monitoring, hypnotized people become more credulous because they are less likely to check the hypnotist's suggestions against what they know to be true. This makes them better able to maintain a 'hallucination' even if it contradicts incoming sensory information.

Altered states of consciousness suggest that normal consciousness operates with or on a selected portion of the information that constantly bombards our senses. For a demonstration of this selection, try the Cheshire cat activity (Activity 15.4). Normal consciousness also involves checking our current mental state against incoming information from our environment and checking our behaviour against our intended goals.

ACTIVITY 15.4

Sit facing a picture of a cat (or a real one if you can persuade it to sit still) on an otherwise blank wall, with another blank wall to your right (see Figure 15.5). Hold the edge of a mirror against your nose, and tilt it so you view the cat picture with your left eye only. Hold up your right hand so that it is reflected in the mirror, the reflection being viewed by your right eye. Move your right hand slowly towards and away from you. With appropriate adjustments to the mirror or to the direction of hand waving, you should experience the Cheshire cat illusion: moving your hand appears to 'rub out' parts or all of the cat (Duensing and Miller, 1979).

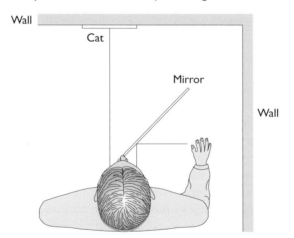

Figure 15.5   Set-up for the Cheshire cat illusion

When you experience the Cheshire cat illusion, your brain is receiving two separate visual images, yet you only see one of them at a time. What does this tell you about consciousness?

Note: If you have difficulty seeing this illusion, try this simpler version. Roll a sheet of paper into a tube and look through it with your left eye while viewing your right hand with your right eye. Hold your right hand against the tube, about 10 cm from your eye. Move your hand slightly to and fro until you perceive a hole in your hand with the same diameter as the tube.

COMMENT

The illusion occurs because the two percepts – the one of the cat and the one of your hand – cannot be fused. Only one percept can be conscious at a time; hence if you are conscious of seeing the reflection of your hand, you will not be conscious of seeing the part of the cat picture that occupies the same apparent visual location as the reflection of your hand. This illusion illustrates the selective and limited-capacity aspect of consciousness. The phenomenon is known as 'binocular rivalry' and has been used by neuroscientists to determine the neuronal activity associated with consciousness of a visual stimulus (e.g. Logothetis and Schall, 1989).

Summary of Section 3

- Consciousness is associated with, and may cause, behavioural control. It helps us override habitual and emotional responses and to learn from our mistakes.
- The effects of mind-altering drugs, and of hypnosis, suggest that normal conscious states involve monitoring and control of behaviour, and selection of incoming information. We are only conscious of a small amount of information at any time.

4   Cognitive theories of consciousness

This section focuses on two theories: working memory and global workspace theory. Baddeley's working memory model is chosen because it is already a widely used model in cognitive psychology (see Chapter 5 on working memory). If it can also say something about consciousness then it could help us integrate our thinking about consciousness with our existing understanding of other aspects of cognition. Baars's global workspace approach is discussed as a contrast, partly because it is the most detailed and comprehensive cognitive model of consciousness currently available and partly because Baars explicitly discusses the hypothetical relationship between consciousness and working memory.

Short-term memory, and later working memory, have often been identified with consciousness. Thus James (1918) described memory generally as a way of bringing back past conscious experiences, but argued that for primary memory there is nothing to bring back because 'it was never lost; its date was never cut off in consciousness from that of the immediately present moment' (1918, p.647). Baddeley (1993) portrays working memory as a conduit to consciousness that serves to bring together information in different modalities from perception and long-term memory, enabling us to imagine novel solutions to problems of evolutionary significance. For example, he suggests that a vivid image of a hunting ground, which included locations where food was found before and locations where danger lurked, would have evolutionary significance as a tool for predicting events and planning action. Working memory thus presents one solution to the binding problem (see Chapter 5, Section 2.3.4), the problem of creating a coherent, unified conscious experience from disparate sensory inputs. (Note though that the binding problem also pertains at lower levels of cognition; we also need to bind together the results of independent shape, colour, motion and location processes, for example.) Baddeley (2000) proposed a new component to the working memory model, called the episodic buffer, as a temporary store for bound information and as an interface between working memory, long-term memory and consciousness. However, the revised model does not specify whether information is conscious by virtue of being stored in the episodic buffer or whether it is conscious only when acted upon by central executive processes. Nonetheless, the wealth of evidence that working memory is involved in conscious cognition, in problem solving and mental imagery for example, suggests that working memory must actually be a cognitive correlate of consciousness.

The hypothetical central executive (see Chapter 5, Section 2.1) of working memory seems particularly closely correlated with consciousness, playing a key role in conscious, strategic activities such as retrieval of information from long-term memory, selective attention and so on (Baddeley, 1996). Baddeley (1986) used Norman and Shallice's (1986) cognitive model of contention scheduling and a supervisory attentional system (SAS) as a model of the central executive. Norman and Shallice's model aimed to explain action selection. They hypothesized that routine responses are selected by a relatively automatic process called contention scheduling, essentially the selection of habitual action schemata by virtue of their high activation level and ability to inhibit competing schemata. Changes in behaviour are effected by an SAS system that increases the activation of a non-habitual action schema so that it 'wins' in the contention scheduling process. The SAS thus serves as an error-correcting mechanism and as the basis for conscious behavioural control, allowing us to respond appropriately in novel situations. Errors in behaviour, such as everyday action slips (e.g. adding milk from habit when intending to make a cup of black coffee) and perseverative behaviours following frontal brain injury (i.e. persisting with an established response when altered conditions mean a new response is needed) are explained as failures of the SAS. Baddeley's adoption of the SAS as a model of the central executive extended its remit from the conscious control of action to the conscious control of cognition generally. However, both models, the SAS and the central executive, are subject to the criticism of postulating little more than a 'homunculus', a little person in the head that tells us which action to do or which memory to retrieve.

Dennett (1991) refers to the homunculus problem as the problem of the Cartesian theatre: it arises from the assumption that there is a cognitive or neuroanatomical module that 'does' consciousness, a location in the brain where consciousness occurs. Dennett's **multiple drafts** theory of consciousness offers a way out of this problem. Dennett argues that it is misleading to think of consciousness as something that suddenly happens, in the sense that stimulus processing works its way up from low-level sensory processes to higher-level cognitive processes and somewhere along the way our representation of the stimulus suddenly enters consciousness. In Dennett's theory, stimuli are not processed and then sent to a consciousness module, they are just processed. Which of many parallel streams of processing we become aware of, and how we experience them, depends on how and when the system is 'probed' by tasks that require particular responses.

Whereas Baddeley argues that working memory is necessary for consciousness, Baars (2002) argues that consciousness is necessary for working memory. All elements of 'active working memory', such as subvocal rehearsal and visual imagery, are conscious. Baars describes consciousness as a **global workspace**, a means of bringing together the products of processing from widely distributed modules. This bringing together – of inner speech, mental imagery, strategic recall, etc. – is necessary for working memory to function. Voluntary control of behaviour is also dependent on consciousness, requiring conscious goals and conscious perception of the effects of our actions. Thus we can learn from our mistakes or avoid emotions biasing our behaviour because our behavioural control processes have access to our knowledge of past mistakes or the causes of our mood swings.

Baars (1997) uses the analogy of a theatre. The unconscious processes of syntax analysis, visual boundary analysis, semantic processing, etc. are the stagehands working behind the scenes in the theatre of consciousness. Although there are actors on the stage, we only see the actor currently performing in the spotlight. Working memory forms the stage of consciousness, representations in working memory are the actors on the stage. Actors only step into the spotlight when chosen by the stage director – likewise the contents of working memory have the potential to become conscious but usually do not do so unless selected by the central executive. Once in the spotlight, the actor can be seen by everyone else: once a representation becomes conscious, it is accessible to other cognitive processes. Thus, consciousness overcomes some of the modularity of mind, enabling us to talk about our ideas, express our feelings, use remembered information to solve problems, and so on.

Baars (2002) draws on many recent neuroscience studies to support his theory. The essence of these findings is that unconscious processing of stimuli activates localized brain regions whereas conscious processing of the same stimuli activates widely distributed brain regions. For example, an fMRI study by Dehaene et al. (2001) showed that processing of masked visual words was associated with activation in early visual cortex whereas processing of visible, unmasked words was also associated with activation in parietal and prefrontal cortex. However, the finding by Zeki and ffytche (1998), of increased but still localized activation with conscious perception, seems to contradict Baars's theory (see Section 2.3). Thus it appears that consciousness is often but not always associated with global brain activity.

Summary of Section 4

- Working memory is closely allied to consciousness, providing a way of binding together information from perception and long-term memory to create conscious, multi-modal representations.
- Although working memory is a cognitive correlate of consciousness, the relationship between working memory and consciousness is unclear. Baars (1997) suggested that working memory serves to select the information that will become conscious. More recently, he has argued that consciousness is necessary for working memory (Baars, 2002).

- Baars sees consciousness as a global workspace, enabling cognitive modules to share information. 'Global access' to conscious information is consistent with findings of widespread brain activity when participants are aware of a stimulus, contrasted with more localized activity when they are unaware of it.

5   Conclusion: what can cognitive psychology tell us about consciousness?

Cognitive psychology has helped to generate hypotheses about the functions of consciousness. For example, studies of errorless learning and of priming have suggested that consciousness helps us control our behaviour by avoiding repetitions of our mistakes and suppressing emotional, rather than rational, responses. However, although consciousness is associated with behavioural control, we have no evidence that consciousness causes behavioural control. Similarly, we have seen that consciousness is associated with limited resource systems like working memory and selective attention, but we do not know whether consciousness plays a causal role in remembering or attending. Thus cognitive psychology has helped us to discover the cognitive correlates of consciousness – that is, those cognitive processes that are always accompanied by consciousness. But a correlation only tells us that two things are related, not that one causes the other. This problem is exemplified by the debate outlined in Section 4 about whether working memory is necessary for consciousness or vice versa. Hardcastle (2000) discusses this problem of correlational data in relation to the search for the neural correlates of consciousness. She argues that there will be many correlates of consciousness, but to explain consciousness effectively we must identify the 'proximal cause', the correlate that is the most important for consciousness. She uses the example of depression: is Fred depressed because he has received bad news or because the level of noradrenaline in his brain has dropped? If people are more likely to become depressed as the result of neurotransmitter changes than as the result of hearing bad news, then neurotransmitter levels are the more important correlate of depression. Hardcastle suggests that it is too early to be able to say which of the many correlates identified so far is the proximal cause of consciousness. Indeed, it is not even clear whether the answer will lie with those who seek to reduce consciousness to particular brain modules or individual neural events, or with those who argue for a dynamic systems approach, who would suggest that consciousness emerges from complex and global interactions of brain processes. In the meantime, cognitive psychology provides us with useful techniques for analysing and researching consciousness. At least, it provides possible solutions to the easy problems of consciousness – attention, recollection, voluntary action and so forth. The problem of why consciousness feels the way it does remains a very hard problem.

Now that you have read this chapter you can reinforce and extend your learning by reading an original journal article associated with it, available online from the DD303 website. Remember, these are original journal articles, so the style is different from this textbook, and don't be too concerned if you can't follow every detail.

Further reading

Baars, B. (1988) *A Cognitive Theory of Consciousness*, New York, Cambridge University Press, and Baars, B. (1997) *In the Theater of Consciousness: The Workspace of the Mind*, New York, Oxford University Press. These books explain Baars's global workspace theory of consciousness.

Blackmore, S. (2001) 'Consciousness', *The Psychologist*, vol.14, no.10, pp.522–5. A succinct overview of interesting issues.

Blackmore, S. (2004) *Consciousness: An Introduction*, Oxford, Oxford University Press. A comprehensive and accessible introduction to philosophical and empirical issues in consciousness studies. Includes interesting practical exercises to help you think about key problems.

Metzinger. T. (ed.) (2000) *Neural Correlates of Consciousness*, Cambridge, MA, MIT Press. An excellent collection of original chapters by leading consciousness researchers. Particularly recommended are the chapters by Hardcastle and ffytche.

Young, A.W. and Block, N. (1996) 'Consciousness', in Bruce, V. (ed.) *Unsolved Mysteries of the Mind*, Hove, Erlbaum. Useful discussion of access and phenomenal consciousness and of what consciousness researchers can learn from neuropsychology.

References

Andrade, J. (1995) 'Learning during anaesthesia: a review', *British Journal of Psychology*, vol.86, no.4, pp.479–506.

Atkinson, R.C. and Shiffrin, R.M. (1968) 'Human memory: a proposed system and control processes', in Spence, K.W. and Spence, J.D. (eds) *The Psychology of Learning and Motivation* (vol.2), New York, Academic Press.

Baars, B.J. (1988) *A Cognitive Theory of Consciousness*, New York, Cambridge University Press.

Baars, B.J. (1997) *In the Theater of Consciousness: The Workspace of the Mind*, New York, Oxford University Press.

Baars, B.J. (2002) 'The conscious access hypothesis: origins and recent evidence', *Trends in Cognitive Sciences*, vol.6, no.1, p.47.

Baddeley, A.D. (1986) *Working Memory*, Oxford, Oxford University Press.

Baddeley, A.D. (1990) *Human Memory: Theory and Practice*, Hove, Lawrence Erlbaum Associates.

Baddeley, A.D. (1993) 'Working memory and conscious awareness', in Collins, A.F., Gathercole, S.E., Conway, M.A. and Morris, P.E. (eds) *Theories of Memory*, Hove, Lawrence Erlbaum Associates.

Baddeley, A.D. (1996) 'Exploring the central executive', *Quarterly Journal of Experimental Psychology*, vol.49, pp.5–28.

Baddeley, A.D. (2000) 'The episodic buffer: a new component of working memory?', *Trends in Cognitive Science*, vol.4, no.11, pp.417–23.

Baddeley, A.D., Emslie, H., Kolodny, J. and Duncan, J. (1998) 'Random generation and the executive control of working memory', *Quarterly Journal of Experimental Psychology*, vol.51A, no.4, pp.819–52.

Baddeley, A.D. and Wilson, B.A. (1994) 'When implicit learning fails: amnesia and the problem of error elimination', *Neuropsychologia*, vol.32, pp.53–68.

Banks, W.P. (1993) 'Problems in the scientific pursuit of consciousness', *Consciousness and Cognition*, vol.2, no.4, pp.255–63.

Bargh, J.A., Chen, M. and Burrows, L. (1996) 'Automaticity of social behavior: direct effects of trait construct and stereotype activation on action', *Journal of Personality and Social Psychology*, vol.71, pp.230–44.

Block, N. (1995) 'On a confusion of a function of consciousness', *Behavioral and Brain Sciences*, vol.18, no.2, pp.227–87.

Chalmers, D. (1996) *The Conscious Mind*, Oxford, Oxford University Press.

Deeprose, C., Andrade, J., Varma, S. and Edwards, N. (2004) 'Unconscious learning during surgery with propofol anaesthesia', *British Journal of Anaesthesia*, vol.92, pp.171–7.

Dehaene, S., Naccache, L., Cohen, L., Bihan, D.L., Mangin, J-F., Poline, J-B. and Rivière, D. (2001) 'Cerebral mechanisms of word masking and unconscious repetition priming', *Nature Neuroscience*, vol.4, pp.752–8.

Dennett, D. (1991) *Consciousness Explained*, Boston, MA, Little, Brown & Co.

Duensing, S. and Miller, B. (1979) 'The Cheshire Cat effect', *Perception*, vol.8, pp.269–73.

Eich, E. (1984) 'Memory for unattended events: remembering with and without awareness', *Memory and Cognition*, vol.12, pp.105–11.

ffytche, D. (2000) 'Imaging conscious vision', in Metzinger, T. (ed.).

Gomez, R.L. (1997) 'Transfer and complexity in artificial grammar learning', *Cognitive Psychology*, vol.33, no.2, pp.154–207.

Hardcastle, V.G. (2000) 'How to understand the N in NCC', in Metzinger, T. (ed.).

Jacoby, L.L., Woloshyn, V. and Kelley, C. (1989) 'Becoming famous without being recognized: unconscious influences of memory produced by dividing attention', *Journal of Experimental Psychology: General*, vol.118, no.2, pp.115–25.

James, W. (1918, first published in 1890) *The Principles of Psychology*, vol.1, London, Macmillan and Co. Ltd.

Knowlton, B.J., Ramus, S.J. and Squire, L.R. (1992) 'Intact artificial grammar learning in amnesia: dissociation of classification learning and explicit memory for specific instances', *Psychological Science*, vol.3, no.3, pp.172–9.

Kunst-Wilson, W.R. and Zajonc, R.B. (1980) 'Affective discrimination of stimuli that cannot be recognized', *Science*, vol.207, pp.557–8.

Levine, J. (1983) 'Materialism and qualia: the explanatory gap', *Pacific Philosophical Quarterly*, vol.64, pp.354–61.

Lieberman, M.D. (2000) 'Intuition: a social cognitive neuroscience approach', *Psychological Bulletin*, vol.126, no.1, pp.109–37.

Logothetis, N.K. and Schall, J.D. (1989) 'Neuronal correlates of subjective visual perception', *Science*, vol.245, pp.761–3.

Marcel, A.J. (1983) 'Conscious and unconscious perception: experiments on visual masking and word recognition', *Cognitive Psychology*, vol.15, pp.197–237.

Marcel, A.J. (1988) 'Phenomenal experience and functionalism', in Marcel, A.J. and Bisiach, E. *Consciousness in Contemporary Science*, Oxford, Oxford University Press.

McElree, B. (2001) 'Working memory and focal attention', *Journal of Experimental Psychology: Learning, Memory, and Perception*, vol.27, no.3, pp.817–35.

Metzinger. T. (ed.) (2000) *Neural Correlates of Consciousness*, Cambridge, MA, MIT Press.

Meyer, D.E. and Schvaneveldt, R.W. (1971) 'Facilitation in recognizing pairs of words: evidence of a dependence between retrieval operations', *Journal of Experimental Psychology*, vol.90, pp.227–35.

Moray, N. (1959) 'Attention in dichotic listening: affective cues and the influence of instructions', *Quarterly Journal of Experimental Psychology*, vol.11, pp.56–60.

Murphy, S.T. and Zajonc, R.B. (1993) 'Affect, cognition, and awareness: affective priming with optimal and suboptimal stimulus exposures', *Journal of Personality and Social Psychology*, vol.64, pp.723–39.

Neumann, R. and Strack, F. (2000) '"Mood contagion" – the automatic transfer of mood between persons', *Journal of Personality and Social Psychology*, vol.79, no.2, pp.211–23.

Nissen, M.J. and Bullemer, P. (1987) 'Attentional requirements of learning: evidence from performance measures', *Cognitive Psychology*, vol.19, pp.1–32.

Norman, D.A and Shallice, T. (1986) 'Attention to action: willed and automatic control of behavior', in Davidson, R.J., Schwartz, G.E. and Shapiro, D. (eds) *Consciousness and Self-regulation*, New York, Plenum.

Reber, A.S. (1967) 'Implicit learning of artificial grammars', *Journal of Verbal Learning and Verbal Behavior*, vol.6, pp.855–63.

Schneider, W. and Shiffrin, R.M. (1977) 'Controlled and automatic human information processing: 1. Detection, search, and attention', *Psychological Review*, vol.84, pp.1–66.

Shanks, D.R. and St John, M.F. (1994) 'Characteristics of dissociable human learning systems', *Behavioural and Brain Sciences*, vol.17, no.3, pp.367–95.

Squire, L.R. and McKee, R. (1992) 'Influence of prior events on cognitive judgments in amnesia', *Journal of Experimental Psychology: Learning, Memory, and Cognition*, vol.18, no.1, pp.106–15.

Zajonc, R.B. (1980) 'Feeling and thinking: preferences need no inferences', *American Psychologist*, vol.35, pp.151–75.

Zeki, S. and ffytche, D.H. (1998) 'The Riddoch syndrome: insights into the neurobiology of conscious vision', *Brain*, vol.121, pp.25–45.

Applying cognitive psychology

Chapter 16

Hayley Ness

1 Introduction

Throughout this textbook you have been introduced to key theories and debates in many interesting areas of cognitive psychology. The questions that the theories and research pose are fascinating. For example, how do we recognize people that we are familiar with? Is it possible to think without language? While research has tended to concentrate on cognitive processing, it is important to remember that cognition does not occur in isolation. Cognitive processing not only changes and develops with age; we also process information in different ways depending on the context we are in. The aim of this chapter is to explore how some of the theories you have looked at earlier in this book have been 'applied' in a number of differing ways. In doing so, it is hoped that you will see links not only between different types of cognitive processing (e.g. perception, memory, attention, etc.) but also across different areas of psychology (e.g. social, developmental and cognitive neuroscience among others). As cognitive psychology has many applications in almost every area of daily life, it is beyond the scope of this chapter to deal with all of them. Therefore we will concentrate on two main areas: (a) memory and the law; and (b) intelligence. While links will be made to the material in this book as well as to other areas of psychology, it is hoped that the issues here will stimulate you to make connections of your own.

2 Memory and the law

2.1 Eye-witness identification

Psychology can learn a great deal from remarkable events. Being a witness to a crime is one such remarkable event. It is also an extremely important event, as the evidence that is provided (the witness's memory of the person or the event) may be used as evidence. As such, it is extremely important that psychologists understand the factors that can impact on the accuracy of cognitive processes and subsequent evidence. One way to do this is to apply existing theoretical and research knowledge. For **eye-witness identification**, theories and research that explain how faces are perceived and recognized are particularly important. In Chapter 4 you were introduced to the Bruce and Young (1986) and IAC models of face recognition (Burton *et al.*, 1990). While these models explain the processes involved in recognizing people that we know well, they can also highlight some of the difficulties involved in eye-witness identification – a situation where the witness is asked to recognise someone they may have seen only once before. For example, at the structural encoding stage of the Bruce and Young model there are two different forms of description: (a) view-centred or pictorial; and (b) expression-independent

or structural. When we have seen a face only once it will be described pictorially; that is, information about the face, as well as about the lighting, clothing and viewpoint, etc., will be specific to that particular instance in time. Furthermore, as it is likely that the witness will have seen the perpetrator only once, for a brief period, an eye-witness's memory of a face will be dominated by the information that takes up most of the image – the hair and face shape. It's only when we see a face more than once, in different contexts and viewpoints, that we start to build up a structural description that allows us to recognize people that we know despite changes in lighting, clothing and hairstyle, etc. (see Chapter 4).

So, when an eye-witness is asked to undertake any form of identification task, their memory of the perpetrator's face will be dominated by the external features (hair and face shape). It will also contain information that is specific to the scene of the crime. Is this necessarily problematic? Encoding specificity theory (e.g. Tulving, 1983; see Chapter 6) suggests that it is. It states that memory will be more accurate if the cues that were available at encoding more accurately match the cues at retrieval. As an eye-witness will be asked to identify the perpetrator in a different location (i.e. a police station) where the context and lighting will be different, this suggests that it will be extremely difficult for an eye-witness to identify the perpetrator accurately. However, we can apply the principles of encoding specificity to help improve the accuracy of the identification process by matching as many of the other cues as possible.

2.2   Eye-witness identification from line-ups

Wells (1978) categorized the different variables that can impact on the accuracy of eye-witness identification from line-ups (identity parades). He initially defined two main variables: estimator and system variables. Wells described **estimator**

variables as factors that impact on accuracy but cannot be controlled for. These are variables that occur at encoding, such as the stress of the crime and viewing distance. While they cannot be controlled for, it is important to understand how these variables impact on identification, so that the effect on accuracy can be estimated. In contrast, **system variables** can be controlled directly. These refer to procedural issues, such as how the information is obtained from the witness. Later, Wells and Olson (2001) added two further categories: suspect-bias and general impairment variables. Suspect-bias variables relate directly to the composition of line-ups: for example, how the line-up is constructed and how the other members of the line-up are chosen. General impairment variables include own-race bias (e.g. Meissner and Brigham, 2001) and own-age bias (e.g. Anastasi and Rhodes, 2006), where it has been demonstrated that we are less accurate at recognizing and identifying faces that are of a different race or age range to our own.

While it is extremely important to understand the impact of estimator and general impairment variables, line-up researchers tend to focus on the system variables – the procedural factors that can directly impact on accuracy. The aim of this research is not only to find the most effective identification procedures; it is also to provide policy guidelines and recommendations to ensure that the most effective procedures are adhered to by all. In England and Wales, psychological research on eye-witness identification has had a huge impact on police procedure, and identification procedures for line-ups have been regulated by the Police and Criminal Evidence Act (PACE) since 1984. These guidelines cover the use of 'live' identification line-ups, video line-ups and photographs, as well as other means of identification such as fingerprints, DNA and shoe impressions.

So, what are the guidelines for conducting line-ups? The recommendations outlined in PACE for 'live' line-ups state that 'The suspect may select their own position in the line' (Code D, p.181) and that 'The identification parade shall consist of at least eight people (in addition to the suspect) who, so far as possible, resemble the suspect in age, height, general appearance and position in life' (Code D, p.180). This description doesn't specify how the line-up members should be presented. A simultaneous line-up, where everyone stands in a line and the witness sees everyone at the same time, is the procedure most commonly seen on films and television programmes. The other method of presenting a line-up is called a sequential line-up. This is where the witness views each person one at a time.

2.3   Simultaneous versus sequential line-ups

So, which method is best? This question has been hotly debated in the literature and a great deal of research has examined the efficacy of both **simultaneous and sequential line-ups**. One of the most effective ways of summarizing research findings is to perform a meta-analysis on the data. A meta-analysis essentially examines as many research articles as possible on a particular topic and draws overall conclusions on the patterns that emerge. Steblay *et al.* (2001) conducted such a meta-analysis on the available line-up research (both published and unpublished). They reported that, overall, identifications using sequential line-ups were more accurate than those using simultaneous line-ups. This led Steblay *et al.* (2001) to conclude that sequential line-ups were more effective than simultaneous line-ups, and they termed this the 'sequential superiority effect'. More recently, other researchers have questioned this conclusion (McQuiston-Surrett *et al.*, 2006). McQuiston-Surrett *et al.* indicate that while the conclusion may be valid when the data are examined overall, different patterns emerge when the data are split.

What does it mean to split the data? Well, in a real-life situation, a witness is told that the perpetrator may or may not be in the line-up. As such it is important to examine what types of identification decision are made when (a) the perpetrator is in the line-up and (b) the perpetrator isn't in the line-up. In research articles these are called **target-present line-ups** and **target-absent line-ups**. A 'correct' decision in a target-absent line-up would be to say that the perpetrator was not there, and a 'correct' decision in a target-present line-up would obviously be to identify the perpetrator. While it is impossible to know if the actual perpetrator is in the line-up in a real-life situation, it is quite straightforward to do in an experimental situation. One of the main reasons why it is important to examine this is because it highlights the different decision-making strategies that are used. It also helps to uncover which line-up method may produce the most accurate identification decision. By splitting the data, McQuiston-Surrett *et al.* demonstrated that identification decisions were more accurate for sequential line-ups only when the perpetrator wasn't there. This means that sequential line-ups appear to reduce the likelihood that an innocent person will be identified. However, it also means that the likelihood of identifying the actual perpetrator when he/she is in the line-up doesn't increase. In contrast, when the perpetrator was in the line-up, the number of correct identifications was higher using simultaneous line-ups. So, when the line-up members are seen one at a time, the likelihood of identifying an innocent person is reduced; however, when the line-up members are seen all together in a line, the likelihood of identifying the actual perpetrator increases. This clearly shows that the two different types of line-up appear to be effective in different ways.

McQuiston-Surrett *et al.* (2006) conducted a full review of the literature. Their results indicate that the debate in the literature regarding the efficacy of sequential vs simultaneous line-ups is highly complex owing to differences in methodology. This is because many research articles adopt slightly different methods to examine this issue and it may be these differences that are influencing identification responses. The authors state that the sequential line-up 'advantage may vary as a function of study methodology in that the effect emerges with some study designs but not with others' (pp.160–1). This problem isn't specific to line-up research. In fact it is a general problem that affects the application of research to real-life issues.

2.4   Decision making in line-ups

Chapter 12 outlines the cognitive theories of decision making, but how does decision making relate to line-ups? Well, decision making is key to line-up identification and much of the debate centres around this issue. When a witness is presented with a line-up they are told that the person they saw commit the crime may or may not be in the line-up. This is to ensure that the eye-witness uses only their memory to make their identification decision and is not influenced by the wording of the instructions provided (a system variable). These are standardized, non-biased instructions that are based on a great deal of psychological research and governed by PACE in England and Wales. Despite these instructions, witnesses still appear to make identification decisions differently, depending on how the line-ups are presented.

So, much of the debate surrounding simultaneous and sequential line-ups centres on how the different modes of presentation alter the ways an eye-witness makes an identification decision.

When a witness is shown a simultaneous line-up, it is thought that they adopt a relative decision-making strategy, by comparing their memory of the perpetrator with each member of the line-up and choosing the person that looks most like them. This means that an innocent person may be chosen from the line-up because they look most like the perpetrator and not because they actually are the perpetrator. This relative decision-making strategy has therefore led researchers to criticize the use of simultaneous line-ups (e.g. Kneller *et al.*, 2001). One reason why this may occur is that even though eye-witnesses are told that the perpetrator may not be in the line-up, the situational context of being asked to attend a line-up may lead to an expectation that the perpetrator is there. Memon *et al.* (2003) suggest that the **relative decision-making strategy** seen with simultaneous line-ups might be influenced by this expectation on the part of the witness. In contrast, when a sequential line-up is adopted, the eye-witness sees each person in the line-up individually. This means that the witness cannot compare the line-up members with each other. Instead, the witness is required to make what is called an **absolute decision** by matching the face in the line-up to their memory of the perpetrator. While there may still be an expectation on the part of the witness that the perpetrator will be in the line-up, using an absolute decision-making strategy with either 'live' or video line-ups (see Box 16.1) may help to reduce the effect of this.

16.1

Video line-ups

Conducting 'live' line-ups is costly and time-consuming (Pike *et al.*, 2002). It is very time-consuming to find volunteers that resemble the suspect on a number of key factors (e.g. age, race, height, hair colour, etc.). Each volunteer is also paid, so 'live' line-ups can be very costly. One way of reducing cost is to use video line-ups. While reducing costs is appealing, the most important factor is whether or not video line-ups are effective. So are they? Valentine and Heaton (1999) examined this by comparing 'live' line-up data from West Yorkshire Police with video line-ups conducted using the Video Identification Parade Electronic Recording (VIPER) system, developed by West Yorkshire Police. The VIPER procedure consists of showing nine-person line-ups. The head and shoulders of each person are shown and the person is seen turning from side to side so that all views of the face are visible. VIPER also contains a database of volunteers, so the process of matching the suspect to volunteers on key criteria becomes much easier. Importantly, it was found that the video line-ups were less biased and fairer than the 'live' line-ups. To examine further whether video line-ups were fair, Valentine *et al.* (2003) examined line-ups that contained volunteers of different ethnic origins (White European and African–Caribbean). In 'live' line-ups there is often difficulty in obtaining volunteers from ethnic minority backgrounds, which can lead to biased line-ups. However, no such bias was reported here. Valentine *et al.*

→

found that there was no difference in fairness for each line-up. Havard and Memon (2009) also examined video identification using the VIPER system. They used both younger (18- to 35-year-old) and older (61- to 83-year-old) adults and manipulated the age of the target face (26 years and 67 years). It was found that in general the younger adults were better at identifying the mock offenders in the line-ups than the older adults. In particular, the older adults were poor when the 'offender' wasn't in the line-up, saying that he was there 70 per cent of the time, compared with 37 per cent for the younger adults. An own-age effect was also found for the younger adults, so they were better at identifying the younger mock offender than the older one. This supports research on the own-age effect in face recognition (e.g. Anastasi and Rhodes, 2006). Interestingly, no own-age effect was found for the older adults. The authors suggest that these results support research which highlights age-related decline in memory. Further research on video identification (Havard et al., 2009) examined children's identification abilities using the VIPER system. Two groups of children aged 7–9 years and 13–15 years were asked to make identifications using either photographs or the VIPER system. It was found that the younger children were as good as the adolescents at making identifications from both video and photographs. It was also found that for the teenagers, using video reduced the number of false identifications. As a result of the large amount of research which has demonstrated the effectiveness of video line-ups, the PACE guidelines have been updated (Section 3.14, Code D) and it is now recommended that a video line-up should be offered first.

2.5 Stress

The impact of **stress** on eye-witness memory would fall under the heading of an estimator variable (Wells, 1978). This is because in a real-life situation it is impossible to control the level of stress experienced by an eye-witness. However, it is important to examine the role that stress plays because in a real-life situation an eye-witness to a crime may be under considerable stress, particularly if the crime is violent. As such, researchers have been studying the impact of stress on both identification and the ability to recall the details of a crime. Unfortunately, while researchers have been examining this area for 30 years, there is still no clear answer and much debate (Deffenbacher et al., 2004).

The **Yerkes–Dodson law** (1908) (see Chapter 14, Section 3.2) indicated that arousal could enhance memory, but that there was an optimal point. If arousal increased beyond this point then memory performance would be negatively affected. This suggests that if an eye-witness experiences stress that falls below the optimal point in the Yerkes–Dodson law, then memory may be enhanced (for more information see the review by Deffenbacher, 1983). Christianson (1992), however, reviewed the literature on stress and memory and argued that the Yerkes–Dodson law was an inadequate measure of emotional stress. He also stated that there was little evidence to support the idea that stress impacted negatively on eye-witness memory. To address this, Deffenbacher (1994) developed a new three-dimensional model containing a cognitive aspect, in order to assess the multidimensional impact of stress on memory. The model contained two variables to predict memory performance: (a) 'cognitive anxiety' or worry; and (b) 'physiological activation'. According to the model, when worry (or cognitive anxiety) is high, this leads to increases in the physiological stress response. These increases initially lead to an increase in memory performance, until the physiological response reaches a point where the activation is so high that there will be a decline in memory performance. This is very similar to Yerkes–Dodson but it contains that all-important cognitive element.

Deffenbacher *et al.* (2004) conducted a meta-analysis on the **effects of high stress on eye-witness memory**. Overall, they reported that stress had a negative impact on identification and recall of the event details. In particular, they found that identification from line-ups was impaired when stress levels were high. However, this impairment was mediated by the type of line-up that was used. When the target was in the line-up, stress reduced the number of times that the target was identified correctly. However, when the target was not in the line-up, stress did not seem to impact negatively on identification decisions. That is, participants were not more likely to identify an innocent person under stress. Interestingly, it was also found that the effect of stress on memory was more than 3 times greater for more ecologically valid studies compared with laboratory-based research.

One ecologically valid study was conducted by Valentine and Mesout (2009). The experiment took place in the London Dungeon and participants were required to wear a wireless heart monitor while they walked through the dungeon. Valentine and Mesout (2009) termed the person that the participants would later be asked to identify as the 'scary person' (p.154). This is because the 'scary person' was wearing stage make-up and a black cloak, and walked in front of each participant, preventing them from walking past, in the Horror Labyrinth. An anxiety questionnaire was also used. After the participants had finished their tour of the London Dungeon, they were informed of the nature of the experiment. Those participants who gave consent were initially asked to recall details of the 'scary person'. They then participated in an identification task, where they were presented with a nine-person line-up and told that the person they saw might or might not be present. The foils in the line-up consisted of other actors from the London Dungeon who resembled the target (e.g. same sex, similar age, similar clothing and make-up). The results indicated that the experiment did increase arousal, as their heart rates were elevated and they scored highly on the anxiety questionnaire. The participants who experienced the greatest amount of arousal recalled fewer correct details of the 'scary person'. Anxiety also impaired identification. For those participants who scored above average on the anxiety scale, only 17 per cent correctly identified the 'scary person', whereas 75 per cent of participants who scored below average correctly identified the 'scary person'.

These results are similar to those obtained by Morgan *et al.* (2004). This US study used an intensely stressful environment – a military survival training camp – to study the impact on eye-witness memory. During the camp 550 participants (military personnel) underwent two forms of interrogation (high- and low-stress). All participants experienced both the high- and low-stress interrogations. These were separated by 4 hours and counterbalanced to reduce order effects. Prior to the interrogations, they underwent 48 hours of food and sleep deprivation. Twenty-four hours after the interrogations, the participants were asked to identify their interrogator from both the high- and low-stress interrogations. The type of identification was manipulated (a 'live' simultaneous line-up, a simultaneous photo spread and sequentially presented photographs). The results were interesting and it was found that while around half of the participants were better at identifying the interrogator in the low-stress, compared with the high-stress, interrogation, many participants performed equally well, with a small number of participants performing better after the high-stress situation. The sequential photo presentation method produced the most accurate results.

2.6   Impact of misleading information

A great deal of research has demonstrated that **misleading information** can greatly impact on the accuracy of both eye-witness identification and recall of the event. For example, Loftus *et al.* (1978) demonstrated that the participants in their experiment could not discriminate between the information they had originally seen and the misleading information that the experimenters had given them. Changing a single verb in a sentence (Loftus and Palmer, 1974) and using presuppositions (Loftus, 1975) have also been shown to influence how participants respond to questions. Misleading information also influences memory for faces (Loftus and Greene, 1980), and more recent research has discovered that people can falsely remember rich episodic memories. For example, Loftus and Pickrell (1995) suggested to participants that when they were 5 years old they had been lost in a shopping mall and had to be rescued. This incident was false but the researchers found that almost a quarter of the participants later reported details about the incident. This finding, that participants can be misled into falsely reporting childhood incidents that did not occur, has also been found by other researchers using similar methods (e.g. Heaps and Nash, 2001).

2.7   Cognitive explanations for the misinformation effect

So, why are people susceptible to misleading information? Researchers have noted several factors that influence susceptibility to misleading information. For example, if there is an increased delay between the witnessed event and exposure to misleading information, the effect is larger (Loftus, 2005). Furthermore, people who distrust their own memories are more likely to accept misinformation than people who feel that their memories are fairly accurate (van Bergen *et al.*, 2009). Associations have also been found between misinformation acceptance and empathy, introversion and imagery ability (Loftus, 2005).

What about memory? Loftus *et al.* (1978) hypothesized that misleading information displaces or transforms the original memory representation. This assumes that memory for the original event is stored as an integrated whole. When new information is received, it is integrated or blended into the previously formed memory. If the new information is inconsistent with some aspect of the original event, the earlier memory may be 'updated' in a way that alters the representation of the original information.

The essence of this hypothesis is that it assumes that individuals would have remembered the original event accurately, had their memory not been 'interfered with' by misleading information. However, Loftus's original interpretation of the eye-witness testimony data was not uncontroversial. Indeed, it initiated an upsurge of debate and experimentation on the nature and causes of the **misinformation effect**.

The controversy surrounding the nature and causes of misinformation effects stemmed largely from a series of experiments conducted by McCloskey and Zaragoza (1985). On the basis of their findings, they argued that there was no loss or distortion of the initially encoded events. Instead, they claimed that misleading post-event information had no effect on the original memory, but simply biased the response; that is, witnesses who are misled remember both the original information and the misleading information. Instead of reporting the original information they follow the suggested information that is presented by the experimenter.

In order to examine whether memory traces were altered by misleading post-event information, Chandler *et al.* (2001) eliminated response-bias and social factors. They posited that if similar (but misleading) post-event information does alter a memory trace permanently, then the effect should still be found after a retention interval. However, the authors reported that while interference effects were found when memory was tested immediately, these effects disappeared over time. This therefore provides no evidence that post-event information permanently alters memory traces.

2.7.1   Source monitoring

Source monitoring accounts have also been put forward to explain the misinformation effect (Johnson *et al.*, 1993). Source monitoring errors can occur when a witness is not able to distinguish between what they have actually perceived and what they have only heard or imagined. This means that a witness may believe that they have witnessed something, when in actual fact they read or heard about it. A core idea within the source monitoring framework is that memories do not have a label specifying the source. Instead, sources are attributed during remembering through a decision process, which usually occurs unconsciously.

The source monitoring framework addresses how memories from different sources are differentiated, and there are three key elements:

*   **Reality monitoring** refers to the ability to discriminate between internally generated memories and externally acquired information.

*   **External source monitoring** refers to discrimination between externally derived sources.

*   **Internal source monitoring** refers to the ability to discriminate between different internally generated sources (Johnson *et al.*, 1993).

One important aspect of source monitoring is that the original memories remain intact and separated but it is the ability to attribute the correct source that is impaired (Reyna and Lloyd, 1997). It is suggested that the factors that affect source attribution decisions are imagery, delay, cognitive development, contextual information, background knowledge, judgement bias and current goals (Reyna and Lloyd, 1997). This may lead a witness to construct a false account of the incident by combining the actual memory with the content of suggestions provided during the process of cross-examination (Loftus, 1997).

2.7.2 Reconstructive memory

ACTIVITY 16.1

Consider this statement: 'A loud screeching sound could be heard shortly after the man ran out of the building clutching a bag full of £20 notes.'

Take a few moments to write down what this sentence might be describing. Write down as much additional information as you need.

COMMENT

What did you write down? Did you say that it was a bank robbery or something else? In order to interpret this sentence you need to use a great deal of pre-existing knowledge. A man running out of a building clutching money could be interpreted as someone who has just been to a bank to withdraw money and is in a rush. However, the fact that the money was in a bag suggests a potential robbery. If it was a robbery, was it a bank or a shop robbery? No information is given about the building, but the fact that he had a bag that contained only £20 notes suggests that it might have been a bank. In addition, the screeching sound could be the sound of the get-away car outside. If we accept that it was a bank, then there must have been other people in the bank – customers and bank tellers. This means that there must have been eye-witnesses. What did the robber do? Rob the bank teller? What did he say? Did he shout? Did he have a gun? Did he have an accomplice? Were customers lying on the ground? As very little information is described, we need to use additional information to infer what might have happened.

Scripts and schemas help us to interpret and remember information. We have different types of script for almost every situation. For example, if I say that I went to a restaurant last night, I don't need to tell you that I entered the restaurant, waited to be seated, looked at the menu and ordered a meal, etc. This is because you will already have a detailed script of the events. Additionally, schemas are knowledge structures that help us to understand information. When we encounter new and incomplete information (such as the sentence above), we use schematic knowledge to 'fill in the blanks'. So if you interpreted the sentence as a bank robbery, all of your associated knowledge about bank robberies (hopefully what you've seen on television and not actually experienced!) would have been activated. As a result you would be more likely to retrieve it. How much schematic knowledge did you use when interpreting the sentence? Did you construct an elaborate story, or did you write only a few key details? As everyone has their own individual schemas, one of the main difficulties with eye-witness memory is that every eye-witness will interpret and remember both events and people differently.

Since Bartlett (1932) many researchers have documented that remembering is a reconstructive process. People do not retrieve a memory as a whole entity, but rather construct or create a memory using the information remaining in memory combined with other related knowledge, or schemata (Hyman and Pentland, 1996). Reconstruction has been demonstrated very clearly, not only in eye-witness memory research (e.g. Zaragoza and Lane, 1994) but also in material from word lists (Roediger and McDermott, 1995), short stories (Bartlett, 1932), songs (Hyman and Rubin, 1990) and personal experiences (Barclay and DeCooke, 1988).

Spiro (e.g. Spiro, 1980) suggested that **memory distortion** is most likely to occur when there are inconsistencies between different sources of information. When a witness is faced with misleading post-event information, they may call up schematic knowledge that is closely related to the false information. This may lead a witness to construct a false account of the incident at the time that the information is encountered and could also lead to a fairly enduring false recollection of the incident, as the information has been integrated into pre-existing schematic or background knowledge.

2.7.3   Misinformation and the social context

While there are many cognitive explanations for the misinformation effect and indeed a debate about what happens to the original memory, it is important to remember that memory doesn't occur in an isolated context. Indeed, memory is embedded within a social context. We perceive, encode, store and retrieve information in a social environment. As such, it is no surprise that social influences impact on what and how we remember information. For example, several researchers (e.g. Echterhoff et al., 2005) have examined the impact of credibility on the misinformation effect. They have found that when the credibility of the misinformation is undermined, the misinformation effect is weakened and sometimes eliminated. This goes against cognitive explanations of memory distortion and highlights the importance of social psychological theories in memory research.

The importance of social psychological explanation is also demonstrated in **memory conformity** studies. While eye-witnesses in the laboratory encounter misinformation via various experimental manipulations (narrative, questions, video, etc.), in a real-life situation an eye-witness may encounter misinformation socially via another eye-witness. Gabbert et al. (2004) examined the impact of co-witness misinformation by asking young (17- to 33-year-old) and older (58- to 80-year-old) participants to view a mock crime video. The participants then encountered misleading information either through discussion with a confederate, or in a written narrative. It was found that the misled group were less accurate than the control group. Furthermore, for both younger and older adults, misinformation encountered socially (via the confederate) was more misleading than misinformation encountered in the text. Gabbert et al. (2007) examined this further by asking pairs of participants to look at slightly different sets of pictures of the same event for the same length of time. Prior to discussion, one person was told that they had seen the pictures for either twice or half as long as their partner. It was found that the participants who believed that they had seen the pictures for half as long were significantly more likely to report information that had been obtained during the discussion; that is, information that they had not actually seen in the pictures.

Similar results have been reported by other researchers. Patterson and Kemp (2006) compared different methods of presenting misleading information (leading questions, media reports, indirect co-witness information and co-witness discussion). They found that the two co-witness conditions had the strongest effect: participants were more likely to report information when it was encountered via another witness. These results were supported by Itsukushima *et al.* (2006), who reported an increased misinformation effect for socially encountered misinformation compared with a written narrative. Patterson *et al.* (2009) also found that the co-witness effect did not diminish after participants had been warned that they might have encountered misleading information.

Garry *et al.* (2008) also examined **co-witness effects** and found that when participants conformed during the discussion, they reported the misleading information 85 per cent of the time. Interestingly, this indicates that 15 per cent of the time participants conformed during discussion but reverted to the correct answer at test. Garry *et al.* suggests that conformity may be more likely when information is not disputed. This supports Wright *et al.* (2005), who conducted three studies using both words and photographs and found that the co-witness effect was larger for unremembered items.

This research clearly shows the importance of social psychological factors in memory. Indeed, Gabbert *et al.* (2003) indicate that while cognitive explanations (e.g. memory distortion or source confusion) may help us to understand some aspects of the co-witness effect, additional social factors may also be important. In particular, they indicate the importance of conformity effects, which may be especially important as the misleading information is provided via a social (face-to-face) interaction. As such, both normative (need for social approval) and informational (desire to be accurate) influences might account for the misinformation effect in these circumstances.

2.8   Memory and the social context

Marsh (2007) highlights that the goal of memory tasks in the laboratory and in a social context are very different. In an experimental situation the goal is often to recall as much information as accurately as possible. So, the goal of recalling information is accuracy. However, Marsh suggests that if someone is 'retelling' an event in a social situation, distortions may occur.

Interestingly, Marsh and Tversky (2004) found that more exaggeration occurred when people retold amusing events, perhaps to exaggerate the humour of the situation and to entertain the listeners. However, when the goal was to give information, the retelling of the event often just contained the key information. So, Marsh (2007) argues that how much information is retold or recalled depends on the nature of the audience. This suggests that while remembering is a cognitive process, it is also a **social psychological process**; an interplay between the speaker and the audience (see Blank, 2009 for an excellent review on the interface between memory and social psychology).

2.9   The cognitive interview

Interviewing a witness is a social interaction. As such the interview process is subject to a whole host of social psychological factors such as normative and informational influence. Furthermore, research has clearly demonstrated that simple manipulations to the way a question is worded can impact on accuracy, and that encountering misleading information via another person produces the strongest effect, so it is vital that the interview process minimizes these effects.

One way to help to ensure that the most accurate information is obtained from a witness is to use the **cognitive interview** (Fisher and Geiselman, 1992). At the start of a cognitive interview, the interviewer builds rapport with the witness prior to the actual interview. The witness is then encouraged to freely recall as much information as possible. During the interview process, the witness is asked to mentally reinstate the context. That is, they are asked to mentally 'go back' to the scene of the crime and describe everything that they can see, hear, smell and touch. They are also asked to recall the information in different orders and from different perspectives.

This method of interviewing has its basis in both cognitive and social psychological research. The method of recalling information is based in particular on the **encoding specificity principle** (Tulving, 1983; see Chapter 6). This principle states that recall will be more accurate when the cues at encoding more accurately match the cues available at retrieval. As a witness will be asked to recall the details of the crime in a different location, the physical, environmental cues will be different. As such, asking a witness to mentally 'travel back' to the scene of the crime and to use multiple retrieval cues (sound, touch, etc.) helps to ensure that there is overlap between the encoding and retrieval environments. Furthermore, building rapport with a witness prior to the interview, and allowing the witness to direct the interview, helps to enhance communication and interaction during the interview process and to reduce the imbalance in power relationships between the interviewer and witness.

Is the cognitive interview effective? A great deal of research has compared the cognitive interview with 'standard' interviews. While the 'standard' interview often varies across different research studies, it has generally been found that the cognitive interview increases both the quality and the quantity of the information that is recalled (e.g. Stein and Memon, 2006). Some studies have reported a small increase in the amount of inaccurate information that is recalled. However, this may be due to the fact that more information is recalled. As the percentage of accurate information increases, so does the percentage of inaccurate information. The cognitive interview has also been shown to be effective with children (e.g. Holliday and Albon, 2004) and elderly people (Wright and Holliday, 2007) and has recently been modified (see Box 16.2).

16.2

The modified cognitive interview

While the cognitive interview is effective, research has demonstrated that police officers often don't fully use the different components of the cognitive interview process (e.g. Memon *et al.*, 1994). One of the reasons for this is that the process is very time-consuming. In order to remedy this, an alternative version of the cognitive interview has been developed (Dando *et al.*, 2009). In this version, instead of asking mock witnesses to mentally reinstate the context, they were asked to draw a sketch of the scene. In their evaluation of this **modified cognitive interview**, Dando *et al.* (2009) found that the interview procedure was quicker and produced just as much accurate detail as the standard cognitive interview. The authors suggest that the drawing aspect of the modified interview may be beneficial as the witness generates their own retrieval cues, without any interference from the interviewer.

2.10 Children as eye-witnesses

Goodman (2006) reviewed the literature on **children's eye-witness testimony** and abuse over four decades (1970s–2000s). She highlighted that while there was little empirical research in this area in the 1970s, research gained momentum after several high-profile cases in the 1980s. Much of the research focused on suggestibility and demonstrated that there were age differences in resistance to suggestibility (e.g. Goodman *et al.*, 1991). The interviewing conditions under which a child may be susceptible to suggestion were also investigated. This led to the development of the National Institute of Child Health and Human Development (NICHD) interviewing protocol with children (Lamb *et al.*, 2000) and a revision of the cognitive interview for use with children (e.g. McCauley and Fisher, 1995).

Research has found that while young children can recall information accurately (Hutcheson *et al.*, 1995), the amount that is recalled is often less than for adults (Deckle *et al.*, 1996) and there are developmental differences in the type of information that is recalled. In general, increases in age-related cognitive function mean that older children process and remember information more effectively than younger children (Gordon *et al.*, 2001). Gordon *et al.* highlight the **fuzzy trace model** of memory developed by Brainerd and Reyna (1990) to explain some aspects of these memory differences. This model suggests that there are multiple memory traces for each event or experience. These traces are represented on a continuum from a verbatim representation to a gist representation. Furthermore, gist representations are more enduring than verbatim ones, which are prone to decay. Gordon *et al.* (2001) suggest that pre-school children encode episodes as a verbatim representation, whereas older children encode both but are inclined to process a gist representation. As verbatim memory traces are more likely to decay than gist, then this may explain why young children (pre-school) recall less information than older children.

The issue of schema and reconstructive processes was discussed earlier with reference to the misinformation effect. Research has also highlighted the importance of pre-existing knowledge in children. For example, Myles-Worsley *et al.* (1986) found evidence over a 5-year period for reconstructive processes in children. They found that the children's memories for events were often combinations of the actual event and prior knowledge of what would normally happen in such circumstances. Knowledge gained after an event has also been shown to affect recall (e.g. Greenhoot, 2000). Importantly, Gordon *et al.* (2001) indicate that stereotyping can impact strongly on recall of an event. They suggest that if a child is told that 'their help is needed in keeping a bad person from hurting other children' (p.167), they may report information that is consistent with a 'bad person' stereotype.

2.11 Socioemotional influences on children's testimony

Emotional and social factors can also influence the accuracy of children's testimony. Bottoms *et al.* (2002) investigated reports that children gave after they had participated in an activity that they were told to keep a secret. Forty-eight 3- to 6-year-olds participated in the study with their mothers. In the study, half of the children were free to play with toys. However, for the other half of the children, while the experimenter told them not to play with the toys, their mothers encouraged them to. They were motivated to conceal their play because the experimenter had told them not to. After the play session, all of the children were interviewed. Half of the children received suggestive questions, while half received specific questions. The results indicated that the older children, who were motivated to conceal their play, withheld more information than the older children who were not given the manipulation. Interestingly, there was no effect of interview, so it was the motivation to conceal rather than the suggestive questions that impacted on the children's recall. For the younger children, the manipulation had no significant difference on recall.

Bottoms *et al.* indicate that older children are more influenced by social context and emotional demands than are younger children. They suggest that while older children may be able to provide more accurate reports, if what children are asked to describe is laden with negative emotional and social demands, as may be the case with family situations, then they may be more motivated to conceal and, thus, no more accurate than younger children (e.g. Goodman *et al.*, 1991).

2.12   Decision making in a jury context

During a trial jurors can often be presented with a huge amount of information, some of which can be very complex. So how do jurors make sense of this information and reach a verdict? Pennington and Hastie (1986) provide a three-stage **'story' model** which helps to describe how jurors understand and interpret the evidence. Stage 1 of the model is an active, interpretive stage, where individual jurors evaluate evidence and form probable 'stories' based both on the actual evidence and on pre-existing knowledge and expectation. In stage 2, jurors generate theories regarding the type of legal decision (verdict) they can make, based on their own understanding of the law and the judge's instructions. Finally, stage 3 is a matching process, where the 'best' story – the one that most adequately explains the evidence – is matched to the appropriate verdict.

While it is important to study decision making in a real jury context, it is against the law in the UK to ask jurors either about any information that relates to the trial, or about how they reached their decision. As such, most of the research on **jury decision making** uses 'mock' jurors and simulated crimes.

Such research (Smith, 1991) has examined how mock jurors make their final verdict decision. In order to reach a decision, jurors have to categorize the information. In Chapter 9, you were introduced to concepts and categories. There you will have learnt that there are two broad theoretical approaches: defining features and prototypes. It is easy to see how these theories apply to the categorization of an object, but how do they relate to juror decision making? At the end of a trial, the judge essentially outlines the 'defining features' of a particular category (e.g. burglary, assault, etc.) when instructing the jury. However, how do jurors categorize the information during the trial? And what impact do the judge's instructions have on the final verdict? Smith (1991) found that during a trial, mock jurors made decisions based on prototypical information regarding crime categories. This conceptual knowledge of crime categories was based on pre-existing knowledge and did not match the legal 'defining features' of the crimes, thus conflicting with the legal instruction given by the judge. Interestingly, the results also indicated that pre-existing knowledge was favoured over the judge's instructions; that is, the legal instructions did not alter the mock jurors' decisions. Further research has demonstrated that pre-existing knowledge influences how mock jurors interpret and understand the evidence. In particular, it has been found that mock jurors 'fill in the blanks' with typical information and that they are more susceptible to typical than untypical misinformation (Smith and Studebaker, 1996).

Interestingly, Tinsley (2000) indicates that jurors reach a decision not during the deliberation stage of a trial but during the trial, with each individual juror actively processing the information and fitting it into an appropriate knowledge framework or schema. This supports a vast body of memory literature stemming from Bartlett (1932) and, in particular, supports the Pennington and Hastie (1986) story model of decision making, which describes how each juror can organize and make sense of the information that is presented. As comprehension and 'sense making' is a reconstructive process that relies heavily on pre-existing knowledge and schemata, it is clear that inconsistencies and distortions will occur, particularly when a juror is faced with inconsistent evidence. One particular issue that impacts on comprehension of the evidence is the way in which it is presented (see Box 16.3).

16.3

Do jurors understand the evidence?

A Home Office report on juror perception (Mathews *et al.*, 2004) found that jurors felt the evidence was not always presented in the clearest way and that 'maps, diagrams, photographs and other visual aids were under-used in courts' (p.3). Furthermore, Tinsley (2000) reports that jurors are often confused by both the nature of the evidence and the way in which it is presented, highlighting a particular difficulty with expert evidence. She states that 'in 6 of the 19 trials in which technical or specialized evidence was introduced, jurors had difficulty in comprehending it, a situation which was often caused or exacerbated by the unduly complicated or ponderous way in which the evidence was delivered' (Tinsley, 2000, p.5).

If the evidence is not presented in a coherent manner, then each individual juror will have a schema that is either distorted or missing vital pieces of evidence. Tinsley suggests that a written factual summary outlining the key pieces of evidence at the start of the trial may provide a coherent framework for each juror to build their schema round. However, this does not remedy the difficulties concerned with the presentation of evidence. Furthermore, the presentation of scientific evidence increasingly involves computer animations and simulations. As Feigenson and Dunn (2003, p.109) state, 'Litigation is being transformed by new technologies of visual communication'. In particular, 'Lawyers are turning to video not only to present evidence...but also to preview their cases... – and even to encapsulate their closing arguments'. While Feigenson and Dunn discuss these issues within a US legal framework, the increasing use of video and computer simulations to illustrate key evidence in UK courts (e.g. in the case of the Angelika Kluk murder) means that a greater understanding of the impact of this form of presentation in UK courts needs to be gained.

ACTIVITY 16.2

At the start of this chapter you were shown a photograph (don't flick back to look at it!). Your task now is to look at the photograph below and decide whether the person you saw is in the line-up. Write down whether or not you think he is there. If you think he is, write down the number.

Now, think carefully about the task you have just completed. What factors impacted on how easy or difficult you found this task? How could the structure of the line-up be improved (system variables)? Did any estimator variables impact on your ability to complete the task accurately?

This section has highlighted just a little of the fascinating research on some of the key issues in psychology and law.

Hopefully, you have been able to see how some of the different areas of psychology (cognitive, social and developmental) interact.

Before you embark on Section 3 of this chapter, take a little time to review the material and see if you can make your own links, both to previous sections of the textbook and to wider psychological research.

Summary of Section 2

- Factors that impact on eye-witness identification have been broadly categorized as system and estimator variables.
- There is debate regarding the most effective way of presenting line-ups, and this debate centres on decision-making criteria.

- There are debates in the literature regarding the effect of emotional stress and arousal on memory. Stress does appear to impact negatively on both eye-witness recall and recognition. However, there are quite large individual differences.
- Research demonstrates that even subtle changes to information can influence the accuracy of eye-witness recall. Cognitive explanations focus on the nature of memory and much debate centres on what happens to the original information.
- Research has highlighted the cognitive and social factors that can impact on children's testimony.
- Cognitive models describe how jurors 'make sense' of evidence during a trial. Research has highlighted the factors that can impact on decision making in this context.

3   Cognition and intelligence

When we think of cognitive psychology, we tend to think of fairly broad questions: How does memory work? How do we learn to read? Implicit within these questions is the issue of generalizability. Researchers develop and test models and theories that apply to most people. While there is an awareness of individual differences, cognitive psychology isn't particularly interested in the individual. However, this doesn't mean that individuals aren't important. Indeed, a whole area of psychology deals with differences between individuals. This research primarily focuses on intelligence and personality, and while it may seem that these issues are very different from the issues tackled by cognitive psychologists, hopefully you will see in the rest of this chapter that cognition is embedded within a great deal of it.

3.1   Definitions of intelligence

What is **intelligence**? This is an impossible question to answer, primarily because there is no single agreed-upon definition. Intelligence has been defined and continues to be defined in many different ways, by many different researchers. However, most tests focus on cognitive abilities and do not take into account social or practical aspects. While there are many different definitions, a broadly accepted definition would include two main factors: (a) the ability to adapt to one's environment (Sternberg and Detterman, 1986); and (b) the capacity to learn from experience.

ACTIVITY 16.3

It is important to remember that definitions of intelligence are often based on Western societal ideals and norms (Gregory, 2007). African cultures, for example, place importance on social aspects (Sternberg and Kaufman, 1998).

- Take a few moments to consider the different cultural and social definitions of intelligence.
- What determines definitions of 'intelligence' in different cultures?

Another difficulty in defining intelligence is that while intelligence tests should seek to measure and understand actual aspects of intelligence (based on what Sternberg and Detterman, 1986 call a 'real' definition), some tests actually define intelligence 'operationally', which means that intelligence becomes whatever that particular test measures. So, rather than attempting to understand the nature of intelligence, some tests confirm their own definition of intelligence.

If we accept a definition of intelligence that emphasizes learning from experience and adapting to the environment (at least in Western cultures) then measures of intelligence (intelligence tests) should capture aspects of learning and adaption. So how well do they do this? Unfortunately, they don't do it very well. Rather than assessing cognitive abilities in differing situations, Gregory (2007) argues that most tests measure learning and adaptability indirectly. Furthermore, while there is agreement amongst theorists that there must be multiple components to intelligence (see Sternberg, 2000), there is no consensus regarding what these cognitive components might be, or how many there are.

3.2   Attention and intelligence

In Chapter 2, you were introduced to some of the key concepts and theories of visual attention. There are many different types of **attentional processing** (e.g. divided, focused, spatial, etc.). As such, it is not unreasonable to suggest that attention is involved in all cognitive tasks. Given this, it is perhaps surprising that while most intelligence tests measure aspects of cognitive processing (e.g. perceptual processing, spatial awareness, memory span, etc.), attention is not defined as a component of intelligence in theories.

However, several researchers have not only noted differences in attentional processing but also suggested that attention is linked to intelligence. For example, Schweizer *et al.* (2005) used a technique called structural equation modelling to examine the relationship between attention and intelligence. They reported that there was a relationship between the scores from intelligence tests and all levels of attentional processing (focused, divided, spatial, inhibition and attentional switching), although the relationship did vary across the measures. The authors also reported overlap between the attentional measures, as well as similarity between some of the attentional measures and measures of cognitive ability. They stated that 'Almost a third of the variance of intelligence was predicted by the whole set of attention measures' (p.607). These results therefore suggest that attentional processing is highly linked to performance on intelligence tests.

More recently, Burns *et al.* (2009) examined the relationship between attention and intelligence. The inspiration for the study came from Carroll (1993), who stated that as attention is involved in all cognitive tasks, it may be extremely difficult to separate out attentional processing from task processing. The aim of the study by Burns *et al.* was both to try to do this and to attempt to understand the relationship between attention and performance on cognitive tasks.

In the study 147 participants were given 17 different tests of attention (e.g. divided sentences, Stroop test, number switch) as well as 14 tests of cognitive ability (e.g. picture recognition, concept formation, Raven standard progressive matrices). Using factor analysis the authors reported a near perfect relationship (0.977) between performance on the cognitive and attentional tests.

ACTIVITY 16.4

What does a correlation of 0.977 mean? Does it mean that differences in intelligence scores are actually differences in attentional processing? Is attention a fundamental component of intelligence? Or does the high correlation just mean that the cognitive tasks contained within the intelligence tests were actually measuring attentional processing, rather than 'intelligence'?

3.3   Working memory and intelligence

From Chapter 5 you will have seen that the working memory model comprises three main elements: the phonological loop; the visuo-spatial sketch-pad; and the central executive. Many researchers have found a relationship between measures of working memory and measures of cognitive ability (e.g. Kane and Engle, 2002). In particular, while the central executive has been the least studied component of the working memory model, it is thought to reflect attentional processing. As individual differences in working memory processing appear to be related to performance on attentional (central executive) tasks (see Kane and Engle, 2002), Schweizer and Moosbrugger (2004) examined the relationship between working memory, attention and performance on intelligence tests. They looked at whether attention and working memory were independent predictors of intelligence. In this study, 120 participants completed two tests of working memory, two attentional tests and two measures of intelligence. Schweizer and Moosbrugger found that, together, the results from the attentional and working memory tests predicted performance on the intelligence tests. A positive relationship was also reported between working memory and sustained attention. As attention is a component of working memory, it makes sense that both factors may be needed in order to predict performance on cognitive tests.

While research has found relationships between working memory and performance on intelligence tests, there is a debate about the extent of the relationship. In particular, Kyllonen and Christal (1990) reported that working memory capacity reflects the ability to reason. As reasoning and problem solving are thought to reflect the **general intelligence construct**, Kyllonen (2002, p.433) states that 'we have our answer to the question of what g [i.e. general intelligence] is. It is working memory capacity'. However, other psychologists have questioned this relationship. Furthermore, Ackerman *et al.* (2005) argue that the relationship between working memory and cognitive ability is more complex than once thought. They conducted a meta-analysis on the relationship between working memory and intelligence and found significant relationships between working memory and both broad and specific cognitive tasks. However, the authors reported a much lower average correlation (0.364) between working memory and g and rejected previous assertions that working memory and g are the same thing. Instead, Ackerman *et al.* critique some of the research methods used in previous research by indicating that high correlations between working memory and cognitive processing tasks may be produced when the cognitive tasks require working memory (they call these 'speeded information-processing tests'). When the cognitive tests are broader in content, the correlations are lower. The authors also highlight the fact that sometimes g is measured using a single intelligence test. Given the complexity of intelligence it is unlikely to be captured by a single test. So, while there are clear relationships between cognitive ability, working memory and attention, the relationships are complex. Given the myriad of tasks and the different types of working memory, attentional and cognitive processing tasks that can be undertaken, it is not surprising that there are complex relationships, perhaps stemming from the lack of any proper definition of intelligence.

3.4   One factor or many?

In the early part of the 20th century, Spearman (e.g. Spearman, 1904) theorized that there were two **multiple components of intelligence**: a general component or factor (g); and other specific factors (s). Spearman spent a great deal of time focusing on the 'general intelligence' construct and believed that it mainly comprised cognitive abilities: making inferences based on past knowledge; drawing analogies; and finding relationships (what Spearman termed apprehension of experience, eduction of relationships and eduction of correlates). The idea that intelligence is a single construct, composed of smaller dimensions (separate cognitive abilities), has been pervasive in the literature and many researchers have sought to define g (see Jensen, 1998 for a review). Indeed, Blair (2006, p.109) states that 'it is beyond question that a single mathematically derived factor can be extracted from tests of diverse mental abilities'. So, if there is a single factor, what might it comprise?

Just because a single factor can be derived from tests, does this mean that the tests are accurately measuring the construct of intelligence? This leads back to the issue of definition. Sternberg (1999) argues that a general factor tends to emerge from data where definitions of intelligence and use of participants (e.g. students) are very narrow. As such, he argues that the construct of a general intelligence factor may be partly a reflection of confirmation bias – those studies that found a general factor were designed to do so. Given the complexity and multidimensional nature of intelligence, it is difficult to see how it could be reduced to a single, general construct. Indeed, as early as 1938, Thurstone proposed that intelligence was made up of seven different components, which could each be measured independently (e.g. reasoning, verbal comprehension and fluency, spatial processing, perceptual speed and memory).

Cattell (1971) also favoured a multidimensional approach, combining the construct of general intelligence with other dimensions to form a three-layered hierarchical theory. In his theory, general ability was at the top, while crystallized abilities (acquired knowledge and its application) and fluid abilities (mainly non-verbal abilities that are thought to be culture-free) were at the next level. Cattell's theory has been extended and revised and is now known as the **Cattell–Horn–Carroll (CHC) theory**. It is based on an extensive body of empirical research and as such it is seen by many as 'the most comprehensive and empirically supported psychometric theory of the structure of cognitive and academic abilities to date' (Alfonso *et al.*, 2005, p.185). The overall structure of the original theory has been retained: it is still a three-layered hierarchical theory. However, the content of the layers has been updated: see Figure 16.1.

The general intelligence construct, g, has been retained in the third layer. Underneath, in layer 2, there are more than 10 broad cognitive abilities. Here, Cattell's fluid and crystallized abilities have been retained, while cognitive abilities

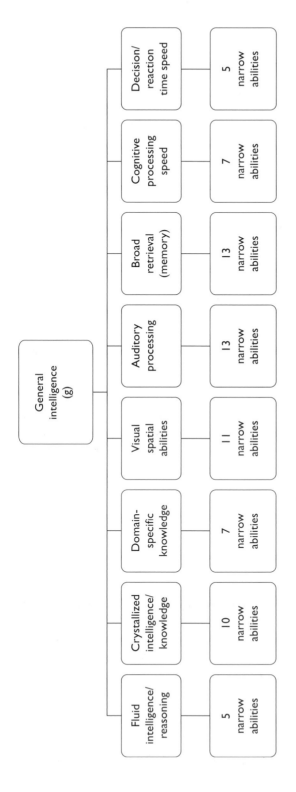

Figure 16.1 Diagrammatic representation of the CHC theory

such as reading and writing, short-term memory and visual processing have been added. Each of the abilities in layer 2 encompasses a set of narrow abilities at layer 1. For example, short-term memory contains three narrow abilities: memory span; working memory; and learning abilities. Currently, the theory contains more than 70 narrow abilities (Alfonso *et al.*, 2005). The theory is well supported by empirical research. For example, relationships have been found between CHC theory and reading achievement (Evans *et al.*, 2001) and mathematical achievement (Floyd *et al.*, 2003) in children and adolescents and it has become highly influential (see Box 16.4).

16.4

Is CHC the way forward?

While the CHC theory is highly influential and supported by a large body of empirical research, McGrew (2009) suggests that researchers shouldn't just accept it as an all-encompassing theory of intelligence. Instead, McGrew argues that the CHC theory should be used as a framework both to describe research findings and to stimulate new research in the field of intelligence.

3.5   Intelligence in context

Sternberg (1999) argues that laboratory tests that examine aspects of cognitive function outside any context cannot properly assess intelligence. He argues that a wider view of an individual is needed, one which captures internal and external experiences, in order to assess and understand the construct of intelligence. Sternberg (2004) calls this 'successful intelligence' to highlight that gaining an understanding of intelligence shouldn't just be about predicting test results in an academic environment; it should be about predicting success in life.

Sternberg's **triarchic theory of intelligence** (e.g. Sternberg, 1999) has three elements to it. The first is the individual's internal world, the second is their experience and the third is their external world. The internal world relates to the individual's cognitive processing; Sternberg says that these processes are constant: they don't change. Experience, however, does vary and mediates cognitive processing. For example, the way in which cognitive processes are used will vary depending upon the situation. Furthermore, the way that processes are applied in different environments and situations will differ between individuals. Similarly, the external world also differs, both within and between different cultures and societies. Sternberg (1999) states that the internal world (cognitive processing) and external world interact and it is experience that mediates this interaction. This means that intelligence tests that assess cognitive processing in one environment aren't fully assessing the complexities of the construct of intelligence. It may also mean that intelligence tests relating to one particular culture or society may not relate to another.

Sternberg developed the **Sternberg Triarchic Abilities Test (STAT)** as a research tool for use in schools and colleges. The aim of the test was to assess abilities that were not included in traditional intelligence tests – more creative and practical abilities as well as cognitive ones. While the test has been designed for use on diverse populations, Sternberg (1999, p.150) states that the test is not 'culture fair' because no test can ever be. He comments that every test is essentially socially constructed and rooted within a particular culture. To investigate the STAT, Sternberg tested 326 students from diverse ethnic and socioeconomic backgrounds. Interestingly, he found that students from lower socioeconomic groups scored more highly in practical and creative elements compared with analytical tasks. In contrast, the upper-middle-class students in his study scored more highly on analytical compared with creative and practical tasks. Sternberg indicates that these differences may reflect the general skills the children had developed during childhood experiences. Interestingly, Sternberg *et al.* (1998) report that no matter what pattern of ability children have (as measured by the STAT), all children benefit from triarchic learning: combining cognitive analytical tasks with practical, experiential tasks benefits learning in all children.

3.6 Emotional intelligence

The construct of **emotional intelligence** was conceptualized at around the same time as researchers were starting to adopt a more multifaceted and multidimensional approach to cognitive intelligence. It has been conceptualized in many ways, but basically emotional intelligence concerns things that are personally relevant to individuals – their emotions, their family and their relationships. Many readers will no doubt be familiar with the broad concept of emotional intelligence, as much has been written about it in the popular press. A great deal of this coverage stems from the work of Daniel Goleman, who has written several books on the topic, as well as numerous research articles. For Goleman, emotional intelligence is separate from cognitive intelligence and comprises a set of skills which can be taught.

3.7 What is emotional intelligence?

Is emotional intelligence as Goleman defines it – a set of learned skills distinct from cognitive intelligence? If we say some forms of intelligence are emotional, then that means that others are not. While traditional definitions of cognitive intelligence have not included emotion, we know, for example from research on memory, that mood and emotion can greatly impact on the way in which information is encoded, stored and retrieved (see Chapter 14 on cognition and emotion). Is emotional intelligence cognitive intelligence with emotion? Or has it been conceptualized as something qualitatively different?

While Goleman brought the construct of emotional intelligence into the public arena, it was actually Salovey and Mayer (1990) who were the first researchers to identify emotional intelligence as a construct, and it was originally defined as a very broad set of abilities. Later, Mayer and colleagues (Mayer and Salovey, 1997; see also Mayer *et al.*, 2008) formalized a **hierarchical four-branch model of emotional intelligence**. The model is based on the premise that emotional abilities fall along a continuum, from what the authors term 'lower-level, fundamental skills' such as emotion perception to 'higher-level skills' that would involve emotion regulation. It essentially combines cognitive processing with emotion. It is also what is termed an 'ability model' as it represents a set of abilities that can be measured (see Figure 16.2 for a diagram of the model).

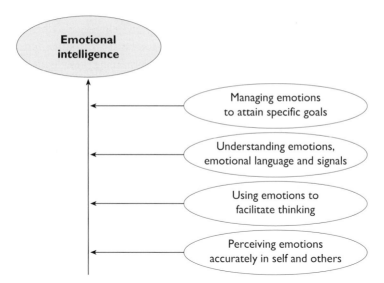

Figure 16.2   A representation of the four-branch model of emotional intelligence

Source: Mayer *et al.*, 2008

There are four levels to the model and within each of these levels there are different abilities. The lowest level in the model is the ability to perceive emotion. Without perceiving and recognizing different emotions, it would be impossible to interpret them and respond to both our own and other people's behaviour. This level concerns the perception of emotion not only in oneself and other people (facial expressions, voices, etc.) but also in music and art. Once the emotion has been perceived it can then be used (level 2). If someone is high in emotional intelligence then they will use emotions to assist cognitive processing. For example, emotions can be used in all sorts of ways to facilitate reasoning, communication and decision making. The third level, understanding emotions, is all about language and thought. It 'involves language and propositional thought that reflect the capacity to analyze emotions' (Brackett *et al.*, 2006, p.781). (For propositions, see Chapter 10, Section 3.3.2.) The highest level concerns the management of emotions and emotional responses. Importantly, this level stresses the role of emotion management in different social contexts. Someone who is high in emotional intelligence will modify their responses and subsequent behaviour to suit their social and interpersonal environment. What is appropriate in one context might not be in another.

This model indicates that if someone is able to perceive emotions accurately and understand and regulate them, then they are highly aware, not only of their own and others' emotions, but also of the consequences of behaviours and emotional responses in differing social circumstances. It may be this awareness that leads to lower levels of stress and higher levels of well-being: being able to 'read' and adapt to social situations and circumstances means that they won't have the frustration and stress that accompanies 'not knowing what's going on'.

We can see that this conceptualization of emotional intelligence is distinct from the construct of personality. It also clearly incorporates cognitive processes (perception, recognition, interpretation and decision making) and applies them directly to emotion. Cognitive–behavioural therapy is based on just this premise, that emotion, cognition and behaviour are inextricably intertwined. In some forms of cognitive–behavioural therapy, patients are encouraged to keep a diary to identify emotions and their associated thoughts and behaviours. It is thought that challenging the cognitive component (negative thought processes), and introducing new behaviour patterns, will impact on emotional processing.

Within each level and ability in the model there are individual differences which can be assessed. In order to measure the differences, the **Mayer–Salovey–Caruso Emotional Intelligence Test (MSCEIT)** was developed. This test provides an emotional intelligence score derived by comparing self-reported responses with pools of responses from experts and members of the general population. Mayer *et al.* (2008) state that the test provides an accurate measure of the concepts described in the model. It also appears to be distinct from other measures of emotional intelligence, IQ and personality (McEnrue and Groves, 2006). In addition, it has been found that the emotional intelligence scores on the MSCEIT increase with age and that the abilities can be learned. Furthermore, research has demonstrated that the MSCEIT can predict a wide range of outcomes (see McEnrue and Groves, 2006). For example, the MSCEIT has been shown to predict stress and leadership potential in workplaces as well as the quality of romantic relationships (Brackett *et al.*, 2005). The model has led to the development of the MSCEIT measurement tool, and Zeidner *et al.* (2008) state that this has made it one of the most influential models of emotional intelligence to date.

Other researchers have, however, questioned the validity of the MSCEIT, as it seems to measure some factors in the model better than others. For example, Palmer *et al.* (2005) found no evidence for the highest level of the model (emotion management), which suggests that there is a disparity between the factors described in the model and what the test actually measures. Furthermore, McEnrue and Groves (2006) also question the external validity of the measure, as no research to date has examined the validity of the test for different cultures, ages or ethnic groups.

Similarly, while the MSCEIT appears to predict a wide range of outcomes, like many tests it is a self-report assessment tool. As such, it could be criticized for failing to capture the complexities of social and interpersonal interaction, which are crucial for the operation of many of the concepts outlined in the model. For example, the perception of emotion may depend on the nature of the relationship between individuals. It may not be possible to know when someone you don't know intimately is experiencing a strong emotion, as they may not express it overtly. Some people express emotion overtly, while others are very guarded. It often isn't until you really get to know people that you can tell if they are stressed or unhappy. Does this mean that someone who doesn't accurately perceive how another person feels lacks emotional intelligence? Many social and individual factors can impact on the perception of emotion. What implications does this have for models of emotional intelligence?

ACTIVITY 16.5

Take a few moments to think about how we, as psychologists, might measure emotional intelligence in social situations, or indeed to decide whether it is something that we can or even should measure. If you think that we could, what would we need to do? How could we include social, cultural and interpersonal factors? Would a quantitative approach be appropriate? Or might it be better to adopt a qualitative or mixed-method approach? Take some time to think about how we might approach this in order to obtain the most useful information.

3.8 Difficulties inherent in emotional intelligence

Although Mayer *et al.*'s framework for conceptualizing emotional intelligence has been influential, emotional intelligence has been conceptualized in many different ways. Just as for cognitive intelligence, there are many differing definitions of the construct. Some definitions, including Goleman's, have been criticized for being over-inclusive, essentially including everything that is not included in tests of cognitive intelligence. Others have defined emotional intelligence as a set of personality traits and abilities (Bar-On, 2005) and as an ability to perceive and manage emotion (Mayer and Salovey, 1997). As such, there is very little agreement regarding a **definition of emotional intelligence**. Researchers have criticized the poorly defined nature of the construct, arguing that a lack of consensus regarding definition, theory and method weakens the area (e.g. Waterhouse, 2006). Others, however, see the lack of consensus regarding definition and theory as a strength, particularly in a research area such as emotional intelligence, which is very young. Cherniss *et al.* (2006) address criticisms posed by Waterhouse (2006) and argue that as there is no clear definition of cognitive intelligence after 100 years of research, why should we expect a clear definition of emotional intelligence after only two decades?

Regardless of the debate, it is clear that the field of emotional intelligence suffers from the same difficulties as that of intelligence in general. Zeidner *et al.* (2008) review the current consensus and controversies in emotional intelligence research. As with standard intelligence tests, different definitions have led to the development of measurement tools that operationally define the construct. So, emotional intelligence essentially becomes defined as the abilities and traits that the individual tests measure. Tests of emotional intelligence also tend to ignore social and cultural contexts, which is surprising given that emotional intelligence relates to how we interact with other people. Furthermore, just as it is unlikely that there is one single general intelligence construct (g), it is doubtful that there is a single emotional intelligence trait. Instead, there does appear to be agreement that it is multifaceted (Zeidner *et al.*, 2008).

Given that emotional intelligence is multifaceted and multidimensional, it has been suggested that emotional intelligence is just a new term for abilities and traits that are already known, for example personality traits and social functioning. So, how similar is emotional intelligence to other constructs such as personality and social functioning?

3.9   Emotional intelligence, personality and mental health

Mixed models of emotional intelligence define it as a much wider construct than ability models (e.g. the four-branch model), encompassing personality, self-perceptions of emotion and 'competencies' that have included communication, empathy, assertiveness and impulsivity. Mixed models have been criticized, not only for including a wide range of factors but also for not justifying why certain factors (e.g. assertiveness) might be classed as 'emotional intelligence' while others are not (see Mayer *et al.*, 2008 for a discussion). The inclusion of many personality factors also means that the boundary between emotional intelligence and personality has not been defined clearly. Interestingly, it has been found that there is a negative relationship between borderline personality disorder and emotional intelligence, so that people who score more highly on personality disorder scales produce lower scores on measures of emotional intelligence and seem to be particularly poor at regulating and managing emotion (Leible and Snell, 2004).

Schutte *et al.* (2006) conducted a meta-analysis and found a positive relationship between health and emotional intelligence, so higher scores on emotional intelligence measures were associated with better health. There was also a relationship between psychosomatic health issues and emotional intelligence and it is suggested that people who score lower on emotional intelligence tests may not regulate emotions properly. A smaller effect was found for physical health and emotional intelligence. Schutte *et al.* (2006) state that the relationships found in their meta-analysis between mental health and emotional health were similar to those reported by other meta-analyses that have compared personality (the 'big five' personality dimensions) and emotional intelligence (e.g. Malouff *et al.*, 2005). In the meta-analysis by Malouff *et al.* a large effect for neuroticism was reported. Similarly, relationships were found between the 'big five' personality dimensions and emotional intelligence. This suggests that there is overlap between **personality and emotional intelligence** (Schutte *et al.*, 2006). Importantly, Schutte *et al.* found that trait measures of emotional intelligence (e.g. the Emotional Quotient Inventory, EQ-i) were more strongly associated with mental health than were ability measures. So while there are relationships to personality, it depends on how the construct of emotional intelligence has been defined.

3.10   Emotional intelligence and social functioning

Emotional intelligence refers to the ability to perceive, understand and regulate emotions in a social environment. Only a very few studies have actually examined it in a social context, but Brackett *et al.* (2006) did just this, using Mayer and Salovey's four-branch theory as a framework. In study 3 they asked participants to engage in a short interpersonal interaction with a confederate, as well as completing emotional intelligence tests (e.g. the MSCEIT and the Self Rated Emotional Intelligence Scale, SREIS, developed by Brackett *et al.*). Each interaction was videotaped and judges evaluated the interactions by responding to Likert-style questions such as 'How confident are you that this participant would work well collaborating with others; is she/he a "team player"?' (p.789). It was found that there was a weak relationship between the SREIS and the MSCEIT, which indicates that the two measures assess different things. There was a relationship between interaction in the observed task and the ability measure (MSCEIT) but it was only for men. No relationship could be found for women. The authors don't know why this is but suggest a number of possible reasons. First, the highest level of the Mayer and Salovey model relates to the management and regulation of emotions. However, the ability to regulate emotions and adapt to interpersonal and social situations is governed by numerous factors. From a social psychological perspective, social norms govern the way that emotion is expressed and managed in different social situations. Similarly, gendered norms impact on emotion management. Parents define and categorize social functioning for children differently depending on their gender (Bacon and Ashmore, 1985). So, it is likely that the factors that underlie the construct of emotional intelligence (e.g. emotion regulation and management) may work differently for men and women.

Interestingly, Brackett *et al.* also found a weak relationship between self-report measures of emotional intelligence and performance. This highlights the difficulty of using self-perception measures to assess behaviour, especially in social situations. This weak relationship may reflect distorted perceptions of behaviour. However, it is perhaps likely that emotional intelligence – a construct which is essentially social (as well as cognitive) – cannot be adequately assessed using self-report questionnaires. As emotion management refers to the ability to respond 'appropriately' in different interpersonal and social situations, it may be impossible to know how we will behave in a given situation. We react differently to people depending on how they react to us. There will be differences in the expression and management of emotion between intimate partners, colleagues and friends. Similarly, other factors such as power, trust and mood will impact on interactions. This means that there is a gap between what many tests of emotional intelligence can assess and how emotionally intelligent people actually act in different social situations. Indeed, as Brody (2004, p.234) states, emotional intelligence tests assess 'knowledge of emotions but not necessarily the ability to perform tasks that are related to the knowledge that is assessed'.

3.11   The workplace

Much has been made of the role of emotional intelligence in the workplace and researchers have claimed that scores on emotional intelligence tests provide better predictions for success in the workplace than scores on standard cognitive intelligence tests (e.g. Dulewicz and Higgs, 1999). It is also thought that emotional intelligence plays a role in effective leadership behaviour (e.g. Palmer *et al.*, 2001).

Nikolaou and Tsaousis (2002) examined the relationship between **occupation, stress and emotional intelligence** by comparing three different groups of mental health professionals – (a) medical/psychological staff, (b) social worker/nursing employees and (c) administrative staff – who were all permanent members of staff. They were all asked to complete the EIQ self-report emotional intelligence questionnaire, an organizational stress measure and the Job Stress Index. It was found that members of staff who scored highly on the EIQ had lower stress scores and higher scores for commitment. The medical/psychological staff members scored significantly higher on emotional intelligence than the other groups. The authors claim that employees in these positions are better at regulating and managing their emotions. However, it's not clear why this group would possess more emotionally intelligent ability than social workers, nurses and administrative workers. It is perhaps likely that other cultural, interpersonal and occupational factors, not reported in the study, may have contributed to these differential findings.

While cognitive and emotional intelligence tests can be useful in the workplace, they can also be problematic. This is because they fail to take into account **cultural and social factors**. As Searle (2003) indicates, businesses that operate globally want to know whether potential employees will be suitable and fit into their organization. They will also want to know whether both potential and existing employees will have the skills and abilities that will enable them to relocate and work effectively within different social and cultural environments. So, tests that are not applicable to different environments have limited utility.

Emotional intelligence has not been defined clearly. Researchers have conceptualized emotional intelligence in many ways, but it can be broadly categorized into two theoretical positions: those that view emotional intelligence as an ability; and those that see it as a trait. As with cognitive intelligence, researchers generally agree that emotional intelligence is complex and multidimensional. It also clearly involves cognitive processing – perception, interpretation and decision making. Importantly, emotional intelligence refers to how we interact with other people and as such it is a social psychological phenomenon. How we behave and interact can be governed by the situational and interpersonal context. Given this, it is surprising that very few researchers have studied emotional intelligence in a social context. It may be that the goal of individual-difference researchers – to measure – is incompatible with gaining a descriptive understanding of the complexities of emotional processing.

Summary of Section 3

- There are disagreements regarding how best to define the concept of intelligence. Now, even the most ardent supporters of a general intelligence construct generally agree that intelligence comprises multiple dimensions.
- If we accept a definition of intelligence that only encompasses cognitive skills and abilities, then it might be possible to say that intelligence tests do measure intelligence. If a broader definition of intelligence is used, however, then the majority of tests are somewhat lacking.
- The relationship between cognitive processing and emotion has not been clearly defined. As such, there is no agreed-upon definition of emotional intelligence.

Further reading

Blank, H. (2009) 'Remembering: a theoretical interface between memory and social psychology', *Social Psychology*, vol.40, pp.164–75. An excellent review that not only puts forward a social psychological framework for 'remembering' but also ties together social psychological theory with social remembering.

Cohen, G. and Conway, M. (2008) *Memory in the Real World* (3rd edn), Hove, Psychology Press. A good general text on memory.

Gregory, R.J. (2007) *Psychological Testing: History, Principles and Applications* (5th edn), Chicago, IL, Pearson. An excellent general text that covers a whole host of issues regarding intelligence testing.

Zeidner, M., Roberts, R.D. and Mathews, G. (2008) 'The science of emotional intelligence: current consensus and controversies', *European Psychologist*, vol.13, pp.64–78. Reviews the current issues in emotional intelligence research.

References

Ackerman, P.L., Beier, M.E. and Boyle, M.O. (2005) 'Working memory and intelligence: the same or different constructs?', *Psychological Bulletin*, vol.131, pp.30–60.

Alfonso, V.C., Flanagan, D.P. and Radwan, S. (2005) 'The impact of the Cattell–Horn–Carroll theory on test development and interpretation of cognitive and academic abilities', in Flanagan, D.P. and Harrison, P.L. (eds) *Contemporary Intellectual Assessment: Theories, Tests and Issues* (2nd edn), New York, The Guilford Press.

Anastasi, J.S. and Rhodes, M.G. (2006) 'Evidence for an own-age bias in face recognition', *North American Journal of Psychology*, vol.8, pp.237–53.

Bacon, M.K. and Ashmore, R.D. (1985) 'How mothers and fathers categorize descriptions of social behavior attributed to daughters and sons', *Social Cognition*, vol.3, pp.193–217.

Barclay, C.R. and DeCooke, P.A. (1988) 'Ordinary everyday memories: some of the things of which selves are made', in Neisser, U. and Winograd, E. (eds) *Remembering Reconsidered: Ecological and Traditional Approaches to the Study of Memory*, Cambridge, Cambridge University Press.

Bar-On, R. (2005) 'The Bar-On model of emotional–social intelligence (ESI)', *Psicothema: Special Issue on Emotional Intelligence*, vol.17, pp.1–28.

Bartlett, F.C. (1932) *Remembering: A Study in Experimental and Social Psychology*, New York, Cambridge University Press.

Bergen, S. van., Horselenberg, R., Merckelbach, H.M., Jelicic, M. and Beckers, R. (2009) 'Memory distrust and acceptance of misinformation', *Applied Cognitive Psychology*, DOI: 10.1002/acp.1595.

Blair, C. (2006) 'How similar are fluid cognition and general intelligence? A developmental neuroscience perspective on fluid cognition as an aspect of human cognitive ability', *Behavioral and Brain Sciences*, vol.29, pp.109–60.

Blank, H. (2009) 'Remembering: a theoretical interface between memory and social psychology', *Social Psychology*, vol.40, pp.164–75.

Bottoms, B.L., Goodman, G.S., Schwartz-Kenney, B.M. and Thomas, S.N. (2002) 'Understanding children's use of secrecy in the context of eyewitness reports', *Law and Human Behavior*, vol.26, pp.285–313.

Brackett, M.A., Warner, R.M. and Bosco, J. (2005) 'Emotional intelligence and relationship quality among couples', *Personal Relationships*, vol.12, pp.197–212.

Brackett, M.A., Rivers, S.E., Shiffman, S., Lerner, N. and Salovey, P. (2006) 'Relating emotional abilities to social functioning: a comparison of self report and performance measures of emotional intelligence', *Journal of Personality and Social Psychology*, vol.91, pp.780–95.

Brainerd, C.J. and Reyna, V.F. (1990) 'Gist is the grist: fuzzy trace theory and the new institution', *Developmental Review*, vol.10, pp.3–47.

Brody, N. (2004) 'What cognitive intelligence is and what emotional intelligence is not', *Psychological Inquiry*, vol.15, pp.234–8.

Bruce, V. and Young, A.W. (1986) 'Understanding face recognition', *British Journal of Psychology*, vol.77, pp.305–27.

Burns, N.R., Nettlebeck, T. and McPherson, J. (2009) 'Attention and intelligence: a factor analytic study', *Journal of Individual Differences*, vol.30, pp.44–57.

Burton, A.M., Bruce, V. and Johnston, R.A. (1990) 'Understanding face recognition with an interactive activation model', *British Journal of Psychology*, vol.81, pp.361–80.

Carroll, J.B. (1993) *Human Cognitive Abilities*, New York, Cambridge University Press.

Cattell, R.B. (1971) *Abilities: Their Structure, Growth and Action*, Boston, MA, Houghton Mifflin.

Chandler, C.C., Gargano, G.J. and Holt, B.C. (2001) 'Witnessing post-event does not change memory traces, but can affect their retrieval', *Applied Cognitive Psychology*, vol.15, pp.3–22.

Cherniss, C., Extein, M., Goleman, D. and Weissberg, R.P. (2006) 'Emotional intelligence: what does the research really indicate?', *Educational Psychologist*, vol.41, pp.239–45.

Christianson, S.A. (1992) 'Emotional stress and eyewitness memory: a critical review', *Psychological Bulletin,* vol.112, pp.284–309.

Dando, C., Wilcock, R., Milne, R. and Henry, L. (2009) 'A modified cognitive interview procedure for frontline police investigators', *Applied Cognitive Psychology*, vol.23, pp.698–716.

Deckle, D.J., Beal, C.R., Elliott, R. and Huneycutt, D. (1996) 'Children as witnesses: a comparison of lineup versus showup identification methods', *Applied Cognitive Psychology*, vol.10, pp.1–12.

Deffenbacher, K.A. (1983) 'The influence of arousal on reliability of testimony', in Lloyd-Bostock, S.M.A. and Clifford, B.R. (eds) *Evaluating Witness Evidence*, Chichester, Wiley.

Deffenbacher, K.A. (1994) 'Effects of arousal on everyday memory', *Human Performance*, vol.7, pp.141–61.

Deffenbacher, K.A., Bornstein, B.H., Penrod, S.D. and McGorty, E.K. (2004) 'A meta-analytic review of the effects of high stress on eyewitness memory', *Law and Human Behavior*, vol.28, pp.687–706.

Dulewicz, V. and Higgs, M. (1999) 'Can emotional intelligence be measured and developed?', *Leadership and Organization Development Journal*, vol.20, pp.242–53.

Echterhoff, G., Hirst, W. and Hussy, W. (2005) 'How eyewitnesses resist misinformation: social postwarnings and the monitoring of memory characteristics', *Memory & Cognition,* vol.33, pp.770–82.

Evans, J.J., Floyd, R.G., McGrew, K.S. and Leforgee, M.H. (2001) 'The relations between measures of Cattell–Horn–Carroll (CHC) cognitive abilities and reading achievement during childhood and adolescence', *School Psychology Review*, vol.31, pp.246–62.

Feigenson, N. and Dunn, M.A. (2003) 'New visual technologies in court: directions for research', *Law and Human Behavior*, vol.27, pp.109–26.

Fisher, R.P. and Geiselman, R.E. (1992) *Memory Enhancing Techniques for Investigative Interviewing: The Cognitive Interview*, Springfield, IL, Charles C. Thomas.

Floyd, R.G., Evans, J.J. and McGrew, K.S. (2003) 'Relations between measures of Cattell–Horn–Carroll (CHC) cognitive abilities and mathematics achievement across the school-age years', *Psychology in the Schools*, vol.40, pp.155–71.

Gabbert, F., Memon, A. and Allan, K. (2003) 'Memory conformity: can eyewitnesses influence each others' memories for an event?', *Applied Cognitive Psychology*, vol.17, pp.533–43.

Gabbert, F., Memon, A., Allan, K. and Wright, D.B. (2004) 'Say it to my face: examining the effects of socially encountered misinformation', *Legal and Criminological Psychology*, vol.9, pp.215–27.

Gabbert, F., Memon, A. and Wright, D.B. (2007) 'I saw it for longer than you: the relationship between perceived encoding duration and memory conformity', *Acta Psychologica*, vol.124, pp.319–31.

Garry, M., French, L., Kinzett, T. and Mori, K. (2008) 'Eyewitness memory following discussion: using the MORI technique with a western sample', *Applied Cognitive Psychology*, vol.22, pp.431–9.

Goodman, G. (2006) 'Children's eyewitness memory: a modern history and contemporary commentary', *Journal of Social Issues*, vol.62, pp.811–32.

Goodman, G.S., Bottoms, B.L., Schwartz-Kenney, B.M. and Rudy, L. (1991) 'Children's testimony about a stressful event: improving children's reports', *Journal of Narrative and Life History*, vol.1, pp.69–99.

Gordon, B.N., Baker-Ward, L. and Ornstein, P.A. (2001) 'Children's testimony: a review of research on memory for past experiences', *Clinical Child and Family Psychology Review*, vol.4, pp.157–81.

Greenhoot, A.F. (2000) 'Remembering and understanding: the effects of changes in underlying knowledge on children's recollections', *Child Development*, vol.71, pp.1309–28.

Gregory, R.J. (2007) *Psychological Testing: History, Principles and Applications* (5th edn), Chicago, IL, Pearson.

Havard, C. and Memon, A. (2009) 'The influence of face age on identification from a video line-up: a comparison between older and younger adults', *Memory*, vol.17, pp.847–59.

Havard, C., Memon, A., Clifford, B. and Gabbert, F. (2009) 'A comparison of video and static photo line-ups with child and adolescent witnesses', *Applied Cognitive Psychology*, DOI: 10.1002/acp.1645.

Heaps, C.M. and Nash, M. (2001) 'Comparing recollective experience in true and false autobiographical memories', *Journal of Experimental Psychology: Learning, Memory, and Cognition*, vol.4, pp.920–30.

Holliday, R.E. and Albon, A.J. (2004) 'Minimising misinformation effects in young children with cognitive interview mnemonics', *Psychology, Crime and Law*, vol.5, pp.101–15.

Hutcheson, G.D., Baxter, J.S., Telfer, K. and Warden, D. (1995) 'Child witness statement quality: question type and errors of omission', *Law and Human Behavior*, vol.19, pp.631–48.

Hyman, I.E., Jr and Pentland, J. (1996) 'The role of mental imagery in the creation of false childhood memories', *Journal of Memory and Language*, vol.35, pp.101–17.

Hyman, I.E., Jr and Rubin, D.C. (1990) 'Memorabeatlia: a naturalistic study of long-term memory', *Memory and Cognition*, vol.18, pp.205–14.

Itsukushima, Y., Nishi, M., Maruyama, M. and Takahashi, M. (2006) 'The effect of presentation medium of post-event information: impact of co-witness information', *Applied Cognitive Psychology*, vol.20, pp.575–81.

Jensen, A.R. (1998) *The g Factor: The Science of Mental Ability*, Westport, CT, Praeger.

Johnson, M.K., Hashtroudi, S. and Lindsay, D.S. (1993) 'Source monitoring', *Psychological Bulletin*, vol.114, pp.3–28.

Kane, M.J. and Engle, R.W. (2002) 'The role of prefrontal cortex in working-memory capacity, executive attention, and general fluid intelligence: an individual differences perspective', *Psychonomic Bulletin and Review*, vol.9, pp.637–71.

Kneller, W., Memon, A. and Stevenage, S. (2001) 'Simultaneous and sequential lineups: decision processes of accurate and inaccurate eyewitnesses', *Applied Cognitive Psychology*, vol.15, pp.659–71.

Kyllonen, P.C. (2002) 'g: knowledge, speed, strategies, or working memory capacity? A systems perspective', in Sternberg, R.J. and Gigorenko, E.L. (eds) *The General Factor of Intelligence: How General Is It?*, Mahwah, NJ, Erlbaum.

Kyllonen, P.C. and Christal, R.E. (1990) 'Reasoning ability is (little more than) working memory capacity?', *Intelligence*, vol.14, pp.389–433.

Lamb, M.E., Orbach, Y., Sternberg, K.J., Hershkowitz, I. and Horovitz, D. (2000) 'Accuracy of investigators' verbatim notes of their forensic interviews with alleged child abuse victims', *Law and Human Behavior*, vol.24, pp.699–708.

Leible, T.L. and Snell, W.E., Jr (2004) 'Borderline personality disorder and multiple aspects of emotional intelligence', *Personality and Individual Differences*, vol.37, pp.393–404.

Loftus, E.F. (1975) 'Leading questions and the eyewitness report', *Cognitive Psychology*, vol.7, pp.560–72.

Loftus, E.F. (1997) 'Creating false memories', *Scientific American*, vol.277, pp.70–5.

Loftus, E.F. (2005) 'Planting misinformation in the human mind: a 30-year investigation of the malleability of memory', *Learning and Memory*, vol.12, pp.361–6.

Loftus, E.F. and Greene, E. (1980) 'Warning: even memory for faces may be contagious', *Law and Human Behavior*, vol.4, pp.323–34.

Loftus, E.F and Palmer, J.C. (1974) 'Reconstruction of automobile destruction', *Journal of Verbal Learning and Verbal Behavior*, vol.13, pp.585–9.

Loftus, E.F. and Pickrell, J.E. (1995) 'The formation of false memories', *Psychiatric Annals*, vol.25, pp.720–5.

Loftus, E.F., Miller, D.G. and Burns, H.J. (1978) 'Semantic integration of verbal information into a visual memory', *Journal of Experimental Psychology: Human Learning and Memory*, vol.4, pp.19–31.

Malouff, J.M., Thorsteinsson, E. and Schutte, N.S. (2005) 'The relationship between the five-factor model of personality and clinical disorders: a meta-analysis', *Journal of Psychopathology and Behavioural Assessment*, vol.27, pp.101–14.

Marsh, E.J. (2007) 'Retelling is not the same as recalling: implications for memory', *Current Directions in Psychological Science*, vol.16, pp.16–20.

Marsh, E.J. and Tversky, B. (2004) 'Spinning the stories of our lives', *Applied Cognitive Psychology*, vol.18, pp.491–503.

Mathews, R., Hancock, L. and Briggs, D. (2004) 'Jurors' perceptions, understanding, confidence and satisfaction in the jury system: a study in six courts', *Findings*, vol.227, London, Home Office.

Mayer, J.D. and Salovey, P. (1997) 'What is emotional intelligence?', in Salovey, P. and Sluyter, D. (eds) *Emotional Development and Emotional Intelligence: Educational Implications*, New York, Basic Books.

Mayer, J.D., Salovey, P. and Caruso, D.R. (2008) 'Emotional intelligence: new ability or eclectic traits?', *American Psychologist*, vol.63, pp.503–17.

McCauley, M.R. and Fisher, R.P. (1995) 'Facilitating children's eyewitness recall with the revised cognitive interview', *Journal of Applied Psychology*, vol.80, pp.510–17.

McCloskey M. and Zaragoza, M. (1985) 'Misleading post-event information and memory for events: arguments and evidence against memory impairment hypotheses', *Journal of Experimental Psychology: General*, vol.114, pp.1–16.

McEnrue, M.P. and Groves, K. (2006) 'Choosing among tests of emotional intelligence: what is the evidence?', *Human Resource Development Quarterly*, vol.17, pp.9–42.

McGrew, K. (2009) 'Editorial: CHC theory and the human cognitive abilities project: standing on the shoulders of the giants of psychometric intelligence research', *Intelligence*, vol.37, pp.1–10.

McQuiston-Surrett, D., Malpass, R.S. and Tredoux, C.D. (2006) 'Sequential vs simultaneous line-ups. A review of methods, data and theory', *Psychology, Public Policy and Law*, vol.12, pp.137–69.

Meissner, C.A. and Brigham, J.C. (2001) 'Thirty years of investigating the other-race effect in memory for faces: a meta-analytic review', *Psychology, Public Policy and Law*, vol.7, pp.3–35.

Memon, A., Holley, A., Milne, R., Köhnken, G. and Bull, R. (1994) 'Towards understanding the effects of interviewer training in evaluating the cognitive interview', *Applied Cognitive Psychology*, vol.8, pp.641–59.

Memon, A., Hope, L. and Bull, R.H.C. (2003) 'Exposure duration: effects on eyewitness accuracy and confidence', *British Journal of Psychology*, vol.94, pp.339–54.

Morgan III, C.A.., Hazlett, G., Doran, A., Garrett, S., Hoyt, G., Thomas, P., Baranoski, M. and Southwich, S.M. (2004) 'Accuracy of eyewitness memory for persons encountered during exposure to highly intense stress', *International Journal of Law and Psychiatry*, vol.27, pp.265–79.

Myles-Worsley, M., Cromer, C.C. and Dodd, D.H. (1986) 'Children's preschool script reconstruction: reliance on general knowledge as memory fades', *Developmental Psychology*, vol.22, pp.22–30.

Nikolaou, I. and Tsaousis, I. (2002) 'Emotional intelligence in the workplace: exploring its effects on occupational stress and organizational commitment', *International Journal of Organizational Analysis*, vol.10, pp.327–42.

Palmer, B., Walls, M., Burgess, Z. and Stough, C. (2001) 'Emotional intelligence and effective leadership', *Leadership and Organization Development Journal*, vol.22, pp.5–10.

Palmer, B., Gignac, G., Manocha, R. and Stough, C. (2005) 'A psychometric evaluation of the Mayer–Salovey–Caruso emotional intelligence test version 2.0', *Intelligence*, vol.33, pp.285–305.

Patterson, H.M. and Kemp, R.I. (2006) 'Co-witnesses talk: a survey of eyewitness discussion', *Psychology, Crime and Law*, vol.12, pp.181–91.

Patterson, H.M., Kemp, R.I. and Ng, J.R. (2009) 'Combating co-witness contamination: attempting to decrease the negative effects of discussion on eyewitness memory', *Applied Cognitive Psychology*, DOI: 10.1002/acp.1640.

Pennington, N. and Hastie, R. (1986) 'Evidence evaluation in complex decision making', *Journal of Personality and Social Psychology*, vol.51, pp.242–58.

Pike, G., Brace, N. and Kynan, S. (2002) *The Visual Identification of Suspects: Procedures and Practice*, London, Crime Unit, Home Office Research, Development and Statistics Directorate.

Reyna, V.F. and Lloyd, F. (1997) 'Theories of false memory in children and adults', *Learning and Individual Differences*, vol.9, pp.95–123.

Roediger, H.L. and McDermott, K.B. (1995) 'Creating false memories: remembering words not presented in lists', *Journal of Experimental Psychology: Learning, Memory, and Cognition*, vol.4, pp.803–14.

Salovey, P. and Mayer, J.D. (1990) 'Emotional intelligence', *Imagination, Cognition and Personality*, vol.9, pp.185–211.

Schutte, N.S., Malouff, J.M., Thorsteinsson, E.B., Bhullar, N. and Rooke, S.E. (2006) 'A meta-analytic investigation of the relationship between emotional intelligence and health', *Personality and Individual Differences*, vol.42, pp.921–33.

Schweizer, K. and Moosbrugger, H. (2004) 'Attention and working memory as predictors of intelligence', *Intelligence*, vol.32, pp.329–47.

Schweizer, K., Moosbrugger, H. and Goldhammer, F. (2005) 'The structure of the relationship between attention and intelligence', *Intelligence*, vol.33, pp.589–611.

Searle, R. (2003) *Selection and Recruitment: A Critical Text*, Basingstoke, Palgrave Macmillan/Milton Keynes, Open University.

Smith, V.L. (1991) 'Prototypes in the courtroom: lay representations of legal concepts', *Journal of Personality and Social Psychology*, vol.61, pp.857–72.

Smith, V.L. and Studebaker, C.A. (1996) 'What do you expect? The influence of people's prior knowledge of crime categories on fact-finding', *Law and Human Behavior*, vol.20, pp.517–32.

Spearman, C. (1904) '"General intelligence", objectively defined and measured', *American Journal of Psychology*, vol.15, pp.201–93.

Spiro, R.J. (1980) 'Constructive processes in prose comprehension and recall', in Spiro, R.J. (ed.) *Theoretical Issues in Reading Comprehension*, Hillsdale, NJ, Lawrence Erlbaum Associates.

Steblay, N.M., Dysart, J., Fulero, S. and Lindsay, R.C.L. (2001) 'Eyewitness accuracy rates in sequential and simultaneous lineup presentations: a meta-analytic comparison', *Law and Human Behavior*, vol.25, pp.459–74.

Stein, L.M. and Memon, A. (2006) 'Testing the efficacy of the cognitive interview in a developing country', *Applied Cognitive Psychology*, vol.20, pp.597–605.

Sternberg, R.J. (1999) 'A triarchic approach to the understanding and assessment of intelligence in multicultural populations', *Journal of School Psychology*, vol.37, pp.145–59.

Sternberg, R.J. (ed.) (2000) *Handbook of Intelligence*, New York, Cambridge University Press.

Sternberg, R.J. (2004) 'Culture and intelligence', *American Psychologist*, vol.59, pp.325–38.

Sternberg, R.J. and Detterman, D.K. (eds) (1986) *What is Intelligence? Contemporary Viewpoints on its Nature and Definition*, Norwood, NJ, Ablex Publishing.

Sternberg, R.J. and Kaufman, J.C. (1998) 'Human abilities', *Annual Review of Psychology*, vol.49, pp.479–502.

Sternberg, R.J., Torff, B. and Grigorenko, E.L. (1998) 'Teaching for successful intelligence raises school achievement', *Phi Delta Kappa*, vol.79, pp.667–9.

Tinsley, Y. (2000) 'Juror decision-making: a look inside the jury room', *British Criminology Conference: Selected Proceedings*, vol.4.

Tulving, E. (1983) *Elements of Episodic Memory*, New York, Oxford University Press.

Valentine, T. and Heaton, P. (1999) 'An evaluation of the fairness of police line-ups and video identifications', *Applied Cognitive Psychology*, vol.13, pp.S59–S72.

Valentine, T. and Mesout, J. (2009) 'Eyewitness identification under stress in the London Dungeon', *Applied Cognitive Psychology*, vol.23, pp.151–61.

Valentine, T., Harris, N., Piera, A.C. and Darling, S. (2003) 'Are police video identifications fair to African–Caribbean suspects?', *Applied Cognitive Psychology*, vol.17, pp.459–76.

Waterhouse, L. (2006) 'Multiple intelligences, the Mozart effect, and emotional intelligence: a critical review', *Educational Psychologist*, vol.41, pp.207–25.

Wells, G.L. (1978) 'Eyewitness-testimony research: system variables and estimator variables', *Journal of Personality and Social Psychology*, vol.36, pp.1546–57.

Wells, G.L. and Olson, E.A. (2001) 'The other-race effect in eyewitness identification: what do we do about it?', *Psychology, Public Policy, and Law*, vol.7, pp.230–46.

Wright, A.M. and Holliday, R.E. (2007) 'Enhancing the recall of young, young-old and old-old adults with cognitive interviews', *Applied Cognitive Psychology*, vol.21, pp.19–43.

Wright, D.B., Mathews, S.A. and Skagerberg, E.M. (2005) 'Social recognition memory: the effect of other people's responses for previously seen and unseen items', *Journal of Experimental Psychology: Applied*, vol.11, pp.200–9.

Zaragoza, M.S. and Lane, S.M. (1994) 'Source misattributions and suggestibility of eyewitness memory', *Journal of Experimental Psychology: Learning, Memory and Cognition*, vol.20, pp.934–45.

Zeidner, M., Roberts, R.D. and Mathews, G. (2008) 'The science of emotional intelligence: current consensus and controversies', *European Psychologist*, vol.13, pp.64–78.

Acknowledgements

Grateful acknowledgement is made to the following sources:

Cover image
Copyright © Dave Ellison/Alamy.

Plates
Plate 1: Tyler, L.K. and Moss, H.E. (2001) 'Towards a distributed account of conceptual knowledge', *Trends in Cognitive Science*, vol.5, no.6. Copyright © Elsevier Science Ltd; *Plate 2:* Henson, R. (2005) 'What can functional neuroimaging tell the experimental psychologist?', *Quarterly Journal of Experimental Psychology*, Section A, vol.58, no.2, Psychology Press; *Plates 6, 7 and 9:* Calder, A.J., Lawrence, A.D. and Young, A.W. (2001) 'Neuropsychology of fear and loathing', *Nature Reviews Neuroscience*, vol.2, no.5, May 2001, Nature Publishing Group.

Table
Table 9.4: reprinted from *Cognition*, vol.13, Armstrong, S.L. *et al.*, 'What some concepts might not be', pages 263–308. Copyright (1983), with permission from Elsevier.

Figures
Figure 1.2: adapted from Tolman, E.C. *et al.* (1948) 'Cognitive maps in rats and men', *Psychological Review*, vol.55, no.4, American Psychological Association, article is now in the public domain; *Figure 1.3:* Copyright © Dale Robins/iStock; *Figure 3.7:* © ADAGP, Paris and DACS, London 2004/Bridgeman Art Library; *Figure 3.12:* © James J. Gibson, *The Ecological Approach to Visual Perception*, Lawrence Erlbaum Associates Inc., New Jersey, 1986, Fig. 2.1; *Figure 3.23:* © Nik Williams/The Swansea Museum 1996, with permission; *Figures 4.11, 4.14 and 4.15:* Marr, D. (2000) *Vision*, Henry Holt and Company, Inc.; *Figure 4.12:* © Succession Picasso/DACS 2004; *Figures 4.16, 4.17 and 4.18:* Marr, D. and Nishihara, H.K. (1978) 'Representation and recognition of the spatial organization of three dimensional shapes', *Proceedings of the Royal Society of London*, B200, pp.269–94. The Royal Society; *Figure 4.24:* reprinted from *Trends in Cognitive Science*, vol.4, J.V. Haxby *et al.*, 'The distributed human neural system for face perception', pages 223–33, Copyright (2000), with permission from Elsevier; *Figure 5.1:* Atkinson, R.C. and Shiffrin, R.M. (1971) 'The control of short-term memory', *Scientific American*, vol.225. By permission of Scientific American; *Figure 10.1:* Reed, D.L. (2004) 'Genetic analysis of lice supports direct contact between modern and archaic humans', *PLoS Biology*, vol.2, November 2004, PLoS Biology; *Figure 14.1:* 'Automatic nervous system' figure from *The Penguin Dictionary of Psychology* by Arthur S. Reber (Penguin Books 1985, third edition 2001). Copyright © Arthur S. Reber, 1985, 1995, 2001; *Figure 14.3(a):* Ekman, P. and Friesen, W.V. (1975) *Unmasking the Face*. Copyright © Paul Ekman; *Figure 14.4, top left:* © J & P Wegner/Foto Natura/FLPA, *top right:* © Jan Pitman/ Associated Press, *bottom right:* © Photodisc Europe; *Figure 14.13:* adapted from Rosenzweig, M.R. *et al.* (1999) *Biological Psychology: An Introduction to Behavioural, Cognitive, and Clinical Neuroscience*, Sinauer Associates; *Figure 15.4:* Baddeley, A. and Wilson, B.A. (1994) 'When implicit learning fails: amnesia

and the problem of error elimination', *Neuropsychologia*, vol.32, no.1. Elsevier Science Ltd; *Figure 16.2:* Mayer, J.D. *et al.* (2008) 'Emotional intelligence: new ability or eclectic traits?', *American Psychologist*, vol.63, no.6, American Psychological Association.

Photographs
Page 574: Copyright © Rich Legg/iStock; page 589: Copyright © Rich Legg/ iStock.

Index